W9-AKC-932

Acclaim for Robert Kagan's

DANGEROUS NATION

"Superb. . . . Kagan's thesis is as compelling as it is sobering."
—*National Review*

"Carefully crafted. . . . An engaging interpretation of American history, made the more so by the author's skill in presenting it. . . . Kagan is able to give fresh interpretations to familiar landmarks of American history." —*The New York Review of Books*

"A superb mix of historical research and political theory."
—*Milwaukee Journal Sentinel*

"Kagan again assumes the stance of *enfant terrible*, assailing the keepers of the conventional wisdom. . . . [His] trashing of orthodoxy [and] . . . systematic dismantling of accepted dogmas is refreshingly provocative. . . . *Dangerous Nation* draws from a deep well of historical scholarship about American foreign relations."
—*The Washington Post*

"Lucid, cogently argued and amply sourced."
—*The Times Literary Supplement*

"Brilliant and absorbing. . . . Many critics of U.S. foreign policy will not need persuading that America is a dangerous nation. . . . *Dangerous Nation* is not aimed at them. It is meant for the general reader, of course, and for those in sympathy with the projection of American power in recent times. . . . There should be something in this project for almost everyone." —*The Wall Street Journal*

"Kagan writes with power and charm. . . . [He] illuminates something very important about the unfolding of American foreign policy and of the American character." —*Commentary*

ROBERT KAGAN

DANGEROUS NATION

Robert Kagan is senior associate at the Carnegie Endowment for International Peace, transatlantic fellow at the German Marshall Fund, and a columnist for *The Washington Post*. He is also the author of *A Twilight Struggle: American Power and Nicaragua, 1977–1990*, and editor, with William Kristol, of *Present Dangers: Crisis and Opportunity in American Foreign and Defense Policy*. Kagan served in the U.S. State Department from 1984 to 1988. He lives in Brussels with his family.

DANGEROUS
NATION

DANGEROUS NATION

ROBERT KAGAN

VINTAGE BOOKS
A DIVISION OF RANDOM HOUSE, INC.
NEW YORK

FIRST VINTAGE BOOKS EDITION, NOVEMBER 2007

The Library of Congress has cataloged the Knopf edition as follows:
Dangerous nation / Robert Kagan. — 1st ed.
p. cm.
Includes bibliographical references.
1. United States—Foreign relations—To 1865.
2. United States—Foreign relations—1865–1921.
3. United States—Territorial expansion—History.
4. United States—Foreign public
opinion—History. I. Title.
E183.7.K34 2006
327.73—dc22   2006045264

Vintage ISBN: 978-0-375-72491-6

Author photograph © The Carnegie Endowment
Book design by Virginia Tan

www.vintagebooks.com

Printed in the United States of America
10 9 8 7 6 5 4 3 2 1

For Tor

The authors of [the Declaration of Independence] set up a standard maxim for free society, which should be familiar to all, and revered by all; constantly looked to, constantly labored for, and even though never perfectly attained, constantly approximated, and thereby constantly spreading and deepening its influence, and augmenting the happiness and value of life to all people of all colors everywhere.

—Abraham Lincoln, June 26, 1857

CONTENTS

DANGEROUS NATION

Introduction

IN 1817 America's minister in London, John Quincy Adams, reported that "[t]he universal feeling of Europe in witnessing the gigantic growth of our population and power is that we shall, if united, become a very dangerous member of the society of nations. They therefore hope what they confidently expect, that we shall not long remain united."[1] In 1819 a congressman returning from a visit to Europe reported that everyone he spoke to "appeared to be profoundly impressed with the idea that we were an ambitious and encroaching people."[2]

Most Americans today would be surprised to know that much of the world regarded America, even in its infancy, as a very dangerous nation. When they think of the nation's relations to the world in the decades before and after the Revolution, the words they tend to conjure are "isolation," "nonentanglement," "neutrality." The early Americans' goal, in the famous words of the Puritan father John Winthrop, was to establish a "city upon a hill" to be emulated by others. Washington's Farewell Address restated this isolationist core of American foreign policy, opposing foreign attachments and expressing the quintessential American yearning for aloofness from a corrupt and corrupting world. The Monroe Doctrine further reconfirmed this tradition of isolation and separation. Or so it is widely believed.

This was not the way others viewed Americans in the seventeenth, eighteenth, and nineteenth centuries, however. Peoples and nations on the North American continent, in the Western Hemisphere, and in Europe considered Americans dangerous for a variety of reasons. First and foremost was their aggressive and seemingly insatiable desire for territory and dominant influence. In the late 1820s a Mexican commission concluded that Americans were a most "ambitious people always ready to encroach upon their Neighbours without a spark of good Faith."[3] The Indian tribes that had been steadily driven back across the continent since the early seventeenth century took the same view, of course. But so did the Spaniards, the French, the Russians, and the British, each of whom in their turn were pushed off lands and out of waterways by what French diplomats described as a "numerous," "warlike," and "restless" American populace. These ambitious Americans were "an enemy to be feared."[4]

But aggressive territorial expansionism was not the only quality that made the young American republic dangerous in the eyes of others. Of equal if not sometimes greater concern was the danger posed by America's revolutionary ideology, as well as by the way its liberal, commercial society seemed to swallow up those cultures with which it came into contact. In 1794 the Spanish governor in Louisiana warned that the spread of the American population and culture, both of them "advancing and multiplying in the silence of peace," were "so much to be feared by Spain as are their arms."[5]

There were many around the world who admired and celebrated the birth of a republic based on the principles of human equality and natural rights. But most of the world's governments were apprehensive. "This federal republic is born a pigmy," the Spanish minister in Paris remarked, but "a day will come when it will be a giant, even a colossus." The source of the new nation's frightening power, the minister believed, was its republican ideology and government. "Liberty of conscience, the facility for establishing a new population on immense lands, as well as the advantages of the new government, will draw thither farmers and artisans from all nations. In a few years we shall watch with grief the tyrannical existence of this same colossus."[6]

Conservative defenders of monarchy and absolutism watched with growing alarm as revolutionary waves rolled back and forth across the Atlantic in the decades following the American Revolution. "If this flood of evil doctrines and pernicious examples should extend over the whole of America," Prince Klemens von Metternich warned, "what would become . . . of the moral force of our governments, and of that conservative system which has saved Europe from complete dissolution?" When President James Monroe announced what would become famous as the Monroe Doctrine in 1823, Metternich apprehended that the Americans, "whom we have seen arise and grow," had "suddenly left a sphere too narrow for their ambition and . . . astonished Europe by a new act of revolt, more unprovoked, fully as audacious, and no less dangerous than" the American Revolution itself.[7]

This gap between Americans' self-perception and the perceptions of others has endured throughout the nation's history. Americans have cherished an image of themselves as by nature inward-looking and aloof, only sporadically and spasmodically venturing forth into the world, usually in response to external attack or perceived threats. This self-image survives, despite four hundred years of steady expansion and an ever-deepening involvement in world affairs, and despite innumerable wars, interventions, and prolonged occupations in foreign lands. It is as if it were all an accident or odd twist of fate. Even as the United States has risen to a position of global hegemony, expanding its reach and purview and involvement across the continent and then across the oceans, Americans still believe their nation's natural tendencies are toward passivity, indifference, and insularity.

This lack of self-awareness has had its virtues. It has sometimes made America's vast power more tolerable to large numbers of peoples around the world, for a nation so unaware of its own behavior may seem less threatening than a nation with a plan of expansion and conquest. But it has also been a problem. Americans have often not realized how their expansive tendencies—political, ideological, economic, strategic, and cultural—bump up against and intrude upon other peoples and cultures. They are surprised to learn that others hate them, are jealous of them, and even fear them for their power and influence. They have not anticipated, therefore, the way their natural expansiveness could provoke reactions, and sometimes violent reactions, against them.

This lack of self-awareness is a problem in another way as well. Not only have Americans frequently failed to see how their actions could provoke reactions from others. They have not even accurately predicted their own responses. The history of America has been one of repeated surprises, not only at the behavior of others but at the behavior of the United States in response to the actions of others. Many Americans have believed they did not care what happened in most of the rest of the world, and yet when events occured, they found that they did care. In the Howard Hawks movie *To Have and Have Not,* Lauren Bacall says to Humphrey Bogart, "I know, I know, you don't give a whoop what I do—but when I do it you get sore." Bogart's Harry Morgan in that 1944 film was meant to be a symbol for an isolationist America coming out of its isolation, but Bacall's line could summarize four hundred years of American foreign policy.

On balance, Americans would be better off if they understood themselves, their nation, and their nation's history better. This applies especially to the early history of American foreign policy. The pervasive myth of

America as isolationist and passive until provoked rests on a misunderstanding of America's foreign policies in the seventeenth, eighteenth, and nineteenth centuries. This book is an attempt to tell a different story that is more about expansion and ambition, idealistic as well as materialistic, than about isolationist exemplars and cities upon hills.

CHAPTER I

The First Imperialists

This is a commonwealth of the fabric that hath an open ear, and a public concernment. She is not made for herself only, but given as a magistrate of God unto mankind, for the vindication of common right and the law of nature. Wherefore saith Cicero of the ... Romans, Nos magis patronatum orbis terrarrum suscepimus quam imperium, we have rather undertaken the patronage than the empire of the world.

—James Harrington,
The Commonwealth of Oceana, 1656

The Myth of the "City upon a Hill": The Americanization of the Puritan Mission

MISPERCEPTIONS about the history, traditions, and nature of American foreign policy begin with the popular image of the Puritans who settled in New England in the 1630s. John Winthrop's hopeful description of the Massachusetts Bay theocracy as a "city upon a hill" is emblazoned in the American self-image, a vivid symbol of what are widely seen as dominant isolationist and "exceptionalist" tendencies in American foreign policy. The Puritan "mission," as the historian Frederick Merk once put it, was "to redeem the Old World by high example," and generations of Americans have considered this "exemplarist" purpose the country's original mission in its pure, uncorrupted form: the desire to set an example to the world, but from a safe distance.[1] Felix Gilbert argued that the unique combination of idealism and isolationism in American thought derived from the Puritans' "utopian" aspirations, which required "separation" from Europe and the severing of "ties which might spread the diseases of Europe to America."[2] The true American "mission," therefore, was inherently isolationist, passive, and restrained; it was, as Merk put it, both "idealistic" and "self-denying . . . a force that fought to curb expansionism of the aggressive variety."[3]

This picture of Puritan America as a pious Greta Garbo, wanting only to be left alone in her self-contained world, is misleading. For one thing, Winthrop's Puritans were not isolationists. They were global revolutionaries.[4] They escaped persecution in the Old World to establish the ideal religious commonwealth in America, their "new Jerusalem." But unlike the biblical Jews, they looked forward to the day, they hoped not far off, when they might return to a reformed Egypt. Far from seeking permanent separation from the Old World, the Puritans' "errand into the wilderness" aimed to establish a base from which to launch a counteroffensive across the Atlantic. Their special covenant with God was not tied to the soil of the North American continent.[5] America was not the Puritans' promised land but a temporary refuge.[6] God had "peopled New England in order that the reformation of England and Scotland may be hastened."[7] As the great scholar of Puritan thought Perry Miller explained many years ago, the Puritan migration "was no retreat from Europe: it was a flank attack." The "large unspoken assumption in the errand of 1630" was that success in New England would mean a return to old England.[8]

The Massachusetts Bay colonists neither sought isolation from the Old World nor considered themselves isolated.[9] The Puritan leaders did not even believe they were establishing a "new" world distinct from the old. In their minds New England and Old England were the same world, spiritually if not geographically. A hundred years after Winthrop's settlement, when the Puritan evangelist Jonathan Edwards spoke of "our nation," he meant both Britain and the British North American colonies. It was a measure of how little the New England Puritans sought isolation from the Old World that their greatest disappointment came when England's Puritan revolution in the mid-seventeenth century abandoned rigid Calvinism, the Puritans' model, thus leaving the Puritans theologically isolated in their American wilderness.[10]

America, in turn, became not a promised land but a burial ground for the kind of Puritan theocracy Winthrop and his followers had hoped to establish. Puritanism died in part because the American wilderness, like the biblical Israel, was a land of milk and honey. The New World was too vast for the Puritans' worldly asceticism. Their rigid theocracy required control and obedience and self-restraint, but the expansive North American wilderness created freedom, dissent, independence, and the lust for land. The abundance of land and economic opportunities for men and women of all social stations diverted too many minds from godly to worldly pursuits. It undermined patriarchal hierarchy and shattered orthodoxy. Those who did not like the way the doctrines of Calvinism were construed and enforced in the Massachusetts Bay Colony had only to move up the Connecticut Valley. Within a dozen years of Winthrop's arrival, Puritan divines were decrying their congregants' sinful desire for ever more "elbow-room" in their New World. "Land! Land! hath been the Idol of many in New-England," cried Increase Mather. "They that profess themselves Christians, have foresaken Churches, and Ordinances, and all for land and elbow-room enough in the World."[11]

The rich lands of North America also helped unleash liberal, materialist forces within Protestantism that overwhelmed the Puritan fathers' original godly vision and brought New England onto the path on which the rest of British-American civilization was already traveling: toward individualism, progress, and modernity. With so many opportunities for personal enrichment available in the New World, the "Protestant ethic," as Max Weber called it, which countenanced the rewards of labor as a sign of God's favor and which demanded hard work in one's "calling" as a sign of election, became a powerful engine of material progress. In a short time, settlers, plantation owners, and the increasingly prosperous and powerful merchants of Boston—the so-called River Gods—came to worship at altars other than those of their Calvinist fathers and grandfathers. The liberal, commercial ethos of these new mercantile groups represented the spirit of a new age, whose "guiding principles were not social stability, order, and the discipline of the senses, but mobility, growth, and the enjoyment of life."[12]

By the early eighteenth century Puritan New England had entered "the emerging secular and commercial culture" of Anglo-America. The New Englanders "relinquished their grand vision of building a city upon a hill," and Puritanism itself melted into the new, modernizing society.[13] The burst of religious revivalism in the early to mid-eighteenth century, termed the Great Awakening, was a monument to Puritanism's failure, a worried response to the increasing secularization of American society and to the spread of Christian rationalism and Deism among colonial elites. From its original pious ambitions, Jonathan Edwards lamented, the Puritans' America had fallen into sin. History had never witnessed "such a casting off [of] the Christian religion," nor "so much scoffing at and ridiculing the gospel of Christ by those that have been brought up under gospel light."[14] Even Edwards's own reactionary revivalism was shaped by the new realities of life in an expansive, modernizing, and free America, for his was a democratized, antihierarchical Puritanism that conformed to the increasingly fluid nature of colonial American society. His effort to stem the tide of liberalism and modernity was futile. As Edwards wrote his treatises on faith and salvation and obedience to God, his fellow British colonials were "beginning to think of themselves as having individual rights that were self-evidently endowments of nature."[15] By the last quarter of the eighteenth century, a foreign observer like the French immigrant Michel-Guillaume-Jean de Crèvecoeur could write of Americans that they "think more of the affairs of this world than of those of the next."[16]

Not only has the original Puritan mission often been misunderstood, therefore, but the rapid absorption and dissipation of Puritanism within the mainstream of colonial American society meant that the Puritan influence in shaping the character of that society, and its foreign policies, was not as great as has sometimes been imagined. Most of America outside of New England had never been under Puritan influence, and by the early eighteenth century even New England was no Puritan commonwealth but a rising center of liberalism and commercialism. In the seventeenth and early eighteenth centuries it was the southern and middle colonies, not New England, that "epitomized what was arguably the most important element in the emerging British-American culture: the conception of America as a place in which free people could pursue their own individual happiness in safety and with a fair prospect that they might be successful in their several quests."[17]

The society and culture that took root in the Chesapeake Bay region had far greater influence on the evolution of American society, and therefore on American foreign policy, than did Puritanism. This colonial America was characterized not by isolationism and utopianism, not by cities upon hills and covenants with God, but by aggressive expansionism, acquisitive materialism, and an overarching ideology of civilization that encouraged and justified both. In Virginia and the other settlements along the Chesapeake Bay that predated the Puritans' arrival in New England, the dreams that drew Englishmen to a rough and untamed country were of wealth and opportunity, not the founding of a new Israel. The boom years that came to Virginia in the middle of the seventeenth century produced no utopia but, at first, an almost lawless capitalism run amok: the "fleeting ugliness of private enterprise operating temporarily without check," a "greed magnified by opportunity, producing fortunes for a few and misery for many," and, of course, the first steps "toward a system of labor that treated men as things."[18] Although gradually this rampant capitalist beast was tamed by the establishment of laws and institutions modeled after England's, the acquisitive, individualistic, modern spirit of liberalism formed the bedrock of American society more than a century and a half before the American Revolution proclaimed liberty and the pursuit of happiness to be the natural rights of all men.[19]

This acquisitive individualism was the powerful engine of an Anglo-American territorial expansion that was neither particularly godly nor especially peaceful and certainly not "self-denying." In the Chesapeake Bay area settled by the Virginia Company and its "adventurers," expansion throughout the tidewater began immediately, stretching up the fertile and accessible valleys of the James, Rappahannock, and York rivers. In the Massachusetts Bay Colony, too, expansion from Boston into the Connecticut Valley and the New England interior began within a few years after the colony's founding. In both the northern and southern colonies, expansion brought the settlers into bloody conflict with Indians—first the Pequot and later the Wampanoag, the Narragansett, and the Nipmuck in the North, and the Susquehanna in the South. In 1637 settlers from Boston and the Connecticut River Valley united in a two-pronged attack that ended in the massacre and virtual extermination of the Pequot. That victory opened up even more territory for expansion and settlement, which in turn led less than four decades later to another, albeit more costly, triumph for the expansion-minded settlers against an alliance of Indian tribes loosely led by the Wampanoag chief whom the Anglo-Americans called King Philip. In Virginia that same year Governor William Berkeley's refusal to launch a war against the Susquehanna resulted in a frontier rebellion led by Nathaniel Bacon and the burning of the Virginia capital of Jamestown. Thereafter in Virginia, as in New England, expansion proceeded apace throughout the latter half of the seventeenth century and into the eighteenth, out into the Virginia Piedmont and the Great Valley of the Appalachians and, in the north, up into Vermont and New Hampshire.

Like most expansive peoples—the Greeks and Romans, for instance—Anglo-Americans did not view themselves as aggressors.[20] In part, they believed it only right and natural that they should seek independence and fortune for themselves and their families in the New World. Once having pursued this destiny and established a foothold in the untamed lands of North America, continued expansion seemed to many a matter of survival, a defensive reaction to threats that lay just beyond the ever-expanding perimeter of their English civilization. The French and Spanish empires were competing with the English for control of North America. And the Indian nations, defending their own shrinking territories and, indeed, their very existence against European aggression, were a constant threat to the settlers' security—at least from the settlers' perspective. Native Americans pushed off one stretch of land, and fearing they would soon be pushed off the next, frequently struck back, both out of vengeance and in the hopes of convincing the settlers to halt their advance and retreat. Settlers under siege, and the governments charged with protecting them, could easily view the Indians as the aggressors and their own actions as aimed at establishing nothing more than a minimal level of security. Attaining even minimal security, however, required an ever-enlarging sphere of control and dominance, for whenever one boundary of security was established, other threats always existed just beyond it. The "original sin" of displacing the first Indians from their lands began a cycle of advance and conquest. As Catherine the Great is supposed to have remarked, "I have no way to defend my borders but to extend them." What has been said of Russia, that it found its security only in the insecurity of others, could be said of colonial Anglo-Americans, too. In the seventeenth and eighteenth centuries, they purchased their security at the price of the insecurity, and often the ruin, of Pequot, Iroquois, and Narragansett, of French and Spaniards, and by the time of the Revolution, of the British, too.

The Expansionist "Mission"

THE SEARCH FOR SECURITY, however, was not the sole motive for expansion. There were other powerful motives as well, and more exalted justifications. The Anglo-American settlers pressed into territories claimed by others in the conviction that they were serving a higher purpose, that their expansion was the unfolding of an Anglo-Saxon destiny. They saw themselves as the vanguard of an English civilization that was leading humanity into the future. The first American exceptionalism was really an English exceptionalism, the first American mission an Anglo-Saxon, Protestant, imperial mission. Even the Virginia Company portrayed itself as more than a purely commercial entity. The company's stockholders insisted theirs was a different kind of commercial enterprise, "the ends for which it is established beinge not simply matter of Trade, butt of a higher Nature."[21] Clearing away the wilderness and implanting English civilization in its place was in their eyes an inherently noble task, as well as being lucrative. While making money for themselves and their London stockholders, the colonists would "bring the infidels and salvages lyving in those partes to humane civilitie and to a setled and quiet govermente." Not for the last time in American history, these early settlers made their way forward in the conviction that enterprise, trade, and the advance of civilization were interlinked. Their civilization, they believed, was beneficial both for those who advanced it and for those upon whom it was advanced.[22] This Anglo-American mission was neither passive nor "exemplarist," however. The settlers moved ever forward; they did not stand still. And they did their converting with their hands, their tools, and their weapons, not by the force of their example.

Nor was the settlers' mission one that isolated them from the rest of the world. They saw themselves spreading European civilization, not escaping it. The settlement of the North American wilderness was in their eyes part of a long process of civilized human evolution, a process that began centuries earlier in the wilderness of Europe. European civilization, too, they recalled, had been born in untamed forests. In their efforts to improve the land on which they settled, Anglo-American colonists provided themselves "with the comforting vision that, notwithstanding their remoteness from the center of history in Europe, they were also incorporated into the historical process as that process had been formulated and sanctioned by Europeans in Europe."[23] "Westward the course of empire takes its way," wrote the Irish philosopher and clergyman George Berkeley in 1726. "The four first acts already past, / A fifth shall close the drama with the day: / Time's noblest offspring is the last.[24]

The Anglo-American colonists were in this respect typical Englishmen. Long before American publicists invented the term in the mid-nineteenth century, the English had developed their own idea of "manifest destiny," derived partly from a sense of racial and cultural superiority, partly from a belief in the superiority of the Protestant religion and in the "perfection" of English political institutions. Along with the idea of destiny came a belief in the right of conquest of backward peoples in the name of this civilization. This was not simple racism; it was civilizationism. Before Englishmen exercised their right of conquest against North American Indians, they had exercised it against Gaelic Irish and Highland Scots, light-skinned peoples who nevertheless, like the Indians, made their living by hunting and fishing, who "seemed to have no settled agriculture or permanent homes," and whom the English therefore conceived to be "of a different and inferior race, violent, treacherous, poverty-stricken, and backward."[25] Sixteenth-century proponents of the colonization of Ireland had justified it as a means of fostering among the Irish an "appreciation for civility so that they might likewise move toward freedom." In the seventeenth and eighteenth centuries Englishmen looked farther across the oceans in their efforts to act as "civilizing agents" for the "barbarous nations."[26] And in the twentieth and twenty-first centuries Americans were still pursuing at least a version of this early English mission, without the aim of territorial conquest but with the same professed purpose of raising "developing" nations up into conformity with advanced civilization.

In the seventeenth and eighteenth centuries, as later, a strong element of nationalist pride was involved. The Anglo-Americans believed they were superior not only to the uncivilized natives but also to other European colonists by virtue of the liberties they enjoyed and the religion they practiced, and by the benefits they could bestow on the Indians. They believed, for instance, that they treated the Indians they encountered more humanely than did the bloodthirsty Spaniards and scheming French Catholics.[27] The notion that Anglo-Americans, by expanding in North America, would be liberating the natives from a brutal Spanish tyranny went as far back as 1584, when Richard Hakluyt entreated Queen Elizabeth's support for the colonial project.

> The Spaniards governe in the Indies with all pride and tyranie . . .
> so no doubte whensoever the Queene of England . . . shall seate
> upon that firme of America, and shalbe reported throughe oute all
> that tracte to use the naturall people there with all humanitie, curte-
> sie, and freedome, they will yelde themselves to her government,
> and revolte cleane from the Spaniarde. . . .[28]

In fact, compared with the French, at least, the Anglo-American colonists were arguably more ruthless and less concerned for Indian ways and interests. But the English believed they were superior conquerors chiefly because their civilization and their religion were superior: French and Spanish Catholic missionaries kept their Indian converts in darkness, because that was the nature of their benighted religion. "The French, they pretend to teach the Indians religion," Jonathan Edwards complained even well into the eighteenth century, "but they won't teach 'em to read. They won't let 'em read the Word of God."[29] The Indians were better off under the tutelage of the superior Protestant faith.

The Anglo-Americans' sense of cultural superiority grew dramatically after the Glorious Revolution in England in 1688, the effects of which rippled across the Atlantic and persuaded "most Englishmen that they lived on an oasis of freedom in a global desert of tyranny." In the North American colonies, as in Britain, people celebrated their unique liberties, both political and religious, and contrasted the perfection of the British "mixed constitution" with the imperfections of the absolutist governments in France and Spain.[30] "To patriotic Englishmen of the eighteenth century," including

Anglo-Americans in the New World, "liberty, Protestantism, and Imperial expansion seemed to be inextricably connected."[31]

The Anglo-Americans were not wrong to believe they had something of benefit to give to others, a way of life that was more prosperous and in some important respects freer, even if the recipients of these benefits often did not agree that this new way of life was preferable to their own. In the end, however, civilization, religion, and even security were justifications for and by-products of conquest and expansion in the seventeenth and eighteenth centuries. Anglo-Americans would not have sought to implant civilization in the wilderness had they not been moved by more self-interested motives, chiefly the desire for land and for all the material, spiritual, and political benefits that came with its acquisition. They did not hesitate when, as was often the case, the drive for ever more land tended to undermine the civilizing mission in both its political and religious forms. Even the most devoted Protestant evangelical missionaries refused to deny themselves a share of the territories occupied by the Indians they were attempting to convert. Nor did they, or could they, deny the waves of Anglo-American settlers who followed them out to the frontiers. This was in contrast to the French Jesuit missionaries who went to live among the Indians. The French Catholics, so disdained by the English Protestants, were more successful in attracting a following among the Indians precisely because they did not ask the natives to save their souls at the expense of losing their homelands.[32]

To say that the Anglo-American settlers were simply greedy would be too narrow. The desire for land was not primarily a desire for profit. Some land speculators made fortunes off the lands they bought and sold. But for the vast majority of settlers, the benefits of expansion were more of a spiritual and political nature. Landownership equaled liberty, both in Lockean theory and in practice. Settlement on the ever-expanding frontier offered unprecedented freedom and independence, and a sense of honor, to hundreds of thousands of families who would otherwise have lived a more dependent and oppressed existence in Europe or crowded in the cities on the Atlantic Coast. The endless supply of land on the continent meant that no one, except the slave, was condemned to spend a lifetime in the employ of someone else. Men earned wages only until they had enough money to buy land and move away. This was the original "American dream," one that Abraham Lincoln was still extolling a century later: the opportunity of every white male American to abandon a wage earner's life for the independent life of the landowner.

What distinguished colonial America from Europe in the eighteenth century, what made it really seem a promised land to settlers, and what attracted an astonishing wave of immigration in the decades before the Revolution was precisely the freedom, the individualism, and the rough equality among peoples that an expanding territory made possible. Contemporary observers such as Crèvecoeur noted in wonder that colonial American society was "not composed, as in Europe, of great lords who possess everything, and a herd of people who have nothing . . . no aristocratical families, no courts, no kings, no bishops, no ecclesiastical dominion, no invisible power giving to the few a very visible one." Adam Smith pointed out that there was "more equality . . . among the English colonists than among the inhabitants of the mother country." And Edmund Burke believed that by freeing people from dependence on employers and landowners, the conditions in North America had fostered "a love of freedom" and a "fierce spirit of liberty" that was "the predominating feature" in the colonial character and was "stronger . . . probably than in any other people of the earth."[33] This quality of colonial existence made America "exceptional," distinguishing the colonies even from the liberty-loving Britons, who were themselves exceptional compared to the rest of Europe.

America's early exceptionalism depended, however, on the endless supply of land on which to settle and build a new life. Unprecedented freedom depended partly on unceasing territorial expansion to open avenues for individual initiative and success. Expansion provided the distance necessary to keep people relatively free from government and ecclesiastical authority.[34] It provided those ineffable but intensely craved human satisfactions: honor and self-respect.[35] For a young man starting out in life in mid-eighteenth-century America—a man such as George Washington—the amassing of land in the yet-to-be-settled West was a chance to achieve a status in society that might otherwise have eluded him.[36] "Land is the most permanent estate," he once wrote, "and the most likely to increase in value."[37] At age eighteen Washington had already become a landowner and land speculator, and he devoted much of the quarter century before the Revolution to adding thousands of acres of western land to his holdings. To one friend down on his luck he relayed advice that showed the importance of land in his mind. "There is a large field before you," he wrote his friend, "where an enterprising Man with very little Money may lay the foundation of a Noble Estate." Look at the fortunes already made in Virginia, he advised. "Was it not by taking up & purchasing at very low rates the rich back Lands which were thought nothing of in those days, but are now the most valuable Lands we possess? Undoubtedly it was."[38] Washington's own national fame was not unrelated to the landed wealth he acquired, for although it often drained him of resources, especially at Mount Vernon, its value allowed him to borrow heavily and then spend generously outfitting his soldiers, lending money to devoted followers in his country, and making his Mount Vernon home a center of Virginia society. Land allowed him to do all the things a prominent gentleman of colonial Virginia was supposed to do.

The material and intangible opportunities offered by land set in motion a cycle of expansion and prosperity in the colonial era. The constant availability of land for settlement pulled workers out of the cities, thus creating a scarcity of urban laborers, which in turn drove wages in the colonies higher than they were in Europe. High wages in the New World attracted more immigrants, who after a few years of employment became new seekers of more land on which to settle. The ever-growing population of land-hungry settlers and the existence of enormous tracts of fertile land east of the Mississippi River, encumbered only by the native inhabitants and their French and Spanish supporters, produced an irresistible pressure for more expansion. This expansionist cycle built up so much momentum in the middle of the eighteenth century that it drove the Anglo-American colonies into a world war. Then, two decades later, it helped drive them to independence.

The "Policy of Savages"

BY MIDCENTURY the most desirable lands within the boundaries of the old colonies had been occupied, or so it seemed to many. The obvious next stage was to expand farther west, beyond the Allegheny Mountains into the rich lands of the Ohio Valley. In the late 1740s those in the colonies who had the influence and the wherewithal to stake a claim to these western lands did so, even if the lands were controlled by others. The Virginia aristocracy dove in with two new joint-stock companies in the late 1740s. One was the Ohio Company, formed by the prominent Virginia politician Thomas Lee, which included among its members the illustrious Fairfax family, as well as the lieutenant governor of the colony, Robert Dinwiddie, and George Washington's older brother, Lawrence. To pull strings in London, the Ohio Company counted the Duke of Bedford among its members. In 1749 George II granted a half million acres of Ohio Valley land to the company, with the stipulation that the shareholders erect a fort and settle at least one hundred families on the forks of the Ohio River. Thus would the interests of the nascent British Empire also be served in its ongoing competition with the French.

One can hardly exaggerate the degree to which American leaders, including future leaders of the independent republic, had a direct, personal interest in this new phase of territorial expansion. Washington was not the only founding father with a stake in the Ohio Valley. Thomas Jefferson was a land speculator by inheritance: his father bequeathed to him and his brothers and sisters a share in the Loyal Land Company, the main competitor of the Ohio Company, which had been "granted" eight hundred thousand acres by the Virginia House of Burgesses.[39] Another prominent Virginian, Patrick Henry, also had speculative interests in western land. Nor was it strictly a Virginia phenomenon. In Pennsylvania Benjamin Franklin served as agent for powerful colonials seeking their own concessions in the Ohio Valley, spurred in part by fear that Virginia would grab everything and leave Pennsylvanians locked out of the West. Connecticut competed for western lands, too, as did Massachusetts, where even evangelical missionaries like Jonathan Edwards were tied up with land speculation, either through their powerful patrons and congregants or, like Edwards, as "owners" of western lands themselves.

The problem was that the British colonies were not alone in wanting the Ohio Valley. The King of France claimed it with equal if not greater justice, for he had actually implanted French settlers, and French forts, on the contested lands. And then, of course, there were the Indians who actually dwelled on the lands that the colonists and their imperial backers were granting to themselves. Any new Anglo-American settlement in the Ohio Valley would come with a struggle and probably war. As American speculators and would-be settlers well knew, therefore, all this land and the great opportunities it afforded could not be obtained without the aid of the powerful British Empire.

Mid-eighteenth-century Anglo-Americans thus became the most enthusiastic of British imperialists. This was no great leap. Most colonists had long been proud and loyal members of the British Empire, despite the tensions and resentments that occasionally flared up between the colonies and the London authorities. By the middle of the eighteenth century, colonial elites, far from seeking separation from the Old World, aspired to be more British in their habits, their manners, and their dress. Washington furnished Mount Vernon with such specimens of English luxury and taste as he could afford. As a young man rising in prominence in Virginia, he yearned for a commission in the British regular army, an achievement that would have laid the basis for a comfortable and successful imperial career. Only lack of influence in London prevented him from attaining this ambition. Benjamin Franklin, too, was "intellectually and culturally . . . an Englishman," who aspired for many years to settle down in England permanently or, failing that, to win a position working for the imperial authorities in the colonies— as a tax collector.[40] Jonathan Edwards considered himself "first of all as a

British citizen." His closest ally in the revival movement on both sides of the Atlantic was the British preacher George Whitefield, and Edwards made no distinction between New and Old England, calling them together "our nation."[41]

Edwards's strong sense of British nationalism provided a window on the way colonists both prided themselves on their Britishness and counted on the strength of the empire to further their interests, both material and spiritual. In the mind of Edwards, and probably of many of his followers, the success of the international Protestant mission depended entirely on the success of the British Empire. Since the accession of the Protestant Hanoverian line to the British throne in 1714, "New Englanders had shed their Puritan outsider image and identified themselves with the Protestant and British cause." Great Britain was the great champion of international Protestantism, and Edwards believed that God worked His will through favored nations and empires. In this sense the New Israel, God's chosen instrument, was not America but the British Empire.[42]

Some scholars have argued that the Anglo-Americans were the earliest and most ardent advocates of the idea of a British Empire, more so than their English brethren across the Atlantic.[43] Certainly the colonists found nothing objectionable in the idea of empire. The word did not connote to them despotic and arbitrary rule by a superior power over weaker and inferior peoples. To the contrary, in the colonists' conception of the British Empire, they were coequal with those who lived in the British Isles—a perception that would take on revolutionary significance in the 1760s when the imperial authorities acted according to a different conception of the relationship between colony and mother country. Before the colonial crisis of the 1760s, most leading Americans were content to pursue their great destiny, both individually and collectively, as Britons.[44] Indeed, the British Empire was the vessel that colonists counted on to deliver them into a prosperous and secure future.

Close identification with the empire was especially desirable when it served immediate expansionist and commercial interests. Anglo-American leaders knew their disunited and jealous colonies were unlikely to succeed in pushing back the French and Indians and capturing the Ohio Valley on their own. The colonies were "like the separate Filaments of Flax before the Thread is form'd," Franklin complained, "without Strength, because without Connection." A colonial union might "make us strong, and even formidable."[45] But that union seemed hopelessly elusive. Failed attempts to organize the colonies into a cohesive force, such as in the abortive Albany Plan of Union in 1754, served only to convince ambitious colonials like

Franklin that they needed the unity, the guidance, and the muscle that only London could provide.

Promoting the idea of empire was useful in the colonists' effort to sway the British public and authorities. Anglo-Americans hoped to give Britons on the other side of the ocean a sense of pride in their imperial mission in North America. The people of Great Britain and the people of the colonies, Franklin suggested in the early 1750s, should "learn to consider themselves, as not belonging to a different community with different interests, but to one community with one interest." The "colonies bordering on the French are properly frontiers of the British Empire," he insisted, "and the frontiers of an empire are properly defended at the joint expense of the body of the people in such an empire."[46]

The idea of a territorial empire on the North American continent was not what most imperialistic Britons initially had in mind in the eighteenth century, however. Before the Seven Years' War with France, their fascination was with maritime empire. Britannia ruled the waves, not the wilderness. Political theorists believed maritime empire better suited to Britain's political economy and its special genius as a commercial nation. And it was compatible with British liberty. Vast landed empires tended toward despotism, or so it was widely believed. Roman republicanism and freedom had been undone by territorial conquest. In the modern era the Bourbons and absolute monarchies on the Continent dreamed of creating a "Universal Monarchy" there. Britain's great destiny lay along a different path, on the oceans. James Harrington offered a compelling vision of a British Empire at once powerful, prosperous, free, and, what would later be of keen interest to revolutionary Americans, republican. His imaginary "Commonwealth of Oceana" would be "a commonwealth for increase," a producer of wealth both for itself and for others, benevolent in its strength and beneficial to all it touched with its commerce. As he put it, quoting Cicero, "[W]e have rather undertaken the patronage than the empire of the world."[47] From the end of the seventeenth through the first half of the eighteenth century, "[t]rade, shipping, the Navy"—not colonization—were the meaning and purpose of empire for most Englishmen.[48]

There was a clash, therefore, between the Anglo-American and the British imperial ideas. A century later, in the middle of the nineteenth century, the British idea of maritime dominance, and even of "tutelary" empire, would inspire such influential Americans as William Seward and James G. Blaine, who wanted nothing more than to emulate the British dominance of the seas and of international trade. They would use language strikingly similar to Harrington's and Cicero's in imagining the United States under-

taking "rather the patronage than the empire of the world." Among the
founding generation, Alexander Hamilton, born on a Caribbean island into
a world of seagoing traders, also hoped to establish a maritime empire modeled after the British. But most of Hamilton's colleagues, such as the Virginians Washington and Jefferson and the Pennsylvanian Franklin, were
determined territorial imperialists who looked westward across the continent for America's destiny. They were repeatedly disappointed by British
unwillingness to support western conquest. In the Treaty of Utrecht of
1713, following the War of the Spanish Succession, the British had agreed
to let France keep its imperial outposts in North America and had established an Indian "buffer" between their respective colonial holdings. The
settlement served the interest of European stability, promising "to confirm
the peace and tranquility of the Christian world through a just equilibrium
of power."[49] In this European drama, North America was a sideshow.

It was no sideshow to the colonists. A "just equilibrium of power" on
the continent was the last thing they wanted. Settlers found the treaty limits
imposed by the British authorities intolerable and made constant forays into
the buffer zone, clashing with Indians, provoking bloody counterattacks,
and repeatedly disturbing British efforts to maintain a stable peace with
France in North America. British imperial commanders reported in frustration that the Anglo-American settlers were "too Numerous, too Lawless
and Licentious ever to be restrained."[50] The Anglo-American colonists
opposed the very presence of France in North America. They detested having a Catholic power as a neighbor. They wanted France's northern territories for themselves and resented French support for Indian tribes that
opposed their expansion. But during the War of the Austrian Succession in
the late 1740s—another war fought chiefly in Europe—British authorities
repeatedly rejected colonial appeals for an invasion of French Canada. On
the one occasion the British did support a foray into Canada, they undid the
colonists' ambitious plans by giving the prize back to France.

That episode was an instructive example of the clash between aggressive colonials and more cautious London ministers. In 1745 the New
England colonists launched an attack against the important French stronghold of Louisbourg, on Cape Breton Island. The expedition, organized by
Massachusetts governor William Shirley, produced unprecedented colonial
unity and determination, particularly among the New Englanders, who mus-
tered four thousand volunteers for the fight. Twenty of Jonathan Edwards's
congregants took part in the siege and capture of the French fortress, inspired
by the motto the evangelical English preacher George Whitefield chose
for their banner: *Nil desperandum Christo duce*. Back in Massachusetts

Edwards led his people in prayers for victory, urging them to purge them-selves of sin, for "[s]in above all things weakens a people at war." (In response to such exhortations, the impious Benjamin Franklin quipped, "in attacking strong towns I should have more dependence on works, than on faith.") The triumph at Louisbourg in 1745 was celebrated on both sides of the Atlantic, but much more so in the colonies. The New England evangeli-cal preacher Thomas Prince prayed that "this happy conquest be the dawn-ing earnest of our divine redeemer's carrying on his triumphs through the Northern Regions; 'till he extends his empire . . . from the river of Canada to the ends of America."[51]

But the rulers of that empire back in London did not share American enthusiasm for driving the French from North America. In the compro-mise peace of Aix-la-Chapelle in 1748, the British returned Louisbourg to France, leaving the colonists again embittered at the mother country's betrayal of their interests.

Embittered but not daunted. In the coming years the colonists redoubled their efforts to enlist British imperial support for continental expansion against the French and Indians. The newly minted Ohio and Loyal Land companies were staking their claim in the Ohio Valley. Edwards's congre-gants in Massachusetts were buying stock in the Susquehanna Company, which sought lands farther north across the Alleghenies. Pennsylvanians were in the hunt for land, too. The colonies, glutted by their growing popu-lation, were an expansionist pressure cooker.

The danger posed by the ambitious Anglo-Americans was not lost on their French and Indian neighbors. The Indians had the most to fear. The buffer zone, their homeland, was being breached, and the delicate bal-ance of power on which their peace and security depended was being upset. In eighteenth-century North America it was the Indians, not the Anglo-Americans, who revered the balance of power. "The great ruling principle of modern Indian politics," one British official observed, was "to preserve the balance between us & the French." But by the 1750s the balance was shifting inexorably toward the British, with their hordes of immigrants and settlers. In 1754, when there were seventy thousand French colonists in all of North America, the Anglo-American population stood at 1.5 million. Nor did the Indians fail to discern the difference between the two imperial forces. The French were interested primarily in trade and secondarily in missionary work. They wanted a firm grip on the waterways that led from the St. Law-rence through the Great Lakes to the Mississippi, and they would expand their holdings in the region if they could. But Louis XIV and Louis XV were preoccupied with affairs in Europe and would not spare the manpower to settle a vast French population in the heartland of North America. The Anglo-Americans did. They wanted to settle new land, and they were settling it at an alarming pace. As one Indian leader told his compatriots, "Brethren, are you ignorant of the difference between our Father [the French] and the English? Go and see the forts our Father has created, and you will see that the land beneath their walls is still hunting ground, . . . whilst the English, on the contrary, no sooner get possession of a country than the game is forced to leave; the trees fall down before them, the earth becomes bare."[52] The onward-rushing British Protestant civilization with its unfettered individualism spelled doom for Indian lands and Indian civilization in a way that the outer reaches of the French Catholic empire did not. In the short run, this meant the French had a better chance of gaining and keeping Indian support. In the long run, it meant the French stood little chance in the imperial battle for control of the continent.

The French worried that they were losing that battle before a shot was fired. The governor of Canada, the Marquis de La Galissonnière, knew that the threat came not from the authorities in London but from the aggressive colonists, whose expansionist desire for land could neither be sated by concessions nor contained by diplomacy. "While peace appeared to have lulled the jealousy of the English in Europe," the governor warned his superiors in Paris, "this bursts forth in all its violence in America; and if barriers capable of staying its effects be not opposed at this very moment, that nation will place itself in a condition to completely invade the French Colonies at the opening of the first war." The power of the English colonies in North America was "daily increasing," and if some means were not found "to prevent it, [it would] soon absorb not only all the Colonies located in the neighbouring islands of the Tropic, but even all those of the Continent of America."[53] A burst of Anglo-American expansion into the Ohio Valley would sever the strategic link between Canadian New France and the French settlements in Louisiana. To prevent this, the French tried to strengthen their grip on the Ohio Valley and to confine Anglo-American settlement to the eastern slopes of the Appalachians. They extended a chain of forts between the Great Lakes and the Mississippi, and they destroyed a Pennsylvania trading village on the Miami River as a message to other Anglo-Americans who dared encroach.

The Anglo-Americans responded with alarm, thus setting a pattern of American behavior that would persist for the next two centuries. American expansionist ambitions had collided with French ambitions, but Americans perceived the French reaction as unprovoked and aggressive, an effort to strangle the colonies, or worse, push them back from their existing frontiers. The French were "drawing a Line along the Borders of our Settlements in every Province, from the mouth of the St. Lawrence, to the Mouth of the Mississippi," warned Archibald Kennedy, a prominent New York official. The colonists were particularly concerned, as Americans would be for the next half century—until the acquisition of the Louisiana territory solved the problem—about the consequences should the French gain full possession of the land between the colonies and the Mississippi. If that happened, one colonist warned, the Anglo-Americans in the southern colonies would have to submit to their rule "or have their Throats cut, and loose all their Slaves."[54] The colonists therefore turned to the British Empire for help. In 1750 the Massachusetts Assembly begged Governor Shirley to use his good offices to convince the king that "we apprehend it impossible, in the present distressed circumstances of the province, to maintain a force necessary for the defence of so extensive a frontier; and therefore we must humbly rely upon his majesty's paternal goodness . . . for assistance."[55]

The most articulate and vigorous lobbyist for aggressive imperial action against France was Benjamin Franklin. He warned of "the Evident Design of the French to Surround the British Colonies, to fortifie themselves on the Back thereof to take and keep Possession, of the heads of all the Important Rivers, to draw, over the Indians to their Interest, and with the help of such Indians added to such Forces as are already arrived and may hereafter be sent from Europe To be in a Capacity of making a General Attack on the Several Governments."[56] His answer was audacious. He proposed planting "two strong colonies of English . . . settled between the Ohio and Lake Erie," that is, in the very heart of the French territorial claims in the *pays d'en haut*. This meant a renewal of Anglo-French war in both Europe and North America, though Franklin did not say as much. The conquest of this new territory would provide a defense to the western hinterlands of Pennsylvania and other colonies and keep France from becoming a growing threat to the British position in North America. It was a preemptive strike that would at once remove a potential threat and conquer for the colonists and for the British Empire a huge portion of rich and fertile land. "The great country back of the Appalachian Mountains, on both sides of the Ohio, and between that river and the Lakes is now well known, both to the English and French, to be one of the finest in North America, for the extreme richness and fertility of the land; the healthy temperature of the air, and mildness of the climate; the plenty of hunting, fishing, and fowling; the facility of trade with the Indians; and the vast convenience of inland navigation or water-carriage by the Lakes and great rivers, many hundreds of leagues around."[57] Within less than a century, he predicted, this rich territory would become a "populous and powerful dominion," and a "great accession of power" to whichever European empire controlled it. He urged the British imperial authorities to seize the moment, to break French power on the continent once and for all, and to capture the great prize.

The core of Franklin's argument was that continued expansion was essential to survival of the colonies, and by extension the empire. The French were aggressive enemies even if they did nothing more than hold their ground. By preventing the onward advance of British settlement, they had placed intolerable limits on colonial population growth. By "preventing our obtaining more subsistence by cultivating of new lands," he argued, "they discourage our marriages, and keep our people from increasing; thus (if the expression may be allowed) killing thousands of our children before they are born."[58] It was incumbent on the British Empire "to secure Room enough, since on the Room depends so much the Increase of her People." There were "already in the old colonies many thousands of families that are ready to swarm, wanting more land. . . . Our people, being confined to the country between the sea and the mountains, cannot much more increase in number." But the "richness and natural advantage of the Ohio country would draw most of them thither, were there but a tolerable prospect of a safe settlement." Franklin's was, in essence, an argument for living space. Within that space the colonies, and the empire, would rise to unparalleled greatness. And the men responsible for this historic achievement would earn lasting fame and the gratitude of posterity. Echoing Machiavelli, Franklin flattered his British audience that "the Prince [or Princes] that acquires new Territory, if he finds it vacant, or removes the Natives to give his own People Room . . . may be properly called Fathers of their Nation, as they are the Cause of the Generation of Multitudes, by the Encouragement they afford to Marriage." Franklin could even envision himself in this historic role, for as he wrote to a friend, "I sometimes wish that you and I were jointly employ'd by the Crown, to settle a Colony on the Ohio. . . . What a security to the other Colonies; and Advantage to Britain, by Increasing her People, Territory, Strength and Commerce."[59]

Instead the task was left to the British Empire. The appeals of Franklin and other colonial leaders for imperial action had finally fallen on receptive ears in London. After decades of relative neglect of North America in favor of preserving a balance of power in Europe, British public opinion in the late 1740s and early 1750s was growing more bellicose. A powerful faction in Parliament wanted more aggressive action against France, which many believed to be on the move in both Europe and North America. Some shared the colonists' unhappiness with the way the last Anglo-French war had ended in the 1740s, especially the return of Louisbourg in the Treaty of Aix-la-Chappelle. The long, stable peace pursued by the ministry of Robert Walpole was losing popularity, and a trio of powerful ministers in the 1750s sought to counter what they regarded as the growing French menace.

The spark that ignited the destructive Seven Years' War, however, came not from any action in London but from the colonies. In 1754 Virginia's governor and influential Ohio Company stockholder, Robert Dinwiddie, dispatched a young colonel of the Virginia militia, George Washington, to the forks of the Ohio River to construct a British fort. On the way to the forks, Washington routed a small force of French and Indians—an attack that resulted in the murder and mutilation of the French commander—only to be defeated and captured in turn by a superior French force at the site of the indefensible Fort Necessity, which Washington hastily erected. The British responded to the bloodshed by launching a four-pronged offensive in North America, including an assault on French positions in Canada. The imperial struggle between France and Britain was under way in North America two years before war began in the European theater.

This was what colonial leaders had been waiting for, and not only the leaders. The launching of full-scale imperial conflict excited and united the populations of the Anglo-American colonies as never before, despite some staggering setbacks in the first years of the conflict. The invasion of the Ohio Valley led by General Edward Braddock, with several regiments of regulars and George Washington as his aide-de-camp, ended in disaster for everyone except the Virginia colonel, who became famous throughout the colonies for his valor despite the slaughter of Braddock and his regulars. Another attack into Canada by forces from New England fared just as badly. But in the campaigns of 1758, 1759, and 1760, the tide began to turn. In part, the sheer power and wealth of the modern British Empire overwhelmed the more backward French. Much like the United States in the twentieth century, mid-eighteenth-century Britain possessed an unmatched capacity for producing warships and cannons, and an equally impressive ability to project military power across a wide ocean. These feats "reflected British superiority in shipping, finance, and organization," which in turn reflected "the more advanced nature of Britain as a capitalist society endowed with far more liquid capital and financial acumen" than France. To some extent, the British won simply by outspending their enemy. The eventual conquest of Canada cost Britain about four million pounds, ten times what the French spent to defend it. As Alan Taylor has noted, "Never before had any empire spent so much money to wage war on a transoceanic scale."[60]

The British also benefited, however, from the power of a colonial population cooperating "in the imperial enterprise with an enthusiasm and a vigor unprecedented in their history." The colonials had long aimed at destroying the French position in Canada, and now with the full backing of the empire they threw themselves into the assault with contributions of men and resources. This was not a war that the colonists watched from a distance. "To a degree virtually unknown in the eighteenth century, every colony north of Virginia . . . experienced the conflict as a people's war."[61] Massachusetts led the way in raising volunteers for the conquest of Canada, and militia from various northern colonies made up a substantial portion of the overall attacking force. Nor was colonial fighting limited to Canada. When the British attacked and subdued the Spanish port city of Havana in 1762, thus removing a main pillar of Spanish power in the Caribbean, North American colonists made up one-quarter of the force.

This "people's war" affected every segment of colonial society. The colonial aristocracy led the battles, the taxpayers paid for the battles, and the plain folk fought the battles. Even the evangelical preachers of the Great Awakening did their part, rallying the faithful, warning against sin, and, most important, converting Indians in the hope of bringing them over to the British side. Jonathan Edwards himself had long been aware of the "immense strategic importance" of building good relations with the Mohawks, and the religious boarding school he established in Stockbridge for the education of Indian children was a deliberate weapon in the imperial struggle. "The only remaining means that divine providence hath left us to repair and secure these Indians in the British interest," he declared, "is this very thing . . . of instructing them thoroughly in the Protestant religion, and educating their children." He had no qualms about mixing the secular, imperial mission with his religious mission. He "never questioned the premise that God used Christian empires to bring his message to unevangelized peoples."[62]

The fall of Quebec in 1759 was a triumphant turning point in the histories of both the colonies and the empire, and so it was understood at the time. The Reverend Jonathan Mayhew, preaching to his excited Boston throng, looked forward to the day when North America would be home to "a mighty empire (I do not mean an independent one) in numbers little inferior to the greatest in Europe, and in felicity to none." Spurred by the conquest, Mayhew's imagination ran wild, although in truth not that wild, as he contemplated the future British American Empire. "Methinks I see mighty cities rising on every hill, and by the side of every commodious port; mighty fleets alternately sailing out and returning, laden with the produce of this, and every other country under heaven; happy fields and villages wherever I turn my eyes, thro' a vastly extended territory."[63] Franklin, too, exulted at the fall of Canada, "not merely as I am a colonist, but as I am a Briton."[64] The citizens of New York raised statues of William Pitt and King George III, and Boston "observed the occasion with an intensity suited to the colony most enthusiastically engaged in the war."[65]

No sooner had the colonists finished celebrating, however, than the disjunction between British and American imperial visions returned to the fore. After the conquest of Quebec a debate opened in Great Britain over whether French Canada should be held or returned to France in the coming peace settlement. Articulate voices in Britain, among them William Burke, brother of the more famous Edmund, made the case for turning Canada back to France. It was filled with harsh criticism of the American colonists' aggressiveness and greed for land. For a variety of reasons, colonial talk of a "mighty empire" in North America did not sit well with all Britons.

Burke worried about the potentially dangerous growth of the British Empire, the fear it might inspire in others, and the arrogance it might inspire in the British people themselves. The "Genius and Dispositions of Nations, as well as Men, is best discerned by the use they make of Power," Burke argued. And the most "rational" ambition for Britain should be to make the nation's power "respectable rather than terrible." Citing Montesquieu, he warned of the fate of Rome, as well as of imperial France and Spain, empires that had decayed and fallen because "they had attained a greater Power than they had wisdom sufficient to direct; for the sake of gratifying the passion of the Day, they lost sight of their lasting Interest."[66] Now Britain stood on the edge of making the same fatal mistake, largely to satisfy the passions and ambitions of its colonists in North America. Why keep Canada? Burke asked. Britain had not launched the war in order to conquer it and did not need it for security. On the contrary, taking Canada from France would only embitter the French and instill a desire for vengeance.

There was another danger, too. If France were driven out of North America, the colonists would have free rein to expand across the entire continent. If "the People of our Colonies find no check from Canada, they will extend themselves, almost, without bounds into the Inland Parts. They are invited to it by the Pleasantness, the Fertility, and the Plenty of that Country; and they will increase infinitely from all Causes." There was "a Balance of Power in America as well as in Europe," Burke reminded his compatriots. Upsetting that balance might prove dangerous to Britain. "A neighbour that keeps us in some Awe, is not always the worst of Neighbours." The colonists' ambitions were dangerous and uncivilized. They needed to be "taught a lesson of Moderation." The idea that one could feel secure "only by having no other Nation near you" was alien and repulsive to the European mind. Yet this was what the colonists demanded. It was the "Policy of Savages."[67]

Burke put his finger on the sharp distinction between the principles of balance and restraint that, in theory at least, characterized the eighteenth-century European order, and the kind of aggressive, immoderate, seemingly limitless expansionism of the Anglo-Americans. If this latter approach was indeed the "policy of savages," then the most articulate and determined savage was Ben Franklin. The Pennsylvanian angrily refuted Burke's points. True, he admitted, the seizure of Canada had not been the initial aim of war. But that was only because the British Empire had lacked the power to demand Canada. Now, in victory, it could. "Advantages gain'd in the course of this war may increase the extent of our rights," by which Franklin meant rights of conquest.[68]

Some historians have described Franklin as a "realist," and if realism means a belief that all nations pursue as much power as they can, and that justice is usually determined by the victor, then he was. But his realism did not extend to a belief in the balance of power, at least not on the American continent; nor did it entail a sense of limit and restraint. He had no interest in balanced coexistence with France. He desired and demanded a level of security for Anglo-Americans that was, as Burke suggested, unheard of in Europe. Security, for Franklin, meant total security. He responded angrily to Burke's suggestion that the French served as a useful "check" on overweening colonial ambitions. "'Tis a modest word, this, check, for massacring men, women and children. . . . We have already seen in what manner the French and their Indians check the growth of our colonies."[69]

Franklin also expressed the kind of ambition, both for the colonies and for the British Empire, that Burke found so appallingly "savage." "No one can more sincerely rejoice than I do, on the reduction of Canada," Franklin wrote. "I have long been of opinion, that the foundations of the future grandeur and stability of the British empire lie in America; and though, like other foundations, they are low and little seen, they are, nevertheless, broad and strong enough to support the greatest political structure human wisdom ever yet erected. I am therefore by no means for restoring Canada. If we keep it, all the country from the St. Lawrence to the Mississippi will in another century be filled with British people. Britain itself will become vastly more populous, by the immense increase of its commerce; the Atlantic sea will be covered with your trading ships; and your naval power, thence continually increasing, will extend your influence round the whole globe, and awe the world!"[70]

This prediction proved accurate, at least in part. Franklin's only error—and it may have been less an error than diplomatic tact—was in prophesying that the British Empire would be the beneficiary of the great North American acquisitions rather than the Anglo-Americans themselves. Thanks to William Pitt, Franklin and his compatriots won the argument over Canada. The warnings of Burke were rejected. Britain kept most of the former French colonies in North America—and within a little more than a decade, lost its own.

Power and Independence

THAT THE COLONIES MIGHT someday break away from the mother country and form their own independent empire had been predicted long before the Seven Years' War began the unraveling. Even in the 1650s James Harrington had described the colonies "as yet babes that cannot live without suckling the breasts of their mother-Cities, but such as, I mistake, if when they come of age they do not wean themselves." In the 1730s a French minister could foresee "one fine morning" when the British colonists, with their own "parliament, governors, soldiers . . . riches, laws, and, what is worse, a naval force," would awaken and ask, "Why should we be dominated by England from Europe? Let us be our own masters and work only for ourselves." It was no secret, either to foreign observers or to Britons and Anglo-Americans, that the presence of France in Canada had always been the greatest barrier to the colonists pursuing this independent destiny. William Burke was not alone in making this point, and Anglo-Americans knew that there was more than a little trepidation in Great Britain after 1759 about removing the French obstacle to colonial ambitions. As Thomas Hutchinson, the governor of Massachusetts, later recalled, this awareness of British concern by itself kindled colonial ambitions. The mere fact that Britons were discussing the danger of colonial independence was "sufficient to set enterprising men [in the colonies] upon considering how far such a separation was expedient and practicable."[71]

What, exactly, turned the colonists, or at least a substantial number of them, from loyal British subjects to rebellious Americans has been the subject of innumerable studies. There is no simple answer. The colonists at the time insisted the issue was taxes and the right to levy them, and if one understands it in the broadest sense, there is no reason to quarrel with the claim. The problem was not only that Anglo-Americans did not want to pay the new taxes and duties that the imperial authorities attempted to impose after the war with France. They also insisted that the way the taxes were levied, by a faraway Parliament in which they were not and could not be represented, violated their rights as Englishmen, and that this was part of a broader effort to impair their liberties and make them "slaves." There was truth in this charge, even if the colonists distorted and exaggerated Parliament's motives and intentions.[72] After the war with France, much of which was fought in North America for the obvious benefit of the colonists and at enormous expense, British ministers considered it reasonable that the colonists should pay a portion of the cost both of the war and of the continuing protection they enjoyed from the empire. But beyond that, British authorities also believed it was high time to put their new "empire" in some order. The colonists had urged them to take the imperial idea seriously, and unfortunately for the colonists they did. As Fred Anderson has noted, "The lessons of the war . . . encouraged both Grenville and Halifax to conceive of the great new empire in strategic terms, as an entity to be directed from Whitehall according to British policy aims." It seemed inconceivable under the new circumstances to "allow the colonies to return to their old, slovenly, parochial ways" and to allow Americans "to benefit from Britain's protection without contributing anything in return."[73] The British authorities in London certainly did not share the colonists' conception of an empire in which all component parts were sovereign and autonomous. Rather, they considered colonial interests subordinate to British imperial interests.

The question of imperial relations was worthy of serious debate. The colonists, however, did not always respond in a serious fashion to British efforts to bring coherence to the situation. One of the more absurd colonial responses also proved to be one of the most significant in shaping Americans' subsequent self-image. Speaking in London before the House of Commons in 1766, Benjamin Franklin declared without apparent embarrassment that the colonists had, in fact, no interest whatsoever in the late war. "I know the last war is commonly spoken of here, as entered into for the defence, or for the sake, of the people of North America," Franklin told Parliament. But "I think it is quite misunderstood." The war had not been fought for colonial interests. It "was really a British war," a "dispute between the two Crowns" of Britain and France in which the colonists had no stake. The colonials had suffered no difficulties in the Ohio Valley before the war, Franklin claimed. They were "in perfect peace with both French and Indians." As for Canada, Franklin insisted, that dispute was also one in which the colonists had "no particular concern or interest." Indeed, Franklin suggested, the people of Great Britain should be grateful to the colonies. Despite the fact that the war over the Ohio Valley and Canada was a matter of utter indifference to the colonists, nevertheless "the people of America made no scruple of contributing their utmost towards carrying it on, and bringing it to a happy conclusion."[74] A sympathetic biographer has noted the extent to which Franklin "falsified history" in this speech, and one can only imagine the reaction of those members of Parliament who remembered Franklin's passionate pleas six years earlier for the conquest and retention of both the Ohio Valley and Canada.[75] But in professing colonial disinterest in the late war with France, Franklin helped lay the foundation for the American myth of innocence and self-abnegation—and did so quite successfully. A few years later Thomas Paine, in his famous revolutionary pamphlet *Common Sense,* repeated the American claim that all the wars fought in North America in the seventeenth and eighteenth centuries had been wars by and for the King of England, not for the colonists, who were ever inclined toward peace.[76] Even two centuries later American historians would still describe early Americans as possessing a "self-denying" idealism, and leading textbook histories of American foreign policy would note that "the British Empire" had spent decades at war in the late seventeenth and eighteenth centuries and that "for the colonies, the cost had sometimes been heavy."[77] Thus did the specious arguments of Ben Franklin and other colonists live on to shape Americans' image of themselves as passive innocents who were continually swept into the wars of others.

The more serious disagreement between the colonists and the mother country, however, was over the terms of empire. The colonists began not by renouncing the empire but by extolling what they claimed to be its virtues. They insisted that the various parts of the empire enjoyed equal rights amounting, in the end, to self-government under the overall rule of the crown. One year before the bloodshed at Lexington and Concord, the Virginia Convention was still committed to "the security and happiness of the British Empire," insisting only that "assumptions of unlawful power" by Parliament were the chief threat to the "harmony and union" of all the peoples within that empire. Jefferson appealed to the king to intervene against one legislature within his realm attempting to subjugate another. This idea of empire was, in a sense, a federal vision, akin to what Jefferson would later imagine as the American "empire of liberty." A century and a half later the British themselves would adopt this idea in the form of the British Commonwealth of Nations. Even at the time of the colonial quarrel some Britons, notably Edmund Burke and Adam Smith, recommended that Anglo-Americans be granted substantial autonomy within the empire, on both political and practical grounds. "The British Empire must be governed on a plan of freedom," Burke argued, "for it will be governed by no other." Smith even imagined that as the Anglo-American portion of the empire grew stronger and richer, London might cease to be the metropolitan center, and "the seat of the empire would then naturally remove itself to that part of the empire which contributed most to the general defence and support of the whole." But few Britons, least of all George III and his ministers, were prepared to accept this loose definition of their empire. The king declared his determination to "withstand any attempt to weaken or impair the supreme authority of this legislature over all the dominions of my crown; the maintenance of which I consider as essential to the dignity, the safety and the welfare of the British Empire."[78]

The idea of an empire of sovereign equals therefore provided no answer to the conflict between the colonies and the mother country. But the argument advanced by the colonists would have lasting significance. It has often been argued that Americans were born anti-imperialists because they revolted from an empire. But the separation from Great Britain left a more complicated and ambiguous legacy. Right up until the outbreak of war, Americans argued for a conception of empire that provided for autonomy and equality among the various parts. They convinced themselves that this was, in fact, the way the British Empire was supposed to operate. The British Empire was itself, in American eyes, an "empire of liberty," and this conception bore a close resemblance to the federative principle on which the continental empire of the United States would be based. The American continental empire would be a federation of equals under a common sovereign, and it is notable that this American federative principle was invented not after the Revolution but in the imperial struggle that preceded it. It meant that in the minds of eighteenth-century Americans, "empire" was not incompatible with "liberty"; and that American territorial expansion, despite what Montesquieu and many Britons might believe, need not be incompatible with the preservation and extension of republican freedom at home and abroad.

Whatever role such disagreements had in bringing about the separation of the colonies from the mother country, there was one important cause of the Revolution that has often been neglected: power. British attempts to put the empire on a more orderly and sustainable footing came at a time when the colonies' own power relative to Britain had grown considerably. Just as observers such as William Burke had warned, the removal of the French from Canada had significantly shifted the balance of power between the colonies and the mother country. As one British pamphleteer had put it during the debate over whether or not to retain Canada, if Britain did acquire it, "we should soon find North-America itself too powerful, and too populous to be long governed by us at this distance."[79] And so it was.

Perhaps just as important was the shift in self-perception among the colonists that was occurring at the same time. It is a truism in human affairs that the weak tolerate many things out of necessity that the powerful will not tolerate because they don't have to. As Theodore Draper has noted, the change in the relationship of power between the colonies and the British imperial authorities created a situation in which imperial impositions that the colonists might once have grudgingly accepted instead became "special grievances" that were "unacceptable to the colonial political consciousness."[80] Looking back from the 1780s, David Ramsay, the first historian of the American Revolution, saw the Anglo-American participation in military attacks on French outposts during the Seven Years' War as the first evidence of the colonies' "increasing importance" and "political consequence"—and the first inkling of their desire for independence.[81] An Englishman traveling through the colonies in 1760 found that the colonists were "looking forward with eager and impatient expectation to that destined moment when America is to give law to the rest of the world."[82] Increasing power created increasing ambition and increasing intolerance for any obstacles that stood in the way.

Anglo-Americans in the two decades before independence were becoming convinced that they were destined for greatness—greatness as part of the British Empire but also, perhaps, as an empire on their own. Some of these great expectations came from the successes against France. But there seemed to be other signs pointing the way. One was the extraordinary economic success of the colonies. Between 1650 and 1770 their gross national product multiplied twenty-five times, increasing at an annual rate of 3.7 percent, with a per capita increase in wealth that was twice that of Britain's. On the eve of the Revolution, Americans had a higher standard of living than any European country. Indeed, it may have been "the highest achieved for the great bulk of the [free] population in any country up to that time." Much of this economic growth came from production and sales entirely within the rapidly growing colonial market and was therefore independent of export sales to England and Europe. The American economy was dependent not upon foreign investment but on the ingenuity and industriousness of the colonials themselves.[83]

Americans saw their economy as the essential engine of the British Empire and its future progress. They believed that Britons across the Atlantic depended on the American economy for their survival, and their conviction was strengthened by the retreat of the imperial authorities in repealing the Stamp Act in 1766. As Ramsay recalled, the lesson to colonists was that "instead of feeling themselves dependent on Great-Britain, she was dependent on them." This realization "inspired them with such high ideas of importance of their trade" that they "conceived it to be within their power, by future combinations, at any time to convulse, if not bankrupt the nation, from which they sprung." This belief, which was shared by Hamilton and many other colonial leaders, later gave Madison and Jefferson the (misplaced) confidence that they could influence British behavior by means of trade embargoes. As Hamilton concluded, the colonies' nonimportation measures showed "how much importance our commercial connexion is to [Great Britain]; and gives us the highest assurance of obtaining immediate redress by suspending it."[84] Nor was this simply an American conceit. The French foreign minister wrote in 1759, "The true balance of power really resides in commerce and in America."[85] A similar judgment led Adam Smith to conclude that in time the seat of empire would move to North America, since that is where the preponderance of wealth would reside.

The colonists were also impressed by the prodigious growth of their population, the result of both immigration and high birth rates. Between 1660 and 1760 it had grown from 75,000 inhabitants to over 1.6 million, an increase of over 1,000 percent. Between 1720 and 1760 Connecticut's population rose from 60,000 to 140,000; Maryland's increased from 60,000 to 160,000; and Virginia's population grew from 130,000 to 310,000.[86] The most amazing statistic, which men like Franklin and Washington and John Adams never tired of repeating, was that the American population was doubling every twenty-five years, much faster than that of any European nation. As Draper has pointed out, this population growth gave Americans a "sense of immanent greatness." Optimism about America's future influenced how they behaved in the present. It "enabled the colonies to defy the greatest empire in the world."[87]

Many colonists believed that although the British Empire had helped them in the past, it had now become an obstacle to their ambitions. Not the least of the colonists' resentments was the ban the British government imposed on further territorial expansion after the war. In order to establish a stable peace with the Indians, who were launching attacks up and down the continent in what was known as Pontiac's Rebellion, the British drew a line from the Great Lakes to Florida and from the Mississippi to the western slope of the Appalachians, and designated all this territory as reserved for the Indians. Beyond this Proclamation Line of 1763, colonial governments were forbidden to grant lands, surveyors were not allowed to operate, no treaties with Indians were to be negotiated, and no land purchases were to be made except by the king's representatives. Settlers living within the zone had to pull up stakes and leave. The great Ohio Valley, which the colonials had long sought, was once again denied them.

As so often in the past, however, the colonists treated the Proclamation Line as one more imperial regulation to be ignored. Speculators speculated, settlers settled, and even ten thousand British regulars could not stop them. But the Proclamation Line did serve as another irritant, another shackle that colonists struggled to throw off. As Washington told a friend, "I can never look upon that Proclamation in any other light . . . than as a temporary expedient to quiet the Minds of the Indians & [one that] must fall of course in a few years especially when those Indians are consenting to our Occupying the Lands."[88] The Proclamation Line was also on the bill of particulars that Jefferson offered in 1774 in his *Summary View of the Rights of British America*. Expressing the nascent "republican" conception of government evolving at the time, Jefferson insisted that "[k]ings are the servants, not the proprietors of the people." George III had "no right to grant lands of himself." That was for the people to decide.[89]

British restrictions on expansion were only one of the grievances that were leading many colonists slowly—and for most, painfully—to the conclusion that their interests might be better served apart from the British Empire. After the Stamp Act crisis, Americans felt their ambitions stymied by British impositions in all aspects of their commercial and political lives. Many, like John Adams, took it personally. "I have groped in dark Obscurity, till of late," Adams complained, "and had but just become known, and gained a small degree of Reputation, when this execrable Project was set on foot for my Ruin as well as that of America in General, and of Great Britain."[90]

This unhappiness with British control was made all the more acute by the colonists' growing sense of self-importance. The victories over France had whetted their appetites for greatness. John Adams speculated, "If we remove the turbulent Gallicks, our people, according to the exactest computations, will in another century become more numerous than England itself. Should this be the case, since we have . . . all the naval stores of the nation in our hands, it will be easy to obtain the mastery of the seas; and the united force of all Europe will not be able to subdue us."[91] Franklin began to speculate that America no longer benefited from membership in the empire: "She may suffer for a while in a separation from it, but these are temporary evils that she will outgrow."[92] The future beckoned. "America, an immense territory, favoured by Nature with all the advantages of climate, soil, great navigable rivers, and lakes, &c. must become a great country, populous and mighty; and will, in less time than is generally conceived, be able to shake off any shackles that may be imposed on her, and perhaps place them on the imposers."[93]

John Trumbull, reciting to the graduating class at Yale in 1770, spun visions of American empire and progress, and at Great Britain's expense.

> In mighty pomp America shall rise;
> Her glories spreading to the boundless skies;
> Of ev'ry fair, she boasts th' assembled charms;
> The Queen of empires and the Nurse of arms.
>
> See bolder Genius quit the narrow shore,
> And unknown realms of science dare t'explore;
> Hiding in the brightness of superior day
> The fainting gleam of Britain's setting ray.[94]

Alexander Hamilton, one of the most ardent promoters of American greatness, prophesied in 1774 that "in fifty or sixty years, America will be in no need of protection from Great-Britain. She will then be able to protect herself, both at home and abroad. She will have a plenty of men and a plenty of materials to provide and equip a formidable navy." As a result, "the scale will then begin to turn in her favour, and the obligation, for future services, will be on the side of Great-Britain."[95]

One striking aspect of this increasing yearning for an independent American greatness was the extent to which Americans—before the Revolution—believed it was their unique liberties that had produced their success and distinguished them even from liberal England. John Trumbull linked cultural greatness with "the unconquered spirit of freedom."[96] Hugh Henry Brackenridge and Philip Freneau, delivering the 1771 commencement address at Princeton, entitled "A Poem on the Rising Glory of America," insisted the muses could sing only "[w]here freedom holds the sacred standard high."[97] In this the Americans believed themselves superior even to the mother country, where the "perfect" English constitution suddenly seemed not so perfect but to have been corrupted by placemen and court intrigue. Franklin expressed the view that would be shared by many future generations of Americans facing many diverse foes: America's special "enthusiasm for liberty" was a source of indomitable power; it "supplied all deficiencies, and enabled a weak people to battle the efforts of the stronger." Franklin sneered at the English, who "have no Idea that any People can act from any other Principle but that of Interest."[98]

Prerevolutionary Americans were convinced that their impending greatness would be measured not only in expansion and prosperity but also in cultural and scientific achievement.[99] They were taught that all the great civilizations of the past had advanced on all fronts simultaneously, with economic, political, cultural, and scientific progress all harmoniously reinforcing one another. Ezra Stiles predicted that the North American continent would be "renowned for Science and Arts."[100] For Brackenridge and Freneau, it was America's destiny to become the "new Athens."[101]

The historical analogy was fitting, though not quite in the way the poets intended. Thucydides relates how the Corinthians described Athens in the fifth century B.C., as a restless people ever on the move, unrelenting in their pursuit of opportunity. They were "incapable of either living a quiet life themselves or of allowing anyone else to do so." If the Athenians aimed "at something and do not get it, they think that they have been deprived of what belonged to them already; whereas, if their enterprise is successful, they regard that success as nothing compared to what they will do next."[102] In the eighteenth century, Americans, too, were in a permanent state of restlessness, driven ever forward and outward by the search for opportunity, accepting momentary delays in achieving their grand ambitions but never abandoning them. By the eve of the Revolution leaders of the colonial rebellion saw themselves no longer as merely the strongest part of the British Empire but as its heirs. Adam Smith observed that the American leaders "feel in themselves at this moment a degree of importance which, perhaps the greatest subjects in Europe scarce feel. From shopkeepers, tradesmen, and attornies, they are become statesmen and legislators, and are employed in contriving a new form of government for an extensive empire, which, they flatter themselves, will become, and which, indeed, seems very likely to become, one of the greatest and most formidable that ever was in the world."[103] In 1776 a prominent South Carolina planter, William Henry Drayton, declared to his fellow Carolinians that "[t]he Almighty . . . has made choice of the present generation to erect the American Empire. . . . And thus has suddenly arisen in the World, a new Empire, stiled the United States of America. An Empire that as soon as started into Existence, attracts the Attention of the Rest of the Universe; and bids fair, by the blessing of God, to be the most glorious of any upon Record."[104]

CHAPTER 2

The Foreign Policy of Revolution

Establishing the liberties of America will not only make that people happy, but will have some effect in diminishing the misery of those, who in other parts of the world groan under despotism.

—Benjamin Franklin, 1782

The American Revolution and the Universalization of American Foreign Policy

BY 1776 the ambitions driving Americans toward their future overwhelming global power were already in place.[1] Aspirations to greatness, visions of empire, and the belief in the exceptional freedoms enjoyed in the colonies all played a part in fomenting the War of Independence with Great Britain. In hindsight, it is hard to imagine how these confident, free, and acquisitive Anglo-American colonists could have long remained subservient to imperial control from London. American independence might have been delayed, perhaps for decades, had the British government pursued a looser style of imperial management after the Seven Years' War, as Edmund Burke, Adam Smith, and others recommended during the colonial crisis of the 1760s and '70s. But some form of colonial autonomy was practically inevitable. The combination of an expanding population, expanding wealth and power, and an expanding sense of colonial rights and freedoms was too potent and explosive a mixture to be pent up.

Whether a more peaceful move toward colonial autonomy would have produced the America we know today is another question. The manner in which the British imperial authorities forced the issue, and the manner in which the Anglo-American colonists responded, had an impact upon the new nation's identity and ideology. It therefore had an impact, as well, on its foreign policy. A struggle for autonomy became a struggle for independence, which in turn became a revolution. American foreign policy, as a result, would also have a revolutionary quality. The American Revolution was more than a separation from the British Empire. It was a separation from the past and a departure into the future. In the course of gaining independence, the Americans invented a new form of politics and social order. They invented the modern liberal republic. They also unwittingly invented a new foreign policy founded upon the universalist ideology that the Revolution spawned.

That the movement for independence took such revolutionary form was less by choice than by necessity. To make a just war for independence, the Americans had to persuade the world, and perhaps also themselves, that their decision to separate from the mother country was legitimate. This in turn required the colonists to abandon traditional theories of government that offered little justification for overthrowing a legitimate sovereign. The idea of a federated empire, with the colonies enjoying autonomy, if not sovereignty, under the crown, was a way station on the road to revolution. When the king himself rejected this interpretation of empire, many colonists believed they had little choice but to take the next step. In their search for justification for breaking free of British control altogether, the colonists turned to the very modern but hitherto untested concepts of the Enlightenment, especially the theories of "natural rights" and the "social compact" propounded by John Locke.

This was no great reach for Anglo-Americans. Like all Britons, the American colonials had long believed they possessed inviolable "natural rights"—even before they appealed to these rights to justify separation from the mother country. The Declaration of Independence stated, following Locke, that if a king or parliament persistently failed to carry out the primary obligation to protect the people in their lives, liberties, and property, then the people had a right to take back sovereign power and form a new government that could protect them. The people could, as the Declaration claimed, frame a new government on such principles "as to them shall seem most likely to effect their Safety and Happiness."[2]

More than two centuries later it is easy to forget what a radical assertion this was, and what a leap into the unknown for the people who asserted it. Just a decade before, Americans had taken immense pride in their Britishness. They had considered themselves the advance guard of British civilization in the New World and had celebrated the victory of British liberties and the British Empire over France. But their allegiance to Britain was inseparable from their enjoyment of those liberties. If the British Crown would not safeguard their natural rights, then they would separate themselves from the crown and from Britain. As Jefferson wrote in a first draft of the Declaration of Independence, "We might have been a free & a great people together. . . . We must endeavor to forget our former love for them."[3] Americans insisted that the rights they enjoyed were not derived from the English constitution, were not merely the product and accretion of centuries of English custom and tradition. They were not the rights of Englishmen. They were universal natural rights, granted by God and enjoyed by all men regardless of nationality, culture, and history.[4] "The sacred rights of mankind are not to be rummaged for among old parchments or musty records," Hamilton declared. "They are written, as with a sunbeam, in the whole volume of human nature by the hand of the divinity itself and can never be erased or obscured by mortal power."[5]

The idea of natural rights was not new. But founding a government and society based on the principle of natural rights *was* new. Until the American Revolution, the principle of natural rights had been "written only among the stars."[6] Such ideas had been mused about all over Europe in the age of Enlightenment, but even the most advanced Enlightenment thinkers had wondered about their practical applicability. No French *philosophe* had yet proposed the overthrow of the French monarchy. The Americans were the first to attempt to vindicate their natural rights in the real world and to erect a nation with universal rights as the foundation. The Declaration of Independence was at once an assertion of this radical principle, a justification for rebellion, and the founding document of American nationhood.

The Declaration of Independence was also America's first foreign policy document. To win foreign support—and, above all, French support—in the war against Britain, the colonists needed to demonstrate their final and irrevocable commitment to fight for their independence. In practical terms, the Declaration provided the international legal basis for France to lend support if it chose. It declared America a sovereign nation, and with that sovereignty came the legal right and ability to form alliances and establish terms of trade with other nations. The United States would "assume among the powers of the earth, the separate and equal station to which the Laws of Nature and of Nature's God entitle them." The Declaration proclaimed that as "free and independent states," the new "united States of America . . . have full Powers to levy War, conclude Peace, contract Alliances, establish Commerce, and to do all other Acts and Things which Independent States may of right do." Some historians have suggested that the Declaration of Independence and the Revolution were an "act of isolation, a cutting of the ties with the Old World, the deed of a society which felt itself different from those which existed on the other side of the Atlantic."[7] Americans did believe they were different, but the purpose of the Declaration was the opposite of isolation. It was to create the legal basis necessary to form alliances with European powers. American independence, from the first, depended on successful diplomacy to secure foreign support. Foreign policy was not merely the "shield of the republic," as Walter Lippmann would later call it. Americans did not form a nation and then embark on a foreign policy to protect and further its interests. They began a foreign policy in order to establish themselves as a nation.

At America's birth, therefore, foreign policy and national identity were intimately bound together, and they would remain so for the next two centuries. Every nation's foreign policy reflects the national idea, however that idea may be defined and redefined over time. Most nationalisms are rooted in blood and soil, in the culture and history of a particular territory. But in the case of the United States, the Declaration of Independence and the Revolution produced a different kind of nationalism, different from that of other nations, and different, too, from the type of British imperial nationalism to which Americans had paid their allegiance before the Revolution. Americans were now tied together not by common ancestry, common history, and common land but by common allegiance to the liberal republican ideology. The principles of the Declaration transcended blood ties and national boundaries. Indeed, it was "only by transcending the English heritage and broadening it beyond the confines of historical-territorial limitation" that Americans were able to "establish their distinctive political existence."[8]

This new universalistic nationalism inevitably shaped Americans' attitudes toward the world, toward their own place and role in that world, and toward what twentieth-century thinkers would call their national interest. The classic definition of national interest—the defense of a specific territory and promotion of the well-being of the people who live on it—was not perfectly suited to a nationalism that rested on a universalist ideology. Americans from the beginning were interested not only in protecting and advancing their material well-being; they also believed their own fate was in some way tied to the cause of liberalism and republicanism both within and beyond their borders. William Appleman Williams once commented, with disapproval, that Americans believe their nation "has meaning . . . only as it realizes natural right and reason throughout the universe."[9] This observation, though exaggerated, contained an important kernel of truth. The new nation, and its new foreign policy, had moved from a British imperial worldview to a universalistic worldview. The British imperial vision that had shaped American thinking in the decades before the Revolution linked imperial expansion, and the resulting material benefits that came to the British people, with the advancement of civilization. This idea persisted in the United States after independence, especially as Americans marched across the continent over the course of the nineteenth century. But the Revolution added a new element, the hope for republican transformation in other lands, even those where Americans had no intention of settling or making money, as a matter of moral and ideological principle. When Thomas Jefferson declared as president, "We are pointing out the way to struggling nations who wish, like us, to emerge from their tyrannies," it was not the old British imperialism he was expressing. It was a universalism that had been produced by the Revolution.

Acceptance of this universal principle would have significant ramifications in coming decades, not all of them welcome to all Americans. Nothing better illustrated the degree to which they were suddenly wedded—indeed, chained—to the universality of the rights they proclaimed than their attitude toward the one issue that put that conviction to its severest test: the issue of slavery. For even the rights of slaves were implicitly acknowledged by the founders. They recognized slavery as evil as a matter of principle but not as a matter of law, thereby setting up a tension that would not be resolved until the Civil War, and not completely even then. But Americans at the time of the Revolution knew their commitment to universal rights might someday compel them to bring practice into conformity with principle. Slaveholders like Patrick Henry, while opposing the abolition of slavery on the grounds of "the general inconvenience of living here without them" and out of fear of what a suddenly liberated army of slaves might do to their former owners and their owners' families, nevertheless felt keenly the hypocrisy of preserving slavery "at a time when the rights of humanity are defined and understood with precision in a country above all others fond of liberty." Thus even Henry, like Jefferson and other Virginians, claimed to look forward to the day "when an opportunity will be offered to abolish this lamentable evil." In the North, where the inconvenience of living without slaves was smaller, ministers railed against "this gross, barefaced, practiced inconsistence," this "self-contradiction," which could not but offend a just God.[10]

The Revolutionary War itself affected the way many Americans viewed slavery. For George Washington, it brought on an acute crisis of conscience, as he and other Americans confronted the mammoth contradiction of a slaveholding people struggling for freedom against their own "enslavement" by the British Empire. The contradiction was especially hard to ignore as it became clear that the survival and success of the Continental Army, chronically short of troops, depended on the enlistment, or impressment, of black soldiers, both free and enslaved. At the Battle of Monmouth, Washington's army included seven hundred blacks. At the Battle of Yorktown, the heroic First Rhode Island Regiment, which captured Redoubt 10, was 75 percent black, led into battle by Alexander Hamilton. "Is it consistent with the Sons of Freedom," General Philip Schuyler asked, "to trust their all to be defended by slaves?" After the war Schuyler, Hamilton's father-in-law, founded the New York Manumission Society. John Laurens, the son of one of America's wealthiest slave traders, asked how Americans could reconcile "our spirited Assertions of the Rights of Mankind [with] the galling abject Slavery of our negroes."[11] In 1779 the Continental Congress actually passed a resolution authorizing the emancipation of slaves who agreed to serve.[12] The plan was crushed in the legislatures of the southern colonies, which decided, not for the last time, that even military defeat was preferable to setting their slaves free.

Nevertheless the Revolution "was a powerful solvent" that "eroded even the adamant foundations of slavery." It drove Washington into a two-decade-long struggle, in his words, "to lay a foundation to prepare the rising generation [of blacks] for a destiny different from that in which they were born." To preserve the union at its birth, he compromised with the South's demand for the tacit protection of bondage in the Constitution. But privately he confided his conviction "that nothing but the rooting out of slavery can perpetuate the existence of our union, by consolidating it in a common bond of principle."[13] Future American conflicts—the Spanish-American War in 1898, the First World War, the Second World War, and even the Cold War—would have a similar effect. All were fought under the banner of freedom and natural rights, first for Americans themselves and later on behalf of other peoples in other lands. But they cast a harsh glare upon the hypocrisies of a nation that proclaimed universal rights yet did not universally honor them.

The tension between the Revolution's universal principles and Americans' selfish interests and prejudices would pose problems in their foreign relations as well. It would reveal the same kinds of hypocrisies and contradictions and create pressures to resolve them. The eighteenth-century world was a world of monarchies and tyrannies. Could the new republic preserve friendly relations with nations that every day trampled the rights Americans claimed were granted to all men? Was the new republic not endangered by powerful empires hostile to the idea of individual liberty? Could the United

States ally with one tyranny in order to protect itself from another? The need for survival answered most of these questions when America was weak and vulnerable. But as it grew stronger and more secure, the problem took a different form. From the Revolution onward foreign peoples would repeatedly rise up against tyrannies, often appealing both to American principles and to the American people for guidance and assistance. As American power grew, so did the potential influence it wielded, and so did the moral challenges and burdens it faced. If the United States maintained friendly relations with tyrannies, many Americans feared they were betraying those struggling for liberty. For better or for worse, Americans believed themselves increasingly implicated in the direction other nations took. "In dreams begin responsibilities," William Butler Yeats once noted, and the American dream of universal rights imposed its own responsibilities.

To make matters more complex, although Americans in the eighteenth century believed in natural rights as a matter of principle, many entertained doubts that other peoples, who did not enjoy the cultural and political blessings of Englishmen, could ever really make good use of the rights with which they were naturally endowed. At home, and especially in the South, most Americans doubted whether blacks were fit to participate in the democracy. There was similar skepticism about other peoples in other lands, and of all skin colors. Some Americans genuinely believed all peoples could benefit from freedom as much as the Anglo-Saxon race did, and they shared the view expressed by Joel Barlow: "If the Algerines or the Hindoos were to shake off the yoke of despotism, and adopt ideas of equal liberty, they would that moment be in a condition to frame a better government for themselves."[14] But many Americans doubted that Catholics, Negroes, and Indians, as well as "Hindoos," were capable of exercising their rights responsibly. Nevertheless, what Americans could not deny was that these rights belonged to all humans, regardless of nationality or race.

Most Americans did not set themselves on a mission to transform the world in their image. The idea of "mission" suggests a positive, deliberate, conscious effort to bring change. Americans' behavior in support of their universal principles abroad was irregular and haphazard, with periods of action and ideological passion punctuating periods of apparent indifference. The vast majority of Americans devoted themselves not to global transformation but to the daily pursuit of their material and spiritual well-being. Most did not aim to change the world, either by example or by intervention. Few Americans then or later consciously worked to ensure that the United States provided a compelling example of republican democracy in the hope that others would emulate it. It was for their own sake that Americans sought to perfect their government's institutions, not for the sake of others. They cheered when other peoples did follow their example, partly because it was encouragement to their own efforts. But few counted the United States a failure on the many more occasions when its example was not followed in other lands. Nor did Americans pursue a consistent, positive mission to "vindicate" their principles abroad. In this sense John Quincy Adams was right when he proclaimed in a July Fourth oration in 1821 that "America goes not abroad in search of monsters to destroy."[15]

Yet when the United States did go abroad for other reasons—as merchants, as diplomats, as religious missionaries, as tourists and adventurers—or even when they learned about the world through newspapers and gossip, they did not find it easy to ignore the "monsters" they encountered. In their dealings with the world they were repeatedly confronted by the question of whether their practices conformed to their stated principles. When Americans' pursuit of material and spiritual happiness thrust them into involvement with other peoples, the principle of universal rights they proclaimed often became part of that interaction. The principle served as a kind of superego looming in judgment over Americans' egoistic pursuits. It pricked their consciences. It called their motives into question, as well as their honor. It forced them to examine and reexamine themselves, much as the institution of slavery nagged at Americans until it was expunged by war. If rights were universal, then what about slaves' rights and women's rights? If rights were universal, then what about the rights of the French people in 1789? What about Latin Americans and Spaniards? What about Greeks and Poles and Hungarians? If the rights of others were being trampled, Americans were forced to confront the question of whether they had an obligation to do something about it. Their answer might frequently be no—just as for seventy years most northerners chose to do nothing to eradicate slavery in the South. But the question itself, like the question of slavery, was hard to avoid. The true American "mission" was a ceaseless effort to reconcile universal principle and selfish interest. Often Americans insisted or wanted to believe that principle and interest were entirely compatible, as sometimes they could be. But whether they were or not, Americans' principles were always there, to inspire them, to bedevil them, to strengthen them, and to confound them in their relations with the external world.

NOTWITHSTANDING THESE COMPLICATIONS, at the dawn of independence Americans embraced the universal implications of their Revolution with enthusiasm and with a proud sense that they had inaugurated a new era in human governance, a *novus ordo seclorum.* "[W]e behold our species in a new situation," wrote David Ramsay. "In no age before, and in no other country, did man ever possess an election of the kind of government, under which he would choose to live. . . . The world has not hitherto exhibited so fair an opportunity for promoting social happiness."[16] "Before the establishment of the American States," Jefferson would later write, "nothing was known to History but the Man of the old world."[17]

It was significant, too, that the Revolutionary War, the American people's first war, was an intensely ideological conflict, which Americans perceived, correctly, as having global ramifications. General Washington constantly reminded his troops that they were fighting for the "blessings of liberty." Many of his soldiers, and their friends and families, did believe that not just their own liberty but liberty for all humanity was at stake in the battle against the British.[18] Benjamin Franklin declared that America's "cause is the cause of all mankind" and that "we are fighting for [Europe's] liberty in defending our own."[19] Indeed, despite the immense popularity of Thomas Paine's rallying cry for independence, *Common Sense,* few Americans shared Paine's insistence that an independent America must become an isolated "asylum for mankind."[20] John Adams believed that Americans had taken up arms "as much for the benefit of the generality of mankind in Europe as for their own."[21] Even more than before the Revolution, Americans saw themselves leading mankind toward a better future. "The progress of society will be accelerated by centuries by this Revolution," Adams wrote. "Light spreads from the dayspring in the west, and may it shine more and more until the perfect day!"[22]

The idea that the Revolution had implications for the rest of mankind, that Americans had become the vanguard of universal human progress, and even that they had thereby gained a purchase on the world's future, was not merely an American conceit—a "harmless arrogance," as one historian has put it.[23] The revolutionary significance of the young republic's birth was felt across the Atlantic and throughout the Western Hemisphere. The historical importance of the Revolution was acknowledged both by those who cheered it and by those who feared it.

Europeans believed "that the American Revolution marked an enormous turning point in the entire history of the human race." There were even many who believed "America would someday, in its turn, predominate over Europe." The Venetian ambassador in Paris predicted that if the new American confederation of states remained united, "it is reasonable to expect that, with the favorable effects of time, and of European arts and sciences, it will become the most formidable power in the world."[24] The

British statesman Thomas Pownall, writing in 1780, declared that the "new system of power" in America was "growing, by accelerated notions, and accumulated accretion of parts, into an independent organized being, a great and powerful empire." Applying the Newtonian view of things common to his age, he argued that North America "is become a new primary planet in the system of the world, which . . . must have effect on the orbit of every other planet, and shift the common center of gravity of the whole system of the European world."[25]

Viewed from Europe, the American Revolution appeared as the first great political victory of the Enlightenment. Enlightenment *philosophes* in France, in Switzerland, in Belgium, in Germany, in the (Dutch) United Provinces, and in England saw in the American Revolution proof that their ideas were not merely theoretically attractive but could be put into practice.[26] In England democratic associations formed, with Charles James Fox singing the praises of the anti-British rebels. In Ireland militias exerted revolutionary pressure for independence. In the United Provinces democrats sought to emulate the model of the American minutemen. And in France and Germany there was "an incredible outburst of discussion, speculation, rhapsody, and argument, a veritable intoxication with the *rêve américain.*"[27] The Abbé Gentil believed it would lead to the "regeneration" of France and the rest of the world. "It is in the heart of this new-born republic that the true treasures that will enrich the world will lie."[28] "What do you think of the success of the Americans?" one Swiss revolutionary wrote to the *philosophe* Isaac Iselin in 1777. "Might it perhaps be from the side of the other continent that we shall see the realization of what you have taught about the history of mankind?" Iselin replied, "I am tempted to believe that North America is the country where reason and humanity will develop more rapidly than anywhere else."[29]

American independence came in the midst of a communications revolution, especially in England but also on the European continent. There was an explosion in the dissemination of the printed word. London's first daily newspaper appeared in 1702; by the end of the century millions of newspapers were sold annually in the city. For the first time in human history, something like a public opinion was coming to play a role in European politics, and essential to the development of this public involvement was the new access to information, both local and international. The United States was the product of this new era, and its influence was the greater because of it. Not for the last time Americans seemed especially well suited to benefit from radical changes in international society and politics, changes that threatened to overwhelm other countries and other forms of government.

The communications revolution of the end of the eighteenth century "under-mined, in Europe, the whole idea of government as a kind of private occu-pation of limited governmental circles." Detailed reports about events in America flooded Europe and helped delegitimize the traditional autoc-racies. The Revolution "inspired the sense of a new era. It added a new con-tent to the conception of progress. It gave a whole new dimension to ideas of liberty and equality made familiar by the Enlightenment." The Revolu-tion "dethroned England, and set up America, as a model for those seeking a better world."[30]

In the Western Hemisphere it stoked the spirit of rebellion against the old Spanish imperium—just as Hakluyt had foretold two centuries before. To be sure, the Latin American revolutions for independence of the early nineteenth century were more directly the product of the French Revolution and of Napoleon's conquest of Europe. But the American Revolution pro-vided the first and, for some Latin revolutionaries, the more compelling example.[31] Francisco de Miranda, one of the most prominent early agitators for the independence of Spanish colonies, wrote during a visit to the United States: "Good God, what a contrast to the Spanish system!" Thomas Jeffer-son, serving in Paris, received a letter from a Brazilian declaring, "Nature made us inhabitants of the same continent and in consequence in some degree patriots."[32] He remarked to John Jay that the Brazilian revolutionar-ies "consider the North American Revolution as a precedent for theirs [and] look to the United States as most likely to give them honest support."[33] Por-tuguese and Spanish Creoles considered themselves "kindred spirits," and though their grievances against Spain were different, they responded to the "intellectual vitality" of the North Americans, to the "daring, bravado, and especially the intensity with which a generation of revolutionaries voiced their cause." Europeans immediately saw the danger that the new nation posed to their holdings in the southern parts of the hemisphere. Even in 1768 a French agent warned presciently of the new North American threat: "I believe not only that this country will emancipate itself from the Crown of England, but that in the course of time it will invade all the dominions that the European powers possess in America, on the main land as well as in the islands."[34]

Nowhere was the overseas impact of the American Revolution more dramatic, of course, than in France. "For France," writes Simon Schama, "without any question, the Revolution began in America."[35] Although its participation in the war began as revenge against the British after the Seven Years' War, aid to the Americans had unintended consequences. It bank-rupted the French treasury, and it also infected segments of the French nobility with dangerous ideas. They had their first "flirtation with armed freedom," and veterans of the war would storm the Bastille. The Comte de Ségur wrote his wife before embarking with the French army for North America in 1782 that "arbitrary power weighs heavily on me. The freedom for which I am going to fight, inspires in me the liveliest enthusiasm and I would like my own country to enjoy such a liberty that would be compatible with our monarchy, our position and our manners."[36] To Jefferson, it seemed clear that the French nation had been "awakened by our revolution. . . . Our proceedings have been viewed as a model for them on every occasion."[37]

Over the course of the next decades, Americans would temper their enthusiasm for the revolutionary impact of their actions, especially in France. Many would come to agree with the observation of Britain's Lord Grenville: "None but Englishmen and their Descendants know how to make a Revolution."[38] In 1811, with Napoleon rampaging across Europe, John Adams regretted his country's role in the monster's creation. "Have I not been employed in mischief all my days? Did not the American Revolution produce the French Revolution? And did not the French Revolution produce all the calamities and desolations to the human race and the whole globe ever since?"[39] Even Jefferson joined Adams in their twilight years in fashioning what became a broad and enduring American consensus that only "moderate" revolutions were good, and "radical" revolutions were dangerous.[40]

Yet this sober view did not prevent Americans from becoming excited every time a new revolution apparently modeled after their own seemed to stir, whether in Latin America, or in Greece, or later in the nineteenth century in Hungary and Poland. At the time of the French Revolution the majority of Americans celebrated the revolutionary stirrings they had inspired abroad. "News of the meeting of the Estates-General in May 1789, the formation of the National Assembly in June, the fall of the Bastille in July, and the Declaration of the Rights of Man and Citizen in August . . . was received with deep exultation in the United States. The very thought that a great and ancient kingdom was acting by our example was stupendous."[41] Even the more "conservative" Americans, some of whom would be mislabeled as "realists" in the twentieth century, welcomed it. Hamilton applauded the French for throwing off their condition of "slavery" and embracing "freedom."[42] In 1792 he wrote, "I desire above all things to see the equality of political rights, exclusive of all hereditary distinction, firmly established by a practical demonstration of its being consistent with the order and happiness of society."[43] Washington expressed his joy in seeing "that the American Revolution [had] been productive of happy consequences on both sides of the Atlantic."[44] Dour northeastern Federalists cheered, from John Jay to John Marshall, Timothy Pickering, Noah Webster, and "virtually the entire Congregational clergy of New England."[45] John Adams alone remained unmoved,[46] but mostly because he believed from the beginning that the French were not going about their revolution in the proper way. Far from not caring to see the Revolution replicated abroad, Adams despaired that the French were not following the American model closely enough.[47]

In Holland, meanwhile, where another American-inspired revolution was unfolding, Adams personally "functioned as a catalyst of revolutionary enthusiasm," even going so far as to encourage democrats in subversion against the prince. On a mission to raise funds for the war against Britain, Adams discovered that the leaders of the United Provinces were, not surprisingly, loyal to London. Only their opponents, the democratic revolutionaries, were prepared to aid the revolution in North America.[48] Later, when things were going badly for the democrats, Adams was anything but indifferent. "I tremble and agonize for the suffering Patriots in Holland," he wrote when it looked like the Dutch republic would be extinguished. "The Prince will be so much master in reality, that the friends of liberty must be very unhappy, and live in continual disgrace and danger."[49] When it came to the struggle between republicanism and tyranny, all American leaders and statesmen were ideologues.

On one level, of course, these overseas revolutions simply flattered American egos. French patriot heroes like the Marquis de Lafayette declared themselves the ideological offspring of George Washington, and revolutionary France was effusive, in the early stages, in claiming the American Revolution as its model. The revolutions overseas offered a kind of retroactive endorsement of the American rebellion against the British. They offered Americans solace that their new republican polity would not exist alone and without allies in a despotic world. "It was that euphoric discovery, the discovery that even the glacial kingdoms of Europe could crack and quickly melt away, that led American mechanics, tradesmen, sailors, lawyers, shopkeepers, merchants, manufacturers, farmers, and laborers to don red cockades and sing 'Ca Ira!' and the 'Marseillaise'; to drink endless toasts to the Rights of Man, the French Republic, and its armies battling the forces of despotism."[50] The coming of the French Revolution was more than merely gratifying to Americans; it was almost essential "in the nourishment it gave to Americans' own opinion of themselves." Prominent Americans linked the fate of republicanism at home with the fate of republicanism abroad. As John Marshall later recalled, "We were all strongly attached to France—scarcely any man more strongly than myself. I sincerely believed human liberty to depend in a great measure on the success of the French Revolution."[51]

This was one consequence of the Americans' embrace of universal principles as the product and justification of their Revolution. The principles of the Declaration linked Americans to the rest of the civilized world and gave them a stake in the direction that world took. They were bound to be a factor in America's relations with individual countries, too, even with allies. Before 1789 "Americans' gratitude to France, even when coupled with the profound anglophobia generated by the Revolutionary War, could not disguise a sense of unease and guilt over being allied with a traditional foe and potent symbol of absolutist rule." As a result, "the United States had a compelling ideological interest in seeing France transformed . . . to reform and liberalize America's principal ally, in conformity with America's Protestant and republican image."[52]

Americans were not alone in believing they had a significant interest in seeing their own ideology prevail in other countries. Enlightenment thinkers throughout Europe agreed. And so did the defenders of absolutism. As Metternich was to ask as the wave of "liberal" revolutions crested in Latin America in the 1820s, "if this flood of evil doctrines and pernicious examples should extend over the whole of America, what would become . . . of the moral force of our governments, and of that conservative system which has saved Europe from complete dissolution?"[53] That was precisely what Franklin had in mind when he predicted to a French colleague in 1782 that "[e]stablishing the liberties of America will not only make that people happy, but will have some effect in diminishing the misery of those, who in other parts of the world groan under despotism, by rendering it more circumspect, and inducing it to govern with a lighter hand."[54]

From Strength to Weakness:
The Birth of "Practical Idealism"

THE NEW AMERICAN NATION that emerged triumphant in the war with the British Empire in 1783 was not in a position to do very much to aid the forces of liberalism and republicanism overseas. In fact, Americans were not in a position to do much of anything except survive. The revolutionary victory, though a vindication of the colonists' long-developing sense of national greatness, produced a strategic calamity from which it would take two decades to recover. The new nation was born weak and vulnerable.

This perilous vulnerability was the direct consequence of success in the war and in the peace settlement that followed. In the Anglo-American Peace of Paris of 1783, the United States acquired control of vast stretches of the land in the Northwest that Britain had wrested from France in the Seven Years' War. The dreams of Franklin and Washington to control the Ohio Valley were realized. The territory of the United States now ran hundreds of miles westward across the trans-Appalachian region to the Mississippi River, and while the Americans failed to acquire the parts of Canada they wanted, their new borders ran to the Great Lakes in the north and southward to the thirty-first parallel.

As would be the case repeatedly in American history, however, successful expansion and the fulfillment of long-held ambitions created new and difficult problems. After 1783 the problem was how to defend the vast new holdings. Spain disputed both the new southern boundary and Britain's unilateral grant to Americans of free navigation of the Mississippi. The Anglo-American settlement fulfilled all but the most grandiose of earlier expansionist ambitions, extending the area of settlement well beyond the Proclamation Line established by Britain after the Seven Years' War, and providing land for many future generations of white settlers. But the new nation lacked the power of the British Empire to keep other nations from pouncing on the newly won prize.

In rebelling from Great Britain the United States had lost a powerful imperial protector and gained a powerful imperial adversary. The favorable terms of the Anglo-American agreement were immediately thrown into doubt by the British refusal to withdraw from the military strongholds they maintained in territories nominally ceded to the United States. A string of forts ran from the St. Lawrence River across the Great Lakes and into the Ohio Valley. Once the outposts of defense against French and Indian forces, after independence they became links in a chain of British containment. Americans who so recently had gloried in the victory of the British Empire over the French in North America now saw the fruits of that victory imperiled by the same British arms and by the same vast global influence this great empire wielded.

The strategic difficulties were exacerbated by the weakness of the government under the Articles of Confederation. The colonies-turned-states, having united just barely enough to defeat the British in war, quickly fell back to their independent and defiant ways. They viewed the new government with the same jealousy and suspicion that they had once aimed at the British Parliament. This was a problem for American statesmen, because preserving the power and autonomy of states and local government generally meant paralyzing the national government's ability to conduct itself forcefully in response to international dangers.

Those dangers were close to home. The most immediate threat was of Indian attack. Here the loss of British imperial protection was compounded by the loss of British imperial finances, since maintaining peace with the Indians had always depended as much on gifts as on arms, gifts for which the bankrupt treasury of the new United States was incapable of paying. Instead the British were paying the Indians to resist the Americans in disputed territories. By 1787 British-backed tribes north of the Ohio River seemed to be uniting for an offensive, while in the south Indians supported by Spain launched attacks all along the Cumberland River. By 1787 Americans along the southwestern frontier "had been reduced to the point of capitulation."[55]

American independence brought similar calamities for maritime and commercial interests. Passage along the vital Mohawk and Hudson rivers became more dangerous. A staggering blow to American commerce came in 1784, when Spain closed the Mississippi to trade, severing the commercial lifeline of the western parts of the country. Overseas, merchant sailors who had been accustomed to traveling throughout the Mediterranean under the protection of the British flag suddenly found that protection removed and were immediately set upon by the pirates of the Barbary powers. Americans asked France to provide protection, but the French would not or could not help.

Worst of all were the harsh British trade restrictions suddenly and somewhat unexpectedly imposed on the United States soon after conclusion of the peace. In the decades leading up to the Revolution, Americans had grown confident that the British Empire would always depend on their commerce, and after the rebellion they expected to benefit from Britain's insatiable desire for American raw materials. On top of that, they expected great new opportunities for trade with the rest of Europe, now that the old imperial trade restrictions were no more. But the British government after 1783 was determined to show that, to the contrary, it was the Americans who were dependent on the British market—a reality that American leaders soon had to acknowledge. "Britain has monopolized our trade beyond credibility," Adams complained from London. "The ardor of our citizens in transferring almost the whole commerce of the country here, and voluntarily reviving that monopoly which they had long complained of as a grievance," had "imprudently demonstrated to all the world an immoderate preference of British commerce."[56] Nor were the nations of Europe as eager to exploit the opportunity of the newly independent American trade as leading Americans had hoped. "We do not find it easy to make commercial arrangements in Europe," Jefferson wrote from Paris. "There is a want of confidence in us."[57]

Franklin and others blamed the British for sullying America's reputation and hence her credit. But even without British connivance, the American victory in the War of Independence had deprived it of all meaningful international support. Spain, with the world's third-largest navy, had been at most a wary ally and now aimed to contain the Americans in the South and Southwest just as vigorously as the British contained them in the North. France also had no interest in seeing its former ally gain an unfettered ascendancy in North America, and it supported Spain's closure of the Mississippi. John Adams feared France would join Britain "in all artifices and endeavors to keep down our reputation at home and abroad, to mortify our self-conceit, and to lessen us in the opinion of the world."[58] John Jay early on recognized, "We can depend upon the French only to see that we are separated from England, but it is not in their interest that we should become a great and formidable people, and therefore they will not help us to become so."[59] A map prepared by the French foreign ministry revealed plans to extend Spain's holdings in the South right up to the Cumberland River; Great Britain would get the greater part of the Northwest; the United States would receive a swatch of territory in the trans-Appalachian area roughly the size of Kentucky. According to this French plan, which Jay was shown, U.S. territory would nowhere touch the Mississippi.

The Europeans hoped to limit not only American territory but also the reach of America's dangerous revolutionary ideology—or so Americans in Europe perceived. The American legation in London reported that the European monarchs "watch us with a jealous eye while we adhere to and flourish under systems diametrically opposite to those which support their governments and enable them to keep mankind in subjection." Richard Henry Lee, president of Congress, was convinced that there existed "a general jealousy beyond the water of the powerful effects to be derived from republican virtue here."[60] This was not mere paranoid puffery. Monarchs on the Continent did fear the liberties taking root in the New World. Even the Americans' erstwhile friends on the European continent did not want to see the republican experiment succeed too dramatically. Documents later released by the French revolutionary government revealed that the monarchy's foreign minister had opposed the ratification of the American Constitution and tried to prevent it, reasoning that "it suits France to have the

United States remain in their present state, because if they should assume the consistence of which they are susceptible they would soon acquire a force and power which they would probably be very eager to abuse."[61]

As serious as these foreign threats was the danger that the American confederation of states might simply break apart. Secessionist tendencies could be found along every frontier. The notorious Kentuckian James Wilkinson was a business partner of the Spanish governor of New Orleans and pledged loyalty to the Spanish king, offering to deliver parts of the southwestern territory into Spanish hands. Other secessionist impulses grew out of desperation. Settlers along the Cumberland River, under constant attack by Indians, had looked in vain to Congress for help and when none was forthcoming turned eventually to Spain. Such were the perilous conditions of settlers in these western and southern frontier territories that, in the view of George Washington, "the touch of a feather would turn them any way."[62] American leaders also feared separatist tendencies in the North, especially in Vermont, believed by many to be in secret league with British Canada. Jefferson and others saw British intrigues behind Shays's Rebellion in western Massachusetts.[63] Jay worried that in the event of war with one or more of the great empires angling for position in North America, some parts of the confederation might be "flattered into neutrality by specious promises, or seduced by a too great fondness for peace" to come to the aid of the others.[64]

AMERICAN FOREIGN POLICY in these years was shaped by a combination of enormous ambition and debilitating weakness. Most American leaders wanted and expected their new nation eventually to take its rightful place among the world's great powers and even to become in time the world's foremost power. But achieving this ambition required prudence and patience, and some sleight of hand. American leaders wanted to achieve great things without taking on great burdens and assuming great risks.

It has often been suggested that Americans possessed an abiding hostility to "traditional diplomacy and power politics."[65] They were determined "to approach foreign relations in terms of the ideal rather than in terms of existing realities."[66] They could not "comprehend the importance of the power factor in foreign relations," and indeed, the "entire colonial experience" had made foreign policy itself "alien and repulsive" to them. After the Revolution, therefore, they naively believed that the very "appearance of their country on the diplomatic scene would be instrumental in effecting a new departure in international relations and would usher in a new and better world," that traditional diplomacy and power politics would "fall at the first blowing of the trumpets of liberty."[67]

The statesmen of the founding era were not unfamiliar with the ways of power politics, however. They were idealists in the sense that they were committed to a set of universal principles, the defense and promotion of which they believed would improve the human condition as well as further American interests. But they were practical idealists. In their moment of weakness they employed the strategies of the weak. They viewed alliances as necessary but dangerous. They denigrated so-called power politics and claimed an aversion to war and military power, all realms in which they were far inferior to the European great powers. They extolled the virtues of commerce, where Americans competed on a more equal plane. They appealed to international law as the best means of regulating the behavior of nations, knowing that they had no other means of constraining the great empires of Britain and France. They adjusted themselves to an unhappy reality that they knew to be very much at odds with their aspirations. They looked forward to the day when, as a more powerful nation, they might begin to shape the world to conform more closely to their ideals. Fortunately for the young United States, the world was configured in such a way as to make this possible.

The Americans at the time of the Revolution were certainly not naïve about the behavior of human beings or about the behavior of nations. "Men I find to be a Sort of Beings very badly constructed," Franklin observed, "as they are generally more easily provok'd than reconcil'd, more disposed to do Mischief to each other than to make Reparation, much more easily deceiv'd than undeceiv'd, and having more Pride and even Pleasure in killing than in begetting one another."[68] Nor did leading Americans believe that the harsh international rules by which the great powers played could be suspended for them.

They did not, for instance, oppose alliances as a matter of principle. They feared unequal alliances that threatened to undermine their sovereignty and make them slaves to the stronger power. They were also wary of making commitments to another power that they could not in safety fulfill. But they were not shy about seeking foreign entanglements when they needed them. Indeed, their very first significant utterance on the subject of foreign policy, the resolution introduced in Congress by Richard Henry Lee one month before the Declaration of Independence, declared it "expedient forthwith to take the most effectual measures for forming foreign Alliances."[69]

Although some Americans, like John Adams, were wary at first of becoming too dependent on a powerful France, they quickly found themselves pleading for a greater entanglement than the French themselves were willing to undertake.[70] Nor did Americans hope to forge a purely commercial relationship with France, as some historians have argued, even at the start.[71] In early 1776 Arthur Lee, the Americans' "secret correspondent" in London, begged Pierre-Augustin Caron de Beaumarchais, the playwright and vigorous champion of the American cause in France, to "consider above all things that we are not transacting a mere mercantile business, but that politics is greatly concerned in this affair."[72] When it appeared that France was unwilling to undertake a full military and political commitment to the Revolution, the Americans forced France's hand by threatening, quite disingenuously, to make peace with Great Britain if a more extensive French commitment were not forthcoming.[73]

Once concluded in 1778, the French alliance struck even conservative Americans as a godsend. John Adams abandoned his caution and embraced the alliance as "a Rock upon which we may safely build." He even hoped the alliance would be permanent: "The United States, therefore, will be for ages the natural bulwark of France against the hostile designs of England against her, and France is the natural defense of the United States against the rapacious spirit of Great Britain against them."[74] Americans did try to set the terms of the alliance so that they would be required to do as little as possible in return for French assistance. This was not because they had a different sense of what "alliance" meant or because they hoped to establish a new system of international relations that transcended power politics.[75] They simply recognized that France's main interest was in striking a blow at the British Empire; the French helped the Americans, but only because it was in their interests to help. They asked only that the United States not make a separate peace with Britain without consultation, which is precisely what the Americans eventually did. By 1782 Adams and his colleagues had abandoned the French "rock" and preferred amicable relations with both European powers. But it was not "a hankering after isolation" that made Americans resist entering traditional military and political alliances with European powers.[76] At a time when the United States was too weak to defend itself from Indian marauders, it was difficult to imagine it coming to the aid of anyone in a major European conflict. "We have neither troops nor treasury nor government," Hamilton soberly noted in 1787. It was this reality that shaped American behavior, not utopian dreams about humanity.[77]

Secrecy and deception were prominent features of American diplomacy from the start. The committee charged with the conduct of foreign affairs before the start of the Revolution, later renamed the Committee on Foreign

Affairs and the forerunner of the State Department, was initially called the Committee of Secret Correspondence. Its first act was to pay an American agent in London, Arthur Lee, to gather secret information on the disposition of the various European powers toward the Anglo-American conflict. At the conclusion of the war, John Jay insisted on conducting negotiations with Spain in secret, chiefly to avoid attacks and interference by domestic political opponents. The treaty negotiated with France in 1778 contained a number of secret clauses, including the one about not concluding a separate peace with Great Britain. This secret agreement, of course, the Americans violated, secretly, as soon as they learned that the British would give them more territory than would France and Spain. So much for the image of American diplomats as poor naïfs, "honest and innocent men" who were no match for Europe's "wily knaves."[78]

Americans understood the intricacies of the European balance of power, and how to exploit it to their advantage.[79] As colonists they had played on British fears and jealousies of France to further their own expansionist ambitions. As rebels they played on French desires for revenge. Manipulating European rivalries was the subject of open discussion in the Continental Congress.[80] John Adams, a great student of the balance of power in Europe, believed that "Nature has formed it. Practice and Habit have confirmed it, and it must forever exist."[81] Jefferson, too, understood that "[w]hile there are powers in Europe which fear our views, or have views on us, we should keep an eye on them, their connections and oppositions, that in a moment of need we may avail ourselves of their weakness with respect to others as well as ourselves, and calculate their designs and movements on all the circumstances under which they exist."[82] In the New World Americans preferred hegemony to a balance of power, but in the Old World they knew a balance served their interests well.

Few Americans believed they could fundamentally change their world, or somehow evade the realities of power politics, by such devices as promoting an international system of free trade. The celebration of what Montesquieu called "sweet commerce" was a staple of Enlightenment thinking on both sides of the Atlantic, and John Adams and others looked to a distant future in which trade could be a solvent of international conflict. But although they may have dreamed, they were under no illusions about their harsh, mercantile world.[83] They were not even faithful apostles of free trade. As British colonials they had been full participants in the mercantilist system; "its acts of trade and navigation had both hindered and helped them." Exporters of raw materials such as tobacco benefited from a large and secure British market. Exporters of manufactured goods generally found ways to skirt the regulations. After independence different segments of the American economy were affected differently by the British restrictions. While tobacco growers suffered, most farmers were not much affected one way or the other. Merchant importers "had not liked the bonds of the Empire when a part of it, but they had enjoyed its privileges, and after the war was over many of them did not think they could survive without them."[84]

Nor could many Americans believe that trade among nations necessarily made for global harmony and peace. They knew that competition for trade produced wars as often as "sweet commerce" prevented them. On this Hamilton and Jefferson were agreed. "Has commerce hitherto done anything more than change the objects of war?" Hamilton asked. "Is not the love of wealth as domineering and enterprising a passion as that of power or glory?"[85] If Jefferson had his way, Americans would "practice neither commerce nor navigation" but would "stand with respect to Europe precisely on the footing of China. We should thus avoid wars, and all our citizens would be husbandmen."[86] Americans knew that whatever their own preferences might be, the world in which they lived was inhospitable to any notion of free trade. Trade restrictions were a fact of life. Adams may have hoped that "[t]he increasing liberality of sentiment among philosophers and men of letters, in various nations," might lead to "a reformation, a kind of protestantism, in the commercial system of the world."[87] But he was not surprised that governments had not followed the philosophers' advice, insisting instead on short-term self-aggrandizement. "National pride is as natural as self-love," Adams noted. "It is, at present, the bulwark of defense to all nations."[88]

Americans were idealists about the future, but in the present they believed the way to shift the balance in their favor was not to convert the world to free trade but to impose trade restrictions of their own. Jefferson and Adams favored retaliatory measures against Britain and despaired that under the Articles of Confederation the Congress lacked the power to impose them.[89] At times Adams expressed a Jeffersonian desire to put a stop to American commerce altogether, for all the trouble it caused. "If every ship we have were burnt, and the keel of another never to be laid, we might still be the happiest people upon earth, and, in fifty years, the most powerful."[90] Commerce, far from being America's answer to the world's problems, often seemed a heavy burden to those trying to preserve the young nation's well-being.

The founders' realism consisted in recognizing that it was an inescapable burden. "Our people have a decided taste for navigation and commerce," wrote Jefferson, "and their servants are in duty bound to calculate all their measures on this datum."[91] Adams agreed that it was vain "to amuse ourselves with the thoughts of annihilating Commerce unless as Philosophical Speculations." The "character of the people must be taken into consideration. They are as aquatic as the tortoises and sea-fowl, and the love of commerce, with its conveniences and pleasures, is a habit in them as unalterable as their natures." Americans would be compelled to form "connections with Europe, Asia, and Africa; and, therefore, the sooner we form those connections into a judicious system, the better it will be for us and our children."[92]

At first Americans sought avenues for commerce abroad for their own sake, therefore, not as a means of changing the world. Too weak and disunited to fight trade wars on their own, they tried to shape international laws to give them the best chance of opening foreign ports for their goods. As a weak nation, the United States sought the same protections against the British navy that many other weak nations sought. "[F]ree ships, free goods, freedom of neutrals to trade between port and port of a belligerent . . . were the principles of maritime practice which were coming increasingly into usage in Europe and which Great Britain, with her surpassing sea power, would not admit as international law."[93] What Americans sought chiefly were not international transformations but some international leverage against the naval superpower of their day.

This desire to constrain the great powers of Europe shaped American attitudes toward international law more generally. It is true that Americans were naturally inclined to a certain legalism, both at home and abroad, as were all British peoples. But their constant appeal to international law owed more to their weakness than to any conviction that all international behavior could be regulated by legal mechanisms. They knew from their reading of the Swiss jurist Emmerich von Vattel that in international law "strength or weakness . . . counts for nothing. A dwarf is as much a man as a giant is; a small Republic is no less a sovereign State than the most powerful Kingdom."[94] Later generations of Americans, less vulnerable to European depredations and possessing more power and influence on the world stage, would not always be so enamored of the constraints of international law.

Finally, there was the American attitude toward war and the possession of the tools of war. Americans tend to think of themselves as a people reluctant to go to war and believe that, especially in the early years of the republic, they differed in this respect from the warlike Europeans. But "[t]he legend of Americans rejecting European attitudes toward war because of their wilderness experience and their idealistic ambitions is . . . built upon myth rather than reality."[95] They had spent more than half of the three

decades from 1754 to 1784 embroiled in full-scale war. Early American
leaders did not believe they had suddenly entered a new era of peace.
Hamilton claimed that "the fiery and destructive passions of war reign in
the human breast with much more powerful sway than the mild and beneficent sentiments of peace."[96] Nor did Americans want to abandon war or the
threat of war as tools to pursue their goals. Jefferson, so often characterized
as the most idealistic in his aversion to power, was as quick as anyone to
reach for the sword in instances where he believed it would work. In the
1780s, infuriated by the attacks of the Barbary powers against American
traders in the Mediterranean, he concluded it would be necessary for the
United States to open the sea-lanes by force: "We ought to begin a naval
power, if we mean to carry on our own commerce."[97] If the Barbary rulers
refused to leave American traders in peace, Jefferson insisted he "preferred
war" as less expensive than the continued payment of tribute. A naval victory in the Mediterranean would "have the defense of honor, procure some
respect in Europe, and strengthen the government at home."[98] John Jay also
favored using force against the Barbary powers and proposed building a
naval squadron of five forty-gun ships to patrol the sea-lanes. "The great
question is whether we shall wage war or pay tribute. I, for my part, prefer . . . war."[99] In July 1787 William Grayson proposed forming an alliance
with European powers "to maintain a permanent naval force that would
guard the Mediterranean for peaceful shipping."[100] Hamilton was not alone
in recognizing, one hundred years before the influential naval strategist
Alfred Thayer Mahan, that the promotion and protection of American commerce overseas would require naval power with a global reach. The revolutionary generation, which had forged a nation by means of war with the
British Empire, "assumed that war was normal, even inevitable, in human
affairs."[101]

Americans had many other occasions to contemplate war, only to be
caught up short by the impossibility of actually waging it. John Adams,
engaged in futile efforts in London to gain British evacuation of the northern forts, wrote a friend that if the posts were not evacuated the United
States should "declare war directly and march one army to Quebec and
another to Nova Scotia."[102] When Spain closed off the Mississippi in 1784,
westerners cried for war and talked of raising ten thousand troops to march
on New Orleans. George Rogers Clark launched an attack on Spanish subjects at Vincennes. Jefferson wrote from Paris that war might indeed be preferable to an unfavorable settlement, and John Jay agreed that the United
States would be justified in going to war to vindicate its navigation rights.[103]
All this talk of war was empty. Neither during the Confederation era nor

afterward did the United States have the strength to fight any of the great powers, even in North America. To pick a fight with one would open the United States to blackmail by the others. A fight with Spain in the South would mean the danger of British pressure in the North. A fight with Great Britain in the North would open vulnerabilities to Spanish pressure in the South. Hamilton, arguing for neutrality between France and Great Britain in 1794, pointed to the central truth that drove American policy throughout the 1780s and '90s. A war with any major European power would be "the most unequal and calamitous in which it is possible for a country to be engaged—a war which would not be unlikely to prove pregnant with greater dangers and disasters than that by which we established our existence as an independent nation."[104]

If Americans eschewed war, then, it was not because they believed war was an obsolete legacy of European monarchs. It was because the option of war was denied them. One should view many of the founders' more utopian declarations in this light. Jefferson might well insist, as he did in a letter to Madison in 1789, that the rule of power and force in relations between nations had been considered acceptable in "the dark ages which intervened between antient and modern civilisation" but was "exploded and held in just horror in the 18th century."[105] This did not stop him from calling for a navy to make war against the Barbary powers. John Adams might argue in 1783, as he did in 1776, that "the business of America with Europe was commerce, not politics or war."[106] But this did not prevent him from embracing a political and military alliance with France at one moment, while at another moment dreaming wistfully of ending commerce with Europe altogether.[107] Americans might look to international law as a salvation, but they recognized, as John Jay noted with regard to navigation rights on the Mississippi, that "even if our right . . . was expressly declared in Holy Writ, we should be able to provide for the enjoyment of it no otherwise than by being in capacity to repel force by force."[108]

There were those who did flirt with utopianism, at least rhetorically. Thomas Paine, the author of *Common Sense,* arguably the most influential political tract ever written, did make the case for both isolationism and an international peace founded on commerce. In his narrowly focused, brilliant piece of revolutionary propaganda, designed to convince the colonists to sever their ties with their king and their beloved British Empire, Paine argued that every problem troubling Americans was the fault of the crown and that merely throwing off monarchical rule would produce a heaven on earth. He declared that all the wars fought in history were the product of dynastic quarrels, and that all the wars fought on the North American continent had been started by the kings and queens of England pursuing their own selfish ends. Americans had only to wrest themselves from the crown, and they would enjoy peace with the entire world. "Our plan is commerce," Paine declared, "and that, well attended to, will secure us the peace and friendship of all Europe; because it is the interest of all Europe to have America a free port. Her trade will always be a protection, and her barrenness of gold and silver secure her from invaders."[109]

An excited populace may well have found Paine's visions of postmonarchic utopia compelling, if only for a moment, before returning to the more difficult world that surrounded them on all sides. But *Common Sense* was not a founding document of American foreign policy. Paine did not conduct American foreign relations after 1776, and those who did—Jay, Adams, Washington, Hamilton, Jefferson, and others—did not consult *Common Sense* for guidance or cite it to justify their policies. On at least one vital question, perhaps the most vital, American leaders ignored Paine entirely. He had argued that independence could be won without foreign alliances, but forming an alliance with France was the very first foreign policy act of the Continental Congress.[110]

Americans believed the world would be a better and safer place if republican institutions flourished and if tyranny and monarchy disappeared. They believed, from Thomas Jefferson to Alexander Hamilton, that free peoples were less likely to make war, especially against other free peoples.[111] They believed commerce tended, on the whole, to draw nations closer together and reduce the likelihood of conflict. In short, they believed in the ameliorative possibilities of Enlightenment liberalism. Even this idealism, moreover, was both practical and realistic. Americans believed a world reformed along liberal and republican lines would be a safer world for their liberal republic, and that a freer and multiplying commerce would make them a more prosperous nation. They were arguably right on both counts. An international order more suited to American interests and institutions would be better for Americans.

In time, Americans imagined, they would help create such an international order. They would play a beneficial role in the world by leading mankind toward a better future. But that time had not yet come. Whatever revolutions Americans hoped their own rebellion might inspire around the world—and they did entertain such hopes—they were too weak to lend a hand to such struggles. Despotism, mercantilism, and war would persist. The strengthening of the republican, commercial, and legal institutions of a liberal international order would have to wait. First the young republic had to overcome its own debilitating weakness.

Nationalism and Foreign Policy:
The Making of the Constitution

ONE OBVIOUS WAY to do so was to strengthen the sinews of the new nation. American weakness gave birth in the mid-1780s to an increasingly fervent nationalism, a widespread, but by no means universal, conviction not only that the nation had to be united but that the power of the national government had to be augmented if the United States was to be secure against foreign attack and internal dissolution and take its rightful place among the great nations of the world. This close relationship between the demands of foreign policy and national security on the one hand, and nationalism and the augmentation of federal power on the other, would prove to be one of the more enduring traits of the American polity. Time and again throughout American history—during the War of 1812, during the Civil War, during the First and Second World Wars, and during the Cold War—nationalist sentiments and domestic demands for a stronger central government would be closely linked with national security challenges and pressures for the more vigorous conduct of foreign policy. In the United States, in the eighteenth century as in the twentieth and twenty-first, a "big" foreign policy generally meant "big" government.

In 1787 the general sense of national insecurity and the apparent helplessness of the young United States to defend and advance its interests and principles in a hostile world became what one historian has called the "major drive wheel" in the movement for increased central government power that culminated in the drafting and ratification of the American Constitution.[112] The loose government structure established to prosecute the Revolutionary War under the Articles of Confederation had proved inadequate to the tasks of war and to preserving national security after the war. As in the colonial era, weak central government and uncooperative state governments plagued the effective conduct of military and diplomatic affairs. Maintaining unity and raising funds during the war had been hard enough. In peacetime, those problems grew unmanageable. The states refused to provide the money for an army to challenge British control of the forts or Spanish control of the Mississippi, or to defend settlers on the frontier from Indian attack. The government could not raise money for a navy to protect merchant sailors in the Mediterranean. Nor would the states unite behind a common policy of retaliatory trade restrictions that might force the British government to lessen its own. At the same time, the states also refused to abide by the terms of the Anglo-American treaty. Some refused to make good on debts to British loyalist creditors, for instance—and the

British used this refusal as a pretext to delay withdrawal of British forces from U.S. territory.

All these deficiencies were mutually reinforcing and had produced a downward spiral of power. Congress derived much of its revenue from western land sales, but land that could not be protected from Indian attack by federal troops was hard to sell. Declining land sales meant lower revenues. Lower revenues meant fewer troops. Fewer troops meant still less protection and even fewer land sales.[113] In addition, settlers left unprotected by the federal government and exposed to Indian attack were inclined to seek succor from other, more powerful quarters, which in turn increased the dangers of secession. Congress before 1787 maintained an army of about seven hundred men, which was theoretically supposed to operate along the entire vast frontier, north, south, and west, and to take the offensive against Indian marauders. This was impossible. The states therefore had to employ their own militias to do the job that the federal army could not do. This in turn exacerbated already dangerous centrifugal forces.

The drive to reform the government and strengthen federal power nevertheless produced a heated debate in the United States, pitting Federalists against Anti-Federalists, who believed the country could be strengthened without significantly augmenting federal power. But on some key matters—the need for more effective taxation, for a military establishment, for the better regulation of foreign commerce, and for the enforcement of treaties—there was "overwhelming consensus."[114] National security and commercial concerns united disparate interests in different sections of the United States. Westerners favored a stronger federal government to protect western expansion. Northerners favored one in order to improve terms of trade overseas. Stronger central government even had solid support in the South. In future decades southern slaveholders would become the most fervent opponents of national power and the most determined advocates of states' rights against the federal government, as they feared that a strong central government controlled by the North would strike at the institution of slavery. And indeed, some of the leading Anti-Federalist opponents of the Constitution in the 1780s were Virginians like James Monroe and Patrick Henry, the latter of whom warned his fellow slaveholders that if proponents of the new Constitution succeeded, "[t]hey'll free your niggers."[115] But Virginia was also home to James Madison, who feared national dissolution absent greater power in the federal government. In the 1780s many southern leaders were afraid of foreign attack and wanted a stronger government for protection. As South Carolina's David Ramsay warned, "If this state is to be invaded by a maritime force, to whom can we apply for immediate aid? To

Virginia and North Carolina? . . . The Eastern states, abounding in men and ships, can sooner relieve us than our next door neighbors."[116] Everyone understood that the institution of slavery made the South vulnerable in times of war. During the Revolution the British had struck terror in southern hearts by promising freedom to slaves who rebelled against their masters.

Not surprisingly, the leading American nationalists and Federalists in 1787 were generally men of experience in military and international affairs. James Madison, John Jay, Alexander Hamilton, Henry Knox, and George Washington—all these defenders of stronger central government had served in diplomatic and military positions at home and abroad, where the weaknesses of the Confederation had been most obvious. Thomas Jefferson, sitting in Paris, shared Anti-Federalist concerns about a strong central government, but he ultimately supported the constitution drafted by his fellow Virginian. The Federalist Papers, written to persuade Americans of the necessity of a new constitution, began with a series of essays on foreign policy by John Jay, who had charge of foreign affairs through most of the Confederation period. As Madison soothingly tried to explain to the Anti-Federalist critics, the operations of the national government would always be "most extensive and important in times of war and danger; those of the state government in times of peace and security."[117]

More was at stake than tangible security and the nation's financial health. For many leading Americans, among the most disturbing consequences of American weakness was that it had deprived the new republic of the respect it deserved from other nations and peoples. Spain thought nothing of closing the Mississippi to American navigation, while in the Mediterranean the Barbary pirates humiliated the young nation by kidnapping and enslaving its citizens. In the courts of the great European powers, American ambassadors were ridiculed for their poverty. The entire world seemed to be sneering at the sorry state of American finances, at the incessant squabbling among the states and between the states and Congress, and at the apparent inability of the United States to stand on its own feet and take a responsible course in world affairs. For Americans, who had an extremely high opinion of their own worth and importance, who believed their Revolution had ushered in a new era, and who were convinced their new nation was destined for a greatness approaching that of Rome and Athens, this lack of international regard was an especially painful rebuke.[118] Federalists seeking to sway public opinion at the various state ratifying conventions argued "that America would be great if the Constitution were adopted, despised if rejected."[119]

The desire to overcome dishonor and humiliation was strengthened by the common American conviction that more was at stake than just national honor. American weakness dishonored not just Americans but republicanism itself. "What a triumph for the advocates of despotism," Washington lamented, "to find that we are incapable of governing ourselves, and that systems founded on the basis of equal liberty are merely ideal and fallacious!"[120] American leaders were acutely aware that the eighteenth-century world of monarchies preferred to see their republican experiment fail. Even allied but monarchical France hoped that the new Constitution would not be adopted, lest the young republic grow too strong and secure and, therefore, too capable of spreading its dangerous liberal doctrines. Since for Americans the national ideology had universal application, restoring or establishing the nation's honor and reputation appeared to be an obligation not just to themselves but also to mankind. In Madison's view, the Constitutional Convention in Philadelphia would "decide forever the fate of republican government." Gouverneur Morris agreed that the "whole human race" would be affected.[121] Defenders of the new Constitution believed that if republicanism was to survive in a hostile world, a republican nation had to be strong and vigorous. This, too, would be a guiding sentiment in American foreign policy for the next two centuries: a strong America was good for the world.

The national strength they sought was necessary not just to meet present dangers. The leaders of the United States were also trying to safeguard the future, to keep the doors open to expansion, progress, and prosperity, to fulfill the promise of greatness, and to ensure the survival and the spread of republican freedom. This was true even of those who opposed the ratification of the very Constitution that had been designed to secure these ends. The Anti-Federalists who battled against a strong central government in the debates of 1787–88 have sometimes been misunderstood as having made a case against greatness, against "empire," and in favor of a pristine isolationism. This would seem to have been the purport of Patrick Henry's speech at the Virginia ratifying convention, when he warned that "the American spirit, assisted by the ropes and chains of consolidation, is about to convert this country into a powerful and mighty empire. . . . [W]e must have an army, and a navy, and a number of things." Not for him this "great and mighty empire," Henry proclaimed. "When the American spirit was in its youth, the language of America was different: liberty, sir, was then the primary object."[122]

It is easy to read Henry's statements as opposing an ambitious foreign policy, until one realizes that the "empire" he was attacking was the thirteen states united under one central government as envisioned in the new federal

Constitution. Employing the arguments of Montesquieu, Henry and other Anti-Federalists insisted that the thirteen states already covered too wide an expanse of territory to be governed by anything other than despotism. Theirs was not an argument about foreign policy, therefore: Henry opposed a "small" America as much as a "large" America, if either was going to be governed by a strong central government.

In fact, the Anti-Federalists did not significantly differ from the Federalists on the fundamental principles of foreign policy, which is one reason they "rarely discussed foreign affairs" when attacking the proposed Constitution. Most favored territorial and commercial expansion. Indeed, many from the southern states were at least as eager to expand American power, influence, and territorial control as their Federalist opponents. Prominent Anti-Federalists like Virginia's James Monroe were powerful advocates of westward and southward expansion. Patrick Henry and other Virginians reviled the agreement John Jay negotiated with Spain, which denied the United States navigation rights on the Mississippi, as an antisouthern conspiracy by northern merchants under the insidious influence of Great Britain. Southern Anti-Federalists warned that under the new Constitution, which required that all treaties be approved by two-thirds of the Senate, the North could always block settlement of new western lands by vetoing treaties with Indians and other foreign powers.[123]

Anti-Federalists were continental expansionists, even more so than many of their northern colleagues, some of whom tended to be commercial expansionists. As one student of Anti-Federalist views has noted, they "took it for granted that as population grew, pioneer farmers would move west in search of virgin lands." They "looked forward to the expansion of the American *people* across the Continent." They "envisioned a succession of new states joining a confederation, rather than being swallowed up into an empire."[124]

Most Anti-Federalists shared the Federalist conviction that the United States, if governed correctly, had a great destiny before it. Charles Pinckney might argue that the "great end of Republican Establishments" was to make people "happy at home"; that "[w]e mistake the object of our government, if we hope or wish that it is to make us respectable abroad"; and that "[c]onquest or superiority among other powers is not or ought not ever to be the object of a republican system."[125] But the Anti-Federalists, for the most part, did not deny that "respectability" abroad was important. They simply denied that it could be achieved only at the expense of the states' sovereign independence. The Massachusetts Anti-Federalist James Winthrop, writing as "Agrippa," proclaimed as proudly as Adams or Franklin that human history had never "produced an instance of rapid growth in extent, in numbers, in art, and in trade, that will bear any comparison with our own country. . . . Two-thirds of the continental debt has been paid since the war, and we are in alliance with some of the most respectable powers of Europe. The western lands, won from Britain by the sword, are an ample fund for the principal of all our public debts; and every new sale excites that manly pride which is essential to our national virtue." All this "happiness," Winthrop declared, "arises from the freedom of our institutions and the limited nature of our government."[126]

The debate between Federalists and Anti-Federalists was the first of what would over the next two centuries be a recurring battle between nationalists on one side and localists and advocates of states' rights against the federal government on the other. This debate would often be characterized as an argument over the proper course of American foreign policy, a debate between isolationism and internationalism, between America as exemplar to the world and America as active shaper of the world, and sometimes, most crudely, as America the "republic" versus America the "empire." But in the 1780s as later, the foreign policy dimension of the debate was inseparable from the argument over governance at home. In the end, the Anti-Federalists lost out to the forces of nationalism that had been rising up even before the Revolution and that crested after independence. The struggle between nationalism and localism throughout American history has been won, more often than not, by the nationalists, and the first great nationalist victory was the federal Constitution itself. It was the Constitution that enabled the young United States to begin conducting the kind of vigorous, expansionist foreign policy its drafters supported.

CHAPTER 3

Liberalism and Expansion

This prestigious and restless population, continually forcing the Indian nations backward and upon us, is attempting to get possession of all the vast continent those nations are occupying between the Ohio and Mississippi Rivers, the Gulf of Mexico and the Appalachian Mountains. . . . If they obtain their purpose, their ambitions will not be limited to this part of the Mississippi.

—Baron de Carondelet, "Military Report on Louisiana and West Florida," New Orleans, November 1794

We desire above all things, brother, to instruct you in whatever we know ourselves. We wish [you to learn] all our arts and to make you wise and wealthy.

—Thomas Jefferson to Jean Baptiste Ducoigne, a Kaskaskia chief, June 1781

Lockean Man and Liberal Expansion

THE UNITED STATES was the world's first modern commercial, liberal republic. The foreign policy that naturally emerged from such a regime was also novel, shaped as it was by the wants and desires of several million free individuals in search of wealth and opportunity, unrestrained by the firm hand of an absolute government, a dominant aristocracy, or even a benevolent constitutional monarch. That diplomatic phrase *raison d'état* had one meaning when a French king, like his colleagues across Europe, could declare *l'état c'est moi* and when the aspirations of the multitude were subordinated, in accordance with divine will, to the interests of the lord of the realm. Foreign policy in the age of monarchy had served the interests of the dynasty. In the age of religious warfare, it had also served the interests of the Catholic Church or its opponents. But what was the meaning of *raison d'état* when the state was nothing more than the secular creation and servant of the people? The foreign policy of a liberal republic could no more be divorced from the principles of liberalism and republicanism than the foreign policy of an eighteenth-century divine-right monarchy could be divorced from the principles of divine right and monarchical legitimacy.[1]

For the leaders and citizens of the new republic, in fact, the nation's foreign policy and its liberal "ideology" were in many respects indistinguishable. The overarching aim of American foreign policy was not merely to protect the nation and its people but also to preserve and protect its unique institutions and its unprecedented liberties—a purpose that by itself influenced the nature and direction of its foreign relations and that distinguished it from other eighteenth-century nations with different forms of government and political economy. American foreign policy was shaped by American liberalism in another way as well. Liberalism in the eighteenth century, and for the next two hundred years, was the main engine of American expansion.

Two centuries later it is easy to forget how novel was the liberal Enlightenment conception both of human nature and of the proper role of a government constituted for the protection of "natural" rights. The old order, which the eighteenth-century apostles of Enlightenment liberalism aimed either to destroy or transcend, had been preoccupied with "intangible goods": "The king had his glory, the nobles their honor, the Christians their salvation, the citizens of pagan antiquity their ambition to outdo others in serving the public good."[2] American leaders and the American people were also concerned with honor and glory, and they wrestled with the tension between private interests and the common good. But modern commercial society, which had emerged in England by the beginning of the eighteenth century and in the United States at the century's end, was devoted as no other before it to the more mundane but, in the liberal view, more universal strivings of human nature. In *The Wealth of Nations,* published in the year of the Declaration of Independence, Adam Smith had attributed to all mankind a continual desire of "bettering our condition, a desire which . . . comes with us from the womb, and never leaves us till we go to the grave." The foundations of the American political economy were erected on this novel, indeed, revolutionary understanding of human nature. Even as they fretted about the dangers of luxury and avarice that a multiplying commerce produced, the members of the founding generation, from Federalists like Hamilton to Republicans like Jefferson and Madison, questioned neither the commercial nature of the American people nor the vast benefits to the nation that would be gained by unleashing the forces of commercial liberalism. Their grand scheme was to harness the material ambitions of men and women into a mammoth self-generating engine of national wealth and power. American foreign policy in the first decade of the republic aimed, above all other goals save the preservation of the nation itself, at feeding the ravenous appetites of a generation of Americans whom Gouverneur Morris recognized as "the first-born children of the commercial age."

Those "first-born children" were an acquisitive people, and indeed they celebrated acquisitiveness as a virtue. The tenets of liberalism exhorted individuals to seek their fortunes and exalted the acquisition of wealth and property not as selfish pursuits but as virtuous ones. The acquisition of property was, in fact, a public as well as a private virtue, essential to the common good. According to Locke, property served as the very foundation of civilized society. The acquisition of new property, for the purpose of improving it and bettering one's own condition, was a liberal ideal. On a vast continent inhabited only by an aboriginal people who, as it happened, did not even believe in property, it was something of an imperative. Nor was the drive for territory the only entangling impulse of liberalism. In the liberal conception of life, "every man," as Adam Smith put it, "lives by exchanging, or becomes in some measure a merchant."[3] When two peoples bordered each other, trade inevitably eroded the boundaries between them. "Proximity of territory invites . . . trade," wrote Hamilton; "the bordering inhabitants, in spite of every prohibition, will endeavor to carry it on."[4] This was certainly true of the Anglo-Saxon Americans who now laid claim to the continent's vast resources.

American liberalism had created a type of man especially well suited both to territorial expansion and settlement and to the penetration of foreign markets. The cult of pioneer individualism, of the self-made and self-reliant man embarking on his own to conquer the wilderness or the open seas, was not unique to the United States. Other cultures had produced their Daniel Boones. But it is doubtful that any nation ever produced so many, or gave them such independence to go where and when they pleased, or more exalted them as national icons. Others marveled at the American pioneer spirit and considered it unique. As even one Englishman observed, "No people are so adapted to encounter the fatigues and privations of the wilderness; none form such efficient pioneers of civilization."[5] Hamilton voiced the common American view that "as to whatever may depend on enterprise, we need not fear to be outdone by any people on earth. It may almost be said, that enterprise is our element."[6]

As Hamilton suggested, it was not the pioneering but what Americans did after hacking through the wilderness that made them such a potent force for expansion and conquest. They were pioneers of civilization in a way that Russian and French fur traders, or even Spanish conquistadors, had never been. In America Daniel Boone blazed the trail, but it was the waves of settlers following him who cleared the land, farmed it, sold its produce, and then moved on to new lands, who turned tracts of wilderness into marketable resources. It was the speculators who bought and sold the land. It was this advance guard of the liberal order that made American territorial conquests both irresistible and permanent.

Liberalism was such a potent engine for expansion in part because a government founded on liberal principles could not easily prevent expansion. As a practical matter, the powers at the American government's disposal were too limited to stem the tide of expansion on the continent. Even the powerful British Empire had been helpless before the hordes of western settlers. To President Washington it was clear that "anything short of a Chinese wall, or a line of troops," would be insufficient to prevent squatters from building homesteads on Indian territories or to keep speculators from buying and selling lands deeded to the Indians by treaty. On the frontiers, many settlers insisted on their freedom to the point of lawlessness. Representatives of the federal government referred to them as "banditti" and "white savages," entirely "averse to federal measures." Rather than be bound by limits imposed in the East, government officials feared, many of the frontier families would prefer to "live under no government" at all.[7]

Even if they could rein in the settlers, however, as a political and ideological matter American leaders would have been hard-pressed to justify doing so. Liberalism's elevation of the individual's interest over that of the state undermined traditional justifications for hemming in individual aspirations, including the aspiration to move onto new lands beyond the national borders. An absolute monarch could more easily justify blocking his subjects' expansionist ambitions, for they possessed few rights he was bound to honor. For a ruler such as Louis XVI or Napoleon, the imperatives of *raison d'état* did not require considering the "rights" of French subjects in New Orleans. The king or emperor could seize territory or abandon it as he saw fit—which is precisely what Napoleon did when he launched and then abandoned his imperial plans in North America in the early nineteenth century, much to the chagrin of the French settlers he left to the mercies of a new government.

American statesmen had much less flexibility. In the new liberal and commercial order described by Locke and Smith and embodied in Jefferson's Declaration of Independence, a government constructed by the people for the purpose of protecting *their* life, liberty, and pursuit of happiness could not easily stand in the way of their efforts to acquire and settle new lands, or to trade in overseas markets. The North American geography invited individual adventure and discouraged government interference. The new republic was situated on a relatively small portion of a vast continent filled with the most fertile and potentially productive lands on earth, lands that in the common view of Americans were simply "empty." The government could not declare on behalf of its citizens that it had no interest in further expansion or impose by fiat sharp limits on their ambitions. Nor could it easily refuse to protect them when they were endangered, even by their own risky and illegal behavior. As the Indian inhabitants learned painfully, land once occupied by American settlers, even extralegally, could almost never be taken back and returned to the Indians by a popularly elected government.[8] The political survival of American leaders depended on their solicitousness to the interests of the increasing numbers of voters spreading out across the western lands and to the merchants of the Atlantic seaboard who hoped to spread out across the oceans.[9]

Not only individual politicians had to worry. The federal government itself risked losing popular support if it hemmed in its citizens. Those Americans who lent their support to the Constitution and the federal government after 1787 did so in part because they believed their interests in territorial expansion and overseas commerce would be better served. The Virginia planters who sought new overseas markets for wheat and other grains; the small farmers of western Virginia who wanted better protection from Indian attacks and government support for their expansionist ambitions; the land speculators in North Carolina who wanted the Indians removed to increase the value of their titles; the shipowners and merchants of Boston and Charleston who wanted greater security, and thus lower insurance rates, for their overseas ventures—all these interests had formed the political base of support for the federal government and for the new Constitution, and they expected in turn that the federal government would look out for them.[10] American leaders rightly feared that if they did not defend and promote expansion, whether against Spanish holdings in the South or against Indian lands in the Northwest, the western populations would turn against the federal government and secede.

Acquiring access to the Mississippi and to western territories became a vital national interest, therefore, but not for what might be regarded as traditional strategic reasons. It was not so much that foreign control of the Mississippi and the western territories could provide a potential launching point for invasions or the means of economic blockade. The reason national leaders like Hamilton believed "the acquisition of those countries [was] essential to the permanency of the Union" was their fear that if foreign nations controlled access to their land and trade routes, the liberal men of the West in their pursuit of happiness might choose to sever their connection with the United States.[11] The problem was the uncontrollable force of liberalism itself.

The leaders of the early republic, of course, had little intention of restraining settlement anyway. On the contrary, inducements to expansionism were embedded in the new republic's legal and institutional structures. American settlers venturing to the frontier carried their rights and their political influence with them. The Northwest Ordinance of 1787, which established the means of incorporating new "territories" into the union, guaranteed western settlers equal rights of self-government and with it the political clout to further their expansionist interests.[12] The ordinance was a foreign policy doctrine every bit as significant as Washington's Farewell Address.[13] It was a consciously designed "machine" of expansion.[14] Bestowing full political rights on the western populations ensured that expansion would become an irrepressible issue in American politics. How the federal government handled such questions as gaining access to the Mississippi or pressing western territorial claims against Spain in the South and Indians in the North became inextricably tied to domestic politics, which often pitted northeastern sectional interests against those of the West. The experience of the 1789 Jay-Gardoqui Treaty, which had so angered western interests that it nearly derailed the ratification of the Constitution, taught American politicians a lesson they never forgot. John Jay's treaty granting Spain exclusive rights to navigate the Mississippi for thirty years all but produced a rebellion in the West. Henceforth western territorial demands would be heeded. When Jefferson embarked on new negotiations with Spain for navigation of the Mississippi, discussions that led eventually to the Spanish-American Treaty of San Lorenzo in 1795, he drew up a lengthy state paper "to demonstrate to voters on the western waters the assiduity of the Secretary of State personally, as well as of the federal government generally, in supporting their one most vital interest."[15] By the turn of the century "the desire for acquisition of Louisiana, or at least part of it, had behind it a broad geographical constituency and had become an important factor in national politics."[16]

The extent to which American statesmen were, and believed themselves to be, servants of the people as they shaped a foreign policy for the nation is an obvious but often neglected fact. Historians have devoted many thousands of pages to describing and contrasting Jefferson's and Hamilton's theories of international relations, for instance. But there were limits on any statesman's ability to determine the broad direction of American foreign policy. That policy was the product of the demands of a dynamic people responding to the opportunities and risks of a vast territory and an international market. This is not to say that American foreign policy was merely the handmaiden of the forces of liberal economic and territorial expansion. The leading statesmen of the day tried to mold public opinion and to channel economic forces in certain directions, sometimes successfully. They took steps to maintain the nation's security, steps the necessity of which the population at large, pursuing their individual ambitions, might not always have been aware. And individual Americans cared about more than money and security. Considerations of honor, ideology, and morality shaped American attitudes toward their place in the world as well. But American leaders could not chart a course in foreign affairs that failed to meet the demands of the people for individual opportunity and gain, even if they wished to do so. For this reason it was, and remains, hard to establish a clear separation between American domestic policy and what is usually considered "foreign policy." American actions abroad as well as at home were dictated to an unprecedented degree by the will of many thousands of interested individuals and groups under the influence of a liberal worldview, rather than by statesmen operating on a separate plane of geopolitical thought.

As a result, there was, and always would be, something unplanned and haphazard in the conduct of American policy with respect to foreign nations. American expansion was consistent, but American policies were not always coherent. Frederick the Great, the quintessential practitioner of eighteenth-century realpolitik, might fashion a grand plan for augmenting his Prussian empire, complete with a list of necessary territorial annexations and preventive wars to be undertaken in a specific sequence and within a certain period of time. American statesmen had general expectations every bit as ambitious as Frederick's, perhaps even more so. But they had few actual plans for turning expectations into reality.

There was scarcely an American in a position of influence in the early years of the republic who did not envision the day when the United States would stretch across the entire expanse of the continent, not only westward but also northward into Canada and southward into Mexico. For American statesmen such as Washington, Jefferson, Jay, and Henry Knox, territorial expansion, increasing national power, and the achievement of continental dominance seemed foreordained. When the United States grew stronger, Hamilton declared, and when the American people were able to make good "our pretensions," they would not "leave in the possession of any foreign power, the territories at the mouth of the Mississippi, which are to be regarded as the key to it."[17] American leaders in the early republic offered few specific designs for accomplishing these objectives, however. Not even in private, and much less in public, did they formulate strategies for expanding American territory up to a certain point, by a certain means, and by a certain date.

American statesmen did, however, take actions aimed at hastening the unfolding of their national destiny. They exploited conflicts in Europe to negotiate advantageous treaties and other arrangements with England, France, and Spain. They made war on Indians when the expanding settler population raised troubles on the frontier. They connived and intrigued with insurgents within the Spanish Empire. Hamilton even conspired with the Venezuelan revolutionary Francisco de Miranda on a plan to liberate all of South America from Spanish rule, though the conspiracy came to naught. Efforts such as these were opportunistic rather than strategic. They fit within a broad expectation of American continental expansion and hemispheric dominance, but they were not part of any specific, detailed strategy for achieving these grand ambitions.

The disjunction between the American people's ambitions and their lack of any plan, much less any of the traditionally recognized means for realizing those ambitions, made it difficult to discern a "foreign policy" of continental expansion in the early republic. This partly explains why it has been so common for subsequent generations to view America's conquest of Indian and Spanish lands not as foreign policy but as an internal, domestic matter.[18] But in so describing early American expansionism, historians and Americans generally have only perpetuated a great liberal conceit: that "peaceful conquest" by an advancing liberal civilization must be seen as being of an entirely different character than other forms of conquest and expansion.

Yet who could doubt that the "peaceful conquest" of neighboring territories by the expanding liberal empire was in many ways a more powerful tool of foreign policy than military strength or diplomatic skill? Certainly not those nations and peoples who had the misfortune of sharing the North American continent with the United States. To both Indians and Europeans, the unplanned "peaceful conquest" of American liberalism appeared more dangerous than any calculated military, diplomatic, or commercial "policy" American statesmen might formulate. As the Spanish governor in Louisiana observed, "Their method of spreading themselves and their policy are as much to be feared by Spain as are their arms."[19] He prophesied doom for anyone who stood in the way of this "new and vigorous people . . . advancing and multiplying in the silence of peace." With or without design, liberal America appeared to have an insatiable appetite for continental conquest. "This prestigious and restless population, continually forcing the Indian nations backward and upon us, is attempting to get possession of all the vast continent those nations are occupying between the Ohio and Mississippi Rivers, the Gulf of Mexico and the Appalachian Mountains. . . . If they obtain their purpose, their ambitions will not be limited to this part of the Mississippi."[20]

How to deal with such a force? Traditional diplomacy proved of limited value. Treaties arranged with American diplomats to stem the expansion rarely worked for long. After all, it was the restive and energetic American people who posed the threat, not the Machiavellian designs of their statesmen. The American government demonstrated time and again that, treaty or no treaty, it was unable and unwilling to hem in its own population. As a result, whether American diplomats always intended it or not, the treaties they negotiated both with Spain and with the Indians were no more than a consolidation of present gains before the onward press of the expanding population broke through to the next frontier.

In fact, American statesmen were often fully aware of the powerful forces working in their favor. Most believed with a deterministic confidence that the triumph of their superior liberal, Anglo-Saxon civilization was inevitable. In the language of the reigning Newtonian paradigm, they frequently expressed their belief that adjacent territories—such as the Floridas—would eventually fall into America's possession like ripened fruit pulled to ground by the force of gravity. Cuba would be drawn in, too, by the powerful attraction of a successful liberal society. This was one reason American leaders truly feared only Britain and France, two powerful nations but, more important, two powerful leaders of advancing Western civilization. The Spanish Empire, on the other hand, appeared to most Americans contemptible and in decline. Jefferson's only fear was that it would be "too feeble" to hold its territories until "our population can be sufficiently advanced to gain it from them piece by piece."[21] Hamilton agreed that problems with Spain and access to the Mississippi would be "arranged to our satisfaction" not through war but "by the natural progress of things."[22] The attractive force of American liberalism would naturally stir the oppressed peoples in the "gloomy regions of despotism" against the Spanish "tyrant" who ruled over them—though Hamilton was also prepared to help that process along, if possible.[23] The Indians, needless to say, were thought to be no match whatsoever.

In this liberal worldview, the triumph of America's civilization over both these inferior peoples did not ultimately depend on the vagaries of European wars, on seismic shifts in the European balance of power, or on other manifestations of "Europe's distress." Given time, the conquest of Spanish and Indian holdings on the continent was inevitable. As Jefferson remarked to James Monroe in 1801, "However our present interests may restrain us within our limits, it is impossible not to look forward to distant times, when our rapid multiplication will expand it beyond those limits, & cover the whole northern if not the southern continent, with people speaking the same language, governed in similar forms, and by similar laws."[24]

This deterministic assumption worked its way into the conduct of American diplomacy. Thus John Jay, even as he had negotiated the terms of a treaty that, much to the consternation of Kentuckians, would have given Spain exclusive control of the Mississippi for thirty years, anticipated that the letter of the treaty would soon be made irrelevant by the continuing migration of the American population into Spanish-held territories.[25] Jay "assumed that within twenty years the fecund and expansive Americans would gain control of the waterway regardless of Spanish objections."[26] Jefferson, in his own later negotiations with the Spanish government, was quick to make use of the uncontrollable settlers and his own government's inability to restrain them as leverage for winning Spain's acquiescence to American demands. To the Spanish minister "he spoke of the difficult task of keeping Kentucky quiet, of his fear that the people there could not be restrained if the federal government did not get for them their desired navigation [of the Mississippi]."[27]

The Spaniards, though possessing the world's third-largest navy and an army that, if ever deployed, would have dwarfed the tiny American forces spread across the frontiers, were nevertheless incapable of withstanding the "peaceful" liberal onslaught. Between the end of the American Revolution and 1800, the Anglo-Saxon population of the trans-Allegheny region grew from 30,000 to 300,000, a good portion of it pressing hard against and infiltrating Spanish holdings in the South and Southwest.[28] The advancing Americans made themselves a vital part of the Spanish colony's economy, producing wheat, tobacco, hemp, corn, whiskey, and beef and exporting it all through the Spanish-controlled ports of Natchez and New Orleans. "Wherever Americans went in Louisiana they appeared to take over."[29] The Spanish government tried just about every available strategy to stem the advance. It employed the time-honored tactic of using the Indians as buffers. It imposed economic restrictions on American trade. Then it tried a different tack, opening Louisiana to American immigration—a desperate stratagem that Jefferson suggested was akin to "settling the Goths at the gates of Rome." He hoped "a hundred thousand of our inhabitants would accept the invitation. It will be the means of delivering to us peaceably what may otherwise cost us a war."[30]

In the end, Spain was forced into a series of tactical retreats, partly due to changes in the alignment of power in Europe but partly in recognition of the hopelessness of resisting the American advance. In the Treaty of San Lorenzo, known in the United States as Pinckney's Treaty, Spain finally recognized the thirty-first parallel as the southern boundary of the United States, opened the Mississippi once again to American traders, and granted them a right of deposit at the port of New Orleans. These concessions only tightened the American economic stranglehold and accelerated the Americanization of the colony. Freed from Spanish restrictions, American flatboats, carrying the produce of western farmers, swarmed the Mississippi, turning Louisiana "into a sphere of American influence" and shattering the colony's allegiances to the Spanish Empire.[31] In 1799 a rebellion in the Spanish-controlled port of Natchez gave the United States an excuse to take possession of the entire region.

American Indian Policy: Power and Responsibility

THE SAME RELIANCE on peaceful conquest, the same tactics of compromise and consolidation followed by further advance, characterized American dealings with the Indians of the Ohio Valley. While they resorted to war more frequently against the Indians than against Spain, American leaders were also more confident that when it came to displacing Indian populations in the Northwest, both time and the forces of liberal expansion were on their side.

In the Indian-controlled regions of the North and Northwest, as in the Southwest, American foreign policy was often shaped by forces beyond the central government's control. Throughout the 1780s and '90s officials in Philadelphia and Washington, eager to avoid costly and often fruitless guerrilla wars with Indian tribes—wars that resulted in some devastating losses for the United States—negotiated treaties and delineated boundaries to try to limit friction between western settlers and the Indians whose land they coveted. Secretary of War Henry Knox expressed the common view in Washington that much of the blame for the violent disturbances along the frontiers of Kentucky and North Carolina could be laid on the "unjustifiable conduct" of white settlers whose "avaricious desire of obtaining the fertile lands" of the Indians had sparked cycles of murder and reprisal.[32] A committee report to Congress in July 1787 insisted it was the "avaricious disposition in some of our people to acquire large tracts of land and often by unfair means" that appeared to be "the principal source of difficulties with the Indians."[33]

How to stop Americans from seizing Indian lands? As Knox laid out the options, "Either one or the other party must remove to a greater distance, or the Government must keep them both in awe by a strong hand, and compel them to be moderate and just."[34] But the latter course was practically difficult and politically next to impossible. The federal government had neither the capacity nor the will to keep white settlers "in awe by a strong hand." Western political pressure virtually ensured that elected officials in Washington would offer the federal government's protection to settlers, even when they intruded into Indian lands in violation of treaties that the government had solemnly negotiated.

The Hopewell Treaty of 1785, for instance, had placed limits on the expansion of North Carolinians onto lands held by the Cherokee. But when white settlement on Cherokee territory continued in violation of the treaty, within six years the federal government simply opened a new negotiation and ratified the expansion by means of a new arrangement, the Treaty of Holston. For all its complaints about the settlers' "unjustifiable conduct," the federal government did not fail to fall in behind them. And one renegotiated treaty made more of them inevitable: "[T]he settlers who had advanced into Cherokee country against federal protests, now found that the federal government had extended the boundary to include them, and those who were left in Indian country by the new line were soon to exert pressure for further cessions."[35] Elected officials in the West, like Governor William Blount of the Tennessee territory, had every reason to seek as much land as possible from the Indians. After all, the settlers whom both Indians and the federal government viewed as unlawful "intruders" were Governor Blount's political constituents.[36]

Rights granted to Indians by treaty, therefore, were steadily eroded, and the treaties proved to be flimsy barriers to the waves of settlers. In this respect American diplomacy with the Indians was contradictory at best, duplicitous at worst. The Northwest Ordinance declared that Indian "land and property shall never be taken from them without their consent"; but it also declared that all the territory from the Ohio River to the Mississippi, much of which was theoretically recognized as Indian land by treaty, "shall remain forever a part of this Confederacy of the United States of America." The last great Indian treaty of the eighteenth century, the Treaty of Greenville, signed in the same year as the Treaty of San Lorenzo with Spain, had no more lasting impact on white settlement than those that had come before. Nor was it intended to. Much of the land the United States guaranteed to the Indians in the Treaty of Greenville had long been promised by Congress to Revolutionary War veterans or had been sold by the federal government to land companies that looked forward to making good on their investments.[37]

American leaders such as Knox, Washington, and Jefferson fully recognized the unfairness with which they and their compatriots dealt with the Indians. Knox, in particular, believed these repeated violations of Indian treaties were a blot on the nation's character. At the same time, however, these same American leaders counted on the constant encroachment of settlers on Indian lands as a central part of their overall aim of achieving dominance in the Ohio Valley. Knox and others expected, mistakenly, that the Indians would simply move away peacefully as white settlements spread and ruined their hunting grounds. As the white population increased and approached Indian boundaries, Knox predicted, "game will be diminished and new purchases [of Indian land] made for small considerations."[38] He and Washington knew their guarantees of Indian land were ultimately meaningless. Over time "the Indians would either be exterminated, retire, or would easily yield land which was no longer useful to them."[39]

Even more than in their dealings with Spanish colonists, American leaders believed that eventual American conquest of Indian territory was preordained, the inevitable consequence of the great disparity between an increasingly modern commercial society and the Indians' primitive ways. The outcome of this dramatic eighteenth-century clash of civilizations, which pitted the powerful new forces of a liberal market economy against a people who still depended for their livelihood on hunting wild game, could never be in doubt. The one by its very existence tended either to transform or obliterate the other. As white settlement advanced, American leaders in Washington believed, the Indians either had to abandon their culture completely and adopt liberal ways, as farmers or traders, or be wiped out. Either way the land would be opened for American settlement, for if the Indian transformed himself into a man of commerce, he, like the Spanish colonist, would inevitably be drawn into the web of the American commercial empire. As President Jefferson told a group of Indians in 1808, in a typical burst of Lockean enthusiasm, "When once you have property, you will want laws and magistrates to protect your property and person. . . . You will find that our laws are good for this purpose; you will wish to live under them, you will unite yourselves with us, join in our great councils and form one people with us, and we shall all be Americans."[40]

American foreign policy on the continent was thus infused with, and inseparable from, American ideology. Americans had brought with them not merely a European culture but a new way of viewing human nature, a view shaped by Locke, by the Scottish Enlightenment, by Adam Smith, and by the new "science" of political economy. Their liberal view of the world made them see land and natural resources as things to be cultivated, improved, bought, and sold. The right of ownership of land, in this view, depended on putting that land to good use. "Man's right and duty to improve on nature's gifts, property's origin in labor and its subsequent regulation by civil society, the role of government in protecting and fostering the different and unequal faculties of acquiring property—all these were accepted by the whites as the bases of civilized life."[41] When squatters illegally seizing Indian territory protested that "all mankind [has] an undoubted right to pass into any vacant country" and that therefore the federal government was "not impowered to forbid them," they were merely giving voice to commonly accepted liberal principles.[42]

This liberal ideology was almost indifferent to race. Americans accorded the decaying Spanish Empire not much greater claim to land on the continent than they accorded the Indian "savages." Hamilton expressed the common view that American citizens were "entitled by nature and compact to a free participation in the navigation of the Mississippi."[43] In fact, such an entitlement could be found nowhere in the strictures of international law that Hamilton was so fond of quoting. The demand for the free use of Spain's land and water resources along the Mississippi "reflected a feeling that Spain's land and its use really should belong to Americans as a natural right." This was evidence not of a European but of a specifically "Anglo-American expansionist ideology."[44] These "first-born children of the commercial age" took a dim view of both Indian and Spanish cultures. Hamilton, along with most Americans, then and later, had contempt for Spanish "indolence" and "supineness."[45] "Feudal lord and Indian chief each displayed an indifference to those concerns that commerce made central for itself. Each disdained what Adam Smith called the 'pedlar principle of turning a penny whenever a penny was to be got.' "[46] Each, therefore, was deemed obsolete in the new commercial era.

But it was the Indians, and especially the Indian male—who made a positive virtue of not "working," as Anglo-Americans understood the term, who rejected the whole notion of property, and who desired neither to better himself nor to "improve" the natural world around him—who stood as a particular object of disdain for Americans, even to those inclined to sympathize with the Indians' plight. Americans could not fathom the Indians' commitment to hold land that in Anglo-Saxon eyes was lying fallow and unused. The land that the federal government bought or forced to be ceded from the Indians was often described as "excess land."[47] Hugh Henry Brackenridge compared the Indians' land claims with those of children who insisted something was theirs just because they saw it first. In Brackenridge's view, no doubt heavily shaped by the fact that he was a politician from western Pennsylvania, land should belong to those who could use it most productively for "the support of the greatest number" and toward "the greatest sum of happiness," by which he meant "the cultivation of the soil." Like many other Americans, he could not respect "any right which is not founded in agricultural occupancy."[48] John Quincy Adams declared that the Indians' claim to the land violated the divine plan.

> Shall [the Indian] doom an immense region of the globe to perpetual desolation, and to hear the howlings of the tiger and the wolf, silence forever the voice of human gladness? Shall the fields and the vallies which a beneficent God has framed to teem with the life of innumerable multitudes, be condemned to everlasting barrenness? Shall the mighty rivers poured out by the hands of nature, as channels of communication between numerous nations, roll their waters in sullen silence, and eternal solitude to the deep? Have hundreds of commodious harbors, a thousand leagues of coast, and a boundless ocean been spread in front of this land, and shall every purpose of utility to which they could apply, be prohibited by the tenant of the woods? No, generous philanthropists! Heaven has not been thus inconsistent in the works of its hands![49]

Americans did not realize, of course, that in setting forth this justification for taking Indian lands, they were giving voice to a revolutionary ideology, that their conception of human nature, of the "natural" workings of the market, and of the value and meaning of wealth and property was "an intellectual construction of the modernizing nations of the West."[50] It was not, as they believed, a universally accepted truth but, in the case of the Indians, an imposition of one set of values upon a people with a very different conception of human nature and social order. Two centuries later this kind of imposition would be given the name "globalization," a process whereby American-style market economics engulfed nearly the entire world and engendered similar resistance from the non-Western cultures it swept across. In the eighteenth century this proto-"globalization" was especially catastrophic in its effects on an Indian culture that would not accept, or was simply unable to accept, the only route left open for its survival. The

American ideology gave the Indians only one choice: "If the Indians chose to join the ranks of the civilized, they were welcome to do so (at least among the enlightened). Becoming Lockean men, however, would be the nonnegotiable condition of their remaining in the neighborhood of the whites."[51]

If the American liberal ideology provided both the impetus and the justification for expansion, however, it also raised troubling questions about the morality of conquest and forced Americans to try to reconcile their territorial ambitions with their liberal and Christian sense of what constituted just and honorable behavior. All great powers in history have at one time or another faced the problem of how to reconcile the exercise of power with principles of morality and justice. Thucydides relates that the Athenians, at Melos, had been content to proclaim that power was its own justification, that conquest of the weak by the strong was simply the natural order of things: "of the Gods we believe, and of men we know for certain, that by a necessary law of nature they always rule where they can." But this was not for Thucydides, and probably not for many Athenians, a very satisfactory justification. The Roman Republic, one of the most aggressively expansionist powers in history, had felt compelled to limit itself, in theory at least, to fighting only "just wars," by which the Romans generally meant wars waged in self-defense or in response to some "unjust" behavior by their adversaries. For the Christian powers of Europe, war and imperial conquest could be justified as furthering Christianity itself, in service to God. For the British, especially in the nineteenth century, some combination of the proselytizing religious mission and the civilizing liberal mission constituted the essential "sinews of empire."[52]

Americans in the early republic also had to reconcile power and conquest with their sense of justice and morality. In addition to the usual difficulties this presented to all strong powers, the Americans had some special problems of their own. A nation whose founding principles proclaimed the universal "natural" rights of all men, not just of Americans, a nation that placed a premium on individual autonomy and national self-determination, a nation whose very existence had been achieved by fighting its way free from an imperial authority—such a people could not easily engage in the conquest of others, peaceful or otherwise, without some arduous self-examination. If all men possessed inalienable rights, what about the rights of Indians whose lands the Americans were seizing and whose very existence as a people was, even as early as the eighteenth century, manifestly in doubt?

To be sure, not all Americans agreed that there was a problem. For many frontier settlers, the Indians were "vermin," a subhuman species possessed of no natural rights that needed to be considered. The hideous tortures that Indians inflicted on victims of all races, including their own, had more immediacy for frontiersmen than for eastern politicians. Removing Indians from the land was simply part of clearing away the wilderness and making the land fit for human habitation and should cause no more pangs of conscience to white settlers than the removal of the snakes and dangerous beasts.

Other Americans, however, including most of the national leaders in Philadelphia and Washington, did not share this view. For Washington, Jefferson, Knox, and many leading members of Congress, the conquest of the Indians did raise troubling questions about the morality of the nation's behavior, questions that demanded some plausible answers that could fit within the liberal American ideology. For one thing, they did not agree that Indians possessed no natural rights. Just as many eighteenth-century Americans, and even many slaveholders, felt compelled to admit that black slaves had rights, at least in theory, so too for men like the secretary of war, Henry Knox, it seemed indisputable that the Indians possessed "the natural rights of man."[53] As such they possessed as well "the right of soil," which could not be taken from them "unless by their free consent, or by the right of conquest in case of a just war."[54] The Indians had "the right to sell, and the right to refuse to sell," and it was incumbent on the United States to respect these "just rights."[55] To ignore them, Knox argued, and to take their land without their consent, "would be a gross violation of the fundamental laws of nature, and of that distributive justice which is the glory of a nation."[56] A report to Congress in 1787 argued that the Indians' resistance to the encroachments of American settlers was both understandable and legitimate: "The Indians appear to act a natural part for men in their situation."[57] Jefferson saw the Indians as men in a primitive state of nature, but men nonetheless, "in body and mind equal to the white man" and lacking only civilization to make them equal in all other respects as well.[58]

Early on in the new republic, American negotiators had approached the Indians much as the Athenians had approached the Melians. In 1785 the American commissioners at Fort McIntosh brushed aside Indian resistance to their territorial claims with a declaration of right based on naked power: "We claim the country by conquest; and are to give not to receive."[59] This answer proved untenable, however, on practical as well as moral grounds. The fact was, the United States had neither the military strength nor the will to drive the Indians out by war alone, an unpleasant realization that soon led the federal government to adopt the more sophisticated approach of tactical compromise and consolidation followed by efforts at peaceful conquest.[60] But neither was the commissioners' cold assertion of the right of conquest entirely acceptable to the American conscience. Two years later a report to Congress, following the line of Knox and Washington, suggested that "instead of a language of superiority and command," it would be both "politic and just to treat with the Indians more on a footing of equality" and to "convince them of the justice and humanity as well as the power of the United States and of their disposition to promote the happiness of the Indians."[61]

At stake for many leading Americans was the question of national honor, and for Americans honor was intimately bound up with the universal principles they claimed to champion. Jefferson was not alone in wishing to show the world how much more justly and benevolently a liberal republic wielded its power. "A nation solicitous of establishing its character on the broad basis of justice," Knox declared, "would not only hesitate at, but reject every proposition to benefit itself, by the injury of any neighboring community, however contemptible and weak it might be."[62] How could the United States distinguish itself from the empires of Europe if it treated the native populations of the New World no better than they did or, indeed, somewhat worse? "If our modes of population and War destroy the tribes," Knox warned in 1793, "the disinterested part of mankind and posterity will be apt to class the effects of our Conduct and that of the Spaniards in Mexico and Peru together."[63] He worried that if the United States persisted in its unjust treatment of the Indians a "black cloud of injustice and inhumanity will impend over our national character."[64]

Washington, Knox, and others believed that treatment of the Indians during the time of the Confederation and before had already put a stain on the nation's reputation. During Washington's administration, therefore, they tried to bring "a new respectability into the conduct of American-Indian relations." Both Knox and Washington "placed far greater emphasis on the morality of American policy than had been common for most of the Confederation period."[65] From the beginning the Washington administration declared its intention to establish peaceful relations with the Indians "on such pure principles of justice and moderation, as will enforce the approbation of the dispassionate and enlightened part of mankind."[66] To the degree that this was accomplished, Knox asserted in 1793, "the reproach which our country has sustained will be obliterated and the protection of the helpless ignorant Indians, while they demean themselves peaceably, will adorn the character of the United States."[67] Knox's successor as secretary of war, Timothy Pickering, shared Knox's discomfort and urged American representatives negotiating the 1795 Treaty of Greenville to seek "peace and not increase of territory."[68]

In their dealings with the Indians, some Americans for the first but not the last time in the nation's history came to the conclusion that with great power comes great responsibility. They felt no similar pangs of conscience when dealing with the Spanish Empire, nor made such tortuous efforts to reconcile their ambition and power with the demands of morality and honor. Their efforts to drive Spain from the North American continent were undertaken without apology. This was no doubt in part because the "peaceful conquest" of Spanish territory did not threaten the very existence of the Spanish people as it did in the case of the Indians. But there was also an unstated presumption that the Spaniards, as Europeans possessed of a powerful empire of their own, could take care of themselves. The contest with Spain was roughly equal. The struggle with the Indians, on the other hand, was profoundly unequal, with the United States holding by far the stronger hand, both in terms of raw national power and by virtue of the Americans' more advanced civilization. There was honor and glory in defeating the Spanish Empire. But while individual Americans might achieve glory in fighting Indians, for the nation as a whole the conquest of a "contemptible and weak" people was devoid of glory. This was certainly Knox's view. "As a soldier, he could see no real honor in an Indian war. He could see only difficulty, expense, and tedious guerrilla warfare. Knox wanted a proud, powerful nation," and this was not to be achieved through the brutal conquest of an inferior race.[69]

What honor there was to be found in dealing with the weak and primitive Indians had to be achieved not through military conquest but through the assumption of responsibility. Inverting the logic of the Athenians at Melos, some leading Americans believed that the very inequality of the relationship imposed certain moral obligations on their nation.[70] Knox insisted that precisely because the United States was "more powerful, and more enlightened," than the Indians, it had acquired a "responsibility of national character, that we should treat them with kindness, and even liberality."[71] In his third annual message to the Congress, Washington asserted that "a system corresponding with the mild principles of religion and philanthropy toward an unenlightened race of men, whose happiness materially depends on the conduct of the United States, would be as honorable to the national character as conformable to the dictates of sound policy."[72]

Given the Americans' ambition for land, an ambition they had no real intention of restraining, and given the impossibility of the Indians preserving their ancestral customs side by side with the new commercial empire, there seemed only one way for Americans to assume their "responsibility" and to fulfill the moral obligations they believed their power imposed upon them. That was to turn the conquest of Indian land into something of positive benefit to the Indians, to bring them what Washington and other Americans unashamedly called the "blessings of civilization." Americans would not renounce their territorial ambitions; nor were they prepared to divest themselves of the power that raised so many difficult questions of honor and morality for a liberal and Christian people. Instead, they tried to reconcile ambition with honor, power with morality, and the solution they arrived at was that of liberalism. They proposed to bestow upon those they had forced to submit to their power and ambition the liberal ideology itself, with all its economic and spiritual benefits. Instead of conquering the Indians, they would be liberating them. How different, Knox declared, "would be the sensation of a philosophic mind to reflect, that, instead of exterminating a part of the human race by our modes of population, we had persevered, through all difficulties, and at last had imparted our knowledge of cultivation and the arts to the aboriginals of the country, by which the source of future life and happiness had been preserved and extended."[73]

For the leaders of the early republic, this moral purpose was to become the "great justification" of their Indian policy: "The Indian would give up his lands to the advancing American farmer, but in return he would receive the inestimable gift of civilization."[74] That the Indians were reluctant recipients of that gift some Americans well understood. As John C. Calhoun put it many years later, this Indian policy was based on the premise that it was "our views of their interest, and not their own, [which] ought to govern them."[75] But neither did some Americans, like Knox and Jefferson, want to believe that the Indians were incapable of being lifted up to civilization. These staunch adherents of the Lockean view of a universal human nature insisted that only bad habits, bad political economy, and bad government limited human possibilities. "Were it possible to introduce among the Indian tribes a love for exclusive property," Knox insisted, "it would be a happy commencement of the business" of civilizing them.[76] In his view, to deny that the Indians could be raised to the level of civilized men was to "suppose the human character under the influence of such stubborn habits as to be incapable of melioration or change." To the modern liberal mind, which saw human history as but a steady climb to enlightenment, this was an insupportable supposition, one "entirely contradicted by the progress of society, from the barbarous ages to its present degree of perfection."[77] The question was not whether the Indians could benefit from the blessings of civilization but whether they could be persuaded to accept the gift the Americans were offering. The settlers of the West probably had a clearer understanding of the difficulties involved in making the Indians see the value of this gift. But Jefferson hoped it would be possible to make the Indians see that the interests of the United States and their own were, in fact, identical. "We, like you, are Americans, born in the same land, and having the same interests," Jefferson told them. "We desire above all things, brother, to instruct you in whatever we know ourselves. We wish [you to learn] all our arts and to make you wise and wealthy."[78]

As Calhoun suggested, many Indians had a different desire and a different conception of their interests, summed up in the statement of Indian negotiators at Detroit in 1793: "We desire you to consider, brothers, that our only demand is the peaceable possession of a small part of our once great country. Look back, and review the lands from whence we have been driven to this spot. We can retreat no farther . . . and we have therefore resolved to leave our bones in this small space to which we are now confined."[79] Others, like the Cherokees, made the effort to become civilized, abandoned hunting for agriculture, and adopted a written constitution modeled after that of the United States. But even this acceptance of the American bargain saved neither the Cherokee people nor the American conscience. The Cherokee "renaissance" that began in 1795 ended with the coming of Andrew Jackson's presidency and an Indian policy more in conformity with western frontier attitudes than with eastern views of enlightened behavior.[80] The mission to bring the "blessings of civilization" to Indians ultimately failed, therefore, and though its spirit lived on well into the nineteenth century, Americans gradually turned to policies of removal and ceased to maintain much more than a theoretical regard for the Indians' "natural rights."

There was, to be sure, a strong measure of hypocrisy even among those eighteenth-century Americans who claimed to value those rights. Both Knox and Jefferson approved making war on the Indians when they refused to cede their lands voluntarily. Jefferson could on occasion express his desire to "give the Indians a thorough drubbing."[81] No one was prepared to sacrifice American territorial expansion to the Indians' demands to do with their lands as they pleased. All leading Americans deliberately averted their gaze from the inherent contradictions of their Indian policy, which simultaneously promised Indians justice while it promised American settlers land.

In fairness to these Americans, the Indians posed a unique problem. Spaniards, French, Russians, and other Western peoples could be absorbed into the American stream without destroying the very essence of their civilizations. Indians could not. But since they could not be transformed into

Lockean men, and since their way of life could not coexist with America's liberal, commercial society, the only way to preserve what remained of Indian society after two centuries of white settlement along the Atlantic Coast was to abstain from further territorial expansion. Even then it is not clear how long such a people would have survived next to the kind of modern, industrial society America was eventually to become. In any event, the Americans, faced with this dilemma, were no more inclined to self-denial than any other people in history. In this respect, at least, they were not exceptional.

Americans remember the Indians and what was done to them. But for some reason the common memory of early American foreign policy today takes little or no account of American Indian policy. Looking back on America's continental expansion from the perspective of the late nineteenth and twentieth centuries, most Americans still view the hardy pioneers of the late eighteenth and early nineteenth centuries as conquering and settling "virgin land" on a "barren continent." There is a degree of racial prejudice in this, of course, or perhaps more accurately, a civilizational prejudice. But this prejudice is also an obstacle to understanding the roots of American foreign policy. Late-eighteenth-century Americans did not, in fact, view their relations with the Indian tribes as strictly domestic. Few accepted the fiction that the territories transferred to the United States by the British at the end of the Revolution were indisputably American. The federal government in Washington conducted endless rounds of diplomacy and entered into numerous treaties with the Indians for land cessions. The treaties were officially deposited at the State Department, like all other international agreements, and had the same legal force, at least in theory, as treaties made with European nations.[82] Secretary of War Henry Knox expressed the federal government's official view that "the independent nations and tribes of the Indians ought to be considered as foreign nations, not as the subjects of any particular States."[83]

After the eighteenth century, and especially by the twentieth century, most of America's relationships would be with weaker nations and, in the case of the Western Hemisphere, where America was to be especially active from the 1880s through the 1930s, with nations whose strength relative to the United States was not much greater than that of the Indians. In dealing with these nations and, as the twentieth century progressed, in dealing with an increasing number of weaker and less developed nations around the world, the United States wrestled with the same conflicts between power and morality, between ambition and honor, and often tried to reconcile them in much the same way—by assuming a "responsibility for all these little states," as Theodore Roosevelt would later describe his Caribbean policy, by offering the blessings of Anglo-American civilization, by spreading the liberal ideology, and by attempting to make others, in Jefferson's words, "wise and wealthy."

Commerce and the Mediterranean

IN THE EIGHTEENTH CENTURY the pursuit of these broad goals was not confined to the North American continent, nor even to the Western Hemisphere. Within the first two decades after independence, the new republic also set out to project its power and influence, and its liberal ways, across the oceans. In the 1780s and '90s overseas trade became a national preoccupation, uniting diverse interests around the country behind policies for promoting expansion of foreign markets. By 1789 the difficult economic straits of the Confederation period had given way to an economic boom, and the return of American prosperity was sparked and sustained to a large extent by a great expansion of foreign trade. Even before the outbreak of war in Europe in 1793, Americans had begun to make their fortunes in overseas commerce. Trade with the British West Indies, though prohibited by British navigation laws, flourished as enterprising American merchants employed all the arts of forgery, bribery, and smuggling to evade the British naval blockade. While trade expanded with traditional partners in Europe, Americans also reached out to new markets in China, South America, the West Coast of North America, and the Mediterranean.

The European war that erupted in 1793 between revolutionary France and the coalition of powers led by Britain proved to be a bonanza for Americans. The war allowed the neutral United States to ship goods to all the belligerent powers, and the need for American goods and shipping only grew as the war devastated European producers and wreaked havoc on European shippers. Grain shortages in Europe created enormous demand for foodstuffs, especially wheat, produced in the expanding North American interior. Between 1790 and 1800, the value of American exports rose from just under $20 million to more than $30 million, while imports rose from $22.5 million to $52 million. The percentage of American exports and imports carried in American ships climbed from less than 40 percent to almost 90 percent. The biggest increase came in the re-export trade, where Americans shipped goods produced in, for instance, the West Indies to the United States and then across the Atlantic. This trade rose from less than a half million dollars to $39 million by the end of the eighteenth century. In the 1790s the United States became a world-class commercial power, thoroughly integrated "into a developing worldwide trading network, centered on the North Atlantic but with tentacles reaching around the globe."[84]

The success of overseas commerce bred popular demands for ever-wider commercial opportunities. Rising fortunes created rising expectations up and down the social ladder as more and more Americans sought to partake in the get-rich-quick scheme of foreign trade. Some Jeffersonians lamented the change but did not see what could be done about it. "The brilliant prospects held out by commerce," one American observer complained, had turned the United States into a nation of gamblers and speculators. "[S]o certain were the profits on the foreign voyages," so steady was the "demand in Europe for foreign merchandise, especially for that of the West Indies and South America," that investing in shipments seemed to be without risk: "The most adventurous became the most wealthy." As a result, "our catalogue of merchants was swelled much beyond what it was entitled to be from the state of our population. Many persons, who had secured moderate capitals, from mechanical pursuits, soon became the most adventurous." A single individual might simultaneously be "concerned in voyages to Asia, South America, the West Indies and Europe."[85]

Even Jeffersonians promoted trade, however. They were particularly eager to open trading opportunities outside the British Isles, to alleviate the American economy's near-total dependence on commerce with a former imperial master too often inclined to impose unpleasant restrictions on American trade. Jefferson and Madison wanted to increase trade with France and other nations on the European continent. They also looked to more exotic locales, to the Mediterranean and to China, for alternatives to the dominant traffic with Britain. Individual investors seeking big profits, meanwhile, required no encouragement or patriotic motivation for their speculative endeavors. They naturally searched across the seas for new opportunities wherever they could find them.

Among the most beguiling of these new opportunities was to be found in China. Before the Revolution American merchants had been effectively blocked from the China trade by British prohibitions on the direct import of foreign goods into the colonies and by the monopoly on Far Eastern trade that the British Crown had granted the East India Company. The Jay Treaty of 1794 opened China to American traders for the first time, and they leaped in with an enthusiasm and willingness to take risks that often exceeded the likelihood of actually turning a profit. Many of those blazing the path to China, like those who blazed the trails to the American West, craved the risks almost as much as the rewards. The "species of men who formed the dramatis personae of the first China voyages"—men such as

Samuel Shaw, Thomas Randall, and Thomas Truxtun—were mostly "Revolutionary War veterans from the Continental army or navy or former privateersmen seeking to replace excitement and danger with adventure and profit."[86] They sailed off to distant ports with the same blend of reckless abandon and Lockean discipline as the settlers who pioneered the vast Indian lands of the Ohio Valley.

Financing these early voyages was a new breed of American entrepreneur, a nouveau riche faithfully pursuing the new capitalist science. Robert Morris, the son of a tobacco importer's agent and émigré from Liverpool, had worked his way from the countinghouse to full partnership in Philadelphia's largest mercantile firm. During the war for independence Morris used both his wealth and his wiles to finance General Washington's military campaign. When the war concluded, he turned his eyes to the opportunities that beckoned in China. He framed his ventures in patriotic terms: in November 1783 he wrote, "I am sending some ships to China in order to encourage others in the adventurous pursuits of commerce."[87] The *Empress of China,* in which Morris owned a 50 percent share, sailed from New York for Canton in February 1784 and returned a year later with exotic Chinese handicrafts for him and his wife and a hefty 25 percent profit on his investment.

Another Philadelphia merchant and shipowner, Stephen Girard, had been born in Bordeaux and at age fourteen gone to sea as a cabin boy. After settling in America after the outbreak of the Revolution, he made a fortune in the West Indies trade before entering the China trade on a grand scale. His ships, suitably named by this Enlightenment merchant the *Rousseau,* the *Voltaire,* the *Montesquieu,* and the *Helvetius,* made more than a dozen voyages to Canton after the turn of the century and produced for Girard one of the largest personal fortunes—he left $7 million when he died—of any American until that time. In 1800 John Jacob Astor, soon to become a "one-man multinational corporation," sent his first shipment of Canadian furs to China, foreshadowing the "audacious globe-girdling scheme that would lead to the founding of Astoria" in Oregon.[88]

The China trade, once inaugurated, quickly became something of a national sensation, if not an obsession. Not only was there money to make, but for the new republic just beginning to stand on its own feet in the world, trade with far-off China was a great national achievement and a source of pride.[89] John Jay saw the voyages as a harbinger of future American greatness built on the selfish pursuit of commerce. "The spirit of enterprise and adventure runs high in our young country," he wrote Philadelphia merchant William Bingham, "and if properly directed by a vigorous and wise government would produce great effects."[90] By the end of 1790, according to one estimate, Americans had sent twenty-eight ships to Canton.[91]

Overseas trade was so popular because so many benefited. The trade boom of the 1790s opened unprecedented opportunities not only for American investors, traders, and shipping interests in northeastern and southeastern port cities, but also for merchants and farmers both along the Atlantic littoral and inland. The China trade, for instance, produced an enormous demand for ginseng, just about the only commodity, other than specie and animal furs, that the Chinese valued but did not produce themselves. As it happened, ginseng was produced in great quantities only in the mountains and forests of the American hinterlands. Thus were the interests of eastern merchants and backcountry yeomen strangely united in the China trade. Indeed, as one historian of Philadelphia's commercial development has noted, "It was the amorphous backcountry regions—the hinterlands—that provided the marketable commodities with which Philadelphia was able to build an international commerce." These included such staples as timber, grain, and milled flour, as well as the more exotic ginseng.[92]

The unparalleled growth in prosperity, in fact, went some way toward softening many of the acute sectional disputes that had pitted East Coast shippers and traders against western agrarian interests. The expanding commerce not only benefited both but also knit them more closely within one market system. Farmers in the West raised crops for the domestic and international markets. Eastern merchants thus supported western demands for more arable land, and western farmers supported eastern demands for access to overseas markets.[93] And the benefits of the trade boom rippled outward. Urbanization of eastern ports increased the demand for laborers to provide needed services to city dwellers. Higher prices for agricultural goods increased demand for farm labor. Increases in national income from customs duties financed roads and turnpikes that linked country to city, lowering the cost of transporting produce to markets, thus spurring even more production and greater efficiency. The growth of private income from the boom in exports provided capital for investment and led to the rapid growth of banking and insurance, laying the basis for continued growth in the economy even after the temporary benefits of the European war stopped flowing into American coffers.[94]

Promoting overseas commerce was the inescapable duty of American statesmen in the new republic, whether they liked it or not. Broad segments of the population supported ratification of the Constitution precisely because they believed it would open such opportunities, and after ratification they expected their government to make good on its promise.[95] Men like Hamilton were happy to oblige. But even those American leaders who worried about the harmful effects on the national character had to admit, as Jefferson did, that "[o]ur people have a decided taste for navigation and commerce . . . and their servants are in duty bound to calculate all their measures on this datum."[96] For the elected leaders of a liberal republic, protecting the citizens' "right" to pursue happiness by trading abroad, and protecting their lives and property from attack when they engaged in such trade, was no less compelling than protecting their "right" to expand onto "unused" land in the West. If the lives and property of Americans trading abroad were "violated on the seas, and in foreign ports," Jefferson argued, the federal government had a responsibility to use its power to defend them.[97]

Trade with the Mediterranean was only one part of America's expanding commercial empire—the British market still commanded the lion's share—but by the 1790s American exports to the Mediterranean and southern Europe, which included fish from New England, flour from the middle states, and rice from the South had made "access to this sea of national importance."[98] Moreover, Jefferson and others looked to the Mediterranean as a place where opportunities might be found to relieve American dependence on the British market.

With new opportunities, however, came new dangers. Before 1783 American merchants plying the Mediterranean had enjoyed the protection of the British flag. The British navy kept at bay the Barbary powers, North African principalities nominally under the control of the Turkish Porte, which made their living by piracy—the eighteenth-century version of "rogue states." After American independence, the British saw no need to continue providing this protective umbrella for American trade, and Americans suddenly became the chief victims of Mediterranean piracy. Insurance rates for Mediterranean voyages soared; profits disappeared; merchants and sailors were seized, enslaved, and physically abused by their captors. The United States experimented with a policy of bribing the Barbary leaders, but the deals did not always hold, and the ransom price kept going up.

A nation zealously committed to remaining aloof from foreign and, especially, European entanglements might have simply withdrawn from further involvement in the Mediterranean, a region four thousand miles away where the machinations of Great Britain, France, and other European powers had combined with the lawlessness of the Barbary states to create a roiling sea of danger, anarchy, and intrigue. The young United States, however, was an ambitious nation zealously committed to overseas trade. And there was also a question of honor. Statesmen and politicians railed against the "insults" the United States was forced to endure. It was bad enough that American merchants and seamen were regularly abused and insulted by the British imperial navy. To be humiliated by Barbary pirates was intolerable.

Few felt this dishonor more acutely than Thomas Jefferson. As early as 1784, from his perch as the American representative in Paris, he argued that the most economical and honorable course for dealing with Barbary piracy was to build a naval squadron that would remain on permanent station in the Mediterranean. He calculated that John Paul Jones, armed with "half a dozen frigates," could "by constant cruising" of the Mediterranean waters cut the Barbary fleets to pieces and thereby "totally destroy their commerce." Jefferson "saw no reason to buy from a weak state what he could achieve with less cost through a limited war."[99]

His plan was not limited to the building of a U.S. "Mediterranean Squadron." He proposed the creation of an international league for the permanent policing of the Mediterranean, with the United States playing a lead role. Jefferson's league would include all the smaller maritime powers of Europe and replicate the "Armed Neutrality" that Russia's Catherine II had organized in 1780 to protect the smaller neutral shippers from attack by the British and French navies. "Each state would contribute a quota of ships, sailors, and capital, and the campaign would be directed by a council of ministers of the confederated states in a European capital under American supervision." The league's international fleet would remain "in perpetual cruise" until the pirates' attacks ceased and "the offensive capabilities of the North African regimes were destroyed." As Jefferson explained, "Such a convention, being left open to all powers willing to come into it, should have for its object a general peace, to be guaranteed to each by the whole." Jefferson anticipated that all the commercial powers of Europe, "except France, England, and perhaps Spain and Holland," would join the proposed league. And he was not far wrong.[100] Portugal expressed interest, and Jefferson received favorable responses from Naples, Venice, Malta, Denmark, and Sweden.[101] Even the French seemed inclined to go along with what Lafayette enthusiastically called the "Antipiratical Confederacy."[102] Jefferson's plan died when the British government expressed its strong, and predictable, disapproval, and the American Congress proved unwilling to pay for even one new frigate.

The problem of the Barbary pirates continued to prey on American statesmen's minds, however. A turning point came after the peace treaty between Portugal and the Dey of Algiers unleashed the Algerine pirates to attack American shipping in the Atlantic. Four days after news of the treaty reached the United States in December 1793, President Washington implored Congress to act. Three months later Congress passed the Naval Act of 1794 providing for the building of four large frigates of forty-four guns each and two of twenty guns. The new American navy was built to fight pirates and to meet the challenge of Algiers.[103]

Before American naval power could be brought to bear in the Mediterranean, the Washington administration negotiated a deal with the Dey, opening the Mediterranean to American shippers in exchange for a ransom of almost a million dollars. But other Barbary states continued to impose new demands, and the most obstreperous of the Barbary rulers, the Pasha of Tripoli, unsatisfied by the bribes offered by the United States, finally decided in 1800 to return to attacks on American shipping. Within a year he formally declared war. In the last days of the Adams administration, the Federalists prepared to launch a punitive expedition against Tripoli. But before it could be carried out, the Federalists were swept from power, and the Mediterranean problem landed back in the lap of the new president, Thomas Jefferson.

Jefferson returned to his earlier dreams of using the new American navy against the Barbary powers and establishing a permanent Mediterranean squadron to police those troubled waters and uphold the principles of international law. He saw only two choices: either "abandon the Mediterranean, or keep up a cruise in it," by which he meant war.[104] In June 1801 a squadron of three frigates and a schooner sailed for Tripoli as the beginning of a naval campaign that would continue without interruption for the better part of four years.

The task the United States had set for itself was daunting. "Four thousand miles from home, and in an area again beset by major war, the American squadron had to deal with the Pasha of Tripoli while at the same time keeping watch on the other restless rulers of a fifteen-hundred-mile stretch of African coast." Between 1801 and 1804 American naval vessels cruised the Mediterranean, intermittently blockading Tripoli, occasionally engaging Barbary corsairs, sinking or capturing some Tripolitan ships, and, in a disastrous setback, losing the frigate *Philadelphia,* which ran aground in Tripoli's harbor. By the time the campaign was three years old, almost the entire U.S. Navy was deployed to the Mediterranean—all five of the remaining frigates, three brigs, three schooners, ten newly built gunboats, and two mortar boats. By the summer of 1804 a portion of this flotilla was firmly ensconced in the harbor of Tripoli (after the dramatic burning of the *Philadelphia* in a commando raid led by Stephen Decatur), bombarding the pasha's fortifications and city at will.[105]

Jefferson supplemented this transoceanic naval campaign with vigorous international diplomacy. His plan for an international league was dead, but he successfully enlisted broad international support anyway. Sardinia-Piedmont and the Kingdom of the Two Sicilies made their ports available and contributed supplies to the American fleet. Sweden and Denmark, frequent victims of Mediterranean piracy, contributed money to pay for the American naval campaign and acted as intermediaries with the pasha.

But what turned the tide in the conflict was an American adventure that defied the modern caricature of the early republic's foreign policy. In 1803 the American consul in Tunis, William Eaton, asked for permission from the Jefferson administration to mount a coup d'état against Qaramanli, the current ruler of Tripoli, and install his brother as the new pasha. Secretary of State James Madison, though acknowledging that Eaton's plan did not "accord with the general sentiments or views of the United States" with regard to meddling in "the domestic contests of other countries," nevertheless concluded it could not "be unfair, in the prosecution of a just war, or the accomplishment of a reasonable peace" to exploit such opportunities when they came along.[106]

In 1805 Eaton and a small group of U.S. Marines led a contingent of four hundred Greek, Levantine, and Arab volunteers and mercenaries across five hundred miles of desert to Tripoli's second city, Derna. Outside the town Eaton appealed to the residents to join their cause in return for a promise of "perpetual peace and a free and extended commerce."[107] Then, with three U.S. Navy vessels pummeling the town from the sea, Eaton and his international band overwhelmed a larger Tripolitan force and drove out the governor. Henry Adams noted almost a century later that Eaton's actions had exhibited an "enterprise and daring so romantic and even Quixotic that for at least half a century every boy in America listened to the story with the same delight with which he read the Arabian Nights."[108]

Eaton failed to take Tripoli, and American intervention did not end piracy in the Mediterranean. But Jefferson's naval campaign was largely successful. No less a figure than Admiral Horatio Nelson considered Decatur's burning of the *Philadelphia* "the most bold and daring act of the age." The pope declared the Americans had "done more for the cause of Christianity than the most powerful nations of Christendom have done for ages."[109] Jefferson took a Hamiltonian pleasure in the way his military venture had earned the respect of the European great powers. The assault on Tripoli had taught Europeans that the United States would not "turn the left cheek when the right has been smitten."[110] It also established the permanent and influential presence in the Mediterranean that Jefferson had long sought. Americans had "no intention of withdrawing again to the western shore of the Atlantic." By the beginning of the nineteenth century the United States had established an "impressive network of commercial and naval representatives in the Mediterranean," with American consuls in Algiers, Tunis, Tripoli, Cádiz, Gibraltar, Málaga, Alicante, Port Mahon, Leghorn, and Messina, and navy agents at Syracuse, Leghorn, Naples, and Malta.[111]

With this foothold in the Mediterranean, American diplomats aimed at more than merely assuring safe conduct for their merchants. Or rather, in trying to safeguard its commercial interests, the United States took a most expansive and typically liberal view of how that might be accomplished. Among the diplomats sent to further American interests in the Mediterranean were some of the leading apostles of American Enlightenment thought. David Humphreys and Joel Barlow, who negotiated peace with Algiers and remained deeply involved in shaping U.S. policy in the Mediterranean thereafter, were diplomats and practical men of the world. But they were also "worldly philosophers" who wrote poems in praise of the "new American Æra" and the power of commerce to enlighten mankind.[112] Even the more prosaic Timothy Pickering, now secretary of state, in his instructions to Eaton while the latter was consul-designate at Tunis, suggested that the "great commerce" of the Tunisians, if ever properly developed, would provide the antidote to their piratical ways. "If ever the states of Barbary lay aside their practice of depredating on the commerce of Christian nations," he opined, "it will probably be owing to an extension of their own commerce, which may convince them where their true interest lies by the greater advantage derived from trade."[113]

As with the Indian in the western territories, the Barbary pirate needed to be persuaded that his interests and those of the United States were actually the same. As with the Indian, the best solution lay in the conversion of the Barbary pirate into a Lockean man. If he refused, it might be necessary to convince him by other means. Jefferson's war against the Barbary powers had been fought not merely to protect American shipping and avenge a wrong. It also had a "pedagogical content": "the attempt to convert the Barbary states to liberal principles and an appreciation of the virtues of legitimate trade could at least be rationalized as an effort to make them see their own best interests."[114]

The American Mediterranean venture was not unique in this respect. On the North American continent, in dealing with Indians and Spaniards, the same blend of self-interested and lofty motives had shaped American behavior, the same combination of force and persuasion had been used to transform peoples into contented and peaceful dwellers in the American liberal order. The chief difference—and an important one—was that Americans never intended to settle themselves in the lands of North Africa and thus did not have to suffer the same moral pangs of displacing a people who refused either to become Lockeans or to make room for Lockean man. That particular problem existed only in North America. But that is why American behavior in the Mediterranean provides such a useful glimpse of what was to be the future of the nation's foreign policy, especially by the end of the nineteenth century, when American territorial ambitions, at least, had dwindled. For even when Americans felt no further need to conquer new territory, by peaceful means or otherwise, they conceived it as both in their interests and in accord with their universalist principles to make liberal converts out of those with whom they did business, preferably by friendly persuasion, by letting the powerful force of commerce work its magic, and sometimes, though rarely, by military intervention.

The principles that guided American foreign policy in the era of the early republic were not isolation and nonentanglement. Few Americans believed they needed to remain separate from what they considered weaker or inferior powers on the North American continent, in Spanish America, in the Mediterranean, or even in most of Europe. American policy in the Mediterranean sought and received consistent cooperation from Sweden and Denmark, from Portugal and the Kingdom of Naples. The smaller European powers, at least, seemed to confirm the views of Americans like Humphreys that the interests of the United States were in alignment with "the common good and int'rest of mankind" and that American liberalism, especially in its commercial form, could provide the basis for an international community based on commonly shared principles. The smaller states of Europe were seen as potential partners, to be summoned to grand coalitions in the service of American commercial interests, whether in the Mediterranean or as a makeweight against the great imperial powers of Europe. Very few Americans worried about the corrupting effect of entanglements with such European nations as Denmark, Sweden, or the Kingdom of the Two Sicilies.

American liberalism was inherently entangling. It sent individuals forth to seek their fortunes, whether on adjacent territories on the continent or in overseas markets. It also profoundly shaped Americans' view of their world. They measured all peoples with whom they came into contact not by the standards of foreign cultures but by what they considered the universally applicable yardstick of liberalism. After Samuel Shaw sailed to Canton to open American commerce in China, he wrote to John Jay reporting his "very unfavorable" impression of the way the Middle Kingdom was ruled. "The laws may be good, but its police is extremely defective. It would shock your humanity, were I to give a sketch of the misery which is here daily exhibited." What most troubled Shaw was that the destitute seemed relatively few in number, and that it was therefore well within "the power of the magistracy amply to provide for them."[115] That Chinese officialdom did not see fit to tend to the poor was clearly the natural consequence of despotic government.

Shaw's outrage was typically American, or rather the typical response of the Enlightenment liberal when confronted with the embedded injustice of premodern societies. Americans "comprehended the world through the assumptions, definitions, and goals of liberal thought"; indeed, it was "their very mechanism of comprehension."[116] They might accept that different cultures ruled themselves differently, but they never really accepted the legitimacy of those differences, and because they did not accept their legitimacy they naturally viewed them as transitory. Thus Alexander Hamilton could imagine the day when South Americans would rise up against the Spanish tyrant; Joel Barlow could imagine what might happen if "the Algerines or the Hindoos were to shake off the yoke of despotism, and adopt ideas of equal liberty." Both men also imagined that the United States might play some role as a catalyst in these overseas transformations. Wherever Americans looked in the world, they saw both the possibility and the desirability of change.

CHAPTER 4

To the Farewell Address and Beyond

I have always preferred a connexion with [Great Britain] to that of any other country, we think in English, and have a similarity of prejudices and predilections.

—Alexander Hamilton, 1794

The Domestic Sources of American Foreign Policy

THE TWO European powers with whom Americans feared entanglement were Great Britain and France. The roots of these fears were primarily domestic and ideological and were related to a great debate that broke out in the United States over the young nation's identity.

Americans shared a common liberal worldview, but in the course of the 1790s there emerged at least two competing conceptions of what liberalism, and what has been called "republicanism," should mean. Not long after the ratification of the Constitution in 1787, a battle erupted between these competing visions. That battle provided the main drama of the young republic, and foreign policy, as always, became one of the principal arenas in which the struggle over the nation's fundamental character was fought.

It is difficult to recapture the apprehension, even paranoia, that gripped the nation's most sober leaders in these early years of the American political experiment. No one was confident that the new republican institutions would survive. There was no clear path to success, and no past record against which to compare the unfolding of events. The emergence of political parties was unexpected and troubling, even to those who helped bring them into being. Each side in the great political conflict tended to suspect the other of the most dangerous and evil motives.

As a result, even as Americans generally sought to maintain peace with the great powers of the age, Great Britain and France, beneath this broad consensus raged one of the most vitriolic and divisive debates in America's history. The titanic debates over such matters as the Jay Treaty with England, the Neutrality Proclamation, and the Quasi-War with France make little sense simply as problems in foreign relations. Their meaning and significance can be understood only within the context of "domestic politics and ideology."[1] The debates were so brutal, in fact, precisely because they were so profoundly ideological. What was at stake, many Americans believed, were not merely matters of war and peace but the very soul of the republic. As would be true throughout the next two hundred years, Americans on all sides of the debate in the 1790s believed that choices in foreign policy had profound domestic implications and ramifications, and that the United States would define itself by the way it conducted its affairs abroad.

The battle over foreign policy in the 1790s derived from a domestic struggle that was already well under way by the time war broke out on the European continent. The issues that divided the nation soon after the formation of the federal government in 1789 concerned Alexander Hamilton's grand scheme for placing the United States on a sound financial footing.[2] His program—which included the funding of the national debt, the assumption by the federal government of the revolutionary debts owed by the states, the creation of a national bank, and the establishment of bounties and tariffs to encourage domestic manufactures—aimed at placing large amounts of capital in the hands of a small number of (mostly eastern) merchants and financiers, those who, in his view, could put it to best use for the financial well-being of the nation. Hamilton's policies were "progressive" and "nationalist" in the sense that they gave power to the federal government to allow it to guide the nation's economy.

His goals ran directly counter to the predilections of James Madison and Thomas Jefferson. And it was around this profound disagreement about the shape of American society and political economy that the nation's first political parties unexpectedly coalesced. If Hamilton's policies were progressive and nationalist, Jefferson and Madison worried more about the dangers of concentrated power in the federal government. The two Virginians feared that Hamilton's program would favor "speculators," "stock-jobbers," and other unscrupulous moneymen who got rich by making informed gambles at others' expense. More fundamentally, they believed that key aspects of Hamilton's program, especially the chartering of a national bank, exceeded the federal government's constitutional authority.

They rejected Hamilton's argument that "implied powers" in the Constitution's "necessary and proper" clause gave the federal government these powers.

The specific measures of Hamilton's program, however, worried Madison and Jefferson less than the master plan that they feared lay behind the measures. What was at stake, they quickly convinced themselves, was not a certain means of financing the national debt but the future of America's republican government and the unique freedoms that it engendered and protected. Under Hamilton's energetic direction, their young republic was taking a form they did not find appealing and that, the more they thought about it, was rather alarmingly different from what they had in mind.[3]

In late 1791 Madison declared the existence of two parties in America: one that favored the "people," their interests, their "republican" spirit, and their liberties, and one that, to the contrary, favored "pampering the spirit of speculation," "unnecessary accumulations of the debt," "arbitrary interpretations" of the Constitution, and above all the "principles of monarchy and aristocracy."[4] This latter was the party of Hamilton. The Federalists represented but a minority of the nation, Madison insisted, but they commanded the allegiance of the most influential men, the men with money. And they had the support of that great enemy of republican liberty, that supreme proponent and defender of monarchy, aristocracy, corruption, and commercial interest: Great Britain.

Even before the conflict between Great Britain and revolutionary France erupted in 1793, Britain and things British had loomed large in the ideological battle that took shape in America after the establishment of the new federal government. Most Americans understandably harbored deep resentments against and profound mistrust of Great Britain. In the western territories settlers saw British machinations behind Indian attacks and resistance to American land claims. Britain's refusal to evacuate western posts, despite its promises in the peace treaty of 1783, seemed further evidence that the British meant to keep a firm and oppressive hand on American throats. On the seas, British impressments of American sailors were a constant outrage, as were continuing British restrictions on American trade. Many American merchants, especially in the South, suffered under British discriminatory trade restrictions and saw British intrigue behind the agreement between Portugal and the Barbary pirates that had such grievous effect on American shipping in the Mediterranean.

Madison and Jefferson, as southerners, were especially prone to anti-British feelings. During the Revolution southern plantation owners had watched the British army destroy their crops and offer freedom to their slaves. Northeastern merchants had a fonder recollection of doing a lucrative business with their English counterparts and wished to see that business resume as quickly as possible after the Revolution. But southerners had sour recollections not only of individual British creditors, to whom they owed crushing debts, but of the entire commercial and financial system that seemed to make Americans dependent for their livelihood on the decisions of a powerful and overbearing mother country. They believed that separation from Great Britain, both political and, as much as possible, economic, was essential to the internal health and longevity of the republic. Madison worried about the "influence that may be conveyed into the public councils by a nation directing the course of our trade by her capital, and holding so great a share in our pecuniary institutions, and the effect that may finally ensue on our taste, our manners, and our form of Government itself."[5] Madison and Jefferson wanted a separation from Great Britain that was "not only political but economic and—above all—moral as well."[6] They planned to effect this separation, to embark on a new era of economic and moral independence, by restricting trade with Britain and expanding trade with other countries, such as France. Madison introduced legislation in the new House of Representatives in 1789 setting up discriminatory duties against British commerce.[7]

When the Senate rejected Madison's plan, thanks in part to the opposition of the commercial and mercantile interests of the northeastern cities, this only proved his claim that the insidious forces of an "English interest" were working to defeat his vision of republican independence. "The body of merchants who carry on the American commerce is well known to be composed of so great a proportion of individuals who are either British subjects, or trading on British capital, or enjoying the profits of British consignments, that the mercantile opinion here, might not be an American opinion; nay, it might be the opinion of the very country of which, in the present instance at least, we ought not to take counsel."[8] When, in the course of the next two years, Hamilton won approval in rapid succession for the measures that maintained and even increased the national debt and established in the country a financial system modeled on that of Britain, it seemed to Madison beyond doubt that "monarchy was just around the corner, that Hamilton and his 'fiscalist,' 'anglocrat' followers were plotting to make an end to republican government in America."[9]

There was a distinct paranoia in these fears of Hamilton and his plans. Hamilton had no intention of restoring monarchy or a hereditary aristocracy in the United States. He was a liberal idealist, too, and did not believe monarchy was possible or desirable in the new nation. But where Jefferson's and Madison's liberal vision led them to seek a break from Britain and the British style of government, Hamilton's liberal vision led him to a strong affinity for what he considered the most successful liberal government the world had ever known or was likely to know.[10] His grand design for the American political economy depended on a close relationship with Great Britain. It depended on British commerce and British finance. Since America's financial health, credit, and future prosperity rested on the revenues that came from tariffs on British imports, he believed, any restrictions on that commerce would destroy his system. The British government would surely retaliate with an embargo of its own on American goods.

Far from seeking to reduce the American dependence on British commerce, therefore, Hamilton aimed to increase and perpetuate it, at least until such time as the United States could grow rich and powerful enough to stand on its own. American relations with Britain had to be kept in good order almost regardless of the insults and depredations the Americans suffered at the hands of the British government. Whatever sacrifices the United States had to make in the short run were well worth it in order to guarantee the long-term financial health of the republic, for it was upon that financial health and the allegiance it inspired among its citizens, especially the wealthiest and most powerful, that the future of the republic depended. Building a closer connection with Britain—a closer economic connection, and even, if necessary, a closer political connection—he believed, was in the best interests of the young nation. The independence sought by Jefferson and Madison was illusory. Until the United States became stronger, such independence could come only at the expense of the republic itself.

Most historians have judged Hamilton's to be the sounder approach to American economic development. The French market could not replace the expansive and well-established Anglo-American commercial relationship. The industrial revolution had not yet transformed France, whose economy remained predominantly agricultural. It was more a competitor than a consumer of American goods. Americans, meanwhile, had a well-developed taste for British-made goods that would be hard to change.

But if Hamilton's was the more pragmatic vision of the American economy, it was not merely pragmatic. He had a vision of America's future—an ideology—every bit as powerful and all-encompassing as Madison's and Jefferson's. The principles of his grand design formed "the core of an entire ideological configuration."[11] Just as a potent Anglophobia lay at the core of Madison's and Jefferson's ideology, so an equally powerful

Anglophilia lay at the heart of Hamilton's. Where Jefferson and Madison and many other Americans saw only monarchy, aristocracy, and corruption, Hamilton saw—as most Britons did, as Montesquieu had, and as most Americans had *before* the Revolution—the splendors of the English "mixed government," the only form of government in human history that offered both freedom and stability. Where Jefferson and Madison believed that the purpose of the Revolution had been to break from England and English ways and to establish a new, distinctly republican system, Hamilton argued that Americans had undertaken their Revolution only "as a refuge from encroachments on rights and privileges *antecedently* enjoyed, not as a people who from choice sought a radical and entire change in the established government, in pursuit of new privileges and rights."[12]

The ideological chasm between Hamiltonian Federalists and Jeffersonian Republicans opened wider once Great Britain and revolutionary France went to war. Although Jefferson supported the neutrality proclamation of 1793, he sought a version of neutrality that did not move the United States closer to Britain at the expense of the Franco-American relationship. And when war with Great Britain threatened to erupt in late 1793 and early 1794, he was not nearly as eager as Hamilton to compromise with the British. He continued to favor commercial retaliation as the best means of persuading London to end its restrictions on American trade and to evacuate the western posts. In time, he believed, the British would see reason. If not, he was prepared to risk conflict.

Although Jefferson has often been depicted as allowing his foreign policy judgments to be clouded by his strong attachment to France—Hamilton once sneered that Jefferson had a "womanish" affection for the French—his affinity for France was chiefly a product of his hatred for England, as the French themselves understood.[13] When the French Revolution triumphed, however, he, like most Americans, saw a natural connection between the two republics. The Declaration of the Rights of Man and of the Citizen, which Jefferson had helped Lafayette to draft, followed the model of the Virginia Declaration of Rights and the American Declaration of Independence, both products of Jefferson's pen. And even when events in France took a turn that seemed anything but liberal, with the arbitrary suspension of rights, the extralegal justice of the guillotine, and the reign of terror, Jefferson was loath to let these disturbing excesses affect his overall judgment. On the contrary, his unflagging defense of the Revolution produced some remarkable statements, as when he declared that rather than see the Revolution fail, "I would have seen half the earth desolated." Whereas Hamilton, Washington, and most Federalists quickly came to view the

French Revolution as utterly unlike the American version—in its radicalism, its violence, and its lack of respect for property and law—Jefferson and many Republicans persisted in the belief, or hope, that the broad similarities of purpose were more important than the differences. Jefferson wanted to believe that "the random violence and careening course of the French Revolution were part of a lamentable but passing chapter in a larger story of triumphant global revolution."[14]

Jefferson's defense of the French Revolution, however, had more to do with his domestic struggle against Hamilton than with his judgment about the bloody struggles occurring among the French people. For whatever Jefferson may have believed about the wisdom and justice of the French Revolution, he saw how its perceived success or failure could affect the development of liberal republican institutions in the United States. "I consider the establishment and success of [the French government] as necessary to stay up our own and to prevent it from falling back to that kind of half-way house, the English constitution."[15] If the Revolution did not appear to succeed in securing the liberties of Frenchmen, Jefferson feared, this would strengthen "the zealous apostles of English despotism here"—that is, it would strengthen Hamilton.[16]

Jefferson claimed that "[t]he liberty of the whole earth was depending on the issue of the contest" between France and Great Britain. If the British-led coalition against France triumphed, it was "far from being certain that they might not choose to finish their job completely by obliging us to change in the form of our government at least."[17] Hamilton and other Federalists retorted that Britain would be too exhausted and have no reason to send its forces across the Atlantic to take on American liberty. But Jefferson's point was that it would not have to. Hamilton and the "British interest" had already launched their conspiracy to bring an end to republican government with British support.

For most of the 1790s Jefferson and his Republican Party seemed to speak for the majority of Americans. Affection for France came as naturally to the American population as enmity for England, thanks to memories of French assistance in the Americans' own revolt against England. After the French Revolution American popular sympathy for France grew enormously. When French armies scored early triumphs in their battles against the European monarchies, many Americans saw a replication of their own revolutionary struggle against monarchical England. So effusively did they welcome the French emissary Edmond Genet, who arrived in the United States in 1793 to win American support, that Genet felt emboldened to appeal to Americans over the heads of the Washington administration.

These pro-French stirrings in the United States seemed to strengthen the Republicans at the expense of the Federalists. "Democratic Societies" formed around the country to defend "liberty and equality" against Hamilton and his presumed monarchist conspirators.[18] Republican newspapers accused President Washington of being under the insidious influence of Great Britain. When Washington, at Hamilton's suggestion, sent John Jay to negotiate an end to Anglo-American hostilities, the Republican press cried treason. When Jay returned from England at the end of 1794 bearing a treaty that even Hamilton found unsatisfying, the floodgates of anti-British sentiment opened. Across the country Jay was burned in effigy, and Republican newspapers railed against the "monarchists" who had sold America's honor to the British king.

Hamilton argued that the treaty, despite its failings, was still better than a conflict with England, and that if the United States could avoid war "for ten or twelve years more," it would be in a stronger position to "advance and support with energy and effect any just pretensions to greater commercial advantages."[19] But Republicans saw the treaty as just another instance of collusion between the cunning British and their American allies.[20]

The Republicans' virulent opposition to the Jay Treaty helped feed in Hamilton a paranoia about his political adversaries that became the mirror image of their paranoia about him.[21] In his more sober moments, Hamilton understood perfectly well that the Republican objections to the Jay Treaty were based less on foreign policy judgments than on domestic political calculations, and that Republicans were using the controversy over the treaty to try to win the presidency for their leader, Thomas Jefferson.[22] But like the Republicans, Hamilton could not help imputing to his opponents a design to seek foreign assistance in overthrowing America's liberal institutions. The Republicans' great success in exciting public anger against the Jay Treaty proved only that they were deliberately turning the precarious republic into a mobocracy modeled on the licentious and illiberal example of the French.

Hamilton and his fellow Federalists feared something was rotten in the soul of their young republic. Simultaneous developments in France and in the United States were too alarmingly similar. In France there was the reign of terror, and in the United States Republicans defended it in the name of liberty. Hamilton did not understand how any American could deny that the French Revolution, however noble its original intentions, had "been stained by excesses and extravagances," by "atrocious depravity," by the "unexampled dissolution of all the social and moral ties," and by the expression of "principles and opinions so wild, so extreme, passions so turbulent, so tempestuous, as almost to forbid the hope of agreement in any rational or well-organized system of government." He predicted that "after wading through the seas of blood," France would find herself "the slave of some victorious Scylla, or Marius, or Caesar." He insisted that there was "more reason to fear that the CAUSE OF TRUE LIBERTY has received a deep wound . . . than to regard the revolution in France in the form it has lately worn, as entitled to the honors due to that sacred and all-important cause."[23] He nevertheless feared, as he wrote Washington, that "the example of France (whose excesses are with too many an object of apology, if not of justification)" had "unhinged the orderly principles of the people of this country."[24] Huge crowds had celebrated the arrival of Citizen Genet, and when Genet called on Americans to commit treason against their government, thousands seemed ready to heed the call. "There are too many proofs," Hamilton wrote in the summer of 1795, "that a considerable party among us is deeply infected with those horrid principles of Jacobinism which, proceeding from one excess to another, have made France a theatre of blood."[25]

Some twentieth-century scholars have praised Hamilton for pursuing the "national interest" in a manner "unencumbered by any ideological or political preferences."[26] But Hamilton's perspective was both ideological and political. This was not a narrow debate over foreign policy. Just like Jefferson and Madison, he considered calculation of the national interest indistinguishable from the ideological and political struggle they were all waging at home over the future course of American government and society. In the "supercharged atmosphere" of the early republic, revolutionary France and England had become "symbols of two alternative futures or fates for the United States."[27] What had erupted in American politics was a struggle not between "realists" and "idealists" but between two competing visions of American liberalism. It was around these two versions of a common liberal ideology that American politics had coalesced in the 1790s. And it was this clash that provided the framework within which the great European war, and America's relations with its two main protagonists, could be comprehended.

The Farewell Address: Politics and Policy

IN THE MIDST of this political and ideological struggle, George Washington, with Hamilton's assistance, began drafting his valedictory statement to the American people. Many Americans over the past two centuries have viewed the Farewell Address as providing a set of maxims for the conduct of American foreign policy that were meant to be strictly construed and applied for all time. But while Washington and Hamilton did wish to lay out some principles they believed would serve Americans well over the coming decades, their chief purposes in the address were immediate and political.

In the summer of 1796 France, outraged at the terms of the Jay Treaty, had begun harassing and capturing American shipping.[28] The Washington administration had learned of French designs to stir secession movements in the West and South. And the French minister in Philadelphia had warned that in the coming election Americans must choose between friendship with France and confrontation, perhaps war—an open call for the American people to defeat the Federalists and elect Jefferson. As Hamilton worked on drafts of Washington's address, he expressed concern that a "dangerous state of things" could soon exist "between us and France" and even suggested that Washington might therefore want to reconsider his plans not to run for a third term. "If a storm gathers," Hamilton asked, "how can you retreat?"[29]

To Hamilton and most leading Federalists, the Republican threat at home looked as dangerous as the French threat from abroad. Washington agreed that Jefferson's followers had dragged him down into the mud with charges of treason and infidelity to republican principles. A deeply wounded president wrote Jefferson that he had "no conception that Parties" could go to such lengths. After he had done his utmost "to preserve this Country from the horrors of a desolating war," he was accused of "being the enemy of one Nation [France], and subject to the influence of another [Great Britain]."[30] To Hamilton, Washington remarked, "The people of this Country it would seem, will never be satisfied until they become a department of France: It shall be my business to prevent it."[31]

That was Washington's primary goal in his Farewell Address. For although it had other purposes, it was very much a political document, aimed at defeating Jefferson's bid for election and with it the dangerous pro-French doctrines of Republicanism.[32] When Washington asked when the address ought to be published, Hamilton replied, "[T]wo months before the time for the meeting of the electors. This will be sufficient."[33]

Subsequent generations of Americans tend to remember only Washington's "great rule" about avoiding foreign alliances, but the principal theme of the address concerned the domestic health of the republic. The president appealed for national unity against partisan and sectional strife, exhorting Americans to frown "indignantly" upon the "first dawning of any attempt to alienate any portion of our country from the rest or to enfeeble the sacred ties which now link together the various parts." Here he was referring specifically to the French conspiracy to induce the West and South to secede and form an alliance with France.[34] He urged the people of the West to shun those who "would sever them from their brethren and connect them with aliens." Defending the Jay Treaty, he asked, had not the federal government opened the Mississippi to the citizens of the West by the recent treaties with Great Britain and Spain, and was this not "decisive proof how unfounded were the suspicions propagated among them of a policy in the General Government and in the Atlantic States unfriendly to their interests"?

Washington turned his rhetorical guns explicitly on the Republicans when he urged his countrymen to reject "irregular oppositions to [the Government's] acknowledged authority" and to resist "the spirit of innovation upon its principles"—by which he meant alterations in the Constitution that would "impair the energy of the system, and thus to undermine what can not be directly overthrown." This was a reference to the attacks Republicans had launched on the constitutionality of Hamilton's nationalist financial plan.[35] He compared the Republicans' demand for less centralized, more democratic republicanism with the bloody and destructive republicanism of the French Revolution. To deprive the government of the necessary "vigor" would make it "too feeble to withstand the enterprises of faction." Factional warfare, unrestrained by a strong government under a strong constitution, would eventually produce a "frightful despotism," as the people, wearying of the resulting "disorders and miseries," sought "security and repose in the absolute power of an individual." Hamilton had predicted despotism in France, and Washington implied that the same fate would befall Americans if Republicans had their way in the next presidential election.

When it came to foreign policy, Washington's warnings against permanent alliances and "inveterate antipathy" toward other nations related directly to the political controversies of the moment. No one reading the address in 1796 could fail to understand what Washington meant: Americans must drop their "inveterate antipathy" toward Great Britain and abandon their "passionate attachment" to France.[36] For among the "variety of evils" that a passionate attachment to one nation produced, Washington argued, was that it gave "to ambitious, corrupted, or deluded citizens (who devote themselves to the favorite nation)" the ability "to betray or sacrifice the interests of their own country without odium, sometimes even with popularity." Meanwhile the "real patriots," Washington observed, "who may resist the intrigues of the favorite are liable to become suspected and odious, while its tools and dupes usurp the applause and confidence of the people to surrender their interests."

Republicans considered such language "a thinly veiled attack on Republicanism and on France, and an effort to influence the upcoming election in favor of the Federalists."[37] And they were right. Who, after all, were the "tools and dupes" of the "favorite" foreign nation, who had somehow managed to "usurp the applause and confidence of the people"? For Washington and Hamilton and their Federalist colleagues, there was no better description of the Republicans' all-too-successful efforts to manipulate the general public's affection for France to serve their own partisan and ideological purposes. And who were the "real patriots," who had resisted the "intrigues of the favorite" and been rewarded only by becoming "odious" in the popular eye? Again, in the Federalists' view, there was no better description of their own valiant but unpopular efforts to steer the nation on the right course.

And now, as Washington released his address to the public, a conflict with France was drawing near. Yet Republicans continued to denounce the Jay Treaty and blamed it for the rise of French hostility. Federalist leaders could well imagine that a Republican victory placing Jefferson in the White House might lead to a wholesale reversal of American policy, a breach in relations with Britain, and a return to closer ties with France, including perhaps a more faithful adherence to the old alliance in violation of the newly approved treaty with Britain.

Thus Washington proffered his famous advice: "It is our true policy to steer clear of permanent alliances with any portion of the foreign world, so far, I mean, as we are now at liberty to do it." This advice aimed specifically and indeed exclusively at France, the only nation with whom the United States maintained a "permanent alliance."[38] Washington declared that "Europe has a set of primary interests which to us have none or a very remote relation" and that it would therefore be "unwise" for the United States to "implicate ourselves by artificial ties in the ordinary vicissitudes of her politics or the ordinary combinations and collisions of her friendships or enmities." But under the circumstances this advice could only be interpreted—and was interpreted, by France, by Republicans, and by Federalists as well—as a warning against forging closer "artificial ties" to France. James Monroe, perhaps the most intemperate Francophile among the top ranks of American officialdom, angrily observed, "Most of the monarchs of the earth practice ingratitude in their transactions with other powers . . . but Mr. Washington has the merit of transcending, not the great men of the antient republicks, but the little monarchs of the present day in preaching it as a publick virtue."[39] When Washington declared that the "great rule" for Americans was to have with foreign powers "as little *politi-*

cal connection as possible," he made it clear that he had France in mind: "So far as we have already formed engagements let them be fulfilled with perfect good faith." But, Washington declared, "[h]ere let us stop."

With the Jay Treaty ratified; with commercial relations with Great Britain all but restored to their prewar footing and the American economy consequently producing an unprecedented national prosperity; and with the French alliance effectively annulled by the French themselves, an American who shared Hamilton's pro-British inclinations could well declare: "Here let us stop." Having linked America's fortunes, as Hamilton believed they had to be linked, to stable relations with Great Britain—at least for a time—it was now not only possible but necessary to declare as a general foreign policy principle that any *further* efforts to "entangle" the United States with European powers were unwise.

There was an explicit caveat to this "great rule," however, and one that Hamilton deliberately inserted into the address. Washington, in his own first draft, had written unequivocally that the United States must "avoid connecting ourselves with the politics of any Nation." But Hamilton proposed, and Washington accepted, a less definitive statement: that the United States should have with foreign nations "as little political connection as possible." Hamilton thereby left the door open for future alliances. While the address admonished Americans to "steer clear" of permanent alliances, it also advised that "we may safely trust to temporary alliances for extraordinary emergencies."

Why the less definitive declarations concerning political connections and alliances? What "extraordinary emergencies" did Hamilton have in mind? Perhaps Hamilton believed that as a general proposition it was unrealistic to expect that the United States would never need "political connections" or even "temporary alliances" with other countries. But Hamilton's concerns were also specific and immediate. By the time of the Farewell Address, Hamilton and other Federalists had already begun to entertain the possibility that some form of political connection or temporary alliance with Great Britain might become necessary and desirable, perhaps sooner rather than later.

By the summer of 1796 Hamilton viewed France as an international menace, a genuine threat to American security and liberty. The expanding naval conflict, he argued in an essay published just four months after the Farewell Address, was not merely a matter of American shipping rights. "[T]he flagrant injuries which we are now suffering from her, proceed from a general plan of domination and plunder." The French aimed at nothing less than "universal domination." Their "specious pretence of enlightening mankind" had proven—just as "well informed and unprejudiced" men had predicted it would—to be merely "the varnish to the real design of subjugating them." By January 1797 he was warning Americans that "the affairs of this country are drawing fast to an eventful crisis."[40]

France had shocked the whole world with its extraordinary successes in the European war. Perhaps no one was more surprised than Hamilton, who in 1794 had predicted that the unstable revolutionary government, then in the throes of the "reign of terror," would quickly succumb to the British-led coalition.[41] But by 1796 the coalition had collapsed. Spain had severed its alliance with Great Britain and, along with Prussia, had signed a peace treaty with France. The French had annexed Belgium, and Napoleon had crushed the Austrian and Sardinian armies in a bold attack on Italy. By the end of 1797 Austria was out of the war, leaving Great Britain alone to face what had swiftly become the mightiest power in Europe. The British, shorn of their continental allies, were tired and on the verge of insolvency. The Bank of England had suspended specie payments. All that remained was for Napoleon to invade and subjugate England, an event much anticipated by many informed Americans. In Hamilton's view, the once inconceivable "possibility of the overthrow of Great Britain" was no longer "chimerical."[42]

Should Britain be defeated, Hamilton declared, the subjugation of the United States by France would not be far behind. With Great Britain "silenced," the Royal Navy could no longer prevent the transportation of France's huge armies across the Atlantic. Hamilton believed that the fate of American liberty had become inextricably tied to the success of British arms in the European war. Nor was he alone. John Adams, though far less enamored of England, nevertheless "believed that Britain shielded the United States from France." Fisher Ames expressed the view of many Federalists when he warned, "The wind of the cannon ball that smashes John Bull's brains out will lay us on our backs."[43] By the summer of 1798 Washington had come to fear that in this "Age of Wonders" an "intoxicated and lawless France," which had seen fit to "slaughter its own Citizens and to disturb the repose of all the World," might well look next to America, and especially at the vulnerable, slaveholding South.[44]

The Federalists' fear of a British defeat at the hands of France was, in part, a simple matter of geopolitics and the balance of power. If France could dominate the entire European continent and neutralize Great Britain, it could then turn its attention to the conquest or domination of North America. Hamilton, characteristically, saw this geopolitical threat entirely through British eyes. "History proves that Great Britain has repeatedly upheld the balance of power [in Europe], in opposition to the grasping ambition of France," Hamilton wrote in April 1798. "[S]he has been more than once an essential and effectual shield against real danger."[45]

But Hamilton's fear of France ultimately derived more from his perception of the character of its revolutionary regime than from past history or from pure balance-of-power calculations. He had never expressed any concern that a total British victory over France could have dire consequences for American security, even though a victorious Britain would have been in an equally strong position to turn its attention to the reconquest of a bumptious nation that had but a decade earlier still been its colony. A British attack on the United States was precisely what Republicans claimed to fear during the debates over the neutrality proclamation and the Jay Treaty.

For Hamilton, the difference between Great Britain and France was a matter of ideology, not geopolitics. It was the difference between the essential liberalism of the British government and the essential illiberalism of the French revolutionary government. He could not believe the liberal British people would ever attack the liberal Americans. They knew Americans were a people who, like themselves, "have a due respect for property and personal security," a people who rested "the foundations of liberty on the basis of justice, order, and law." They saw Americans as "sincere republicans, but decided enemies to licentiousness and anarchy," unlike the French. More importantly, he argued, any British government that tried to attack America would be regarded by the people as harboring "a malignant and wanton hostility against liberty, of which they might themselves expect to be the next victim." Even the most corrupt Parliament could not wage a long and difficult military campaign without support from the "majority" of the population.[46] It was not the vast oceans that protected America from Great Britain, therefore. It was the institutions and spirit of British liberalism.

Despotic revolutionary France was a different matter. It was "marching with hasty and colossal strides to universal empire," Hamilton warned, and he saw a direct link between French domestic tyranny and French imperial expansionism. The "five tyrants of France, after binding in chains their own countrymen, after prostrating surrounding nations, and vanquishing all external resistance to the revolutionary despotism at home," had determined that "peace would not prove an element congenial with the duration of their power."[47] Prefiguring the argument advanced a century and a half later by George F. Kennan about another revolutionary despotism, the Soviet Union, Hamilton argued that French leaders were driven to expansionism abroad by fear of their own lack of legitimacy at home.[48] Britain's liberal institutions could be relied on to restrain British leaders, but the "secret mourning voice of [France's] oppressed millions" could not stop France's revolutionary tyrants. With its rulers seeking "to confirm their usurpation and extend the sphere of their domination abroad," revolutionary France had become a self-generating, expansionist "engine of despotism and slavery." "Who that loves his country," he publicly demanded, "would not rather perish than" submit to "such men *and such a system?*"[49]

Fear of the French "system," and not simple balance-of-power calculations, lay at the heart of Hamilton's concern, just as in a later period in American history fear of communism, and not simply the reach of Soviet power, lay at the heart of so much of American anxiety during the Cold War. Indeed, it was here among the founding generation, on both sides of the Hamiltonian-Jeffersonian split, that Americans first displayed a tendency to shape foreign policy around a genuine fear of domestic subversion by a foreign power preaching an antiliberal ideology.

And just as future American anticommunists would fear their nation might be all too susceptible to communist subversion, so Hamilton doubted his fellow citizens could be trusted to meet the French threat. He and other Federalists feared that the United States might be ripe for a French-backed insurrection. The Republicans were "ready to *new-model* our Constitution under the *influence* or *coercion* of France, to form with her a perpetual alliance, *offensive* and *defensive,* and to give her a monopoly of our trade by *peculiar* and *exclusive* privileges."[50] Washington shared Hamilton's fears. He argued in the Farewell Address that the United States was vulnerable to France because American society and political institutions were vulnerable. The "spirit of faction," by which he meant the Republican faction, was opening the door to French conquest. The "divisions among us," Hamilton warned, would increase the likelihood of an invasion, for "it would be believed that a sufficient number [of Americans] would flock to the standard of France to render it easy to quell the resistance of the rest."[51] Washington agreed that French aggression had been practically "encouraged . . . by a party among ourselves," a party "determined to advocate French measures under *all* circumstances."[52]

Hamilton and other leading Federalists preferred to wage war with France rather than to accept a negotiated compromise, for to make concessions would only strengthen the pro-French faction at home. They made a pretense of favoring negotiations with France, but only to show the American public that they were not warmongers. Washington agreed that it was wise to support negotiations with France, because their likely failure would prove the administration's case.[53] When failure came, Hamilton would push for war. Those who believed "we ought to bear any thing from France rather than go to war with her," he declared, were engaging in treason.[54] Washington agreed that the coming contest with France would reveal "who are true Americans."[55]

In this increasingly desperate mood, Hamilton became convinced that resisting the full extent of the French menace required combating internal as well as external threats. This conviction proved to be his undoing. He proposed nothing less than the establishment of a fifty-thousand-man army, to be led by him. The primary, stated purpose of this new standing army would be to fight France and Spain in the South. But the ancillary purpose, which he occasionally made explicit, would be to overawe domestic opponents of the federal government. Federalists, without Hamilton's approval, then passed the Alien and Sedition Acts to squelch foreign influence on American politics and root out treasonous behavior. As would later be the case in the 1940s and '50s, the threat posed by a powerful nation with a foreign ideology regarded as hostile to and subversive of American liberalism led to illiberal extremes in squelching its alleged supporters within the United States.

Hamilton's fears of the French had obvious diplomatic implications. For if the French threat justified contemplating war, if it justified the creation of a standing army, if it justified, for many Federalists, the Alien and Sedition Acts, then it justified closer cooperation with Great Britain and even an alliance. Britain was the font and bulwark of Anglo-Saxon liberalism. Its "destruction," Hamilton pointed out, had become the "direct object in view" for France's leaders. If the French succeeded, this would seal America's own fate.[56] If war with France came, Hamilton, Secretary of State Pickering, and other Federalists believed, a closer connection and even a tacit alliance with England could not be excluded. As President Adams remarked, it would be "the height of folly for a people . . . not to secure the assistance and defense that may be derived from another nation engaged in the same common cause."[57]

In response to the undeclared Quasi-War with France, in fact, the United States and Great Britain established an undeclared quasi-alliance. The Federalist administration of John Adams and the British government under William Pitt worked out a scheme of "common action and mutual assistance in the military field" that would not be equaled until the First World War.[58] British assistance included the provision, free of charge, of cannons and shot for American harbor defense, a gift historians have described as the first "lend-lease," as well as the purchase by the United States of vast amounts of military supplies that American industry was as yet incapable of producing.[59] More significant was the extensive cooperation between the Royal Navy and both the newly built American navy and the American merchant fleet, which had been so badly harassed by French marauders. As early as January 1797, just four months after Washington delivered his Farewell Address, the British government offered the United States the Royal Navy's protection for American commerce. Within a year American merchant ships began sailing in convoys under the protection of British naval vessels—the kind of help Britain gave only to its military allies.[60] Between the American and British navies there was an explicit division of labor. Because the Royal Navy was challenging the French everywhere else, the tiny American fleet was able to concentrate almost entirely in the Caribbean. Admiral Nelson's defeat of the French fleet in the Battle of the Nile in August 1798 shifted the balance in the Quasi-War significantly in America's favor.

Even in the Caribbean, where the United States lacked naval bases of its own, large British forces stationed on Jamaica and Martinique allowed American naval vessels to operate freely.[61] The two governments also worked closely to carry out a common policy toward the slave rebellion led by Toussaint L'Ouverture against French plantation owners in Santo Domingo. The result was an Anglo-American agreement recognizing Toussaint as the leader of an independent Santo Domingo (so much, again, for the alleged American doctrine of nonintervention in the internal affairs of other nations) and limiting trade with Santo Domingo exclusively to the United States and Great Britain. Secretary of State Pickering considered the United States "bound" by its commercial interests and by "considerations of political Safety against what may justly be called a common enemy" to act "in perfect concert with Great Britain."[62]

Anglo-American cooperation occurred not just on the seas. In the American West and in Canada the British and Americans shared intelligence on French intrigues, and agreed on joint military action against French efforts to stir up trouble among the Indians or to launch filibustering expeditions against the United States from Canada. In Europe, Gouverneur Morris and William Vans Murray provided the British both intelligence and analysis of the political situations in France, in Prussia, and in Austria-Hungary.[63]

Then there was the question of Spanish America. Just a month before the publication of Washington's address, Spain had concluded the Treaty of San Ildefonso, making her a formal ally of France and completing the revolution in Spanish diplomacy begun a year earlier that had transformed Spain from ally to enemy of Great Britain. Hamilton had long mused about the possibility of seizing Louisiana and the Floridas from Spain. When

Spain joined arms with France in 1796, Hamilton was ready to move. "If a universal empire is still to be the pursuit of France," he declared, "what can tend to defeat the purpose better than to detach South America from Spain, which is only the channel through which the riches of Mexico and Peru are conveyed to France?"[64] He suggested that Britain be asked to send a naval force to America to seize "the Floridas, Louisiana, and South American possessions of Spain" should France and Spain declare war jointly on the United States.[65]

A bold plan for Anglo-American cooperation crossed Hamilton's desk in early 1798 in the form of correspondence from Francisco de Miranda, the Venezuelan patriot who had fought in the American Revolution, had intrigued in France during the French Revolution, and now sought British and American assistance in a grand scheme to liberate Latin America from the Spanish Empire. Miranda's plan, which he laid before both British and American officials in London, "called for an alliance of Britain, the United States, and the Spanish-American colonies against France and Spain." In practical terms this meant a joint Anglo-American expedition, "with Britain furnishing the fleet and the United States the troops." The reward for the United States would be possession of Louisiana and the Floridas.[66] Prime Minister Pitt liked the idea, telling Miranda, "We should much enjoy operating jointly with the United States in this enterprise." Rufus King, the American minister in London, and Secretary of State Pickering liked the idea, too. King hoped President Adams would agree to cooperate with Great Britain in the liberation of South America and "by great and generous deeds lay deep and firm the foundations of lasting accord between [the] rising Empires" of the "New World."[67] Perhaps Europe could not be rescued from French tyranny, but this was "no reason why America should perish likewise."[68] Hamilton was enthusiastic, too. As he told Secretary of War James McHenry, his proposal for a large army was not merely to defend against a French attack. "Besides security against invasion," he suggested in the summer of 1799, "we ought certainly to look to the possession of the Floridas and Louisiana, and we ought to squint at South America."[69] As to Miranda's plan for liberating South America, he told King, "I wish it much to be undertaken." The goal, he said, foreshadowing many decades of American aspirations for Latin America, was "the independence of the separate territory, under a moderate government, with the joint guaranty of the co-operating powers, stipulating equal privileges in commerce." His chief concern was that American public opinion was "not quite" ready for such a venture, though he asserted, "we ripen fast."[70]

What Hamilton principally hoped to see ripen was popular support for cooperation between the United States and Great Britain. He hoped that negotiators between the two powers would soon begin to agree on a plan of action: "A fleet of Great Britain, an army of the United States, a government of the liberated territory agreeable to both co-operators, about which there will be no difficulty."[71] Hamilton wanted to make sure that the United States took the leading part in any invasion. He assumed that command of the forces would "very naturally fall upon me."[72] His son later recalled that he entertained hopes that "his name would descend to a grateful posterity, as the Liberator of Southern America."[73]

In the end, Miranda's plan came to naught. President Adams, much to Hamilton's consternation, was already intent on negotiating a settlement with France, had no wish to become embroiled in a dispute with Spain, was jealous of Hamilton and frightened by his plans to build and lead a large army, and was sufficiently troubled by the revolution in France not to want to engage "myself and my country in most hazardous and expensive and bloody experiments to excite similar horrors in South America."[74]

Even so, discussion of Miranda's proposal in both capitals showed a common desire to cooperate wherever possible against their common foe. "Only formal allies could have done much more for one another than did the United States and England at this time."[75] Hamilton and most of his Federalist colleagues drew the line at a formal alliance with Great Britain. Partly they feared that American public opinion, even at the height of anti-French feeling, would never accept an alliance with the British monarchy. Partly they realized that the British, though desirous of a formal alliance, would provide all the assistance the United States needed even without one. Partly they worried that should France conquer Britain, the United States would be locked in an alliance with the losing side in the world war. And should France successfully foment a revolution in Britain, implanting a "wild democracy" of the kind that had taken root in France, there would then be "the danger of reviving and extending that delirium in America."[76]

If they shied away from formal alliance, however, Federalist leaders believed they were engaged in common struggle with Britain against a dangerous, ideologically driven enemy. They saw the war between Great Britain and France neither as a remote European broil, nor as a struggle between equally evil powers that, from the American view, could best end in a draw. Rather, they saw the war as a momentous clash of opposing ideologies with direct consequence for liberalism and republicanism both abroad and at home. On this much, at least, they and their Republican opponents agreed.

It would have been remarkable, in fact, had Americans believed that their foreign policy could be divorced from their ideology, or that foreign affairs and domestic affairs could be isolated from each other. Certainly none of the European powers of the late eighteenth century entertained such delusions. The American and French revolutions had permanently blurred any distinction between relations among states and political developments within states—if such a distinction had ever existed. The French Convention in 1792 declared that France would support all peoples seeking to overthrow monarchy, and even before it made good on that promise, France's revolutionary principles stirred challenges to monarchical regimes throughout Europe and in Great Britain. The government of William Pitt, fearful of infection at home from the revolutionary virus, repressed the London Corresponding Society established in 1792 as a working-class reform movement. He suspended habeas corpus and drove the radical democrat Joseph Priestley into exile. In Austria, Prussia, and Russia, fears of the spreading influence of the French Revolution put an end to the "enlightened absolutism" of Joseph II, Frederick II, and Catherine II and inaugurated a prolonged era of conservative reaction.

For all the European powers, foreign policy aimed at distinctly ideological goals. Pitt declared Britain's war aims to be not merely the defeat of France but the restoration of the French monarchy. The three absolute monarchies of eastern Europe partitioned Poland in 1793 and 1795, eventually wiping it off the map, partly to quash liberal reforming efforts by Polish aristocrats, which they feared could undermine their own despotic rule. Given the highly ideological nature of American society and politics, it would have been strange if Americans, alone among the great and middle-sized powers in the revolutionary era of the late eighteenth century, had decided that ideology should play no part in the formulation and conduct of their foreign policy.

In the end, the disasters that both Federalists and Republicans feared throughout the 1790s were averted. After the Battle of the Nile, when Admiral Nelson destroyed the French fleet, fears of a French invasion of Britain, much less of North America, subsided. President Adams, for a variety of reasons, not the least being a desire to clip Hamilton's wings, chose a path of negotiation and conciliation with France. The Convention of Mortefontaine brought an end to the Quasi-War *and* to the French alliance. Adams's peacemaking wrecked Hamilton's plans for a large standing army and put an end to the quasi-alliance with Britain. Ironically, it was not France that did in the Federalists and elevated Jefferson and the Republicans into the presidency, but the Federalists themselves. In the election of 1800 the party split into factions led by Adams and Hamilton, giving the presidency to Jefferson and inaugurating the next era in American foreign policy.

THE NATIONAL DEBATES of the 1790s, however, had revealed a great deal about the character of early American foreign policy. In later years politicians and historians would argue that American policy toward Britain and France, and Washington's pronouncements in his Farewell Address, expressed a national desire for complete separation and independence from Europe and the rest of the world. Political entanglements with other nations and concern about their domestic institutions were to be no part of American foreign policy.

But in the 1790s American fears of entanglement were selective. Few Americans saw the need to keep away from what they considered weaker or inferior powers on the North American continent, in Spanish America, in the Mediterranean, or even in most of Europe. But even when it came to the two great powers, France and Great Britain, Americans disagreed about the dangers of entanglement. When Republicans warned against entanglement with foreign powers in the 1790s, they meant entanglement with Great Britain. They had much less fear of entanglement with France, especially with revolutionary France. Jefferson later became a convert to a general policy of nonentanglement only when he saw that the promise of republicanism in France had been crushed by Napoleon. When Federalists warned against entanglement, on the other hand, they meant entanglement with France. They had no similar fear of entanglement with Great Britain.[77] "I have always preferred a connexion with you," Hamilton told one British agent, "to that of any other country, we think in English, and have a similarity of prejudices and of predilections."[78] By the 1790s few Americans any longer shared the view expressed by Thomas Paine in the 1770s that America should separate itself entirely from *all* of Europe. Nonentanglement was a selective tactic, not a grand strategy.

The same could be said about other aspects of American foreign policy in this era. Although Hamiltonians and Jeffersonians alike often claimed to oppose interfering in the internal affairs of other nations, both looked approvingly on plans to do just that, whether in the Western Hemisphere or on the coast of North Africa. While both Hamiltonians and Jeffersonians understood the principle of the balance of power and recognized the benefits to the United States of preserving such a balance in Europe, their ideological differences led them to assess the threats to the balance of power differently.

Although both Hamiltonians and Jeffersonians agreed that the United States should avoid war with the great powers, Republicans were sometimes inclined to risk war with Great Britain, and Federalists were sometimes inclined to risk war with France. Although Hamilton and Jefferson both supported the principle of free trade, in practice Hamilton opposed trade embargoes against England but favored them against France, while Jefferson opposed them against France but favored them against England. And although both Hamilton and Jefferson believed that a nation's honor had to be preserved at almost any cost, Hamilton was willing to suffer some dishonor in pursuit of better relations with Great Britain, while Jefferson was willing to suffer some dishonor in order to maintain good relations with France.

Even on so fundamental a matter as independence, it would be a mistake to believe that the goal of establishing American independence and freedom of action in the world superseded all other goals. Hamilton was prepared to increase American dependence on Great Britain for a period of time so that the nation might eventually grow strong enough to assume an even more forceful and complete state of independence in the future and also so that American society and its economy might follow a more British style of evolution. Jefferson, for his part, was prepared to accept greater dependence on France in order to achieve what he considered a more important independence from Great Britain, and to avoid replication of the British system that he abhorred.

The point is not that American leaders were hypocrites. It is that their judgments on matters of foreign policy were shaped primarily by their visions for what America should become, both at home and abroad. These visions of America's future were the polestars by which Americans navigated their way through the foreign policy crises of their day.

The Call to Greatness

IF THE 1790s were a time of division and turmoil in both domestic and foreign affairs, a time in which principles of foreign policy were applied inconsistently by the competing factions of American politics, there were nevertheless some significant areas of consensus. Indeed, there was a recognizable grand strategy that Americans pursued fairly consistently. It concerned America's future as a great world power.

That America was a nation of "great destinies" was one matter on which there was no disagreement among Jeffersonian Republicans and Hamiltonian Federalists. All agreed with Hamilton that the United States in the 1790s was "the embryo of a great empire."[79] To be sure, Americans had somewhat different visions of precisely the form national greatness should take. Jefferson's "empire of liberty" was an empire of mammoth territorial expanse. As he wrote James Monroe in 1801, "However our present interests may restrain us within our own limits, it is impossible not to look forward to distant times, when our rapid multiplication will expand itself beyond those limits, and cover the whole northern, if not the southern continent, with a people speaking the same language, governed in similar forms, and by similar laws; nor can we contemplate with satisfaction either blot or mixture on that surface."[80] His fellow Virginian, George Washington, also looked west. As Woodrow Wilson later wrote of the Farewell Address, "It was [Washington's] way of fulfilling the vision that had long ago come to him, of a nation spreading itself down the western slopes of the mountains and over the broad reaches of land that looked toward the Mississippi."[81]

Hamilton characteristically looked in the other direction, across the Atlantic toward England and Europe.[82] His grand vision was of an America that could take its place alongside Great Britain as one of the world's great powers. Indeed, this aspiration for great-power status was almost inseparable from his conception of how America's economy, society, and political institutions should be organized. The former was the essential prerequisite to the latter.[83] To fulfill its destiny and become a great power, he believed, the United States had to pursue two closely related objectives. First, it needed to build a navy large enough to defend its far-flung overseas trade and to deter other great powers from using their naval strength to force the United States to bend to their will. To be a great world power, the United States had to "have all the accoutrements of world power: a vital domestic industry, a healthy world trade, and, to protect that trade and the national integrity, a naval fleet." For this reason, "Hamilton had long held that a peacetime standing navy was a necessity for a nation aspiring to greatness."[84] He even envisioned the day when the United States, like Britain and other maritime empires, would hold overseas colonies.[85]

A large peacetime navy was an essential accompaniment to Hamilton's second purpose: to make the United States the dominant power not just on the North American continent but in the whole of the Western Hemisphere. The United States should "aim at an ascendant in the system of American affairs."[86] He hoped the United States would grow strong enough "ere long, to become the arbiter of Europe in America."[87] Hemispheric dominance would be the means by which the United States established not only its independence from Europe but also its greatness as a world power. "Let Americans disdain to be the instruments of European greatness!" he exhorted in *The Federalist*. "Let the thirteen States, bound together in a strict and indissoluble union, concur in erecting one great American system, superior to the controul of all trans-atlantic force or influence, and able to dictate the terms of the connection between the old and the new world!"[88] As early as 1787 Hamilton foreshadowed the hegemonic pretensions of the Monroe Doctrine and of Henry Clay's panhemispheric "American System."[89]

Expectations of future world power permeated Washington's Farewell Address as well.[90] The first president never expected America to remain in the weak and perilous circumstances of 1796. It just needed time and peace, and that was what he had tried to provide it. The whole thrust of his foreign policy, from the neutrality proclamation onward, had been "to endeavor to gain time to our country to settle and mature its yet recent institutions, and to progress without interruption to that degree of strength and consistency which is necessary to give it, humanly speaking, the command of its fortunes." "If we remain one people, under an efficient government," he predicted, "the period is not far off when we may defy material injury from external annoyance; when we may take such an attitude as will cause the neutrality we may at any time resolve upon to be scrupulously respected; when belligerent nations, under the impossibility of making acquisitions upon us, will not lightly hazard giving us provocation; when we may choose peace or war, as our interest, guided by our justice, shall counsel."

That day, he believed, was no more than a few decades away. Although they were deliberately vague in the Farewell Address, elsewhere in their writings and statements Washington and Hamilton gave a more precise sense of how long it might be before the United States could "command its own fortunes." At about the time the address was being prepared, Washington wrote to Hamilton his conviction that "[t]wenty years peace with such an increase of population and resources as we have a right to expect; added to our remote situation from the jarring power, will in all probability enable us in a just cause, to bid defiance to any power on earth."[91] A year earlier Hamilton had suggested that if the United States could avoid war "for ten or twelve years more," it would acquire the "maturity," a "state of manhood," and the "growing prosperity" to enable Americans to "take a higher and more imposing tone" in dealing with foreign nations.[92] In 1798 he wrote to a colleague that despite America's current difficulties, it would "erelong, assume an attitude correspondent with its great destinies—majestic, efficient, and operative of great things. A noble career lies before it."[93]

American ambitions for empire and greatness were more than just a drive for power. As with all other important matters with which Americans concerned themselves, American ambitions carried ideological and moral implications.[94] Jefferson's continental empire was to be an "empire of liberty," uniting people under the banner of liberalism, "governed in similar forms, and by similar laws." The empire Hamilton hoped to emulate was the British Empire, which Britons and their American sympathizers considered to be an empire "that stood high for liberty."[95] But for Americans, more than for Britons, belief in universal rights was the essence of their national identity and therefore had to be a defining characteristic of their participation on the world stage. When their power grew to approximate Britain's, as almost all Americans fully expected it would, Hamiltonians and Jeffersonians alike expected to wield that power on behalf of liberal principles.

CHAPTER 5

"Peaceful Conquest"

The universal feeling of Europe in witnessing the gigantic growth of our population and power is that we shall, if united, become a very dangerous member of the society of nations.

—John Quincy Adams, January 17, 1817

The American Ideology of Expansion, 1800–1823

AS THE VISIONS of Washington, Hamilton, and Jefferson made clear, Americans entered the nineteenth century not with cloistered modesty but with grand dreams of national expansion. Under the circumstances, this was a confidence bordering on hubris. They could not even count on access to the vital waters of the Mississippi. Yet American leaders from every region of the country and representing every political stripe shared a common belief that most if not all of North America, including Canada, Mexico, and the islands of Cuba and Puerto Rico, formed the "natural" dominion of the United States. In 1801 a leading Federalist journal declared, "It belongs of right to the United States to regulate the future destiny of North America. . . . The country is ours; ours is the right to its rivers and to all the sources of future opulence, power and happiness."[1] John Quincy Adams, from the Federalist Northeast, coveted the Floridas and the territories of the Pacific Northwest, convinced that "the whole continent of North America" was "destined by Divine Providence to be peopled by one nation . . . in one federal Union."[2] Henry Clay, the leading statesman of the Republican West, had his eyes fixed on Texas and also on parts of Canada. Andrew Jackson, soon to become the hero of the American frontier, was by 1806 already looking forward to the conquest of Mexico.[3] Thomas Jefferson, John Calhoun, John Quincy Adams, Henry Clay, and Andrew Jackson all shared the conviction that the islands of Cuba and Puerto Rico must someday fall into American hands. Gouverneur Morris, assessing the mood of his countrymen in 1803, declared that "all North America must at length be annexed to us—happy, indeed, if the lust for dominion stop there."[4]

Decades before the phrase "manifest destiny" entered the foreign policy lexicon, this "lust for dominion" was an almost unstoppable force in American politics. Americans believed it their right and their destiny to spread across the land. They were the vanguard of human progress. If possible, they would civilize those who stood in the way. If necessary, they would remove them. But either way the land would be taken and settled.

The "lust for dominion," when married to the transforming power of American liberalism, doomed Indian civilization on the continent. After 1800, as before, policy toward the Indians remained suffused with the moral purpose—sometimes sincere, sometimes merely rhetorical—of advancing Anglo-Saxon civilization among savage peoples. "In time," President Jefferson told the Indians, "you will be as we are."[5] But hunger for land, expressed through an increasingly democratic politics, overwhelmed most benevolent plans. Even those Indians who tried to follow the white man's course found little protection from frontiersmen pursuing their "natural" right to "unused" lands and demanding the aid of their elected representatives in obtaining those lands for American settlement. White settlers petitioned their politicians, demanding to know how the federal government could "gratify" the demands of a "heathen" Indian population, when American citizens who wanted to "improve the country" and who voted were prevented "even from inJoying a small Corner" of the vast land. Under this unceasing pressure, Jefferson frankly explained to Indian leaders, it would be necessary "from time to time" to "procure gratifications to our citizens" by taking away more swaths of Indian territory.[6]

The policy of Indian "removal" is normally associated with the famed Indian fighter Andrew Jackson, but Jefferson pushed the Indians off hundreds of thousands of square miles of territory. When he took office, most of Tennessee was in the hands of the Cherokees and Chickasaws. Most of Georgia was divided between Cherokees and Creeks. Creeks, Choctaws, and Chickasaws occupied nearly all of the future states of Mississippi and Alabama. What would later become Florida was mostly in the hands of the Seminoles. And in the West, Indians occupied substantial portions of what would later be the states of Indiana, Illinois, Arkansas, and Missouri. By the time he left office, Jefferson had acquired for the United States nearly two hundred thousand square miles of this territory and had flanked the remaining Indian-held lands with established white settlements on the east and west.[7]

Jefferson hoped the Indians would learn that it was "in their interest" to give away their "surplus and waste lands" and work on "improving those they occupy."[8] But when they did not learn, he was prepared to be ruthless. "The backward will yield, and be thrown further back," he warned. "These will relapse into barbarism and misery, lose numbers by war and want, and we shall be obliged to drive them, with the beasts of the forest into the Stony mountains."[9] What choice was there? As John Quincy Adams had declared, "Shall [the Indian] doom an immense region of the globe to perpetual desolation, and . . . silence forever the voice of human gladness? . . . No, generous philanthropists! Heaven has not been thus inconsistent in the works of its hands!"[10]

This early-nineteenth-century idea of expansion had implications beyond the Indians. Other peoples who stood in the path of progress would require removal, too. Frequently, to be sure, a powerful element of racism was involved in this conviction. Three decades later, the man who invented the phrase "manifest destiny" would warn that the "Mexican race" must "amalgamate and be lost, in the superior vigor of the Anglo-Saxon race, or they must utterly perish," just like the Indians.[11] But feelings of racial superiority were not the cause of American expansion in the early nineteenth century. Racism was a justification, and only one of many.

The Indians were not the sole obstacles to American progress. So, too, were Spaniards who held lands on the continent that American settlers coveted. So, too, were the French, who early in the century acquired Louisiana from Spain with the aim of re-creating their lost empire in the Western Hemisphere. So, too, were the Russians, who laid claim to lucrative territories along the Pacific Coast. And so, too, were the British, fellow Anglo-Saxons, who controlled Canada and parts of the Pacific Northwest and strongholds in the Caribbean. In the first quarter of the nineteenth century all four European powers watched their territorial holdings become targets of American expansion. Their fairer complexions did not protect them. For just as Americans from Jefferson and John Quincy Adams to Andrew Jackson believed it contrary to God and nature's plan for Indians to roam on vast, fertile lands without cultivating and "improving" them, so after the turn of the nineteenth century Americans also regarded it as unnatural for any foreign power to hold territory on the North American continent. It was a "physical, moral, and political absurdity," Adams proclaimed, "that such fragments of territory, with sovereigns at fifteen hundred miles beyond sea, worthless and burdensome to their owners, should exist permanently contiguous to a great, powerful, enterprising, and rapidly growing nation."[12]

Spain was the first victim of Adams's law of geopolitical physics. By 1800 the stage was set for the "peaceful" dislodging of Spanish control of the vast territory of Louisiana. Thanks to Spanish policies encouraging settlement in the 1790s, more than half of the population of upper Louisiana was American-born. American settlers were also dominant in West Florida. In lower Louisiana and New Orleans the Americans, though a minority, were a powerful force in the region's economy and government. Americans were making their way west of the Mississippi, settling in the Missouri country and in Texas; traders and cattle ranchers were scouting out the vast southwestern territory right up to and even beyond the borders with Mexico.[13]

As Spanish governors learned the hard way, these American immigrants were unruly and dangerous guests, "an alien element within an alien culture."[14] When they got into trouble, American settlers could count on support from their kinsmen across the border, including from a federal government that rarely passed up an opportunity to gain sway over Spanish territory. Thus in 1797 American settlers rebelled against Spanish authorities in Natchez, and when the Spaniards withdrew their meager forces from the northern posts, the United States took possession of the region and organized it as the new Mississippi territory. This seizure proved to be only a prelude to the absorption or conquest of all Spanish lands on the North American continent.

The Spaniards saw what was coming. As a resident of Spain's vast territory warned, Louisiana would "never cease to be the object" of American ambitions: "Their position, the number of their population, and their other means, will enable them to invade this province whenever they may choose to do so."[15] And indeed, as New York Federalist Rufus King explained, Americans "looked without impatience to events which, in the ordinary course of things, must, at no distant day, annex this country to the United States."[16]

The Americans could be patient so long as no other power threatened to take what they insisted rightfully belonged to them. When Napoleon took Louisiana back from Spain at the turn of the century, playing the usual imperial game of trading territories, the Americans acted as if some aggression had been committed against them. When they aimed at something and did not get it, as the Corinthians said of the Athenians, "they think that they have been deprived of what belonged to them already." American politicians rose up in anger and fear at the prospect of French control of New Orleans and Louisiana, especially after the Spanish suspended the American right of deposit at the mouth of the Mississippi. Congress debated a resolution to send fifty thousand militiamen to seize New Orleans. Hamilton and other Federalists, reviving their favorite project from the 1790s, called for military action against France and Spain and a formal alliance with Great Britain. President Jefferson declared that if France took New Orleans, "we must marry ourselves to the British fleet and nation."[17]

The uproar helped convince Napoleon that taking New Orleans and Louisiana was a risky proposition. Even if Jefferson's threats were hollow and his diplomacy inept, French and Spanish officials worried about the "numerous, warlike, and frugal" American population, which they considered "an enemy to be feared."[18] Perhaps the president himself did not really want war, one anxious Spanish diplomat reported back to Madrid, but "in three months the clamor of the Federalists, the impulse of public opinion, and party policy will force the President and Republicans to declare War against their wish."[19] French officials warned Napoleon that any foreign government in Louisiana would be dependent on American goodwill in peacetime and be at America's "mercy in the first war with England."[20] Some of his advisers believed France simply could not "maintain itself in Louisiana against the will of the United States."[21] When Napoleon ultimately decided to abandon his plans for North American empire and to sell Louisiana to the United States, part of the reason was the disastrous conquest of the island of Santo Domingo, where thousands of French soldiers fell to yellow fever. But fear that the American people would not long tolerate foreign control of Louisiana influenced his thinking. "I will not keep a possession which will not be safe in our hands," he told his advisers, "that may perhaps embroil me with the Americans, or may place me in a state of coolness with them."[22] Better to sell Louisiana to the Americans and cement a friendship with a "numerous, warlike" people who might prove useful in a war with Great Britain.[23]

The United States thus gained the measureless expanse of Louisiana, doubling the size of the country without firing a shot. Many Federalists, including Hamilton, reversed themselves and opposed the Louisiana Purchase when it became Jefferson's triumph. But for most Americans it was a kind of immaculate conquest. "The treaty which we have just signed has not been obtained by art or dictated by force," Robert Livingston proudly declared.[24] The *National Intelligencer* boasted, "We have secured our rights by pacific means" and proved that "truth and reason have been more powerful than the sword."[25] The federal government informed the newly incorporated, wary, and generally unhappy people of New Orleans that it was their "peculiar happiness" to be coming under the rule of "a philosopher who prefers justice to conquest."[26]

Americans at the time, and over the next two centuries, either denied or ignored the extent to which fear of America's growing power or its persistent demand for control of the Mississippi Valley had influenced the French decision.[27] They viewed themselves as passive and pacific, seeking only to be left alone and wishing to stay out of other people's business, and the peaceful acquisition of Louisiana strengthened this self-perception. But other powers saw a very different set of American qualities. They saw an aggressive power with an insatiable appetite for land and a remarkable willingness to employ force to get its way. Jefferson, according to one French observer, betrayed "an ambition of conquest."[28] A Spanish minister considered the famous transcontinental expedition of Meriwether Lewis and William Clark not as a benign scientific exploration but as Jefferson's gambit "to perpetuate the fame of his administration" by "attempting at least to discover the way by which Americans may some day extend their population and their influence up to the coasts of the South Sea [Pacific Ocean]."[29]

To outside observers, the best proof of the Americans' aggressive nature came after the Louisiana Purchase. Instead of accepting their territorial windfall and turning inward to concentrate on the development of this magnificent bounty of new land, Americans took their vast gains merely as an invitation to still further expansion. "Since the Americans have acquired Louisiana," one French diplomat complained, "they appear unable to bear any barriers round them."[30]

Indeed, no sooner had the United States acquired the vast territories of Louisiana than it began to press Spain to give up the Floridas as well. This was not a defensive response to a perceived threat, for after 1803 the Spanish posed no threat to the United States. They were helpless to prevent the crumbling of their tenuous foothold in North America. Their present ally, France, had retreated from North America, and their past and future ally, Great Britain, had its hands full with the war in Europe. American officials looked at Spain not with trepidation but with confidence and a sense of superiority based on power. "What is it that Spain dreads?" James Madison asked at the end of 1803. "She dreads, it is presumed, the growing power of this country, and the direction of it against her possessions within its reach. Can she annihilate this power? No. Can she sensibly retard its growth? No."[31] American statesmen agreed it was time for Spain to face the reality that its holdings in North America were, as John Quincy Adams pointed out, contrary to nature. Spain should accept its fate and America's destiny. "The United States [was] a rising and Spain a declining power," James

Monroe reasoned. Of what value could Florida be to Spain, therefore, since "at no distant period we should acquire it"?[32]

American settlers launched uprisings against the local Spanish authorities in West Florida, and in the summer of 1810, aided by their compatriots across the border, they marched on Baton Rouge, seized the Spanish fort, declared themselves the independent Republic of West Florida—complete with a "lone star" flag—and asked to be annexed to the United States. President Madison promptly sent in American troops to occupy the territory up to the Perdido River, explaining to foreign governments that the upheavals in Spanish territory had created "a great uncertainty . . . in that quarter."[33] By the following year American forces controlled all of West Florida except for the city of Mobile and its garrison of Spanish troops. Mobile fell to the Americans in 1813, in the midst of war with Spain's ally, Great Britain.

The territory known as East Florida fell a few years later. In 1811 Congress passed a "no transfer" resolution warning that the United States would not sit idle were Florida to pass into the hands of another European power. The "no transfer" principle may have sounded defensive to American ears, but it was tantamount to planting the American flag in Florida. The resolution authorized the president to take East Florida should any "existing local authority" prove ready to cede it. Seven years later, no such accommodating "local authority" having materialized, General Andrew Jackson, battling for Indian lands in the South, was sent across the Florida boundary to repulse attacks from resisting Seminoles. The bigger target, though, was Florida. President Monroe wrote Jackson that his pursuit of the Seminoles "will bring you on a theatre where you may possibly have other services to perform. Great interests are at issue. . . . This is not a time for repose . . . until our cause is carried triumphantly thro'."[34] Jackson's triumph was swift, and Pensacola fell.

The Spanish minister, Luis de Onis, angrily protested to Secretary of State John Quincy Adams that "the war against the Seminoles" had been "merely a pretext for General Jackson to fall, as a conqueror, upon the Spanish provinces . . . for the purpose of establishing there the dominion of this republic upon the odious basis of violence and bloodshed."[35] Adams just as vigorously defended Jackson's actions, insisting that Spain, and England, were entirely to blame for the outrages that had forced America's hand in Florida. In 1819 he held a gun to his Spanish counterpart's head. "If we should not come to an early conclusion of the Florida negotiation," he warned, "Spain would not have the possession of Florida to give us."[36]

Nor was Adams content merely to take the Floridas. Negotiating from strength, he demanded that Spain also cede a large stretch of territory along the northwestern Pacific Coast. De Onis at first expressed shock that he would try "to dispossess us also of the whole Pacific Coast which belongs to us," but then gave in.[37] The treaty of 1819 gave the United States not only the Floridas but all Spanish territory in the Pacific Northwest above the forty-second parallel as well.

This was certainly aggressive behavior on the part of the very young nation. Yet American expansionism in the first two decades of the nineteenth century, from Louisiana in 1803 to East Florida in 1818, was also haphazard. The paradox was that although Adams and other American leaders had a clear vision of continental empire, they had no specific plans to obtain it. On the contrary, they were often surprised to be acquiring ever more of the continent more quickly than they had thought possible. Adams noted this in reflecting on his own work in acquiring Spanish territory in the Northwest. The Louisiana Purchase, he wrote, had made it "unavoidable that the remainder of the continent should ultimately be ours." But even so, it was only "very lately that we have distinctly seen this ourselves; very lately that we have avowed the pretension of extending to the [Pacific Ocean]."[38] This was not empire acquired in a fit of absentmindedness, but neither was it acquired by careful design. Each acquisition brought a new horizon and new ambitions. The fulfillment of one desire produced another. Perhaps the most accurate description was that it was empire attained by determined opportunism.

American expansion did follow a recognizable pattern, even when there was no conscious design behind it, and it was often the product of private initiative. Certainly from the outside American expansion looked like a concerted government "project." As one Mexican official observed, the process would begin with private Americans "introducing themselves into the territory which they covet, upon pretense of commercial negotiations, or of the establishment of colonies, with or without the assent of the Government to which it belongs." The American-born population would grow until it outnumbered everyone else. Then the Americans would begin demanding their democratic "rights" from local authorities. When the authorities refused, as they had to, the Americans would start stirring up trouble, often with local Indian tribes. It was only a matter of time before the United States government stepped in, insisting its interests were affected by the trouble on its borders. Then began the diplomatic negotiations, which invariably resulted in new territorial agreements favorable to the United States. Of course, sometimes the United States skipped all these steps and simply invaded the territory, "leaving the question to be decided afterwards as to the legality of the possession, which force alone could take from them."[39] Such was the case with Jackson's raid on East Florida and Adams's subsequent negotiation of the Transcontinental Treaty to ratify the conquest. Mexican leaders considered the Americans to be a "most ambitious people, always ready to encroach upon their Neighbours without a spark of good Faith."[40]

Nor did outsiders have any difficulty predicting the course of American expansion. As early as 1812 the Spanish minister in Washington warned his government that the United States intended eventually to take Texas, New Mexico, California, and some of the northern provinces of Mexico as well. "This project will seem delirium to any rational person," he mused, "but it certainly exists."[41] He saw the workings of "manifest destiny" long before it became an expansionist rallying cry: "The Americans believe themselves superior to all the nations of Europe, and see their destiny to extend their dominion to the isthmus of Panama, and in the future to all of the New World."[42]

Spain was not alone in its concerns. The British government viewed growing American power, and growing American ambition, with the same appalled apprehension. Lord Liverpool, the British prime minister and no friend of the United States, called the seizure of West Florida "one of the most immoral acts recorded in the history of any country." British diplomats such as Stratford Canning were repeatedly shocked by American efforts to take lands in the Pacific Northwest that Britain, Russia, and Spain had already claimed. The British themselves had beaten back American attempts to seize Canada, most recently during the War of 1812. At Ghent in 1814, where American and British negotiators wrangled over a peace agreement to end that war, the British at first demanded exclusive control of the Great Lakes. They regarded it as an essential precaution against an American aggressiveness that had been all "too clearly manifested by their progressive occupation of the Indian territories, by the acquisition of Louisiana, by the more recent attempt to wrest by force of arms from a nation in amity the two Floridas, and, lastly, by the avowed intention of permanently annexing the Canadas to the United States."[43] Only that prodigious expansionist, Russia's Tsar Alexander I, seemed to take a more empathetic view of American behavior. As he remarked, smiling, to John Quincy Adams, "One keeps growing bit by bit in this world" (*On s'agrandit toujours un peu, dans ce monde*).[44]

Americans were often surprised by their international image as a grasping nation. A congressman returning from Europe in 1819 reported with dismay that in England and France everyone he spoke to "appeared to be profoundly impressed with the idea that we were an ambitious and encroaching people."[45] This struck many Americans as unfair. Yet at the same time many felt pride in their nation's growing size and power. The British, Adams recalled, had once sneered at Americans as a "peddling nation," having "no God but gold." Now the British wanted to "alarm the world at the gigantic grasp of our ambition." He knew which reputation he preferred. "If the world do not hold us for Romans they will take us for Jews, and of the two vices I would rather be charged with that which has greatness mingled in its composition."[46] The other great powers of the world should become "familiarized with the idea of considering our proper dominion to be the continent of North America. From the time when we became an independent people it was as much a law of nature that this should become our pretension as that the Mississippi should flow to the sea." Until the nations of Europe recognized that the United States and North America were "identical," he believed, "any effort on our part to reason the world out of a belief that we are ambitious will have no other effect than to convince them that we add to our ambition hypocrisy."[47]

Ambition and opportunism had produced power and security, which in turn produced more ambition and opportunism. The Louisiana Purchase had opened the door to further acquisition of Spanish territories in Florida and along the Gulf Coast and removed one imperial power, France, with at least a plausible chance of hemming the United States in. By securing American control of its hinterlands, that acquisition bolstered American security and gave it the confidence to take on another imperial power, Great Britain, in the War of 1812. The end of that war left the third and weakest imperial power, Spain, holding out alone against the United States while the British settled boundary disputes and abandoned their Indian allies in the Northwest. Four years after the war Adams's Transcontinental Treaty opened up the rest of the continent to settlement. He spent the rest of his time as secretary of state laying the groundwork for further expansion into both the Northwest and the Southwest. It was "not imaginable," he declared, "that in the present condition of the world, any European Nation should entertain the project of settling a Colony on the Northwest Coast of America." America's right to control that region was unquestionable and "absolute"; it had been "pointed out by the finger of Nature."[48] As for the Southwest, although Adams abjured the immediate acquisition of Texas, he foresaw the day when the "inhabitants" of Texas would "exercise their primitive rights, and solicit a union with us."[49]

Nor did American statesmen in the early nineteenth century limit their ambitions to the continent. Once the Floridas were secured and a strong claim to the Northwest staked out, leading Americans looked immediately to Cuba and Puerto Rico as the next logical acquisitions. No one made a stronger case for the eventual acquisition of the extracontinental isle of Cuba than Adams. Noting Cuba's "commanding position with reference to the Gulf of Mexico and the West India seas," its "situation midway between our southern coast and the island of San Domingo," and the "safe and capacious harbor of Havana," which the Florida coastline lacked, he envisioned Cuba not only as a defensive outpost to shield the Floridas but also as an ideal place from which the United States could widen its influence, particularly its commercial influence, in the Caribbean. He believed that Cuba held "an importance in the sum of our national interests, with which that of no other foreign territory can be compared, and little inferior to that which binds the different members of this Union together." Perhaps the United States was not yet ready to seize Cuba, but he considered it impossible "to resist the conviction" that within "the short period of half a century" the annexation of Cuba to the United States would be "indispensable to the continuance and integrity of the Union itself." Cuba and Puerto Rico were "natural appendages to the North American continent," and just as with the territories bordering the United States on the continent, he saw "laws of political as well as of physical gravitation" at work pulling them toward the mainland. Those laws of political gravity operated on the United States, too. If "an apple severed by the tempest from its native tree cannot choose but fall to the ground, Cuba, forcibly disjoined from its own *unnatural* connection with Spain, and incapable of self-support, can gravitate only towards the North American Union, which by the same law of nature cannot cast her off from its bosom." He declared a "no transfer" policy with regard to Cuba, warning that the United States had both the "right" and the "power to prevent" the transfer of Cuba to another great power, that is, Great Britain, and would do so, "if necessary, by force."[50] This was only a prelude to the eventual annexation of Cuba, whenever the time was deemed right. For when Britain's George Canning proposed an agreement among France, Great Britain, and the United States renouncing any intention of seizing Cuba, Adams refused.

The Monroe Doctrine of 1823, which Adams played an essential role in formulating, aimed to keep America's expansionist options open for the future. In 1823 Canning approached the United States with a proposal for a joint Anglo-American declaration against efforts by any nation to gain "possession of any portion" of the Spanish colonies.[51] The declaration was aimed at France and the so-called Holy Alliance of eastern absolutist powers—Russia, Austria, and Prussia—but Adams correctly suspected that

Canning wanted to block future American expansion in Texas and in Cuba as well.[52] Adams opposed making any such promise. "We have no intention of seizing either Texas or Cuba," at least not at present, but "we should at least keep ourselves free to act as emergencies may arise, and not tie ourselves down to any principle." President Monroe's famous statement of December 1823 opposed only "European" efforts to form new colonies in the Western Hemisphere. The United States did not promise to respect the territorial integrity of Spanish lands. Within two decades after the Monroe Doctrine's promulgation, the United States began the process of annexing Texas and, a decade later, made serious attempts to acquire Cuba as well.

War and Nationalism

AMERICA IN THE FIRST QUARTER of the nineteenth century was expansive not only in a territorial sense. As national confidence grew with the acquisition of more land and more security, Americans took an increasingly expansive view of their role in the world, beyond territorial boundaries. Oddly enough, it was the nearly futile War of 1812 that boosted American confidence and brought to the fore qualities in the American character that had been submerged during the trying decades of the 1780s and '90s. If the acquisition of Louisiana and the ratification of the Transcontinental Treaty determined the physical contours of the American continental empire for the remainder of the century, the War of 1812 both revealed and significantly shaped the character of the nation that was to inhabit it.

Although the United States had embarked on a great period of expansion, in the first decade of the nineteenth century many Americans worried about the health of what was still a comparatively new nation. The nervousness was partly a product of the expansion. Some worried that increased territory would make the nation ungovernable or prone to tyranny. Other concerns were less theoretical. The United States after the turn of the century remained buffeted between the two superpowers of the Napoleonic era as they fought for dominance and survival. Americans felt overawed and oppressed by a British fleet that prosecuted the war against France in ways that inevitably victimized neutral American shipping. It also became the victim of both French and British blockades that made American shippers fair game to privateers and warships on both sides.

President Jefferson, who shaped American policies at home and abroad through the first decade of the nineteenth century, managed both to inspire Americans with a new sense of power and confidence and to make them doubtful about their future. In his first term he had scored the greatest triumph of America's short history in acquiring Louisiana without a shot being fired. It was not surprising, therefore, that he hoped to settle America's crisis with Great Britain and France by means of "peaceful coercion" as well. Like many Americans of his era, he believed the two superpowers were so dependent on their access to the American market that a determined embargo would be sufficient to force them to back off. Added to this was Jefferson's governing philosophy, which opposed the accumulation of debt and the levying of taxes. Although Jefferson's actions as president often contradicted this philosophy and seemed to hew more closely to Hamilton's, he did oppose spending money on the kind of navy that would have been required to challenge the British. Yet at the same time he refused to accommodate British policies he considered humiliating and damaging to the young American republic. The result was a policy, not uncommon in American history, in which hopes ran ahead of realities and in which means did not match ends. Jefferson attempted to win concessions from Britain that only a war could gain, but without fighting a war. The result was a failure both in foreign policy and in domestic politics.[53] By the time James Madison assumed the presidency in 1809, Jefferson's hope that "peaceable coercions" could influence both England and France had been thoroughly discredited, Republicanism was in crisis, and national unity itself was threatened.

The perils that Americans perceived in these years were as much internal as external. Many carried over from the eighteenth century the feeling that their experiment in republican government was still just that, an experiment whose success remained uncertain. The dwindling but still significant ranks of Federalists believed Jeffersonian republicanism threatened all that had been achieved under the reign of Washington and Adams. Within Jefferson's own party, "Old Republicans" like John Randolph were dismayed at Jefferson's adoption of so many Hamiltonian policies, especially the augmentation of federal power at the expense of the states. Even among Jefferson's most ardent supporters there was concern that the United States and republican government might prove inadequate to the foreign and domestic challenges.

These fears were compounded by the apparent inability of the Jefferson and Madison administrations to do anything about a number of issues stemming from the war in Europe and the overbearing dominance of the British navy. British impressment of American sailors was painful to Americans and politically hazardous for elected politicians unable to protect their constituents. British and French trade restrictions were onerous, if sometimes evaded. And troubles with Indians along the western and northern frontiers were for the most part blamed on British intrigue.

Americans with differing perspectives generally agreed that the republic was at risk. For leaders of the Republican Party, the failure of Jefferson's and Madison's efforts at peaceful coercion of Great Britain threatened the party's reputation in the country, opened the door to a Federalist comeback, and thereby threatened republicanism itself.[54] Madison believed if the government did not take firm action against Great Britain, "the effect will be felt on the principles of our govt. as well as on the character of those who administer it."[55]

The same democratic pressures that compelled the federal government to defend settlers and pioneers, even when they strayed across recognized boundaries into foreign lands, also put democratically elected leaders under pressure to protect the rights and persons of Americans captured on the high seas. The Declaration of Independence declared the national government responsible for protecting individuals' life and liberty. This raised an issue like impressment, by itself no particular threat to the safety of the country, to the level of a significant national interest. Calhoun insisted it was a republican government's obligation to "protect every citizen in the lawful pursuit of his business." If the government performed this role, the citizen would feel at one with the government, would believe "that its arm is his arms; and will rejoice in its increased strength and prosperity."[56] If not, the government would lose the people's allegiance. And what could be a greater threat to the national interest of a democracy than that? For many leading Americans it was the intangible questions raised—questions about national character, national honor, and the health and vigor of the republic— that weighed more heavily in the calculation of the "national interest" than the practical issues of impressment and trade restrictions. Money and territory were one thing, but American leaders like Henry Clay argued that adopting a passive policy toward Great Britain was forfeiting "a nation's best treasure, honor."[57]

Many Americans genuinely worried that failure to respond adequately to British depredations had already damaged the reputation of republican government both at home and abroad. Europe, they feared, viewed American society as driven entirely by commerce, greed, and the love of luxury, without patriotism or civic virtue.[58] Secretary of State James Monroe remarked with some passion to a French diplomat that while "[p]eople in Europe suppose us to be merchants, occupied exclusively with pepper and ginger," in fact "the immense majority of our citizens . . . are . . . controlled by principles of honor and dignity."[59] Such protestations revealed inner anxiety. "The inordinate pursuit of commerce," Philip Freneau fretted, "has rendered us effeminate" and laid the United States open to conquest by presumably more virile European powers. Henry Clay worried "that we shall become enervated by the spirit of avarice unfortunately so dominant" and asked, "Are we to be governed by the low groveling parsimony of the countingroom?"[60]

For the first but not the last time in U.S. history, Americans voiced concern that their commercial republic could not survive the challenges of a world dominated by powerful armies and navies. The love of commerce, they feared, was incompatible with the martial temperament that a nation needed to compete with other nations. Americans worried that as commercial men they lacked what the ancient Greeks had called *thumos,* a patriotic spiritedness that made men put the honor of their nation ahead of personal comfort and luxury and that made citizens willing to sacrifice all for their country. This anxiety would run through the entire course of American history.

There was, of course, a partisan tinge to these comments by Republican leaders, for it was chiefly Federalist commercial interests in New England who complained that confrontation with Great Britain was disastrous to their trade. But by the summer of 1812 no less a Federalist stalwart than the aging John Adams allied himself with the Jeffersonian Republicans in support of war with Great Britain. Like Clay and others, the former president "endorsed the military struggle for reasons that ultimately transcended any strategic quarrel with Great Britain. He interpreted the conflict as a trial of American virtue, as a test of her republican citizens' capacity for disinterested support of the common good."[61] President Madison in 1812 justified the war in similar terms: "To have shrunk under such circumstances from manly resistance would have been a degradation blasting our best and proudest hopes." Had the United States shied away from war, "it would have struck us from the high rank where the virtuous struggles of our fathers had placed us, and have betrayed the magnificent legacy which we hold in trust for future generations."[62]

Why did the challenge to America's honor, its virtue, and even its virility seem so much greater to these political leaders in 1812 than it had in the 1790s, when most had counseled forbearance in the face of similar mistreatment by both France and England? One difference lay in Americans' changing perception of themselves and of their place in the international hierarchy. What had been barely tolerable to the weak, newborn republic in the 1790s was becoming intolerable to the expanding continental empire of the first decade of the nineteenth century. The old tactics of diplomacy, forbearance, and even embargo—the tactics of the weak—could no longer sal-vage national honor. As Calhoun put it, negotiations and peaceful coercion alone "might suit an inconsiderable nation," but it was "improper for us."[63]

Some in the United States Congress were actually eager for war, hoping it would toughen a people made soft by luxury. The United States, they believed, could not be a strong nation if it lacked a strong martial character. Men as different in temperament as Calhoun and John Quincy Adams agreed that Americans should "rejoice at the acquisition of those national qualities necessary to meet the vicissitudes of war."[64] Clay thought that among the greatest benefits of a war would be "the re-production and cher-ishing of a martial spirit among us."[65]

There was a striking similarity between this way of thinking about war in 1812 and the perspective of the generation of Americans who came of age in the 1880s and '90s and were best represented by that great propo-nent of national vigor and virility, Theodore Roosevelt. Just as Roosevelt, John Hay, Henry Cabot Lodge, and John Quincy Adams's descendants Henry and Brooks Adams would later worry that Gilded Age avarice was sapping the nation's soul and strength, so the "War Hawks" of 1812 feared that the love of luxury—by which they meant Federalist love of British trade—cast doubt on the durability of the republican system. And just as the men of Roosevelt's time would seek to replicate the glories of their fathers' generation, which had fought in the Civil War, the second genera-tion of Americans at the time of the war with Great Britain yearned to repli-cate the martial glories of *their* revolutionary fathers. When Roosevelt's friend Henry Adams wrote his history of the early nineteenth century, he understood well the feelings that animated Clay, Calhoun, and his own grandfather, John Quincy Adams. "If war made men brutal," he remarked in reflecting on the War of 1812, "at least it made them strong; it called out the qualities best fitted to survive in the struggle for existence. To risk life for one's country was no mean act. . . . War, with all its horrors, could purify as well as debase; it dealt with high motives and vast interests; taught courage, discipline, and stern sense of duty."[66] For leading War Hawks in 1812, war with England was a means of forging the new nation's iron. "No man in the nation desires peace more than I," Clay declared. "But I prefer the troubled ocean of war, demanded by the honor and independence of the country, with all its calamities, and desolations, to the tranquil, putrescent pool of ignominious peace."[67]

These intangible, incalculable, but nevertheless potent forces helped impel Americans to war in 1812. One proof of their importance relative to the practical matters at issue was that in the settlement that ended the war,

Adams, Clay, and Albert Gallatin failed to win from their British counter-parts significant concessions on any of the concrete issues over which the war had been fought: impressment, trade restrictions, and redrawing of boundaries. Even so, and despite the fact that the war had generally gone badly for the United States, almost leading to secession by the Federalist-dominated states of New England, Americans nevertheless emerged from the War of 1812 as if from a great victory. Fighting the world's strongest navy to a draw was accomplishment enough for most Americans. The Bat-tle of New Orleans, where General Andrew Jackson led a small American force to smashing victory over a much larger British contingent, though it came after the conclusion of negotiations at Ghent, gave Americans a memorable martial triumph. It was enough so that the *Niles' Weekly Reg-ister* could boast that the United States "now stands in the first rank of nations."[68]

This was not mere patriotic chest thumping. Even if the negotiators at Ghent failed to win British concessions on impressment and other issues, the war did have an impact on British policy at the broadest level. Ameri-cans' willingness to fight, even for the intangible cause of honor, proved a stimulus to better Anglo-American relations. At the conclusion of the war the foreign secretary, Lord Castlereagh, made improved relations with Washington part of his larger effort to build an era of peace and stability after the grand calamity of the Napoleonic wars, and British governments thereafter sought to avoid conflicts with the United States. Indian tribes north of the Ohio River, deprived of British support, gave up vast stretches of land in the years immediately following the war, permitting a huge west-ward migration of the American population. The Anglo-American détente that followed the conclusion of the war in 1815, meanwhile, was a disaster for Spain. England's withdrawal as a reliable ally against the United States helped to convince the Spaniards that they could not resist American demands for territory in 1819. Americans may or may not have gone to war in 1812 in order to carry out expansionist goals, and many did view Canada as a worthy prize of war. But the war certainly helped open the door to fur-ther expansion. Trying to contain American continental aspirations after the war with Great Britain, John Quincy Adams observed, would be like "opposing a feather to a torrent."[69]

Just as the war itself was fought largely for reasons having little to do with foreign policy as traditionally understood, so the most significant effects of the war were to be found not only in the realm of international relations but also in the realm of national development and national charac-ter. Like other American wars, the War of 1812 was a catalyst for change, both accelerating trends that predated the war and providing the spark to propel the country in new directions.

The requirements of fighting the war expanded the role of the federal government and exposed deficiencies in the operation of federal power under the old Jeffersonian Republican scheme—much as the Revolutionary War had pointed up the deficiencies of the Articles of Confederation. The end of the war in 1815 brought calls for augmented national powers even from Republicans.[70] James Madison, Jefferson's staunch colleague in the struggle against Hamiltonian policies in the 1790s, now all but embraced the Hamiltonian system. His Republican administration called for the charter of a new national bank, sought federal monies to encourage the building of roads and canals, and proposed moderate tariff protection for domestic manufactures that had flourished as a result of America's lucrative neutrality during the Napoleonic era but that were about to be swamped by more efficient British manufactures now that the flow of transatlantic commerce was freed again.

All of these measures, long favored by Federalists but opposed by leading Republicans, had gained support largely as a result of the war. America's shaky financial situation during the conflict had led to desperation as the federal government ran out of money to keep the war going, and a poor domestic transportation system had hindered military operations. Support for a tariff on manufactured goods grew because many Americans believed the United States needed greater independence from British imports if it was to maintain its standing as a strong, independent nation. This view could be found not only in the North, where American manufactures were most heavily concentrated, and not only in the West, where Henry Clay championed the tariff to nurture domestic manufactures and pay for roads and canals as part of his "American System," but at first even in the South, where leaders like Calhoun agreed that independence from British commerce was essential to national power and honor.[71] Both Calhoun and Andrew Jackson, who would later become the champions of small government and fiscal restraint, were confirmed nationalists during and after the war, supporting not only expenditures on the army and navy and on roads and canals, but even tariffs for the protection of domestic manufactures.[72]

The turn to Hamiltonian protectionism for domestic manufactures did not mean a turn away from overseas trade. On the contrary, the experience of confrontation and war with England had made converts out of most Republicans, who had once worried about the effects of commerce on republican institutions but had since discovered that America's extraordinary prosperity depended on both strong domestic manufactures and an expanding international commerce. With American farmers already producing more than the domestic market could absorb, and with Americans eager to lessen their heavy reliance on the British market, the War of 1812 spurred the federal government to redouble efforts to open access to foreign markets. Indeed, in the years following the war with Britain, the federal government explicitly took on the task of promoting overseas commerce.

Active promotion of commerce required further expansion of American military strength, especially the navy. This, too, was a novel course for Republicans, for according to old Jeffersonian principles there was no greater threat to republican government than a standing army or a large peacetime navy. Jefferson himself had violated this principle by maintaining a permanent naval presence in the Mediterranean, however, and after the war with Great Britain fears of a permanent military establishment temporarily subsided. In 1816 Congress passed a huge naval appropriations bill to build nine seventy-four-gun ships of the line—equal to most of the warships in the British navy's inventory—as well as twelve forty-four-gun frigates and batteries for coastal defense. Secretary of War Calhoun established new military academies for the training of professional officers, modeled after similar institutions in Europe. More remarkable still was the unprecedented decision by Congress to appropriate money for continuing the naval buildup in future years—a million dollars a year for a decade. John Quincy Adams believed that the "most profitable lesson" of the war had been the need to keep the nation in "a state of permanent preparation for self-defense." Madison insisted, "We must support our rights or lose our character." National honor was "national property of the highest value."[73]

A small but vigorous minority fought against this avalanche of support for an expanding federal government, reprising the battle fought by the Anti-Federalists in the 1780s and foreshadowing many similar battles over the coming decades. Die-hard "Old Republicans" like John Randolph and John Taylor of Caroline had opposed the war against Great Britain precisely because they understood that war and ambitious policies abroad would mean bigger, more centralized government at home. Taylor had railed against this "metaphysical war" and predicted that "this war for honour, like that of the Greeks against Troy," would end in "the destruction of the last experiment in . . . free government." After the war Randolph tried to shame his fellow Republicans into opposing Madison's grand betrayal of old Republican principles. "Gentlemen must either stop on the good old Virginia ground," he declared, "or they must . . . go into Federalism." If his colleagues were "prepared for this system of internal taxation, this system of patronage, this vast Army and Navy, and the point of honor . . . it is hardly worth while to keep up the old distinction."[74]

The voices of Randolph and Taylor were almost drowned out, however, in the national enthusiasm for a bigger, more active federal government, a stronger military, and a more vigorous foreign policy. Many Republicans did venture into Federalism, just as Randolph complained. Convinced that the federal government had been too weak to defend the nation and republicanism itself, a new breed of "National" Republican leaders like Henry Clay "began to support the continuation of many old Federalist policies under Republican auspices," selling the old Hamiltonian ideas with a more democratic, less elitist, and therefore more successful political rhetoric.[75] "A new world has come into being since the Constitution was adopted," Clay argued in response to Taylor's and Randolph's insistence on adhering to the old principles of strict construction and weak central government. "Are the narrow, limited necessities of the old thirteen states . . . as they existed at the formation of the present Constitution, forever to remain a rule of its interpretation? Are we to forget the wants of our country? . . . I trust not, sir. I hope for better and nobler things." Even many Old Republicans who clung to Jeffersonian tenets almost as doggedly as Randolph had nevertheless concluded that those hallowed principles had been inadequate to meet the crisis of 1812. "No man dislikes . . . [a national debt] more than I do," North Carolina senator Nathaniel Macon said, "[a]nd I dislike taxes as much as I do a national debt." But Macon did not hate debt and taxes as much as he hated impressment, "and before I would acknowledge the right of Great Britain to impress American citizens, I would bear as much of both as I could without complaining."[76] War Hawks like Calhoun insisted that the nation's "fame, prosperity, and duration" were at stake in the passage of postwar nationalist legislation. Would Congress, he asked, "go on in the old imbecile mode" and let the nation "travel downward"? Or would it "act on an enlarged policy" of promoting "the prosperity and greatness of the nation"? One Virginia congressman, urging Congress to adopt higher taxes to pay for the naval buildup, declared he was not ashamed "to speak of national glory. . . . I love national glory." The Virginian president James Monroe, a passionate opponent of Hamiltonian Federalism in the 1790s, now declared that with a new government-sponsored transportation system, the American republic could cease being a "small power" and become, at last, a "great" power.[77] This victory for the Federalists ironically came just at the moment when the Federalists had destroyed themselves as a viable national party by their opposition to the war. The War of 1812 thus inaugurated a new era of nationalism in American politics, a nationalism that might fairly be called "progressive."

Support for war and support for the progressive nationalist agenda had gone hand in hand. The leading War Hawks of 1812—Henry Clay, John Calhoun, John Quincy Adams—were also the leading advocates of a stronger federal government and of a more vigorous American nationalism, and all in the service of what they called progress. They believed in the benefits of change or, at the very least, in the necessity of adapting to change. Men like Randolph were generally skeptical of "progress," especially the kind of liberal capitalist evolution the United States seemed to be undergoing. John Taylor of Caroline wrote treatises assailing a liberal, capitalist order where the market reigned supreme. Clay, Adams, and for the moment Calhoun, on the other hand, were the apostles of American liberalism and of market capitalism. Clay, whose home state of Kentucky was shipping its produce across the globe, was the representative of a new western entrepreneurial spirit.[78] Adams, a Federalist turned National Republican, represented the commerce-loving Northeast. The South Carolinian Calhoun saw both profit and honor in a stronger government at the core of a stronger nation. Much like their descendants in the Republican Party at the end of the nineteenth century, these men represented the "progressive element" in the National Republican Party.[79] Having emerged victorious from the war they helped start, "they were now anxious to exercise with wartime vigor the peacetime power of an activist capitalist state."[80]

Supreme Court justice Joseph Story, writing shortly after news of peace reached the United States, spoke for many of these progressive nationalists as he laid out the grand prospect that now opened before them: "Let us extend the national authority over the whole extent of power given by the Constitution. Let us have great military and naval schools; an adequate regular army; the broad foundations laid of a permanent navy; a National bank; a National system of bankruptcy; a great navigation act; a general survey of our ports, and appointments of port wardens and pilots; Judicial courts which shall embrace the whole constitutional powers; National notaries; public and National justices of the peace, for the commercial and national concerns of the United States."[81]

From 1815 through the beginning of the administration of John Quincy Adams in 1825, these nationalists controlled the presidency and the Congress. The apogee of the nationalist dream may have been reached in Adams's first annual message in 1825, when the new president spoke in visionary terms of his plans for a national university, government-sponsored scientific explorations, the creation of new government departments, the fostering of internal improvements, and even the building of a national astronomical observatory, a "lighthouse of the sky."[82] The "great object of the institution of government," Adams declared, "is the improvement of the condition of those who are parties to the social compact." Rebutting the charges of Randolph and other Old Republicans, Adams insisted the government's "duty" was not only to build canals and roads; it was also to foster the "moral, political, intellectual improvement" of society. The end of government, Adams declared, was "the progressive improvement of the condition of the governed."[83]

Along with this early progressive approach to governance in the public sector came a burgeoning movement of progressive social reform in the private sector, the forerunner of the great and more famous reform era of the early twentieth century. Most of the reform movements that were to dominate the nineteenth century and even much of the twentieth—the temperance movement; the simultaneous drives for prison reform, education reform, and health reform; the early glimmerings of a women's rights movement; the first overseas missionary societies; and most significantly the first organized antislavery efforts—had their origins around the time of the war with Great Britain, a period that witnessed "one of the most fervent and diverse outbursts of reform energy in [American] history."[84]

The war was a powerful if indirect source of this energy. The expansion of the federal government, the emergence of a national consciousness, and the growing conviction that national problems required national solutions had relevance beyond the fighting of wars and the building of roads, canals, and observatories. Drunkenness and the condition of prisons and schools were increasingly seen as national problems, too, and though they might not be problems for the federal government to solve, they seemed to be appropriate targets for national reform movements.

The war was only one of several impetuses to early-nineteenth-century reform, however. The growing American capitalist system, the "market revolution," combined with an expanding ethic of individualism and a rebirth of religious fervor, all produced a powerful drive for amelioration of the human condition. The very success of the economy in the first two decades of the century, the riches that flowed to Americans from overseas commerce, generated both the public problems that needed to be addressed by reformers and the private wealth to finance their reforming efforts.[85] Chief among these problems was the growth of cities, especially the burgeoning seaports of the East, where poverty, disease, and vice shocked many Americans' sensibilities. As with the later reform movements at the end of the nineteenth century, early-nineteenth-century reform was partly a reaction to the unsettling changes of a rapidly growing and changing economy. It also reflected, however, the ambitions of an increasingly prosperous people who believed in the possibility of improvement, both personal and collective.

The faith in progress and improvement was not limited to the material world but also applied to the human soul. The religious revival that swept across the nation in the first two decades of the nineteenth century, the early phase of the Second Great Awakening, both sparked and reinforced the impulse to reform. New England's Lyman Beecher and other clergy put a new twist on the old Puritan theology and preached that "good deeds were the mark of godliness and that the millennium was near." Their religious revival movement took the ambitious American's desire for self-improvement and pointed it outward at American society and beyond, to the world. Confident in the possibility of progress and in the capacities of the human will, Americans assumed "the world did not have to be the way it was and that individual effort mattered." A growing national consciousness reinforced the message of religious revivalists, whose attempts to spark reformist zeal could not have succeeded had their followers not been able "to look beyond the borders of their communities and regard a sin in one part of the Union as a matter of concern for all Americans."[86]

The new theology was distinctly American and suited to an era of progressive nationalism and reform.[87] "The ardent worshipper and inventive manufacturer, the radical reformer and propulsive do-gooder," were all shaped according to "a dominant American mold."[88] Alexis de Tocqueville, traveling through the United States in 1831, found "a form of Christianity which I cannot better describe than by styling it a democratic and republican religion." American preachers were always showing their congregants "how favorable religious opinions are to freedom and public tranquility," to the point where it was often difficult to see whether "the principal object of religion is to procure eternal felicity in the other world or prosperity in this."[89]

The decades after the War of 1812 have rightly been called an "age of nationalism." Albert Gallatin believed that Americans had emerged from the conflict possessing "more general objects of attachment with which their pride and political opinions are connected. They are more Americans; they feel and act more as a nation."[90] But it is important to recognize what form this "nationalism" took in the United States. It was not the blood-and-soil nationalism then emerging in Europe. The new European nationalisms of the early nineteenth century "emphasized permanency and continuity, a glorious past of a homogenous nation in ancestral lands."[91] In the post-Napoleonic reaction against revolution, European leaders sought to steer nationalist feelings back toward the crown and the church. The restored Bourbon monarchy in France spoke of "nationalizing the monarchy and of royalizing the nation."[92] But Americans had no ancient myths to glory in, no monarch or church to serve as the symbol of the national spirit. American nationalism derived more from a common commitment to certain liberal, democratic, and republican ideals than from historic attachments to the land or to an individual personification of the nation. This meant that American nationalism possessed a moral component. It also gave American nationalism a supranational, universalistic quality.[93] For Americans, the unifying theme of the nation was that they were to be the vanguard of human progress.[94] Their nationalism naturally led them to look beyond the national boundary.

That is why the burgeoning nationalism of the early nineteenth century manifested itself in international as well as in domestic affairs. For the progressive nationalists leading America, as for their Old Republican opponents, domestic improvements and active involvement in world affairs— big government and big foreign policy—were two sides of the same coin. In his presidential address in 1825, John Quincy Adams directly linked government-sponsored "improvement" at home to an enlarged role on the international stage. "The spirit of improvement is abroad upon the earth," Adams argued. "Liberty is power," and the nation "blessed with the largest portion of liberty must in proportion to its numbers be the most powerful nation upon the earth." Henry Clay's "American System" was a grand plan for government-subsidized roads and canals and for the nurturing of domestic industry, "a vision of progress, a bold reformulation of the relationship between government and society." But his American System had an important foreign policy component as well. His first use of the phrase came in a speech about American policy in the Western Hemisphere, when he called upon his countrymen to "place ourselves at the head of the American system," which included the newly independent states of Latin America. The domestic and foreign elements of the American System were linked in a material sense. His desire for an expanding American commerce independent of British influence led him to look south and to a growing hemispheric trade. It was in America's "power to create a system of which we shall be the centre," he declared. The United States would "become the place of deposit of the commerce of the world."[95] But even more than these commercial advantages, Clay's American System, in both its domestic and its hemispheric manifestations, embodied the spirit of progressive nationalism and aimed at that ineffable goal of national greatness.

The link between the domestic and the foreign realms could be found in

Monroe's December 1823 message to Congress. Today it is remembered only for its enunciation of the so-called Monroe Doctrine, just as Washington's Farewell Address is remembered only for its warning against foreign entanglements. But like Washington's address, Monroe's annual message was devoted chiefly to domestic matters. In just a few paragraphs Monroe demanded that Europe cease colonizing in the Western Hemisphere and asserted America's predominant interest in that part of the world; in the remainder of his lengthy message, he advanced the rest of the republican nationalist agenda.[96] Monroe pointed with pride to the expansion of the navy, which was "steadily assuming additional importance" for American policy, especially in "the West Indies and the Gulf of Mexico." He praised those "patriotic and enlightened citizens" who saw the need for such domestic "improvement" as the building of more roads and canals, along which "troops might be moved with great facility in war" and by means of which the produce of the West might find a market in the East. He called for a further review of the tariff to give more "protection to those articles which we are prepared to manufacture, or which are . . . connected with the defense and independence of the country." As was true of Clay, Adams, Calhoun, and other American nationalists at the end of the first quarter of the nineteenth century, Monroe's confident, progressive, and expansive foreign policy doctrine meshed with his confident, progressive, and expansive domestic policies.

Every aspect of the new nationalism pointed Americans outward. As before, the drive for foreign markets in which to sell American goods naturally inclined Americans to involve themselves overseas and not only, they believed, for their own gain. Americans steeped in the thought of Adam Smith believed international trade was a moral as well as a material issue. Many shared John Quincy Adams's conviction that commerce was "among the natural rights and duties of men" and that it was the "duty" of nations to trade, "not from exclusive or paramount consideration of [one's] own interest; but from a joint and equal moral consideration of the interests of both." Trade was a way of advancing civilization. To trade with the peoples of the Levant was to make them converts to Western civilization. To open China to American trade was to open it to American liberalism. Adams railed at the Chinese for refusing to trade on equal terms with the West, not merely because this denied Americans income but because China's exclusionary policies hindered human progress. At the end of the nineteenth century American demands for an "open door" to trade in the Far East explicitly blended together the desire for profit and the high-minded goals of advancing Western civilization. At the end of the twentieth century Americans were more convinced than ever that global trade yielded global democracy and global peace. But these ideas had been fully formed in the early nineteenth century.[97] Even when deploying the navy to protect their own merchants, Americans believed they acted "less as nationalists than as self-appointed agents of the international commercial society."[98]

The religious revivalists looked beyond national borders, too. The Congregationalist Lyman Beecher, in addition to stirring up revivalist fervor among easterners, helped found the American Board of Foreign Missions in 1810 to spread the gospel to heathen lands. Before the end of the decade Baptists, Methodists, and other Christian denominations founded their own missionary movements. By the 1820s American missionaries were bringing not only Western religion but also, as they saw it, American civilization to the unenlightened in China and in the islands later to be called Hawaii, as well as in India and the Levant.

Historians have often suggested that the idealism of American foreign policy derived from this so-called missionary tradition.[99] But American missionaries were themselves part of, and were strongly influenced by, a much broader American tradition.[100] The missionary movement was only one manifestation of a widespread conviction that Americans should carry the "blessings of civilization" to others and that these blessings were spiritual as well as political and economic in nature.[101] Americans believed the spread of commerce would civilize, uplift, and liberalize mankind. They also believed the spread of republican government would raise mankind to a higher state of perfection. And religious Americans believed the spread of the Christian gospel was essential to the spread of civilization. Where American missionaries differed was in their desire and willingness to go abroad solely for the purpose of spreading the gospel and winning converts, while other Americans went abroad for other reasons and then added as a justification their genuine conviction that they were also benefiting others. Nevertheless Americans of all persuasions generally agreed that religion, commerce, and republican government were mutually supporting and that it was hard to have one without the other two. The missionaries saw little distinction between spreading the gospel and spreading American liberty. As Tocqueville observed, "The Americans combine the notions of Christianity and of liberty so intimately in their minds that it is impossible to make them conceive of one without the other."[102] These were all different expressions of the same conviction, that American principles were universally applicable, universally beneficial, and universally desired.[103]

The nationalist enthusiasm of the immediate postwar period crossed sectional, class, and generational lines. Even the seventy-eight-year-old John

Adams, the normally dour conservative skeptic, could be swept up in it. Writing to Jefferson in 1813, Adams predicted, "Many hundred years must roll away before we shall be corrupted. Our pure, virtuous, public spirited, federative republic will last forever, govern the globe and introduce the perfection of man."[104] America by 1820 was a Prometheus unbound, ready to bring knowledge and freedom to the world. The ebullient mood of Americans manifested itself in the widespread popular support for the independence of Latin American states struggling against the Spanish Empire and in popular enthusiasm for the Greek independence movement. More broadly it took the form of hostility to those powers in the world that opposed essential elements of the American creed.

CHAPTER 6

A Republic in the Age of Monarchy

*On Andes' and on Athos' peaks unfurled, the self-same standard
streams o'er either world!*

—Lord Byron

America and the Global Ideological Struggle
of the Post-Napoleonic Era

IT WAS COINCIDENCE that as Americans were becoming more confident
in their power and in their liberal convictions, in Europe the defeat of
Napoleon and the arrangements of the victorious allied powers at the Congress of Vienna in 1815 ushered in a period of conservative reaction. In the
East, Russia's Tsar Alexander and Austria's Prince Metternich defended the
divine right of monarchs against the revolutionary forces of liberalism and
constitutionalism; in France archmonarchists and the restored Bourbon
dynasty curried favor with the absolutists of Moscow and Vienna who held
the key to France's return as a great power. In the constitutional monarchy
of Great Britain the experience of the French Revolution and Napoleon's
aggression had frightened English aristocrats into staunch defense of monarchical legitimacy. America's fellow liberals in Europe were an endangered
species, and absolutism was in the ascendant. The clock appeared to have
been turned back a century: "Europe in 1815 was in the control of kings,
nobles, and priests as it had not been since the Age of Louis XIV."[1]

For an increasingly open and democratic America, post-Napoleonic
Europe offered an appalling spectacle. Just as many Americans were
becoming more committed than ever to the Enlightenment ideals of human
progress and individual rights, European elites were turning sharply away

from those ideals, disillusioned by the bloody revolution in France and by the twenty years of devastating war that had followed. European monarchs and their defenders vigorously denied that a government derived its power from the people, denied the existence of "natural rights," and denied that the purpose of the state was to secure those rights and the freedom of the individual. Such rights as existed were privileges granted to the people by their sovereign. Written popular constitutions like that of the United States were dangerous and inferior to the organic social arrangements of the monarchies.

After 1815 the absolutist monarchies of Europe, fearful of the liberal contagion, launched a repression more systematic and extensive than any attempted by the monarchies of the ancien régime, giving an early foretaste of the totalitarianism that would emerge full-blown in the twentieth century. In Russia, in the Austrian Empire, in Prussia, and in the German Confederation, secret police compiled detailed dossiers on figures suspected of liberal sympathies. Agents of the state listened to and reported on private conversations, opened mail, and kept close track of citizens traveling abroad. Governments controlled and heavily censored the press. In Austrian-controlled Lombardy the works of Dante were abridged to remove dangerously suggestive passages. In the United States the state was expanding to build roads and canals and to achieve John Quincy Adams's vision of "the progressive improvement of the condition of the governed." In Europe, the state was expanding its administrative power to snuff out all the flickering flames of liberal reform and revolution.[2]

Repression could be found even in the birthplace of constitutional liberalism, Great Britain. In 1819 government forces killed protestors in what became infamous in liberal and democratic circles as the massacre of Peterloo. To stifle radicalism, the conservative Tories who dominated the Cabinet and Parliament passed the Six Acts. The Duke of Wellington, hero of Waterloo, hoped passage of the repressive legislation would help "the whole world . . . escape the universal revolution which seems to menace us all."[3]

More worrying to the Americans were the foreign policies of the absolute monarchies. For Russian and Austrian absolutists, repression of dissidents at home was of no use if liberal reform and revolution flourished just across the border or indeed anywhere in the Western world. When the stirring of liberalism in Germany threatened Austria's shaky despotism, Metternich sought and was granted by the other European powers a right to intervene and organize the Confederation of Germany under Austrian domination. With the Carlsbad Decrees of 1819, Austria seized control of

German politics, imposed press censorship, intimidated university professors and students, and forced liberal resistance underground. In Italy the Kingdom of the Two Sicilies was bound by a secret treaty with Austria not to enact liberal reforms. Alexander's army of agents and ambassadors were actively involved in the politics of countries throughout Europe. In France the Russian ambassador meddled constantly, "setting up and pulling down ministries" as it suited the tsar's predilections.[4] The American minister in Paris, Albert Gallatin, reported, "Ever since the restoration of the Bourbons, there was nothing, even the smallest details, in which [the tsar's] Ambassadors did not interfere in France."[5]

In 1820 Europe plunged into turmoil. Revolutions broke out in Italy and in Portugal and, a year later, in Greece. In Spain military forces that had been assembled to suppress the rebellious colonies of America turned instead against the crown and forced King Ferdinand to accept a democratic constitution. Assassination plots against kings and ministers were uncovered in France and even in England. In Russia a military rebellion in one of Alexander's elite regiments had to be put down. Outbreaks of liberalism and revolution or anarchy seemed to be everywhere. In response, the Eastern powers, styling themselves the "Holy Alliance," proclaimed the right to "deliver Europe from the scourge of revolution" and to enforce the principles of monarchical legitimacy.[6] Nations that had "undergone a change of government, due to revolution," would be dealt with by force.[7] To American ears the words were ominous.

The United States was unavoidably a protagonist in this Cold War–style global confrontation. "All the restored governments of Europe are deeply hostile to us," John Quincy Adams wrote his father from London in 1816. "The Royalists everywhere detest and despise us as Republicans. . . . Emperors, kings, princes, priests, all the privileged orders, all the establishments, all the votaries of legitimacy eye us with the most rancorous hatred."[8] Europe viewed the Americans as "the primary causes of the propagation of those political principles which still made the throne of every European monarch rock under him as with the throes of an earthquake." This ideological hostility, combined with America's prodigious growth and equally prodigious appetite for more land, more trade, and more power, made the continental monarchies eager to see the United States brought down. "The universal feeling of Europe in witnessing the gigantic growth of our population and power," Adams related in 1817, "is that we shall, if united, become a very dangerous member of the society of nations. They therefore hope what they confidently expect, that we shall not long remain united. That before we shall have attained the strength of national manhood our Union will be dissolved, and that we shall break up into two or more nations in opposition against one another."[9]

EUROPEAN ABSOLUTISTS were not wrong to view the United States as dangerous. The republic was an inspiration to revolutionaries in Europe and Latin America, and American leaders and citizens actively supported liberal revolution, materially in the case of Spanish America, rhetorically in the case of Europe. As far back as 1811 President James Madison had insisted that the revolutionary events "developing themselves among the great communities which occupy the southern portion of our own hemisphere and extend into our own neighborhood" could not be ignored. An "enlarged philanthropy" and "an enlightened forecast" required the United States to "take a deep interest in their destinies."[10] This conviction grew stronger after the conservative counterrevolution in Europe. As John Quincy Adams wrote his father, "[T]he republican spirit of our country not only sympathizes with people struggling in a cause so nearly, if not precisely, the same which was once our own, but it is working into indignation against the relapse of Europe into the opposite principle of monkery and despotism."[11] Many believed that as reactionary Europe prepared to crush liberalism and republicanism, an independent and republican South America could join the United States as a formidable counterweight in the New World. Henry Clay proposed that "a sort of counterpoise to the Holy Alliance should be formed in the two Americas, in favor of national independence and liberty."[12]

After 1815, with Clay in the lead, support for Latin independence from Spain became a wildly popular cause in the United States. It was, according to the French minister in Washington, "the only cause popular here."[13] Enthusiasm was greatest in the West, where hostility to Spain ran highest and where the desire for southern markets for western produce was most keen. But Clay appealed to honor and principle as well as to interest. How could Americans "honorably turn away from their duty to share with the rest of mankind this most precious gift"?[14] The "patriots of the South" were "fighting for liberty and independence—for precisely what we fought for." He asked Americans to recall how much it had meant to learn "that France had recognized us." The "moral influence" of America's recognition of the Latin nations, Clay believed, would be "irresistible."[15] Alexander Hamilton had proposed that the United States make itself the "arbiter" of the New World in its dealings with the Old. Clay believed it even more important to play that role against an aggressive, reactionary Europe. "We should become the centre of a system which would constitute the rallying point of human freedom against all the despotism of the Old World. . . . Let us become real and true Americans, and place ourselves at the head of the American system."[16]

Although Clay spoke of an "American system," his approach to the world was driven more by ideology than by geography. Support for the Latin patriots "would give additional tone, and hope and confidence, to the friends of liberty throughout the world."[17] And when the Greeks rose up against their Turkish rulers in 1821, Clay urged Americans to proclaim their support for that "nation of oppressed and struggling patriots in arms." To those who warned that this might anger Europe, he asked, "Are we so humbled, so low, so despicable, that we dare not express our sympathy for suffering Greece, lest, peradventure, we might offend some one or more of their imperial and royal majesties?" The United States should not force its principles on another people, Clay believed, but "if an abused and oppressed people willed their freedom," the United States had an obligation to help.[18]

With American public opinion solidly behind Clay on the question of Latin America, in 1817 President Monroe began edging toward recognition of Latin independence by sending a fact-finding commission to South America. When Adams assumed his post as Monroe's secretary of state, the president directed him to begin preparing the way for recognition of the government in Buenos Aires, which had declared its independence in 1816. As part of this effort, Adams repeatedly asked Great Britain to join the United States on that path, hoping thereby to separate the British from the Holy Alliance and to protect the United States from Europe's wrath.

Adams himself was unenthusiastic about the cause of Latin independence, at least at first. Both the Adamses, father and son, shared a deep skepticism that Spanish-Americans as a race, and Catholics as a religion, were capable of supporting republican government. While Americans' sympathy with the "patriots of S. America" was "natural and inevitable," John Adams wrote his son in early 1818, the "Roman Religion" was "incompatible with a free government" and served only to perpetuate the "General Ignorance" of the Spanish-Americans.[19] Jefferson agreed that history offered "no example of a priest-ridden people maintaining a free civil government."[20] The senior Adams agreed with his son that "the relapse of Europe into the principles of monkery and despotism" was an "awful and direful and rueful subject of consideration . . . portentous of calamities beyond the reach of all human calculation." It was "enough to make the best Christians pray for another Voltaire." But the answer was not to be found in Spanish America.

"Monkery" and ignorance ruled there, too. John Quincy Adams expressed his opinion that the Spanish-Americans did not possess "the first elements of good or free government. Arbitrary power, military and ecclesiastical, is stamped upon their education, upon their habits, and upon all their institutions." He had "little expectation of any beneficial result to this country from any future connection with them, political or commercial."[21] Clay refused to accept this judgment. It was "the doctrine of thrones that man is too ignorant to govern himself," he responded. "Self-government is the natural government of man."[22] But Adams dismissed Clay's idea of an "American system." "As to an American System," he said, "we have it; we constitute the whole of it; there is no community of interests or of principles between North and South America."[23]

Adams had other reasons for opposing what he regarded as hasty American recognition of Latin American independence, and for opposing Clay. The Transcontinental Treaty he negotiated with Spain, which he hoped would catapult him into the presidency, had yet to be ratified by that country. He feared that recognizing Latin independence prematurely would anger Spain and delay or even prevent ratification. Domestic politics were on Clay's mind, too. He passionately believed in recognizing the Latin republics, but he was also using the issue to further his own presidential ambitions. He would have been happy to see Adams's treaty go down in flames. He claimed that the treaty gave away too much territory to Spain anyway, and the United States could seize whatever it wanted, with or without a formal agreement. Adams, to save his treaty, marshaled every argument he could to fend off Clay's attacks.[24]

On July 4, 1821, Adams delivered a passionate Independence Day oration in which he famously declared that America "goes not abroad, in search of monsters to destroy." It is "the well-wisher to the freedom and independence of all," but the "champion and vindicator only of her own." "She well knows," Adams continued, "that by once enlisting under other banners than her own, were they even the banners of foreign independence, she would involve herself beyond the power of extrication, in all the wars of interest and intrigue, of individual avarice, envy, and ambition, which assume the colors and usurp the standard of freedom. The fundamental maxims of her policy would insensibly change from liberty to force. . . . She might become the dictatress of the world. She would be no longer the ruler of her own spirit."[25]

These sentences would be cited many times in the twentieth century as perhaps the most powerful and articulate warning ever uttered against the dangers of idealism in American foreign policy. Adams's sentiments had been shared by Americans in previous decades and would be adopted by future opponents of expansion and intervention. It is a mistake, however, to view Adams as a nineteenth-century spokesman for twentieth-century realism. For unlike twentieth-century realists, Adams believed in the primacy of ideology in international affairs.

Indeed, those who read or heard Adams at the time barely noticed his comparatively brief appeal for American restraint. What they remembered and enjoyed most was his virulent assault on monarchy and absolutism and his aggressive celebration of republicanism. He lashed out at Great Britain, always a popular July Fourth theme, describing English history as a seven-hundred-year struggle between the "oppression of power and claims of right." The American Revolution, on the other hand, had been a victory for the "claims of right," for the principle of universal natural rights for all men. Rather remarkably, given his position as secretary of state, Adams called on the peoples of Europe to make their own revolutions. He exhorted "every individual among the sceptered lords of mankind: *'Go thou and do likewise!'*" The Russian minister was appalled, writing back to his government that Adams's speech was at once a "virulent diatribe against England" and a "miserable calumny on the Holy Alliance." He also noted what he regarded as the stunning hypocrisy of Adams's boast on behalf of the United States' commitment to universal natural rights: "How about your two million black slaves . . . ? You forget the poor Indians whom you have not ceased to spoil. You forget your conduct toward Spain." But what angered the Russian minister most about Adams's address was that it seemed to him "an appeal to the nations of Europe to rise against their Governments." How else to take Adams's exhortation "Go thou and do likewise!"?[26]

Adams may have been playing to public opinion, trying to compensate for his unpopular position on Latin recognition. But there was nothing insincere about his focus on the great divide between the principles that animated the American republic and those that were championed by the European powers and especially by the members of the Holy Alliance. Adams, like the vast majority of his contemporaries both in the United States and throughout Europe, viewed the international system through an ideological lens. He believed the rise of the Holy Alliance had produced what former president James Madison called "the great struggle of the Epoch between liberty and despotism."[27] He also shared the widespread conviction on both sides of the Atlantic that the nature of a nation's government—whether constitutional monarchy, absolutist monarchy, or republic—determined the direction of its foreign policy and its foreign allegiances. National security and national ideology were indissolubly linked.

That was certainly the view of the absolutist European powers, who after 1820 had become increasingly alarmed at the revolutionary stirrings on both sides of the Atlantic. The military uprising against the Spanish king in 1820, the success of independence movements in the Spanish colonies, and their recognition in 1822 by the increasingly powerful and ambitious American republic had convinced Tsar Alexander to turn the Holy Alliance into an active instrument of absolutism against international liberalism. In the spring of 1823 France invaded Spain in order to restore Ferdinand to the throne and also, as the French government proclaimed, "to inspire a salutary fear among the revolutionaries of all countries."[28] France's war, supported by Alexander, aimed explicitly to defend the universal principle of absolutist legitimacy. "Let Ferdinand be free to give to his people institutions which they cannot hold but from him," France's king had declared.[29]

The French invasion of Spain immediately raised the question of Spain's rebellious colonies in the New World. The revolution in Spain, Alexander had declared, was an offense to "the peoples of the two hemispheres"—in the Americas as well as in Europe. To the absolutist rulers on the Continent, it appeared that the liberal contagion, just then being stamped out in Naples and Spain, was spreading out of control across the Atlantic. It was no sideshow. In November 1823 Alexander described Spain's colonial problems as the "great affair" of the day. He insisted that the Holy Alliance not "depart from principle," that the defenders of monarchy should be as unwilling "to sanction a revolution in America" as they had been in Europe.[30] After France had crushed the constitutionalists in Spain, the Russian government sent a message to the United States reaffirming the legitimist principles of the Holy Alliance and warning the young republic against any further efforts to aid the rebellious Spanish colonies. On August 30, 1823, the Russian minister delivered a circular to Adams celebrating the conservative compact of the European powers and their establishment of a "new political system" based on monarchical legitimacy. All of Russia's statements were, in Adams's view, "an 'Io Triumphe' over the fallen cause of revolution, and with sturdy promises of determination to keep it down." The tsar was "bearding us to our faces upon the monarchical principles of the Holy Alliance."[31]

Officials in Russia, France, and Spain were not content with rhetoric and remonstrances. Russia's influential ambassador in Paris believed the autocratic powers should join forces to place Bourbon princes on thrones in the Latin American states, and in 1823 the French foreign minister, François de Chateaubriand, conspired with Spain and Austria to "establish in America large monarchies governed by princes of the house of Bourbon."[32] According to the plan, France would put its navy at the Spanish king's service to transport the European royalty across the ocean, and French troops would help place them on their New World thrones. The plan became well known both in London and in Washington. John Quincy Adams reported that in Mexico and in Buenos Aires France was already "intriguing to get a monarchy under a Prince of the House of Bourbon."[33] The British prime minister, George Canning, considered the threat of a French expedition to reconquer Spain's former colonies serious enough that in October 1823 he warned the French government that any such action would lead to war with Great Britain.

American statesmen could hardly escape the combined geopolitical and ideological challenge posed by the Holy Alliance. Once the treaty with Spain had been safely ratified, even Adams threw himself into that struggle, taking up the very "banners of foreign freedom and foreign independence," in both Latin America and in Europe, that he had claimed were so dangerous. In May 1823 he drafted instructions to the ministers assigned to the five new Latin nations that the United States had finally recognized. In words that could have been drafted by Clay, he noted that "the emancipation of the South American continent" had opened "to the whole race of man prospects of futurity, in which [the United States] will be called in the discharge of its duties to itself and to unnumbered ages of posterity to take a conspicuous and leading part." It was the duty of the United States to establish the foundations of relations with South America upon "principles of politics and of morals" that were "new and distasteful to the thrones and dominations of the elder world." These principles, moreover, were not limited in their reach to the Western Hemisphere but were "coextensive with the surface of the globe and lasting as the changes of time." He asked the ministers to support the republican principle against any local "hankering after monarchy."[34] He hoped that "a Constitution emanating from the people and deliberately adopted by them will lay the foundations of their happiness, and prosperity on their only possible basis, the enjoyment of equal rights," and he urged his ministers to "promote this object" as best they could. The United States and South Americans shared a set of common interests: "that they should all be governed by Republican Institutions, politically and commercially independent of Europe."[35]

The nature of a country's constitution, Adams explained, determined the course of its foreign policy. "The European alliance of Emperors and Kings have assumed, as the foundation of human society, the doctrine of unalienable *allegiance*. Our doctrine is founded upon the principle of unalienable *right*. The European allies, therefore, have viewed the cause of the South Americans as rebellion against their lawful sovereign. We have considered it as the assertion of natural right. They have invariably shown their disapprobation of the revolution, and their wishes for the restoration of the Spanish power. We have as constantly favored the standard of independence and of America."[36]

It was over the question of "natural right" that Adams and his colleagues believed the world divided, and the division was not geographically determined. Beginning in 1818, Americans hoped Great Britain might become an ally in the struggle against absolutism, for even in the last days of Castlereagh's stewardship it had become clear that British policy was diverging sharply from that of the Holy Alliance. The course of Britain's policy, like those of the Continental powers, was shaped by the nature of its constitution. Although Castlereagh had created the European alliance to safeguard the postwar peace in Europe, and although many leading Britons feared revolution almost as much as Metternich and Alexander did, nevertheless England remained a liberal constitutional monarchy. They might fear "monster Radicalism," but they had their own view of the proper relationship between the sovereign and the people—and it was different from Alexander's and Metternich's. When France's restored Bourbon king, Louis XVIII, declared that the people of Spain had no right to make their own constitution and could only be granted one by the crown; when Alexander declared that constitutions were legitimate only if bestowed by a sovereign's "benevolence"—these assertions of divine right outraged English sensibilities. Even after the horrors of Napoleon, the English could not hold the same unequivocally hostile view of "revolution" as the eastern autocrats did. Their own "'glorious revolution of 1688' was the palladium of their present freedom and the source of their present dynasty."[37]

Alexander's attempt to turn the European alliance into an international police force to stamp out liberalism, therefore, had begun to alienate the British. Even Castlereagh, who desired at almost any cost to preserve comity among the European great powers, insisted that such interventions violated "first principles" and were "contrary to the sense of [the British] people." Castlereagh's successor, George Canning, warned still more bluntly that if the British government got involved "with great despotic monarchs, deliberating upon what degree of revolutionary spirit may endanger the public security," then the British people would soon come to "look with great jealousy for their liberties."[38] When France invaded Spain, over Canning's strenuous objection, he publicly expressed his hopes for the Spanish constitutionalists' triumph.

The shift in British foreign policy was noted even in Anglophobic America. In June 1823 John Quincy Adams observed in his diary that "Great Britain had separated herself from the counsels and measures of the [Holy] alliance. She avowed the principles which were emphatically those of this country, and she disapproved the principles of the alliance, which this country abhorred." Britain's change of course opened the door to Anglo-American rapprochement and possibly significant international cooperation. "This coincidence of principle, connected with the great changes in the affairs of the world, passing before us," seemed to him "a suitable occasion for the United States and Great Britain to compare their ideas and purposes together, with a view to the accommodation of great interests upon which they had heretofore differed."[39] Britain's minister in Washington reported to Canning that the "course which you have taken in the great politics of Europe has had the effect of making the English almost popular in the United States."[40]

Canning, like Adams, saw an opportunity, and in the midst of the crisis brought on by France's invasion of Spain in 1823 he made a tantalizing offer to the United States. He proposed to Richard Rush, the American minister to London, that the two nations issue a joint statement declaring that the United States and Great Britain would together oppose any effort by France, or by any other power, to take control of the former Spanish colonies in the Western Hemisphere. Thus would Canning call "the New World into existence to redress the balance of the Old." "What do you think your Government would say to going hand in hand with England in such a policy?" Canning asked Rush.

Canning's proposal was tantamount to a military as well as political alliance, for although he doubted France or the Holy Alliance would test Anglo-American resolve given "the large share of the maritime power of the world which Great Britain and the United States share between them," nevertheless there was always the possibility of war. In a toast to one American diplomat, Canning celebrated the rebirth of Anglo-Saxon solidarity: "The force of blood again prevails, and the daughter and the mother stand together against the world."[41]

The common view of American foreign policy in this era, and of the Monroe Doctrine set forth three months later in response to Canning's proposal, was that it aimed at separating and isolating the United States and the Americas from Europe. Yet President Monroe and the majority of his closest advisers seriously considered accepting Canning's proposal for a virtual alliance between the United States and Great Britain. When Monroe received communication from Rush concerning Canning's proposal, he summoned his cabinet and privately solicited the advice of former presidents Madison and Jefferson. In posing the question for them, Monroe made his own inclinations apparent. "Has not the epoch arriv'd," Monroe asked Jefferson, "when G. Britain must take her stand, either on the side of the monarchs of Europe, or of the U States, & in consequence, either in favor of Despotism or of liberty . . . ?"[42]

Both Jefferson and Madison agreed the epoch had arrived and were enthusiastic about embracing Canning's offer. Jefferson considered Canning's proposal the most significant event that had occurred since the Revolution, and as Adams reported, he was "for acceding to the proposals, with a view to pledging Great Britain against the Holy Allies."[43] Madison also favored the Anglo-American declaration and even argued that it should be expanded. Not only should Britain and the United States warn France against action in the Western Hemisphere, but they should also condemn France's intervention in Spain and declare their support for Greek independence—a comprehensive assault on the polices and principles of the Holy Alliance. Anglo-American "cooperation" on these matters, Madison suggested, was "due to ourselves and to the world. . . . With the British power and navy combined with our own we have nothing to fear from the rest of the nations and in the great struggle of the Epoch between liberty and despotism, we owe it to ourselves to sustain the former in this hemisphere at least."[44] Jefferson and Madison's views were seconded in the cabinet by Secretary of War Calhoun. Calhoun favored giving Rush "a discretionary power to act jointly with the British Government in case of any sudden emergency of danger."[45] President Monroe agreed. Only Adams objected.

The desire to make league with Great Britain against the Holy Alliance was all the more striking given the poison pill that Canning had included in his proposal. For Canning had also suggested that the United States and Great Britain both promise not to take possession of any portion of the former Spanish Empire in the Western Hemisphere for themselves. This required the United States to renounce any intention of ever acquiring Cuba and Texas. Jefferson, Madison, and Calhoun were all prepared to concede on this point as well, despite the fact that all three shared Jefferson's view that "Cuba would be a valuable and important acquisition to our Union."[46] Adams ultimately prevailed, and Canning's proposal was rejected. But it was remarkable how strong was the view among Monroe's closest advisers and among America's leading statesmen that a virtual alliance with Great Britain against the ideological menace of the Holy Alliance was worth the price of these significant territorial gains.

Ideology and Expansion: Toward the Monroe Doctrine

CANNING'S PROPOSAL instead provided the impetus for the presidential statement of December 1823 that would become famous as the Monroe Doctrine. Monroe began drafting his declaration at a time when many Americans were intently focused not only on events in the Western Hemisphere but also on events in Europe. Over the previous two years they had seen France invade Spain to crush revolution and Austria invade Italy. They worried about the Holy Alliance and hoped to bring Great Britain to the side of liberalism. In 1823 Americans were in an uproar over the revolution in Greece, where an independence movement was trying to break free of the control of the Turkish sultan.

The Greek drama, in particular, was tailor-made to appeal to Americans and to liberals everywhere. The stirrings of the Greeks recalled for Western Enlightenment liberals the glories of the ancient birthplace of democracy. Philhellenism was rampant among liberals on both sides of the Atlantic. Monroe was personally moved by the spectacle of the Greek Revolution, and in his message a year earlier had spoken of "the reappearance of [the Greek] people in their original character." The fact that the modern heirs of Greek democracy were fighting to liberate themselves from what was widely regarded as one of the world's more odious despotisms made the struggle between good and evil starker in liberal eyes, and the Manichean quality of the contest was further highlighted by the fact that the Christian Greeks were fighting Muslim Turks.

Finally, there was the humanitarian issue. Although both sides committed unspeakable barbarities in this prototypical Balkan "ethnic conflict," it was the horrors inflicted upon Greek by Turk that caught the imaginations of liberals in America and Great Britain and throughout Christian Europe. A century and a half before political scientists discovered the so-called CNN effect, in which the transmission of televised images of human atrocities could fire public opinion to the point of forcing an administration's hand, a similar phenomenon was created merely by transmission of the printed word, even when that transmission took several weeks. Thus American Christians, like Christians everywhere, were shocked and sickened when they learned that the Greek patriarch in Constantinople had been hanged in his sacred robes on Easter Sunday, his body later dragged through the streets and dumped into the Bosporus. The following year there were reports of a massacre of Greek men, women, and children on the island of Chios. Upward of twenty-five thousand had been slaughtered by the Turkish army, and another forty thousand or more sold into slavery—or so it was reported.[47] The term "ethnic cleansing" had not yet been invented, but for Turks and Greeks alike, the war was driven to extremes by ethnic and religious hatred. On both sides of the Atlantic, liberals raised funds to aid the Greek victims as well as the Greek rebels, and they put pressure on their governments to take a firm stand against the Turks.

Americans were especially attracted to the Greek cause because the revolutionaries made a direct and specific appeal to American principles. The Greek declaration of independence in 1822 was modeled on Jefferson's; the Greeks proclaimed a republican form of government; and the Senate of Calamata begged the "fellow-citizens of Penn, of Washington, and of Franklin" not to "imitate the culpable indifference" of Europe and refuse aid to "the descendants of Phocion and Thrasybulus." The Greeks regarded the United States as "nearer than the nations on our frontiers"; they would "cement an alliance founded on freedom and virtue." The Harvard professor Edward Everett, in an influential article in the *North American Review,* wrote that "such an appeal from the anxious conclave of self-devoted patriots . . . must bring home to the mind of the least reflecting American, the great and glorious part, which this country is to act, in the political regeneration of the world."[48]

Liberals on both sides of the Atlantic saw the Greek Revolution and the Latin American independence movements bound up together as part of the same worldwide revolutionary struggle. "On Andes' and on Athos' peaks unfurled," Lord Byron wrote, "the self-same standard streams o'er either world!"[49] Leading American politicians asked how the United States could support the struggle for freedom and republican government in the Western Hemisphere yet ignore the same struggle occurring in Europe. Daniel Webster, preparing to launch his famous public campaign to support the Greek effort, insisted that "we have as much Community with the Greeks, as with the inhabitants of the Andes, & the dwellers on the borders of the Vermilion Sea."[50] Everett called on Monroe to pursue the same policy toward Greece that he had recently carried out toward the Latin American republics: send a commission of investigation to discover the state of affairs and then, when the commissioners reported, "as they must," that Greece had achieved its independence, recognize the new government and send an American minister. In the great school of nations, Everett declared, "liberty is the lesson, which we are appointed to teach."[51]

Was it not America's "duty to come forth, and deny, and condemn" the Holy Alliance and its "monstrous principles"? Webster asked. "Where, but here . . . are they likely to be resisted?" Opponents of his resolution on behalf of the Greeks ridiculed the idea of offering mere moral support, since he explicitly ruled out more forceful aid. But Webster insisted there was some value in making a "moral cause." The rise of a liberal public opinion in the world was already presenting "the most formidable obstruction to the progress of injustice and oppression." Public opinion was a form of power, too, and one he believed Americans could wield with great effect. Asking whether "the expression of our own sympathy" would do the Greeks any good, Webster answered: "I hope it may. It may give them courage and spirit. It may assure them of public regard, teach them that they are not wholly forgotten by the civilized world, and inspire them with constancy in the pursuit of their great end."[52] But whether it did or did not help, he believed it was "due to our own character, and called for by our own duty. When we shall have discharged that duty, we may leave the rest to the disposition of Providence."[53]

When Monroe was contemplating his presidential message at the end of 1823, the Greek cause had already become a sensation in the United States. Funds for the revolutionaries were being raised in American cities; newspapers were filled with reports of the revolution's progress; for a time, the Greek issue garnered more national attention than the pending presidential contest.[54] By March 1823 Great Britain under Canning's leadership had already recognized the Greeks as belligerents, partly as a result of mounting public pressure in England.[55] Leaders in the Monroe administration believed that the United States should do no less and probably a good deal more. Albert Gallatin, the hero of Jeffersonian Republicans, returned from Paris seized with the Greek cause. He not only favored recognition of Greek independence but wanted to send an American naval squadron to put some force behind American declarations. John Calhoun supported Gallatin's proposal.[56] Adams thought the idea mad, but he shared their conviction that great issues of direct relevance to the United States were at stake in the Old World, whether or not there was anything the United States could or should do about them.

President Monroe himself was a great believer in two mutually reinforcing ideas: that the fate of republicanism in Europe directly affected the safety of republican principles at home, and that the United States, in turn, could and should be an important source of encouragement to liberals and republicans on the European continent. The United States had spurred a republican movement in Latin America, he believed, and in the 1820s the American example was "producing another great movement in Europe," visible in Spain, in Portugal, in Italy, and in Greece.[57] As a radical Jeffersonian Republican in 1796, he had once dismissed Washington's warning against foreign entanglements as nothing more than a declaration of the Federalist Party's pro-British, "monocrat" prejudices. He long afterward felt the United States had violated its own principles, and harmed its interests, by not giving more assistance to the French Revolution. A quarter century later he was more tempered in his views of that revolution and more cautious in his proposals for American involvement, but he still saw purpose in aiding republican causes, both in the Western Hemisphere and in Europe.

Monroe believed that there was no way to separate the ideological struggle in Europe from the conduct of American foreign policy. "The movement in Europe," he wrote in 1821, "forms an issue between most of the sovereigns and their subjects, & the United States are regarded as the natural ally of the one & enemy of the other." He "saw the United States as less strong when republicanism in Europe was at low ebb."[58]

On several occasions in the early 1820s Monroe had wanted to make a public declaration of American support for European liberalism and to condemn the Holy Alliance for stamping out revolution and reform on the Continent. In 1821 he had discussed with Adams the idea of condemning Metternich's use of force to crush constitutionalism in Italy.[59] In his annual message of 1822, he had expressed "strong hope" that the Greeks struggling to break free from Turkish rule would succeed and "recover their independence." In 1823 he believed the time had arrived to "take a bolder attitude . . . in favor of liberty" than had been possible in the past.[60]

In his own first draft of the December 1823 message, therefore, Monroe intended to speak out forcefully, not only on the subject of Greece but about all the conflicts in Europe. His draft contained a general warning to Americans that their beloved republican institutions were under siege around the world and that their own security was directly implicated in the global ideological struggle. He intended to denounce France and the Holy Alliance for the invasion of Spain and the crushing of constitutional liberalism there. He even planned to recognize Greek independence, recommending to Congress that an American minister be dispatched immediately.[61] These were not the sentiments of a man eager to build an impregnable wall between two geographical "spheres." Monroe's desire to take a stand on the ideological struggle in Europe was enthusiastically supported by the majority of his cabinet, by Gallatin, by Secretary of War Calhoun, and by Secretary of the Navy Samuel Southard. Outside the cabinet it had the support of Clay and Webster and other leading members of Congress, of ex-presidents Jefferson and Madison, and judging by reports in the press, of a substantial portion of the American public.

Adams, however, insisted that Monroe tone down his original draft, which seemed to him a "summons to arms . . . against all Europe, and for objects of policy exclusively European." Monroe's message, he said, "would at once buckle on the harness and throw down the gauntlet. It would have the air of open defiance to all Europe."[62] He worried that Spain, France, and Russia would sever relations, or worse, and that the United States would be engaged in a "quarrel with all Europe."[63] If Monroe insisted on making pronouncements in support of republicanism and revolution in Europe, moreover, Adams suggested Europeans would be justified in asking on what grounds the United States proposed to prohibit Europe from meddling on behalf of monarchism in the Western Hemisphere. He proposed that Monroe make "earnest remonstrance against the interference of the European powers by force with South America, but to disclaim all interference on our part with Europe; to make an American cause, and adhere inflexibly to that."[64]

Monroe finally agreed, but only up to point. He struck from his text the explicit recognition of Greek independence and softened the language of global ideological struggle. Nevertheless, even in the final draft of his message, the president had a good deal to say about events in Europe. He expressed the "strong hope" that the Greeks would "succeed in their contest and resume their equal station among the nations of the earth." There was good cause to believe that the Turks had already "lost forever all dominion over them" and that Greece would "become again an independent nation." That was "the object of our most ardent wishes."[65]

Nor did Monroe refrain from commenting on events in Spain. The revolution and France's invasion showed that Europe was "still unsettled." He expressed concern at the interposition "by force" in Spain's internal affairs and openly wondered whether the Holy Alliance might feel free to intervene elsewhere "on the same principle," that is, the principle of defending monarchical legitimacy. This was a question "in which all independent powers whose governments differ from theirs are interested, even those most remote, and surely none more than the United States." Put in plain language, the United States considered European intervention to crush constitutionalism in Spain a threat to its own security. For this and other reasons, he declared, the United States could not help but be concerned in European affairs. "Of events in that quarter of the globe, with which we have so much intercourse and from which we derive our origin, we have always been anxious and *interested* spectators."[66]

For a message purportedly abjuring any desire for entanglement in Europe, this was a fairly forward expression of American interest in European affairs. Monroe followed these statements by insisting, in the phrases most commonly cited by future generations, that it remained American policy "not to interfere in the internal concerns" of the European powers and to recognize as legitimate whatever government happened to be in de facto control. But European monarchs could be forgiven for doubting the sincerity of this disclaimer. Monroe's statements on behalf of the Greeks and the Spanish liberals constituted precisely such interference. His message was not a declaration of hemispheric isolationism. In important respects, it was a statement of international republican solidarity.[67]

Adams's efforts to tone down the more inflammatory statements did not succeed in masking this fundamental purpose. Contemporary observers understood that Monroe had made only a tactical concession to Adams. Daniel Webster, who learned the background of the message from Calhoun and other members of the administration, explained that since Monroe planned to take "pretty high ground as to *this Continent,*" he was "afraid of the appearance of interfering in the concerns of the *other continent* also."[68] Foreign observers also understood Monroe's intent. The defenders of absolutism in the other hemisphere read Monroe's statements on behalf of republicanism as applying to Europe as well as to the Western Hemisphere. To Metternich, Monroe's declarations were an indication of an American self-confidence bordering on arrogance, an unmistakable sign that the citizens of this once-small republic, "whom we have seen arise and grow," had "suddenly left a sphere too narrow for their ambition and have astonished Europe by a new act of revolt, more unprovoked, fully as audacious, and no less dangerous than the former." Having upset the old order with their Revolution a half century ago, the increasingly powerful Americans were now prepared to set "altar against altar," to "foster . . . revolutions wherever they show themselves," to give "new strength to the apostles of sedition, and reanimate the courage of every conspirator."[69] Disregarding Monroe's declaration abjuring involvement in Europe, Metternich understood that the American president's purpose was to give aid and comfort to republicanism everywhere. Indeed, even from their very different vantage points, Monroe and Metternich saw their world in much the same light: for both men the global ideological struggle knew no natural, geographical boundaries.

The real purpose of Monroe's message, in fact, was not to draw geographical distinctions. It was to draw ideological distinctions. It was the "political system of the allied powers" of Europe to which Americans objected. That system was "essentially different" from America's, and it was different because of the profound differences "in their respective governments." Monroe warned, therefore, not only against colonization and acquisition of territory in the Western Hemisphere but also against "any attempt" by European powers to extend "their system" to "any portion of this hemisphere." Henceforth Americans would consider the implantation of despotism in the Western Hemisphere "dangerous to their safety."[70] The United States, according to John Quincy Adams, needed "to avow that it stood apart from Europe." But "this stand," he made clear, rested "on the differences in political principles which guided governments in Europe and in the United States." Indeed, he believed there was no other principled reason why the United States should demand European abstention in the Western Hemisphere. America's republican principles were the "foundation . . . for our justification of the stand we are taking against the Holy Alliance, in the face of our country and of mankind."[71]

Some twentieth-century diplomatic historians have singled out the American people for being unusually "moralistic" or "ideological" in their approach to foreign affairs. The oft-repeated characterization of Americans in this era is that their view of the world, in addition to its alleged isolationism, was also replete with "elements of self-righteousness and moralism." This gave "to American discussion of foreign affairs a distinctive coloring," as compared with that of the Europeans. There was, according to this view, something irresponsible, even childish about American attitudes. Isolated as they were from "the struggles of Europe," Americans could safely pronounce "moral judgments on the right and wrong of every revolt, every alliance, and every government." Europeans, on the other hand, because they "faced constant danger of rivalry near at hand," allegedly had to be more "cautious and limit themselves to vital interests."[72] While other nations defined security in a "traditional and restricted manner, as largely a function of the balance of power," Americans uniquely defined security as a function of the "internal order maintained by states, that is, as a favorable ideological balance."[73]

Yet there was nothing uniquely American in the view that ideology, security, and foreign policy were all closely related. In the early nineteenth century it was the European autocracies that had pronounced judgments on the right and wrong of every revolt, every alliance, and every government. The search for a "favorable ideological balance" in Europe and the Western

Hemisphere was foremost in the minds of Alexander and Metternich and a constant subject of concern in London. Canning even declared, after the promulgation of the Monroe Doctrine, that "the effect of the ultra-liberalism of our Yankee co-operators, on the ultra-despotism of Aix-la-Chapelle allies, gives me just the balance that I wanted."[74] If Americans saw international politics as consisting of a great struggle between the forces of monarchy and despotism and the forces of republicanism and liberalism, they were not alone. The French foreign minister, Chateaubriand, still nursing ambitions to put Bourbon princes on Latin American thrones, expressed hope that even the British would see the danger of Monroe's statement. "Mr. Canning," he believed, "can have no more desire than I to favor military uprisings, the sovereignty of the people, and all the pretty things which Mr. Monroe says to us about the actual governments." Chateaubriand preferred to imagine that "temperate monarchies established in America, more or less allied with the mother Country, would be a good result for England and for us."[75]

Nor was Chateaubriand entirely mistaken in his impression of British preferences. British and American interests were hardly consonant. Britain considered trade with Latin America vital to its economic interests and feared American commercial expansionism. Officials in London as well as in Washington assumed that in order to gain sway in Latin America, it was important and perhaps even necessary to affect the shape of government adopted by the new Latin nations.

Canning's foreign policy toward the Western Hemisphere was subtle and complex. He saw a three-way competition for hemispheric influence, one that involved Britain, the Continental powers, and the United States. Canning's foreign policy both in Europe and beyond aimed at striking the correct ideological balance that favored British interests. He wanted to steer a middle course between the two nineteenth-century evils, between radical revolution and "simple democracy," on the one hand, and "simple Despotism" on the other. With its perfectly mixed constitution, he believed, England lay in the "temperate zone of freedom" and ought to serve as the model to be emulated everywhere. In matters of foreign policy, he observed, this required Great Britain to walk along "a plank which lay across a roaring stream" and to resist attempts that "might be made to bear us down on one side or the other."[76]

This vision applied as well in Latin America. Just as the French, Russian, and Spanish governments believed Bourbon dynasties would be loyal to the absolutist regimes on the Continent, so British diplomats believed constitutional monarchies modeled on that of Great Britain would prove most loyal to London. All the European powers, Britain included, feared that if the new nations of Latin America remained republics, they would quickly come under the influence of the increasingly self-confident republic to the north. Lord Liverpool expressed the common British concern that "if we allow these new [Latin] states to consolidate their system and their policy with the United States of America, it will in a very few years prove fatal to our greatness, if not endanger our safety." In trade, the Americans had become "more formidable rivals to us than any nation which has ever yet existed." Their goal was to supplant British commerce "in every quarter of the globe, but more particularly in the seas contiguous to America." If the Latin Americans adopted republican governments, they would give "a decided preference in their ports to the people of the United States over ourselves," and the trade "of these extensive dominions will be lost to us, and it will, in great measure, be transferred to our rivals."[77]

Canning's concerns about the spread of republicanism in the Western Hemisphere went beyond commercial interests. "The great danger of the time," he believed, was "a division of the World into European and American, Republican and Monarchical; a league of worn-out Gov[ernmen]ts, on the one hand, and of youthful and stirring Nations, with the Un[ited] States at their head, on the other."[78] Great Britain, geographically, politically, and ideologically, existed astride the two worlds. Its special role was to be the great mediator between young America and old Europe. In Latin America this required steering new governments toward constitutional monarchy, the middle path. Britain's fondest hopes lay with Simón Bolívar, the Great Liberator of northern South America. Canning's minister in Bogotá favored Bolívar as a constitutional president-for-life, to be succeeded by a European constitutional monarch of Britain's choosing. This would ensure that the country remained "in the hands of a friendly power in case of any future war with either the United States or France."[79] Canning saw Mexico as a particularly useful place to build a barrier against American hegemony. His plan was simple: "*We* slip in between; and plant ourselves in Mexico . . . and we link once more America and Europe."[80]

Latin leaders agreed that whether they chose a British-style monarchy, a Bourbon prince, or a republican regime would go a long way toward deciding whether their state was likely to be friendly to Great Britain, France, or the United States. Bolívar opposed republican government for a variety of reasons, not least being his fear that the Latin "Albocracy" would be overrun by the dark-skinned masses. "Wholly representative institutions," he had decided, were "not suited to our character, customs, and present knowledge."[81] He worried that the United States seemed "destined by Providence to bring on America a plague of miseries under the name of Liberty!" He preferred England as "our example,"[82] for as he remarked to the British minister, "how infinitely more respectable your nation is, governed by its Kings, Lords, and Commons, than that which prides itself upon an equality which holds out little temptation to exertion for the benefit of the State."[83] Bolívar's hostility to North American–style republicanism also had other sources. He feared South America was destined either to fall under the hegemony of the northern power or to become a victim of reactionary absolutism in Europe, unless some powerful nation from outside the hemisphere acted as a counterweight. The British fleet was reason enough to seek British friendship. The interests of South America, Bolívar declared, "pointed to the expediency of securing the friendship of Great Britain in preference to that of any other Nation."[84]

No one saw Canning's ideological and geopolitical challenge more clearly than John Quincy Adams. With Adams at the helm throughout the 1820s, first as secretary of state and then as president, the Anglo-American competition in the Western Hemisphere was incessant, and it frequently took the form of republicanism versus monarchy. In Mexico British and American ministers vied to gain predominant influence within the divided political elite. The American minister, Joel Poinsett, was instructed by Washington to encourage republicanism, and he did so zealously, to the point where the British minister complained that Poinsett, with the full support of the American government, engaged "in a constant and active interference with the internal affairs of the new State." Mexican politics were divided between Liberals and Conservatives, and in the mid-1820s that cleavage took the form of a rivalry between two Masonic lodges, one founded by Poinsett, the other sponsored by the British chargé d'affaires. Not surprisingly, the Conservative faction, which included Mexico's old mining and landowning aristocracy, as well as its Catholic priests and its high-ranking military officers, looked to the more conservative and aristocratic Britain for support. The Liberals, made up of Creoles and the mestizo middle class, generally looked to the more democratic, bourgeois, and progressive Americans. British diplomats complained that on any question that arose in Congress "in which the interests of England came into competition with those of the United States," Poinsett was able to "obtain a majority in both chambers against us."[85]

Similar battles were fought in Colombia and the neighboring states of South America. American ministers found Simón Bolívar hostile to republicanism, hostile to the United States, warlike, and despotic, a "second Caesar." William Henry Harrison, famed Indian fighter and future president of the United States, arrived in Bogotá with instructions from Secretary of State Henry Clay to seek occasions to express America's "ardent hope" that Colombia's turmoil would "terminate in the establishment of constitutional government." Harrison instead found Bolívar and the British in close alliance, with the British government "eagerly embracing every opportunity to increase its influence." The Colombian people, on the other hand, seemed to Harrison democratic and "extremely desirous to tread in our footsteps." When Bolívar insisted the Colombian people were not ready for republicanism, Harrison said the problem was their "cursed government" and the "intolerant character of their religion."[86] Harrison soon got himself ordered out of the country, accused of fomenting insurrections.

Indeed, most American ministers were at one time or another reprimanded or sent packing because of their meddling on behalf of opposition forces against the central government. As they tried to plant democratic and republican ideals in Latin America, they were often frustrated by what seemed a lack of fertile soil, as well as by stiff competition from the British. Nor did the United States refuse to recognize Brazil in 1824, even though it was a monarchy.[87] Few, however, gave up hope of the eventual progress of the South American peoples toward liberal republicanism. The American minister to Peru wrote Henry Clay in 1827 that while it might be true that Peruvians were as yet "ill-equipped" to support free government, it was equally true that they "never will be quiet under a despotism." The "spirit of the age," he wrote, "has its influence here as elsewhere," and while it might take many years of trial and error, the "representative system, more or less purified, must eventually triumph."[88]

By the end of the first quarter of the nineteenth century, the United States appeared launched on a trajectory whose course and destination could be roughly predicted. John Quincy Adams and others had sketched the outline of continental empire and cast their eyes beyond the continent as well. The Monroe Doctrine propped open the door to further territorial expansion and staked a claim to American hegemony in the Western Hemisphere. As American power and influence grew, so did Americans' tendency to press their own principles on the world around them. And in a world where geopolitics and ideology were deemed inseparable, the spread of American-style government offered a reconciliation of power, self-interest, and principle. It was not hard to imagine—and both Americans and foreign observers already did imagine—that the United States would continue growing in size and power, would continue expanding its influence in ever wider arcs, would continue demanding a greater say in the affairs of other nations, and would continue to have an ever more revolutionizing effect on the world. A writer commenting in the *Edinburgh Review* of June 1818 on America's "marvellous empire" asked, "Where is this prodigious increase of numbers, this vast extension of dominion, to end? What bounds has Nature set to the progress of this mighty nation? Let our jealousy burn as it may; let our intolerance of America be as unreasonably violent as we please; still it is plain, that she is a power in spite of us, rapidly rising to supremacy."[89] This was, after all, the natural career of a burgeoning great power. Nothing was likely to arrest this many-pronged expansion except, as some foreign observers hoped and expected, the destruction or dismemberment of the United States from internal causes.

CHAPTER 7

The Foreign Policy of Slavery

> *A dissolution of the Union for the cause of slavery would be followed by . . . a war between the two severed portions of the Union. It seems to me that its result might be the extirpation of slavery from this whole continent; and, calamitous and desolating as this course of events in its progress must be, so glorious would be its final issue, that, as God shall judge me, I dare not say that it is not to be desired.*
>
> —John Quincy Adams, 1819

The "National Interest" of Slavery

THE UNITED STATES AFTER 1825 did not proceed along the path charted by Monroe, Adams, and Clay, however. Soon after Monroe and Adams launched the nation on a bold course of hemispheric leadership, both commercial and ideological, and announced to the world that the United States had a special interest in the fate of republicanism abroad, on both sides of the Atlantic, the United States suddenly pulled back. For almost two decades after the Monroe presidency, the nation seemed to turn inward, slowing expansion on the continent and muffling expressions of solidarity with struggles for republican liberty in both the Old World and the New. Then, just as suddenly, in the mid-1840s the nation embarked on an unprecedented burst of expansionism in what historians would call the age of "manifest destiny," annexing Texas, confronting Great Britain in the Oregon territory, and seizing from Mexico the vast portion of lands that now make up the southwestern United States all the way to California on the Pacific Coast.

How to explain the fits and starts of American foreign policy in the first half of the nineteenth century? A coherent narrative of this era has for the most part eluded diplomatic historians.[1] But that is perhaps because they have given too little prominence to the issue that dominated American politics and society in the decades before the Civil War: the issue of slavery. If a nation's foreign policy reflects the nature of its polity, then American slavery must be as much a part of the narrative of nineteenth-century American diplomacy as American democracy and American capitalism.[2]

From before the birth of the republic through the first two decades of the nineteenth century, American foreign policy reflected the dominant characteristics of the American polity as an increasingly powerful liberal society, expanding its influence, enhancing its security, seeking opportunities for its enrichment, and gradually but determinedly imposing its will and its beliefs on the world around it. But the United States was not only a liberal, democratic republic. It was also a nation of slaveholders. Therefore it was also, in part, a racial despotism. The United States had been born with a split personality: with a principled commitment to human equality and natural rights as embodied in the Declaration of Independence, and a practical commitment to the defense of the institution of slavery as embodied in the Constitution.

Two decades into the nineteenth century this split personality emerged in more striking form than it had in the years of the early republic. The United States began to resemble two separate and mutually antagonistic societies, with divergent ideologies and two distinct and ultimately clashing conceptions of the national interest. Just as the evolution of British policy in the early nineteenth century reflected its unique status as both a hereditary monarchy and an increasingly democratic liberal government, so in an even more dramatic way did American foreign policy reflect its own mixed regime. The course of American foreign policy from the 1820s until the Civil War, the moments of passivity and the moments of exuberance, the turning in upon itself and the unprecedented outward thrust—all this was shaped primarily, though not exclusively, by the struggle over slavery.

The republic was scarcely a decade old when the question of slavery first intruded in a dramatic way into American foreign policy calculations. In 1791 a slave revolt erupted in Haiti, and for the next decade slaves massacred their masters in a civil war that culminated in the independence of a new republic in 1804. Sympathetic Americans called it the "black republic." In the late 1790s, during the Quasi-War with France, President John Adams lent American support to the Haitian rebels and their charismatic leader Toussaint L'Ouverture, both as a means of thwarting French power in the Western Hemisphere and because northern antislavery Federalists generally sympathized with Toussaint's cause. But the Haitian revolt sent shudders through the slaveholding South, and soon after the Virginia slaveholder Thomas Jefferson succeeded Adams in the White House, he reversed course. After first encouraging Toussaint's drive for independence in the hope of dampening French imperial ambitions and convincing Napoleon to give up his drive for a foothold on the North American continent, Jefferson followed slaveholder demands and turned against Toussaint. He refused to grant recognition to the independent Haitian nation, even though, as Garry Wills notes, this went against Jefferson's usual insistence that the United States should accord recognition to whatever government happened to be in power in another nation.[3]

Many southerners feared an independent Haiti run by former slaves more than they feared Napoleon. When the slave insurrection first erupted, both Washington and Jefferson had lamented what Washington called "a spirit of revolution among the blacks." The danger that such a spirit would spread to the slaves of the American South seemed too great. The leaders of the Haitian Revolution offered to help liberate slaves elsewhere in the hemisphere by the same violent means that they had liberated themselves, and southern slaveholders feared that it was only a matter of time before the Haitian infection spread to their own plantations. Jefferson's son-in-law, John Wayles Eppes, warned that a slave victory in Haiti would "bring immediate and horrible destruction to the fairest portion of America."[4]

Sure enough, after the abortive Prosser Gabriel slave rebellion of 1800 and another uprising in 1802, Virginia slaveholders claimed to uncover plots of insurrection allegedly involving thousands of slaves who had been directly inspired, or so it was widely believed, by emissaries from the "black republic." In 1802 Jefferson wrote to Rufus King that the "course of things in the neighboring islands of the West Indies appeared to have given a considerable impulse to the minds of the slaves" in the United States and that as a consequence of events in Haiti "a great disposition to insurgency" had "manifested itself among" the slaves in the United States.[5] Fears of Haiti, and of "another Haiti" emerging elsewhere in the Caribbean or even on the North American continent, never subsided in the slaveholding South. Twenty years later South Carolinians learned to their horror that Denmark Vesey, a free black who conspired to lead another slave rebellion, had been in contact with Haitian blacks and had expected a Haitian invasion to aid his uprising.[6]

For American slaveholders, no "national interest" was more vital than the prevention of a domestic slave uprising. During the Revolutionary War, when Charleston, South Carolina, was threatened by British invasion, local slaveholders faced a choice between arming their slaves to help in the struggle or letting Charleston be sacked. They chose defeat at British hands over the risk of a slave uprising. Indeed, many southern slaveholders preferred to forgo independence altogether if the price was emancipation. From their point of view, such a victory was no victory at all. As Henry Wiencek writes, in the eighteenth century as in the nineteenth, "the planters regarded the preservation of slavery as the bedrock of their . . . society and economy. If the United States had won independence but put slavery on the road to extinction, then they would have lost the war. The planters were prepared to see their region fall to the British before they would arm three thousand slaves."[7] Fall it did, and when the British threatened to expropriate their slaves unless they swore an oath of allegiance to George III, "the majority of South Carolina planters, including former leaders of the Revolution, foreswore their allegiance to the Patriot cause and solemnly pledged loyalty to the British crown."[8]

Fear of a slave rebellion concentrated the minds of slaveholders and their protectors in Washington as no purely economic or geopolitical interest possibly could. To the American slaveholder, whose bondsmen worked his plantation, lived in his house, cooked his meals, helped his wife, and reared his children, even the smallest slave revolt meant domestic slaughter. Nat Turner's "uprising" in Virginia in 1831 numbered no more than sixty slaves and was quashed in less than two days. But in those forty-eight hours Turner and his men decapitated mothers sleeping in their beds and babies in their cribs, and the entire slaveholding South went into a frenzy. This comparatively minor episode filled the southern imagination with dread at the prospect of the catastrophic race war that could be unleashed if slaveholders ever let down their guard—another Haiti, but on an even more horrific scale.

How to prevent "another Haiti" from erupting in the United States, therefore, became a question of primary importance in the early nineteenth century—surpassing other economic and strategic concerns—and it bedeviled slaveholders right up until the Civil War ended slavery altogether. For as the handful of southern slave uprisings seemed to reveal, it was not enough to control the movement of slaves and free blacks within the United States. In Haiti, after all, the uprising had begun with free blacks, inspired by the French Revolution, demanding their rights. Only later did the contagion of freedom spread to the slave population. In the United States, therefore, both enslaved and free blacks alike had to be walled off from foreign influence. When Congress moved to open trade with Toussaint's forces in 1799, Jefferson expressed the slaveholders' anxiety that even trading with Haiti was too dangerous. If the Haitian "combustion can be introduced among us under any veil whatever, we have to fear it."[9] During Jefferson's second term Congress passed a general embargo against Haiti, for to trade with the Haitians, one southern congressman warned, would be "a sacrifice on the altar of black despotism and usurpation."[10] Exports to Haiti worth almost $7 million in 1806 fell to $1.5 million in 1808, with the bulk of profits directly transferred to America's top commercial competitor, Great Britain.[11] Protecting U.S. slaveholders required more than a sacrifice of trade. Sometimes important strategic interests had to be sacrificed, too. When Jefferson turned against Toussaint, he indirectly supported Napoleon's attempt to subjugate Haiti, even though the island of Santo Domingo was a stepping-stone to French control of New Orleans.[12]

Slavery shaped American foreign policy, above all, by producing an acute national vulnerability that was recognized in both the North and the South. Any foreign power at war with the United States could see the advantage of sparking a slave insurrection. During the Revolution the British had raised a panic in the South by offering freedom to slaves willing to fight against the American colonial rebellion, and tens of thousands of slaves had seized the opportunity to escape their masters.[13] In the War of 1812 British strategy envisioned a landing on the Gulf Coast to encourage armed uprisings by both Indians and slaves.[14] In any war between the United States and Spain, British and French officials believed, black slaves from Cuba could be offered freedom and sent to the South to encourage a slave insurrection.[15] And of course it was an American, Abraham Lincoln, who would most effectively exploit the southern weakness and who understood the military and strategic blow that could be struck by emancipating the slaves.

Even without such threats, the risk of leaving slaves unguarded in time of war was too great for southerners to tolerate. During the colonial era each southern state's militia became "an agency to control slaves, and less an effective means of defense." During the French and Indian War Virginia had devoted more resources to policing its slave population than to patrolling the frontier and thus left settlers' families more vulnerable to Indian attack.[16] Many northerners agreed with Timothy Pickering's scathing comment that the South would be worse than useless in "case of foreign war," since even the mighty Virginia would have to "keep at home half her force to prevent an insurrection of her Negroes."[17]

But slaveholders felt their security endangered even when no European empire threatened. Isolated and hapless Haiti was one danger. Closer to home were the minuscule settlements of free blacks living in the nominally Spanish but virtually ungoverned Floridas, just south of the great slaveholding states of Georgia and the Carolinas and close by the slaveholding territories of Louisiana and Mississippi. During the War of 1812 British forces in Florida had recruited, armed, and trained a contingent of four to five hundred runaway slaves and free blacks at Prospect Bluff, along the Apalachicola River in the Florida panhandle. After the British withdrew in 1815, the blacks took over the British position, and it became known in the United States as "Negro Fort." Armed with guns, ammunition, and several cannon, the inhabitants of the fort created a tiny pocket of black freedom carved out of the wilderness of a white-dominated continent. Outside the fort's walls, families farmed and raised cattle on their own property.

It is hard to imagine how a few hundred settlers scattered along the banks of the Apalachicola posed a threat to the United States. But for southern slaveholders, even this small community of free black families, independent of white control and living and working on their own property, constituted a living "symbol of slave insurrection."[18] In 1816 the Madison administration dispatched a gunboat to reduce Negro Fort. Secretary of State John Quincy Adams justified the attack and subsequent seizure of Spanish Florida by Andrew Jackson as national "self-defense," a response to alleged Spanish and British complicity in fomenting the "Indian and Negro War."[19] Adams even produced a letter from a Georgia planter complaining about "brigand Negroes" who had made "this neighborhood extremely dangerous to a population like ours."[20]

Haiti and Negro Fort illustrated one important difference between the foreign policies of slaveholding and nonslaveholding America. Both shared strong expansionist inclinations, but the South had an additional and sometimes decisive motive for acquiring neighboring territory. Northerners might yearn to expand into Canada to deny the British a possible launching point for invasion, to exploit Canadian land and resources, to enhance American prestige, or to fulfill America's "manifest destiny" to control the whole of the North American continent. But by 1800 northerners did not fear that the mere existence of Canadians across the border threatened the stability of their social, economic, and political institutions. Southern leaders, however, worried that even a small, impoverished island of rebel slaves in the Caribbean or a parcel of Florida land occupied by a few hundred blacks could threaten the institution of slavery.

The slaveholding South had this much in common with the despotic regimes of nineteenth-century central and eastern Europe and, for that matter, with the totalitarian societies of the twentieth century. For the slaveholders, as for the absolutist powers of Europe, the mere existence of free nations in close proximity constituted a potentially fatal threat. The slave-holder might wield absolute authority on his own land, but he could not control what happened beyond his boundaries, could not prevent his slaves from looking to neighboring lands for escape and sanctuary, could not stop both blacks and whites across the border from promulgating doctrines of freedom and abolitionism that could infect his slaves with dangerous ideas. In an age of advancing liberalism, the despotic ruler could not easily coun-teract the magnetic attraction of freedom. He was always under siege.

The "national interest" of both the European despot and the American slaveholder, therefore, lay in diminishing the areas of freedom around them. Dangerous pockets of liberty had to be destroyed. When this was impossible, rulers and slave owners had to wall off their fiefdoms to keep out dangerous outside influences. Such had been the purpose of the Holy Alliance, of Metternich's quashing of liberal movements in Germany and Italy. Such were the aims of tsarist Russia when it sent its armies into Poland in 1830 and Hungary in 1848. And such were the aims of southern planters, who used their influence in Washington to get federal assistance whenever they feared encirclement by free territories, or worse, by lands where former slaves had been emancipated. As the South over the course of the first half of the nineteenth century grew more fearful about the security of its slave society, the "defensive" impulse toward expansion became more urgent, culminating in the 1840s in the southern drive for the annexa-tion of Texas and in the 1850s in the effort to purchase Cuba and build a southern empire in the Caribbean.

It is easy to lose sight of this uniquely southern influence on American foreign policy in the first two decades of the nineteenth century. Early-nineteenth-century American expansionism was hardly a southern inven-tion: the United States was a determinedly expansionist power irrespective of the South's special concerns. The aim of acquiring all the territory along the Gulf Coast had maintained broad national support as far back as Hamil-ton and had been endorsed by Federalists until the hated Jefferson achieved Hamilton's vision. Hunger for land and for the economic opportunities it afforded remained fervent throughout the nation. In the 1820s America's leading expansionists, John Quincy Adams and Henry Clay, were neither "true" southerners nor advocates of slavery.[21]

But in the course of the first two decades of the nineteenth century, a schism between the free North and the slaveholding South opened wide to reveal vastly different perceptions of what the United States was becom-ing as a nation and therefore how it should conduct itself in the world. The clash produced by this schism dominated American politics throughout the antebellum era. It was also the decisive factor shaping the conduct of American foreign policy between the 1820s and the start of the Civil War.

The Civilization of Progress and the "Civilization of Antiquity"

IN THE LATE eighteenth and early nineteenth centuries the divergence of interests, motives, and character in the slaveholding and nonslaveholding sections of the United States had been muted by the fact that in both the North and South slavery was thought by many to be on its way out as an important institution in American life. The northern states had mostly abolished slavery by the end of the eighteenth century.[22] The states of the Upper South, where slavery had served the tobacco economy, were being gradually drained of slaves. The booming cotton industry in the Deep South created a huge demand for slaves, and slaveholders in the Upper South found it more profitable to sell their slaves "down the river." Many expected this southward drain to culminate in the eventual termination of slavery in the United States. At the beginning of the century it was still possible for Thomas Jefferson and like-minded southerners to hope that the enslaved population would dwindle and gradually disappear—or at least it was possible for them to express such hopes, whether or not they really believed such a thing would come to pass. These hopes had been embodied in the Northwest Ordinance, which banned slavery in the new territories of the Ohio Valley, and in the decision to permit the ending of the slave trade in 1808. Oliver Ellsworth of Connecticut was not alone in anticipating that "slavery, in time, will not be a speck in our country," although those who actually dwelled in the South, such as Virginia's George Mason, had what turned out to be a more realistic view of slavery's future. Slavery would expand westward, Mason predicted, driving the price and demand for slaves ever higher.[23]

Still, the moral and ideological perspectives of the North and the South were not as strikingly different in the early years of the republic as they would later become.[24] During these years there was general agreement in both the free North and the slaveholding South that slavery contradicted American principles of human freedom and equality. In postrevolutionary America, a slave-state politician like Maryland's William Pinkney could publicly insist that his fellow southerners should "blush at the very name of Freedom" so long as they continued to enslave blacks who were "in all respects our equal by nature."[25] Southerners often depicted slavery as an unfortunate burden that had been foisted upon the United States, as Jefferson had charged in the Declaration of Independence, by the hated British. The appeal to a common liberal morality softened sectional differences.

The compromises struck by the Founding Fathers limiting the spread of slavery, however, began to unravel at the start of the nineteenth century. The Louisiana Purchase, that great strategic and economic bonanza that solidified America's fate as the dominant power on the North American continent, also set the nation on a course toward sectional conflict. For the acquisition of vast lands in the South and Southwest also opened up new regions of the country where slavery could be implanted successfully and thus threatened to upset the fine balance struck between North and South in the Constitution.[26] Not only would new slave states be added to the Union, but the Constitution's three-fifths clause would give southerners greater representation in the House of Representatives and in the Electoral College than any nonslave states that might be carved out of the vast Louisiana territory. Northern senators tried to pass a law barring slavery from the new territories, therefore. And many northern Federalists opposed the acquisition altogether, fearing not only the spread of slavery but an irrevocable tilt in the political balance away from Northeast-based Federalism and toward South-based Jeffersonian Republicanism. Josiah Quincy argued that Louisiana's French and Spanish subjects possessed "habits, manners and ideas of civil government" that made them unfit for "republican institutions." Another northerner, foreshadowing arguments that would be advanced throughout the nineteenth century against southward expansion, objected to incorporating into the United States this "Gallo-Hispano *omnium gatherum* of savages and adventurers." Samuel White of Delaware predicted with what may at the time have seemed hysterical exaggeration that if "this new, immense, unbounded world . . . should ever be incorporated into this Union . . . [it] will be the greatest curse that could at present befall us."[27] In the North incorporation of the Louisiana territories gave birth to a fear that would increase over the coming decades, that an ever-expanding "slave power" in the South was threatening to dominate the federal government.

But Louisiana was too rich a plum to be handed back. The national strategic and economic advantages to be gained appeared to outweigh the seemingly distant risk of sectional conflict. Nor did it prove possible to limit the spread of slavery into the southern portions of the new territory. Planters and investors would not be attracted to the new lands if they could not bring slaves to work them. As John Quincy Adams remarked, in words he would no doubt later wish to take back, "Slavery in a moral sense is an evil; but as connected with commerce, it has important uses."[28] Thus did America's slave territories expand rather than contract.

Then came the cotton boom in the South. At the end of the eighteenth century increased demand in England, following the invention of steam-powered machines for spinning cotton into fabric, and increased ease of production, following Eli Whitney's invention of the cotton gin, produced an explosion in the South's cotton industry. In 1790 the United States produced just 3,000 bales of cotton a year; by 1810 annual production had risen to 178,000 bales, and that was just the beginning of a surge that would have the United States producing more than 4 million bales a year on the eve of the Civil War. Meanwhile the cotton gin also made slavery more profitable, and the new Louisiana territories offered inviting acreage for cotton planting and a lucrative market for slaves sold down river from the Upper South. Earlier predictions that the slave population would decline with the abolition of the slave trade proved wildly off the mark. Between 1790 and 1810 the slave population in the United States increased by 70 percent to over one million, but during the remainder of the antebellum period it more than tripled.[29]

Together these new circumstances transformed American slavery from an economically dubious proposition into a profitable business. There were times in the antebellum years when the South's cotton-driven economy grew faster than the North's more diversified economy. Not surprisingly, southerners who in the 1780s and '90s had been willing to consider and even to welcome the demise of slavery—if some way could be found to save white owners from the wrath of freed slaves—were by the early nineteenth century more enthusiastic about defending their slave society. Moral qualms were tempered in the rush to exploit the lucrative possibilities of King Cotton.

The rejuvenation of the slave economy in the early decades of the nineteenth century set the South off on a pattern of economic development different in some significant respects from what the North was experiencing. Both regions were full and active participants in the growing worldwide capitalist market. Both took part in the "market revolution" of the early nineteenth century. But the southern slave economy was a hybrid: capitalist in some respects, but in other respects something different.[30] Adam Smith and other free market advocates had long insisted that slavery, by eliminating both the competition for labor and the worker's incentive to increase productivity in return for higher wages, violated the laws of the market.[31] The southern planter society, although it operated in the world market, was "in its spirit and fundamental direction . . . the antithesis of capitalism."[32] It was, as Eugene Genovese has put it, a unique "social class," with its own "discrete material interests, moral sensibility, ideological commitment, and social psychology." Those class interests and sensibilities "clashed with those of the dominant class of the larger capitalist world."[33]

In recent decades historians have debated just how different the political economies of the North and South really were.[34] But contemporary observers were certainly struck by the contrast between northern and southern economic, political, and social development. To Alexis de Tocqueville, a trip west along the Ohio River between free Ohio and enslaved Kentucky revealed two different worlds. On the Kentucky side "the population is sparse; from time to time one descries a troop of slaves loitering in the half-deserted fields; the primeval forest reappears at every turn; society seems to be asleep, man to be idle." On the Ohio side "a confused hum is heard, which proclaims afar the presence of industry; the fields are covered with abundant harvests; the elegance of the dwellings announces the taste and activity of the laborers; and man appears to be in the enjoyment of that wealth and contentment which is the reward of labor."[35]

Statistics supported Tocqueville's observations. The North was more urbanized, with several great cities swelling in population, while the South was more rural and thinly populated. The North was more industrialized, especially in the Northeast, where domestic manufactures had blossomed during the protracted conflict with England. The southern economy was built almost entirely around the production and export of cash crops like cotton and tobacco. Tocqueville noted that it was "only the Northern states that are in possession of shipping, manufactures, railroads, and canals."[36] In the South, where the interests of plantation owners predominated, their one-dimensional economy required little domestic infrastructure.

New York's William H. Seward, traveling through Virginia in 1835, saw "an exhausted soil, old and decaying towns, wretchedly-neglected roads, and, in every respect, an absence of enterprise and improvement," all of which he attributed to slavery.[37] The southern antislavery politician Cassius M. Clay had explored New England in his youth and came back awed by its greater prosperity, despite a soil and natural resources notably inferior to those of his own state of Kentucky.[38] In the North he saw "industry, ingenuity, numbers and wealth," and also an astonishing degree of social mobility. "The northern laboring man could, and frequently did, rise above the condition [in] which he was born to the first rank of society and wealth." Clay claimed he "never knew such an instance in the South."[39]

These were no doubt exaggerations. Seward was a northern opponent of the southern "slave power" and Clay a southern apostate. But even loyal southerners, especially in the Upper South, noted the effects of slavery on their region's economic development. George Washington lamented in 1796 that land prices in Pennsylvania were higher than in Maryland or Virginia, despite not being of superior quality, because Pennsylvanians had passed laws "for the gradual abolition of slavery."[40] James McDowell, Jr., governor of Virginia, lamented that the "improvidence," "inactivity," and "apathy" engendered by the slave labor system was responsible for "our desolated fields, our torpid enterprise, and . . . our humbled impotence."[41] Except in times of high cotton prices, there appeared to be a growing gap between an increasingly rich and industrialized North and a South whose economy was stagnant and backward. By the 1820s the North was already in the early stages of developing a modern capitalist economic system and what Marxists would call a bourgeoisie and an accompanying bourgeois ethic, morality, and ideology. The southern economy, though participating actively in the capitalist world, was nevertheless dominated not by a bourgeoisie but by an antibourgeois class of slaveholders, whose interest in preserving their status as masters often ran counter to their interest in their region's economic development.[42]

Decades before the Civil War observers believed they could see a "national difference of character" between North and South.[43] The North was the world's incubator of that modern breed of human, the liberal democratic capitalist, always on the move and on the make, looking for the "main chance" to become wealthy and to rise above his station. In the North, Tocqueville noted, labor was associated with "prosperity and improvement." But in the South labor was "confounded with the idea of slavery," and poor white men who worked feared being compared to black slaves. The southern plantation owner, meanwhile, lived in "idle independence, his tastes are those of an idle man."[44] Kentucky's Henry Clay commented in 1798 that slavery harmed not only the slave but also the master, "by laying waste his lands, enabling him to live indolently, and thus contracting all the vices generated by a state of idleness."[45] In fact, most southern slaveholders owned only a few slaves and generally worked hard themselves. But this was not true of the southern political elite. John Quincy Adams, in a frank exchange with John Calhoun, made the characteristic northern observation that "this confounding of the ideas of servitude and labor was one of the bad effects of slavery." Calhoun, speaking for the South, "thought it attended with many excellent consequences."

Southerners steeped in the agrarian tradition neither envied the North its big cities, which they considered dirty and dangerous, nor wished to emulate the North's frenetic pace of life. The large plantation owners who dominated southern society and politics preferred the slower, gentler rhythms of the South. Even if the North was surpassing the South in wealth and industry, defenders of southern institutions viewed northern society as capitalism run amok. From the southerners' quasi-aristocratic perspective, the northern capitalists were vulgar strivers who valued money above all else and who had abandoned the simple republican virtues upon which the nation had been founded. Northern workers who toiled in the capitalists' service were "wage slaves," to be pitied for their mistreatment and feared for the radicalism that their mistreatment was likely to engender. Where northerners valued success, individualism, drive, and self-improvement, southerners, or at least the dominant class of southern planters, generally valued honor, family, and community. This was especially true in Calhoun's South Carolina, where the planter class was especially aristocratic both in its style of life and in its political institutions.

Northerners, in turn, found southern pretensions to superior virtue appalling and false. To John Quincy Adams, the southerners revealed "at the bottom of their souls pride and vainglory in their condition of masterdom. They fancy themselves more generous and noble-hearted than the plain freemen who labor for subsistence. They look down upon the simplicity of a Yankee's manners, because he has no habits of overbearing like theirs and cannot treat negroes like dogs."[46] As even the Virginian George Mason once put it, "Every master of slaves is born a petty tyrant."[47]

These distinctions may have been caricatures, but they also reflected real differences. To a foreign observer such as Tocqueville, the contrast between the two Americas illustrated the distinction between a civilization of modernity and "the civilization of antiquity."[48] The North was embarked on a voyage into the future, driven by the relentless machine of liberal capitalism. The South was steadfastly clinging to the old ways, determinedly preserving the structures, institutions, and psychology of an older era based on the institution of slavery. "Southern slave society," according to Genovese, was essentially aristocratic and "could never fully assimilate bourgeois ideology and morals."[49] When Tocqueville wrote about "Americans," he meant the North, "the regions where slavery does not exist." The slaveholding South, in Tocqueville's view, did not represent America's future.[50]

By the end of the first quarter of the nineteenth century, these two economic and social systems were producing two distinct worldviews. In the North, where slavery had been abolished, a "free-labor" ideology emerged extolling the virtues of work, celebrating social mobility and change, and seeking equality of opportunity, if not of results, for all. The northern idea of "free labor," which would eventually form the ideological foundation of the Republican Party's challenge to the southern "slave power" in the 1850s, was a comprehensive vision of advancing civilization. Northerners saw themselves as "a dynamic, expanding capitalist society, whose achievements and destiny were almost wholly the result of the dignity and opportunities which it offered the average laboring man."[51] This doctrine of progress was aptly suited to a northern world where industrialization and roads and canals were taming nature and where even human nature seemed capable of improvement. Northern men of affairs, though disagreeing about many things, generally "cohered around an imagined enterprise of improving the material environment, reforming a flawed people, and putting the United States in the vanguard of history."[52] "Progressive improvement in the condition of man," John Quincy Adams believed, "is apparently the purpose of a superintending Providence."[53]

The increasingly capitalist North was the natural home for America's burgeoning progressive reform movements. The evangelical fires of the Second Great Awakening swept across the entire nation, North and South, but only in the North did they produce the powerful impulse to social reform. In the late 1820s and 1830s the evangelical Protestant leader Charles G. Finney encouraged northerners to aspire to perfection in themselves and to work for the reform of society so that it, too, might approach nearer to the perfection that could be found in God's heavenly kingdom. True Christians, Finney insisted, were committed "to the universal reformation of the world."[54]

Evangelical Protestantism also breathed fire into the northern antislavery movement. Northern abolitionists never constituted more than a tiny portion of the population, but their condemnation of slavery fit well not only with the precepts of perfectionism but also with the more broadly shared free-labor ideology. Abolitionists insisted that southern slavery was a "relic of barbarism," whereas the North, with its "mixture of farming, commerce, and industrial growth," was clearly advancing along "the course of civilization and progress."[55] Even conservative northerners who abhorred the abolitionists' extremism generally agreed that slavery was immoral, not only or even primarily because of what it did to blacks but because it was antithetical to northern whites' aspirations for themselves and for American society. "If slavery is not wrong then nothing is wrong," the young Abraham Lincoln declared, and a majority of northerners agreed. For the northern celebrants of free labor, slavery "both offended liberal morality and impeded capitalist progress."[56] When these northerners looked south, they saw a society that "seemed to violate all the cherished values of the free labor ideology." The South was a drag on America's destined progress, both materially and morally. As the years passed, the free-labor North increasingly came to view the South as a threat to civilization itself.[57]

The slaveholding South took a very different view, of course. If the North was moving along the path toward modern liberal capitalism, the slaveholding South did not want to follow. Indeed, it could not follow without transforming southern society to fit the northern mold, which meant ridding itself of slavery, with all the monumental risks that this entailed. During the revolutionary era southern political leaders had stood at the vanguard of worldwide Enlightenment thinking, "questioning the morality of slavery, enunciating doctrines of equal rights, and challenging the traditional Puritanism of New England with liberal religious views."[58] In 1800 a "belief in progress and commitments to reform or radicalism were no more prevalent in the North than in the South."[59] But by the end of the first quarter of the nineteenth century the South was hunkering down into a defensive, conservative rejection of the North's vision of human progress.

As the North became a breeding ground for reform movements of all kinds, the South became "the home of religious and social orthodoxy."[60] In the South Protestant evangelical ministers stressed individual piety, not social reform and perfectionism. A society dominated by slaveholders understandably viewed all social reform movements with suspicion.[61] Southern intellectuals cited the proliferation of radical-sounding "isms" in the North as sure evidence of a society that was losing its moorings. "Where will all this end?" asked South Carolina's James Henry Hammond. Southern slaveholders feared it would end with the abolition of their southern institutions.[62]

As time passed, and as the threat from the North grew more ominous, defenders of the southern way of life insisted that amid the revolutionary and dangerous changes sweeping Europe and the North in the 1830s and '40s, only the South could be counted on as, in the words of another South Carolinian, "the conservator of law and order—the enemy of innovation and change—the breakwater which is to stay that furious tide of social and political heresies now setting towards us from the shores of the old world." While the North worshiped at the shrine of progress, the South viewed the idea of progress with ambivalence and suspicion. While the North flirted with notions of human perfectibility and the progressive possibilities of social and institutional reform, the South approached the world with a skeptical realism. "Southerners, who came into daily contact with the harsh reality of human cruelty and suffering, knew better than to believe in such fairy tales."[63]

The Missouri Crisis

DURING THE FIRST TWO DECADES of the nineteenth century a number of forces kept a lid on the burgeoning sectional conflict. The conflict with Great Britain over trade and impressment distracted attention from diverging interests. The ebullient nationalism of the years following the War of 1812 was fed equally from North and South and West, uniting the major politicians of the day, the South Carolinian Calhoun, the Kentuckian Clay, and the Bostonian Adams along with the Virginia dynasty of Madison and Monroe, behind the progressive nationalist project.

But the inevitable confrontation between the two Americas burst into the open in 1819, the direct consequence of the early expansionism that most Americans had so enthusiastically endorsed. The roots of the crisis lay in the Louisiana Purchase, which had opened new southern and western territories to settlement by slaveholders and nonslaveholders alike. When the Missouri territory applied for statehood, a New York congressman, James Tallmadge, Jr., proposed barring the introduction of new slaves and freeing all existing slaves born after admission once they reached age twenty-five. Much to everyone's surprise, Tallmadge's proposals to halt the westward spread of slavery into the Louisiana territories won almost unanimous support in the North. As John Quincy Adams observed, passage of Tallmadge's amendments "disclosed a secret": there was a powerful and widespread animosity in the North against the "Southern domination which has swayed the Union for the last twenty years."[64]

For many northerners, the Missouri battle was about the political and sectional balance of power, not about southern slavery.[65] The prospect of more slave states entering the Union, their disproportionate influence guaranteed by the Constitution's three-fifths clause, the apportionment of Senate seats, and the allocation of electoral votes stirred fears among northeastern politicians that had been quieted since the original Louisiana Purchase.[66] But the issue of slavery itself was unavoidable. Northern support for Tallmadge's proposal "came accompanied with an anti-southern moral attack" by abolitionists and nonabolitionists alike. Northerners were suddenly suggesting that "the South was too depraved to expand."[67]

Southern politicians responded bitterly. Some pleaded for understanding, defending slavery not on principled but on practical grounds. Jefferson lamented that "we have the wolf by the ears, and we can neither hold him, nor safely let him go. . . . Justice is in one scale, and self-preservation in the other."[68] But pleas for understanding soon gave way to angry defiance. And the moral qualms about slavery that Jefferson expressed, which for decades had signaled that the southern gentleman planter existed in the same moral universe as his northern compatriot, gave way to a stout southern defense of the institution. By forcing the South to defend its very right to exist, the Missouri crisis gave birth to a potent sectional political consciousness.[69]

The Missouri crisis revealed the full depths of division between the slaveholding and nonslaveholding sections of the United States, radicalizing northerners and southerners alike. The vicious intersectional debates of 1819 prompted Jefferson's famous exclamation that the country had been awakened as if "by a fire bell in the night" to the horror of civil conflict and disunion.[70] Forty-two years before the firing on Fort Sumter, Calhoun and Adams, like Americans across the country, weighed the possibility of civil war.

John Quincy Adams underwent a radical conversion during the Missouri crisis, becoming an abolitionist in his heart if not yet in his politics. Throughout most of his career in government, as minister to Russia and Great Britain and later as secretary of state, he had done little to impinge on the constitutional rights of the slaveholders. He faithfully represented slaveholder interests in demanding indemnification from the British government for slaves "abducted" by British forces after the peace of Ghent. He employed the State Department's good offices to help southerners trying to extradite slaves who had escaped to Canada. During the debates over Jefferson's purchase of the Louisiana territory, he broke sharply with his fellow New Englanders in opposing restrictions on the spread of slavery in the new lands. Around the time of the Missouri crisis, however, Adams's "personal squeamishness" about slavery began to affect his conduct of foreign policy. As Samuel Flagg Bemis has put it, "Adams's inner convictions on slavery and politics first began to crystallize during the debates in Congress over the admission of Missouri into the Union." Adams wrote in his diary, "[T]he present question is a mere preamble—a title page to a great tragic volume."[71]

In the privacy of his diary, Adams traced the roots of the crisis to the "dishonorable compromise with slavery" in the Constitution, a "bargain between freedom and slavery" that was "morally vicious" and "inconsistent with the principles upon which alone our revolution can be justified." As Lincoln was to do four decades later, Adams looked not to this flawed American Constitution but to the Declaration of Independence, with its promise of human equality, for ultimate guidance. That declaration of equality, he predicted in 1820, was "the precipice into which the slaveholding planters of this country sooner or later must fall."[72] Foreshadowing his own future as an antislavery crusader in Congress, the secretary of state declared—though for the moment only to himself—that a "life devoted to" the extirpation of slavery from the union "would be nobly spent or sacrificed."[73]

Two decades earlier Washington had prophesied that "nothing but the rooting out of slavery" could "perpetuate the existence of union, by consolidating it in a common bond of principle."[74] Adams now foresaw that the rooting out of slavery might put an end to the Union. Realist that he was, he did not flinch at the implications of a principled stand against slavery. With eerie prescience he described the nation's destiny in a spirit and language that would later be adopted by his moral and ideological heir, Abraham Lincoln. "If slavery be the destined sword of the hand of the destroying angel which is to sever the ties of this union," he wrote,

> the same sword will cut in sunder the bonds of slavery itself. A dissolution of the Union for the cause of slavery would be followed by . . . a war between the two severed portions of the Union. It seems to me that its result might be the extirpation of slavery from this whole continent; and, calamitous and desolating as this course of events in its progress must be, so glorious would be its final issue, that, as God shall judge me, I dare not say that it is not to be desired.[75]

Adams's conception of the "national interest" rested on a moral foundation, for even the destruction of the nation was preferable to the perpetuation of slavery—that "great and foul stain upon the North American Union."[76] As the years passed, more and more northerners would find themselves equating the national interest not with territorial expansion, economic growth, or even national defense but with the containment or abolition of southern slavery. America "goes not abroad, in search of monsters to destroy," he declared in his much-quoted address on July 4, 1821. No, the monsters that needed to be destroyed were not abroad but at home, or so he had concluded at this point in his life. When he declared in that same speech that America was the well-wisher to the liberty of others but the "vindicator" only of her own, his point, lost on succeeding generations of historians and commentators, was that American liberty had in fact not yet been vindicated. This was the great task that lay ahead. A terrible conflict to rid the nation of slavery must precede any championing of liberty abroad.

The Missouri Compromise, which permitted Missouri to enter the Union as a slave state but prohibited slavery above latitude 36°30', temporarily settled the crisis. But it did not settle the fundamental conflict between North and South. It left a bitter taste in southern mouths, for as Nathaniel Macon complained, merely by the act of compromising with northern congressmen the South had acknowledged "the right of Congress to interfere and to legislate on the subject." That violated a cardinal southern principle since the nation's founding that "the institution of slavery should not be dealt with from outside the South." Henceforth southerners would be on their guard against northern interference in any form. They would be on guard, too, against any interpretation of the Constitution that permitted the federal government to intrude on the sovereign rights of the states to manage their own affairs. As Richard H. Brown has noted, in Jefferson's day "the tie between slavery, strict construction of the Constitution, and the Republican party was implicit, not explicit. After Missouri it was explicit." Southerners believed that "if the loose constitutional construction of the day were allowed to prevail, the time might come when the government would be held to have the power to deal with slavery." The Missouri Compromise also convinced many leading southerners that the slaveholding South would have to expand westward if it was to survive within the Union. The limits codified in the Missouri Compromise gave many southerners claustrophobia. They feared being "dammed up in a land of slaves," as Spencer Roane put it. Thomas Ritchie, the influential Richmond newspaper publisher, insisted that "[i]f we are cooped up on the north, we must have elbow room to the west."[77] The Missouri Compromise practically guaranteed a conflict between North and South over Texas, should that Mexican territory ever become ripe for the plucking.

After the Missouri crisis it was no longer possible to pretend that the United States was a single nation with a single set of national interests. Although politicians in both North and South worked hard over the next two decades to suppress the issue of slavery in the national debate lest it drive a deeper wedge between the northern and southern wings of both national parties, the society of slaveholders would henceforth be in conflict with the society of free labor.

At times the sectional conflict would be subsumed by other prominent issues—such as Andrew Jackson's war against the Bank of the United States and the Jacksonian democratic revolution more generally. But it was clear to far-seeing observers like Adams and Jefferson that the ideological conflict between North and South would never go away. The "North-South geographical line," Jefferson warned, "coinciding with a marked principle, moral and political, once conceived and held up to the angry passions of men, will never be obliterated; and every new irritation will mark it deeper and deeper."[78]

Slavery and Foreign Policy "Realism"

THE EXISTENCE SIDE BY SIDE of two societies with conflicting perceptions of interest and values, with fundamentally different views of what kind of country the United States should be, and with an increasingly suspicious if not hostile view of each other could not fail to affect the conduct of American foreign policy. On many fundamental issues, of course, Americans shared a common view of their nation's relations with the outside world. They shared an expansive vision of America's destiny and a passion for new territory as a source of economic opportunity and individual autonomy, as proof of their nation's greatness, and as validation of the American political experiment. Southern slaveholders, like their northern compatriots, saw their nation as a beacon for republican freedom in the world, even if this required them to ignore their own suppression of black freedom at home. They sought the extension of American trade, supported the search for markets, and believed in the transforming effects of a free international commerce.

But the increasingly stark differences between slaveholding and free-labor America manifested themselves in foreign policy matters both great and small. Northerners and southerners differed on what to do about the international slave trade. They differed in their reactions to overseas revolutions. They differed in their attitudes toward the nations of the Western Hemisphere. And they differed profoundly on matters of territorial expansion.

John Quincy Adams as secretary of state, and later as president, offers a useful measure of what was happening to the United States, for in many ways he personified the national dilemma. In 1819, as the Missouri crisis was exploding, he was busy negotiating with Spain over the terms of the Transcontinental Treaty and the cession of Spanish territory in North America. But even as he pursued one material conception of the "national interest" by expanding American territory in the South and West, his policies were already being shaped by another, moral conception of the "national interest," preventing the spread of slavery. The final sticking point in the negotiations with Spain concerned the precise delineation of the southwestern boundary. Adams did something strange and, to someone not privy to his inner thoughts, out of character. He settled for a boundary at the Sabine River, thus excluding the vast portion of what would later become the state of Texas. Publicly he argued that Spain would not have conceded more, a claim that was later proved false, much to his embarrassment.[79] Privately he revealed other concerns. "As an eastern man," he told one Illinois senator, "I should be disinclined to have either Texas or Florida without a restriction excluding slavery from them."[80] Territorial self-denial was not normally part of Adams's makeup. As secretary of state he had waged a "tenacious struggle for every square inch and every watercourse in the Northwest."[81] But in the Southwest he loosened his grip and let new territories escape. Southerners would never forgive him for giving up Texas. In the presidential campaign of 1824 Virginia's representative John Floyd excoriated him for ceding to Spain territory that might have become "two slaveholding states" and thus swindling "the Southern interest" out of four senators.[82] Once elected, the tortured Adams tried to purchase Texas—he later dubiously claimed that it would have been an abolitionized Texas—but he failed.

Adams was not alone, however, in viewing southwestern expansion as contrary to the national interest and indeed as a threat to the nation's survival. President Monroe, though a Virginia slaveholder, agreed that Texas was poison, as would Andrew Jackson and Martin Van Buren during their presidencies. The problem was not that taking Texas was beyond American capacities in the 1820s and '30s. As Monroe told Jefferson, "[N]o European power could prevent" the United States from taking as much Spanish land as it wanted. Instead the difficulty was "altogether internal, and of the most distressing and dangerous tendency." The "further acquisition of territory, to the West and South," threatened to "menace the Union itself" because it would open another sectional struggle over slavery.[83] Under the circumstances, Monroe believed, expansion was contrary to the national interest, not because Texas was worthless but because the divided nature of the American polity made it indigestible. The United States could not expand because it could not decide what kind of nation it wanted to be.

This was not the first time that Americans had faced this problem. From the earliest days of the republic, debates over the conduct of American foreign policy had occurred within the context of a larger debate over the identity of the nation. In the 1790s the differing perspectives of Hamiltonian Federalists and Jeffersonian Republicans on the struggle between Great Britain and France were shaped by differing aspirations for the development of America's political economy. During and after the years of conflict with Great Britain, which had produced calls for secession by New England Federalists, leading to their unraveling as a party, those particular schisms largely vanished. A common view of America's foreign relations derived from a commonly accepted vision of U.S. nationalism during the ascendancy of the National Republicans. But the growing North-South divide had now produced differing conceptions of the nation, and the reinterpretation or fracturing of U.S. nationalism inevitably led to different views of America's role in the world.

In the decade after the Missouri crisis the chief domestic victim of the sectional confrontation was the progressive nationalist project that had united political leaders in both North and South since the War of 1812. Southern fears for the institution of slavery were not the only cause of the American System's decline. The economic panic of 1819 and the ensuing hard times stirred antagonism toward that key Hamiltonian institution, the Bank of the United States, and raised angry suspicions about the relationship between the federal government and the wealthy men who ran and benefited from the bank. Southerners were hostile to the American System's protective tariffs, which helped northern manufacturers at the expense of southern exporters. The grand bargain implicit in Clay's American System was that the Northeast got protectionist tariffs, while the West got money for internal improvements, chiefly roads and canals. The South got little out of the deal and became increasingly resentful of what many regarded as a corrupt bargain. John Quincy Adams's narrow Electoral College victory over Andrew Jackson in 1824 enraged many in both the North and the South, who saw Adams's presidency as the illegitimate product of an electoral "corrupt bargain" between Adams and Clay, who just happened to be the two leading advocates of a greater federal role in the nation's "improvement."

But the national reaction against the progressive nationalist project, which culminated in Jackson's landslide election in 1828, could not have acquired its overwhelming strength without the impetus of the South's deep and growing insecurity about its ability to preserve slavery in the face of northern pressures.[84] The national coalition assembled by New York's Martin Van Buren "had its wellsprings" in the Missouri crisis. It was Van Buren's genius to see in southern insecurities the chance to rebuild the old Jeffersonian Republican national coalition. In the South the dispute over Missouri had produced a strong reaction against the progressive nationalism of the National Republicans and shifted the balance of political power to "a hardy band of Old Republican politicians who had been crying in the wilderness since 1816." As a result of the Missouri crisis Old Republicans won elections "in state after Southern state, providing thereby a base of power on which a new strict construction party could be reared." Van Buren promised these southerners a national political party that would once again "be responsive to the South" and that would "maintain its identity in relation to the opposition as a states' rights–strict construction party."[85] In Van

Buren's conception, every plank of the Republican nationalist agenda must become a target and a means of uniting the new party.

Southerners needed no prodding. By 1820 the collection of internal improvements, tariffs, and other federal programs of the American System became the target of southern leaders who saw in the program not only political corruption but also a direct threat to slavery and southern interests. The voices of Old Republicans like John Randolph, drowned out in the nationalist fervor of the postwar years, found a new and eager audience among southern slaveholders worried about a possible northern assault on slavery.[86] Southern politicians who had flirted with progressive nationalism during and after the war with Great Britain now shifted course and adopted an exaggerated version of old republican principles: strict construction of the Constitution, jealous guarding of states' rights against the federal government, and retrenchment and parsimony in federal spending. Every program of the American System—from the national building of roads and canals, to the protective tariff, to the establishment of a national bank, to spending on the military—came under attack. If Congress could "make canals," Nathaniel Macon warned, "they can with more propriety emancipate."[87] In 1823 a strong advocate of southern rights, Duff Green, purchased the *St. Louis Inquirer* to promote Andrew Jackson for president, "fearing that John Quincy Adams and his 'federal party' were conspiring to form a northern antislavery coalition that would emancipate the slaves and prostrate the South."[88]

The combined southern and Van Burenite attack on the American System destroyed Adams's presidency almost before it began. Adams's message to Congress in December 1825, proposing a far-reaching program of national "improvements," complete with astronomical observatories, a national university, a naval academy, an extensive system of roads and canals, explorations of the Pacific Coast, and a federal commitment generally to the "improvement of the condition" of the governed—all this was far too much for an increasingly anxious South to swallow. Adams's message, Macon declared, "seems to claim all power to the federal Government."[89] Southern members of Congress, with support from northern opponents of Adams led by Van Buren, defeated proposals for the establishment of a naval academy and a national university.[90] Calhoun's planned increases in the army and navy were decimated. A unified bloc of southern senators opposed a plan for a scientific exploration of the South Seas on the grounds that such a national project violated the principles of strict constitutional construction. After the Missouri crisis, even the idea of nationalism came under assault. One influential South Carolina senator claimed that the very term "national" was "a new word that had crept into our political vocabulary . . . a term unknown to the origin and theory of our Government."[91]

The southern-led counterrevolution had an immediate and powerful impact on American foreign policy, for the American System had always possessed an important foreign policy dimension. Progressive nationalism had been a powerful engine behind the expansive foreign policies of Adams, Clay, and Monroe. The role President Monroe had outlined for the United States in his famous message to Congress in 1823 "could be fulfilled only by a vigorous nation."[92] The rejection of the nationalist domestic program spelled doom for the far-reaching goals of the nationalists' foreign policy.

The first sign of the impending struggle came with the defeat of Daniel Webster's resolution on Greek independence at the beginning of 1824. Arrayed on the side of Webster's proposal to help the Greeks in their struggle against Turkey, in addition to southern progressive, nationalist Republicans like Clay, Madison, Monroe, and still John Calhoun, was a who's who of northern nationalists, progressives, philanthropists, and missionaries, people like William Henry Harrison, Edward Everett, and Samuel Gridley Howe.[93] On the other side, representatives of merchants who traded with Turkey joined the inchoate Jacksonian coalition of northerners rebelling against the National Republican ascendancy and the representatives of the increasingly conservative South led by John Randolph.

It was Randolph, the staunchly conservative apostle of Old Republicanism, the spokesman for states' rights, the antinationalist opponent of the War of 1812, the defender of the slave states' prerogatives, who made the most eloquent case against Webster's resolution. Employing arguments that would in the twentieth century be called "realist," Randolph lampooned and excoriated Webster's "crusade," his "Quixotic" attempt to embroil America in the internal affairs of Europe, and above all his lack of concern for purely American "interests." Members of Congress had been sent to Washington "to guard the interests of the People of the United States," Randolph declared, "not to guard the interests of other people."[94]

Randolph also revealed the sectional roots of this foreign policy "realism." How could the United States condemn the "enslavement" of Greeks by their Turkish masters, he asked, while Americans held blacks in bondage? The problem was not the hypocrisy. The real danger was that the nation might decide to square practice with principle. How long, Randolph asked, before the moral condemnation of Turkey was turned with equal force against the South? He suggested that the United States was better off not interfering in the internal affairs of other nations, lest the North one day decide to interfere in the internal affairs of the South.[95]

The question of interfering in the internal affairs of others had taken on new importance in the South since the Missouri crisis. Georgia's governor, George M. Troup, was among many southerners who had begun to complain that the North was engaging in "officious and impertinent intermeddlings with our domestic concerns."[96] For those who wished to preserve the southern institution of slavery against the increasingly powerful and moralistic North, expressions of American moral purpose abroad were dangerous. Too often it seemed to southerners that this moralism in foreign policy went hand in hand with moralistic opposition to slavery at home. It was no coincidence that Secretary of State Henry Clay, from lightly enslaved Kentucky, was both the driving force behind a moralizing American foreign policy and the leading spokesman for the gradual emancipation of slaves and their removal to an African colony. In 1798 the young Clay had written in favor of abolition in his own state of Kentucky: "All America acknowledges the existence of slavery to be an evil."[97] In an address to the American Colonization Society in 1825 he called slavery the "deepest stain," the foulest "blot," and the "greatest of human evils." To free "the unhappy portion of our race doomed to bondage," he declared, echoing Adams, would be a greater accomplishment than "all the triumphs ever decreed to the most successful conqueror."[98] For southern slaveholders, the connection was clear. With people like Clay running around the halls of government in Washington, adhering to the principle of noninterference and nonintervention was safer, domestically as well as internationally.[99]

For southerners and other opponents of the American System, the trajectory of American foreign policy since the war with Britain had become dangerous. This included the Monroe Doctrine, that most potent expression of American international ambition and ideological exuberance. Coming on the heels of the Missouri crisis, Monroe's December 1823 message had struck many southerners as fraught with risks. The danger of slave rebellion demanded, at the very least, that the letter and spirit of the Monroe Doctrine had to be applied very selectively in the Western Hemisphere. It was one thing to encourage independence in Colombia. It was another thing to stir up revolution in Cuba and Puerto Rico, where the ratio of black slaves to white masters was so great that what began as a revolution could easily become a massive slave rebellion—"another Haiti."[100] The Creole slaveholders in Cuba opposed independence from Spain for precisely this reason, and they communicated this fear to worried American plantation owners, who in turn communicated it to their representatives in Washington. Even Clay took a cautious path as secretary of state when it came to dealing with movements for Caribbean independence in the mid-1820s. Although personally sympathetic to Cuba's liberation, he faithfully represented slaveholder interests in stability. If "at this premature period" Cuba moved toward independence, Clay declared, "one portion of the inhabitants of the Island, as well as their neighbours in the United States . . . would live in continual dread of those tragic scenes which were formerly exhibited in a neighbouring island."[101] When the United States learned that Colombia and Mexico were contemplating an invasion of Cuba to liberate Spain's last significant colony in the New World, American officials opposed the project, at considerable cost to relations with both Latin powers and to their own ringing declarations on behalf of hemispheric independence and solidarity.

The Monroe Doctrine also became a victim of the broader counter-revolution against nationalism, federal power, and the American System. The very boldness of the president's declaration had been unsettling to southerners worried about a federal government becoming too dominant in the setting of national policy. Senator Macon warned that Monroe's 1823 message was a "strong measure and of a prerogative nature," while John Floyd of Virginia criticized it as "violating the spirit of the Constitution."[102] If a president could assume such powers to shape American policy abroad, he could turn those powers against the South.

Given these southern fears, it was not surprising that the northern anti-slavery president, John Quincy Adams, and his antislavery secretary of state, Henry Clay, met fierce southern opposition in Congress when they attempted to strengthen and expand the Monroe Doctrine in 1825. The battleground for this doctrinal struggle was the Bolívar-inspired Congress of Panama scheduled for the following year. Bolívar had invited the United States to attend, and Adams and Clay believed that the conference offered a chance to entrench American principles of international behavior among the "sister republics" of the Western Hemisphere. They believed Monroe had committed the United States, if not to a hemispheric alliance, then at least to the support of common hemispheric principles. Clay, in a moment of political indiscretion, had even referred to Monroe's "memorable pledge" of 1823.[103] If they had their way, the Monroe Doctrine would blossom into a policy of Pan-Americanism and lead to the creation, as Daniel Webster put it, of a great "American family of nations."[104] Clay even proposed a policy of "good neighborhood," by which he meant a common hemispheric commitment to the principles of freedom and self-determination and, of course, free commerce.

These ambitious plans to strengthen and deepen the Monroe Doctrine collided with southern hostility and the Van Buren coalition, now bolstered by the inclusion of Adams's vice president, John C. Calhoun. The political and intellectual evolution of Calhoun in the early 1820s was another striking example of how the slavery issue, brought to a head by the Missouri crisis, shaped the thinking of Americans on a large number seemingly unrelated issues. During the first Monroe administration he had undertaken to carry out so many Hamiltonian programs, including a national bank and a large peacetime army and navy, that Old Republicans regarded him as a traitor. Van Buren summed up the common view when he described his views on the "Federal Constitution" as "latitudinarian in the extreme."[105] His foreign policy views were of a piece with the progressive nationalism of his domestic policies. As Monroe's secretary of war, he had supported the ideological and territorial ambitions of the Monroe Doctrine and had sought to go further in recognizing Greek independence and even sending U.S. naval vessels to put force behind American words. He had joined Jefferson and Madison in favoring a virtual alliance with Great Britain against the monarchies of Europe.

Political changes in the South after the Missouri crisis, however, and especially in Calhoun's home state of South Carolina, helped lead him after 1824 to adopt a very different stance on all these issues, foreign and domestic. In South Carolina a series of victories by Old Republicans had driven the National Republicans from office, imperiling his political future in the state. The Old Republicans were linking up with Van Buren's followers in the North under the Jacksonian banner, thus threatening his national aspirations as well. Whether out of political calculation, therefore, or because the increasing virulence of the North-South conflict forced him to become more distinctly "southern," Calhoun wheeled and renounced the Hamiltonian doctrines he had once endorsed. Like the Old Republicans, he drew an explicit link between nationalism and slavery. A strong federal government, he now warned, could fall into the hands of abolitionists. It was therefore necessary to "turn back the Government to where it commenced operations in 1789 . . . to take a fresh start, a new departure, on the State Rights Republican tack."[106] He joined forces with the emerging Jacksonian movement, and he told Van Buren that he intended to make the issue of the Panama conference the first great battle against Adams and Clay.[107]

In retrospect it is hard to comprehend how a proposal to send ministers to a conference in Panama could have become a highly divisive issue in American politics. But opponents of Adams and Clay saw their hemispheric ambitions as the foreign policy dimension of the hated American System.[108] For most southerners, the preeminent issues at stake were slavery and race relations. Senator Robert Y. Hayne of South Carolina, who would become famous in 1830 for debating Daniel Webster over the question of nullification, began the attack by expressing southern fear "that the Panama Congress would discuss the suppression of the slave trade and the independence of Haiti." He asked whether representatives from a black nation should be allowed to sit as equals with white Americans and "answered his own question in a thundering voice: not while there were southern votes in Congress to prevent it."[109] Calhoun also expressed concern that the Panama conference would resolve to recognize Haiti. It was "not so much recognition simply," he explained, "as what must follow it. We must send and receive ministers, and what would be our social relations to a Black minister in Washington? . . . Must his daughters and sons participate in the society of our daughters and sons?" Such considerations "involve the peace and perhaps the union of the nation."[110] Southerners worried that recognition of Haiti would encourage other slave rebellions elsewhere in Latin America and maybe even in the United States.[111]

There was also the more fundamental question of the Constitution. Van Buren wanted to establish his national party on the basis of strict construction, and he wanted to use the Panama conference as an ideal place to stake out this position. He did so by forging a link between the Constitution and the injunctions of Washington's Farewell Address, insisting that just as the Constitution must be strictly and narrowly interpreted, so should the foreign policy principles enunciated in the Farewell Address.

Adams's proposal to send ministers to the Panama conference thus sparked the first national debate about the true meaning of America's foreign policy "tradition." The basic parameters of that debate would remain the same throughout the nineteenth and twentieth centuries, even though its roots in the debate over strict construction and slavery would be forgotten. Did Washington's Farewell Address bind the nation against foreign entanglements everywhere? Did it bind it forever? Had Washington set the country on a course of isolation, or did he propose husbanding American resources until its power was great enough to assume a commanding position in the world?

Adams and Clay, setting forth the arguments that would later be repeated by William Seward, Theodore Roosevelt, Woodrow Wilson, and a host of other twentieth-century internationalists, insisted that Washington had never intended to bind future generations of Americans to the principles he had pragmatically set forth in 1796. Nonentanglement had been a tactic, not a timeless principle. "The counsel of Washington," Adams declared, "was founded upon the circumstances in which our country and the world around us were situated at the time." But to "compare our situation and the circumstances of that time with the present day" was to see that a new policy was called for.[112]

One change, Adams argued, was in the makeup of the governments in Central and South America. In Washington's day, "we were the only independent nation of this hemisphere, and we were surrounded by European colonies, with the greater part of which we had no more intercourse than with the inhabitants of another planet." Thirty years later those European colonies had become eight independent nations, "seven of them Republics like ourselves, with whom we have an immensely growing commercial, and must have and have already important political, connections; with reference to whom our situation is neither distant nor detached."

The other revolutionary change was the growth of American power. In the thirty years since Washington delivered his address, Adams noted, "our population, our wealth, our territorial extension, our power—physical and moral—have nearly trebled." Washington had predicted that the period was "not far off" when the United States would be strong enough "to choose peace or war, as our interest, guided by our justice, should counsel." That time had come. Adams believed that growing American power and the changing ideological complexion of the world beyond American shores justified and even compelled greater international involvement. If there were nations in the world "whose political principles and systems of government" were "congenial with our own," they would have an "action and counteraction upon us" to which "we can not be indifferent if we would." And if the United States had the "physical and moral" power to risk involvement with them, it ought to do so.

Adams's opponents in the Congress rejected this logic. Washington's nonentanglement principle was "universal and immutable, acknowledging no distinction of time or place."[113] His warning against foreign connections was the sole principle that must guide foreign policy, and both the Monroe Doctrine and American participation at the Panama conference violated that principle. They denied that Washington had implied that when America became strong, "we may go abroad and form foreign alliances." Washington's dictum could no more be modified by future generations than could the timeless principles embedded in the Constitution. "To be represented at a congress of Independent confederated nations," Andrew Jackson declared, "is an event . . . the framers of our constitution never thought of."[114] Van Buren introduced resolutions in the Senate declaring that even a "conditional acceptance" of the Panama invitation would depart "from that wise and settled policy by which the intercourse of the United States with foreign nations . . . [had] hitherto been regulated."[115] Calhoun declared that Adams's Panama proposal put "the liberties of the country . . . in danger."[116]

The attack on the Panama conference was also an attack on the Monroe Doctrine, and it culminated in a congressional resolution sponsored by James Buchanan, congressman from Pennsylvania, supporter of Jackson, and future secretary of state and president. Appropriating the language of Washington, Buchanan declared that it was "the settled policy of this Government, that, in extending our commercial relations with foreign nations, we should have with them as little political connexion as possible." Therefore the United States could not be party "to any joint declaration for the purpose of preventing the interference of any of the European Powers with their independence or form of Government, or to any compact for the purpose of preventing colonization upon the continent of America."[117] Had it passed, the Buchanan resolution would have officially gutted the Monroe Doctrine, less than three years after its promulgation.

Even though Buchanan's resolution was narrowly defeated, the effect of the great debate over the Panama conference on the direction of American foreign policy after 1825 was significant. It marked "the end of the first epoch in the development" of the Monroe Doctrine. Instead of concluding, as Adams and Clay wished, with the inauguration of a policy of Pan-Americanism, the first quarter of the nineteenth century ended with the doctrine weakened if not eviscerated.[118]

Many twentieth-century diplomatic historians have commented that after the promulgation of the Monroe Doctrine, the United States simply drifted, as if its leaders had never intended to do much to back up their bold declaration. "The United States, far from assuming responsibilities in South America, abstained."[119] But this abstention was the product not of U.S. timidity or indifference, nor of careless enunciation of a doctrine Americans had no real intention of implementing. Rather, it was the product of an American political conflict, in which opponents of the American System both in its domestic and foreign policy manifestations scored a victory.

America the Rogue State:
The South Confronts the British Antislavery Crusade

THE ELECTION of Andrew Jackson and his southern-dominated political coalition in 1828 halted the advance of the American System, and it had other far-reaching effects on American politics and society. It spurred and rode a new democratic revolution, in which the voice of the "common man" made itself heard distinctly for the first time in American politics.

This democratic, egalitarian revolution posed its own problems for southern planters, as it did for many northern conservatives who also feared the radicalization of democratic politics, especially when tides of Irish and German immigrants washed onto American shores less than two decades later. The Jacksonian movement strengthened the northern tendency to celebrate individualism, individual rights, and the "self-made" man, while in the South it threatened to erode the dominance of the planter aristocracy. The Jacksonian democratic revolution also had a distinct impact on the conduct of American foreign policy, making public opinion, including that of the millions of new European immigrants, a more potent force in both national and international affairs. Perhaps most significant was the powerful egalitarian impulse of the Jacksonians, which, in the North at least, added to the growing hostility to the antiegalitarian and antidemocratic planter aristocracy in the South. In the late 1850s many leading northern Jacksonians would migrate into the Republican Party and become the greatest enemies of southern slavery.

But for the moment Jackson's victory was a victory for the South. Southern slaveholders had succeeded in wresting control of the federal government from the likes of Adams and Clay. They would not face a hostile northern president again until Lincoln. For the remainder of the antebellum period, southern leaders, or northerners like Buchanan who accommodated to southern views, would control the upper reaches of government, including, at crucial moments, the offices of the president and secretary of state.

The Jacksonian triumph scarcely put an end to southern fears, however, or to the conflict between the free-labor North and the slaveholding South. In the 1830s abolitionists, though still a beleaguered minority even in the North, became an increasingly important factor in national politics. The incendiary abolitionist William Lloyd Garrison founded his newspaper, *The Liberator*, in 1831 and with the support of rich northern philanthropists began an unremitting attack on the South's peculiar institution. John Quincy Adams entered Congress in 1831 and started his own second career as an antislavery crusader, fighting the slaveholding "monsters" at home. Southern politicians, provoked by the northern abolitionist minority, launched a counteroffensive that in turn offended majority opinion in the North. Southern congressmen insisted that antislavery petitions sent to Congress by northern constituencies had to be blocked—the so-called gag rule. Southerners demanded that abolitionist literature and speeches produced in the North and sent by mail to the South had to be confiscated at the Mason-Dixon Line, on the grounds that such material, when it reached the ears of slaves, threatened to incite revolt. And as the North increasingly became a haven for runaway slaves, southern slaveholders demanded the enforcement of fugitive slave laws requiring the federal government and northern citizens to aid in the return of southern "property."

The South's efforts to control the speech and actions of northerners sparked far more northern outrage than the abolitionists ever managed to incite. "When issues changed from black slavery to white republicanism, from an unfortunate institution on the other section's turf to unacceptable ultimatums about a common democratic government, Yankees stiffened into anti-southern postures." But the southern attempt to control northern behavior, however ill-advised, was the product of the same concerns that made southerners worry about Negro Fort. The slaveholders' despotism was threatened by free territory not only along its southern borders but also on its northern and western borders. What made the threat all the more ominous was that the lightly enslaved border states of Kentucky, Maryland, and the rest of the Upper South were also the home of antislavery politicians like Cassius M. Clay and James Birney. As William W. Freehling has shown, southern anxieties about the reliability of the "less committed, less enslaved hinterlands lying close to the free North" were a principal motive behind efforts to enforce discipline throughout the nation.[120]

The South became increasingly despotic, and not only toward slaves and free blacks. Preserving the southern master's authority over his slaves required control of white behavior, too. A nineteenth-century version of mild totalitarianism, not unlike that practiced by the absolutist courts of central and eastern Europe, eroded southern democracy. Strict limits on freedom of speech and thought were backed up by threats of violence. In the Deep South discipline was enforced through the selective lynching of whites deemed hostile to the slave regime.[121] Antislavery agitators, when they were not hanged, were tortured, tarred and feathered, and driven from southern towns. Kentucky's Birney was forcibly expelled from the South and became a living martyr to the antislavery cause as well as the North's first antislavery presidential candidate. In the Upper South and in the North, southern slaveholders tried to extend their coercive authority by legislative means. There too the effort to "shutter off" their "exposed northern boundary" required "anti-republican impositions on northern whites," which exacerbated northern fears of a southern slave power that aimed to destroy the North's free-labor civilization.[122]

Like other quasi-totalitarian regimes in both the nineteenth and twentieth centuries, the South's paranoia led it naturally toward expansion and conquest as a means of eliminating threats posed by free territories on its borders. The Missouri Compromise of 1820, though it averted disunion and protected slavery below latitude 36°30', was no triumph for southern slave-holders. They feared that no slave state could survive encircled by free states, and the prohibition against the westward expansion of slavery above 36°30' threatened the permanence of slavery in Missouri and the rest of the border South. These fears gave birth to a southern conviction that slav-ery must continue to expand westward, northward, and, most promisingly, southward toward the tropics of Latin America and the Caribbean.[123]

The South's defensive expansionism was also driven by a well-grounded fear that the forces of history were working against the institution of slavery. By the 1820s it was in a state of worldwide decline. Many of the new republics in the Western Hemisphere abolished slavery upon achieving independence from Spain. When Mexico abolished slavery in 1829, the South was suddenly surrounded on three sides by free territory. And when Great Britain emancipated the slaves in its Caribbean colonies in the 1830s, the South was all but isolated in the hemisphere. Only Brazil and the Span-ish colonies of Cuba and Puerto Rico stood with the South in upholding an institution that increasingly seemed a relic of antiquity in a modernizing world. The fact that the driving force behind the international antislavery movement was Great Britain, the world's most advanced industrial society and most powerful empire, made the South especially fearful.

By the third decade of the nineteenth century British foreign policy had undergone a transformation beyond what even Adams and Clay were advo-cating in the United States. As in the United States, the shift was rooted in Britain's own political transformation. Its politics were becoming more democratic after the 1820s. The Reform Bill of 1832 opened the limited franchise to a broader segment of the population. In foreign policy Brit-ain became a defender and promoter of liberal principles in Europe and throughout the world. Lord Palmerston, the dominant figure in British for-eign policy in the mid-nineteenth century, spoke unblushingly of Britain's special role. "We stand at the head of moral, social and political civiliza-tion. Our task is to lead the way and direct the march of other nations." Under Palmerston, Britain supported constitutionalism and liberal reform in Belgium, Italy, Greece, Poland, and on the Iberian peninsula.[124] Critics at home and abroad charged Palmerston with pursuing a "quixotic policy" that "subordinated immediate British interests to general causes."[125] But like Monroe, Adams, Clay, and others in the United States, Palmerston believed that the spread of liberalism served British interests.[126]

This new, more liberal Great Britain had its own version of "manifest destiny": its supreme mission, Palmerston and many other Britons believed, was to expand its influence to all corners of the world and, in the process, bring the blessings of civilization to backward and benighted peoples. Nineteenth-century British imperialism was more universalist than the seventeenth- and eighteenth-century version had been. It was more like American foreign policy in this respect, and indeed may even have been influenced by the universalism of the American Revolution. The progressive Palmerstonian of the early Victorian era believed in a "universalist notion of progress based on British cultural norms, applicable to all societies across the globe." Palmerston's policy of "world bettering" was the moral basis on which empire, and the economic rewards of empire, could be newly justified.[127] Like many Americans, Palmerston saw free trade and capitalism as the main engine of Britain's benevolent expansion. Capitalism was a "moral force," and free trade encouraged "moral regeneration, allowing economically 'backward' nations to develop their resources and throw off outdated elites."[128] And just as Americans had sometimes found it necessary to bring enlightenment to Barbary rulers and others through the cannon's mouth, the far more powerful Britain of Palmerston's day believed British naval power was a necessary adjunct to commerce in the civilizing mission. The "half-civilized governments such as those of China, Portugal, Spanish America," Palmerston once remarked, required "a dressing every eight to ten years to keep them in order."[129]

British policy under Palmerston suggested the course American foreign policy might have taken in the mid-nineteenth century had there been no southern slaveholders, and no southern realism, to check the liberal exuberance of the free-labor North. For like the American North, increasingly capitalist Britain had divested itself of slavery by the 1830s. And like some in the North, Great Britain had embarked on a crusade to stamp out slavery in those corners of the Western world where it still flourished.

The powerful antislavery movement in Great Britain that had begun to shape British foreign policy at the beginning of the nineteenth century contained the same social and economic forces that spurred the antislavery politics of the North. A vocal minority of Protestant evangelicals, referred to by their critics as the "Saints," had started agitating against slavery as far back as the 1780s. Their leader, William Wilberforce, preached the doctrines of personal and national redemption that would later be taken up by Finney and other American evangelicals. Through good works, Wilberforce declared, "we may, I may, become holy."[130] Such teachings helped spur in Great Britain, as later in the American North, a wide-ranging reform movement to treat the social ills of an advancing industrial economy: temperance, prison and education reform, and, above all, abolitionism.

For British evangelicals, as for their American counterparts, "slavery and sin were regarded as synonymous, equally individual and national evils to be rooted out."[131] And the British antislavery movement, again like its counterpart in the American North, drew strength from the fact that Britain was a rising capitalist power with an evolving liberal ideology hostile to the idea of slave labor.[132] The moral case against slavery meshed well with the interests and the ethos of Britain's capitalist classes. When Wilberforce and his followers succeeded in convincing the House of Commons to abolish the slave trade in 1806, Lord Chancellor Thomas Erskine declared it "our duty to God and to our country, which was the morning star of enlightened Europe and whose boast and glory was to grant liberty and life, administer humanity and justice to all nations, to remedy that evil."[133]

From the early nineteenth century onward, British leaders, spurred by an aroused public, devoted vast time and energy to stamping out the international slave trade. They came up against many of the same obstacles that other international humanitarian efforts would face in the twentieth century. They had to convince other governments to sacrifice their sovereignty and, in some cases, their economic interests to a cause that few felt as strongly about as the British.[134] They had to set up new international mechanisms for monitoring and enforcing the slave-trade ban. Castlereagh established a permanent conference of the European powers in London "to be a center of information, as well as of action, about trading slaves."[135] The British Foreign Office established a special department exclusively devoted to the slave trade. In 1842 the British foreign secretary, Lord Aberdeen, could announce with pleasure that antislavery diplomacy had been established as a "new and vast branch of international relations."[136]

The hardest task was establishing an international police force to patrol the seas and seize slave ships. In practice, the naval muscle had to be provided almost entirely by Great Britain, which possessed the world's largest navy and near total command of the seas. But British naval vessels still needed permission to stop and search suspected slave ships flying the colors of other nations. This raised hackles in foreign capitals, where critics suspected the British of attempting to extend their already impressive international hegemony under the cover of humanitarianism. But most of the European powers eventually agreed.

The United States did not. During the first four years of the Monroe administration, when progressive nationalists still dominated a Congress led by Henry Clay, and when the secretary of state was the closet abolitionist John Quincy Adams, the United States did cooperate in a limited way. In 1819 Congress authorized President Monroe to send armed vessels to the

African coast to join the British in patrolling for slave ships. In 1820 Adams persuaded Congress to declare that participants in the slave trade were pirates punishable under American law. But the sticking point was Britain's demand that its naval officers be allowed to stop and search vessels flying the American flag. This stirred memories of the British practice of stopping and boarding American vessels for the purpose of impressing alleged British citizens—a principal cause of the War of 1812.

The real problem, however, was the South. The American minister in London, Richard Rush, whose father had been a leading northern abolitionist, told Castlereagh that American opposition to any agreement on the right of search was due to the "peculiar situation and institutions of the United States."[137] When John Quincy Adams negotiated a treaty allowing British search of American vessels under certain circumstances, and a joint convention for suppression of the slave trade in 1824, southern senators crippled the agreement with amendments, including the exemption of American territorial waters from any scrutiny. The British backed out in disgust.

Far from cooperating with the British antislavery crusade, the United States demanded British protection for American slave owners. In 1822, after the Denmark Vesey conspiracy was uncovered along with its alleged Haitian connections, frightened South Carolina legislators enacted a law requiring that all black sailors, regardless of nationality, be imprisoned while their ships were docked at Charleston. This violated an Anglo-American agreement giving sailors of both countries free access to their ports. But when a justice on the U.S. Supreme Court ruled the South Carolina law unconstitutional, the legislature simply ignored the ruling, arguing that "the duty of the state to guard against insubordination or insurrection among our colored population . . . is paramount to all laws, all treaties, all constitutions. It arises from the supreme and permanent law of nature, the law of self-preservation."[138]

The United States also demanded that runaway or accidentally liberated slaves be returned to their American masters. When American ships forced by wind or weather into British ports in the West Indies lost slaves, who then sought their freedom in Britain's emancipated colonies, Americans demanded compensation. An American démarche to Palmerston actually requested that Great Britain refrain from "forcing" freedom upon "Americans slaves" who might be "forced by stress of weather or unavoidable contingency within British Colonial Ports." It demanded that Britain place the slaves in prison "for temporary safe keeping" until their owner could arrange to have them shipped home.[139] Palmerston replied that a policy of forcing freed slaves back into bondage "would be so entirely at variance with every principle of the British Constitution" that no British government would dare propose it to Parliament and no British troops could be expected to carry it out.[140]

America's refusal to allow its ships to be searched for slaves stymied British efforts to suppress the illicit trade. Even though the slave trade had been banned in the United States after 1808, American sea captains took a big part in it. Many American ships fitted out as privateers during the War of 1812 became slaving ships after the war, carrying captured blacks from Africa to Brazil and Cuba. Sea captains of other nationalities immunized themselves from British search and seizure by flying the U.S. flag. The American colors, much to the indignation of the British, became the shield behind which Portuguese, Spanish, and Brazilian slave traders carried on their business.[141] After repeated failures to enlist American cooperation in the international effort to suppress the trade, Palmerston wrote in exasperation that he could not believe "the Government of Washington can seriously and deliberately intend that the flag and the vessels of the Union shall continue to be, as they now are, the shelter under which the malefactors of all countries perpetuate with impunity crimes which the laws of the Union stigmatize as piracy and punish with death."[142] The United States, however, did not budge. So long as slavery existed in the United States, and so long as slaveholder interests controlled important levers in the federal government, the British would not be permitted to search American ships. This was less a principled demand for sovereign immunity than a practical demand for the protection of American slave owners. For the United States eventually did drop its demand for sovereign independence on the high seas—in 1862, after the secession of the South and the same year as the Emancipation Proclamation.

Despite American success in warding off British restrictions, the constant pressure of the British antislavery crusade nevertheless put great strain on the internal contradictions of the American polity. The antislavery movement in the North drew sustenance from British policies. Northern abolitionists rejoiced at Britain's emancipation of the slaves of the West Indies, and even Britain's marginal advances against the international slave trade strengthened their belief that slavery could eventually be eradicated if the forces opposed to it summoned the will. Even that erstwhile Anglophobe John Quincy Adams came to view Britain as an ally in the struggle against the southern slavocracy.[143]

To southern slaveholders, meanwhile, a hostile antislavery world seemed to be closing in, and Great Britain was behind it all. Mexico, which had abolished slavery and which after 1830 had come to view the United

States as a menacing aggressor, had turned to Great Britain for protection and was becoming a British satellite in the Western Hemisphere. The British seemed bent on turning the vital Gulf of Mexico into a British lake. Canada was under British control in the north. The Oregon territory gave Britain a foothold in the Northwest. California, owned by pro-British Mexico, bounded the United States on the west: "The whole constituted a noose around the republic."[144] Americans in both North and South expressed concern about British policies in the Western Hemisphere, but the South was especially alarmed. For lying behind the geographical encirclement, many southerners feared, was Britain's grand ideological design. In 1843 President John Tyler's secretary of state, Abel P. Upshur, one of the South's leading defenders of slavery, warned John C. Calhoun that "England is determined to abolish slavery throughout the American continent and islands."[145]

The Annexation of Texas: A "Southern Question"

CALHOUN NEEDED no convincing. By the early 1840s he and other southern leaders had already identified a two-pronged conspiracy to destroy southern slavery. The northern antislavery movement, led in Congress by John Quincy Adams, was attempting to undermine slavery from within. First northern politicians limited its spread, and then they used the North's growing power to strike at slavery where it was weakest—in the Upper South. External support for the antislavery cause came from Great Britain, which intended to contain slavery on America's southwestern frontier and then weaken it by establishing emancipated territories where slaves could flee the slaveholders' control. How long could the slaveholding South hold out against this two-pronged attack?

The question, Calhoun and Upshur believed, would be decided in Texas. Ever since Adams and President Monroe had failed to demand Texas from Spain as part of the territorial settlement of 1819, the disposition of that northern Mexican state had been a contentious issue in American politics. Throughout the late 1820s and '30s successive American presidents had balked at acquiring Texas, believing the issue too explosive to inject into an American politics already fractured by the sectional dispute over slavery. Even Andrew Jackson had been timid. Americans provided substantial assistance to the Texans in their war for independence against Mexico in 1835 and 1836, but Jackson rejected the Texans' urgent request for annexation, fearing it would damage the electoral prospects of his chosen successor, Martin Van Buren. For the next four years President Van Buren opposed annexation, reflecting the sentiments of his northern political base and attempting to avert a national crisis. Van Buren's whole political strategy, which had worked so brilliantly over three successive elections to unite a national Democratic Party, depended on not exacerbating schisms that would again divide the party along geographical lines. He struggled to keep slavery out of the national conversation, therefore, and to concentrate on economic and political issues that transcended the North-South divide. His greatest fear was a repetition of the Missouri crisis and any revival in the North of the "clamour" against "Southern Influence and African Slavery," which Van Buren knew would spell the death of the Democratic Party in the North.[146] Then when the anti-Jacksonian Whig Party finally took the White House in 1840, in the person of William Henry Harrison, the new president and his secretary of state, Daniel Webster, also continued to resist annexation in deference to the wishes of the party's dominant northern constituency.[147]

But the Texas question could not be evaded forever, and powerful forces came together in the early 1840s to produce the inevitable explosion. In the North, hostility to the southern slave power reached a new plateau as congressional debates over the "gag rule" pitted Adams and other northern antislavery politicians against southerners determined to prevent even the discussion of slavery in Congress. Meanwhile Adams and others kept their eyes on Texas, waiting in almost eager anticipation for a southern attempt to bring it into the Union. Then the real battle against the slavocracy could begin. In Texas itself the struggle for independence and security against an angry and menacing Mexico was forcing the new republic's leaders to cast about for support wherever they could find it. Most Texans wanted to join the United States, but after repeated rebuffs Texan leaders were starting to look to Great Britain. The British, meanwhile, wanted to turn Texas into a buffer against further American southward expansion and had offered to serve as a friendly mediator between Texas and Mexico.

All this looked ominous to the South, and growing anxiety about the domestic and international forces massing against the institution of slavery brought to the fore a group of leaders determined to raise southern consciousness about the impending threat to their way of life.[148] Two of these extremists, Upshur and Calhoun, would follow Webster as secretary of state in the Tyler administration and take matters into their own hands.

The historical accident that set the match to this combustible mix was the death of William Henry Harrison months after taking office and the rise of "His Accidency," John Tyler, to the presidency. Harrison had been a northerner and a nationalist in the mold of Clay and Adams, determined to leave the Texas issue alone. Tyler was a Virginian, a slave owner, a Democrat, and like many of that description, anxiously impatient. Before becoming president, he had railed against the northern abolitionist movement and the threat it posed to southern institutions and southern lives: "It invades our hearth, assails our domestic circles, preaches up sedition, and encourages [slave] insurrection."[149] Within months of assuming the presidency, he was at war with the nationalist Whigs in Congress led by Clay over the latter's efforts to put the American System back in place. From then on he desperately searched for allies, and he found them in the South. In 1843, when Webster resigned as secretary of state, the Tyler administration became the vehicle for southerners determined to save their civilization from the worldwide antislavery movement.

The leading figures in the Tyler administration after 1842—the president himself, his second secretary of state, Abel Upshur, and Upshur's successor, John Calhoun—all epitomized the South's anxiety at the adverse domestic and global trends. Upshur's first annual report as secretary of the navy in 1841 called for a naval buildup, warning that in a war with "any considerable maritime power," that is, Great Britain, the enemy would stir up a slave insurrection.[150] This was only the first of many occasions when the usual southern opposition to big government spending was abandoned in the interest of saving slavery. Calhoun as secretary of state wanted American diplomacy to be conducted by men "completely identified with the South."[151] He objected when untrustworthy northerners were sent to London and Paris to serve as ambassadors, believing with some justice that the northern antislavery movement was making common cause with the British and with antislavery government officials in France.

In 1843 Duff Green, a devoted follower of Calhoun and ardent defender of southern interests—John Quincy Adams called him the "ambassador of slavery"—believed he had uncovered a British plot to abolitionize Texas and, after that, the United States. The British prime minister, Lord Aberdeen, had offered the Texan government support against Mexico in return for the abolition of slavery. Aberdeen, according to Green, had even offered to provide Texas a loan to defray the costs of emancipation. Green insisted that Aberdeen's goal was nothing less than to incite "rebellion and servile war in the South by purchasing and emancipating the slaves of Texas."[152]

There was a kernel of truth in Green's otherwise exaggerated charge. Aberdeen had no plans for abolishing slavery in the United States. But antislavery forces in Parliament had long viewed Texas as a vital battleground in the struggle for abolition in the Western Hemisphere. Texans had agitated for independence, after all, partly to reestablish slavery after Mexico had abolished the institution in 1829, and British abolitionists had sided with

Mexico during the independence struggle, pouring money into Mexican bonds and helping finance Mexico's purchase of warships for use against Texas. After Texas achieved independence in 1836 and reinstituted slavery, the new republic became the main transfer point for slaves shipped from Africa via Cuba to the slave market in New Orleans. Texas thus became a symbol of the slave traders' defiance of Britain's antislavery crusade. Even the cautious Aberdeen could not ignore pressures from Parliament to try to put an end to slavery in the Lone Star Republic.[153] When asked in the House of Lords by the antislavery leader Lord Brougham if there was not a "very great chance" that Texas would abolish slavery in exchange for Mexican recognition, Aberdeen answered that "every effort on the part of Her Majesty's Government would lead to that result."[154] Great Britain was "constantly exerting herself to procure the general abolition of slavery throughout the world."[155]

Nervous southerners had reason to be alarmed. It didn't actually matter whether Aberdeen was truly committed to abolishing slavery in Texas. The mere threat of abolition could be enough to discourage people from owning slaves or bringing them into Texas. Over time slavery might become untenable in the republic.[156] Whether the British forced abolition upon Texas immediately, therefore, or simply made it impossible for slavery to survive in Texas, the result would be the same: more free territory on the borders of slavery, a haven for runaway slaves and would-be insurrectionists, "a sort of Hayti on the continent," as one worried Texan wrote to Calhoun.[157] If Texas were lost, Upshur feared, southern slavery could not "exist surrounded on all sides by free States."[158]

In April 1844 Calhoun, who had become secretary of state after Upshur's death, declared that he regarded "with deep concern the avowal" that Britain was "constantly exerting herself" to abolish slavery throughout the world. An emancipated Texas would "expose the weakest and most vulnerable portions" of the slave South's "frontiers." In a speech that was calculated to inflame the South and certainly succeeded in inflaming the North, Calhoun vigorously defended the institution of slavery as a positive blessing to the "negro race." The enslaved black race had been elevated in its "morals, intelligence," and "civilization." In preserving slavery, Calhoun declared, the United States was "acting in obedience" to racial "obligation."[159]

Calhoun's declaration brought the sectional conflict over slavery to the fore again after twenty years of being assiduously suppressed by American political leaders. Other southern politicians, including Tyler, had tried to portray the annexation of Texas as being in the interest of the whole nation. But Calhoun deliberately revealed what many northerners already suspected—that the chief motive behind annexation was the defense of southern slavery. Calhoun, like Upshur, hoped to radicalize the South and prepare it for the arduous defense of its institutions against the northern onslaught. If this led to the fracturing of the two national parties along sectional lines, so much the better. As Upshur declared, Texas had to be made a "Southern question, and not one of Whiggism and Democracy."[160]

Calhoun and Upshur were right about one thing: northerners couldn't be trusted. As the Van Buren presidency had shown, no northerner of either party would commit unreservedly to the defense of slaveholder interests in Texas. Even a confirmed nationalist and continentalist like John Quincy Adams would make common cause with the British against the South's vital interests in Texas. In 1843 two leading American abolitionists, on their way to the World Antislavery Convention in London to celebrate the tenth anniversary of British emancipation in the West Indies, stopped in Massachusetts to seek Adams's counsel. Urging that they meet with Aberdeen and encourage him to press for abolition in Texas, Adams declared that "the freedom of this country and of all mankind depends on the direct, formal, open, and avowed interference of Great Britain to accomplish the abolition of slavery in Texas."[161]

This was a rather extraordinary statement coming from the man who had once devoted decades of government service to American continental expansion, who had worked tirelessly to push Great Britain and every other European power off the North American continent, and who had been the primary architect of Monroe's policy of preventing European interference in the Western Hemisphere. It was a measure of how fervently Adams and other northerners had come to believe that America's overriding "national interest" no longer lay in continental expansion, or even in the expulsion of European influence from the continent, but in the containment and eventual abolition of slavery in the United States. Adams was more than willing to see expansion thwarted and foreign influence on the continent enhanced in the service of what he had come to believe was a higher moral imperative.

In truth, Adams no longer conceived of the United States as a single nation. The South and its slaveholding oligarchy had become the enemy, far more to be feared than the liberal, crusading Great Britain. Adams's view mirrored that of Calhoun and Upshur and the southern extremists they represented. They, too, no longer thought of the "national interest" as something indivisible, something that could be divorced from sectional interests. The interests they sought to preserve and advance were the South's interests. The annexation of Texas, as Secretary of State Upshur had insisted, was a "Southern question."

For most leaders in both North and South, questions of national aims and national interests became inseparable from the sectional conflict over slavery, and although that conflict was frequently played out beyond American borders, the victory that each section sought was at home, not abroad. For both northerners and southerners, external expansion aimed primarily at redressing the internal balance of power. From the debate over Texas annexation to the equally passionate arguments over the cession of Mexican territory later in the decade to the struggles over the annexation of Cuba in the 1850s, the continent of North America, including Mexico and the islands of the Caribbean, became a vast battleground for what might best be described as an imperial competition between the two sections. From the 1840s to the outbreak of the Civil War, the sectional conflict *was* America's foreign policy. Or, to be more precise, it was America's two foreign policies.

CHAPTER 8

Manifest Destinies

Slaveholders of America, I appeal to you. Are you really in earnest when you speak of perpetuating slavery? Shall it never cease? Never? Stop and consider where you are and in what day you live. . . . This is the world of the nineteenth century. . . . You stand against a hopeful world, alone against a great century, fighting your hopeless fight . . . against the onward march of civilization.

—Carl Schurz, 1860

Northern Containment, Southern Expansion: America's Two Foreign Policies

THE MAN WHO carried out the annexation of Texas and the most prodigious expansion of territory in American history, and who came to symbolize the era of "manifest destiny," was James K. Polk. Although a southerner from Tennessee and the owner of more than one hundred slaves, Polk often expressed bafflement at his countrymen's preoccupation with the slavery issue. His territorial ambitions were not limited to lands where slavery could spread. He sought California, an unlikely stronghold for slavery for which he was prepared to go to war with Mexico, and Oregon, where slavery was almost unimaginable and for which he was rather less inclined to go to war with Great Britain. The Democratic Party platform he ran on in 1844 called both for the "re-annexation" of Texas and the "re-occupation" of the Oregon lands up to the 54°40' latitude, an ambitious continental agenda that appeared to serve national rather than sectional interests. His election in 1844 is often regarded as a popular referendum on manifest destiny. Between 1845 and 1848 the United States under Polk's leadership expanded by more than one million square miles and laid claim to every inch of territory from the Atlantic to the Pacific north of the Rio Grande and south of the forty-ninth parallel. Small wonder that these vast acquisitions have been viewed as a national project, the result of the determined will of a growing nation "as restless as a caged leopard and as charged with latent energy."[1]

Often lost in this picture of national consensus and calculated pursuit of the "national interest," however, were the divisive sectional politics of the era—a politics from which Polk, more than anyone, directly benefited. President Polk owed his presidency to southern influence. The most important issue in the 1844 campaign was the southward expansion of slave territory, and Polk, the original "dark horse" candidate, would never have won the Democratic nomination had it not been for the "southern question" of Texas. In the summer of 1844 the presumptive Democratic nominee was Martin Van Buren. But when Van Buren made known his opposition to Texas annexation, southern Democrats abandoned him and searched for someone willing to defend southern interests. They found Polk. In the general election Polk won only the narrowest of victories over the Whig candidate, Henry Clay. Again, the southern drive for Texas played a big part. Clay's opposition to the annexation of Texas hurt him in the South, but in the North Clay—along with the antiannexationist Liberty Party candidate, James K. Birney—won a narrow majority over Polk.[2] If the 1844 election was a referendum on Texas annexation, the South voted overwhelmingly yes, the North voted narrowly no, and Polk was the winner.[3]

It did not surprise anyone, therefore, when President Polk tilted his policies southward, following the direction of the party that had catapulted him into the White House. Thus Texas annexation was approved in early 1845. In January 1846 Polk sent American troops into the disputed zone between the Nueces River and the Rio Grande. When Mexican troops came across to challenge them, he declared war on Mexico in May of that year, and by the time the war was finished, the United States had acquired millions of square miles of new southwestern territory. Polk's drive for northwestern territory, on the other hand, was a good deal more restrained. The Democratic Party's election plank demanding "all of Oregon" quietly vanished once Polk was elected, and Polk accepted a compromise boundary at the forty-ninth parallel, giving the British what northerners such as John Quincy Adams insisted was by rights American territory north of that line.

Some twentieth-century historians have divined in Polk's disparate policies—aggressive war southward, compromise and restraint northward—a consistent, sensible view of the "national interest." Looking back on America's territorial acquisitions from a modern perspective, with memories of the sectional conflict dimmed if not lost altogether, most Americans would agree that the acquisition of Texas, as well as of Oregon and California, "were so obviously in the American interest . . . that any policies designed to extend the territories of the United States to the Pacific" should have faced "little opposition."[4]

Yet Polk's policies did face significant opposition, precisely because there was so little agreement on what constituted the "American interest" in the 1840s. Much to Polk's professed disgust and disappointment, Americans in both the North and the South insisted on viewing all questions of expansion and foreign policy as part of the great struggle over the future of slavery. Polk's contemporaries did not all view him as an impartial steward of American foreign policy focused intently on the "national interest." The southerners who placed him in office hoped he would serve southern interests, and the northerners who opposed him believed he amply rewarded southern hopes.

Polk's actions, in fact, opened deep and enduring sectional rifts in both of the national parties. Texas annexation and the subsequent acquisition of Mexican territory after the war "undercut prospects that [northern] Democrats could long remain Democrats or that Southern Whigs could long remain Whigs." By speeding the transformation of the two parties into sectional parties—with Democrats representing the South and Whigs representing the North—Polk's expansionism "carved inexorable ruts a long way down the road to disunion."[5] It is a sign of how unhelpful, even distorting, our modern understanding of the national interest can be. Polk may have gained some immensely valuable territory for the United States, territory that would eventually serve the nation well and even be the pillar on which its future global power rested. The price, however, was steep, insofar as Polk's acquisition hastened the nation toward dissolution and a devastating civil war.

When Polk sought to reap the harvest of his war with Mexico, northern bitterness produced the first major sectional eruption since the Missouri crisis of 1819. Once again it was a northern member of a southern president's party who set match to tinder. In 1846, as Polk prepared to negotiate with Mexico for the cession of territory encompassing the future states of California, Nevada, New Mexico, Utah, and parts of Wyoming and Colorado, a northern Democrat, David Wilmot, introduced legislation banning the extension of slavery into any of the new territories that might be acquired. Wilmot's famous "proviso" was partly an effort to shield northern Democrats from their angry constituents. It "expressed Northern Democrats' fear that further appeasing Southerners would hand Whigs the North."[6] But the Wilmot Proviso, like the Tallmadge amendments twenty-seven years before, brought to the surface the sectional tensions over slavery that had been deliberately suppressed by Presidents Jackson, Van Buren, and Harrison, and by both major parties before 1844. The northern Whig editor Horace Greeley called it "a solemn declaration of the United North against the further extension of Slavery under the protection of our Flag."[7] John Calhoun warned that if the Wilmot Proviso were approved, the South would be "at the entire mercy" of the North, "a mere handful" of slave states "forever" imprisoned behind a wall of free states.[8] Polk's Democratic Party split down the middle: northern Democrats voted almost unanimously for the proviso; a solid phalanx of southern Democrats voted against it.[9] It passed in the House and was blocked in the Senate.

Polk's war against Mexico and his acquisition of the Southwest thus "triggered the release of forces of sectional dissension" that had long simmered just beneath the surface of American society. His decision to fight in Mexico upset the uneasy balance that had existed between North and South since 1820, and "the acquisition of a new empire which each section desired to dominate endangered the balance further."[10] Polk may well have wanted to acquire California, New Mexico, and other northern Mexican territories neither to extend nor to contain slavery but simply to control the Pacific Coast and open the door to the trade of the Orient. But for most northerners and southerners, the extension of American territory in the Southwest was preeminently an issue of slavery. In 1837 Daniel Webster had warned, "He is a rash man, indeed . . . who supposes that a feeling of this kind is to be trifled with or despised."[11]

After 1846, as the national parties gradually dissolved into sectional parties, the specter of sectional conflict doomed all attempts at compromise over the new territorial questions created by Polk's expansionism. The Compromise of 1850, engineered by the northern Democrat Stephen Douglas and the Kentucky Whig Henry Clay and supported by Daniel Webster, Millard Fillmore, and other conservative Whigs trying to preserve the Union and the national Whig Party, only served to infuriate both northern antislavery Whigs and southern slave expansionists. California (as well as New Mexico and Utah) was permitted to enter the Union without restrictions on slavery, thus violating Wilmot's principle. Nevertheless, Californians voted to enter as a free state, thus dashing southern hopes of a new and powerful slave state to balance northern free-state power. The Compromise of 1850 was only a temporary truce.

The acquisition of vast stretches of southern and western territory forced both sections to address the issue that they had evaded in the two decades since the Missouri crisis. The compromise of 1820 had established an uneasy gentlemen's agreement between North and South based on preservation of the status quo. The North would not interfere with slavery in the states where it already existed. But neither would slavery be permitted to expand any further. While abolitionists in the North had always called for immediate emancipation, after 1820 the consensus among northern politicians was that the institution of slavery should be left alone in the South if only because the price of destroying slavery would be the destruction of the nation itself. Nevertheless, a cardinal principle of even the more conservative northerners was that southern slavery had to be contained within its existing boundaries. As Lincoln put it, "toleration by necessity where it exists, with unyielding hostility to the spread of it."[12]

Although many northerners were indifferent to southern slavery, for Lincoln and many others this northern containment strategy was not intended to be neutral regarding the future of slavery in the United States. In the North as in the South there was a common assumption that slavery "required expansion to survive, and that confinement to the states where it already existed would kill it."[13] Most northerners believed, and many southerners feared, that in time the natural deficiencies and internal contradictions of the archaic slave system would produce its natural and peaceful demise. The experience of the Upper South, where slavery had been gradually giving way to the forces of the capitalist market system and where the slave population had dwindled accordingly, offered northerners hope and southerners cause for despair that this natural evolution away from slavery might occur throughout the South. In the struggle between the civilization of modernity and the civilization of antiquity, many northerners believed, there could be only one outcome. The North's confidence in the superiority of its free-labor system argued for patience, and containment.

In the two decades before the Civil War, northern superiority seemed to be visible in any number of social and economic indicators. The census of 1850 showed that since 1840 population growth in the free states had exceeded that in the slave states by 20 percent. Migration from slave states to free states exceeded by three times the flow in the other direction, and seven-eighths of all foreign immigrants to the United States—numbering in the millions at midcentury—settled in the North. The increase in the northern population was related to the greater demand for labor produced by a burgeoning industrial economy that was growing faster than the southern agriculture-based economy. While the northern economy was becoming increasingly self-sufficient, moreover, with a growing pool of northern consumers to buy northern-made products, the South's economy was becoming increasingly dependent on the North and on Great Britain for both export markets and investment capital.[14] The South did not even have the capacity to turn its own cotton into fabric—there were more machine-driven looms in Lowell, Massachusetts, than in the entire South—which meant that northern merchants and industrialists reaped as much profit from cotton as did southern plantation owners. In time, many northerners believed, the North's superior economy and growing population would force the South to abandon its failed economic system and adopt northern ways. At the very least an increasingly populous, free North would amass greater power in the electoral system while the contained slave South grew ever weaker. Lincoln, in his famous debates with Stephen Douglas, insisted that the formula for slavery's extinction had already been discovered by the founders, who tried to contain slavery's spread with the deliberate intention of eventually putting an end to it. Lincoln prophesied that slavery would "become extinct, for all time to come, if we but re-adopted the policy of our fathers."[15]

The northern strategy for the gradual and peaceful defeat of southern slavery resembled the strategy of containment set forth by George F. Kennan and other Americans a hundred years later at the dawn of the Cold War. Just as Kennan believed the Soviet Union's totalitarian system bore "within it the seeds of its own decay" and that Western containment of Soviet expansionism would in time force the Soviet system either to mellow or to collapse under the weight of its own contradictions, so northern political leaders believed the peaceful containment of slavery was the surest and safest route to its destruction.[16] "Slavery has within it the seeds of its own destruction," David Wilmot insisted. "Keep it within given limits . . . and in time it will wear itself out."[17] In both the mid-nineteenth and the mid-twentieth centuries, confidence in the North's, and later America's, superior political and economic system seemed to offer a strategy for victory without the risk of catastrophic war.

There were some in the North, of course, who opposed the containment strategy, just as during the Cold War many Americans questioned the policy of containing the Soviet Union. On one side, northern abolitionists demanded a more aggressive strategy for undermining slavery in the South. William Lloyd Garrison denounced gradualism as tantamount to accepting slavery "in perpetuity." When in history, he asked, had a despotic aristocracy like the southern planters ever peacefully given up power? On the other side was the influential group of northern merchants and industrialists, mostly Whig Party leaders in the Northeast, who profited immensely from the South and its cotton. These conservative "Cotton Whigs" naturally objected to all antislavery efforts, whether gradualist or immediatist, as disastrous both to the Union and to the national economy.

Many northerners of lesser means feared that the consequence of ending slavery in the South would be a flood of black migrants to the North to compete with white laborers and drive down wages. After 1846 this fear produced increasing support for the free-soil movement. Free-soilers were not all fervent opponents of slavery on moral grounds and did not propose to end southern slavery. But they favored containment. They insisted that the new territories of the West had to be kept open for settlement by free labor. If slavery were permitted in the new territories, the free-soil editor and poet William Cullen Bryant warned, free labor would not settle there, since wages would be artificially suppressed by the presence of slaves. But if slavery were kept out of the new territories, free labor would swarm in, and "in a few years the country will teem with an active and energetic population."[18] "Peaceful conquest," the primary tool used to push British, French, Spanish, and Indian peoples from the continent, would now be put to use in the imperial battle with southern slavery over control of the West. Although there were heated disagreements in the North over the best strategy for dealing with slavery, and although motives differed even among those who agreed on the strategy, the consensus that had emerged by the 1840s was for containment.

At times, however, this strategy would take on the aspect, certainly in southern eyes, of an aggressive containment, designed both to contain slavery from without and to undermine slavery from within. One antislavery politician from Ohio expressed what southerners feared was, in fact, the real northern plan: "We will establish a cordon of free states that shall surround you; and then we will light up the fires of liberty on every side until they melt your present chains and render all your people free."[19] This approach, too, would be echoed by Americans in the next century, in the waning years of the Cold War.

Small wonder that many southern leaders viewed even more accommodating northern attitudes with alarm. Mainstream opinion in the North professed to want only to preserve the status quo achieved by the Missouri Compromise of 1820 and to leave slavery alone where it existed. But southerners understood as well as their northern compatriots that the status quo established in 1820 was fraught with danger for slavery, especially if some influential northerners were bent on a more aggressive antislavery policy. Although southerners reviled the abolitionists, they knew that their problems with the North extended beyond the radicals.

At the most fundamental level, southerners generally agreed that containment of slavery over time likely spelled doom for the institution and the southern way of life. Thanks to the rapid growth of the North, "the long-standing sectional equilibrium within the Union was disappearing and the South was declining into a minority status."[20] The growing North was only part of the problem. In the Upper South the commitment to slavery was dwindling. Albert Gallatin Brown of Mississippi pointed out that New York and Pennsylvania had once been slave states, too, but had sent slaves southward and then freed the remainder. "Virginia, Maryland, and the border states are now undergoing the same process," Brown warned.[21] Maintenance of the preponderant power of the slaveholders—even within the South—required the acquisition of new slave states where slavery was known to be viable. If southern expansion was blocked by the North, James Hammond of South Carolina warned, the North would "ride over us rough shod" in Congress, "proclaim freedom or something equivalent to it to our slaves and reduce us to the condition of Hayti." Southern security, Hammond declared in 1846, lay in "equality of POWER. If we do not act now, we deliberately consign . . . our children to the flames."[22] Territorial expansion was necessary, therefore, if only to bring new slave states into the Union to make up for the declining power of slavery within the South itself.

Many southern slaveholders believed slavery had to expand if it was to remain viable both economically and politically. "With Cuba and St. Domingo," one southern newspaper prophesied, "we could control the productions of the tropics, and, with them, the commerce of the world."[23] As for Mexico and the territories of the Southwest, these might not be hospitable to large-scale plantation agriculture, but slaves had been successfully employed in mines in Africa and South America, and Mexican territories were believed to contain rich deposits of gold, silver, and other valuable minerals.[24] Mississippi's Brown spoke for many when he declared, "I want Tamaulipas, Potosi, and one or two other Mexican States; and I want them all for the same reason—for the planting and spreading of slavery."[25]

Beyond politics and economics, the southern elite faced the perhaps even more frightening prospect of being penned up forever in what seemed an increasingly claustrophobic space inhabited by a burgeoning population of poor whites and enslaved blacks. The South will be "smothered and overwhelmed by a festering population that was forbidden to migrate," exclaimed one South Carolina congressman, "pent in and walled around on exhausted soil—in the midst of a people strong in idleness" and bent on "revolt and murder." Without a "safety valve" to siphon off both black slaves and poor whites looking for opportunity, the South would soon confront the most "awful calamity . . . in the widest stretch of the imagination."[26] The annexation of new territories, declared one of the leading promoters of southern expansion, was necessary for "our very existence."

The South's "superabundant slave population" could not remain penned up "within their present limits." New land must "operate as a safety valve" until "the Providence of God shall provide some natural and safe way of getting rid of this description of people."[27]

Most southerners favored expansion in order to save slavery, however, not to end it. Some southern Whigs dissented from the expansionist mainstream, for a time, in the interest of preserving national party unity. Some southern extremists like Calhoun feared that expansion beyond Texas would distract the South from the main task of defending their rights against northern tyranny; they doubted Mexico was a promising home for slavery, in any case; and they viewed expansionist efforts as "pleasing deceits . . . to quiet the South in the progress of the North to mastery in the Union."[28] Although Calhoun had agitated for Texas, he had come to believe that the South's destiny lay in protecting its sovereign rights within the Union, not in territorial expansion. But by the mid-1840s the dominant view among slaveholders and their representatives in Washington was that the South had to expand to survive. Some of the reasons had to do with intangible fears no less important than the material ones. As Martin Van Buren understood, prohibiting slavery in the new territories carried with it "a reproach to the slaveholding states. . . . Submission to it would degrade them."[29] Ever since the Missouri crisis slaveholders had argued, and had no doubt largely persuaded themselves, that the institution of slavery was both necessary *and* a positive good. They had built an entire ideology around the idea that slavery was the best possible organization of human society, for both whites and blacks. To acquiesce in containment would be to abandon this carefully constructed worldview and to adopt the northern view that slavery was, in fact, evil—too evil to be allowed to spread.[30] For reasons of politics, economics, honor, and ideology, many southerners had come to believe that if the North insisted on containing the spread of slavery, the southern states must equally insist on its expansion. And if the North succeeded in using its superior power to block southern expansion, the southern states, in order to preserve their civilization, would have no choice but to secede. When Abraham Lincoln was elected fourteen years later, on a platform promising not to end slavery but only to contain it, they did.[31]

What had emerged in the America of the 1840s was not a unifying spirit of confidence and a consensus on the nation's destiny, therefore. Rather there was a fierce clash between two diametrically opposed visions of that destiny, which in turn produced two distinct foreign policies aimed primarily not at the external world but at each other. Northern foreign policy from the 1840s until the Civil War was focused on the containment and eventual, peaceful extinction of southern slavery. Southern foreign policy centered on breaking through the barriers the North was trying to erect. The struggle was for power and survival at home, not for power or influence on the world stage. For all the talk about "manifest destiny," the nation's destiny had become subsumed by sectional destinies. The sectional conflict had turned the United States in on itself, not because Americans were isolationist or introspective but because until the question of slavery was settled, until the question of the national identity was settled, it was impossible to reach a common understanding of the nation's role in the world. The idea of a national interest, if it has any meaning at all, presupposes the existence of a common national purpose. But in the two decades before the Civil War, the United States as the world's greatest slave republic contained two well-defined and thoroughly antagonistic ideologies. How could such a nation agree on a common definition of the national interest?

The concept of manifest destiny, in fact, deliberately skirted the problem, which was why it was so useful. Its advocates tried to argue that expansion itself, whether slave or free-soil, was both in the national interest and part of the American mission to bring enlightenment to the benighted. But few in either section really agreed. Northerners embraced manifest destiny insofar as it meant the expansion of free territory. Southerners embraced it only when it meant the expansion of slave territory. The irony was that the notion of manifest destiny, so often viewed as an innovation of this era, actually drew what strength it had from the sentiments of an earlier time in American history, before the question of slavery had reared up as an insoluble national conundrum. But by the 1840s it had become absurd, a politician's trick, to talk of America's civilizing mission and the beneficent spread of its political institutions, when southerners insisted that among the blessings they would bring to newly absorbed peoples was slavery.

The drama of American foreign policy in the 1840s was not the unfolding of a single manifest destiny, therefore, but clashing visions of that destiny in the North and the South, which explains the fits and starts of American expansion in this period. The same dynamic of imperial competition between North and South that drove American expansion also limited it. The "Era of Manifest Destiny" began when it did because, in 1843, extremist southern slaveholders, unexpectedly finding themselves in control of the nation's levers of power, decided that the preservation of slavery and southern civilization required the immediate annexation of Texas. And what David M. Potter has called the "ebb tide of Manifest Destiny" came not when American restlessness had ceased, the leopard was sated, and youthful romanticism had faded. The Democratic administration of

Franklin Pierce came into office in 1853 bursting with expansionist enthusiasm, determined to pick up where Polk had left off. But Pierce and his team
of "Young Americans" were thwarted at every turn—in Cuba, in Mexico,
and in Central America—not by external resistance or by lack of means,
and certainly not by any lack of expansionist fervor, but by a North that had
itself become charged with new passion for the containment of slavery.

The Southern Dream of Tropical Empire

THE CATALYST for that renewed northern determination was, fittingly, a
battle not over foreign policy or manifest destiny but over the future of
slavery in the American heartland. In 1853 the rising young star of the
northern Democracy, Stephen Douglas, introduced legislation to organize
the Nebraska territory, a large swath of the old Louisiana Purchase west of
Missouri and Iowa, into a new state. Douglas's aims were fully in keeping
with northern expansionist ideology: he hoped to run a transcontinental
railroad linking the nation's heartland with the new states on the Pacific
Coast, with a terminus, of course, at Chicago in his home state.

But the Illinois senator's grand expansionist scheme collided with
southern slaveholder anxieties. The Nebraska territory lay north of 36°30'
and therefore under the terms of the 1820 compromise would have had to
enter the Union as a free state. Missouri's powerful senator David R. Atchison, "the most outspoken defender of southern rights in the Senate," declared
that he would sooner see Nebraska "sink in hell" than allow it to join the
Union on those terms. Missouri, he feared, would be "surrounded . . . by
free territory," and with the "emissaries of abolitionists around us" slavery
in the state would soon be at risk.[32] Southern leaders demanded that the
Nebraska territory be organized without any restrictions on slavery, and
Douglas, ambitious not only for expansion but also for southern support in
the coming presidential election, acquiesced. His Nebraska Act in 1854
organized the territory into two new states, Nebraska in the north along the
border with Iowa, and Kansas in the south along the border with Missouri,
with the implication that the latter might, like its neighbor, choose slavery.
Employing the doctrine of "popular sovereignty," which in the Compromise of 1850 had allowed the residents of California and other former
Mexican territories to choose whether to enter the Union as free or slave
states, Douglas proposed to leave it to the people of both territories to
decide for themselves. This was still not good enough for Atchison and his
southern colleagues. They offered their support for Douglas's proposal only

when he agreed to include in it an explicit repeal of the thirty-four-year-old Missouri Compromise.

Douglas's Nebraska Act proved a decisive turn on the road to civil war. The repeal of the Missouri Compromise was more than northern Whigs, and most northern Democrats, could stand. Not only did it mean a southern breakout from northern containment; to many northerners, most notably Abraham Lincoln, it seemed a first step toward the eventual introduction of slavery throughout the nation. While the Missouri Compromise had placed slavery on the path to eventual extinction, Lincoln warned, the Nebraska Act put it "on the high road to extension and perpetuity."[33] Douglas and some conservative northern Whigs like Daniel Webster might argue that the laws of nature would keep slavery out of regions that were climatically inhospitable to large-scale plantation farming, but Lincoln and other northerners disagreed. As modern nineteenth-century liberals convinced of mankind's ability to mold and conquer nature, they refused to be calmed by what Lincoln called this "lullaby argument." Surely Kansas could be made as fit for slavery as neighboring Missouri. But beyond that, who could be sure a way might not be found to extend slavery northward? The cotton gin had revived a dying slave institution in the 1790s. Some new human invention might make slave labor profitable beyond the cotton plantation.

The only reliable bar to slavery in the North, Lincoln believed, was the moral conviction that it was evil and the codification of that moral principle in American law. Douglas's "popular sovereignty" offered no escape from moral choice. If blacks were men, and Lincoln insisted that even southerners acknowledged they were, then they possessed natural rights equal to those of all other men. To deprive them of those rights was despotism, not self-government.[34] Lincoln, like John Quincy Adams at the time of the Missouri crisis, appealed for ultimate guidance not to the American Constitution but to the Declaration of Independence. "Our republican robe is soiled," he declared in 1854. "Let us repurify it. . . . Let us re-adopt the Declaration of Independence. . . . If we do this, we shall not only have saved the Union; but we shall have so saved it, as to make, and to keep it, forever worthy of the saving."[35]

The Nebraska Act passed Congress, thanks to the reluctant backing of the Democratic president, Franklin Pierce, and to the Democrats' strict party discipline. But the act gave "the coup de grace to the intersectional two-party system."[36] The Whig Party fractured and disintegrated, never to reappear. For northern "Conscience" Whigs like William Seward, the party was "now manifestly no longer able to maintain and carry forward, alone and unaided, the great revolution that it inaugurated"—the revolution, that is, against the slaveholders.[37] The Democratic Party fared little better. Nearly half of northern Democrats in the House broke ranks to oppose the measure; the rest were almost all cast out of office by angry voters. In the wake of the passage of Douglas's legislation, northern Whigs, northern Democrats, and members of the Free-Soil Party joined to form the Republican Party. The new party's platform was built around opposition to the Nebraska Act, restoration of the Missouri Compromise, and above all the rigid containment of southern slavery.

The North-South imperial conflict in the meantime moved from the halls of Congress to the fields of Kansas. Seward was among the first to declare war. "Since there is no escaping your challenge," he told southern senators, "I accept it in behalf of the cause of freedom. We will engage in competition for the virgin soil of Kansas, and God give the victory to the side which is stronger in numbers as it is in right."[38] Southerners responded in kind. "We are playing for a mighty stake," Missouri's Atchison declared. "If we win we carry slavery to the Pacific Ocean, if we fail we lose Missouri Arkansas Texas and all the territories."[39] There followed a proxy war for control of the territory or, more specifically, for control of the voting process that would determine the slave status of the new state. Northeastern merchants provided money and arms to farmers from neighboring states to settle in Kansas and vote for a free-soil constitution. Atchison led an invasion of "border ruffians" from Missouri, urging them to "mark every scoundrel among you that is the least tainted with free-soilism, or abolitionism, and exterminate him."[40] By early 1856 Kansas was divided, with two territorial governments representing the slave- and free-state interests. In May of that year pro-slave Missourians, armed with five cannons, attacked the free-soil "capital" of Lawrence, destroyed two newspaper offices, and burned the home of the free-soil governor. The South cheered the "Sack of Lawrence" and cheered again two days later when South Carolina congressman Preston Brooks, furious at a vituperative antisouthern speech given by Charles Sumner, split the Massachusetts congressman's head open with his cane on the Senate floor. Northerners outraged by "Bleeding Kansas" and "Bleeding Sumner" howled for retaliation, and in the dead of night on May 24, 1856, John Brown, a northern abolitionist guerrilla in Kansas, seized five pro-slavery settlers from their cabins and executed them with an axe. The conflict between North and South had turned bloody on the nation's midwestern periphery. In the end, violence in Kansas gave way again to diplomacy in Washington, and much to the South's fury, Kansas entered the Union as a free state.

Blocked in the north, the South now turned back to what had always seemed the more promising region for slave expansion, the tropics. Southern foreign policy in the late 1830s and early 1840s had produced the annexation of Texas and the acquisition of territory in northern Mexico. Having been robbed of California, however, southern foreign policy in the 1850s aimed next at the acquisition of Mexican territory south of the Rio Grande. During Polk's war against Mexico in the mid-1840s, the strongest support for taking and incorporating all of Mexico had come from Democrats in the Southwest who saw in Mexico "tropical turf for slaveholders."[41] A conviction that Mexican territory could be hospitable to slavery combined with the usual southern fear that free Mexican territory posed a risk to American slave states on Mexico's borders. Indeed, no sooner had the United States acquired Texas than southerners began demanding a more aggressive policy toward Mexico. The more southern slavery expanded, the more it had to expand to defend recently acquired slave territory. "Negroes are running off daily" to Mexican territory, one Texan complained. "Something must be done for the protection of slave property in this state."[42]

Southerners often spoke the language of manifest destiny, insisting that "[o]ur people will go South among the Mexicans and Spaniards, and will carry with them the love of our civilization and our liberty."[43] But the civilization they intended to carry with them was a southern civilization that included bondage. Southerners warned of the danger of European meddling in Mexico, and to justify expansion Presidents Polk, Buchanan, and others even resurrected the very Monroe Doctrine that Buchanan and other Jacksonians had tried to eviscerate in the 1820s. But the European meddling they chiefly feared, as earlier in Texas, was meddling against slavery. Mississippi's John Quitman warned that Mexico was a "waif" that would eventually be conquered by "some stronger power"—that is, by an abolitionist Great Britain or France.[44] Some southerners demanded transit rights across Mexican territory to build a transcontinental railroad to compete with northern rails pushing across the Great Plains. Some wanted to carve new slave states out of Mexico to balance the new free states coming into the Union in the Northwest. And some were already looking ahead to possible disunion and wanted Mexican territory to enhance the power of a future independent southern confederacy.[45]

Under southern pressure, successive U.S. administrations in the late 1840s and '50s worked to acquire more of Mexico. The Whig administrations of Zachary Taylor and Millard Fillmore, following the antislavery dictates of their powerful northern constituents, were predictably less ardent in their pursuit of more southern territory than the southern-dominated Democrats. It took the Democratic administration of Franklin Pierce to compel Mexico to give up more territory for a southern transcontinental railroad. Under the Gadsden Treaty of 1853, Mexico ceded fifty-four thousand square miles of additional territory in what became southern Arizona and southern New Mexico, in exchange for an American payment of $10 million. The Gadsden Purchase was the quintessential product of the North-South imperial conflict, in this case the race to the Pacific; "the pro-slavery element in Congress was struggling to get the railroad built through southern territory in order to hamper the settlement along the northern routes of free-soil farmers."[46] But it did not slake the southern thirst for Mexican territory. From 1857 through 1860 Democratic president James Buchanan pressed Mexico for still more land cessions, arguing that the "great laws of self-preservation," by which he meant the preservation of slavery, required further expansion.

Southern slaveholders were even more determined to annex Cuba. From the end of the Polk administration to the election of Lincoln in 1860, acquiring Cuba became a primary southern preoccupation. These distinctly southern ambitions were portrayed, of course, as timeless national ambitions, with some justification. The desire for Cuba had roots stretching back to the early days of the republic. Jefferson had foreseen the day when Cuba would fall "like a ripe fruit" into the American lap. John Quincy Adams had insisted that the law of gravity would inevitably draw Cuba into the American orbit, and that the United States could not refuse it when it came. Viewed simply as a matter of territorial and economic interests, the case for the acquisition of Cuba was as strong as that for many other American territorial acquisitions.

Whatever reasons might normally have driven the United States to seek Cuba, however, in the 1850s it was widely understood in both the North and the South that the driving force behind the Cuban annexation movement was the southern slaveholding interest. It was no accident that America's pursuit of Cuba was most ardent when the southern-dominated Democratic Party held the White House. The South's desire to increase its power within the Union blended with the fear that slavery might soon be abolished in Cuba if the United States did not act quickly. An island led by emancipated slaves—another Haiti, less than a hundred miles from American shores—would pose a grave threat to American slavery.

This fear was more justified in the case of Cuba than it had been in Texas. British diplomatic pressures against Cuban slavery "reached an all-time high in the early 1850s," when Lord Palmerston issued a "virtual ultimatum" to Spain insisting that it abide by its agreements to suppress the lucrative slave trade. British officials thereby hoped, among other things, to head off American expansionist ambitions, for as Palmerston pointed out to the Spanish minister in London, emancipation of Cuban blacks "would create a most powerful element of resistance to any scheme for annexing Cuba to the United States, where slavery exists."[47] The Spanish government appeared to be taking British pressure seriously,[48] and from the late 1840s onward southern slaveholders grew increasingly desperate to preempt the British plot. In 1848 Polk's secretary of state, James Buchanan, worked on a plan to purchase Cuba from Spain for $100 million. But the Spanish government was not interested in selling, and the plan was shelved by the Whig administrations of Zachary Taylor and Millard Fillmore and their secretary of state, Daniel Webster. The South would have to wait until the Democrats controlled the White House again to make another attempt at Cuba.

Between 1849 and 1852 southerners placed their hopes in the Cuban "filibuster," Narciso López, who like other Creoles favored Cuba's annexation to the United States precisely to prevent emancipation of its slave population. Despite Fillmore's efforts to preserve American neutrality, López's four expeditions received vital support from the South, including assistance from Mississippi's governor, John Quitman. López's capture and execution by the Spanish government in 1851 infuriated the South, and Fillmore's timid approach to expansionism in Cuba and Mexico became a prominent issue in the 1852 campaign and damaged southern Whigs. When Franklin Pierce was elected, carrying thirteen out of fifteen southern states, the "Democrats' latest northern man with southern leanings"[49] declared in his inaugural address that "[t]he policy of my administration will not be controlled by any timid forebodings of evil from expansion. . . . [O]ur attitude as a nation and our position on the globe render the acquisition of certain possessions not within our jurisdiction eminently important for our protection."[50]

The election of Pierce placed southern expansionists and their northern supporters more firmly in control of American foreign policy than at any time since the days of Tyler, Upshur, and Calhoun. Jefferson Davis, who eight years later would become president of the Confederacy, was named secretary of war. The remainder of the cabinet, and much of the American diplomatic corps in Europe, was filled by men with a willingness to look out for southern interests and a proven commitment to Cuban annexation. The dispatch to Madrid of Louisiana senator Pierre Soulé, one of many southerners who had contemplated secession after the Compromise of 1850, was a sign of the new administration's "commitment both to expansion and, more generally, to an easing of Southern nationalists' concerns."[51] The Virginian John Y. Mason was named minister to France. And although the minister to Great Britain, James Buchanan, the secretary of state, William Marcy, and the minister to Portugal, John O'Sullivan, were northerners, they were reliable party men willing to accommodate the South on matters of vital southern interest such as Cuba.

In the North defenders and promoters of Cuban annexation spoke the language of trade and manifest destiny, but in diplomatic channels the Pierce administration made clear that the main issue was slavery. The "deep and vital interest" of the United States, Buchanan explained to British officials, concerned "the condition of the colored population" in Cuba. The island was "within sight of our shores and should a black Government like that of Hayti be established there, it would endanger the peace and the domestic security of a large and important portion of our people." If a slave uprising occurred in Cuba as a result of British policies, Buchanan warned, "no human power could prevent us from interfering in favor of the Creoles."[52] Buchanan's argument was not the "spread-eagled" idealism of manifest destiny. It was blunt southern realism: the foreign policy of self-interest and self-preservation.

The South's worst fears soon began to materialize. After the execution of Narciso López, former governor Quitman put himself in charge of filibustering efforts to liberate Cuba and attach it to the United States. A veteran of the war with Mexico, an opponent of the Compromise of 1850, and one of the earliest advocates of southern secession, Quitman aimed not only to prevent the emancipation of slaves in Cuba but to bring it into the Union as "a means of strengthening the South" by adding a new slave state to balance California.[53] As Quitman made plans for the invasion of Cuba, he had the full support of several members of Pierce's cabinet.[54]

News of Quitman's plan, however, pushed the Spanish government to take extreme measures. In 1853 Spanish authorities in Cuba bent to British pressure and promised to crack down hard on the slave trade. More alarming still for the American South, the Spanish colonial government embarked on a partial emancipation of Cuban slaves, decreeing that all slaves brought into Cuba after 1835—a large portion of the total slave population—should be freed. The captain-general of Cuba then announced his intention to transform the slave system into a system of free labor. He encouraged racial intermarriage and organized newly freed blacks into a militia. Quitman suddenly faced the prospect that an "invasion of Cuba might involve grim fighting against embattled slaves defending their new freedom."[55]

The so-called Africanization program in Cuba sent the South into a panic, and southerners regardless of party united behind immediate annexation to prevent emancipation. The radical secessionist Quitman warned that the creation of "a negro or mongrel empire" near the southern border would inspire slave revolts throughout the Deep South.[56] Even Whigs who had opposed southward expansion, like Georgia's Alexander Stephens, took fright at the prospect of another Haiti. "We must and will have [Cuba]," Stephens declared. "We can not permit them to go on with their policy of filling it with Africans first."[57] Politicians across the South called for war. Mississippi senator John Slidell, the chairman of the Senate Foreign Relations Committee, proposed an outright repeal of the neutrality laws in order to make way for Quitman's private invasion of Cuba. The *Richmond Enquirer* declared in the summer of 1854 that "the acquisition of Cuba is the only measure of policy in regard to which the people of the South may feel any special and present interest."[58] The Pierce administration agreed. Assistant Secretary of State A. Dudley Mann, a Virginian and close friend of Jefferson Davis, wrote a southern congressman that Cuba was "essential to the South both in a political and geographical point of view."[59]

Unfortunately for the Pierce administration, the northern wing of the Democratic Party would not, could not, support an intervention to save slavery in Cuba. Especially after passage of the Nebraska Act had inflamed northern opinion against the "slave power," Cuban annexation was political poison for northern Democrats. Therefore Pierce backed away from armed aggression against Cuba and looked for another alternative.[60] In the fall of 1854 Secretary of State Marcy instructed Pierce's proannexationist ministers in Europe—Buchanan, Soulé, and Mason—to propose a strategy short of war for gaining Cuba from Spain, preferably by purchase but if necessary by finding some other means to "detach" the island from Spanish control. Buchanan and his colleagues went a bit further. In a diplomatic memorandum that became famous as the Ostend Manifesto, they warned that if Cuba were Africanized "with all its attendant horror to the white race," Americans would be "unworthy of our gallant forefathers" not to intervene. If Cuba "endanger[s] our internal peace and the existence of our cherished Union," then "by every law human and Divine, we shall be justified in wresting it from Spain, if we possess the power."[61] The Ostend Manifesto expressed the essence of the southern foreign policy of expansionism abroad in defense of slavery at home.[62]

When news of the memorandum leaked into the press, it became an election-year cause célèbre, providing a significant new plank in the platform of the recently founded Republican Party. Six years later, in the election of 1860, Abraham Lincoln was still railing against the Ostend Manifesto as a "highwayman's plea" worthy only of "shame and dishonor."[63] So furious was the assault from embarrassed northern Democrats that the Pierce administration had to disown the Cuba plan in order to maintain party unity. But it was too late. Damaged in part by the manifesto, though more by the Kansas-Nebraska Act, Democrats were trounced throughout the North in the 1854 congressional elections.

Pierce's decision to support the Nebraska bill, on the one hand, while retreating from an aggressive Cuba policy, on the other, struck many southerners and their northern sympathizers as a bad bargain. Few southerners believed slavery was likely to take hold in Kansas—despite the best efforts of some southern toughs to seize control of the territory. But Cuba was certain to join the Union as a valuable new slave territory. Secretary of State Marcy complained that the "Nebraska question has sadly shattered our party in all the free states and deprived it of the strength" that "could have been much more profitably used for the acquisition of Cuba."[64]

The South didn't give up, however. For southerners the failure to acquire Cuba was proof of the North's determination to crush their power. After the abortive annexation efforts of the early 1850s, no northern Democrat aspiring to the party's nomination for the presidency could afford to be on the wrong side of Cuban annexation and Caribbean expansion more generally. In 1856 Buchanan rode to the top of the Democratic ticket partly on the strength of his role in shaping a pro-southern policy toward Cuba.[65] Mississippi's Senator John Slidell, a leading backer of Cuban annexation and the earlier filibustering efforts, later a prominent official in the Confederate States of America, became his campaign manager. Buchanan ran in 1856 on a platform calling for American "ascendancy in the Gulf of Mexico"—a euphemism for the acquisition of Cuba and for other southern imperial visions.[66] In 1859 he asked Congress for $30 million to begin negotiations with Spain.

Cuba remained a paramount issue right up to the outbreak of the Civil War. Indeed, for an increasing number of southerners, it became the price for continued allegiance to the Union. It was to be a vital down payment on a future slave empire stretching southward into the Caribbean, Central America, and beyond. Alexander Stephens declared that "we are looking out toward Chihuahua, Sonora, and other parts of Mexico. Where are to be our ultimate limits, time alone can determine. But of all these acquisitions, the most important to the whole country is that of Cuba."[67] In early 1860 an Alabama newspaper declared, "Our India lies in the tropics. There will we find inexhaustible sources of wealth and power, which none can wrest from our grasps." The editors wanted to "surround the Gulf of Mexico with great and prosperous States, all bound to us by the ties of interest and identity of institutions."[68] Louisiana's governor insisted that if Cuba were annexed to the United States, Havana "would speedily become the great entrepot of southern commerce, and in a few years be the rival of New York itself. . . . And she would be a southern city, a slaveholding city."[69] In 1854 the *Richmond Enquirer* noted, "These two great valleys of the Amazon and the Mississippi" were "possessed by two governments of the earth most deeply interested in African slavery—Brazil and the United States." Between those two valleys lay a vast region "under the plastic hand of a beneficent Providence." How was that region to developed? "With black labor and white skill."[70]

During the secession crisis after Lincoln's election in 1860, Cuba became a key intersectional bargaining chip. Stephen Douglas, desperate to court southern favor without alienating his northern supporters, saw Cuba and southern expansion as the "glue" to unite "warring Democratic factions."[71] As late as December 1860 Douglas was proposing a plan to bring Mexico into the Union as a slave state in order to keep the South from seceding.[72] The bipartisan and bisectional congressional committee established to negotiate a compromise also fastened on Cuba as the best means of pulling the South back into the Union. The famous Crittenden Compromise, devised by the Kentucky Whig John J. Crittenden, aimed to satisfy the North by reestablishing the Missouri Compromise and its prohibition of slavery above 36°30'. Among its many concessions to the South, the Crittenden plan also proposed to guarantee slavery in perpetuity in all territories south of that latitude, territories "now held, or hereafter acquired." This "hereafter clause" was the vital concession to the South, for it officially opened the way for annexation of Cuba, and of other tropical lands, as new slave territory.

A number of northerners, including Seward, seemed prepared to consider this compromise as a way to avert secession and war. But President-elect Lincoln rejected it. From Springfield, Illinois, he instructed his supporters, "Entertain no proposition for a compromise in regard to the *extension* of slavery."[73] Accepting the "hereafter clause," Lincoln insisted, would "lose us everything we gained by the election." Acceptance of the clause would be followed by "[f]ilibustering for [territory] South of us" and then by the organization of new slave states in the tropics. The "hereafter clause" would "put us again on the high-road to a slave empire." If the North surrendered on this point, Lincoln declared, "it is the end of us."[74] Lincoln was willing to compromise on other issues. He even permitted Seward to strike a deal preserving the Fugitive Slave Law. But Lincoln demanded that Seward make "no compromise which *assists* or *permits* the extension of slavery."[75]

Lincoln's stand on the "hereafter clause" just about destroyed any chance for compromise with the South in the difficult winter of 1860–61. His willingness to take that stand reflected his commitment to the northern strategy of containment. Few Americans were more passionately devoted to preservation of the Union than Lincoln. But like John Quincy Adams four decades earlier, Lincoln would risk secession and even war rather than countenance the transformation of the Union, Jefferson's "empire for liberty," into an empire for slavery. And that was the future that Lincoln and other northerners envisioned if southern expansion were permitted.[76]

It is, of course, impossible to know with certainty what course the South might have taken had Lincoln agreed to the "hereafter clause" in the Crittenden Compromise or, alternatively, had he permitted the South to secede and establish itself as an independent nation. But there can be no doubt about the ambitions of the South's leaders. Even before the secession crisis Jefferson Davis and others had begun to view Cuba, Mexico, and Central America as vital to the security and economic viability of a new, independent southern nation and empire. Davis commented on the "indispensable" importance of Cuba to a South "formed into a separate confederacy."[77] Some southerners even argued that secession from the Union was necessary precisely to free the South to make the territorial acquisitions that were blocked by the North. A seceded South, they argued, could "extend her institutions over Mexico, Cuba, San Domingo and other West India Islands and California, and thereby become the most powerful Republic that ever the sun shone upon."[78] When the Confederacy was born, its constitution opened the way for the acquisition of "new territory" and explicitly remedied the defect in the Constitution of the United States and in the old Northwest Ordinance by declaring that in any new territory that might be acquired "the institution of Negro slavery, as it now exists in the Confederate States, shall be recognized and protected by Congress and by the Territorial government."[79]

The outbreak of war prevented the South from pursuing this destiny. To avoid alienating the European powers and prevent their siding with the North, southern leaders had to set aside expansionist plans during the war. Nor could the South spare the forces required to invade Cuba and Mexico while it was locked in mortal combat with the North. "The dream of a Caribbean empire became one of the first casualties of the Civil War."[80] But this does not mean that the South would not have returned to its dream after a Civil War victory.

There could not be much doubt that a South permitted to remain in the Union would have pursued its dream of a slave empire, wielding the full power of the federal government with the sanction of Crittenden's "here-after clause." The southern policy of slave expansion toward the tropics would have become the national policy. One can only speculate what role the United States, thus constituted, might have played in world affairs as it reached the pinnacles of power at the end of the nineteenth century, or won-der "what the twentieth century would be like if the United States had entered it as first and foremost of totalitarian powers."[81] And indeed, no less a figure than Adolf Hitler would later reflect on the road not taken by the United States and lament that "the beginnings of a great new social order based on the principle of slavery and inequality were destroyed by [the Civil War], and with them also the embryo of a future truly great America."[82]

CHAPTER 9

Beyond the National Interest

The rights asserted by our forefathers were not peculiar to themselves. They were the common rights of mankind.

—William Seward

We are not engaged in a Quixotic fight for the rights of man. Our struggle is for inherited rights. . . . We are conservative.

—Jefferson Davis

The Foreign Policy of the North: Beyond Slavery

ABRAHAM LINCOLN and many other northerners were determined not to permit this particular manifest destiny to unfold. Rather than allow the Union to become an all-powerful vehicle for slave expansion, which they saw as but the first step toward the eventual submission of the North to southern dictates, Lincoln and others were prepared to fulfill John Quincy Adams's apocalyptic vision and fight a war to purge the nation of its "great stain of evil." Only with the creation of a new Union committed to the principles of the Declaration of Independence, Lincoln believed, could the United States fulfill its true destiny in the world. "Liberty has yet her greatest warfare to wage in this Hemisphere," John Quincy Adams had declared.[1] Struggles for liberty elsewhere depended on the triumph of liberty at home.

Not all northerners agreed that slavery was an insuperable obstacle to the achievement of America's destiny. Northern Democrats like Stephen Douglas, Lewis Cass, and John O'Sullivan made their peace with southern slavery and pursued their vision of the national destiny as if nothing in the condition of American society hindered them. If American expansion meant slave expansion, so be it: Cuba and Mexico were worthy prizes for the nation, even with slaves. If building a great transcontinental railroad along a northern route required repealing the Missouri Compromise, then let it be repealed. These northern Democrats hoped they could have it all: the advancement of northern civilization and northern dreams for their constituents, and the protection and advancement of southern slave civilization for their powerful fellow party members in the South. O'Sullivan's manifest destiny perfectly encapsulated a grand national vision that deliberately evaded the conflict over slavery. He frankly admitted that for reasons of party unity he had no choice but "to stand aloof from the delicate and dangerous topic of Slavery and Abolition."[2]

For most northerners, however, and especially for northern and border-state Whigs, the problem could not be so easily wished away. Most northern Whigs believed it was impossible, and certainly undesirable, for both northern and southern civilization to advance together in equal measure. If national growth also meant the growth of slavery, it would be better if the nation did not grow at all.

This was one source of what many historians have misinterpreted as the "conservative" attitude of many northern and border-state Whigs toward expansion and toward the conduct of American foreign policy generally.[3] While the Democratic Party, dominated by slaveholder interests, became in the 1840s and '50s the party of enthusiastic expansionism, the northern-dominated Whigs preferred "a diminished profile in international affairs" and warned "against the perils of empire-building."[4] "Our augmentation is by growth, not by acquisition," Daniel Webster declared, "by internal development, not by external accession."[5]

The Whigs of the 1840s and early 1850s were, in some respects, the more conservative of the two national parties. Although their nationalist liberalism was by definition more progressive than the Democrats' agrarian, states' rights conservatism, the Whigs also harbored a conservative mistrust of what seemed to them the dangerously radical, class-based democracy of Jacksonianism. During the Jacksonian era many Whigs became concerned with maintaining an "ordered liberty," the protection of property from the mob, and the defense of an organic society based on the "harmony of interests."[6]

But on matters of foreign policy, Whig conservatism owed less to conservative principles than to the unique circumstances of the time. The Whigs were constrained, just as the North as a whole was constrained, by the politics of sectional rivalry. If the national Whig Party threw its support behind southern slave expansion, the northern, antislavery wing of "Conscience" Whigs would revolt and splinter the party.[7] But if national Whig policy tilted toward this powerful northern wing's ideal of expansion, supporting territorial growth but insisting that new territory come into the Union only as free states, then southern Whigs would either have to break party ranks or be crushed by southern Democrats claiming that they were traitors to southern slaveholder interests. The option of embracing O'Sullivan's manifest destiny in all directions was simply not available to the northern-dominated Whigs as it was to the southern-dominated Democrats.

For Whigs the safer answer to sectional division was to oppose territorial expansion altogether: no new territory in the South, where it might lead to the admission of slave states and thus alienate northern Whig voters; but no aggressive pursuit of territory in the Northwest, either, since northern expansion of free territory without compensating southern expansion of slave territory would destroy the Whig Party in the South. John Quincy Adams and other "Conscience" Whigs might belligerently clamor for "All of Oregon" in the 1840s, therefore, even as they opposed a southern war of conquest for Mexican territory. Their antislavery position was more important to them than the health of the Whig Party. But mainstream Whigs interested in party unity, and also in national unity, opposed the aggressive pursuit of the Oregon territory with almost as much vigor as they opposed the conquest of Mexico. The peculiar result was that the aggressive "All of Oregon" policy contained in the Democratic platform of 1844, specifically designed to appeal to the North, was eventually defeated by an alliance of northern Whigs and a united South. Northern and border state Whigs joined southerners in both parties who, as the Georgia Whig Robert Toombs put it, didn't want "a foot of Oregon or an acre of any other territory, especially without 'niggers.'"[8] In the end, Daniel Webster and Henry Clay joined hands with Toombs and John C. Calhoun in opposing an aggressive Oregon policy. But this said more about the imperatives of party and slavery politics than about Whig attitudes toward expansion.

There was nothing inherently antiexpansionist in the doctrines of northern Whiggery. Whigs in both North and South in the 1840s and early 1850s argued that it was better to consolidate and improve the nation within existing boundaries than to expand it: "You have a Sparta," declared Webster. "Embellish it!"[9] But the idea that the American "Sparta" could not improve and expand at the same time—could not develop "qualitatively" across time and "quantitatively" across space—reflected a change of heart for Whigs like Webster. In the 1810s and '20s Adams, Clay, and Webster had believed that building the American System at home was entirely consistent with territorial expansion and an ambitious, ideological foreign policy.

Indeed, they were two sides of the same progressive nationalist coin. Clay and Webster reversed their views in the 1840s because the kind of expansion the Democrats were promoting was slave expansion, and that kind of expansion, in their eyes, *was* the enemy of national improvement. For Whig devotees of the northern free-labor ideology, the expansion of slavery damaged the economic health of the nation and weakened the moral fiber of the people. The problem with manifest destiny in the 1840s and '50s, as New Hampshire's John Hale explained, was that it "always traveled south."[10]

Northern Whigs expressed few qualms about northern expansion, where slavery was unlikely to take hold. Charles Sumner of Massachusetts believed that the United States was "bound to extend its institutions and its government over the entire North American continent," and he spent most of his political career, before and after the Civil War, eyeing Canada as a great prize to be annexed to the United States as soon as circumstances permitted.[11] John Quincy Adams berated Polk for ceding the British too much territory in Oregon, even as he excoriated him for taking too much territory from Mexico. Nor, Adams claimed, did he necessarily oppose southern expansion, if it could be achieved without expanding slavery. During the controversy over Texas annexation, when his opponents reminded him of his efforts as president to purchase Texas, he responded that he had never objected to "the acquisition of Texas" itself. Indeed, he thought it might bring great advantages to the nation, so long as it was "purged from that foul infection."[12] Webster, though opposed to the annexation of Cuba under the prevailing circumstances, nevertheless regarded the island much as John Quincy Adams and Jefferson had, as "large and important" in terms of commerce and for the United States "the most interesting portion of the Spanish empire."[13] William Henry Seward opposed southern efforts to acquire Cuba, but not because he didn't want Cuba to become part of the United States. It was the "immediate and early annexation" of Cuba that Seward opposed, for "until slavery [has] ceased to counteract the workings of nature in that beautiful island," he could never support its annexation.[14]

Far from being philosophically opposed to expansion, the northern Whig Party of the 1840s was home to some of the most ambitious Americans of that or any other generation—and none more so than the leading "Conscience" Whig and Republican Party stalwart, William Seward. A disciple of John Quincy Adams, he entertained expansionist ambitions that exceeded even Adams's bold vision. He predicted in 1853 that the "borders of the federal republic . . . shall be extended so that it shall greet the sun when he touches the tropics, and when he sends his gleaming rays toward the polar circle, and shall include even distant islands in either ocean."

Looking north, he congratulated Canadians for "building states to be here-after admitted to the American union." Looking to Russian settlements in the Pacific Northwest, he predicted that they " 'will yet become outposts' of the United States," as indeed they did when he acquired Alaska in 1867. Looking southward, he imagined a day when the capital of the new American empire might be located somewhere in Mexico.[15]

Seward was an unabashed American expansionist, and like Alexander Hamilton and other nationalists of the early republic, he looked to the ever-expanding British Empire as a model to be emulated. Americans and Britons, he pointed out, were "of the same stock, and have the common passion for domination." Gauging America's economic growth in the 1850s, he frequently insisted the time had come for the United States to take its rightful place as the world's dominant power. The American people were "entering on a career of wealth, power and expansion." The first step was to gain mastery of the continent, but this was only a prelude to achieving global hegemony. "Control of this continent" was to be "in a very few years the controlling influence of the world."[16]

In the 1840s and '50s, northerners with an expansive vision of America's role in the world believed that the nation's vocation, and the ultimate source of its global power, lay in an expanding global commerce. Seward believed that "the nation that draws the most materials and provisions from the earth, fabricates the most, and sells the most of productions and fabrics to foreign nations, must be, and will be, the great power of the earth." The belief in the power of commerce to tame the world was as old as the republic, of course, but whereas for the founding generation American global dominance through commerce was little more than a dream, for men of Seward's generation it was an approaching reality. The United States by the 1850s was clearly on its way to becoming one of the world's foremost economic powers. The aim of American foreign policy, Seward declared in 1853, should be mastery of "the commerce of the world, which is the empire of the world."[17]

Seward envisioned a form of American imperium that would be welcomed by weaker foreign nations. American global influence need not depend on the perpetual military subjugation of overseas colonies. That aspect of the British imperial model he rejected as both immoral and impractical. While the use of force might sometimes be necessary to gain American traders equal access to foreign markets, America's real and lasting influence would come through the power of trade itself—"political supremacy follows commercial ascendancy." Just as commerce united Americans across sectional and partisan divides and attracted their allegiance to the federal government, so commerce could attract distant peoples to the United States and bring them within the sway of American influence. For instead of being victims of American conquest, they would be partners in American prosperity. Instead of becoming mere colonial subjects, as they were in the British Empire, American commercial dominance would "spare their corporate existence and individuality" and thus make them voluntary recipients of American power and protection. As American commercial influence widened, this natural attraction would only increase, until the United States had achieved a true and lasting "commercial hegemony."[18]

Unlike southern imperialism, which was driven toward aggressive conquest by defensive anxiety for the future of slavery, Seward's approach was more patient, reflecting the northern civilization's confidence in its own superiority and inevitable triumph. The United States, he argued, was "sure to be aggrandized by peace" more successfully than by war. He rejected the South's "lust of conquest, this seizing the unripened fruit, which, if left alone, would fall of itself."[19] His commercial approach to empire did not mean the United States could sit back passively and await its imperial destiny—sometimes force would be necessary to pry loose the hinges of locked doors—but it did mean that most gains could be accomplished by the steady, peaceful expansion of trade.

For Seward, as for John Quincy Adams and many other northerners, the most inviting target for American commercial expansion was Asia. With the acquisition of California and Oregon, the United States had become "practically the only real Power there is that dwells upon the Pacific Ocean."[20] Almost half a century before Brooks Adams, Alfred Thayer Mahan, and Halford Mackinder declared that the future of human civilization depended on the outcome of the imperial struggle for control of China, Seward and other Whigs had already concluded that Asia was the "new theatre of human activity." If the United States could extend its power "to the Pacific ocean and grasp the great commerce of the east," he predicted, it would become "the greatest of existing states, greater than any that has ever existed."[21] For the moment, Great Britain occupied this lofty perch atop the new international economic order. Britain was "completing a vast web of ocean steam navigation, based on postage and commerce, that will connect all the European ports in the West Indies, all the ports of Asia and Oceania, with her great commercial capital. Thus the world is to become a great commercial system, ramified by a thousand nerves projecting from the one head at London."[22] Seward's goal was to meet and surpass the British, in a "competition depending not on armies nor even on wealth," where the British were still superior, "but directly on invention and industry," which were America's strengths.[23] And the battleground would be Asia. Seward believed the path to greatness lay "through the Manillas, and along the Indian coast, and beyond the Persian gulf, to the far-off Mozambique."[24] Having once gained control of the trade of Asia, the United States, fortunately situated between Asia and Europe, would become the nexus for the commerce of the entire world, with New York City—not London—at the center of it all.

To the extent that northern Whigs were able to carry out any foreign policy in the two decades before the Civil War, it was the expansion of American commerce, especially in Asia. This was the policy least constrained by sectional schism. Pressures for commercial expansion came not only from the Northeast but also from southern and western farmers in search of markets for their produce. Andrew Jackson negotiated more trade treaties with foreign powers in every corner of the world than John Quincy Adams, and he was quick to use American naval power to express disapproval when he felt the United States was being unfairly treated.[25] Still, it was the northern-dominated Whig administrations that gave the most emphasis to commercial expansion, especially in Asia, and it was the Whigs who accomplished the most. Even the hapless Tyler administration managed to fulfill some of Seward's grand ambitions. Following Great Britain's thrashing of China in the Opium War of 1841–42, a conflict in which the United States stood firmly behind the British, Tyler dispatched Caleb Cushing to negotiate favorable terms of trade with China. The Treaty of Wanghia, signed in 1844, gave the United States most-favored-nation trade status in China and became the cornerstone of America's "Open Door" doctrine a half century later.[26] The Cushing mission set the stage for the later opening of American trade with Japan. In 1842, when the Hawaiian government felt its independence threatened by Great Britain and France, Tyler applied the noncolonization principles of the Monroe Doctrine to the Pacific and marked Hawaii off as an American protectorate in all but name. Northern foreign policy, like American foreign policy in the coming century, aimed at the creation of a vast global network of communication and trade, with some key strategic outposts in places like Hawaii. As secretary of state after the Civil War, Seward would obtain the Midway Islands as another link in the chain stretching out to the Asian market.

The case of Hawaii, however, showed how even northern ambitions for commercial expansion could be blunted by the sectional conflict. Hawaii lay below 36°30' latitude and therefore, under the terms of the Missouri Compromise, could enter the Union as a slave state. In 1854 the native

Hawaiians therefore demanded that they be allowed to bypass the normal territorial phase and be admitted immediately as a state with "the same rights, civil, political, and religious, as are enjoyed by" the state of Massachusetts—in other words, without slavery.[27] This was unacceptable to the southern-dominated Pierce administration, and northern Whigs opposed Hawaii's admission under any other conditions. So the idea of Hawaiian annexation was killed. It would be resurrected in the 1870s, when the issue of slavery had disappeared. This was one reason why Seward and many other northerners considered southern slavery the great obstacle to America's destiny. If the curse of slavery could be eradicated, Seward's ambitions were practically limitless.[28] But until then America's fulfillment of its destiny would have to wait.

The slavery question also affected attitudes toward matters of war and peace. Southern slaveholder society had produced a people that highly esteemed personal honor, familial loyalty, and the martial virtues. The South was disproportionately represented in the nation's military academies, and southerners made up the bulk of the force that fought in Mexico, despite the fact that the South's population was much smaller than the North's.[29] For many northerners, meanwhile, the experience of the Mexican War—a war of conquest for the expansion of slavery—left a sour taste, as did the South's sometimes belligerent quest for Cuba. Even northern expansionist Democrats like John O'Sullivan hoped the United States could achieve its conquests by "moral agencies" and commerce and, like Seward, believed this would "beget a community of interest between" the United States and other peoples.[30] Stephen Douglas declared that the United States had a "mission to perform . . . of progress in the arts and sciences" and even "in the development and advancement of human rights throughout the world."[31] In the North the reformist movements of the 1820s and '30s had produced a small but potent strand of pacifism, a phenomenon that was almost nonexistent in the South. The northern pacifist movement included many abolitionists, like William Lloyd Garrison, and some "Conscience" Whigs, like Charles Sumner. Their pacifism would be put to its severest test by the Civil War, when many abandoned the pacifist creed out of the necessity of fighting the slave power. But in the two decades prior to the secession crisis, the Mexican War, the aggressive southern expansionist pretensions of the Ostend Manifesto, and the various southern-backed filibustering expeditions had presented no similar conundrum. Faced with a South bent upon extending slavery in the Western Hemisphere by violent means, northern Whigs in the 1840s and '50s could denounce slavery and war in the same breath. "I abhor war, as I detest slavery," Seward declared in 1846. "I would not give one human life for all the continent that remains to be annexed."[32]

Whether Seward and many of his colleagues would have opposed wars of conquest in the absence of slavery cannot be known. But Henry Clay had welcomed the War of 1812 partly as a chance to seize Canada from the British. John Quincy Adams had supported Jackson's military conquest of the Floridas in 1818, and he did not seem to shy away from war with Great Britain for control of "All of Oregon" three decades later. But in general northerners tempered by the experience of southern aggression in the 1840s looked to other, less violent means of national aggrandizement. Most agreed with Seward that "the sword is not the most winning messenger that can be sent abroad."[33]

Finally, the slavery question had a powerful effect on the moral tenor of mid-nineteenth-century American foreign policy, including that of many northern Whigs. It helped explain the otherwise baffling shift in attitudes by onetime advocates of foreign policy moralism such as Clay and Webster. In the 1810s and '20s they had championed what Webster called America's "duty" to provide moral and perhaps even material support to those struggling against despotism abroad, whether in Greece or in the Western Hemisphere. Their foreign policy views in those days were of a piece with their views on slavery. Clay would declare in one breath that to free "the unhappy portion of our race doomed to bondage" would be a greater accomplishment than "all the triumphs ever decreed to the most successful conqueror."[34] And in the next he would speak of America's obligation to give "tone, and hope, and confidence to the friends of liberty throughout the world."[35]

But in the 1840s and early 1850s, as Clay and Webster chose the path of compromise with slavery at home and worked to preserve both party and Union from sectional schism, they also abandoned their earlier penchant for moral causes abroad and adopted a foreign policy stance closer to the principles of what had hitherto been chiefly a southern realism. As a practical matter, it had become almost impossible even to discuss moral and ideological issues without stirring up a sectional quarrel. Antislavery "Conscience" Whigs called for an ideologically expansive policy abroad not only because that was their preferred approach to the world but precisely because it drew attention to the immorality at the core of American society. With northern abolitionists and "Conscience" Whigs ever on the lookout for opportunities to point up the immorality of the South's institutions, discussions of good and evil abroad invariably became indictments of the evils of the South. National Whig Party leaders had to turn away from moral causes abroad in the interest of party and national unity. For Webster, embrace of the Compromise of 1850 had meant the abandonment of "a lifelong opposition to more slave territory."[36] Webster's earlier foreign policy moralism had to be abandoned, too, in the interest of intersectional peace. "God knows that I detest slavery," the Whig president Millard Fillmore declared, "but it is an existing evil, for which we are not responsible, and we must endure it." As one historian has noted, "It was this fundamental realism . . . that shaped the president's political philosophy" in foreign policy as well.[37]

The sectional and political divisions over the moral content of American foreign policy came to the fore when liberal revolutions briefly raged across Europe beginning in 1848. The growing divide between Whig Party leaders and "Conscience" Whigs was exposed during the extraordinary visit of the Hungarian revolutionary leader Louis Kossuth in 1851. The charismatic Kossuth led the uprising against the Hapsburg Empire in 1848, but three years later the Hungarian revolt was being crushed by the absolutist regimes of Austria and Nicholas I's Russia. Kossuth had escaped, been imprisoned and then released by the Turkish sultan, and in 1851 fled to the United States, where he hoped to win American assistance, both moral and material, in his fight for Hungarian independence.

To many Americans, Kossuth symbolized the worldwide struggle against despotic oppression. When he landed in New York, a quarter of a million people gathered along Broadway to cheer him. Signs hung from buildings along the parade route read, U.S. TO RUSSIA: MIND YOUR OWN BUSINESS, and HIS VISIT REMINDS US OF OUR NEGLECTED DUTY TO FREEDOM AND THE PEOPLE OF EUROPE.[38] Both political parties immediately embraced Kossuth, fearing that to do less would damage their electoral prospects in 1852, and for a time his procession across the country actually eclipsed the issues of slave expansion, the Fugitive Slave Law, and the Compromise of 1850 as national obsessions. The House of Representatives welcomed him in open session, an honor previously given only to Lafayette.

Most diplomatic historians have treated the Kossuth affair narrowly, as an instance where Americans debated whether to intervene in Europe. That they did not intervene is variously assumed to be a sign of their inherent isolationism or their "realist" rejection of moralism in foreign policy. But the uproar over Kossuth was not about either of these issues. As Seward once remarked, "Every question, political, civil, or ecclesiastical, brings up slavery as an incident, and the incident supplants the principal question. We hear of nothing but slavery, and we can talk of nothing but slavery."[39] The furor over Kossuth was not about what America should do abroad but about what it should be at home.

The response to Kossuth and his appeal for American assistance differed sharply across sectional lines. Enthusiasm for the Hungarian cause, and for the cause of European revolution generally, was confined almost entirely to the North. Among the first to seize on the visit to strengthen their own case within the United States were the northern abolitionists and their sympathizers among the "Conscience" Whigs. Abolitionists, for a time, took to calling Kossuth the "William Lloyd Garrison of Hungarian liberty."[40] Charles Sumner made the visit the subject of his maiden speech in the Senate and declared in deliberate double entendres that Kossuth had fled "the house of bondage" and that his arrival on American free soil was an "emancipation."[41] Seward declared that the United States should "solemnly protest against the conduct of Russia . . . as a wanton and tyrannical infraction of the laws of nations" and warned that the United States would not be "indifferent to similar acts of national injustice, oppression, and usurpation, whenever or wherever they may occur."[42]

Even the more moderate Abraham Lincoln offered a resolution supporting a universal right of self-determination at a "Kossuth meeting" in 1852. In an early echo of a doctrine that would later be associated with Woodrow Wilson but that really derived from Locke, Lincoln declared it was "the right of any people, sufficiently numerous for national independence to throw off, to revolutionize, their existing form of government, and to establish such other in its stead as they may choose." This, after all, was what Americans had done in 1776. The United States was not compelled to support such movements, Lincoln argued, but could demand that despotic nations like Russia had no right to suppress them. It could also do more than demand: "To have resisted Russia in that case, or to resist any power in a like case, would be no violation of our own cherished principles of nonintervention, but, on the contrary, would be ever meritorious, in us, or any independent nation."[43]

Northern Democrats, including O'Sullivan's "Young America" movement, supported Kossuth with equal fervor. When critics suggested that such a policy violated the principles of nonentanglement and nonintervention contained in Washington's Farewell Address, northern Democrats, echoing Adams, Clay, Webster, and other advocates of ambitious foreign policies in the 1820s, insisted that Washington's principles no longer applied to a great and powerful nation like the United States. Senator Isaac P. Walker of Wisconsin declared, "What was our policy in our infancy and weakness has ceased to be our true policy now that we have reached man-hood and strength."[44]

Southern leaders viewed the northern Kossuth mania with suspicion. Calhoun argued that expressions of moralism in foreign policy violated the national government's sacred trust with its citizens and were an abuse of the Constitution. National leaders were supposed to defend the rights of citizens, not foreigners, Alabama's Jeremiah Clemens insisted. Nothing could "excuse or extenuate the guilt of him who idly perils a nation's welfare" by pursuing moral crusades abroad.[45] Southerners appealed for adherence to America's "traditional" policy of nonentanglement and nonintervention and to the timeless principles Washington had set forth in his Farewell Address. Lurking behind these protests was fear of the northern threat to slavery.[46] "They want to get this Government to commit itself to a principle which can hereafter be applied to internal concerns," warned the *Baltimore Clipper.*[47] If the South supported interference abroad, the *New Orleans Bulletin* cautioned, "we will be the first who will be interfered with. . . . Of all the people upon the earth's surface, the Southern people are the last to think of, much less attempt to enforce, doctrines of this character."[48] For "men bred to the ways of slavery and intellectual tyranny," the doctrine of realpolitik "was the only rational approach to foreign policy."[49]

For Whig leaders trying to hold party and nation together, the Kossuth affair was a nightmare. President Fillmore declared that America's "true mission is not to propagate our opinions, or impose upon other countries our form of government, by artifice or force," but rather "to teach by example, and show by our success, moderation and justice, the blessings of self-government and the advantages of free institutions."[50] Henry Clay, on his deathbed, met with Kossuth and, after expressing ardent personal sympathy for the Hungarian's cause, begged him "for the sake of my country" not to press his appeal.[51] But Whig leaders were out of touch with a northern population that was becoming more radical, and more moralistic, with each passing year. In 1852 a pro-Kossuth resolution passed the Senate by a single vote. The dominant sentiment in the North was reflected in a new alliance that brought together northern Democrats, "Conscience" Whigs, and Free-Soil Party members, led by Salmon Chase. On the other side, southerners from both parties joined more conservative Whigs and the Fillmore administration. The vote was a microcosm of the shifting political currents. Whig leaders like Webster, whose support of the Compromise of 1850 had left them isolated and mistrusted in the North, could no longer speak for the majority of their constituents on matters of domestic or foreign policy.

The 1852 election, in fact, marked the last time the Whigs would offer a candidate for the presidency. After the Nebraska crisis of 1854, the Whig Party disintegrated. The future lay with the "Conscience" Whigs who voted for the Kossuth resolution along with Chase and one of the northern Democrats. In a few years this northern coalition would come together again to form the new Republican Party, a party based entirely in the North, rejecting fundamental compromise with southern slavery, and representing the distinctly northern view of the nation's future—and the nation's foreign policy.

The Republican Party and the "Apple of Gold"

"THE RISE of the Republican party," Daniel Walker Howe has observed, "reflected the rise of the reforming impulse within Whiggery at the expense of its conservative aspect."[52] In many ways the Republican Party only revived a progressive, reformist spirit that had long been suppressed by the sectional conflict over slavery. On matters of both domestic and foreign policy, leaders of the new party like Lincoln and Seward drew their inspiration from the earlier generation of progressive nationalist reformers, from John Quincy Adams and the young Henry Clay, who had championed the American System. After Adams's death in 1846 Seward declared, "I have lost a patron, a guide, a counselor, and a friend—one whom I loved scarcely less than the dearest relations, and venerated above all that was mortal among men."[53] Lincoln, the transplanted Kentuckian, had reserved his veneration for Harry of the West, calling Clay "my beau ideal of a statesman," and had remained devoted to his Kentucky elder until the early 1850s, when Lincoln's refusal to accept further compromises with the South led him to break with the Great Compromiser. Lincoln had then turned to John Quincy Adams for inspiration.

Like most Whigs, both Lincoln and Seward had remained consistent supporters of the American System throughout the Jacksonian era, favoring federal support for internal improvements and a strong federal bank and, more broadly, sharing Adams's view that the "great object of the institution of government" was "the improvement of the condition of those who are parties to the social compact." Seward, even more than Lincoln, had been an ardent reformer throughout his long career in New York politics. As the state's governor beginning in 1839, he had promoted state aid for the building of roads and canals, the creation of a board of education, anticorruption measures in the cities, prison reform, and the reform of treatment of the insane.[54] He was considered a champion of the rights of ethnic voters, particularly the Irish, who were generally treated with disdain by mainstream

Whigs. He protected fugitive slaves, and he was as close to being an abolitionist as the constraints of practical politics allowed. In 1848 Seward declared, "Our lot was cast in an age of revolution—a revolution which was to bring all mankind from a state of servitude to the exercise of self-government—from under the tyranny of physical force to the gentle sway of opinion—from under subjection to matter to dominion over nature."[55] The quintessential northern liberal, Seward possessed a "comprehensive vision of modernization" in which "political freedom, public education, and technological progress were all synthesized."[56]

The pursuit of these projects had for decades been blocked by a wary South influenced by a slaveholder class that had sought self-preservation by pulling the nation in another direction. The new Republican Party essentially declared an end to compromise and called for the final fulfillment of the promise of the American System. Although the Republican Party was itself based on a bargain between northern Whigs and northern Democrats, which required some compromises on economic matters, the party platform nevertheless called for an increased tariff, internal improvements, and federal aid for the building of a transcontinental railroad.[57] The Republican program advanced "a progressive, energetic . . . democratic form of capitalism" that would become the American model in the decades after the Civil War. "The Republicans became a party unambiguously in support of modernization."[58] The lack of southern influence even allowed these northerners to resume their natural inclination to seek more territory. The Republicans set aside Whig trepidations about expansion and embraced westward settlement and the incorporation of new states into the Union, north and south. They also gave voice to the old moralistic spirit in foreign policy.

But if Republican leaders took up the old progressive nationalist program, in one important respect they also moved beyond it. For the new Republicans, unlike the nationalist Republicans of the Monroe era, were a party consciously formed in opposition to slavery.[59] John Quincy Adams had been among the first American leaders to make the radical observation that the Union was not an end in itself but only the means to realizing the promise of the principles of natural rights and human equality set forth in the Declaration of the Independence. He was also among the first to argue that the American Constitution, that "morally vicious . . . bargain between freedom and slavery," was "inconsistent with the principles upon which alone our revolution can be justified." Four decades after Adams penned those words in his private diary, his ideological heirs, Lincoln and Seward, made this the central political doctrine of their northern antislavery party.

Lincoln elevated the Declaration of Independence over the Constitution as the true expression of American nationhood. He likened it to an "apple of gold" framed by a "picture of silver"—the Constitution and the Union. But he declared that the "picture was made for the apple, not the apple for the picture."[60] The United States could not have achieved its great power and prosperity "without the Constitution and the Union," but these were not the "primary cause of our great prosperity." There was "something back of these, entwining itself more closely about the human heart. That something, is the principle of 'Liberty to all'—the principle that clears the path for all—gives hope to all—and, by consequence, enterprize, and industry to all."[61] Seward, in his maiden speech in the Senate denouncing the Compromise of 1850, declared that there was a "higher law than the Constitution," a law that guaranteed to all men the enjoyment of the "natural rights" bestowed by the "Creator of the Universe." The United States had a great destiny before it, but the "security, welfare, and greatness of nations" depended not on material success alone. It also depended on their promotion of "the security of natural rights, the diffusion of knowledge, and the freedom of industry." Slavery was "incompatible with all of these."[62]

Breaking from a long Federalist and Whig tradition of antipathy toward Thomas Jefferson, Lincoln celebrated what he believed was Jefferson's incomparable contribution to the nation's founding. He called on Americans to "re-adopt the Declaration of Independence" and to rededicate themselves to Jefferson's Enlightenment conviction that "all men are created equal." As Harry Jaffa has noted, he also subtly transformed Jefferson's original meaning to fit the great struggle of his own day. Jefferson had conceived of "just government mainly in terms of the relief from oppression." His Declaration had put forth a Lockean justification for American independence: the British Crown and Parliament had forsaken their governing legitimacy by denying Americans their natural rights, and so Americans were justified in waging a revolution for independence to restore those rights. Lincoln, facing very different circumstances in the late 1850s, appealed to natural rights to justify a "second American revolution," this time not against an imperial master but against the domestic institution of slavery. He turned Jefferson's "negative, minimal" requirement of government, that it must not deprive citizens of their natural rights, into a positive requirement that government must actively defend and promote those rights.[63] As John Patrick Diggins has put it, Lincoln set forth the Declaration's doctrine of equality "as a moral imperative rather than as a scientific postulate." The principle of equality enunciated in the Declaration, Lincoln declared, was to be "constantly looked to, constantly labored for, and even though never perfectly attained, constantly approximated and therefore constantly spreading and deepening its influence, and augmenting the happiness and value of life to all people of colors everywhere." Borrowing from the religious "perfectionism" whose spirit had so infused northern thought since the Second Great Awakening, he exhorted: "As your Father in Heaven is perfect, be ye also perfect." He believed in a concept of equality "that was as much a *duty* of the community as a *right* of the individual and as much the end product of historical striving as a condition preceding history."[64]

Nothing could have been further from the principles of southern realism than this. And indeed, Lincoln's appeal to Americans' responsibility to fulfill the promise of the Declaration, not only for themselves but for all men everywhere, was a deliberate refutation of the doctrine of self-interest that underlay the South's defense of slavery. For despite the insistence of Calhoun and his followers that the institution of slavery was a positive good for white masters and black slaves alike, ultimately the South's defense rested on self-interest. Everyone knew that slavery existed in the South not because whites felt an obligation to enslave blacks, but because plantation owners believed they needed slaves to work under conditions that free men would not tolerate.

In his appeal to a higher morality than the Constitution, Lincoln rejected the doctrine of self-interest as the sole guide to human action and also as the sole guide to national action. It was not enough to pursue the national interest. It was not even right to pursue the national interest if the nation itself had departed from the principles of the Declaration. What Lincoln hated most about Douglas's Nebraska Act, he said, was that it assumed there was "no right principle of action but *self-interest*."[65] He and Seward both insisted that the "right principle of action" was not self-interest but justice—and justice was to be found only in the Declaration's principle of equal rights. Because all men enjoyed equal rights, all men had a duty to defend those rights not only for themselves but for others—even for black slaves.[66] This was a step beyond Locke's contractual understanding of the relations among citizens and between citizens and their government. It was a call for moral responsibility.

The revolutionary implications of Lincoln's message were well understood by the leaders of the South. It was with some justice that prominent southerners insisted after the outbreak of the Civil War that they were not the "revolutionists" but were "resisting revolution." Jefferson Davis perceptively contrasted the revolutionary progressive idealism of Lincoln's

North with the conservative realism of the South: "We are not engaged in a Quixotic fight for the rights of man," Davis exclaimed. "Our struggle is for inherited rights. . . . We are conservative."[67]

Just as southern realism had a foreign as well as a domestic dimension, so Lincoln's rejection of self-interest as the only guide to action and his appeal to moral responsibility had significance beyond the domestic conflict over slavery. If the "central idea" of the American nation was to be found not in the Constitution or in the Union but in the Declaration of Independence's promise of equal rights, this meant that at the core of American nationhood was a set of universal principles that transcended national boundaries. The Constitution and the Union were compacts that applied only to those who had voluntarily consented to them in 1787 and who continued to be bound by them seven decades later. The Declaration of Independence spoke of rights and obligations that were universal.

Lincoln, Seward, and other Republicans did believe that their struggle for freedom at home served the cause of freedom everywhere. They believed the "stain" of American slavery prevented the United States from fulfilling its role as the exemplar of republican democracy for peoples struggling against despotism the world over.[68] They worried, as Charles Sumner put it, that slavery had degraded "our country" and prevented "its example from being all-conquering." Lincoln feared that the mere existence of slavery deprived "our republican example of its just influence in the world," and it enabled "the enemies of free institutions to taunt us as hypocrites." It was in this spirit that Lincoln at Gettysburg called the United States "the last best hope of earth," whose success or failure would determine "whether any nation so conceived and so dedicated can long endure."

But Lincoln's emphasis on moral responsibility, on the community's duty to further human equality, also bore within it a more far-reaching implication: that the United States had to be more than just a beacon of hope. The Declaration's commitment to equality was, Lincoln insisted, "an abstract truth, applicable to all men at all times."[69] If Americans had a positive duty to further this abstract truth at home, to meddle in the affairs of the South even at the risk of civil war and national destruction, could this obligation extend beyond the nation's boundaries as well? If self-interest alone was not a sufficient guide to national action, if it was not an acceptable justification for northern passivity while slavery flourished in the South, could self-interest alone be the appropriate guide to action in a world where despotism flourished? If what made Americans a nation was not a common territory, common blood, or even a common Constitution but rather a common commitment to universal principles, then where was the logical limit to their moral responsibility?

Lincoln never addressed these questions directly, in part because before assuming the presidency he rarely discussed matters of foreign policy. On one of the rare occasions when he did, in his resolution supporting Kossuth in 1852, he expressed a conviction that moral responsibility and principled altruism, not mere self-interest, should be a guide for the nation as well as for the individual. He argued that it would have been "meritorious" for the United States to intervene against Russia to prevent the crushing of the Hungarian Revolution—meritorious not because intervention was in America's selfish interest but because it advanced a universal "right" of any people "to throw off" unjust rule. His understanding of American nationhood contained within it a sense of moral obligation, that a nation founded on the principle of universal human equality had a responsibility for "spreading and deepening" its influence for "all people of colors everywhere."[70]

Lincoln and his fellow Republicans were not the first Americans to speak of an obligation to support others struggling for freedom around the world. During the years of the early republic, Jeffersonians had argued for American assistance to a revolutionary France besieged by European monarchs, while Hamiltonians had proposed linking America's fortunes to the defense of a liberal Britain besieged by a despotic France. In the 1810s and '20s Monroe and Clay had called for American assistance to revolutions in Europe and in the Western Hemisphere, and Webster had spoken of America's "duty" to support the struggle for freedom abroad. But in these earlier instances, the case for aiding republicanism and liberalism abroad as a matter of principle was also advanced as a matter of self-interest and self-defense. The United States of Jefferson's and Hamilton's day was a weak and vulnerable republic in a hostile sea of monarchies; the conquest of European liberty by powerful monarchs could be but the prelude to the physical conquest of American liberty. Even in the days of Monroe and Clay, leaders on both sides of the Atlantic believed the global struggle between republicanism and despotism must eventually spill over into the Western Hemisphere. When Monroe declared in 1823 that the United States was an "interested spectator" of the political struggles in Europe, he really did mean that the nation had a profound interest in the outcome.

Lincoln's political doctrine seemed to go a step beyond even this broad ideological definition of interest. To be sure, the global struggle between monarchy and republicanism continued in his own day. The liberal revolutions that briefly spread across Europe in 1848 had been crushed, and another long period of conservative reaction had settled in across the Continent. When Lincoln declared in 1863 that the United States was the "last best hope of earth" for free government, it was events in Europe over the previous decade that gave his plea such poignancy. But his reformulation of the American political creed, his assertion of a positive obligation to advance the principles of the Declaration, added a new dimension to this old understanding of America's role in the world.

What Lincoln only implied, other Republicans openly avowed. "The rights asserted by our forefathers were not peculiar to themselves," Seward declared, "they were the common rights of mankind."[71] The United States had not just the opportunity but the duty "to renovate the condition of mankind," to lead the way to "the universal restoration of power to the governed" everywhere in the world.[72] For Seward, soon to become Lincoln's secretary of state, this was America's true destiny: not empire in the traditional sense of rule by conquest, but "empire and liberty." And this was why he believed so passionately that slavery had to be destroyed. To fulfill the nation's historic responsibility, he believed, Americans had to "qualify ourselves for our mission."[73]

CHAPTER 10

War and Progress

The rapid increase of the means of communications throughout the globe have brought into almost daily intercourse communities which hitherto have been aliens and strangers to each other, so that now no great social and moral wrong can be inflicted on any people without being felt throughout the civilized globe.

—Hamilton Fish, April 30, 1873

The "Second American Revolution"

FEW NORTHERNERS BELIEVED, even in 1860, that embarking on that mission would first require a war against the South, much less what turned out to be the bloodiest and costliest war in American history. Few anticipated that the mere election of Lincoln on a platform of containment would drive the South to secede. Certainly until the firing on Fort Sumter in 1861, few northerners harbored aggressive intentions toward the South. Most hoped, with Lincoln, that the containment and eventual elimination of southern slavery could be accomplished peacefully, ground down under the steady weight of the North's economic, political, and moral superiority. Most northerners believed, right up until the outbreak of war, that the South would simply have to acquiesce and accept that its only course lay along the path toward modernity that the North had blazed. The German immigrant and Republican leader Carl Schurz expressed a common northern view when he half-challenged, half-exhorted the South in 1860: "Slaveholders of America, I appeal to you. Are you really in earnest when you speak of perpetuating slavery? Shall it never cease? Never? Stop and consider where you are and in what day you live. . . . This is the world of the nineteenth century. . . . You stand against a hopeful world, alone against a great century, fighting your hopeless fight . . . against the onward march of civilization."[1] Like Americans of future generations, who would find baffling the refusal of other nations to give up their hopeless struggles and adopt American ways and American principles, northerners mostly ignored the fact that the South could not possibly join its "onward march," that southern slaveholders could not enter the North's "hopeful world" without betraying everything they believed, and, in their eyes, risking annihilation at the hands of their former slaves.

The South's decision to secede, though incomprehensible to many northerners, was logical. To accept Lincoln's victory, and with it the victory of the northern view of America's future, was incompatible with the survival of southern ideology. And there was logic, too, in the North's refusal to permit the South to form its own independent nation. For the preservation of the Union—the "picture of silver"—was essential to Lincoln's hopes for the survival of republican government rededicated to the principles of the Declaration. To acknowledge the sovereignty of the states as superior to that of the federal government was to put an end to the nation and to the notion of popular government. "We must settle this question now, whether in a free government the minority have the right to break up the government whenever they choose."[2] For Seward and other Republicans, "the integrity of the Union, important as an end in itself, was also a prerequisite to the national greatness Republicans felt the United States was destined to achieve."[3] Seward's vision of an empire of freedom depended on a consolidated, prosperous, continental Union, cleansed of the stain of slavery, which would form the essential base from which America's global hegemony would emanate.

In the end, therefore, and much to many northerners' surprise and chagrin, the North had to go to war to realize its vision of America's destiny. The election of Lincoln led the southern states to secede. When southern forces attempted to seize Fort Sumter, and when Lincoln determined to defend it by force, the war began.

At the beginning both sides embarked upon what each believed was a limited war for limited ends. The Confederacy fought to be left alone to enjoy its new independence, much like the original thirteen colonies when they separated from the British Empire. President Lincoln fought to restore the integrity of the Union against an unlawful rebellion, insisting he was simply using military means to quell an uprising "too powerful to be suppressed by the ordinary course of judicial proceedings." But early southern victories and northern defeats led to a massive escalation in the war, and not only on the battlefield. Northern war aims took revolutionary and even messianic form when Lincoln delivered his Emancipation Proclamation two years into the conflict. To win the war and make the goals of the war consistent with the principles of the Declaration that he had stated to be the essence of American nationhood, Lincoln freed the slaves. He justified it as "a military necessity," but in striking at slavery he also knew he was striking at "the heart of the rebellion," the underpinning of the southern way of life.[4] After 1862 the northern war aim became not merely the defeat of rebellion. The war for the Union became a war for justice, a moral crusade for liberty.

John Keegan has called the Union and Confederate armies among the most "ideological" armies in human history.[5] James M. McPherson, in a study of the letters of more than six hundred Union soldiers, has discovered that while not all cared about the ideological issues at stake in the war, a substantial number did believe they were fighting for a moral and ideological cause beyond themselves. A good many soldiers shared Lincoln's conviction that the struggle for freedom at home was a struggle for freedom the world over. As they wrote family members back home, "the liberty of the world" had been "placed in our hands to defend." If the North succeeded, "then you may look for European struggles for liberty," but if it failed, "the onward march of Liberty in the Old World" would be "retarded at least a century."[6]

Like Lincoln, some northern soldiers saw the war as necessary not only to keep the flame of liberty burning in the Union but also to advance the universal, abstract principles of the Declaration for all men everywhere. By the last years of the war, "most Northern soldiers had broadened their conception of liberty to include black people"—a huge leap for northern whites whose racism was often no less fervent than that of their southern compatriots. While a sizable minority of Union soldiers greeted Lincoln's Emancipation Proclamation with hostility after it was announced in January 1863, McPherson estimates that twice as many favored it. "A good many Union soldiers" embraced the new war aim of freeing the slaves "with an ideological fervor they had not felt for the cause of restoring the Union with slavery still in it."[7] As one Pennsylvania captain wrote, Lincoln's action had made the war no longer a contest "between North & South; but a contest between human rights and human liberty on one side and eternal bondage on the other."[8] Another Pennsylvanian wrote, "[E]very day I have a more religious feeling, that this war is a crusade for the good of mankind."[9] Some northerners shared Lincoln's view that the war was a noble and worthy cause precisely because it was *not* a war fought exclusively for interest. "This is not a war for dollars and cents," one Indiana captain wrote, "nor is it a war for territory—but it is to decide whether we are to be a free people."[10] And by "we" he did not mean himself, for he was already free, but those in bondage in the South.

Many northern idealists eagerly embraced a justification for war that went beyond self-interest. The decision to go to war had been a difficult one for most northerners. Throughout the 1840s and '50s northern Whigs and Republicans had portrayed themselves as the party of peace against the aggressive, militaristic slave power Democrats. For northerners who had opposed the aggressive southern expansionism of the Mexican War and the efforts to acquire Cuba by force, for reformers who blended abolitionism with pacifism, for commercial liberals who preferred that America wield its power through trade rather than through force of arms, a "moral crusade" was perhaps the *only* acceptable justification for war.

Lincoln recognized perhaps better than anyone the problems inherent in such a crusade. In 1862 he noted that "[i]n great contests each party claims to act in accordance with the will of God" and that "both may be . . . wrong." It was "quite possible that God's purpose is something different from the purpose of either party."[11] But Lincoln did not let theological doubt deter him. Uncertainty about God's intentions did not absolve men and leaders from deciding to go to war, and he was prepared to press forward and let God decide who was right, on the battlefield.[12]

The ideological nature of the conflict, as well as the evolving technology of warfare, helped determine the brutal, horrific manner of the struggle. When the war became ideological, it also became a "total" war waged not only between combatants but between and against peoples.[13] The gentleman's war that the Union general George B. McClellan had wanted to fight—waged, as he told Lincoln, "upon the highest principles known to Christian Civilization"—reflected not only McClellan's military training but also his preference for a nonideological conflict.[14] As Ulysses S. Grant later reflected, McClellan "did not believe in the war." He and other early Union generals "let their ambivalent attitude toward the conflict influence their military performance."[15] The northern generals who prosecuted the war most effectively, and most ruthlessly, had more understanding of its ideological purposes. Grant, though not a vigorous opponent of slavery, nevertheless perceived that "he was engaged in a people's war, and that the people as well as the armies of the South must be conquered, before the war would end." "We are not only fighting hostile armies," William Tecumseh Sherman declared, "but a hostile people, and must make old and young, rich and poor, feel the hard hand of war, as well as the organized armies."[16] Sherman was no more opposed to slavery than Grant. But he understood that the South was fighting for a way of life and that the people of the South would not surrender until they concluded that the loss of their civilization was preferable to the horrors of war. Therefore the North must "make the war so terrible . . . [and] make them so sick of war that generations would pass away before they would again appeal to it."[17]

Grant and Sherman did make the war terrible, with Lincoln's full support. "Fondly do we hope—fervently do we pray" for the speedy end of the war, Lincoln proclaimed in his second inaugural address. But he did not shrink from the alternative. If God willed that the war must continue "until all the wealth piled by the bond-man's two hundred and fifty years of unrequited toil shall be sunk, and until every drop of blood drawn with the lash, shall be paid by another drawn with the sword," then Lincoln would devastate the South and its people. "The judgments of the Lord, are true and righteous altogether." The Union's conduct of the Civil War would remain, for American commanders in both world wars of the twentieth century, "the model of a great war . . . a war of 'power unrestrained' unleashed for 'complete conquest.' "[18]

The Civil War, like most of America's major wars, transformed the nation's government and society in ways both tangible and intangible. The exigencies of total war and national mobilization produced a revolutionary expansion of the power of the federal government beyond what even Clay and Adams had contemplated. Between 1861 and 1865 Lincoln's administration enacted the tariffs, the federally chartered banking system, and the federal improvement programs of the old American System. For the first time in American history the federal government began direct federal taxation, created an internal revenue bureau to collect the taxes, and inaugurated a national currency. It instituted a national draft to fill the ranks of the army. To assist blacks freed from bondage in the course of the war, it created the Freedmen's Bureau, "the first national agency for social welfare." The Civil War produced a victory for a government committed to what Adams had called "the progressive improvement of the condition of the governed." The southern states had "invoked the negative liberties of state sovereignty and individual rights of property (i.e., slave property) to break up the United States." Lincoln invoked the "positive liberty of reform liberalism, exercised through the power of the army and the state."[19]

The impact of the Civil War on American foreign policy was equally profound. The Civil War was America's second great moral war, but unlike the Revolution it was a war of conquest. The North liberated the oppressed segment of the South's population and subjugated the oppressors. It established a decadelong military occupation of the South's territory, abolished the despotic institution of slavery, and attempted to establish reformed political and economic systems that would prevent a return to the old ways.

The Civil War was America's first experiment in ideological conquest, therefore, and what followed was America's first experiment in "nation-building." When Grant accepted Lee's surrender, the South lay in ruins. The southern economy was destroyed, and an entire generation of men had been killed, maimed, or incapacitated. The Confederate government was vanquished, so the U.S. Army became "the sole source of law and order in occupied areas." Army provost marshals were de facto governors of southern civilians, regulating every aspect of life, from arresting suspected "rebels" to distributing food and clothing. During the war Lincoln had established loyalist governments in some of the occupied states, but even these were dependent on and subordinate to the military department commanders.[20]

To the North, the defeated South was, in the argot of the twentieth century, an underdeveloped nation.[21] Its underdevelopment, its backwardness, exemplified by the archaic institution of slavery, many northerners believed, had been responsible for the horrendous conflict that had almost destroyed the entire nation. Now the North, having subdued the rebellion and punished its leaders, had the task not only of standing the conquered land back on its feet, but of curing it of the evils that had led to war, which in turn meant dragging it forcibly into the modern world. As James Russell Lowell poetically put it in his series *The Biglow Papers,*

> Make 'em Amerikin, an' they'll begin
> To love their country ez they loved their sin;
> Let 'em stay Southun, an' you've kep' a sore
> Ready to fester ez it done afore.[22]

Conquest of the South gave northerners the opportunity—or, depending on one's point of view, saddled it with the burden—of accomplishing the task that had eluded northern statesmen in the antebellum years. "Why cannot the best civilization be extended over the whole country," Ralph Waldo Emerson had asked in 1862, "since the disorder of the less-civilized portion menaces the existence of the country?"[23] After the war ended, this remained the fundamental question: how to re-create the South in the North's image?

Northern aims during Reconstruction comprised a typically American blend of humanitarianism, moralism, acquisitiveness, and strategic self-interest. The federal government provided humanitarian aid, through the military, both during and after the war. The Freedmen's Bureau, run by the "Christian soldier" General O. O. Howard, distributed millions of rations and built schools and hospitals for both blacks and whites. Northern philanthropists raised almost $3 million for southern relief in the two years following the war.[24] Northerners also saw opportunities for themselves in this civilizing project. Capitalists saw opportunities for profit. Missionaries saw a chance to win converts. Republicans saw a chance to win votes. Nationalists wanted to strengthen the sinews of the nation. Internationalists, like Seward, saw the South's restoration as the key to world power. To most southerners, Reconstruction seemed more like exploitation and imperialism.[25] And, indeed, consensus broke down in the North over just how far nation-building should go. How far should southern society and its economy be transformed to suit the North? How should former rebel leaders be treated—should they be barred from politics or allowed back into the new southern governments? How much constitutional protection did the former Confederate states enjoy? How long should American troops remain an occupying force in the South? And most difficult and controversial of all, how much northern power should be exerted on behalf of the freedmen? Opinion varied widely in the North, and it was not easy to separate moral and ideological passions from political interests. The hapless northern Democrats, suffering under the stigma of the "party of rebellion," opposed any reconstruction plan that gave rights to the freedmen, especially the right to vote, for granting such rights would turn a whites-only Democratic southern electorate into a bastion of black Republican voters. Most Republicans, on the other hand, wanted to give blacks the vote, on the plausible assumption that they would vote for the party that had liberated them. For many Republicans, the insistence on preserving their ascendancy went beyond simple partisanship. They believed, with more than normal justification, that the interests of the party and the interests of the nation were the same. "The safety of this great nation," one party leader declared, depended on continued Republican dominance over the "rebel" Democrats.[26]

Republicans nevertheless divided over both means and ends. Those who demanded the most thorough transformation of the South were the so-called Radical Republicans, led by the powerful House Republican leader Thaddeus Stevens. They included in their ranks Charles Sumner, the powerful chairman of the Senate Foreign Relations Committee, as well as future secretary of state James G. Blaine and future presidents James A. Garfield and Benjamin Harrison, all of whom supported the expansive use of federal power to guarantee the civil liberties of the freedmen in the South, including the right to vote, to fight southern reaction and intransigence, and to ensure that the old leaders of the Confederacy never returned to power. In Stevens's view, the southern states were conquered provinces of the United States, "like clay in the hands of the potter," and it was the North's "duty to take care that no injustice shall remain in their organic laws." The abolitionist George W. Julian insisted that before the South could rejoin the Union, it needed to be made safe for the freedmen, safe for whites loyal to the Union, safe for northern immigrants, and "safe for Northern capital and labor, Northern energy and enterprise, and Northern ideas to set up their habitation in peace, and thus found a Christian civilization and a living democracy amid the ruins of the past." Only "the strong arm of power, outstretched from the central authority here in Washington," could effect such a transformation.[27]

Against this Radical Republican view was arrayed a powerful bloc of moderate and conservative northerners with a more modest vision. Hostile to the vast expansion of federal power inherent in the Radicals' program and unwilling to shoulder the financial burden required to keep large numbers of federal troops in the South indefinitely, conservative northerners were also reluctant to force northern democracy upon the South "at the point of the bayonet." Senator John Sherman of Ohio spoke for many when he asked, "What becomes of the republican doctrine that all governments must be founded on the consent of the governed?" It was a paradox that would confront the United States as an occupying power time and again over the coming century and a half. How far could liberty be denied to an occupied people in the effort to implant liberty among them? And there were other vexing issues. While most northerners were hostile to the southern "planter aristocracy," many were also hostile to Radical Republican plans for redistributing southern land and wealth to the former slaves. Northern capitalists objected because they wanted the South to move "as quickly as possible along the economic road marked out by the North, through aid to railroads, industry, and agricultural diversification."[28] And while Republicans all agreed that slavery had to be abolished, not even all the Radicals agreed that the federal government should use its military power to enforce the newly freed blacks' rights, in particular their right to vote.

From 1865 through 1877 the North's southern policy careened among these competing visions of Reconstruction, never settling on one course and never really satisfying anyone. Most historians agree that Reconstruction failed for the most part. It certainly failed American blacks, who despite the promises of the Fourteenth and Fifteenth amendments did not begin to reap most of the benefits of freedom until another eighty years had passed. The Radical Republicans' legislative victories were undone by a recalcitrant South that refused to give up white supremacy and quickly established new means of segregation, discrimination, and oppression. While northerners and their Republican leaders spent vast amounts of time, energy, and resources on Reconstruction, their efforts proved inadequate to the mammoth task. Most were ultimately unwilling to shoulder the far heavier burdens that probably would have been necessary to give substance to their proclaimed ideals and to enforce northern demands against a South determined to resist. The occupying force was too small to compel southern compliance with northern dictates, even during periods when the Radicals were in charge. As would frequently be the case in American foreign policy, there was a large gap between ends and means, which exacerbated the moral gap between the desire to impose justice by coercion and the desire to respect the South's right of self-determination.

Contrary to many southern-inspired histories of Reconstruction that painted the era as one of rampant political corruption and perfidy, the politicians of the era were not much more venal or less high-minded than usual. Their battles, though almost incomprehensible today, were for the highest possible stakes. Decisions taken on matters of Reconstruction would determine the meaning and purpose of the American nation, as well as the electoral prospects of both national parties, and everyone knew it. The first Reconstruction president, Andrew Johnson, was impeached and nearly removed from office by Radical Republicans in Congress because they considered his lenient southern policy a betrayal of the purposes of the war. Johnson survived by a single vote in the Senate, but the struggle produced a virtual congressional coup d'état. For a time in the late 1860s the Congress not only made the laws but also executed them, through a U.S. Army that unofficially pledged its fealty to the legislature and against the president, at least in the conduct of southern policy. The possibility of a return to war was never far from people's minds. When the Republican Rutherford B. Hayes won the disputed election of 1876 over Democrat Samuel Tilden, many in the capital worried that the Democrats might resort to arms.

IN SUCH CIRCUMSTANCES it was not surprising that American foreign policy in the decade following the Civil War had an erratic quality. Radical Republicans in the Senate supplemented their assault on President Johnson's executive powers at home by exercising to the fullest their constitutional role on matters of foreign policy. They blocked almost every treaty negotiated by Johnson and his secretary of state, William Seward, on issues great and small, regardless of the merits, because they feared that ratification of international treaties would hand the president and his beleaguered administration desperately needed political victories.[29] Such calculations helped doom the Anglo-American Johnson-Clarendon Convention, a perfectly reasonable settlement of outstanding Civil War claims negotiated in 1867.[30] Even the one treaty passed by the Senate during the Johnson years— the annexation of Alaska—stirred controversy and left reluctant Republican backers worried lest their approval appear an endorsement of the hated Johnson.[31] For five years after the Civil War, presidents and cabinet officers who found themselves out of favor with Republican leaders in Congress on policy toward the South could accomplish little in any realm of policy, foreign or domestic.

The politics of Reconstruction destroyed any hope Seward might have had of personally implementing the grand vision of American foreign policy he had laid out before the war. The antislavery leader of the antebellum years took a lenient approach to the conquered South after the war, arguing that the freed slaves would "find their place" and that the North "must get over this notion of interfering with the affairs of the South."[32] He may have hoped that bringing the national conflict to a rapid and painless end would allow the United States to turn its attention outward again, or he may simply have tailored his views to match those of the border state president he served.[33] But Radical Republicans condemned Seward as an apostate and accused him of abetting the "usurper" President Johnson. In the 1866 congressional elections Republicans ran on a platform attacking the "Seward-Johnson Reaction."[34] Sumner in particular considered Seward a traitor to the cause of black freedom, and as chairman of the Senate Foreign Relations Committee he opposed almost every foreign policy initiative Seward brought him. James Blaine, who shared Seward's expansive approach to American foreign policy, nevertheless opposed his efforts to acquire naval stations in the Caribbean in part because he was angry about the secretary of state's "lenient approach to the former Confederate states."[35] President Grant, who later tried to annex Santo Domingo, opposed the purchase of the smaller and less controversial Danish West Indies because it was "a scheme of Seward's."[36]

Beyond the political warfare that stymied most foreign policy initiatives, the experience of the sectional conflict affected the way many Americans felt about their nation and its role in the world long after that conflict was settled. History did not start afresh after Robert E. Lee's surrender at Appomattox. For the generation that lived through it, the Civil War would forever remain the most important event of their lives. Theirs was, as Oliver

Wendell Holmes, Jr., later said, a generation "touched by fire." Just as World War II cast its shadow over American foreign policy for a half century after its conclusion—President George H. W. Bush, elected in 1988, had served as a pilot in the war—so the Civil War's influence on Americans persisted well into the beginning of the twentieth century. President William McKinley, elected in 1896 and again in 1900, had served as a major in the Union army, and in the nine presidential elections between the end of the Civil War and the election of Theodore Roosevelt in 1904, every Republican presidential candidate except one had served as an officer in the Civil War.

A living symbol of the continuing fixation on the sectional conflict and the issues of slavery and black rights was Charles Sumner, the onetime scourge of the slave power who after the war helped lead the Radical cause from his perch as chairman of the Senate Foreign Relations Committee. Probably no member of Congress in American history ever wielded more influence over foreign policy. But foreign relations were not Charles Sumner's principal concern. In the late 1860s and early 1870s he was still fighting the battle against slavery and its consequences; he fought for the rights of the freed slaves and against the men who would deprive them of those rights. As committee chairman, Sumner evaluated and approved nominees for overseas posts strictly on the basis of their stance on national issues before, during, and after the war, to the point where his Senate colleagues protested his "propensity . . . to reduce every discussion, no matter what may be its subject, to the general head of slavery." An exasperated Secretary of State Hamilton Fish once asked Sumner, "How long is the rebellion to last?"[37]

The foreign policy question to which Sumner devoted most of his energies during the Reconstruction era, and on which he repeatedly frustrated the designs of two administrations, was the settlement of outstanding claims against England from the Civil War—the so-called *Alabama* claims. Most Americans, even the more viscerally anti-British politicians, focused chiefly on gaining British compensation for the economic damage done by Confederate commerce raiders operating with impunity out of British ports. That constituted a sizable claim, eventually determined by a commission of arbitration to amount to over $15 million. Sumner cared more about justice than about compensation, however. He wanted to punish Britain for its pro-Confederate actions and sympathies during the Civil War. Had it not been for British sympathy with the South, he believed, the rebellion would have quickly collapsed. England's actions had prolonged the war, therefore, and exacerbated the suffering of the American people. But in Sumner's eyes, British sins were even greater than that. Once the leader of the worldwide antislavery crusade—the hope and inspiration of the American antislavery movement and of Sumner himself—the British government during the Civil War had sold its soul for cotton. By its "flagrant, unnatural departure from that anti-slavery rule which . . . was the avowed creed of England," Sumner charged, the British government had "opened the gates of war" and then fanned the flames of destruction.[38] What kind of financial settlement could compensate for such a historic moral betrayal? Sumner toted up the cost at something in excess of $2 billion (more than $25 billion in today's dollars), but he was prepared to accept Canada in lieu of a cash payment.

Sumner's passion for the issues of slavery and black rights also shaped his views on what became in the decade after the Civil War the perennial question of Santo Domingo. Whether to annex Santo Domingo (later the Dominican Republic) to the United States or, less ambitiously, to lease Samana Bay as a port for American warships, became one of the biggest foreign policy controversies of the Reconstruction era. But the hullabaloo over Santo Domingo had little to do with strategic or economic considerations. Senior American naval officers wanted Samana Bay partly because Confederate raiders during the Civil War had revealed the nation's vulnerability to attacks against its commerce and hence the desirability of acquiring what Seward called "island outposts" in the Caribbean for both military and commercial reasons.[39] Merchants and West Coast politicians who favored building a transisthmian canal to secure easier passage between the Atlantic and Pacific viewed the island outposts as useful for defending and supplying the ships that would carry American trade through a Nicaraguan or Panamanian passage.[40] The Dominican leader of the time, who eagerly sought either annexation or protectorate status to defend against his Haitian neighbors, held a dubious plebiscite that allegedly registered popular support for annexation. In the United States President Andrew Johnson supported the acquisition, as did Seward. President Grant was enthusiastic; Hamilton Fish was much less so but willing to go along. The normally cautious senator and later secretary of state Frederick T. Frelinghuysen supported annexation, as did most leaders of the Republican Party, including the powerful Radical leader Thaddeus Stevens. As Johnson put it in his annual message to Congress in December 1868, in a line drafted by Seward, "Comprehensive national policy would seem to sanction the acquisition and incorporation into our Federal Union of the several adjacent continental and insular communities."[41] Future generations of diplomatic historians, adopting the rhetoric and arguments of Grant's opponents, have generally described the proposed Santo Domingo annexation as a "scheme," a corrupt little affair driven by shady characters with dollar signs in their eyes. It certainly was partly that—the desire for personal profit had played a role in this as in every previous and future acquisition of new American territory, from the Ohio Valley to Louisiana to Florida and Texas to Alaska to Hawaii. Still, many observers at the time believed there was merit in the idea,[42] and but for the determined opposition of Sumner, Grant's treaty for annexing Santo Domingo "might have slipped through the Senate almost uncontested."[43]

Instead, Sumner managed to build enough opposition in the Senate to deny Grant the two-thirds majority required to pass the treaty. Some of this opposition was purely partisan, and so was some of the support. But what ultimately killed the proposal was a combination of lingering sectional animosities, disagreements over what to do with the South, and the question of race. The defeat revealed the subtle changes that had come to American attitudes about foreign policy, and particularly about territorial expansion, as a result of the long sectional crisis and the Civil War.

Race and racism were a significant factor for many opponents of annexation, though for a variety of different and sometimes contradictory reasons. A powerful bloc of political leaders simply opposed adding the darker-skinned population of Dominicans to the already large population of African-Americans. This group included Thomas F. Bayard, the Democratic senator from Delaware and future secretary of state under Grover Cleveland. He had opposed the Fourteenth and Fifteenth amendments, which granted rights to "ignorant and semi-barbarous" freed slaves,[44] so it was not surprising that he opposed incorporating what he called this "semi-barbarous . . . population of black cut-throats," these "descendants of African slaves" whose "attempts at self-government" had produced nothing but a "chaotic mass of crime and degradation" and "a series of blood-stained failures." Perhaps "a strong-handed and just-minded white ruler would be the greatest blessing that Heaven could bestow." But that was no role for the United States. A "fiat of nature" had decreed that Americans would be "unable to elevate such a race as inhabit that island to the level of our own." On the contrary, he feared that "if a level is to be achieved at all it will only be by dragging us down, and not by bringing them up." The view that American democracy would be poisoned by the incorporation of non-white populations, that America would suffer grievously from the admission of all these "niggers," was popular in the South, but it was also the view of a certain set of East Coast intellectuals, like the editors of *The Nation* and *Harper's Weekly,* who described the Dominican people as a "radically alien and essentially perilous element."[45]

Other northerners had a different concern. James G. Blaine opposed southward expansion, but not so much because of what the incorporation of nonwhite peoples would do to the United States. What Blaine feared was the expansion and enlargement of the South itself. The South, in his view, had never truly changed. It was still dominated by former Confederates with no real loyalty to the Union, by plantation owners waiting for the chance to reestablish slavery in some new guise, and by Democrats determined to overthrow the Republican ascendancy. He feared that expansion south of the Rio Grande "might too readily reestablish a Southern ascendancy in the Union."[46]

Fears of a resurgent South enjoyed remarkable vitality in the northern states long after the war ended, and they manifested themselves in a widespread hostility to all southward expansion. Missouri senator Carl Schurz warned that annexation of Santo Domingo would be the start of a renewed southern imperialist drive that would eventually swallow Haiti, Mexico, Central America, and then the entire hemisphere "down to the isthmus of Darien."[47] Under the pretense of taking "fraternal care of the colored people," southerners migrating to the Caribbean islands would soon be pressing the natives "forcibly into the service of their eager appetites." They might not call it slavery, but the tropical sun, under which no one would work voluntarily, would "breed slavery and despotism in a thousand disguises."[48]

Schurz saw in the rise of the Ku Klux Klan and the wave of lynchings across the South "the old spirit of violence, the old impatience of adverse opinions, the old propensity to use force in preference to patient reason, and all those disorderly tendencies which are still so evident in alarming transgressions." The struggle between North and South had been no "mere historical accident" but the inevitable clash of "two different currents of civilization developed under different natural influences." He doubted whether Americans would "ever be able to become completely masters of the disease." He therefore opposed any expansion of the nation's southern domain. "[H]ave we not enough with one South? Can we afford to buy another one?"[49]

Finally, there was Sumner, the nation's leading champion of black rights before and after the Civil War, a man who asked to be buried in a black cemetery, perhaps the least racist man in America in his day. Sumner opposed annexation of Santo Domingo not because he wanted to keep blacks away from whites but because he wanted to keep whites away from blacks. He wanted to preserve one place in the hemisphere where blacks could rule themselves free from white domination. An "ordinance of Nature," he claimed, a "higher law" had set aside the island of Santo

Domingo for the "colored race" as a place where blacks could live free.[50] The formerly enslaved blacks had earned this sanctuary from oppression with their sweat and blood and tears, and now former Confederates were scheming to take it away from them. Sumner feared that annexation of Santo Domingo would soon lead to American encroachments on Haiti, his beloved "Negro Republic," whose very existence was a monument to the antislavery struggle. To Sumner, still fighting against the southern slave power, Dominican annexation was another attempt to "subjugate a distant Territory to Slavery," and Grant was another James Buchanan.[51] He wished that Grant had spent half "the time, money, zeal, will," and personal effort protecting southern blacks from the Ku Klux Klan as he had trying to "obtain half an island in the Caribbean."[52]

The Senate's rejection of Santo Domingo's annexation offered a glimpse into how the Civil War had redirected American foreign policy. The South, which in the 1840s and '50s had been the engine of American southward expansion, was now prostrate and oppressed and no longer interested in acquiring new lands filled with "niggers." The northern Republicans who dominated American politics after the war, meanwhile, brought to the Congress, the White House, and the State Department a perspective significantly shaped by long years of opposing the slave power. To many leading northerners, the Civil War had been fought precisely to prevent the South from expanding its territory, from annexing Santo Domingo, and from buying or conquering Cuba, more of Mexico, and parts of Central America. Containment of the southern expansionist drive had been the unifying principle of the Republican Party at its founding. Opposing territorial manifest destiny, when it aimed southward, was an established Republican Party tradition. After the Civil War this strain of opposition to southern territorial expansion continued to influence Republican policies. Even in the 1880s Blaine would recall that the nation's territorial acquisitions prior to the Civil War had "all been in the interest of slavery."[53]

The Republican Vision

AS BEFORE THE WAR, there were exceptions to Republican opposition to territorial expansion. Many who opposed expansion southward still looked longingly northward.[54] Schurz saw in the northern territories "a magnificent field . . . for our ambition of aggrandizement" and mistakenly hoped, along with many others, that the Canadian people would happily choose annexation to the United States if given the opportunity. It "fills my soul with delight when I see events preparing themselves which will lead the whole continent north of us into our arms."[55] With its white, predominantly Anglo-Saxon and Protestant population, Canada could be absorbed without injecting a tropical, dark-skinned poison into the nation's bloodstream. Yearning for northern territorial expansion was another party tradition, going back to the days when Republicans sought new northern states to counterbalance the South's drive for new southern states. Blaine applauded Seward's acquisition of Alaska because looking "northward for territory, instead of southward, was a radical change of policy."[56]

Some leading Republicans still wanted to acquire naval stations and "island outposts," such as Samana Bay, or a port in Haiti or the Danish West Indies, both for the protection of the American coastline and American shipping and for the defense of an eventual canal. When the era of Reconstruction passed, Republican policy makers would return to these plans again. The purchase or lease of naval stations from which to promote and defend commerce had always been considered by northern Whigs and Republicans to be morally superior to the southern desire for territory in which to implant slavery. Grant's plans for Santo Domingo had failed in part because they had crossed the line from seeking a harbor to annexing an entire foreign population and thereby had acquired an excessively southern flavor.

Finally, there was the question of Hawaii, which had long been an object of first Whig and then Republican ambitions in the antebellum years. In the 1840s the annexation of Hawaii had been blocked by the sectional struggle, partly because the Hawaiian population, fearing enslavement, had insisted on admission to the Union as a nonslave state. It was another measure of how much Republican policies after the Civil War continued to be shaped by prewar attitudes that the acquisition of Hawaii, despite its large, dark-skinned, "mongrel" population, remained high on the agenda of Blaine and most Republican leaders, even those who rejected expansion into the tropics south of the Rio Grande.[57]

These exceptions did not prevent Republican leaders after the Civil War from insisting, and believing, that the Union victory had put an end to the nation's territorial expansionism and certainly to expansion by military conquest. Any island outposts would be acquired not by force of arms but by purchase or by voluntary annexation. A strain of pacifism had been linked to the antislavery movement in the antebellum years, and although onetime pacifists like Sumner had abandoned it in the great moral crusade against the slave power, the ideal of a world without war returned after Appomattox. Even President Grant, in his second inaugural address, expressed his conviction that "our great Maker is preparing the world, in His own good time, to become one nation, speaking one language, and when armies and navies will not longer be required."[58]

The mainstream Republican view, before and after the war, was that in most cases, as Seward put it, "the sword is not the most winning messenger that can be sent abroad" and that the way to acquire global influence and power befitting a great nation was by the spread of commerce, modern technology, and American principles of government. Seward, Blaine, and other Republicans hoped eventually to place the United States at the center of that system and to exert global influence not by force and conquest but through the erection of a system of mutual dependence. "Heretofore nations have either repelled, or exhausted, or disgusted the colonies they planted and the countries they conquered," Seward noted. But America would "expand, not by force of arms, but by attraction."[59]

The postwar turn away from territorial expansionism was no turn toward isolationism. Republican leaders envisioned an enormous increase in American influence, commercial, political, and moral. They believed the United States, purged of slavery and slave power imperialism, stood on a higher moral plane. The path was clear for the United States to play the role it had always been destined to play, as a great power—indeed, the greatest of world powers—wielding its benevolent influence across the globe. These Republican aspirations promised a far greater expansion of global influence than anything the Democratic South would have imagined or considered desirable before the war. As Jefferson Davis had insisted, the South had not been "engaged in a Quixotic fight for the rights of man. . . . We are conservative."

The Republicans were not conservative, either in their domestic or in their foreign policies. For most of the half century after the Civil War, the Republican Party remained very much the party of the North, and to its devoted followers, it was more than a mere political organization. It was the party that had saved the Union, had saved freedom itself, and had done so by massing national power and directing it against an evil uprising led by southern rebels, who happened to be Democrats, and over the determined resistance of traitorous northern "copperheads," who also happened to be Democrats. In every election Republican politicians "waved the bloody shirt" in national campaigns, never letting the voters forget that the Democrats had been the "party of rebellion." In 1893 a leading Republican like Senator Henry Cabot Lodge would still insist that his party was "the party of progress that fought slavery standing across the pathway of modern civilization," while the Democrats, "the party of conservatism," had "clung to slavery."[60] When Wilson was elected as only the second Democratic president in sixty-two years, Lodge and Theodore Roosevelt would frequently disparage him by comparing him to James Buchanan. The Republican Party's very identity derived from its role in the great moral crusade of the Civil War.

That war had been, in Lodge's words, an "overshadowing experience" that had left him and many others of his generation "with profound convictions which nothing can ever shake."[61] For three decades after the war the cause of the Union still inspired both voters and politicians, who equated it with freedom, progress, and true Americanism. Republican presidential candidates tended to be not only veterans of the Union army but antislavery leaders before the war and Radical Republicans after it. President Garfield, elected in 1880, had served as a major general in the Civil War, had been elected to Congress by the intensely abolitionist Western Reserve of Ohio, was a Radical Republican in the struggle to impeach Andrew Johnson, supported all the Republican civil rights bills, and until the day he died remembered the Democratic Party in the North as "the cowardly peace party" and the South as a "bastard civilization." The platform of 1880 reminded voters that the Republican Party had "transformed 4,000,000 human beings from the likeness of things to the rank of citizens."[62]

The Republicans were, in the context of their times, progressive. In their domestic policies they remained, as before the war, the party of the "active state."[63] Belief in a strong federal government took the form of interventionist measures to reform the South during Reconstruction and then of high protective tariffs and large federal government expenditures. The famously free-spending "Billion-Dollar Congress" of 1890 was a Republican Congress. Republican leaders like Blaine resurrected Henry Clay's American System and called for "constructive action" by the federal government, "improvement of the nation's waterways, the encouragement of foreign commerce, and a national protective-tariff system that would band together all sections and occupational groups."[64] President Garfield endorsed a national Department of Education, the Smithsonian Institution, and a federal census. Republicans in Congress promoted "basic scientific inquiry through the Coast and Geodesic Survey, special commissions, western and polar exploration, agriculture experiment stations, and land grants for education."[65] As Blaine and other Republicans never tired of arguing, the "phenomenal" progress the United States had enjoyed since the end of the Civil War had "required the broad measures, the expanding functions which belong to a free Nation."[66] The northern triumph in the Civil War itself had in the Republicans' view vindicated their faith in strong government. It had "compelled the most influential northern intellectuals, publicists, and politicians to subscribe to the ideal of a powerful, unified, purposeful nation."[67]

The Civil War had also affected Republican attitudes toward foreign policy. The American people, Lodge insisted, had awakened "to a full realization of the greatness of the work in which they had been engaged and of the meaning and power of the nation they had built up." Salvation of the Union had created a "beneficent power," he told audiences in 1882, "and think of the good which it means to humanity! . . . [W]e have a great mission and a great work as a nation." That greatness would be measured "by whether the United States actually stood for something in world affairs."[68] For leading Republicans like Theodore Roosevelt, the Civil War was the standard against which all other American endeavors must be judged. Although he was only three when war broke out, little "Teedie" had prayed for God to "grind the Southern troops into powder," and although his mother was a southerner and his maternal uncles fought for the South, Roosevelt never doubted that the "right was exclusively with the Union people, and the wrong exclusively with the secessionists."[69] Slavery had been "a grossly anachronistic and un-American form of evil," and Roosevelt lionized both Lincoln and Seward for having brought about "its destruction."[70] "Had I been old enough," Roosevelt would often say, "I would have served on the northern side."[71] For Lodge, who "believed so strongly in the righteousness of the Northern cause that he long found it difficult to look on Southerners as his moral equals," the war would appear as "a struggle where the onward march of civilization was at stake."[72]

Both Lodge and Roosevelt believed that the war had provided the supreme test of Americans' willingness to sacrifice for a higher cause. Whether in the struggle against complacent materialism at home or against lassitude, pacifism, and isolationism in relations with the world, they would appeal again and again to memories of the Civil War to inspire Americans. "As our fathers fought with slavery and crushed it, in order that it not seize and crush them," Roosevelt would declare, "so we are called on to fight new forces."[73] Decades after Lincoln defined American nationalism as inherently infused with international moral responsibility, Lodge would insist that for America to fulfill its destiny and become a great power, it would have to accept its global duties.[74] When war with Spain approached over the struggle for the independence of Cuba, he appealed to the moral logic of Lincoln. To those who argued that Americans had neither the responsibility nor the right to interfere in Cuba, even in a just cause, Lodge retorted, "[T]he proposition that it is none of our business is precisely what the South said about slavery."[75]

The Republican vision of a more active and moralistic American foreign policy was not confined to a small group of northeastern intellectuals and politicians. By far the most popular and dominant political figure from the late 1870s to the early 1890s was James G. Blaine, the "Plumed Knight" who won the Republican presidential nomination in 1884, despite being implicated in a scandal, and was a leading contender in both 1880 and 1888. Republicans in all parts of the country seemed ready to "give their lives to elect him," one contemporary reported. He was "a great party leader, superbly attuned to the men and measures of his time."[76] This consummate politician presumably knew what many Republican voters wanted when he appealed for an expanded American role in the world, as he never ceased to do throughout his political career. In the antebellum years he had been a Lincoln supporter, a founder of Maine's Republican Party, a fierce opponent of slavery, an admirer of John Quincy Adams, a longtime supporter of Clay's American System, and a disciple of Seward. The Civil War had been a war for progress, he believed, and throughout the ordeal he "retained his faith in the future greatness and destiny of the United States." His internationalism "confirmed and complemented his already firmly held sense of American mission—a belief that the United States and the American people should assume a more active role in global affairs and in the improvement of the world."[77] He served twice as secretary of state in the early 1880s and early 1890s under two Republican presidents, James Garfield and Benjamin Harrison, who shared his foreign policy vision and believed it accorded with the general views of the party faithful.

For Republicans, the appeal for a more vigorous and moralistic foreign policy reflected the fact that the party faithful after the Civil War did view the world through a moral and ideological lens, both at home and abroad. House Foreign Affairs Committee chairman Nathaniel P. Banks wanted America "to be the grand disturber of the divine right of kings, the model of struggling nations, the best hope of the independence of states and of national liberty."[78] Banks tended toward florid rhetoric, but his sentiments were not far from the mainstream views of politicians, government officials, and commentators. President Grant in his second inaugural address expressed his "conviction that the civilized world is tending toward republicanism, or government by the people through their chosen representatives, and that our own great Republic is destined to be the guiding star of all others.''[79] There was more sentiment than policy in such pronounce-ments, but policy would eventually catch up with sentiment.

The forceful abolition of slavery had a lot to do with shaping this moral-istic sensibility. Through the ordeal of the Civil War the United States had morally regenerated and purified itself—at least in the eyes of many north-erners and Republicans. It had also taught them a new lesson, that war could serve what they regarded as just and moral ends. As Lincoln changed the meaning of the Declaration into a positive requirement to further human rights, so the Civil War provided the example of an aggressive war of con-quest to implant American principles in a civilization that had manifestly rejected them. It was an example of power wielded in the service not only of self-interest or material gain but of ideals.

Among the first expressions of America's new foreign policy moral-ism after the Civil War was a strong objection to slavery in the Western Hemisphere. Scarcely a year had passed after the collapse of the Confed-eracy when Secretary of State Seward began protesting Spanish laws that required black American sailors to post bond before going ashore in slave-holding Cuba. Foreign observers may have been astonished to see the United States condemning as unacceptably immoral the institution that until recently had thrived within its borders. Until 1865 states like South Carolina had demanded that black British sailors not post bond but actually be held in prison while ashore. Nevertheless Seward proclaimed "the great change of the political relations between the races in this country" now made it the government's "duty" to ensure that other countries did not discriminate between Americans "of different birth, extraction, or color." American moralism extended beyond the protection of black citizens abroad. Slavery anywhere was denounced, and antislavery forces were applauded and encouraged. During the Civil War the once-feared "black republic" of Haiti was recognized by the United States. After the war even the more con-servative Hamilton Fish, Seward's successor, condemned Cuban slavery as contrary to "those rights of man which are now universally admitted." When Spain did free several thousand slaves in 1873, Fish spoke of a new era in which immorality anywhere concerned everyone everywhere. "The rapid increase of the means of communications throughout the globe," Fish declared, sounding like a twenty-first-century human rights advocate, "have brought into almost daily intercourse communities which hitherto have been aliens and strangers to each other, so that now no great social and moral wrong can be inflicted on any people without being felt throughout the civilized globe.''[80] This was the universalistic and moralistic language of the antebellum Republican Party, which as a result of the Union victory had become the language of American foreign policy. Even a moderate like Fish now spoke of international moral obligations.

"Civilization as Ideology"

AMERICANS DID NOT EMBARK on a positive "mission" to change the world after the Civil War. There was no grand strategy for global reform, nor any deliberate policy to remake any specific country in the liberal mold. But when events or their own actions brought Americans into contact with "great social and moral wrongs," they responded with protest, sometimes with diplomatic interference, and occasionally with force, depending on the circumstances. Even when the United States took no particular action at all to address perceived wrongs, Americans formed attitudes toward other countries and peoples that affected their judgment at critical moments. There is more to a nation's foreign policies than invasions and annexations or the acquisition of territory and markets. The attitudes that Americans developed toward the rest of the world provided the context in which they acted. And sometimes the actions came long after the attitudes were formed.

One example was the evolving American attitude toward tsarist Russia. During the Civil War most Union supporters had viewed Russia favorably, mistakenly believing the tsar had intervened on the Union's side when the Russian fleet, looking for a place to hide from the British and French, decided to put in at New York harbor. "God bless the Russians!" Navy Secretary Gideon Welles had exclaimed.[81] Northern antislavery leaders had also developed a high opinion of Alexander II, the "Tsar Liberator" who freed the serfs two years before Lincoln freed the slaves.

Soon after the Civil War ended, however, this goodwill evaporated, and the reason had little to do with matters of commerce or security. When Russia sold Alaska in 1867, it backed out of the Western Hemisphere and for the next three decades posed less danger to perceived American interests than any of the other great powers. Yet from the 1860s onward a large number of Americans came to despise Russia on grounds that were moral, humanitarian, and ideological.

American hostility to the Russian government grew out of its treatment of its Jewish population. Starting in the 1860s Alexander II began enforcing old anti-Semitic regulations, and tsarist authorities, refusing to distinguish between Russian Jews and American Jews, abused and sometimes arrested the latter for doing proscribed business while in Russia. In the late 1860s the issue came to dominate Russian-American relations, thoroughly sour-ing American attitudes toward the tsarist government over the next three decades.

The steady prominence of the issue revealed, among other things, the evolving nature of the American polity after the Civil War, especially the role of new immigrant groups. In the 1860s prominent American Jews wielded significant influence in an increasingly democratic system that was more easily swayed by "the demands of domestic interest groups," of which the Jews were one of many.[82] Simon Wolf, Oscar Straus, Jacob Schiff, and others had easy access to presidents, cabinet officers, and congressmen, partly because these successful businessmen had money to spend on campaigns, partly because the large numbers of Jews who settled in northeastern cities—numbers that rose as Russian anti-Semitism worsened—sent members of Congress to Washington who looked out for their interests. William Seward, the longtime New York politician, needed no enlightening about the issues that concerned Jews. But Grant, whose anti-Semitic comments during the Civil War had come back to haunt him in the 1868 campaign, bent over backward to reassure Jewish leaders that he was concerned about the treatment of Jews in Russia, Romania, and anywhere else they were oppressed.

It was not just a matter of votes and money. American officials were genuinely appalled by the persecution of Jews in Russia, especially of Jews who happened to be American citizens. As they wrestled with this frustrating issue over the decades—and they rarely made much headway with the determinedly anti-Semitic tsarist authorities—they constantly recurred to a common conviction: that Russia's behavior was contrary to "the spirit of the age," by which they meant the spirit of liberalism and progress. President Grant declared it was "contrary to the spirit of the age to persecute anyone on account of race, color, or religion." When pogroms broke out in Russian-controlled Romania, Hamilton Fish ordered joint protests by American and European consuls. The United States made "no distinction" among its own citizens on the basis of religion, he noted, and therefore "naturally believes in a civilization the world over which will secure the same universal views."[83] Blaine even approached the British with the idea that the two nations should make league with "other Powers whose service in the work of progress is commensurate with our own" to put pressure on Russia so that it "may be beneficially influenced by their cumulative representations."[84]

Blaine knew that a nation's repression of its own people was not normally "a fit matter for the intervention of another independent power." But he believed that the United States had "a moral duty" not only to its own citizens but also "to the doctrines of religious freedom we so strongly uphold, to seek proper protection for those citizens *and tolerance for their creed,* in foreign lands."[85] The United States must therefore "urge upon Russia action in consonance with the spirit of the age."[86] This break from recognized diplomatic practice, claimed the normally fastidious Fish, was justified because the "grievance adverted to is so enormous as to impart to it, as it were, a cosmopolitan character in the redress of which all countries, governments, and creeds alike are interested."[87]

When Alexander II was assassinated in 1881, a nervous and angry Alexander III abandoned his father's tentative political reforms and further tightened enforcement of anti-Semitic regulations. A new wave of pogroms swept across Russia, and in the 1880s two hundred thousand Russian Jews passed through Ellis Island, doubling the Jewish population in America.[88] The arrival of these Russian Jewish refugees—who to the American public appeared desperate, dirty, and, compared to the settled and prosperous German Jewish population, quite alien—produced a "spontaneous outcry" across the nation, "not confined to Jewish centers or to Jewish pressure groups."[89] Blaine protested to the Russian government that its oppressive policies were now directly affecting the United States, "upon whose shores are cast daily evidences of the suffering and destitution wrought by the enforcement of the edicts against this unhappy people."[90] President Benjamin Harrison picked up this theme in his annual message to Congress in 1891, insisting that Russia's "banishment" of Jews was "not a local question." When Russia forced people to leave the country, he argued, they had to go somewhere. A report commissioned by Harrison concluded: "To push these people upon us in a condition which makes our duty of self-protection war against the spirit of our institutions and the ordinary instincts of humanity calls for a protest so emphatic that it will be both heard and heeded."[91] American protests were heard, but they were not heeded. By the early 1890s Russian consuls in the United States were interrogating Americans seeking visas to find out if they were Jews, a practice President Grover Cleveland condemned as "an obnoxious invasion of our territorial jurisdiction."[92]

By then the difficulties between the two countries extended beyond the Jewish problem. Under Alexander III's stern autocratic reign, thousands of dissidents, radicals, and political opponents, both real and imagined, were arrested and sent to internal exile in the prison system of Siberia, the forerunner of the Soviet Union's gulag archipelago. Life there was brutal, and when word of its horrors spread in the United States, American hostility to Russia reached new heights.

Americans in the television age have always had difficulty believing that their nineteenth-century forebears knew or cared what was going on in the world, with no televised images in their living rooms to show them. But in the late 1880s hundreds of thousands of Americans learned about the political prisons in Siberia thanks to the work of George Kennan, a relative of the Cold War era's George F. Kennan, who traveled through Siberia for several months and produced a series of articles published by the *Century* magazine over a three-year period beginning in 1888. His vivid depiction of the Siberian prison system produced a national sensation. The *Century* reached more than two hundred thousand paid subscribers, and between 1889 and 1898 Kennan delivered more than eight hundred lectures to an audience of close to a million. "His stories of the cruel, barbarous treatment of the exiles by the Russian Government were extremely thrilling and pathetic," one contemporary reviewer reported. "They tended to rouse within his hearers a feeling of revenge against the monarchy that inflicts such horrible treatment on her prisoners—feelings that are only known to people who enjoy liberty in the 'land of the free,' under the 'stars and stripes.' "[93] At one lecture, Samuel Clemens, better known as Mark Twain, exclaimed, "If such a government cannot be overthrown otherwise than by dynamite, then, thank God for dynamite!"[94]

Kennan's reports blackened Russia's image and fixed the tsarist despotism as a perennial bogeyman for both parties. The Democratic Party platform in 1892 called on the American government "in the interest of justice and humanity . . . to use its prompt and best efforts" to stop "these cruel persecutions in the dominions of the Czar and to secure to the oppressed equal rights." When Russia suffered a famine in 1891, William Jennings Bryan opposed sending relief, in part because it was "one of the most despotic of nations."[95] Mary E. Lease, the radical midwestern populist who urged farmers to "raise less corn and more hell," wrote a book in 1895 warning of "the establishment of a world-wide Russian despotism."[96] A West Virginia congressman asked, "Can we have a friendship between tyranny and liberty; between Asiatic despotism and modern civilization; between the inertia of barbarism and the spirit of progress?"[97]

Elite northeastern Republicans were just as hostile as prairie populists. In 1891 the Boston-based American Society of Friends of Russian Freedom included Julia Ward Howe, author of the "Battle Hymn of the Republic," William Lloyd Garrison, Mark Twain, the Reverend Edward Everett Hale, John Greenleaf Whittier, and Lyman Abbott. Hard-headed Wall Street Republicans like Elihu Root had nothing but "scorn and contempt" for Russia.[98] Henry Cabot Lodge noted that while Russians appeared "on the surface and in external things" to be "like us," their ideas, their "theory of life," and their "controlling motives of action" were "utterly alien." As far as Lodge was concerned, Russians and Americans had "no common ground, no common starting place, no common premise of thought and action."[99] Theodore Roosevelt believed that Russians hated and feared "our political institutions" and therefore were natural adversaries. For Roosevelt, the only hope was that Russia would modernize and leave despotism behind. "While he can keep absolutism," Roosevelt speculated, the Russian would "possess infinite possibilities of menace to his neighbors." Only liberalization would make Russia less threatening.[100]

The United States did not go to war with Russia in the nineteenth century. But anti-Russian sentiment helped stir rather remarkable American anxiety about Russian encroachments in remote Manchuria at the turn of the century, and Americans roundly applauded Japan's devastating attack on the Russian fleet in 1904. A goodly portion of Americans' sense that Russia posed a grave strategic threat in those years derived from their perception that it was a backward and therefore dangerous despotism lacking the civilized morality consonant with the "spirit of the age."

Americans applied this measuring stick to all nations and peoples that came into their line of sight. Sometimes their judgments about who measured up were dubious, their perceptions distorted by being refracted through the lens of America's own circumstances and experiences. For instance, Bismarck's Germany enjoyed overwhelming American support for a brief time during and just after the Franco-Prussian War of 1870–71. Northerners, Republicans, and the U.S. government they controlled were grateful for Prussia's pro-Union leanings during the Civil War and for German immigrants' contribution to the northern cause. It helped that Germany's opponent was France, since northerners hated France for its pro-southern sympathies (many southerners and Democrats took the opposite view, of course) and for attempting to implant a European monarch in Mexico. The French invasion force had departed only three years before the war with Prussia. It helped, too, that the ethnic German population in the United States outnumbered the French immigrants by fifteen to one and was a crucial Republican voting bloc in several states.[101]

These factors would have weighed less in the scales had not many Americans also convinced themselves that Bismarck's newly unified Germany would be a beacon of liberalism in Europe. Its federal constitution looked on the surface to be much like the American federal constitution. Bismarck in the early years often allied himself with the German National Liberal Party, and Protestant America applauded his Kulturkampf against the powers and privileges of the German Catholic church, while it lasted. One American observer happily declared that the prevailing "tendency in Europe" was toward "the American system of separating church and state."[102] The U.S. minister in Berlin, the historian George Bancroft, predicted the new German Empire would be "the most liberal government on the continent of Europe." It was "the child of America," its very birth inspired by the Union victory. Hamilton Fish agreed that the Germans were copying the American Constitution and American-style liberalism, and President Grant in an address to Congress in February 1871 applauded "the adoption in Europe of the American system of union under the control and direction of a free people." German success could not "fail to extend popular institutions and to enlarge the peaceful influence of American ideas."[103]

Many Americans viewed the Franco-German conflict not in geopolitical terms, as a struggle between great powers, but in ideological and civilizational terms, as a struggle between liberalism and tyranny, progress and reaction. If Germany was the alleged outpost of American-style liberty in Europe, Napoleon III's France was the exemplar of imperial despotism. Charles Sumner accused the French emperor of using war with Germany as a pretext to "overthrow parliamentary government so far as it existed" and to "re-establish personal" rule. Napoleon was guilty of "disloyalty to republican institutions." "Considering the age, and the present demands of civilization," Sumner declared, "such a war stands forth terrific in wrong."[104]

As in pre–Civil War days, when they were divided over the visit of the Hungarian revolutionary Louis Kossuth, Americans projected their own political, ideological, and even religious disagreements onto the European canvas. Protestant leaders insisted the Prussian war against France was between enlightened faith and benighted Catholicism, while Irish Catholics, who tended to be Democrats, supported Catholic France. So did most southern whites. "The people of the Southland, among them General Robert E. Lee, saw in the French defense of homes and country a parallel to their own recent experience."[105] (The editors of the pro-Republican *Harper's Weekly,* in turn, pounded home a favorite Republican theme, that the Democratic Party had "no sympathy with liberty in Europe because it has been the relentless enemy of liberty in the United States.")[106] The *New York Times* described the Franco-German conflict as a struggle for the future between the "Latin" and "Teutonic" races. "The Latin races have done their part—and not always an inglorious one—in the world's history," the *Times* commented. "Now more earnest and moral and free races must guide the helm of progress. Protestantism and parliamentary government must lead European advancement."[107]

"Latin" and "Teutonic" were code words for distinctions that were more ideological than racial. When the French Second Republic was born in the midst of the war, Americans for a brief moment saw their own image reflected again and temporarily warmed even to Catholic, "Latin" France. In December 1870 Grant told Congress that "[w]hile we make no effort to impose our institutions upon the inhabitants of other countries, and while we adhere to our traditional neutrality in civil contests elsewhere, we can not be indifferent to the spread of American political ideas in a great and highly civilized country like France."[108] But a majority of Americans remained more confident of Germany's than of France's commitment to liberty, especially after they observed the radicalism of the Paris Commune. The French, for their part, could not forgive Americans for abandoning them to Prussian militarism. Victor Hugo, in his *L'année terrible,* "wept for an America which abandoned France during its agonizing crisis and strangely manifested its republican solidarity by stooping so low as to kiss the heel of the German Caesar."[109]

Americans' high expectations for a liberal Germany were indeed severely disappointed over the coming decades, as the imagined promise of liberal constitutional government soon devolved into the reality of conservative rule under the ever-shifting Bismarck and the kaiser. The early caricature of a peaceful, progressive, liberty-loving Germany metamorphosed into a very different caricature, of "Kaiser Bill" and an "autocratic, militaristic, rude, presumptuous Germany." Nasty trade battles in the 1880s helped this transformation along, and by the 1890s many Americans hated and feared the kaiser's Germany as much as they hated and feared the tsar's Russia. In both cases American perceptions of these nations as somehow backward, hostile to progress, despotic, and therefore aggressive shaped their strategic judgment. They provided the ideological backdrop for the confrontation between the United States and Germany over the tiny islands of Samoa in the 1880s and cast in a more sinister light Germany's tentative and mostly feeble probes in the Caribbean. One German historian suggests that the American hatred was the product of dashed expectations, that Germany had been caught in a "Manichean trap": the Americans had designated Germany as a good, "freedom-loving European state" and had expected it to "emulate the historic mission of the United States by promoting the progress of liberty throughout history." When it failed to live up to these high expectations, they decided it was evil.[110] When that perception took hold, even millions of ethnic German voters could not, and would not, prevent the breakdown in relations. The German government found to its dismay that most German-Americans were more American than German.

Americans made Manichean distinctions in Asia, too, and looked for signs that their model of political and economic progress was being emulated by others. They searched "to find in progressive Chinese and Japanese," and later in progressive Koreans, "an image of progressive Americans." By the late 1860s a sturdy consensus had formed around the proposition that the progressive force in Asia was Japan, while China was a bastion of backwardness and barbarism. The ancient Chinese civilization, with its confident sense of superiority and apparent lack of interest in the outside world, including the "modern" world of Europe and America, made it contemptible in the eyes of most Americans. The Chinese "will hear of nothing outside the 'Middle Kingdom,'" an American observer complained in 1871, and this made them a "cold, snaky, slow, cowardly, treacherous, suspicious, deceitful" people. Even Americans friendly to China agreed that it was "too proud to learn." For most others, China was simply inert, held back from civilization by a "deadening conservatism," its government and society "palsied," "corrupt," "degraded," and "enfeebled."[111] A sympathetic American living in China expressed admiration for its ancient civilization but not for the "eunuchs in the palace," the "pink buttoned censors who read the stars," and "all that mass of thieving treacherous, cowardly conniving adventurers which surround the throne and live an insectivorous, parasitic existence on this venerable and august monarchy."[112]

Japan, on the other hand, appeared to be everything China was not. Beginning in the late 1860s, when the restoration of the Meiji emperor produced a determined effort to copy Western ways and institutions, Americans looked upon Japan as a model of progress in Asia. They admired its people's "eagerness to adopt new ideas." The fact that Americans took credit for "opening" Japan, with Admiral Oliver Hazard Perry's expedition in 1853, enhanced their paternalistic fondness. A memorandum prepared for congressional committees in 1872 explained that "the Japanese people not only desire to follow, as far as possible, in all educational and political affairs, the example of the Americans, but . . . they look upon them as their best friends, among the nations of the globe." A best-selling American travelogue in the 1870s reported that Westernization and modernization had "taken Japan out of the ranks of the non-progressive nations" and "out of the stagnant life of Asia." Japan's advancement toward civilization practically removed it from its racial category in American eyes. The Japanese were increasingly viewed less as true Asians than as honorary Anglo-Saxons, "more Western than Asian."[113] Or rather, more American. With their "vigor, thrift, and intelligence," the Japanese were "a bright, progressive people—the Americans, so called, of Asia."[114] The strikingly different ways

Americans viewed Japan and China had much to do with seeing their own reflection in the former but not the latter: "Japan was, and China was not, becoming like America."[115]

Americans viewed conflicts among the Asian nations much as they viewed European conflicts, as contests between progress and reaction. This perspective often outweighed narrow strategic calculations and was independent of economic calculations. Americans regarded China as weak and contemptible, and they recognized that Japan was a rising power destined to be a force in East Asia, where Americans also hoped someday to be a force. American interests were more likely to clash with a rising Japan than a prostrate China. Yet they rooted for Japan in the Sino-Japanese War of 1894–95, precisely because it was strong and progressive and China was backward and pitiful. To the American mind, it was China's backwardness that was threatening while Japan's modernization was reassuring. "The American Minister to China advised the Secretary of State that Japan was only doing for China what the United States had done for Japan: bringing Western civilization." American journalists, analysts, and businessmen saw the Sino-Japanese War as "a contest between barbarism and civilization."[116] Elihu Root held out hope that Japan would become "the England of the Orient, with a constitutional form of government, a freedom from excessive territorial ambition, and a desire to promote stability and equality of commercial opportunity in a troubled area."[117] Some Americans even compared Japan's struggle against benighted China with the battle against slavery in the United States.[118] When Japan attacked and sank the Russian fleet at Port Arthur ten years later, Americans applauded again. Oscar Straus, already hostile to Russia, expressed a common view when he declared that "Japan is certainly battling on the side of civilization." Roosevelt agreed: "The Japs have played our game because they have played the game of civilized mankind."[119]

There were those who warned that Japan's adoption of Western institutions might not necessarily lead them to become either Western or friendly. A prominent American who worked for the Japanese government noted, "A country is not necessarily free because it has a form of government similar to that of other nations whose people are free."[120] Some Americans may have been taken aback when they read journalists' accounts of the seizure of Port Arthur, where Japanese soldiers partook in an "orgy of slaughter and torture" against the civilian population, killing and mutilating as many as two thousand defenseless men, women, and children.[121] And even as Americans applauded Japanese victories over China and Russia, some felt a tinge of concern that Japan might turn out to be too powerful, too modern, and therefore a threat to American interests in the Pacific. Roosevelt at times professed to be "fully alive to the danger from Japan." And he worried about how the Japanese really felt about the United States in their heart of hearts. "I wish I were certain that the Japanese down at bottom did not lump Russians, English, Americans, Germans, all of us, simply as white devils inferior to themselves . . . and to be treated politely only so long as would enable the Japanese to take advantage of our national jealousies, and beat us in turn."[122] But such fears were generally overwhelmed by the perception that Japan stood for progress and by the pervasive American conviction that progress was always and everywhere in the interests of the United States.

American attitudes toward European and Asian powers revealed how after the Civil War the ideas of progress and civilization provided organizing principles for American thinking about foreign relations. This view was inherited from the Enlightenment and enjoyed an old pedigree in America. The founding generation had shared the prevailing Enlightenment faith in liberal progress, as well as the popular belief that the seat of civilization had over the centuries traveled west, from ancient China to Rome to Great Britain and finally to America. This almost deterministic belief in progress could be seen during the antebellum years, chiefly in the North, where John O'Sullivan's *Democratic Review* declared that "the history of humanity" was the "record of a grand march . . . at all times tending to one point—the ultimate perfection of man," while the American *Whig Review* defined progress in terms of the advance of civilization toward "the complete harmonious development of man in all his appropriate relations to this world."[123] After the Civil War, a war fought for progress against slavery "standing across the pathway to civilization," the belief in the advance of civilization became even more firmly rooted. Thanks to the work of Charles Darwin and his popularizers, it also acquired the aura of scientific "truth" in an age when reverence for science was growing. Herbert Spencer, whose work was probably more widely read in America than Darwin's, extended evolutionary theory to human societies and also provided a new gloss of scientific authority to the old Enlightenment idea, well articulated by Edward Gibbon, that human societies progressed on a developmental continuum from savagery to barbarism to civilization and then eventually, like Rome, to decay. Darwin's theory of evolution presented a dire challenge to theologians—though some, like Josiah Strong, managed to blend Darwinism and Christianity in their worldview—but it fit well with American ideas of progress that were rooted not in religion but in the secular ideas of the Enlightenment.

This fusion of old and new theories about human progress produced what one historian has called an American "ideology of civilization." Americans evaluated other nations and their relationship to the United States according to where they stood on the continuum of progress. Some nations were marching forward smartly, some were stumbling, and some, like China, were inert. The Russians, Roosevelt explained, "are below the Germans just as the Germans are below us . . . [but] we are all treading the same path, some faster, some slower." It was a means of understanding the direction the various nations and peoples in the world were taking and relating it to what Americans regarded as their paramount interest: the global achievement of civilization, which was to say, Western liberal civilization. The central issue of international relations was the fact that, as Roosevelt told Andrew Carnegie, "the peoples of the world have advanced unequally along the road that leads to justice and fair dealing."[124]

For Americans in this era, these notions were not idle philosophical musings. The ideology of civilization offered a fairly coherent if not unerring guide to America's relations with other nations and peoples. The division of the world into the civilized and the barbarous "carried with it a clear moral differential. . . . There were good powers and bad powers." These moral judgments often blurred into strategic judgments. Russia, a bad power, had to be watched carefully and beaten back when necessary, preferably by someone else. Japan, a good power, could expand at Russia's and China's expense without causing much concern.[125] Americans equated progress and civilization with peace and their own national security. They believed, along with many European liberals, that the more advanced, liberal, and commercial a people were, the more attuned they would be to modern concepts of justice and morality and the less inclined to war and aggression. Hence the popular American expectations of a more peaceful Germany after 1871 and of a peaceful Japan after the 1860s. The more backward and despotic nations were also the more dangerous—Russia, China, and as the expectation of budding liberalism faded, Germany. They were dangerous both because their concepts of justice and morality were less developed and because they retained the martial spirit characteristic of societies in the "barbaric" stage. "Opening" other nations to commerce was in American interests, therefore, not only because there was money to be made but because in time commercial penetration would hasten the progress of backward peoples toward civilization. They would become more liberal, more commercial, and therefore less threatening to the United States and to the civilized world in general. The spread of civilization was important not so much to accept a "white man's burden" but because it would bring "order worldwide through the spread of morality and the reinforcement of virtue."[126] For some Americans, like Roosevelt, civilizing the world's barbaric peoples was all the more urgent because, according to the same reigning evolutionary paradigm, advanced liberal commercial societies like the United States were in danger of losing the martial spirit necessary to defend themselves. The world had to be made safe for civilized peoples.

The late-nineteenth-century American view of progress has often been misunderstood as simple racism, because Americans of that era frequently used the language of race to describe the differences not only among Asians, Africans, and white Europeans but also among "Teutonic" Germany, "Latin" France, "Slavic" Russia, and any number of other nationalities and cultures. But while many if not most Americans did hold racist views, they were also attentive to differences in development that were not dependent on race. The Asian race in Japan could rise to the heights of civilization, while the Asian race in China remained mired in barbarism. This was not a static and hierarchical view of the world that fixed some races and peoples permanently at the top or at the bottom. It was an internationalized version of the American dream: every nation and people had the inherent capacity to advance to the highest stages of civilization if given the freedom and opportunity to do so. Theodore Roosevelt "saw no reason why all men could not eventually become civilized."[127] The problem was not necessarily race or nationality so much as history and institutions. Antiquated institutions produced backward societies. Bad governments stood in the way of political and economic progress. And centuries of bad government might require centuries to overcome. America, in this view, was not so much an exception as simply ahead of everyone else. It was ahead in part because it was young and had not needed to overcome a long history of backwardness, and in part because it was the inheritor of British civilization, which had already made the long march up from savagery and barbarism.[128] Anglo-Saxonism was not only about race; it was also, and more importantly, about history, civilization, and progress. The American example "revealed that if only others saw the light and made the same effort, they too could enjoy the benefits of freedom and civilization."[129]

This universalistic and moralistic belief in progress distinguished Americans from most other peoples around the world, even to some degree from the liberal British. The sharpest contrast was with the Chinese, with their ancient Confucian view of "an eternal political order." While the Americans' view of progress made them look expectantly to other cultures and societies, anticipating and hoping for their evolution toward civilization, the Chinese were secure in their belief in a fixed hierarchy of which they were at the summit.[130] The difference between the American and the Chinese perspectives was the difference between a nation founded upon universal principles and a people who considered their own culture unique and not transferable to others. Americans considered the Chinese hopelessly backward and out of step with the spirit of the age. But in fact it was the American perspective that was the more unusual, the more distant from the general view of humanity at the time, and also the more revolutionary in its implications. Most of the nations and peoples in the world in the late nineteenth century actually stood closer to the Chinese view of eternal order than to the American view of eternal progress. Even Europeans, despite repeated revolutions and a growing movement toward liberalism in some countries, still had a more organic and fixed view of society and were less sure of the benefits of progress. Americans were by far the most extreme in their universalism and in their belief in the inevitability and desirability of change.

Even American optimism about progress was not unqualified, however. While backward societies could be led toward civilization by the more advanced nations, many believed there was a limit to how quickly this process could be accelerated. Civilization took time, even centuries. And this raised a conundrum for Americans. Were backward peoples capable of self-government? Many Americans in the latter part of the nineteenth century, as in the latter part of the eighteenth century, believed they were not. But just as before, this view clashed with the American belief in universal natural rights. In the 1810s Henry Clay had responded to such arguments—advanced in those days by people like John Quincy Adams—by declaring that all humans were capable of self-government and that only despots argued otherwise. He had insisted that God would not have created a race incapable of enjoying liberty. Sixty years later this contest between theories of progress and the belief in universal rights was still being fought out. The new scientific discoveries regarding evolution could be understood to suggest that less evolved peoples, while enjoying the same capacity for eventual civilization, nevertheless could not be considered as fit for self-government so long as they were in a backward stage of development. Josiah Strong insisted that "Clay's conception was formed before modern science had shown that races develop in the course of centuries as individuals do in years, and that an underdeveloped race, which is incapable of self-government, is no more a reflection on the Almighty than is an underdeveloped child who is incapable of self-government."[131] Theodore Roosevelt could and did argue the issue from both sides. At one moment he argued that even the English race in the time of Cromwell "were not fit yet to govern themselves unaided." Fitness for self-government was "not a God-given natural right" and could not be "grasped in a day by a people only just emerging from conditions of life which our ancestors left behind them in the dim years before history dawned." Yet on other occasions he argued that it was impossible to deny human beings their natural rights. The southern argument that blacks were "not fit to exercise political rights," for instance, could not be "advanced in good faith . . . by any man who honestly believes in our American theory of government."[132] Probably the majority of commentators and intellectuals as well as the majority of Americans believed that not all peoples were ready for self-government and had to be guided to it over time, while a minority believed it was immoral to suggest that any peoples were not "ready" for democracy and needed the guidance of more advanced peoples. But the whole argument took place within a common paradigm of progress and civilization.[133]

The nineteenth-century belief that the United States was the advance agent of civilization and morally superior to all others coexisted, of course, with a pervasive domestic racism that was hardening into the apartheidlike system of Jim Crow in the South. As Americans condemned pogroms in Russia and Romania in the 1880s and '90s, hundreds of innocent blacks were lynched, mostly but not exclusively in the South, tortured, and killed, their dead bodies sometimes torn to pieces by crazed white mobs. On the West Coast it was Chinese immigrant workers who were savagely beaten and murdered in great numbers. "Dead, my reverend friends, dead," wrote Bret Harte of one murdered Chinese immigrant in San Francisco. "Stoned to death in the streets of San Francisco, in the year of grace 1869 by a mob of half-grown boys and Christian school children."[134] Some Americans cringed at the hypocrisy of the nation's foreign policy moralism. Secretary of State John Hay, questioning Roosevelt's eagerness to denounce Russian pogroms in 1903, noted the record number of lynchings in America that same year and asked whether the United States really could cast the first stone. For all that the Civil War had changed, Americans' professed belief in progress and the capacity of all humans to achieve civilization in the world at large was still contradicted by American treatment of blacks, Indians, Asians, and other minorities at home as well as women. James Blaine insisted that "the majesty and might of a nation" were measured "by no standard so accurately as by the degree of protection given to their citizens or subjects."[135] But even Blaine, who fought for black rights, which fortuitously coincided with Republican political interests, could turn a blind eye to the mistreatment of Chinese immigrants on the West Coast when politics required it.

Hypocrisy did not stand in the way of moralism, however. Many Americans were aware of their own nation's failings, but most nevertheless extolled what they regarded as its superior institutions and enlightened worldview. Those who did not share that worldview were to be assisted and converted, criticized and sanctioned, and in the case of the South militarily defeated and reconstructed. This powerful impulse to reform had its roots in the universalist ideology of the Declaration of Independence. But the Civil War gave birth to new and more potent aspirations. As William Seward insisted, the war had a "positive moral and political significance," producing what he and other leading Americans considered "a homogenous, enlightened nation, virtuous and brave, inspired by lofty sentiments to achieve a destiny for itself that shall, by its influence and example, be beneficent to mankind."[136] Even in the age of Seward it was clear to foreign observers as well as to some Americans that their belief in progress, their constant evaluation and measurement of societies and civilizations against their own ideals, and their disapproval of those that refused to conform to the spirit of the age would upset the status quo if and when Americans accumulated sufficient power and influence and the desire to use them to shape the world more to their liking.

CHAPTER 11

From Power to Ambition,
from Ambition to Power

America while she was united ran a race of prosperity unparalleled in the world. Eighty years made the Republic such a power, that if she had continued as she was a few years longer she would have been the great bully of the world.

—J. A. Roebuck, in the British House of Commons,
June 30, 1863

The Rise to Security

AS IT HAPPENED, the America that emerged from the Civil War was more powerful and influential than ever before. Despite a destroyed South, a mammoth national debt, and ongoing political and sectional strife, the United States was a burgeoning giant and was recognized as such by observers in Europe, in Asia, and above all in Latin America and the Caribbean. By the end of the 1870s, despite the travails of depression, the United States was already among the richest countries in the world. Its population was booming, fed by masses of immigrants from Europe. Compared to the small, fragile republic that had struggled for survival a century earlier, America had become a great continental power. Northerners who had once opposed the vast extension of territory produced by Polk's war against Mexico now celebrated the prodigious national power and wealth those conquests had produced. Benjamin Harrison in his inaugural address in 1889 noted the "happy contrasts" between the America of his day "and that weak but wisely ordered young Nation that looked undauntedly down the first century, when all its years stretched out before it." The original thirteen states had been "weak in everything except courage and the love of liberty," but now, with "thirty-eight populous and prosperous States," the United States was a leviathan.[1]

America's power could be measured not only by wealth and population but also by the relative safety Americans enjoyed within their borders. The United States was far more secure than at any time in its past. Thanks in part to the great expansion of territory between 1800 and 1848, it had become too large, too rich, and too heavily populated to be an inviting target for invasion even by the world's strongest powers. The conflict over slavery had delayed the impact of this new geographic and demographic reality, since a nation at war with itself was always at risk. But after the Civil War America was almost invulnerable to serious attack. Its ports could be blockaded and coastal cities seized, but there was no strategic nerve center whose capture could force American capitulation, and the country's internal market meant it could survive an extended blockade if necessary. As a British chief of military intelligence put it, "a land war on the American Continent would be perhaps the most hazardous military enterprise that we could possibly be driven to engage in."[2] Except for the need to protect Canada, an increasingly difficult assignment, British policy aimed at appeasing the United States, not challenging it. After the Civil War that policy "was based on an assumption that the preponderance of power in North America lay with the republic."[3]

American predominance had begun to encompass the Western Hemisphere. For a brief period during the Civil War, some European powers had taken temporary advantage of America's distress to make new inroads in the New World. Spain had briefly reannexed Santo Domingo in 1861, and two years later France's overthrow of President Benito Juárez and installation of a Hapsburg archduke as emperor of Mexico had fulfilled a decades-old French dream of placing a friendly prince on that Latin American throne. But after the North's victory in 1865, Grant ordered General Sheridan with fifty thousand troops to the Mexican border, and a combination of the evident willingness of the United States to go to war against the French, with almost a million Americans still under arms, and the valiant struggle of Mexican forces against Maximilian, helped put an end to that most dramatic of European military adventures. Subtler forms of encroachment continued, as European governments pursued commercial interests in a part of the world where they had, after all, been active for four centuries. But they were politically and militarily in retreat. Bismarck was highly solicitous of American concerns and assured Hamilton Fish, "We have no interest whatsoever in gaining a foothold anywhere in the Americas, and we acknowledge unequivocally that, with regard to the entire continent, the predominant influence of the United States is founded in the nature of things and corresponds most closely with our own interests."[4] Only Spain did not concede American control, clinging to Cuba and Puerto Rico as the last vestiges of its once-vast Latin American empire. But that empire was in the terminal stage, and Spain after 1865 had no ambitions beyond the preservation of its few remaining possessions and its national honor.

America's growing dominance in the Western Hemisphere in the last third of the nineteenth century owed much to the fact that the great powers, especially Great Britain, were increasingly distracted by challenges elsewhere in the world. By the 1880s the Anglo-Russian competition in Central Asia, the "Great Game," was under way. The international scramble for China was in its early stages, and the colonial competition in Africa was hot. In Europe itself the rising power of Germany increasingly preoccupied both Britain and France. The world's great powers were not merely distracted—they were irrevocably entangled in the grand geopolitical struggle that would shape the twentieth century, produce two world wars, and ultimately give rise to the global hegemony of the United States.

Americans did not owe their position in the late nineteenth century only to the great-power struggle, however, or to the existence of two vast oceans and a friendly British navy. Oceans offered little protection in the era of steam, and even in the age of sail they had been no barrier to foreign conquest. The Western Hemisphere was as accessible as China and the African jungles and could just as easily have been the target of an "imperial scramble." The British as late as the 1840s had been anything but friendly in their competition with the United States in Central and South America. If Great Britain and other European powers no longer sought to challenge the United States in the Western Hemisphere, it was because the growth of American territory and power had gradually foreclosed opportunities and temptations. British statesmen "no longer dreamed of securing San Francisco," and they had little choice but to acknowledge American "supremacy in the Caribbean area."[5]

Americans had not acquired this supremacy passively but from the beginning had worked to change the political and strategic equation in the hemisphere. They had conquered, prospered, and populated their way out from under the shadow of European power. By their economic, political, and at times military aggressiveness, they had steadily raised the price of competition higher than the nations of Europe wanted to pay. They had demanded special prerogatives in what they had considered their own backyard since the days of Jefferson and Hamilton, and they had done so with notable belligerence. Even before the Civil War, Lord Palmerston had complained, "These Yankees are most disagreeable Fellows to have to do with about any American question: They are on the Spot, strong, deeply interested in the matter, totally unscrupulous and dishonest and determined somehow to carry their Point."[6] These Yankee traits became even more pronounced after the Civil War, so much so that Britain's efforts to maintain its traditionally dominant position in Central America rapidly gave way "to a resigned acceptance of U.S. hegemony."[7]

Leading Americans not only recognized the favorable shift in the balance of power, they gloried in it. The purchase of Alaska in 1867 prompted Charles Sumner to exult, "One by one they have retired—first France, then Spain, then France again, and now Russia."[8] By the early 1880s many Americans already understood, as Blaine did, that "a new power relationship existed" between America and the European powers and that the United States "was rapidly becoming the nation to be reckoned with in the Western Hemisphere." Even with regard to Great Britain Blaine boasted, "we can defy her, and we are today the only power on the globe that can . . . and we can do it with just as much dignity or just as much insolence as we choose to employ."[9]

From Power to Ambition: The Western Hemisphere

GROWING POWER affected the United States' conduct of foreign policy in a number of ways. For one thing, it expanded Americans' sense of what constituted their national interests. As a general principle, a nation's perception of its interests is not static but expands and contracts along with perceptions of its power and ability to shape its environment. A common trait of rising powers throughout history, whether ancient Athens, nineteenth-century Germany, late-nineteenth-century Japan, or late-twentieth-century China, is their expanding sense of both interests and entitlement, and the rising power of the United States in the last decades of the nineteenth century was no exception.

One example of America's expanding perception of interests after the Civil War was the evolution of attitudes toward control of a prospective transisthmian canal. When Americans had first taken an interest in the idea back in the 1820s, Henry Clay had set forth a rather modest claim. The canal would not be an exclusively American project but would be shared by many nations. Clay's biographer cites this stance as an example of his "extraordinarily enlightened view of how the United States should conduct its foreign relations not only with Latin America but with the rest of the world."[10] But Clay's modest plan also reflected America's incapacity in

1826 to insist on exclusive control. That position remained fundamentally unchanged even after the acquisition of Texas, the Southwest, California, and Oregon in the Mexican-American War, as well as the discovery of gold in California. These acquisitions greatly increased the importance of rapid transportation from the Atlantic Coast to the Pacific and thus the value of a canal route linking the two more closely. Nevertheless, in 1850 the United States negotiated the Clayton-Bulwer Treaty with Great Britain stipulating that neither side would attempt to fortify or to exercise exclusive control over a canal and guaranteeing the canal's neutrality. The agreement reflected the disparity of power between the British Empire and the United States of the time, "a second-rate power, torn by a violent slavery controversy."[11] Even as late as 1867 the United States, politically fractured by the struggle between President Johnson and the Radical Republican Congress, was not insisting on "exclusive domination of the canal."[12]

No sooner had the United States begun to make itself whole again, however, than American leaders began looking for more. "Perfect neutrality" was no longer acceptable. When President Grant took office in 1869, his demand was simple: "an American canal, on American soil."[13] Ten years later, when the French entrepreneur Ferdinand de Lesseps, the builder of the Suez Canal, proposed to repeat his feat in the Western Hemisphere, President Rutherford B. Hayes announced that "the policy of this country is a canal under American control." The House of Representatives passed a resolution demanding immediate abrogation of the Clayton-Bulwer Treaty.[14] Hayes and then Blaine insisted that any transisthmian passage must be considered de facto American territory, "virtually a part of the coast line of the United States"[15]—a stance reminiscent of Hamilton's claim in the 1790s that the Mississippi River belonged to the United States by natural right.[16] In late 1884 Blaine's successor, Frederick Frelinghuysen, negotiated a treaty with Nicaragua giving the United States exclusive rights to build and control a canal in return for U.S. protection of Nicaragua against foreign powers. The agreement was never ratified because opponents did not want to bind the United States to defense of that Central American nation, but the secretary of state's willingness to ignore the restrictions of the Clayton-Bulwer Treaty was a sign of growing American impatience and assertiveness.

The evolving stance reflected American power and confidence but also its declining tolerance for any challenge to its predominance within the hemisphere. The De Lesseps venture did, of course, pose some theoretical risk for the United States. The company was backed by considerable French capital, and there was a remote possibility that France would demand control over its investment. But the danger of French seizure of the canal was small,[17] and the United States had accepted far greater risks in 1850. By the 1870s and '80s a stronger America was less willing to accept risks, simply because it was stronger. Because they believed they could demand full control of a canal, Americans refused any longer to accept partial control. The irony was that they were much more interested in demanding an exclusive right to control any canal than they were in actually building one. The desire for hemispheric primacy was a stronger motive than the desire for commerce. The United States, Blaine told the British, would not "perpetuate any treaty that impeaches our rightful and long-established claim to priority on the American continent." Blaine's friend Andrew Carnegie put the matter bluntly: "America is going to control anything and everything on this continent—that's settled."[18]

As such statements suggested, growing power produced an interesting blend of confidence and an impatience that sometimes bordered on anxiousness. It seemed as if the more powerful and secure Americans became, the more intolerant they were of the obstacles, both real and imagined, that stood in their way. Great Britain was, of course, regarded as the prime obstacle. From the end of the Civil War until the last years of the nineteenth century, Americans complained that they were being constrained and suffocated by British power on all sides. Henry Cabot Lodge claimed to fear that Great Britain had encircled the United States with "a cordon of forts and bases of supply for a navy manifestly for use in case of war."[19] In fact, the majority of British "forts and bases" Lodge pointed to had been erected before the Declaration of Independence and had long since fallen into a state of neglect, and the British had all but given up trying to contain the United States in the Western Hemisphere.[20] Americans' feelings of being hemmed in were the product not of British pressure but of their own expanding sense of interest and entitlement.

Americans were also stung by the way Europeans had exploited their weakness and divisions before and during the Civil War. Many blamed Seward for soft and passive policies toward the French occupation of Mexico and in response to Spain's attacks on Chile and its reannexation of Santo Domingo. When Grant took office in 1869, Blaine expressed hope that American diplomacy would be "rescued from the subservient tone by which we have so often been humiliated in our own eyes and in the eyes of Europe, and the true position of the first nation of the earth in rank and prestige will be asserted; not in a spirit of bravado or with the mere arrogance of strength, but with the conscious dignity which belongs to power, and with the moderation which is the true ornament of justice."[21]

The new consciousness of power after the Civil War made some Americans impatient to realize old ambitions. Slavery had been vanquished, the Union had been saved, and the continent had been conquered. These accomplishments seemed to have placed the United States on the threshold of greatness. But "while we were engaged in this great work," Lodge complained, "other things have been neglected." Americans had "heeded too little the importance of . . . putting the United States in the place where they belong in the great family of nations."[22]

This impatience was felt most keenly with regard to the Western Hemisphere. Alexander Hamilton had long ago declared that the key to American greatness lay in erecting "one great American system, superior to the controul of all trans-atlantic force or influence, and able to dictate the terms of the connection between the old and the new world."[23] In the 1820s Monroe and Clay had set out to establish a Pan-American "family of nations," a "good neighborhood" among the "sister republics" of the Western Hemisphere. But the project had unraveled almost immediately due to the burgeoning sectional crisis. "Threescore years have passed," Blaine declared. "The power of the Republic in many directions has grown beyond all anticipation, but we have relatively lost ground in some great fields of enterprise." One of these was the establishment of a sound relationship with the "sister republics" in the hemisphere. The word Blaine and Presidents Garfield and Harrison repeatedly used to describe what they sought in the hemisphere was "friendship." Blaine lamented the "lost ground" of six decades during which America's once "ardent friendship with Spanish America" had "drifted into indifference if not coldness."[24]

As a northern Republican, Blaine naturally blamed the sixty-year deterioration of hemispheric relations on southern imperial expansionism prior to the Civil War. The nations of South America, Central America, and the Caribbean had indeed come to fear southern expansionism from the 1840s onward, as they watched Polk swallow the northern parts of Mexico, William Walker attempt to colonize Central America, and the authors of the Ostend Manifesto claim the right to seize Cuba by force. The Confederate constitution's explicit endorsement of imperial expansion gave peoples south of the Rio Grande good reason to wish for a Union victory in the Civil War. The victory of Lincoln, the North, and Blaine's Republican Party was at first greeted with cheers throughout the hemisphere.[25]

Blaine and like-minded Americans after the Civil War saw a vast difference between the old territorial aggression and the hemispheric leadership they hoped to provide. He believed that an abolitionized, purified, regenerated America had the moral standing to provide leadership that would be welcomed by the "sister republics." As he put it, "Friendship and not force, the spirit of just law and not the violence of the mob, should be the recognized rule of administration between American nations and in American nations."[26]

As Americans returned to old ambitions of benevolent hemispheric leadership, the need for it seemed to them to be greater than ever. In the days of Monroe, Clay, and Adams hopes for the new "sister republics" ran high. The peoples of Latin America were emerging from their long colonial subordination to Spain, and most were proclaiming themselves republics like the United States. Some Americans were skeptical, but many were optimistic. If the Latin peoples were not as far advanced as the North Americans, they were also not so far behind. In the early nineteenth century the per capita income of Mexico was almost half that of the United States, and the population of Mexico City was larger than that of any North American city. But after decades of colonial struggle against Spain, followed by decades of domestic political turmoil, Mexico had emerged in the 1870s with a per capita income about one-seventh that of the United States. The North American national income was thirty-five times higher than that of Mexico.[27] Some Latin nations, notably Chile, were doing better, but most were not.

Latin America's failed economies were not the only problem. Since independence the region had been rife with war, both between and within states, and in Blaine's time the conflicts had been particularly bloody and destructive. The War of the Triple Alliance, pitting Brazil, Argentina, and Uruguay against Paraguay, lasted from 1865 to 1870, claimed fifty thousand dead in Brazil, and wiped out almost the entire adult male population of Paraguay. The War of the Pacific from 1879 to 1883 pitted Chile against Peru and Bolivia and produced high casualties, the devastation of Peru, and the permanent enfeebling of Bolivia.[28] Rebellions, coups, and civil wars were constantly erupting throughout Latin America and the Caribbean. To American eyes the region was a boiling cauldron of violence. One American senator colorfully described the Dominican Republic as "a land of throes and convulsions . . . a volcano of human passions and a river of human blood," and this was the common view of all the lands south of the border.[29]

Americans who bothered to think about the matter attributed Latin America's economic and political backwardness to two causes: Catholicism and the Spanish colonial heritage. In a largely Protestant America it was widely assumed that Catholicism produced despotism and was incompatible with democracy. William Prescott, in his popular histories of the conquests of Mexico and Peru, contrasted the conquistadors, whom he described as brutal proselytizers of the Catholic faith in South America, with the Puritan divines and their followers who settled North America: "What a contrast did these children of southern Europe present to the Anglo-Saxon races who scattered themselves along the great northern division of the western hemisphere!" While the Protestant settlers pursued freedom and independence, the Spaniards pursued only vainglory, driven by an "aristocratic set of values," a desire for royal favor, and a belief that conquest and conversion were God's will.[30] This American fixation on the Catholic origins of Latin backwardness was not new. Thomas Jefferson had disdained Spanish-Americans as a "priest-ridden people," and both John Adams and his son John Quincy Adams believed the dominance of the Catholic Church made it impossible for them to sustain liberal government.[31]

In the latter part of the nineteenth century, American contempt and hostility also fastened on Spain, a country and a people widely regarded as having a brutal past and a naturally cruel temperament. The historian Francis Parkman in 1865 described the conquering Spaniards of the sixteenth century as "bigotry incarnate." Popular novels exploited the centuries-old "Black Legend" of a cruel, rapacious Spain committing unspeakable atrocities against a defenseless Indian population. According to the government envoy and writer William Elroy Curtis, whose articles and books in the 1880s both informed and reflected a common American view, the Spanish colonial era had been one long "carnival of murder and plunder." In the global struggle between progress and reaction, Spain with its absolutist monarchy was well out of step with the spirit of the age. It was the "backwash of European civilization," and its heavy reactionary hand strangled progress in Latin America. Mexico's history, according to Curtis, was one long struggle between "antiquated, bigoted, and despotic Romanism, allied with the ancient [Spanish] aristocracy . . . on the one hand, and the spirit of intellectual, industrial, commercial, and social progress on the other." Of Ecuador he observed that "until the influence of the Romish Church is destroyed, until [non-Spanish] immigration is invited and secured," that country would remain "a desert rich in undeveloped resources."[32]

The idea that Spain was to blame for Latin America's backwardness was not limited to North Americans but was widely shared throughout Latin America itself. The influential Cuban writer and thinker José Martí declared that the great task of the era was "to overcome the result of three centuries of colonial 'darkness' and 'poison' left by Spain." It was not enough to remove the Spanish colonial presence from Cuba; the Cuban people also had "to get it out of our habits."[33] Many Mexican and Central American leaders expressed similar sentiments and looked to the open, modernizing United States as an alternative model to Spain's stifling traditions.

From the North American point of view, Latin backwardness not only produced instability, endemic violence, and oppression but deprived both the Latin peoples and the Americans of the vast riches that lay locked up in their abundant but undeveloped territories. Seward declared it America's role to cure the "disorganization, disintegration, and anarchy" he saw plaguing the hemisphere. This would offer "to mankind," and to the United States, "the speediest and surest means of rendering available . . . the natural treasures of America." President Grant, defending his plan to annex Santo Domingo, had insisted it would advance "the welfare of a downtrodden race" and of a people who were "not capable of maintaining themselves . . . [and] yearn[ed] for the protection of our free institutions and law, our progress and civilization."[34] During the Civil War Congressman Henry Winter Davis, one of Blaine's mentors, had called on the United States "to lead the sisterhood of American republics in the paths of peace, prosperity, and power."[35] These lofty goals, as well as the more prosaic ones of making the United States the dominant economic and political power in the hemisphere, required the eventual removal of Spanish power and influence.

Cuba was the place where these American impulses twice came together. The first time, in the late 1860s and early 1870s, it almost brought the United States and Spain to blows. The second time, a quarter century later, it produced the Spanish-American War. Both clashes were the product of Cuban rebellions against Spanish colonial rule. In 1868 Cuban rebels launched what proved to be a ten-year revolt against Spain. A large and vocal Cuban émigré population established revolutionary "juntas" in New York, Washington, Philadelphia, and Tampa, popularizing their cause by sponsoring concerts, issuing bonds in the name of the new "Republic of Cuba," and holding mass meetings. Their cause was popular in the United States, especially after Creole militias sponsored by the Spanish colonial authorities committed the first great atrocity of the conflict, firing into a crowded Havana theater and killing and wounding dozens of men, women, and children.[36] This and other "butcheries" were graphically reported back in the United States by Charles A. Dana's *New York Sun* and other early tabloids. In April 1869 majorities of both parties in the House of Representatives passed a resolution advising President Grant that Congress would support recognizing the Cuban rebels as belligerents. Grant was inclined to do so, even though it risked conflict with Spain. "If there come war," he insisted, "we must try and be prepared for it." The secretary of war, John A. Rawlins, who died while in office, pleaded from his deathbed for "poor, struggling Cuba" and vowed, "Cuba must be free. Her tyrannical enemy must be crushed."[37]

Secretary Fish, who wanted no war with Spain, did his best to slow the drive for recognition of the rebels. But there was no ignoring the political ferment across the United States demanding Cuban independence, and it was hard to quell passions that had more to do with hostility to "barbaric" Spain than with economic or any other tangible interests.[38] Fish tried to force Spain to make concessions to American public opinion. He offered a $100 million indemnity guaranteed by the United States in return for Cuba's freedom, with the vague threat of war if Spain refused. He beseeched the Spanish government to enact humane reforms on the island, including the abolition of slavery, in the hopes that this would cool anti-Spanish sentiment in Congress. "The United States have emancipated all the slaves in their own territory," Fish pointed out, in "recognition of those rights of man which are now universally admitted." Now Spain must do the same, because the whole "civilized world" was "looking to see liberty as the universal law of labor."[39] Fish even drew up a plan to impose economic sanctions in the form of high discriminatory duties on all goods imported from slaveholding countries, including Cuba, Puerto Rico, and Brazil.

Unfortunately for Fish, Spain preferred to face bankruptcy or lose Cuba honorably in a war rather than dishonorably sell it into independence.[40] Nor was anti-Spanish opinion in the United States prepared to accept a settlement that left Cuba in the hands of what Republican senator Oliver P. Morton called Spain's "atrocious and satanic barbarism." Horace Greeley summoned the spirit of his idol Henry Clay in appealing for the completion of Latin America's liberation from Spanish oppression. Even Fish concluded, after Spain had rejected every offer of American mediation and "assistance," that Cuban independence was both right and inevitable. He was appalled by the "horrible butchery" and insisted the slaughter of men, women, and children made it "evident that Spain cannot govern [Cuba], in fact that Spain has not for some time past been able to control it." Therefore, Fish asked, "[s]hould not then the nominal supremacy of Spain over the colony be denounced by other Powers—even if not renounced by her?"[41]

The Grant administration stopped short of such a dramatic step, but while the United States officially stayed out of the Cuban conflict, unofficially Americans provided substantial aid to the rebels. Former high-ranking officers from both the Confederate and Union armies organized filibusters. One Confederate general, Thomas Jordan, traveled to Cuba in May 1869, became chief of staff of the rebel army, and within a month led the rebels to a victory over a large Spanish force. A Union army colonel organized the formation of the "First New York Cavalry Cuban Liberators" and prepared to set sail for Cuba in the summer of 1869, only to have his ship captured and taken into custody by a federal marshal.[42] Cuban exiles in the United States raised funds to buy arms and supplies and found ways to ship them to the rebels, often with the active assistance of the U.S. Navy. In 1869 the navy sold a Confederate blockade-runner to a wealthy Cuban-American, who then hired an American captain to sail its cargo of arms and supplies to Cuba. The *Virginius,* another former Confederate blockade-runner, began running guns to Cuban rebels in 1870 under an American flag. Twice when Spanish ships of war approached the *Virginius,* U.S. naval vessels protected it and helped it escape capture.[43] Spanish authorities could be forgiven for believing that rebel vessels like the *Virginius* operated with the consent if not the support of the American government. They arrested and executed Americans caught aiding the rebels, therefore, which only further inflamed public opinion in the United States and on more than one occasion led to the dispatch of American warships into or near Cuban waters.[44]

The confrontation remained hot over the course of four years, and as one historian has suggested, "[p]ublic sentiment was such that any event like the *Maine* explosion would have made war inevitable."[45] War did almost erupt in 1873 when the infamous *Virginius* was finally captured by a Spanish warship and towed into the harbor at Havana. The Spanish colonial authorities swiftly executed the expedition leader, the ship's American captain, and an additional fifty-one crew and passengers, including a number of U.S. citizens. An angry American public demanded satisfaction and a final end to Spanish "barbarism" in Cuba. As one southern editor commented, "On no occasion for a quarter of a century have the people of all sections of the Union been so united upon a question as upon this of launching the power of our government against the Cuban authorities."[46] The Grant administration sent Spain an ultimatum and readied for war. The secretary of the navy ordered shipyards into full production and an increase in the number of enlisted men by ten thousand. American troops gathered at Fortress Monroe and other posts along the Gulf Coast, preparing to launch an invasion.[47] The Mediterranean Squadron sped back across the Atlantic to the waters around Florida, and for a time the entire U.S. Navy—with the exception of the East India Squadron operating in the Pacific—gathered at Key West, a fleet of some thirty ships carrying more than four hundred guns. The twelve American ships in the Pacific, meanwhile, stood prepared to attack "the Spanish possessions in that quarter," that is, the Philippines, since as far back as

1855 American naval plans had called for the seizure of Manila in the event of a Spanish-American war over Cuba.[48]

What might have gone down in history as the Spanish-American War of 1873, complete with an attack on the Philippines, was averted by a last-minute Spanish apology, which Secretary Fish readily accepted. The secretary of state had never wanted war with Spain, and his caution was reinforced by concerns throughout the Grant administration that the navy might not be up to the challenge. The crisis ended, passions cooled on both sides, and the Cuban rebels eventually put down their arms in return for a Spanish promise to grant Cuba autonomy. But the *Virginius* affair both reflected and hardened the deep animosities and conflicting ambitions that characterized relations between Spain and the United States in the Western Hemisphere. For Americans, the memory of Spanish brutality remained vivid for the next quarter century: the hero of a best-selling novel in 1897, when asked about his past, replied, "My Father, Miss Hope, was a filibuster, and went out on the *Virginius* to help free Cuba, and was shot, against a stone wall." A popular history of American politics written after the turn of the century expressed the view that conflict between the United States and Spain had become "inevitable ever since the Cubans rose in 1868 . . . and since Spanish soldiers shot down the crew of the *Virginius* at Santiago. From that moment, Spain and the United States were like two railway engines heading toward each other upon a single track. A collision between them could not be avoided." As Caleb Cushing put it a year after the *Virginius* affair, "The question of Cuba still remains, palpitating, to be settled, no one knows how, perhaps by some unforeseen accident."[49]

WHEN BLAINE BEGAN seriously contemplating American policy in the Western Hemisphere in the 1870s, it was not war he sought. Rather, he aimed to establish a more peaceful and stable hemispheric order and end what he and other Americans regarded as an endless cycle of violence that had begun during the Spanish colonial era. "The Spanish-American States are in special need of the help," Blaine believed. "They require external pressure to keep them from war; when at war they require external pressure to bring them to peace."[50] The United States, in his view, was well suited to provide this help. Not only was it a powerful republic dedicated to freedom, but because it no longer coveted territory, it was also a disinterested power, concerned only for the general well-being of the hemisphere. It therefore had "the right to use its friendly offices in discouragement of any movement on the part of neighboring states which may tend to disturb the balance of power between them."[51]

There was also a matter of responsibility, and of honor. Blaine and like-minded American leaders considered that by making itself the supreme, disinterested arbiter of the hemisphere, the United States was fulfilling the obligations that history and power imposed: "Blaine believed that the United States was destined to be a great power and wanted it to begin acting like one."[52] Americans had to accept the "responsibility of great trust" that came with its position as the hemisphere's leading nation.[53] To fulfill this duty, the United States had to offer the peoples of the hemisphere the benefits of its power and its advanced civilization. The earnest President Harrison told Blaine in 1889, "I am especially interested in the improvement of our relations with the Central and South American States. We must win their confidence by deserving it."[54]

That the assumption of this "responsibility" in the hemisphere served American interests Blaine never denied and never felt it necessary to deny. Like Clay, Blaine aimed to protect and advance American commercial interests in the hemisphere, especially against the leading competitor, Great Britain. He did not like "to see England winning great commercial triumphs in a field that legitimately belongs to the United States, and which the United States could readily command if she would."[55] If Americans did not build closer commercial ties with their neighbors, Blaine feared "the equivalent of a commercial alliance against us." If "Spanish-American friendship is to be regained, if the commercial empire that legitimately belongs to us is to be ours, we must not lie idle and witness its transfer to others."[56] Nor did American diplomats welcome European assistance in bringing peace and order in the hemisphere, even when that assistance was proffered in a friendly and cooperative spirit. Their policy was rigidly unilateralist. The order they sought was an American-dominated order.

The desire for peace and the sense of American responsibility for stability and tranquillity were intertwined with tangible interests, therefore, above all the broad interest in hemispheric primacy. But it seemed to Blaine, as it would seem to many American leaders throughout the nation's history, that interest, principle, and responsibility were all related. Blaine wanted to improve friendship with the Latin nations so he could increase access to their markets. But he also wanted to increase American commerce in the hemisphere so that he could foster regional prosperity, strengthen Latin-American friendship, and make the United States the arbiter of hemispheric affairs. He wanted to keep European influence out so that American influence would predominate. But he also believed, along with most other

Americans, that European influence in the hemisphere, whether Spanish, French, or British, had always been pernicious not only for the United States but for its neighbors, and that the Europeans brought monarchy, despotism, and conflict to peoples that needed and sought freedom and peace.

It was not absurd to imagine that many in the hemisphere might welcome American friendship, influence, commerce, and even on occasion intervention. The growing power of the northern republic made it an attractive partner for those seeking support against foes at home and abroad, and throughout the nineteenth century the nations of Latin America and the Caribbean frequently looked to the United States for help against aggression from neighbors or to shield them against pressures from Europe. Central American leaders in the 1820s sought annexation by the United States as preferable to incorporation by Mexico.[57] Peru and Bolivia sought America's assistance against Chile in the War of the Pacific. Chile itself had sought U.S. military assistance against Spain in 1867, demanding that the United States enforce the Monroe Doctrine, and many Chileans never forgave the United States for standing aside and letting the Spanish navy bombard and destroy Valparaiso. Guatemala's dictator Justo Rufino Barrios admired the United States as "the epitome of progress" and importuned American support, first in his efforts to unify Central America under his own rule, then against Mexico in the struggle over a disputed border.[58] The leader of the Dominican Republic sought American protection against Haiti and even offered his nation up for annexation. Venezuela asked to be made an American protectorate in 1883 and repeatedly pleaded for American assistance in interminable boundary disputes with Great Britain.

Governments and their opponents welcomed American intervention in their domestic conflicts as well. One faction of Nicaraguans had embraced William Walker and even elected him president, preferring rule by the American "grey-eyed man of destiny" to rule by their political rivals. A prominent Nicaraguan priest called Walker "the tutelary Angel of Peace, and the North Star of the aspirations of an afflicted people."[59] The Brazilian government welcomed an American naval blockade against Brazilian rebels in 1894. Chile's President José Manuel Balmaceda sought American power to counterbalance British support of his opponents in the Chilean congress. Colombia sought American protection against domestic rebellions in Panama in return for granting Americans transit rights across the isthmus. Cuban rebels persistently lobbied for American assistance in their on-again, off-again struggle against Spanish colonial authorities, while leading Latin nations, including Mexico and Peru, encouraged the United States to help liberate Cuba from Spain.

Most political leaders in the hemisphere, especially in the Caribbean basin, sought American dollars and investment, either to modernize their countries or to enrich themselves or both. Central American nations jockeyed to be designated the preferred route for a canal and fought one another over unsettled boundaries that determined control of ports or lucrative plantations that might attract American investors. Mexico was the country least likely to welcome American intervention in any form, inasmuch as it had been the principal victim of that intervention. But even Mexican leaders believed that American financing and technological know-how were vital to their nation's progress and eventual survival. Mexico's Liberals, who dominated the nation's politics from the 1850s through the long authoritarian rule of Porfirio Díaz, believed their humiliating military defeat at the hands of the North Americans was the consequence of their backwardness. They had been defeated by a "superior political and economic system," while their own "captivity in tradition and privilege," the inheritance from Spanish colonial rule, had produced weakness and vulnerability. Mexico, therefore, "needed to emulate the Anglo-Saxon nations."[60]

The trick for a country like Mexico was to attract American investment without "being swallowed up by the United States." The Liberals wanted a "special economic relationship" that would produce "all the fruits of annexation without any of the dangers." Mexico would accord U.S. investors "a dominant position" in the economy, with "free rein to develop Mexico 'from without'" and with the understanding that the Americans would pay off Mexico's mountainous debt to European creditors. President Benito Juárez instructed his minister in Washington to promote Mexico as an attractive investment for bankers and railroad magnates, hoping "the lure of rich mines in northern and central Mexico would induce them to fund the construction of a railroad system."[61] Porfirio Díaz granted Americans two important railroad concessions connecting Mexico City with Ciudad Juárez and Laredo, thus sealing "the fate of the Mexican economy as complementary to that of the United States."[62]

The irony was that the Mexican invitation to American economic imperialism was ahead of American thinking. When the Liberal government of the late 1850s invited the United States to assume the commanding position in the Mexican economy, the southern-dominated administration of James Buchanan wasn't interested. The slaveholding South wanted Mexican territory to expand slavery, not access to the Mexican economy to expand opportunities for northern investors. Even after the Civil War the administrations of Grant and Hayes were more interested in stopping Mexican bandits from crossing the Rio Grande than they were in economic penetration.

For two years they refused to recognize Díaz's government, long after he had taken effective control of the country, and Hayes sent American troops to the border with instructions to chase bandits into Mexico without Díaz's consent, thereby reawakening Mexican fears of American aggression. In time the American investors did arrive, and the policies pursued by Juarez and Díaz achieved their goal. Americans soon owned more than 60 percent of total foreign investment in Mexico.[63]

Increased commercial ties between the United States and its Latin neighbors contributed to the prosperity of Mexico and others. It did not, however, always produce the stability or hemispheric "friendship" that Americans sought. In Central America the lure of American investment actually produced conflict, as various local caudillos battled to attract dollars.[64] In Mexico it produced an independent and at times defiant foreign policy. Porfirio Díaz built his rule upon a nationalism that sprang from fears and resentments of American power, promoting himself as the defiant protector of Mexican sovereignty, even as he sold mining and railroad concessions to North American investors.

The desire to emulate the North American model of progress and prosperity, moreover, was hardly universal among Latin Americans. Mexico's Conservatives had for decades opposed the "Protestant United States" and supported "Catholic Europe" as their model, as they demonstrated by their support of the Hapsburg emperor. The United States threatened Mexican society "both by its push for land and by its espousal of liberty and juridical equality . . . [which] attacked the existing social order." A common criticism in Latin America, in Europe, and in the United States itself was that Americans were greedy and base. Financial success and material comfort meant more to them than honor and religious devotion. Many of the most prominent Latin writers, including Martí, Nicaragua's Rubén Darío, and the Uruguayan José Enrique Rodó, criticized the materialistic, grasping, selfish "American way of life."[65] The Chilean intellectual Benjamin Vicuña Mackenna disparaged American leaders as lacking "honor, patriotism, or intelligence" and suffering from "depraved selfishness." In America, he asserted, "mercantilism" corrupted everything, "religion, family, the tomb, the marvels of creation." Nor did all observers agree that the Anglo-Saxon race was necessarily destined to triumph over the Latin race. To many proud descendants of Spain, their civilization, with its roots in the glory of ancient Rome, was clearly superior to that of the barbarian hordes from which the Anglo-Saxons were descended. "To see the typical Yankee," wrote one Chilean, "is to see the old Saxon." And just as "Rome triumphed over the barbarians by virtue of its superior culture and morality, Catholic,

Hispanic Chile would vanquish the materialism and greed of Anglo-Saxon, Protestant America."[66]

But this confidence in Hispanic and Catholic cultural superiority mingled with a more potent fear that the greedy northern barbarians would overwhelm them, as they had long ago overwhelmed Rome. To these critics, the grasping, avaricious nature of American society was of a piece with the northern power's record of aggressive territorial expansionism. In the 1880s Latin Americans had not forgotten that the United States seven decades before had been more eager to take Florida from Spain than to recognize the independence of the struggling Latin republics, notwithstanding all of Clay's and Monroe's grandiose rhetoric. Chile's early-nineteenth-century founding father, Diego Portales, had warned his countrymen after their liberation from Spain, "Take care not to escape one domination to fall under another!" True, American territorial aggression seemed to be a thing of the past after the Union victory, and most Latin Americans no longer feared military conquest. But despite Blaine's claims that the North's victory in the Civil War had wiped the slate clean and made America a morally pure and disinterested arbiter in the hemisphere, many harbored understandable doubts about the great northern power, the "boa constrictor which fascinates us and unwinds its tortuous sinews."[67] These lingering fears and antipathies were formidable obstacles to the kind of open system of friendship and commerce Blaine and other American statesmen hoped to build. The Mexican leader who followed Juárez into power in the 1870s articulated a common view that competed with Juárez's and Díaz's vision of Mexican-American economic integration. Between the two countries he wanted a barrier—or as he put it, "between strength and weakness, the desert."[68]

An even greater obstacle to Blaine's grand ambitions, however, was that other prominent nations in the hemisphere had ambitions of their own. Mexico, especially under Díaz, believed it had the right and perhaps even the duty to extend its own hegemony over the nations of Central America. The United States did not own a monopoly on condescension and racism. Just as North Americans looked at Latin America as backward, so Mexicans looked at Central Americans with a similar blend of disdain and paternalism. Mexican diplomats described Central America's capitals as "squalid snake pits, its countryside . . . untamed wilderness, its rulers . . . despotic barbarians . . . and its people . . . backward, uneducated 'Indians.'" In an effort to foment an "official nationalism," Díaz played an "assertive role" in Central America, calculating that a "paternalistic posture toward weaker, poorer Central American nations like Guatemala could show off alleged and real benefits of Porfirian modernization."[69]

Central America, meanwhile, had its own assertive leaders, and one of them, the Guatemalan strongman Justo Rufino Barrios, aimed both to challenge Mexico over a disputed border area at Chiapas and to unite Central America under his own leadership. Mexico resisted, partly out of fear of being squeezed between a militarily potent Barrios and the northern colossus and partly to assert its own hegemony. Barrios, in turn, looked to the United States for help, and in 1881 he invited Washington to serve as mediator in the border dispute, appealing to the United States "as the natural protector of the integrity of the Central American territory."[70]

For Blaine, the brewing crisis showed why the United States had to play the role of disinterested arbiter in the hemisphere: to stop the senseless and destructive wars that plagued the region. American policy makers had generally supported Central America's reunification, partly to end the recurrent wars among them, partly to help them resist pressures and intervention by the European powers, and partly to provide stability in a region where a canal might be built. Blaine wanted to prove that the United States was indeed, as he put it, "the natural protector of Central American territory," and he promised Barrios that the United States would do everything possible to strengthen the "indispensable and natural union of the republics of the continent." To the Mexican government, he declared that the United States was "the founder, . . . the guarantor and guardian of republican principles on the American continent." Its "now established policy" was to "refrain from territorial acquisition." It therefore had not only the "right" but a "moral obligation" to prevent aggression and territorial conquest by others. Offering some "amicable counsel," he warned that "should disrespect be shown to the boundaries which separate [Mexico] from her weaker neighbors, or should the authority of force be resorted to in establishing the rights over territory which they claim," this would constitute "a menace to the interests of all." On the other hand, if Mexico and the United States worked together "in cordial harmony," they could persuade "all the other independent governments of North and South America to aid in fixing this policy of peace for all the future disputes between nations of the Western hemisphere."[71]

The Mexican government, furious that Blaine seemed to be taking the side of Guatemala in the border dispute, responded that there was "nothing . . . to arbitrate," adding pointedly that its "position with regard to the United States" made it especially "desirous to avoid sanctioning in any way the right of conquest."[72] It followed by sending troops to the Guatemalan border, and the standoff ended with a settlement that favored the Mexican position and embarrassed Blaine. The episode contributed to a reputation, fastened on him by Democratic Party critics and Republican rivals, as "Jingo Jim." But war with Mexico was the last thing on Blaine's mind. He had wanted to establish orderly principles of behavior in the hemisphere, principles that would be commonly enforced under the leadership of the United States, the "ultimate arbiter of peace and guardian of republican principles."[73]

This search for order was not to be confused with an effort to maintain the status quo. It required revolutionary change in the hemisphere, an assertion of American influence, and an acceptance by the region's other powers of this new, American-dominated system, which had implications for their foreign as well as their domestic policies. As the confrontation with Mexico showed, such revolutionary change was likely to be resisted when it conflicted with the interests and ambitions of other powerful players. The irony was that Mexican leaders welcomed and even pleaded for American economic "imperialism." What they could not tolerate was the American demand for a peaceful and stable order arbitrated by the United States.

The same was true of Chile, the aspiring hegemon of South America. The Chileans were a proud, self-confident people, with a sense of national destiny much like that of the North Americans. As the first of the newly independent Latin peoples to establish internal order and a fairly stable republic, the Chileans regarded themselves as "an exemplar of progress." They also considered themselves racially superior to their Bolivian and Peruvian neighbors—they were "like Rome, a white enclave in a colored continent," and felt justified in imposing their "own vision of international order" on their region. Chile's military triumph over a Peruvian-Bolivian confederation in the 1830s had further whetted these ambitions, as had the expansion of an industrializing economy that easily dominated the less developed economies of Peru, Bolivia, Ecuador, and even for a time Argentina. Chile also gradually established itself as the leading naval power not only of South America but of the Western Hemisphere. During the 1860s and '70s, and well into the 1880s, the Chilean navy was more powerful than that of the United States.[74]

In 1879 another war broke out pitting Chile against Peru and Bolivia, and with total dominance of the seas Chile easily routed its two neighbors. Within months it had seized Bolivia's only port and had invaded Peru, occupying the mineral-rich provinces of Tarapaca and Arica, as well as the capital city of Lima. A crippled Bolivia lost vital access to the ocean and would never regain it. Thousands of Peruvians died in the fighting, and the nation's economy was destroyed. When the fighting stopped, Chile demanded the permanent cession of the most valuable portions of Peru as indemnity.

American officials sympathized with the defeated powers. President Garfield wrote in his private diary of "the sad condition of Peru, and our duty to prevent her destruction." Blaine complained that Chile's domination of Peru's provisional government and seizure of its most valuable territory "amounted to the extinction of a state." He wanted to keep Peru in one piece, to preserve its "territorial integrity," in the interest of ensuring the "peaceful maintenance of the status quo of the American Commonwealth . . . the very essence of their policy of harmonious alliance for self preservation." He therefore urged Chile to accept a monetary indemnity for the seized territory, insisting this would make for a "more permanent peace." In some respects, Blaine did not really believe that the problem was Chile. With typical North American condescension, and in apparent ignorance of the history of the region, he could not believe Chile was the real aggressor. It was "an English war on Peru, with Chili [*sic*] as the instrument," Blaine insisted. The Chileans "would never have gone into this war one inch but for the backing of British capital."[75]

Blaine's ignorance of Chile's ambitions, as well as its sense of honor and destiny, wound up costing him, and Peru, dearly. American diplomats, after rejecting a proposal of joint mediation from the British, French, and Germans, encouraged Peru's president to stand firm against Chile's demands. When he did, the Chileans simply arrested him, seized Peru's treasury, and challenged the United States to do something about it. They knew, as did the Americans, that the U.S. Navy, several thousand miles from its home ports, would have a hard time against the powerful Chilean navy operating in its own waters.

But Blaine, again, had no thought of going to war. He warned Chile that the United States would "hold itself free to appeal to other republics of this continent to join it in an effort to avert consequences which cannot be confined to Chile and Peru." This sounded like a threat of war, but it was a threat of a conference. Blaine hoped a "congress of American republics" could, through "moral suasion," force Chile to relent. In November 1881, therefore, the Arthur administration issued invitations to the hemisphere's republics for a conference to be held early in 1882, the "sole purpose" of which was "to seek ways to prevent wars between the American states." But before the conference could be held, Blaine was out of office. Back in the United States, his enemies once again crowed about "Jingo Jim," while in Chile the people celebrated another smashing victory over Peru and Bolivia, made all the sweeter by the humiliation of the North American bullies. As one of Blaine's more astute diplomats had predicted, the outcome was that "we have offended everybody by our interference without securing a single advantage to either [Chile or Peru] or ourselves."[76]

The failures in Central and South America did not deter Blaine or his supporters from pursuing their goal of hemispheric solidarity under American leadership. Through the mid-1880s Republican leaders, including William McKinley, worked in Congress to convene Blaine's inter-American conference, and in 1888 a reluctant Cleveland administration sent out the invitations. Blaine returned to office in time to preside over the 1889 Pan-American Conference, which lasted six months. All but one of the seventeen invited nations attended. In his opening address Blaine insisted that every nation would have an equal say and that the conference would "seek nothing, propose nothing, endure nothing that is not, in the general sense of all the Delegates, timely and wise and peaceful." His goal was "international friendship" and the orderly regulation of closer "personal and commercial relations of the American states, south and north" so that everyone could gain "the highest possible advantage from the enlightened and enlarged intercourse of all."[77]

Closer commercial ties and greater access to Latin American markets were certainly important goals for Blaine and even more so for the congressional sponsors of the conference. The Latin delegates were treated to a six-week railway tour of the American industrial heartland—the idea being to impress upon the visitors the vitality of the American economy, and upon local American industrialists the value of Latin markets. Blaine wanted to create a hemisphere-wide customs union to strengthen regional trade at the expense of the Europeans, an idea the leading Latin nations rejected. The Argentine delegate objected to a Pan-Americanism that excluded Europe, especially Catholic Europe. "I do not forget that Spain, our mother, is there . . . that Italy, our friend, is there, and France, our sister." Instead of "America for Americans," he proposed, "[l]et America be for mankind."[78]

For Blaine, however, as for Harrison, the overarching goals of the conference were more political than economic. The big prize they sought was establishment of a permanent international arbitration tribunal, to be based in Washington, that would adjudicate all future hemispheric conflicts. And they wanted to make resort to the tribunal compulsory, for the United States as well as for its neighbors. Not for the last time in its history, the United States proposed to erect an international institution that would help keep the

peace and thereby serve American interests in stability, but without requiring constant American exertions. The most powerful Latin nations, however, especially Argentina, Mexico, and Chile, saw the proposal as another
manifestation of America's hegemonic ambitions, an attempt to limit their
freedom of action, to constrain the use of their power to further their ambitions and to defend their interests as they saw them. They insisted on a
clause permitting any nation to reject arbitration if its national independence was threatened, and in the end only about half of the delegations
agreed even to this watered-down proposal.[79] All agreed to the building of
a hemispheric railway system, with funding to be provided by American
investors.

Blaine declared victory. "We hold up this new Magna Carta," he
declared in his closing address, "which abolishes war and substitutes arbitration between the American Republics, as the first and greatest fruit of the
Inter-American conference." This was, of course, a significant exaggeration. Blaine had worked throughout the conference to avoid "any appearance of coercion," had attempted to treat the other nations as equals and
thereby "overcome Latin suspicions of Yankee intentions." But this proved
beyond his or probably anyone's capacity. A long history of territorial
expansion was hard to erase. Even harder to overcome was the enormous
disparity of power between the United States and most of its neighbors, and
the fears and resentments this disparity engendered. While welcoming occasional North American protection and financing, the Latin nations did not
welcome and would not endorse an all-encompassing American hegemony.
Astute observers like Sáenz Peña recognized the North American ambition
for what it was. Looking back on the conference years later, he recalled
"[t]he masterful audacity of James Blaine, who was undoubtedly more intense than [Theodore] Roosevelt." Blaine had wished "to make of America
a market, and of the sovereign states, tributaries." But, the Argentine noted,
"[t]he idea, economic in form, was essentially political. . . . A brilliant and
haughty spirit speaks and commands one hemisphere in the name of the
other hemisphere, gives orders to Europe in the name of America."[80]

That was indeed part of what Blaine had in mind, following a line of
ambition that went back to the days of Hamilton and Jefferson. Sáenz
Peña's description of Blaine's aspiration was a perfect paraphrase of Hamilton's hope, expressed a century earlier, that the United States would "aim at
an ascendant in the system of American affairs"[81] and become the "arbiter
of Europe in America."[82] But Blaine and the presidents he served, as well as
the diplomats who served him and a sizable portion of Republican Party

leaders and opinion makers, also hoped and believed they were bringing something of benefit to the inhabitants of their "American system." That, too, was an old ambition.

From Power to Ambition: Asia and the Pacific

THERE WERE TIMES when American leaders gave voice to similar ambitions in Asia and the Pacific. President Garfield declared in 1881 that the United States should become "the arbiter" of the Pacific, "the controller of its commerce and chief nation that inhabits its shores." At the very least Garfield hoped the United States would become a "power to be reckoned with."[83] Blaine declared that American interests in the Pacific were "steadily increasing," and the United States could not "accept even temporary subordination" of its expanding role.[84] Commodore Robert Shufeldt, one of the more influential Americans in Asia in the 1870s and '80s, envisioned the day when the entire Pacific would become "the commercial domain of America."[85]

Like American ambitions in the Western Hemisphere, these ambitions were not new. American interest in the trade of the Orient went back to the eighteenth century, when the first trading ships of the new republic set sail for China, and dreams of the bounty of the Asian market had mesmerized traders ever since. But over the course of the nineteenth century territorial expansion on the North American continent had placed the United States in an increasingly strong position to realize old aspirations. When the United States acquired California and full title to Oregon after the Mexican-American War, it became one of only three major powers with a coastline on the Pacific. Seward's purchase of Alaska in 1867 strengthened the American position in the Pacific by removing Russia from the Northwest. He also acquired the Midway Islands west of Hawaii, and in the 1870s the United States acquired from Samoan leaders the rights to a naval station in the harbor of Pago Pago.

Then there was Hawaii itself. In the early 1840s Secretary of State Daniel Webster and President John Tyler had thrown the mantle of the Monroe Doctrine around Hawaii, declaring it off limits to other powers. Annexationist movements grew up both in the islands and in United States, but their plans foundered on the rocks of the slavery issue. The quest for Hawaii resumed after the Civil War. Seward negotiated a reciprocity treaty in 1867 to stake the American claim until, as President Andrew Johnson put it, the people of Hawaii "voluntarily apply for admission to the Union."[86] The Radical Republican anti-Johnson Congress rejected that treaty but in

1875 passed another negotiated by Hamilton Fish, who aimed to "bind these islands to the United States with hoops of steel." When Blaine took office in 1881, he argued that the islands belonged "by the operation of political necessity" within America's sphere of influence.[87]

By the 1880s Hawaii had become a virtual "economic colony" of the United States. Hawaiian products sold to the United States, mostly sugar, constituted 99 percent of all the island's exports, while the United States supplied three-fourths of all Hawaii's imports. American-born settlers, the sons and daughters of missionaries and whalers, had over the years become a dominant economic and political force on the islands. Over time the "American" and other influential light-skinned merchants in Hawaii agitated for political rights and a political system more closely attuned to their political and economic interests. The "capriciousness, extravagance and corruption" of the native Hawaiian monarchy, they believed, were not consistent with "a modern system of property and economics."[88] In 1887 these influential property owners forced King Kalakaua to establish a parliamentary government that placed significant power in their hands. When Queen Liliuokalani acceded to the throne in 1891 and began efforts to rewrite the constitution to restore power to the crown, the stage was set for political conflict.

The enormous economic, political, and military power of the United States heavily influenced the course of Hawaiian politics at every stage. American trade enriched and strengthened the light-skinned property owners at the expense of the native royalty. American interest in annexation, consistently expressed from the days of Webster through the time of Seward and Blaine, encouraged the repeated blossoming of annexationist movements on the islands. And America's growing interest in the Asian market made Hawaii increasingly attractive. Even President Cleveland urged Congress to renew the reciprocity treaty on the grounds that "those islands, in the highway of Oriental and Australasian traffic, are virtually an outpost of American commerce and a stepping-stone to the growing trade of the Pacific."[89] When Congress approved the new treaty in 1887, it added a demand for exclusive rights to use the mouth of the Pearl River as a possible American naval station.

By the time of the Benjamin Harrison administration, Blaine and others were eager to seize the next opportunity. In 1889 the United States landed seventy marines from the USS *Adams* to prevent a coup in favor of the queen. Harrison ordered a warship to remain on permanent station in Hawaiian waters, and he appointed as consul in Hawaii a determined annexationist. "Hawaii may come up for decision at any unexpected hour," Blaine

observed in 1891, "and I hope we shall be prepared to decide it in the affirmative."[90] The hour came two years later. In 1893 Queen Liliuokalani challenged the constitution, and the property owners responded by overthrowing
her. The American consul ordered the landing of 150 marines, ostensibly to
protect American life and property but with the intended effect of protecting the new Hawaiian government. The overthrow of the monarchy was
successful, a provisional republic was established, and the republic's leaders immediately requested annexation to the United States.

Whether the United States was complicit in fomenting the coup against
the queen or intervened by force to bring about an overthrow of the monarchy are interesting questions but in important respects are beside the point.
America's power and evident interest in annexation encouraged the coup.
When it came, the United States provided de facto military support to the
new government. Then in a matter of weeks, and in the waning days of his
presidency, President Harrison rushed a treaty of annexation before Congress for ratification.

Events in Hawaii followed a familiar pattern of American expansion,
stretching back to the days when an "American" population overthrew the
Spanish government of West Florida, declared it a republic, and sought
annexation to the United States. President Harrison claimed, as had President Madison eight decades before, that disturbances in Hawaii had placed
American interests "in serious peril." The overthrown monarchy had been
"effete," "weak," and "inadequate," and the task of the United States was
now to seize the opportunity that had been afforded.[91] The only difference
was that Hawaii lay a thousand miles off the American coast.

Prior to 1898 this was the outer limit of American territorial ambitions
in Asia and the Pacific. No American official in a position of responsibility
called for the acquisition of territory on the Asian mainland. Not even those
who would later be labeled "imperialists" looked to the Philippines or to any
other part of the island chain that ringed Asia as desirable American acquisitions, much less as possible colonies. Even the acquisition of Hawaii had
more to do with defending American interests in the Western Hemisphere,
including the as-yet-unbuilt transisthmian canal, as well as those of the light-
skinned Hawaiians, than it did with extending American power toward Asia.

American ambitions in Asia were not as great as in the Western Hemisphere. There was no equivalent of the Monroe Doctrine or of Pan-
Americanism or of the century-old ambition to make the United States the
region's "arbiter." This was not because Americans believed Asians did not
need uplifting or that the United States was not uniquely suited to play such
a role. Rather, it was because the United States possessed nothing like the

power and influence in Asia that it at least theoretically enjoyed in the Western Hemisphere. The latter had been ceded as an American sphere of influence by the great European powers. But in Asia the United States was among the weakest of the Western powers. Indeed, it had historically relied on the power of others to provide what entrée and influence it did have, its diplomats following in the wake of British gunboats and piggybacking on treaties, especially in China, that were the product of British power.

Americans did not expect or, for the time being, even desire to compete for predominance in Asia. Instead, they hoped to turn their relative weakness into an advantage and to exert influence of a softer, more attractive variety, contrasting themselves with the more muscular and, on occasion, bullying Europeans. They hoped to take advantage of their lack of past territorial conquest and evident lack of future territorial ambition to win the trust and friendship, and commerce, of such Asian powers as China, Japan, and Korea, and to use American commerce and technological know-how to assist their progress upward to civilization. But they would do so without attempting to exert hegemony.

Asian leaders often wished the United States were more ambitious. They actively sought to involve America in their affairs—often more ardently than the American government wished to become involved. They had none of the Latin American concerns that they were inviting a "boa constrictor" into their homes. Compared with Great Britain, France, Germany, and Russia, the United States appeared to the Asians relatively harmless and disinterested. But it was strong enough to be a potentially useful ally. The leading Asian nations, above all China and Japan, agreed with Garfield that the United States was becoming a power to be reckoned with. Even before the Civil War Chinese government observers regarded the Americans as "one of the three or four major nations of the West."[92] The Chinese were not always impressed by their mental acuity—a Chinese imperial commissioner in the 1840s advised the emperor to speak to American envoys in a manner that was "simple and direct" and "clear and obvious," for if he was too "deep" the Americans "would probably not even be able to comprehend" what he was saying.[93] But they generally regarded the Americans as "respectful," "compliant," and "peaceful" and in this respect different from the other Western "barbarians."[94] In 1861 a Chinese leader "singled out the United States as a country whose people were 'pure-minded' and of 'honest disposition.' "[95] Much of this positive feeling had to do with the Chinese perception throughout the nineteenth century that the United States, alone of the great Western powers, posed no threat "to China, its ruling house and established order."[96] And if in addition to being unthreatening, the Americans lacked the Europeans' cunning, all the better. The question, one Chinese official explained, was "how to control them and make them exploitable by us."[97]

There were a number of ways in which Asian leaders sought to "exploit" the Americans. One was as a model of economic and technological modernization; another was as a source of financing; yet another was as a source of training and technology for their antiquated navies. Li Hung-chang, a modernizer and the most influential Chinese leader from the 1870s through the mid-1890s, eagerly sought American financial and technical assistance in the building of mines and railroads. Among the many virtues of the Americans from Li's point of view was that businessmen "did not receive the close support from their government that their European counterparts enjoyed," which meant there was less risk of confrontation with the American government. Li considered the United States "to be the least avaricious and, hopefully, the most useful of the barbarian nations."[98] In fact, American entrepreneurs received so little help from their government in the form of subsidies and political support that they proved mostly unwilling to invest in China and thus disappointed Li's plans. Less disappointing was the assistance provided by Commodore Shufeldt to the Chinese navy, also at Li's request, to strengthen it against burgeoning challenges from Europe and Japan.[99]

The Chinese were not nearly as interested in American-style modernization, however, as were the Japanese. In 1860, even before the Meiji Restoration, an embassy of more than seventy samurai traveled to Washington to ratify a commercial treaty but also to get a good look at the rising American power. They came back impressed by American science and technology, marveling at everything from railroads and weaponry to gaslights and flush toilets.[100] After the Meiji Restoration in 1868, Japan's new modernizing leaders traveled to the United States to observe its economy, society, and political institutions. The head of the delegation, speaking in the House of Representatives, declared: "We came for enlightenment and we gladly find it here. . . . In the future an extended commerce will unite our national interests in a thousand forms, as drops of water will commingle, flowing from our several rivers to that common ocean that divides our countries."[101] Soon hundreds of Japanese students were studying in the United States, and they "returned home to make the history of early Meiji Japan, founding schools, publishing newspapers and books on world history and geography, introducing new techniques in farming and in industry, and becoming diplomats, generals, and admirals."[102]

Much like the Mexicans, the Japanese came to learn Western ways, in part so that they might resist Western power. The secret of that power, they had determined, was economic modernization and also, within limits, political liberalization. For some Japanese officials, "the United States represented the ultimate in political and economic modernization." The British had the military power, but the United States "exemplified what the Japanese considered to be characteristics of the modern state."[103]

Asian leaders also viewed the United States as a potentially important partner in the geopolitical competition then emerging, chiefly between China and Japan but also involving some of the European powers. The Chinese, watching and worrying about the rise of a Westernizing Japan, looked to the United States to balance and check Japanese power. Washington loomed large in the strategic calculations of Li Hung-chang, who sought active American intervention in no less than four different crises involving China's neighbors between 1879 and 1895, "sometimes as a putative ally, sometimes as a would-be intermediary." In 1879 he called on former president Grant to mediate a dispute with Japan over the Liuchiu Islands (Ryukyu, in Japanese). In the early 1880s and again in the 1890s Li invited the United States into Korea as a means of preserving Chinese suzerainty against the aggressive designs of both Russia and Japan. He also sought American help against the French in Indochina. Li looked to the United States because he believed it was powerful and thus "might significantly strengthen China's international position," and also because "of all the major powers of the day only the United States posed no clear peril to China's territory or to the safety of her tribute states." As Li explained to the cloistered Koreans, "America, which faces directly on the Pacific, has no intention of invading the territory of others there."[104] Soon the Koreans themselves were looking to the United States, both to help them modernize and to fend off pressures from China, as well from Japan and Russia, both of whom looked to seize control of parts of the Korean peninsula for themselves.

The American government was cautious about involving itself too deeply, partly because American officials knew they were weak compared to the European powers, and partly because despite the lure of the Asian market they did not consider the commercial interests large enough to warrant a more active role. In 1890 American exports to China amounted to $3 million, which was 0.3 percent of total U.S. exports worldwide. A decade later Americans were exporting $15 million worth of goods to China, which still amounted to only 1.1 percent of total exports.[105] Some American entrepreneurs dreamed of selling four hundred million cotton shirts to four hundred million Chinese consumers, as well as to the Japanese and Koreans. But no one was making that much money yet, and neither the U.S. government nor American envoys placed the highest priority on Asian commerce.

Such involvement as Americans did undertake in Asia, both officially and unofficially, had more to do with perceptions of morality, honor, and responsibility, and with the continuing American preoccupation with progress and civilization, of which commerce was an important but subordinate component. American officials were pleased that Asian leaders considered the United States a disinterested arbiter, operating on a higher moral plane than the European powers, for that was exactly how Americans saw themselves. When Li Hung-chang sought American mediation in the 1879 dispute with Japan, Secretary of State William Evarts responded that his government would provide its "good offices" if Japan agreed. After all, he pointed out, the United States was the world's most "prominent advocate of arbitration." It was only fitting that the "wise counselors" of both Asian nations would turn to the United States for such help.[106]

Such friendly assistance provided an opportunity, Americans believed, to hasten Asia's advance toward modern civilization. Former president Grant gladly accepted the role of mediator in the Sino-Japanese dispute for this reason, and also because he was flattered to be asked. He did not believe that East Asia was as important strategically or commercially as the Western Hemisphere was, at least not before a canal was built. But "what had captured Grant's imagination was the imminent development of modern civilization in Asia and the role the United States might play not only in planting the seeds of progress but also in maintaining a propitious environment for the seed to germinate and take root."[107] Part of this role was to keep the Asian powers from fighting one another; and part of it was to protect them, as much as the United States could, from the aggression of the Europeans. Grant expressed the desire to get Japan and China out from under the burdensome treaties they had been forced to conclude with the European empires, although these treaties also governed their relations with the United States. "With a little more advancement in modern civilization," he wrote a senior Chinese official, both nations "could throw off the offensive treaties which now cripple and humiliate them, and could enter into competition for the world's commerce."[108]

Grant hoped they in turn would view the United States as "the most friendly of the powers," and by and large they did.[109] Five years later, when China again turned to the United States for help in resisting French demands in Indochina, the American minister, John Russell Young, "used the opportunity to lecture the Chinese on the necessity of adapting Western ways for self-defense" and on the links that could be forged between "an ancient China and a youthful United States" traveling "hand in hand along the path of progress."[110] By offering the United States not only as a source of progress and civilization but as a disinterested, principled alternative to the greedy Europeans, American leaders and envoys hoped to gain some advantage in both countries, including commercial advantages. But they were also convinced that they had something of benefit to offer these Asian peoples, the means of helping them move from barbarism to civilization. American diplomats like Hamilton Fish sought "to pursue a policy of moral force—to encourage material development" and the "increase of trade" that would both enrich Americans and make such development possible.[111]

America's involvement with Korea beginning in the 1870s showed how such motives could shape policy, often more than considerations of tangible material interests. Korea, justly known as the "hermit kingdom," had long shunned contact with the outside world and accepted its status as a "tributary" state to China. In the late 1860s, however, American diplomats in China reported that Korea was now regarded by the Chinese as "independent" and that it was interested in negotiating treaties with the United States as well as with other powers. This information proved inaccurate in the case of China, which didn't really consider Korea "independent" as Americans understood the term, and premature in the case of Korea, which was not interested in opening itself to the outside world. Nevertheless, in 1871 Fish dispatched Frederick Low to Korea, accompanied by several gunboats commanded by the head of American naval forces in the Far East, with instructions "to secure a treaty for the protection of shipwrecked mariners and a commercial treaty." But when the American ships reached the mouth of the Han River, they were warned to stay away. Low disregarded the warnings, and when his ships were fired on from a Korean fort, the American guns leveled it. Low demanded an apology from the Korean government, and when none was forthcoming, he attacked the remaining Korean positions, killing every last defender. Low and his colleagues wrote home admiringly of how the Korean troops fought to the bitter end, dying "at their posts of duty heroically and without fear." The Korean government, for its part, condemned the Americans for their "barbarous" and unprovoked attack.[112]

The incident was ironic in two respects. The self-proclaimed disinterested and peace-loving Americans had introduced themselves to Korea by killing its people. Yet the Koreans then responded by deciding that they had no choice but to open themselves to the world in order to acquire the means to defend themselves from such attacks. Korean leaders, led by the young

King Kojong, realized "how helpless and weak their proud nation was against an attack by 'barbarians,'" and they determined that Korea had to modernize. In 1876 Korea entered into a treaty with Japan, and six years later Commodore Shufeldt negotiated a treaty opening relations between Korea and the United States. It was primarily a commercial treaty, but it contained a clause that promised, "If other powers deal unjustly or oppressively with either government, the other will exert their good offices, on being informed of the case, to bring about an amicable agreement, thus showing their friendly feeling." In the decade to come, this American promise of "good offices" would take on much more significance than American policy makers back in Washington imagined.[113]

When the first American minister arrived in Seoul in 1883, the Korean king "danced for joy." He sent a delegation to the United States to get a better understanding of American society; one prominent delegate, upon returning, declared, "I was born in the dark; I went into the light; and I have returned into the dark again. I cannot as yet see my way clearly, but I hope to soon." The king's hope was that the United States would support Korea's independence against an overbearing China, defend it from the aggressive designs of other nations, and assist him in the modernization of his country. With little prodding from American envoys, he invited American businesses into Korea. Thomas Edison won the exclusive right to install and operate electric lights, and the king promised that American proposals to build railways and telegraph lines would be "favorably considered" and the companies granted "a liberal franchise."[114] Partly he believed his nation's survival depended on opening opportunities for American commerce, both to modernize and to strengthen. But partly he wanted to ensure that the Americans would remain interested enough in Korea to provide protection against Japan and China. Along these lines the king asked the United States to provide an adviser to his foreign ministry to help draw up treaties with England and Germany, and to serve as an intermediary to begin negotiations with Russia and France. Like China's Li Hung-chang, he also requested military advisers to help improve the fighting capability of the royal army.

The king also provided royal subsidies to American missionaries, whom he and other Korean progressives considered a "civilizing" influence in their country, allowing them to open schools and hospitals. American diplomats in Korea invariably warned the missionaries against heavy-handed proselytizing, and the missionaries generally obeyed, concentrating more on temporal than on spiritual assistance. In fact, they had a powerful impact on Korean life, introducing modern medical practices and establishing some of the better secondary schools and colleges in the country. Their successes further convinced Americans that Korea was, in the words of one diplomat, "susceptible to progress and improvement and worthy of the assistance she may receive, and needs, from the Western nations that recognized her as a sister."[115]

From the beginning of the new relationship, the Americans serving in Korea—whether diplomat, businessman, or missionary—strongly and even passionately supported the king and his goals of independence and modernization. This made them hostile to China, which they believed was trying to keep Korea in a state of backwardness, and they vigorously upheld American official policy, which recognized Korea as sovereign and not part of China's tributary system, even though the United States was virtually alone in this view. The British made no pretense of concern for Korea's independence. Japan recognized Korea's independence, but only because the Japanese hoped to take it for themselves. Shufeldt understood from the beginning that Korea would become "the battlefield of any war between China and Russia or Japan," and he believed the United States should be willing to offer "protections against the aggression of surrounding powers."[116]

Official Washington was a good deal more cautious than its envoys, repeatedly warning them not to commit the United States to any defense of Korean sovereignty. But the mere fact that the United States recognized Korean independence produced entangling complications. Secretary of State Thomas Bayard, in a note attempting to restrain one zealous American minister, insisted that "the Government of the United States has no concern . . . beyond that of a friendly state which has treated Corea [*sic*] as independent and sovereign and hopes to see her position as such among nations assured."[117] Even this seemingly harmless statement could turn into a large commitment if the U.S. government sincerely intended to continue treating Korea as "independent and sovereign." And indeed these vague, principled commitments in Korea proved difficult for American officials to ignore. As the inevitable international competition over Korea heated up, the little codicil in the 1882 treaty offering "good offices" loomed large, if only in the American conscience.

The big crisis came in 1894, when instability and disorder spread throughout Korea, inflamed in part by a combination of Japanese and Chinese meddling. The instability prompted China and then Japan to send troops, and King Kojong immediately appealed to the United States for its help and "good offices," pursuant to the treaty. Neither President Grover Cleveland, now in his second term in office, nor his new secretary of state, Walter Q. Gresham, were looking to deepen American involvement overseas. They had no "expectations of promoting the insignificant American trade with Korea." Yet they felt compelled to respond to the king's plea. Cleveland was especially concerned about protecting American missionaries in Korea who might be endangered by the spreading violence. Yet he and Gresham also felt obligated to do something to help Korea itself. "Acting under a stipulation in our treaty with Korea," Cleveland later told Congress, "I felt constrained from the beginning of the controversy to tender our good offices to induce an amicable arrangement" of the conflict.[118]

The president began by dispatching the cruiser *Baltimore* to the port city of Chemulpo (later renamed Inchon). The idea was to protect American lives in Korea, but in the view of American observers the *Baltimore*'s arrival also had a "salutary moral effect" on the rebellion, which promptly collapsed. The State Department meanwhile instructed the American minister, "in the view of the friendly interest of the United States in the welfare of Korea and its people," to make "every possible effort for the preservation of peaceful conditions." Back in Washington Gresham confronted the Japanese minister, accusing Japan of seeking an excuse for war with China. When the minister candidly admitted that this was true, and that in fact the Japanese government was provoking war in order to quell domestic opposition by "arousing the patriotic sentiment of our people," Gresham was outraged. He sent an angry note to Japan, criticizing it for refusing to withdraw its troops from Korea and expressing "hope that Korea's independence and sovereignty will be respected." Gresham warned the Japanese that President Cleveland would be "painfully disappointed should Japan visit upon her feeble and defenceless neighbor the horrors of an unjust war."[119]

Gresham's warning did not have much more effect than had similar warnings by Blaine to Mexico and Chile. The Japanese continued their military operations and eventually seized and imprisoned King Kojong. The Cleveland administration ordered nearly fifty heavily armed marines from the *Baltimore* to move in and protect American lives. Japanese forces were in control of the city and could have provided protection, but Cleveland and Gresham did not want to legitimize the Japanese occupation by calling for their assistance. As one historian summarized their actions, "Inspired by concerns of justice and humanity rather than self-interest, Gresham and Cleveland responded spontaneously to sudden demands to save missionaries and aid a pitiful and helpless little country."[120]

These American concerns for "justice and humanity" had consequences, and not only in Korea. During the Sino-Japanese War that followed, the United States again provided its "good offices" to protect Japanese interests in China, as well as Chinese interests in Japan. But American assistance to the Japanese stirred up violent resentment among the Chinese population, and soon President Cleveland had reason to worry that American missionaries in China were actually in greater danger than those in Korea. He dispatched two gunboats to Chinese waters and augmented the size of the Asiatic squadron, preparing to protect American missionaries from Chinese attack.

All this involvement in the Far East resulted primarily not from American commercial ambitions or from narrow national security interests but from moral and humanitarian concerns and a sense of obligation stemming from an offer of "good offices" more than a decade before. American trade with Asia was a small fraction of its overall trade with the world. Between 1850 and 1890 American exports to Asia amounted to only 5 percent of its total exports.[121] American involvement in Asia in the late nineteenth century stemmed from a blend of material interests on the one hand, and intangible and abstract ambitions and sentiments on the other, with the latter frequently outweighing the former.

Nor was American involvement in these crises unpopular, either at home or abroad. European powers, and especially Great Britain, urged the United States to get more involved and actively mediate between Japan and China. In the United States peace groups proposed participation in an "international police force" to end the conflict and guarantee Korea's independence. Both opponents and supporters of the Cleveland administration called for deeper involvement, on the grounds that the United States was uniquely suited to play a helpful role. The pro-Cleveland *Review of Reviews* opined that "from the very inception of this Oriental contest," it had been clear that "it was the manifest duty of the United States, as a long-time friend and disinterested neighbor, to attempt to restore harmony."[122] The Cleveland administration held back, but only a decade later, in another war involving Japan in Northeast Asia, President Theodore Roosevelt would accept the role of mediator and win the Nobel Prize for Peace.

Even in tiny Samoa, insignificant material interests blended with moral and humanitarian concerns and a sense of responsibility to produce unwanted confrontations and crises. America's material interest in Samoa had never been substantial. The islands stood across the path of transpacific travel and through much of the nineteenth century had been a port of call for American whalers. The tribes and foreign settlers who lived there had seemingly forever been engaged in internecine struggles, with the various factions often looking to outside powers for help and offering their accessible harbors as inducement. In 1872 an American naval commander, without advance authorization but encouraged by the owner of an American steamship line, concluded such an arrangement on behalf of the United States. In return for exclusive access to the harbor of Pago Pago, he promised a Samoan chief the "friendship and protection of the great Government of the United States of America."[123] The Senate never acted on that treaty, but a few years later a prominent Samoan traveled the four thousand miles to Washington to seek support. While the American public read with fascination of the envoy's extensively tattooed body, Secretary of State Evarts modified the old agreement, promising that in return for rights to a naval station at Pago Pago, the United States would provide its "good offices" to mediate in any conflict between Samoa and foreign powers.[124] The following year the Samoans concluded similar agreements with both Germany and Great Britain, each of which received its own rights to Samoa's harbors. The United States, interested not in dominating Samoa but only in ensuring that no other power did, accepted a tripartite arrangement for joint protection of the islands and recognized the appointment of King Malietoa Laupepa, whose friendly feelings for the United States were well known in Washington and in Berlin.

Problems began in the mid-1880s, when Germany started demanding greater control of the islands commensurate with its larger commercial interests. After years of putting off pressures for overseas colonies, Bismarck was shifting course to mollify domestic critics. As he saw it, the Americans had Hawaii; the British had Fiji, Australia, and New Zealand; and the Germans could take tiny Samoa. Powerful German businessmen began moving against King Malietoa, arming and financing a rebellion in support of a rival chieftain who would be friendlier to German control.

In 1885 the emerging Samoan "crisis" fell into the lap of President Cleveland and Secretary of State Bayard. Of course, it need not have been a crisis for American foreign policy, unless they chose to make it one. The United States could allow Germany to have its way in Samoa, as the British were fully prepared to do. Both Cleveland and Bayard were generally inclined to caution in foreign policy and sought to pull the United States back from what they regarded as the overly ambitious policies of the Garfield-Arthur administration. For Secretary of State Bayard, however, there were some principles at stake. One was the existing agreement among the three powers to keep Samoa independent and open to the navigation and commerce of all. Germany was clearly trying to change the rules. By the mid-1880s the American honeymoon with Germany was over. To Bayard it was "unquestionable" that Germany had "of late years given evidence of a disposition to cherish schemes of distant annexation & civilization in many quarters of the globe," including, he suspected, in the Western Hemisphere.[125] Even minor economic and strategic interests deserved some defense, therefore, even if they were thousands of miles away in the South Pacific. Neither Bayard nor Cleveland was prepared to roll over in the face of what they regarded as German bullying.

Another principle Bayard wanted to uphold was the independence and autonomy of the Samoan people free from "foreign interference." This was, of course, another way of preventing Germany from dominating Samoa. But Bayard also believed that the islanders had the right to rule themselves and that the United States and the other Western powers should help them acquire the ability to do so. "My only intention," Bayard insisted, was "to bring peace and order and civilization to the island by means of a native autonomy, and to use the native material for its own advancement by instructing the people in the arts of peace and good morals so that they could assist themselves." An American commissioner sent to study the situation in 1886 reported that without outside assistance the natives would be unable to "construct or maintain a government which will enforce authority or command respect." His British counterpart used stronger language, calling the Samoan people "excitable," "credulous," "thieves by instinct," "lazy," "consumed" with "mutual jealousy," "incapable of unity of action" or of sustaining "any form of government worthy of the name." However, both believed that with guidance from the civilized powers the natives could be "taught to rule themselves and coalesce in all matters concerning their common weal." Bayard agreed and hoped the concerted efforts of the three Western powers might "assist them in forming a civilized government." He favored elections for the king, who would serve a limited term, and for a House of Representatives. The British commissioner had given him a volume containing the laws and regulations by which the Fiji Islands were administered, and Bayard was impressed by the "unmistakable line of morality, good faith and benevolence running through this simple system of government which should commend it to all just-minded men." If the same could be achieved in Samoa, he exclaimed, "I would be delighted." Expressing his gratitude to the British commissioner, Bayard declared, "The forces of good and the forces of evil are at work in this world, but I recognize in you a valuable ally of the former."[126]

The "forces of evil" in Berlin were not especially worried about the rights of the natives. Bismarck objected to giving "the savages" much influence over the shape of the Samoan constitution, and German negotiators wanted the elected king to be approved by the outside powers. Bayard refused. He wanted "a native election, free, and unawed" by foreign influence. The idea was "not to obliterate the rights of the islanders, but to assist them in forming a civilized government." Worried that the Germans wanted to impose an "autocratic government, based on mercantile interests," he proposed naming an American arbiter to settle disagreements. Because U.S. interests were minimal, he reasoned, an American would have a greater ability to be "disinterested and impartial."[127]

Both the German and the British governments considered Bayard's solicitude for the islanders vaguely absurd. Lord Salisbury advised indulging him, believing that events would soon "convince even America of the impossibility of maintaining native governments in the Pacific Ocean." Bismarck's elder son, Count Herbert Bismarck, was not so sure. He spoke of "dreamers in America who imagined an eventual republican brotherhood" and warned Salisbury that among their dreams was "a linking up of the various Australian Colonies with the United States." Salisbury remarked, "[W]e must keep a sharp eye on American fingers."[128]

By 1887 the Germans had grown impatient with the wrangling and dispatched four warships to Samoa, demanding indemnities and apologies from Malietoa for various alleged offenses. The Germans insisted the king perform an *ifu*, which required him "to crawl upon his stomach towards the German consul as a token of abject apology." When Malietoa hesitated, the Germans landed seven hundred marines, ravaged several villages, took control of Apia, seized Malietoa, and recognized another chieftain as king. The Samoan government, trusting "in the love of the United States of America toward this weak people," appealed for help, citing the 1878 treaty. The Germans, for their part, demanded that American officials provide no support for Malietoa "moral or other—that would induce him to prolong the conflict"; instead, they should "inform him of the futility of objecting to German rule."[129]

American officials were outraged. Bayard answered that "the first allegiance of this Government was to right and justice, and . . . we owed it to ourselves to consider what were the rights of the natives in Samoa." When he learned that the Germans had "burned down native villages, destroyed fruit trees on which these poor people were dependent for their food, it filled me with pain." The American consul was even more upset, cabling Bayard, "My sympathy for this people is great, and is not lessened by a strong feeling of personal chagrin at the course of events here." He appealed for forceful action "in behalf of these people," insisting the "present troubles would never have come upon Malietoa had it not been for his friendship with the United States." Back in Washington Secretary of the Navy William C. Whitney was "outraged" at what he considered a "national disgrace," which he blamed on Bayard.[130] Republicans pounced on Bayard for weakness in the face of the German challenge, and the press of both parties condemned Germany's mistreatment of the islanders. In January 1889 the *New York World*'s headline read, GERMAN TYRANNY IN SAMOA.[131]

Bayard, however, was determined to avoid war with Germany. He would do what he could "to secure a measure of justice and fair treatment to these innocent and unhappy islanders," but unfortunately there was little he could do "without placing in useless jeopardy the vaster interests of our own countrymen." War with Germany would be a terrible thing, he warned, and indeed a senior naval officer reported, "If we go to war with Germany there is an extreme probability that the German fleet may threaten to shell New York. . . . We have practically nothing with which to drive the enemy away, and it would take a long time to build anything suitable for that purpose." Bayard declared, "If peace can be had with honor and without war, what malediction should pursue the man that leads a people into strife?" He hoped events in Samoa might take a turn for the better, reporting to Cleveland in the fall of 1888 that "the poor natives" seemed to have risen up against "the ruler set up by Germany in place of poor Malietoa!" But he concluded wryly, "I suppose a German gunboat will give them another Ruler."[132]

Unfortunately for Bayard, 1888 was an election year, a segment of the American public was aroused, and the attacks on him escalated. The "ruthless nature of German rule," he complained, seemed to have many "would-be imitators in this Country." President Cleveland, under pressure at home and angry at German behavior, dispatched three warships to Samoa to "protect American interests" in the ongoing fighting. In his message to Congress in January 1889 he portrayed his policy as one of tough resistance to German pressures: "I have insisted that the autonomy and independence of Samoa should be scrupulously preserved according to the treaties made with Samoa by the powers named and their agreements and understanding with each other. I have protested against every act apparently tending in an opposite direction, and during the existence of internal disturbance one or more vessels of war have been kept in Samoan waters to protect American citizens and property."[133]

In early 1889 the port of Apia was crowded with foreign warships—three American, three German, and one British—and many foresaw a conflict erupting through miscalculation or misunderstanding. Then on March 15 a typhoon struck, destroying or running aground all but the British ship, with the loss of fifty American and ninety German sailors. The magnitude of the tragedy temporarily overshadowed the international confrontation, and later that year James Blaine, back as secretary of state in the Harrison administration, reached a settlement with Bismarck that temporarily preserved tripartite cooperation on Samoa. The Republican press, revealing the changed attitude toward Germany, depicted it as a victory for the "Plumed Knight" over the "Iron Chancellor."

As one historian has commented, there was "something remarkable about the determination of the United States to go to the very brink of hostilities with Germany rather than yield negligible commercial and questionable strategic advantages in faraway Samoa."[134] It was true that even the most ardent American expansionists did not consider the islands a critical American outpost,[135] and Bayard could honestly declare that the United States had "no policy of annexation or protectorate whatsoever in Samoa or anywhere else." But he and other Americans saw Germany as a bully and felt both sympathy and responsibility for the Samoans. America's "object," he insisted, "was to be perfectly humane and kind to the natives of those islands, and assist their autonomous government." He saw himself as a "political Missionary to the unclad Samoans" and wanted to be remembered for the "really hard work" he had done to "befriend this scanty band of Islanders against the plundering traders of America, Germany, and Great Britain." "Civilization has had a rough side to them," he remarked, "and I am not sure whether they will survive its blessings."[136]

From Ambition to Power: The New Navy

THE EXPERIENCE IN SAMOA led some Americans to question the wisdom of such involvements abroad. When Grover Cleveland returned to the White House four years later, he wanted to pull out of Samoa altogether. He believed the whole mess showed how even innocent promises to provide "good offices" could produce dangers. Many other Americans, however, including some Democrats, drew a different lesson from Samoa and from similar troubles abroad. To them, the skirmishes and confrontations in the Western Hemisphere, in East Asia, and in the southern Pacific suggested the problem was not excessive involvement abroad but insufficient power.

When the United States confronted Germany over Samoa, or Chile over Peru, or when it was necessary to send warships to Korea and China to protect missionaries, it did so with a navy that was barely adequate to the task. Even a reluctant Cleveland had found himself dispatching warships at moments of crisis and wishing he had more to send. As a result, those who put their fate in American hands, whether Peruvian presidents, Korean kings, or Samoan chieftains, did not fare well, and ardent suitors like Li

Hung-chang and King Kojong came to view America as unreliable.[137] More upsetting to many Americans was the fact that second-rate powers like Chile could insult and defy the United States with impunity. The tangible interests at stake in places like Samoa and Peru might be comparatively minor, but there was also a question of honor and respectability, which a majority of Americans in both parties regarded as valuable commodities for any great nation. The desire to play a more dominant political and economic role in the hemisphere, to have greater influence in more distant lands, and to be regarded and treated by other powers with respect helped spur one of the most portentous developments of the late nineteenth century: the building of a new, more capable, and more powerful American navy.

Beginning in the 1880s leaders in both Republican and Democratic administrations began hesitantly, inefficiently, but steadily trying to increase U.S. naval power. Before 1880 the navy had been a victim of the long sectional conflict. During and just after the War of 1812 there had been broad national support for maintaining a strong and effective naval presence. Monroe wanted a "strong naval force" capable of keeping "the Barbary Powers in awe" as well as policing "along the southern Atlantic Coast, [and] in the Pacific and Indian Oceans."[138] John Quincy Adams declared it "the destiny and the duty of the confederated States to become in regular process of time and by no petty advances a great naval power." But in the late 1820s the naval buildup became the target of the rising Jacksonian movement and of slaveholders worried about the federal government's expanding powers. An 1827 bill for the "gradual improvement of the Navy" was defeated by the Jacksonian opposition,[139] and in his first inaugural address President Jackson, insisting that "the bulwark of our defense" was the national militia, called for an end to the building of large naval ships.[140] After the financial panic of 1837, Martin Van Buren insisted that the United States "required no navy at all."[141] During the remainder of the antebellum era, the United States fell behind European, Asian, and even some Latin American powers both in number and size of ships and in naval architecture.

The Civil War produced a vast naval buildup, and in the last year of the war the Union navy comprised some seven hundred vessels, displacing half a million tons and carrying almost five thousand guns. When war ended, however, this large navy was rapidly dismantled. Washington politicians were preoccupied by Reconstruction and anxious about the federal budget deficit. Within five years the navy shrank to fewer than two hundred vessels mounting thirteen hundred guns, and most of the ships were unfit for service. Only a couple of dozen fighting ships were in commission, and most of their guns had become obsolete in an era of advancing technology. Secretary of the Navy Gideon Welles attempted to bring order and reform, but the Navy Department became so embroiled in the Radical Republicans' attacks on President Andrew Johnson that "administration of an intelligent and consistent naval policy became virtually impossible."[142]

Most Americans and even many naval officials were only dimly aware of the dismal state of the fleet. In the 1870s and early 1880s, however, a series of events sent shocks through the naval community. The first was the 1873 confrontation with Spain over the *Virginius*. When the American fleet assembled off the coast of Florida it was in a "laughable . . . condition"— "two modern vessels of war would have done us up in 30 minutes," Rear Admiral Robley "Fighting Bob" Evans later recalled. "We were dreadfully mortified over it all."[143] America's leading naval officer, Admiral David Dixon Porter, lamented that there was "not a navy in the world that is not in advance of us as regards ships and guns."[144] While Britain and France were building steel navies and ever larger battleships, some of which they sold to smaller powers like Japan and Chile, the American fleet was almost entirely wooden. As Alfred Thayer Mahan exclaimed, "We have not six ships that would be kept at sea in war by any maritime power."[145]

The sobering awareness that the United States could have lost a naval confrontation with Spain spurred early demands for naval reform and rebuilding within the top ranks of the service, and the start of a quiet campaign of lobbying sympathetic members of Congress. Commodore Foxhall A. Parker, after watching the fleet maneuver slowly and clumsily off Key West for a month, began pushing for a new American navy based on "artillery-vessels," or battleships. He delivered his proposal to the members of the U.S. Naval Institute at the Naval Academy at the end of 1874, an organization founded hurriedly in the wake of the *Virginius* crisis to advance "professional and scientific knowledge in the Navy." His audience included most of the officers who would help design the "new navy" and then lead it into battle against Spain in 1898.[146]

Little was done to address the problem in the 1870s. President Hayes was preoccupied with ending Reconstruction and holding his fracturing party together, and he faced a Democrat-controlled Congress throughout most of his term. The transformation of the navy into a "European-style force ready for combat with the navies of other major powers" began in 1881.[147] That year the first post-Reconstruction Republican president, James A. Garfield, came into office along with Republican majorities in both houses of Congress. A naval planning board appointed by Garfield's secretary of the navy immediately, and impoliticly, called for the construction of sixty-eight new ships, many to be made of steel and driven by steam. This proposal far exceeded what Congress was willing to spend, and the administration adopted a much more modest plan for four ships. Two years later a Republican Congress—flush with new surpluses from the high Republican tariff and a relatively healthy economy—authorized construction of the first ships of the new navy, the small steel "protected cruisers" *Atlanta,* *Boston,* and *Chicago,* and a dispatch vessel, the *Dolphin*—the so-called ABC ships.[148] These steel cruisers represented no great revolution in American naval capability or in naval doctrine. Nonetheless, Congress had voted to build new warships for the first time since the Civil War.[149]

The American public's evident enthusiasm "fueled bipartisan political support for a 'new navy.'"[150] So did the vast sums of money spent by the federal government. The naval buildup of the 1880s was heavily influenced by financial interests and partisan politics. Federal dollars went to shipyards that were controlled by supporters of one party or the other and that tended to employ only reliable party men. When control of the Congress changed hands, therefore, as it did frequently, one party often pared back or rejected what the other party had proposed. When the executive branch changed hands, as it did in four consecutive elections—1884, 1888, 1892, and 1896—the new administration's secretary of the navy usually began with a thorough housecleaning. Despite the partisan warfare, however, the buildup continued and accelerated throughout the 1880s and into the early and mid-1890s. Between 1885 and 1889 the otherwise parsimonious administration of Grover Cleveland added two more "protected cruisers," the *Baltimore* and the *Olympia,* and two "armored cruisers" later reclassified as the battleships *Maine* and *Texas.*[151] In 1890 President Benjamin Harrison, with Republicans once again in control of both houses of Congress, won appropriations for three modern, first-class battleships—the *Indiana, Massachusetts,* and *Oregon*—costing an unprecedented $3 million each and considered roughly equal to the top-line battleships in the British fleet.[152] A fourth battleship of this class was authorized in 1892, and three more were authorized in 1895, during Cleveland's second administration.

There was more to the buildup than new ships and money. In the early 1880s American naval doctrine and naval architecture still lagged behind those of the world's great naval powers, but by the mid-1880s changes in naval doctrine were beginning to take shape. Rear Admiral Stephen B. Luce, "the intellectual link between Foxhall Parker's early musings about American battle fleets and Alfred Thayer Mahan," was the pivotal figure in the transition from a naval doctrine centered on small ships for coastal defense and commerce raiding to one centered on large groups of battle-ships for controlling the seas.[153] In 1885 the navy recommended construc-tion of one large "sea-going armored vessel" and wound up getting two from Congress that year, two more the next, and one larger "armored cruiser" in 1888. It was in the first year of the Harrison administration that the United States turned decisively toward a battleship fleet. The deadly forces of nature played a part when the typhoon at Apia pulverized the wooden-hulled American pacific squadron that Cleveland had sent to keep an eye on the Germans at Samoa. That year Secretary of the Navy Ben-jamin Tracy delivered a report to Congress calling for two fleets of battle-ships, one for the Atlantic and one for the Pacific.

Tracy's 1889 report put the battleship at the heart of the U.S. Navy and shifted naval doctrine from passive coastal defense to an aggressive, offen-sive strategy. "A war, though defensive in principle," he argued, "may be conducted most effectively by being offensive in its operations."[154] The shift was controversial. Many Democrats argued that an offensive strategy ran contrary to American traditions and would likely lead the United States to war. Members of Congress representing coastal districts worried that their constituents would be left vulnerable to attack. Republicans therefore emphasized the new navy's defensive purposes, authorized only three new battleships, legislated that the new ships' cruising radius must not exceed five thousand miles, and described them as "seagoing coastline battle-ships."[155] But this oxymoron could not hide the reality that the United States was building itself a navy with offensive capabilities and an offensive doc-trine. As the critics pointed out, such a navy could be used for aggressive purposes, regardless of the original defensive intentions. It was capability that mattered.

Thus did the United States begin a naval rearmament program during the 1880s, a time of peace when the nation faced no menacing threat from abroad and enjoyed more security than ever before in its history and also more security than any other great power of the time. It was a decade that began with President Rutherford B. Hayes declaring, "Our relations with all foreign countries have been those of an undisturbed peace."[156] Under these circumstances the complex and varied motives behind the naval buildup revealed a good deal about Americans' evolving and somewhat contradic-tory attitudes toward their place in the world, their hopes and their fears, as well as how they wanted and expected others around the world to view the United States.

Supporters of a stronger navy did insist that the threats from abroad were increasing. Congressman Henry Cabot Lodge warned in 1891 that the British were aggressively encircling the United States with "a cordon of forts and bases of supply" intended for use in a future war.[157] Officials warned of blockades and bombardments of coastal cities by Great Britain, Germany, and even Chile. They also worried that the European powers were carving up vast portions of the world, jockeying for territories in Africa and Asia and jostling for position in the Middle East, and they could begin carving up pieces of South and Central America as well. A mere four years after President Hayes's soothing assessment, President Arthur was admonishing Americans, "The long peace that has lulled us into a sense of fancied security may at any time be disturbed."[158] Some historians have depicted the era as one of "vanishing security" and the new navy as "a defensive answer" to Europe's worldwide "imperial scramble."[159]

But America's security was not really vanishing. The threat of European imperial aggression in the Western Hemisphere was remote, as critics of the naval buildup pointed out. European powers in this era were never shy about proclaiming their desire for new colonies. The British were expanding in southern Africa openly and unapologetically, and often by force, as in their brutal war against the Zulus in 1879. The French were taking their share of Africa by means of public treaties with African rulers. The Germans made no secret of their yearning for a "place in the sun" in the South Pacific. The Belgian king Leopold II did not conceal his desire for the Congo—*"Il faut à la Belgique une colonie."*[160] But in the Western Hemisphere they expressed no such ambitions. Europeans, including the Germans, avoided crossing swords with the United States and invariably backed down at the first sign of American displeasure.

It is not that the concerns expressed by some Americans were disingenuous or even irrational. The world in the 1880s did seem an increasingly violent and dangerous place. The average reader of American newspapers knew of British military actions in the Transvaal and Egypt, of Russia's war against Turkey, of French and Belgian plans to colonize the Congo, and of German ambitions in the South Pacific. It was prudent for Americans to be on their guard against the possibility that these well-armed powers could someday turn their attention back to the Western Hemisphere. When the British landed a small force at Corinto, Nicaragua, to settle a minor dispute in 1895, who could be sure whether this was a brief aberration from the general retreat of British power from the hemisphere or the beginning of a new phase of aggression? When the Germans sniffed around the Caribbean, who could say with confidence that they might not try to grab an island or two for themselves, just as they were attempting to do in Samoa? American hypersensitivity was itself a deterrent to imperial probing, for it reinforced the European perception that it was not worth the trouble to meddle.

Yet it would be a mistake to imagine that the naval buildup was chiefly a response to threats or even perceived threats from Europe. In the late 1870s and throughout the 1880s, when naval officers and their supporters argued for more warships, the potential adversaries they most frequently cited were not naval heavyweights like Great Britain and France but the fading middleweight Spain and the bantamweight Chile. Later generations of Americans, accustomed to worrying only about other global powers and superpowers, may find it hard to believe that the naval buildup of the 1880s was more a response to fears of Chile than of Great Britain. But in 1884 Maine's respected Senator Eugene P. Hale warned there was "nothing whatever to prevent Chile" from "burning and destroying" the cities of the American Pacific Coast,[161] and in 1891 Secretary of the Navy Benjamin Tracy made the case for a continuing naval buildup by noting, among other dangers, that the Chilean warship *Esmeralda* had appeared "without warning, close to the California coast."[162] It was a source of concern, as well as embarrassment, when Americans "suddenly realized" that not just Chile but "several South American republics had been acquiring warships, any one of which single-handed could probably destroy the entire United States Navy."[163] Naval officials also professed to be worried about China, whose navy was at the time the equal of America's, and about Japan, whose navy was tiny but beginning to grow under the Meiji reformers.[164] They considered even the Haitian navy "a potential rival."[165] And then there was Spain, which from the time of the *Virginius* to the outbreak of war in 1898 was cited as a potential military adversary by American naval planners.

Concerns about war with the likes of Spain, Chile, and Haiti did not reflect a primarily "defensive" search for security against foreign aggression. Naval planners did not fear that Spain would launch an unprovoked attack on the United States. The "cloud of war . . . hanging darkly on the horizon" was Cuba.[166] But there could be no war over Cuba unless Washington started it, for a conflict with the United States over a vulnerable colony two thousand miles from Spanish harbors was the last thing Spain wanted. As Hamilton Fish had understood, if the United States wished to avoid war, it need only refrain from meddling in Cuban affairs. Those who imagined the possibility of war with Spain were calculating that the United States might not refrain—which displayed a pretty good understanding of their own country. The same was true in the case of Chile. No one believed that the Chileans sought a conflict with the northern behemoth. Conflict would come because the United States intervened in Chile's affairs or tried to block Chile's regional aspirations—as Blaine had attempted to do in 1881—in the service of the hemispheric "order."

Haiti was on the list of potential threats because the Harrison administration sought a naval base and found itself at odds with an uncooperative Haitian ruler—when he resisted, Tracy dispatched a fleet of gunboats that conducted target practice within earshot of Haiti's inhabitants. Japan and China were on the list because the United States had embroiled itself in Korea and because American missionaries in Asia might require protection—especially when American actions inflamed local opinion against them. War with Japan could erupt over Hawaii, but that too would be a product not of unprovoked Japanese aggression but of American desires to control and eventually annex the Hawaiian kingdom. When in 1889 American naval officials warned of the possibility of the German fleet sailing into New York harbor, it was because the United States was at that moment confronting Germany over Samoa some four thousand miles away.[167]

If many influential Americans believed the United States needed a bigger navy, in short, it was largely because of American ambitions, both material and intangible. The wide range of foreign entanglements, stemming from a vast array of motives and impulses, seemed to many to require an increase in the overall amount of power the United States could bring to bear on any number of situations. Americans needed a bigger navy because they aimed for a certain U.S.-dominated "order" in the Western Hemisphere, because they had growing commercial interests and ambitions in Latin America and in Asia and worried they would be nudged out by stronger imperial powers, because they felt sympathy for the fate of the natives in Samoa and had promised to help them, because they had vaguely committed the nation to Korean "independence," because they supported Cubans struggling against Spanish tyranny, and because they wanted to be able to protect American citizens abroad in all situations where they came into conflict with foreign powers over one issue or another. As President Garfield's secretary of the navy, William Chandler, explained in 1881, a strong navy "quickens the nation's powers and infuses life and vigor into its international relations."[168] A dozen years later Grover Cleveland's secretary of the navy insisted that the navy had to be strong enough "to give weight to whatever policy it may be thought wise on the part of the government to assume."[169]

Although it was gradually turning toward an oceangoing battleship fleet, the main focus of American attention remained the Western Hemisphere. In 1884 Senator Hale warned that although the United States had "gone on for years safely with a dwindling navy, . . . [t]he man is blind who does not realize that at any time the United States may be called upon to maintain propositions with regard to the American continent, with reference to its influence, with reference to its control, with reference to its transit, upon which the American people are substantially of one mind."[170] The new navy, according to a report by the House Naval Affairs Committee, would be used to pursue "affirmative policies" in the hemisphere.[171] If the United States was to attain what Secretary of the Navy Chandler called its "natural, justifiable and necessary ascendancy in the affairs of the American hemisphere," it could hardly do so while its navy was inferior to Chile's.[172] During the Harrison administration, Blaine and the president concluded that the United States could not "win a commanding influence in the Western Hemisphere merely by setting an example of moral and peaceful conduct or even by more vigorous commercial enterprise." It also needed military power.[173]

Some Americans admitted that the United States did not need a larger navy to defend itself from attack. A report by the navy's policy board in 1890 stated frankly that Americans did not have to fear "encroachments upon our territory." Strategically and even economically, the United States was "self-contained to a greater degree than any other important nation."[174] Not even the British posed much of a threat, despite their vast naval power. With an increasingly powerful Germany on the Continent, Britain would be very reluctant to "detach all her effective navy from her own coast for distant operations." The prospects of a war with Great Britain or with any other European power were "at a minimum."[175]

If American security was threatened, the members of the policy board argued, it was not because other powers were advancing against American interests but because the United States was "certain to reach out and obstruct the interests of foreign nations."[176] They had in mind commercial interests, but their analysis applied to other tangible and intangible interests, too. If some leading Americans sensed their security was vanishing, it was not so much because the world was closing in around them but because they were pushing out into the world in pursuit of a whole spectrum of commercial, strategic, ideological, and moral interests. The policy board's undiplomatic point was that war could come as a result of American, not foreign, actions. Indeed, the point was too blunt for American ears, and it brought angry condemnations from both ends of the political spectrum.[177] The idea that the United States might itself be the instigator of conflict by virtue of its expansive polices ran too violently against the popular perception of American innocence and passivity. Foreign observers, however, would have had little difficulty recognizing the soundness of the policy board's argument.

Americans in the 1880s and '90s were exhibiting a common attribute of rising powers. Growing power produced an expanding sense of interest and entitlement. But as perceived interests expanded, so did perceived threats and the perceived need for even more power to address them.[178] Some of these interests included such intangible and often elusive matters as honor, prestige, and respect in the international arena. These are not so easily measured as commercial and other material interests, but in human affairs they are often more potent motives for action. They played a significant part in the naval buildup of the 1880s and early 1890s. Americans wanted to be accorded the respect due to a great nation. Especially in their own hemisphere, they wanted to be recognized as the dominant "arbiter" both by their neighbors and by the European powers. Some have called this a nationalist "egoism," but if so it had a long and distinguished American pedigree. George Washington had once declared that "there is a rank due to the United States among nations, which will be withheld, if not absolutely lost, by a reputation of weakness."[179] Many late-nineteenth-century Americans from both parties and of varying ideological dispositions agreed. Navy Secretary Chandler complained in 1881 that the United States had been "unable to make such an appropriate display of our naval power abroad as will cause us to be respected."[180] Navy Secretary Tracy sought to shame members of Congress when he pointed out that the United States stood only twelfth among the world's naval powers, below Austria-Hungary, Turkey, and China, and that despite the naval improvements of the previous eight years the country remained "at the mercy of states having less than one-tenth of its population, one-thirtieth of its wealth, and one-hundredth of its area."[181]

The need to gain the world's respect was not just a matter of pride or vanity but had practical aspects as well. "What do the nations of the earth care about your moral power after you leave your own shores?" a Florida senator asked in 1884. "All that they respect when the emergency arises is a decent display of public force."[182] According to this view, American missionaries in China would not be protected by America's reputation for disinterested benevolence. If other nations believed the United States lacked the power to make good on its commitments, they were more likely to raise a challenge, even in the Western Hemisphere. Lodge combined the practical and the intangible when he argued, "Weakness, fear, and defenceless-ness mean war and dishonor. Readiness, preparation, and courage mean honor and peace." Alexander Hamilton had once argued that to be a great world power, the United States needed the accoutrements of a great world power, and among these was a first-class navy. A century later Lodge would argue that national dignity and national greatness, as well as the preservation of an honorable peace, required a return to "our old and successful naval policy of always maintaining a small but highly efficient fleet, which led the world in naval architecture, in ordnance, and in equipment."[183]

Nations always seek respect, especially self-respect, but for rising powers it can seem a more urgent issue. Americans, though mostly confident, were sensitive to perceived signs of disrespect partly because they touched on doubts they had about themselves. A brief confrontation with Chile in 1892 showed how a blend of confidence and insecurity could produce surprising manifestations of belligerence.

Relations between the two nations had never quite recovered from Blaine's intervention on Peru's behalf at the conclusion of the War of the Pacific. But by the late 1880s the comparatively friendly government of José Balmaceda was in control in Santiago, and in 1891 a civil war erupted between Balmaceda and his opponents in the Chilean congress. The rebels received unofficial but open backing from the British navy and British civilians, victims of Balmaceda's efforts to tax and assume ownership of nitrate production controlled by British investors. In Washington, not surprisingly, the rebellion immediately took on the appearance of a British power play against the putatively pro-American Balmaceda.[184] Adding fuel to the fire was the fact that the U.S. minister to Santiago, Patrick Egan, was an Irish immigrant and widely viewed as hostile to Britain and its Chilean allies and an active supporter of the Chilean president. In the course of the conflict both Egan and the U.S. Navy were accused by the rebels of helping Balmaceda, first by seizing a ship loaded with rebel arms purchased in the United States, then by sheltering Balmaceda's supporters at the American legation in Santiago. When the rebels drove Balmaceda from office and took control of the Chilean capital, their followers among the Chilean public were seething with anger at the United States. President Harrison had dispatched the USS *Baltimore* to Valparaiso harbor to protect American citizens if necessary. When the ship's captain released the crew on an ill-advised shore leave, a barroom brawl in the True Blue Saloon turned into a riot in which two Americans sailors were killed and more than a dozen others were seriously wounded.

From the moment he received word of the attack, Harrison "viewed the affair as an insult to the U.S. uniform and an unprovoked outrage," which he blamed on Chilean authorities. He sent a stern note to the Chilean government demanding an explanation and an apology, but the Chileans, equally sensitive to signs of disrespect, considered the note insulting and rejected it. Harrison commented to Blaine, "[T]he trouble with these people . . . seems to be that they do not know how to use victory with dignity and moderation; and sometime it may be necessary to instruct them." Harrison's response showed the degree to which he considered the United States to have been defeated by the rebel victory in Chile. And his comment about "these people" reflected the common North American prejudice that Latin Americans were hot-blooded and violent. In his annual message to Congress in December 1891, he lamented that the fall of Balmaceda had "brought about a condition which is unfortunately too familiar in the history of the Central and South American states."[185]

That comment could not have been better designed to offend the Chileans, who considered themselves the vanguard of white civilization in Latin America and entirely unlike the backward "Indians" of Central America. The Chilean foreign minister assailed Harrison's statements as "erroneous or deliberately incorrect" and promised to uphold "the right, the dignity, and the final success of Chile, notwithstanding the intrigues which proceed from so low and the threats which come from so high." James Blaine, despite the moniker "Jingo Jim" bestowed on him by his critics, was once again eager to avert war and preserve the modest achievements of his Pan-American conference of two years earlier. He tried to calm both his president and the Chileans. To the latter he insisted, "I do not want difficulties or questions, only peace and good friendship." He even recalled Patrick Egan, a loyal Blaine supporter for more than a decade, in the interest of pacifying Santiago. But this only further infuriated Harrison. When the Chilean government released the results of its investigation of the incident, which laid equal blame on both sides, the president's anger boiled over.[186]

In December 1891 Harrison informed Congress he would call on it "for such action as may be necessary" should the Chileans fail to respond appropriately to his demands. Meanwhile he told Navy Secretary Tracy to prepare for war, which Tracy proceeded to do with energy and enthusiasm, putting dockyards on a seven-day week, purchasing large quantities of coal, ordering the preparation of all available warships for action, and negotiating for base rights at Montevideo, Uruguay. Foreign observers had no doubt that Harrison would go to war; some suspected it was a tactic to get himself reelected. The British Foreign Office, far from savoring the prospect of a conflict, urgently warned the Chileans to be conciliatory and to apologize immediately. "Fighting Bob" Evans, now at Valparaiso in command of the *Baltimore,* wired Washington that while the Chilean mob was for war, "sensible men" realized it would be suicidal.[187] Within days the Chilean government offered up a formal apology, which Harrison accepted with a discernible air of disappointment.

The whole episode surprised many foreign observers, including no doubt the Chileans. A bemused Bismarck, fresh from his own encounter with American belligerence over Samoa, wondered why "a nation as powerful as the American Union did not show more moderation and respect for a nation as small as Chile."[188] The whole incident revealed a bevy of American sensitivities, prejudices, ambitions, and insecurities.[189] There was the perception of British intrigue. There was the disdain for hot-blooded Latins who needed to be put in their place and "instructed" by a more civilized Anglo-Saxon power. Perhaps above all there was deep resentment at the mistreatment and lack of respect shown to sailors wearing the uniform of the U.S. Navy, a worrying indication that the Chileans, with their own powerful navy, were not sufficiently cowed by American superiority. Nor were these responses limited to one hotheaded president and his hawkish navy secretary. If observers considered the whole affair a political ploy to gain Harrison's reelection, it was because his bellicose stance was so obviously popular. There were occasions when even the more restrained Grover Cleveland would respond angrily to perceived insults from other powers, and even contemplate going to war to restore American honor.

For some Americans there was in all this a question of national character. What kind of nation was the United States, they asked, if its citizens could give so little regard to preserving a respectable level of military power and the will to use it? "Gilded Age" America, they worried, seemed to have become obsessed with the selfish pursuit of wealth and personal gain and possessed too little of what Mahan called the "masculine combative virtues."[190] Oliver Wendell Holmes, Jr., the famed jurist and Civil War veteran, worried that Americans in their "snug, over-safe corner of the world" sought only material comfort and worshiped only "the man of wealth." Modern philosophers declared that "war is wicked, foolish, and soon to disappear." Americans had lost their "faith in the worth of heroism."[191] The prevailing theory of civilization, which posited a final stage of decadence, made some Americans worry that their commercial republic, precisely because of its commercial nature, lacked the "martial virtues" necessary for survival. Henry Adams, in his account of the War of 1812, observed, "If war made men brutal, at least it made them strong. . . . War, with all its horrors, could purify as well as debase; it dealt with high motives and vast interests; taught courage, discipline, and stern sense of duty."[192] For Lodge and many others, the experience of the Civil War had only strengthened the case. This was a generation of Americans "who had seen the value of militarism at first hand and who had been forced, with Lincoln, to acknowledge that it was upon the progress of our arms that all else depended."[193] Holmes, who had fought and been wounded three times in the Civil War, observed, "War, when you are at it, is horrible and dull. It is only when time has passed that you see that its message was divine." He spoke of a faith, "true and adorable," that "leads a soldier to throw away his life in obedience to a blindly accepted duty."[194] Later historians have treated this celebration of war and of "masculine, combative virtues" as a novel development of the late nineteenth century. But martial "virtues" had been extolled and celebrated in similar language and with equal conviction by Henry Clay, John Calhoun, James Madison, John Quincy Adams, and others at the time of America's second war with Great Britain.[195]

Whatever the blend of motives that lay behind the naval buildup, by the early 1890s many leading Americans believed they had ample evidence that naval power could be a most useful aid to diplomacy. When Chile retreated from confrontation in 1892, Harrison, Tracy, and a number of Republicans, including Lodge and Roosevelt, were convinced that the rapid mobilization of the navy was the reason.[196] The thesis seemed validated again a couple of years later, when Cleveland's secretary of the navy ordered the South Atlantic squadron to Brazil to break a rebel blockade of Rio de Janeiro. The assistant secretary of the navy, William Gibbs McAdoo, who would later go on to become Woodrow Wilson's secretary of the treasury, exulted that the United States had finally become "a factor in the affairs of our neighbors" because it had "put into Brazilian waters the most powerful fleet which ever represented our flag abroad." He predicted that "constant upheavals" in East Asia as well as in Latin America would again require the United States to bring naval power to bear.[197]

Other nations could be forgiven for judging the United States to be a most unpredictable and difficult power, especially in the Western Hemisphere but also in faraway places like Samoa. Because American concerns tended to be general rather than specific, because their goals were often intangible rather than material, it was not always clear to others what Americans would care about, what would offend them, and what would provoke a belligerent response. The United States, lacking any clear strategic design, was alternately passive and belligerent in ways that foreign observers sometimes found baffling.

Historians have found it baffling, too, and have characterized American foreign policy in this era as "halting and unassertive," lacking coherence and direction, "composed of incidents, not policies—a number of distinct events, not sequences that moved from a source to a conclusion."[198] It is true that American foreign policy in the 1880s, and well into the 1890s, proceeded by fits and starts. Treaties were signed, then were abandoned or not implemented, then were taken up again. The annexation of Hawaii was sought and then rejected. A deal with Nicaragua for an American-built canal was signed and then discarded. Americans sought to acquire rights to Pearl Harbor in Hawaii but did not take the necessary steps to dredge it and make it usable.[199] Americans demanded exclusive control of a transisthmian canal and even contemplated measures necessary to defend such a canal once built, but seemed in no hurry to build it. One of the few constants in these years was, in fact, the naval buildup.

The apparent incoherence of American foreign policy had much to do with domestic politics and the fact that the White House changed hands so often in this era. It may also have been due to the wild swings of boom and bust in the American economy. The economy was sunk in depression from 1873 to 1878, from 1882 to 1885, and from 1893 to 1897, during which the government generally ran deficits. In the intervening boom years it generally ran surpluses, which permitted a freer attitude toward spending on the tools of foreign policy.

But the seeming inconsistency of American foreign policy in these decades also reflected American ambitions and insecurities. Although the overall thrust of American foreign policy was expansive, it nevertheless had a reactive quality. This was, again, because of the general, intangible, almost abstract nature of many American ambitions. The desire to gain respect, for instance, did not always demand a positive policy. Whether the United States enjoyed sufficient international respect to satisfy Americans' growing pretensions depended mostly on the behavior of other nations. If other nations did not challenge or "insult" the United States by, for instance, beating up its sailors in a bar, there was nothing the United States need do to defend its honor. Similarly, if other nations did not challenge American primacy in the Western Hemisphere, Americans were not moved to ask whether their primacy was universally acknowledged. If other nations did nothing to upset the peaceful "order" Americans valued, then the United States did not need to take steps to impose or defend it.

Nor did most Americans quite understand the effect that their claim to regional primacy, their demand for a certain kind of order in the hemisphere, and even their offers of "good offices" and "friendly" assistance could have on other nations and peoples. The report of the navy's policy board in 1890 was so offensive to Americans in part because most were scarcely conscious that they were reaching out and obstructing the interests of foreign nations. They were unaware of their intrusion into Chilean politics, for instance, or of the way their actions threatened Chile's own ambitions, and therefore they were unaware of the hostility that American behavior engendered among a large faction of the Chilean political elite. But when American sailors were killed in barroom brawl by an angry Chilean mob, Americans demanded satisfaction. Most did not have strong opinions about Samoa, or quite understand how their offer of "good offices" and concern for the natives might entangle them in a conflict with other powers. But when the kaiser raised a challenge, many Americans wanted their government to respond vigorously and reassert a claim they had hitherto barely noticed.

American attitudes toward defending certain principles in the hemisphere, maintaining "propositions," had a similar reactive quality. Americans were not missionaries in the sense that they worked consistently and tirelessly to promote independence, self-determination, democracy, or even order throughout the hemisphere. On the contrary, American statesmen and the public could go for years without giving such matters much thought. However, when actions and events violating Americans' moral sensibilities and principles were thrust before their eyes, they sometimes demanded action. Those who clamored for war with Spain in 1873 took little notice of the Cuban problem after 1878, when the struggle for independence foundered. It was only when civil war broke out again and the conflict reached new heights of brutality, as it did in 1895, that Americans demanded their government do something. American "jingoism," to use the favored pejorative of late-nineteenth-century critics and future historians, almost always came in response to some perceived challenge to U.S. influence or to its principles or both, and therefore to its honor, in those parts of the world where Americans had determined that they were to be predominant or at least to have a say.

The expansive-reactive quality of American foreign policy, and the vagueness of American foreign policy goals, did determine the comparatively limited size and pace of the naval buildup. In 1896, a decade and a half into the creation of the new navy, the United States possessed a total of five battleships with another seven under construction. The British navy, in comparison, had forty-five battleships with twelve under construction. France had twenty-nine battleships, Germany twenty-one, Italy thirteen, and Russia ten with eight under construction. Even in 1901, when the American buildup was twenty years old and accelerating, there were only seven battleships in commission with eleven more under construction.[200] By contrast, when Germany launched its own naval buildup in 1898, the first navy bill authorized seventeen battleships, eight armored cruisers, and thirty-five other ships. There was a vast difference in the magnitude of these two buildups, therefore, and a significant difference in the arguments and rhetoric used to justify them. While American navalists labored to avoid the appearance of "jingoism" as they argued for their buildup, the Germans felt no similar constraint. Foreign Minister Bernhard von Bülow, urging adoption of the bill in the Reichstag, insisted that Germany needed "a place in the sun" and faced a clear-cut choice: "Either world power or demise"; or as Admiral Alfred von Tirpitz put it, "life or death."[201] The Americans were more confident than the Germans that the forces of history were on their side. Unlike the Germans, they did not have to challenge the world's greatest naval power in its home waters in order to achieve their objectives. They need only build a navy sufficient to stare down Chile in a crisis or give Spain pause in a possible conflict over Cuba.

For all their inconsistency and incoherence, the advocates of a naval buildup accomplished what they set out to accomplish. The historical consequences of the peacetime buildup that began after 1881, modest as it was, should not be underestimated. Opponents of a stronger navy were right to predict that increasing American naval power would increase the chances that this new power would someday soon be used. Even with only a moderately improved navy, Harrison was far more willing to go to war against Chile in 1892 than Garfield and Blaine had been in 1881. If Harrison was more bellicose, part of the reason may have been his personality, but another explanation was his greater confidence in American military prowess. Grover Cleveland, hardly an aggressive, bellicose president, nevertheless showed a greater willingness to employ gunboat diplomacy in his second term than in his first, and this had something to do with the greater power at his disposal. Finally, and most significantly, the United States might not have gone to war with Spain in 1898, and therefore would not have acquired a colony in the Philippines, had it not possessed a navy deemed capable of readily accomplishing those tasks.

Historians have often located the origins of the rise of America to world power status and the imperial surge at the turn of the century in the early 1890s. But the navy that President William McKinley sent into battle in 1898 was not conceived in the 1890s.[202] It was not a response to the great depression of 1893, to a "psychic crisis" that followed, or to the "closing of the frontier." It was authorized by Congress between 1881 and 1892, in response to ambitions and insecurities that had begun to emerge in the years following the Civil War.[203]

CHAPTER 12

Morality and Hegemony

Every nation, and especially every strong nation, must sometimes be conscious of an impulse to rush into difficulties that do not concern it, except in a highly imaginary way. To restrain the indulgence of such a propensity is not only the part of wisdom, but a duty we owe to the world as an example of the strength, the moderation, and the beneficence of popular government.

—Walter Q. Gresham, April 1894

It is no answer to say that this is all in another country, belonging to another nation, and is therefore none of our business. . . . It is specially our duty, for it is right at our door.

—William McKinley, April 1898

The Democracy's Dissent

THE NAVAL BUILDUP of the 1880s and early 1890s certainly had its opponents. Critics insisted that no external threat required such a prodigious rearmament. They warned that the building of oceangoing battleships would tempt Americans to abandon their "traditional" policy of "aloofness from world affairs" and seek conflict with other nations. As one congressman put it during the debate over battleship appropriations in 1890, if such a fleet were created, "then I would not be responsible for the peace of the United States for twelve months."[1] Carl Schurz argued in 1893, in opposing the annexation of Hawaii, that the United States was already secure: "[I]n our compact continental stronghold we are substantially unassailable . . . we can hardly get into a war unless it be of our own seeking."[2]

Schurz had a point. The United States was relatively secure, and if the American people could be satisfied with their continental dominance and their already substantial foreign commerce, then they did not need a much bigger navy, and certainly not the two-ocean battleship fleet that proponents of the naval buildup had begun advocating in the late 1880s. The buildup was the product of the same forces that seemed to be leading the United States into ever greater foreign entanglements, but to opponents, these foreign entanglements were unnecessary. They expanded American obligations and the threat of conflict with other great powers in regions far removed from American shores and American interests.

The main challenge to this ambitious, expansive foreign policy and the accompanying drive for power came from the Democratic Party.[3] Democratic opposition to Republican expansionism in the 1880s and early 1890s was not merely a matter of partisanship. Throughout most of the last two decades of the nineteenth century, leading Democratic politicians and policy makers, ably represented by two-term president Grover Cleveland, did not share Republican enthusiasm for expansion and national greatness on the world stage. Indeed, both times Cleveland took office, in 1885 and again in 1893, his explicit aim was to reverse what he, his advisers, and Democratic Party leaders in general believed was a new, dangerous, and even immoral course in foreign policy.

Just as Republican attitudes toward America's proper role in the world were closely related to their views of domestic policies and the role of the national government in the affairs of the people, so it was for the Democrats. If the Republican Party throughout the last half of the nineteenth century was the party of federal power and the active state, of "nationalism," the Democratic Party remained in the 1880s and early 1890s the party of states' rights, local control, and suspicion of federal power. The party's policies and principles reflected the fact that its political center of gravity remained in the southern states. No Democrat could win the party's presidential nomination without southern support, and in the general election no Democratic nominee "had a chance of victory without the support of the Solid South."[4] Democratic power in Congress, especially in the Senate, was also based on the southern electorate, just as it had been before the Civil War.

This southern orientation alone made for a contrast with the Republicans, for while the northern-based Republican Party associated itself with the Union's triumph in the Civil War, the abolition of southern slavery, and the military defeat of the "rebel" South, the outlook of the southern-dominated Democratic Party was shaped in part by bitter southern memories of defeat in the Civil War and of military occupation during Reconstruction. In the twentieth century it would often be said that Americans had never suffered the horrors of foreign invasion and conquest. But as C. Vann Woodward has pointed out, this was not true of the South. The region that once called itself the Confederate States of America had learned what it was like to be on the receiving end of the American way of war. It had lived through "an experience that it could share with no other part of America . . . the experience of military defeat." It had learned "the un-American lesson of submission," and it was the special kind of political and ideological submission that Americans were especially inclined to try to impose.[5] Since the end of that occupation, southern leaders had aimed to restore the South's economy, to win a measure of economic and political independence, to restore white supremacy and "home rule," and to gain freedom from federal, which was to say northern, dictates.[6] Not surprisingly, it was the common view in the South, as one southern leader put it, that "[n]o man has the right or duty to impose his own convictions upon others." And this view dominated the Democratic Party, just as the South did. In the 1880s Democratic leaders liked to quote Albert Gallatin's dictum: "We are never doing as well as when we are doing nothing."[7]

Southern Democrats particularly objected to northern efforts to use the federal government's power to force them to permit blacks to vote. Southern racism combined with party interests in this case, since it was northern Republican strategy to empower blacks, who would almost certainly vote Republican. Southern Democrats exerted every energy to defeat these efforts, and they succeeded. Between 1870 and 1880 the black population of Louisiana grew 33 percent while the number of Republican votes declined by 47 percent. The numbers in Mississippi were even more striking.[8] The central southern mission of the last three decades of the nineteeth century was to deprive blacks of all political and economic rights—as Senator Ben Tillman later put it, "We took the government away. We stuffed ballot boxes. We shot them. We are not ashamed of it"—and the national Democratic Party supported the South at each step.[9]

If Republicans celebrated Lincoln and the Civil War, therefore, and looked back fondly to the nationalist tradition of Clay and Hamilton, Democrats looked back to the era of Jackson and adhered to the Jeffersonian principle that the federal government "governs best that governs least." In the 1880s and '90s another old battle between these competing traditions emerged over that most intrusive form of government regulation of the national economy, the protective tariff. For the devastated South, which lagged far behind the North in industrialization and manufacture and depended instead on exports of crops chiefly to the European market, the high Republican tariff appeared both unfair and disastrously inhibiting to southern livelihoods still recovering from the war. To a small but growing number of northerners, too, including some Republicans, it was also a source of mammoth political corruption, as manufacturers' associations and industrial tycoons poured money into lobbying campaigns to maintain high tariffs on their products. For leading Democrats, reducing the tariff was the highest national priority, far more important than any question of foreign policy.

Cleveland was a stolid and consistent defender of these Democratic principles. In both terms, he entered the White House determined to pare back federal power to the minimum. That meant sharp reduction of the Republican tariff, the elimination of Republican budget surpluses—which he and other Democrats considered an outrageous federal seizure of tax-payers' money—the preservation of the gold standard, and the restoration of what old-line Democrats regarded as the "fiscal orthodoxy" that had prevailed before the Civil War. The "simple and plain duty which we owe the people," Cleveland declared, "is to reduce the taxation to the necessary expenses of an economical operation of the government, and to restore to the business of the country the money which we hold in the Treasury through the perversion of governmental powers."[10] While Blaine and other Republicans might look back approvingly on President John Quincy Adams's declaration that the purpose of government was "the progressive improvement of the condition of the governed,"[11] Cleveland, following a different tradition, insisted that, on the contrary, "the lesson should be constantly enforced that though the people support the Government, the Government should not support the people."[12]

On the question of black rights, and particularly black voting rights, Cleveland supported the position of southern whites. He had opposed even moderate Republican Reconstruction as an ugly amalgam of "federal bayonets, Republican carpetbaggers, and 'Black Rule,' " and he believed the question of black rights was "a matter best left to the South."[13] In his campaign for reelection in 1888 he opposed Lodge's bill authorizing the federal government to protect southern black voters against fraud and intimidation—what southerners disparagingly called the "Force Bill"—while the Republican candidate, Benjamin Harrison, made defense of black rights a prominent campaign theme.

Cleveland chose for his cabinet men who shared these views. His secretary of state in his first term, Thomas F. Bayard, had been a vigorous defender of southern and states' rights during Reconstruction, an equally vigorous opponent of what he called Republican efforts to manipulate the votes of "ignorant and semi-barbarous" blacks—he opposed the Fourteenth and Fifteenth amendments—and a devotee of Cleveland's fiscal orthodoxy, especially the gold standard, the defense of which was among the principal aims of his diplomacy.[14] In Cleveland's second term his first secretary of state was Walter Q. Gresham, a onetime Republican who had broken with his party in part because of his opposition to the Republican tariff, which was the main reason Cleveland chose him. His second secretary of state, Richard Olney, was a conservative lawyer who had proven his conservatism with his tough response to striking workers as Cleveland's attorney general.

Democratic attitudes toward foreign policy were closely aligned with the dominant mood of the South, and most southern leaders were in a decidedly antiexpansionist mood for the better part of three decades after the Civil War. Most of the leading architects of the "New South" sought to "modernize the South without resorting to expansion and conflict." Although a few prominent southerners, such as Alabama's powerful senator John T. Morgan, sought to revive old dreams of tropical expansion in order to build new markets for southern produce, most " 'forward-thinking' southerners" in the decades after the Civil War considered the national market sufficient to absorb the South's limited productive capability.[15] Economic expansionism, in their view, was a northern vice.

Many southerners also found the expansionism and occasional bellicosity of Republican foreign policy morally disconcerting, all too reminiscent of what they considered northern aggressiveness and tyranny during the Civil War and Reconstruction. One of the most prominent of the New South's leaders was Georgia's James Blount, a colonel in the Confederate army who was elected to the House of Representatives when Georgia reentered the Union in 1872 and who remained in office for the next eighteen years, rising to the influential chairmanship of the House Foreign Affairs Committee. Blount's own "moralism" in foreign policy, as well as his opposition to expansion and the annexation of foreign territories, was very much the product of his experience under the hated "Republican rule." Northern military occupation of the South had been an immoral and humiliating denial of the rights of white southerners, he believed, as well as an enormous and unnecessary drain on the nation's resources. Now, in the post-Reconstruction era, overseas expansion was being championed by the very same northern leaders who sought to oppress the South—men like Blaine, Garfield, Harrison, and Lodge. As Blount saw it, aggressive Radical Republicanism had been transformed into aggressive overseas expansionism, and he placed himself squarely in opposition to the trend. "As a Victorian-era advocate of the New South, he worked quietly and steadily to incorporate . . . lessons about the evils of Yankee aggression into the critical foreign-policy developments of his time." He opposed federal subsidies for shipbuilding and the expansion of overseas diplomatic posts. "As a former Confederate and a product of the Reconstruction South, [Blount] believed he had great sensitivity to the flaws of a self-righteous and aggressive America." The foreign policy he sought would be based on "a respect for self-determination, a sensitivity to traditional American notions about self-government, and an opposition to subjugation of a weak people by a stronger one." The changes Blount sought in his New South were based on economic diversification and self-reliance and "hinged on minimal connections with the world beyond."[16]

This southern perspective, which blended devotion to the principle of self-determination with a tendency toward isolationism, found reflection in the ideology of the national Democratic Party and helped shape Democratic foreign policy throughout the 1880s and early to mid-1890s. Cleveland's restrained view of the federal government's role in domestic policy was complemented by an equally restrained view of the goals and purposes of American foreign policy. In contrast to his Republican predecessors and successors, Cleveland aimed not at increasing but at reducing American overseas involvement. His policy was "neutrality," Cleveland declared in his first inaugural address, "rejecting any share in foreign broils and ambitions upon other continents and repelling their intrusion here."[17] In both Democratic administrations, from 1885 to 1888 and then from 1893 to 1896, Cleveland's foreign policy, insofar as he articulated one, aimed chiefly to halt or undo what the previous Republican administrations had begun or completed. A dominant theme of Democratic Party thinking and popular rhetoric was that the Republican administrations of Garfield, Arthur, and Harrison had led the United States in a dangerous departure from hallowed American traditions. A supporter of Bayard's appointment as secretary of state saw, after four years of Republican leadership, "a foreign policy looming up in the distance at variance with national traditions and involving enormous expenditures and no end of jobbery." Bayard, it was hoped, "could put his heel upon it and save us . . . from entanglements of that kind."[18]

Bayard tried. Among the Cleveland administration's first acts in 1885 was to withdraw the Frelinghuysen-Zavala Treaty from Senate consideration, on the grounds that building an American canal through Nicaragua in return for an American guarantee of Nicaragua's security constituted "an absolute and unlimited engagement" by the United States, in violation of the principles of neutrality and nonentanglement.[19] Bayard shared Blaine's desire for peace and stability in the hemisphere, and he shared, too, Republican hopes for expanding American commercial opportunities. But these goals need not lead the United States to expansion or entanglement. "The prosperity and independence of the Central American States we very much desire," Bayard declared, "but no entangling alliances with them or any other power."[20] The Cleveland administration abandoned several trade and reciprocity agreements that the Arthur administration had negotiated with Central American and Caribbean nations, partly because they interfered with the Democrats' primary goal of reducing the Republican tariff, but also because Cleveland feared "they represented the beginnings of a policy of establishing economic protectorates in the Caribbean."[21] The administration buried the treaty ratifying the Berlin Convention concerning the Congo, which the Arthur administration had helped negotiate, on similar grounds.

Extricating the United States from foreign entanglements was not always easy, however, especially for a man like Bayard, who, as the Samoan affair showed, had genuine concerns for the fate of peoples who looked to the United States for help, a commitment to the principle of self-determination, and a strong desire to uphold what he considered America's honor against a variety of global bullies. President Cleveland also had a strong sense of honor, both personal and national. He did not enjoy the attacks launched on him by Republicans and even by some Democrats for what critics charged was a foreign policy of retreat and weakness. The Samoan affair showed how hard it was for even a determined administration to limit or curtail American involvement abroad.

The second Cleveland administration, beginning in 1893, made an even more determined effort to change course in foreign policy. The new secretary of state, Walter Q. Gresham, though himself a onetime Republican, aimed to halt and reverse what seemed to him the dangerous expansionist and warlike course taken by Harrison and Blaine over the previous four years. The belligerence and complications over Samoa, the near war with Chile, the accelerating naval buildup and turn to a battleship fleet, and above all the attempted annexation of Hawaii struck Gresham as grave departures from what he called "the conservative teachings of the founders of our government." He declared himself "opposed to a large army and navy" on the old Jeffersonian grounds that a growing military establishment would endanger republican government. A "splendid naval establishment," as he sarcastically called the Republican-inspired naval buildup, was not "consistent with the early policy" of the republic. He spoke contemptuously of "what is sometimes termed a magnificent or splendid

Administration" and was determined to "do something toward bringing the people back to a proper view of things."[22]

Like Bayard, and like Carl Schurz, Gresham's opposition to the Republicans' expansive policies stemmed chiefly from his concern about their likely effect on the American polity. Expressing a worldview whose lineage could be traced back to John Randolph and the Old Republicans of the early nineteenth century, and before that to the Anti-Federalists of the 1780s, he insisted that "[p]opular government" could "not long survive under such a policy." Americans should "stay at home and attend to their own business"; otherwise "they would go to hell as fast as possible."[23]

The most egregious Republican policy remained the tariff, but in Gresham's mind, as in Cleveland's and that of many other Democrats, high tariffs and the political corruption they spawned seemed inseparable from Republican expansionism and navalism. They were all symptoms of the same disease. That was why Gresham believed that continuing on "a career of foreign acquisitions and colonization" would be "disastrous" for America's republican institutions, and why he considered it essential that the Cleveland administration pursue a "conservative" foreign policy to match its conservative domestic policy. All foreign entanglements were dangerous. Even reciprocal trade agreements were objectionable because they entangled the United States in an international economic web and reduced its independence. He insisted that domestic legislation—that is, tariff reform—was "preferable to an international agreement."[24]

His aim was to isolate the United States as much as possible so as to allow it to enjoy its republican freedoms without the risk of an overbearing federal government and an oversize military. He sought to roll back the more overt forms of Republican expansionism, such as the annexation of Hawaii. And he was acutely aware that even apparently innocuous and limited forms of American involvement overseas could prove entangling and therefore had to be nipped in the bud.

The best example of this danger could be seen in Samoa, where an early and seemingly innocent promise of "good offices" had entangled the United States and even brought it to the brink of war. Cleveland in his first annual message in 1893 declared that the Samoan difficulties "signally illustrate the impolicy of entangling alliances with foreign powers" and the folly of departing from an American tradition of isolation "consecrated by a century of observance." For Gresham, Samoa was a prime example of "the evils of interference in affairs that do not specially concern us."[25]

In one of the more thoughtful critiques of the Blaine school of American foreign policy, but also of Bayard's moralist interventionism, Gresham warned that "[e]very nation, and especially every strong nation, must some-times be conscious of an impulse to rush into difficulties that do not con-cern it, except in a highly imaginary way. To restrain the indulgence of such a propensity is not only the part of wisdom, but a duty we owe to the world as an example of the strength, the moderation, and the beneficence of popu-lar government."[26]

Cleveland's and Gresham's desire to extricate the United States from Samoa derived in large measure from their displeasure with the recent course of events in Hawaii.[27] Even before Cleveland took office, Democrats had begun taking steps to slow down and if possible stop the annexation of Hawaii that Harrison had embarked upon in his last weeks in office. The driving force behind the effort to block the annexation treaty came from a powerful southern Democrat, Kentucky congressman James B. McCreary, who had replaced James Blount as chairman of the House For-eign Affairs Committee. Working closely with the southern members of the incoming Cleveland cabinet, McCreary persuaded the new president to postpone consideration of the treaty and appoint a fact-finding commis-sion to look into the circumstances surrounding the overthrow of Queen Liliuokalani and the American role in that civil conflict. Cleveland agreed and, at McCreary's suggestion, appointed as head of the commission none other than the prominent and recently retired southern Democrat James Blount.[28]

Most historians believe that Cleveland and Gresham had not yet decided what they wanted to do about Hawaii. But the appointment of Blount, a well-known New South opponent of expansion and annexation, showed which way they were leaning. Blount had already stated that he did "not like the looks" of the Hawaiian affair. Three southern friends of his were in Cleveland's cabinet—the secretary of treasury, the interior secretary, and the secretary of the navy—and all three "personally opposed America's ter-ritorial expansion" and knew that he "shared their sentiment."[29]

Blount's report on the Hawaiian situation and the behavior of Harrison's minister, John L. Stevens, was predictably censorious. He concluded that the United States had intervened forcefully and improperly to aid the over-throw of the queen and install a mostly white, pro-annexationist govern-ment in Hawaii that did not have the support of the nonwhite majority. He may have exaggerated popular opposition to the new government, but he probably did not exaggerate the significance of the American role in aiding the overthrow of Queen Liliuokalani. Nor was he alone in decrying this form of intervention as a novel departure from American traditions, no mat-ter how often the United States had undertaken similar efforts in decades past. A majority of Democrats were eager to criticize the late Republican administration in any case.

But Blount and other southerners had their own reasons to find the Harrison administration's behavior disturbing. It was all painfully reminiscent of Blount's experience "as a white southerner of the Reconstruction days—defeated, occupied, removed from national and regional authority by invading Yankee soldiers, politicians, and capitalists." His opposition to Hawaiian annexation derived in part from his principled commitment to self-determination, his "sensitivity to traditional American notions about self-government," and an "opposition to subjugation of a weak people by a stronger one." As the historian Tennant McWilliams notes, "There was much in his past as a Civil War and Reconstruction southerner to make him look at the world in this way."[30]

Gresham, armed with Blount's report, sought to remedy the evil wrought by President Harrison. He and Cleveland insisted that the pending annexation of Hawaii be canceled and the treaty set aside, a proposal agreed to by the Democrat-controlled Congress. Southern newspapers took the lead in applauding. As the *Charleston News and Courier* noted, "It will go hard with [the Republicans] to give up Hawaii; it went hard with them to get out of the South."[31]

Gresham wanted to go even further. The circumstances of Queen Liliuokalani's overthrow, he believed, had "created a moral obligation on the part of the United States to reinstate her." There was logic to his argument. If the United States had wrongly and contrary to the wishes of the Hawaiian population overthrown the queen, as Blount had determined, then the wrong continued so long as the queen remained out of office and the "fraudulent" government that overthrew her remained in power. Gresham believed the United States had an obligation to remove it and restore the queen. "Should not this great wrong be undone?" he asked. To critics who objected that restoring the queen was at the very least impractical, he responded: "There is such a thing as international morality."[32] Moreover, if the pro-annexation government remained in power in Hawaii, the Democrats' defeat of Harrison's annexation treaty would be a hollow and short-lived victory. How long before persistent Hawaiian entreaties were finally accepted by a more accommodating Republican administration? Indeed, on July 4, 1894, the Republic of Hawaii proclaimed its independence, and four years later under the Republican administration of William McKinley it was annexed to the United States.

Gresham's perception of international morality and his opposition to entanglements abroad presented the Cleveland administration with a quandary, however. The United States had been complicit in the removal of the queen. To restore her would require it to be complicit in another change of government in Hawaii. The new government would not overthrow itself, especially after the queen promised to behead its leaders as soon they surrendered. Gresham hinted he would support another coup, even with force if necessary, to put the queen back on her throne, and as a sign of tacit encouragement for another coup, Cleveland ordered the American warship stationed at Honolulu to depart Hawaiian waters, indicating that the United States would not come to the aid of the current Hawaiian government.[33] But neither Hawaiians nor the U.S. Congress showed much interest in going along with this plan for a second American-inspired change of government.

Gresham's defense of the principle of self-determination was running afoul of his commitment to nonintervention, and these two principles would frequently collide over the course of American history. To restore self-determination to a people robbed of it by past American policy required another intervention that would, arguably, rob it again. Gresham's and Cleveland's desire for an American foreign policy of abstention and nonentanglement seemed to require only further intervention and entanglement. How could any administration extricate the United States from this cycle of intervention? Isolationism and retrenchment were a difficult course on which to try to place a nation that had been persistently expanding for more than a century, often at the expense of the self-determination of other peoples.

It was especially difficult because, despite the Democratic critique of the excesses of the Harrison administration, both Republican and Democratic leaders could see that popular opinion was broadly hostile to the Cleveland administration's course. The same outcry that had greeted Bayard's forbearing policy toward Samoa now greeted Gresham's Hawaiian policy, though with even greater force. Not only Republicans but leading Democrats attacked him for proposing to overthrow the new "republic" in Hawaii and restore a corrupt monarchy. Neither the House nor the Senate, both controlled by the Democrats, "would back the administration in any interference to restore the Queen." Senator Morgan appealed to the Monroe Doctrine in declaring that when a "crown" or "scepter" falls in "any kingdom of the Western Hemisphere," it must never be restored, "no matter how virtuous and sincere the reasons."[34] Republican politicians and newspaper editors, meanwhile, had a field day. Illinois senator Shelby Collum, whose political career stretched back to the Civil War, called Blount's lowering of the flag over Honolulu "no less treasonous than Confederate soldier

William B. Mumford's removing the American flag flying over Yankee-occupied New Orleans."[35] Henry Cabot Lodge condemned Cleveland's "policy of retreat and surrender." In a widely read article entitled "Our Blundering Foreign Policy," published a year later, he accused the administration of abandoning American interests and principles in the Pacific. As Gresham's biographer notes, the secretary of state's policies on both issues proved politically "disastrous." The Hawaiian affair, in particular, "handed the Republicans an easily exploited issue and further weakened Cleveland's leadership of the Democratic Party."[36]

Despite Cleveland's desires to pull back from the world, in fact, the momentum of American power and ambition was difficult to slow. Even Gresham could not always resist the temptation to wield American influence abroad. He had barely taken the reins at the State Department when he stepped into the middle of a boundary dispute between Colombia and Costa Rica, proffering America's "good offices," insisting the dispute be referred to arbitration in Washington, and thereby earning the enmity of the Colombians, much as Blaine had angered the Chileans a decade before.[37]

And despite Gresham's derisive comments about the "splendid naval establishment," the naval buildup accelerated under the enthusiastic stewardship of Cleveland's secretary of the navy, Hilary Herbert, one of several influential Americans who really were influenced by the writings of Mahan.[38] Cleveland sent gunboats to Korea and to China to protect American missionaries, and within a year of taking office he dispatched a much larger fleet of warships to intervene in a civil war between alleged "republicans" and alleged "monarchists" in Brazil. Assistant Secretary of the Navy William Gibbs McAdoo, holding the office that Theodore Roosevelt would occupy three years later, sounded very Theodore Roosevelt–like when he boasted to a Democratic Party rally of the physical and emotional "stimulus" that came from "the sight of that splendid squadron . . . carrying our flag with pride over decks cleared for action, as it steamed up the Bay of Rio." The Cleveland administration had given "notice to the world that . . . we were keenly alive to our expressed declarations, that all the Americas are for Americans, and that our sympathies are of right and do naturally belong to those who believe in a republican form of government."[39]

Then in 1895 President Cleveland and his second secretary of state, Richard Olney (Gresham had died), suddenly pushed for a resolution to a long-simmering and somewhat obscure dispute between Venezuela and Great Britain over the precise location of the western border of British Guyana. The Venezuelans, for whom the matter was not obscure, had repeatedly appealed to Washington to help them, in the spirit of the Monroe

Doctrine. In 1894 they had hired a retired American diplomat, William L. Scruggs, to plead their case. Aware that "not one American in ten thousand had even heard of the boundary question," Scruggs published a pamphlet with the deliberately explosive title "British Aggressions in Venezuela, or The Monroe Doctrine on Trial." The pamphlet gained a wide circulation, and its warnings were repeated by newspapers across the country.[40]

Cleveland, already politically vulnerable as a result of the depression and the disastrous Democratic losses in the 1894 elections, for which he was blamed, quickly found himself on the defensive. Britain was widely hated in the West and South, two Democratic strongholds where his support had collapsed. Critics had in the past accused Cleveland of being a British stooge—an indiscreet letter from the British ambassador indicating that London favored him over Harrison had hurt him in the 1888 election. Now here were alleged "British aggressions" against Venezuela, and Republicans and even many Democrats wanted to know what he intended to do about it. Lodge warned that if the president would not uphold the Monroe Doctrine, it would be "the duty and the privilege of the next Congress to see that this is done."[41]

Cleveland took up the dispute in the spring of 1895 in order to silence domestic critics and defuse the crisis.[42] He could not have believed that British refusal to settle the boundary dispute in 1895 constituted a new act of aggressive imperialism. British stubbornness on this question went back decades. Nor did Cleveland care a whit about Venezuela's claims in the matter. His goal was to avoid confrontation and pursue his conservative foreign policy. "Disturbed at the rising tide of jingoism," he hoped to get out in front of the building pressures for a confrontation with England before the newly elected and overwhelmingly Republican Congress convened in December and forced his hand. The blunt-spoken Olney may not have been the best person to defuse a conflict, though. Two decades of "soft words and tactful language," he believed, had "undermined respect for the United States" in Britain and throughout the Western Hemisphere. He therefore "proposed calling the London government up short" and demanded that the British submit the dispute to arbitration. In his lawyerly fashion he assembled what amounted to a ten-thousand-word legal brief on the Venezuelan matter that would, however, be remembered for only one sentence: "Today the United States is practically sovereign on this continent, and its fiat is law upon the subjects to which it confines its interposition." His note went down in history as the "Olney Corollary" to the Monroe Doctrine.[43]

The irony was that the author had little affection for the doctrine, and his president had even less. The Monroe Doctrine had never found much favor among conservatives and Democrats. Back in the 1820s John Randolph had vowed he would not risk "the safety and independence" of the United States to defend South Americans from Europeans.[44] President Andrew Jackson had never invoked the doctrine or even mentioned it in public. And neither had any other Democratic president, except James K. Polk, who invoked it to justify his demand for British territory in the north and Mexican territory in the south. Since the Civil War conservative Democrats had viewed the doctrine as a rhetorical shield behind which Republicans like Blaine attempted to expand American involvement throughout the hemisphere. Olney was "disturbed by the penchant of jingoes for invoking it to block European powers from punishing Latin American states for various offenses . . . or to promote the expansion of United States interests in Central and South America."[45] Cleveland in his first term never mentioned the Monroe Doctrine.[46] He told Bayard he "knew it to be troublesome" and had no "clear conception or information" about it, though he knew it had been a doctrine of intervention, not abstention. But now political weakness and Scruggs's successful lobbying had pushed him into a corner. The Venezuelans, the Republicans, many Democrats, and the national press all insisted the doctrine was at risk. Over Olney's objections, Cleveland "insisted that in taking its stand" on the Venezuelan matter, "the administration must squarely vindicate the Monroe Doctrine."[47]

A reluctant Olney took care to define what exactly was being vindicated. He was "anxious to dispel the wilder pretensions of domestic jingoes."[48] He shared the concern of John Bassett Moore, a confidant of Bayard's, that many Americans, especially Republicans, seemed to believe "that the Monroe Doctrine committed us to a kind of protectorate over the independent states of this hemisphere, in consequence of which we are required to espouse their quarrels, though we cannot control their conduct." Olney wanted to refute this notion. In his note to the British he insisted that the doctrine did not "establish any general protectorate by the United States over other American states"; it did not "contemplate any interference in the internal affairs of any American state or in the relations between it and other American states"; and it did not "justify any attempt" by the United States "to change the established form of government of any American state or to prevent the people of such state from altering that form according to their own will and pleasure." The Monroe Doctrine had but a "single purpose and object," to ensure that "no European power or combination of European powers shall forcibly deprive an American state of the right and power of self-government and of shaping for itself its own political fortune and destinies."[49]

Olney later boasted to his brother that the doctrine had never before been "so carefully defined and so narrowly restricted."[50] He was right. Even the line for which his note became notorious was embedded in a conservative appeal for a foreign policy of passivity and even isolationism. When he declared that the United States was "practically sovereign on this continent" and its "fiat was law," he was not celebrating expansive hegemony but admonishing Americans to cherish the unique security and freedom they enjoyed in their isolated corner of the world. The nation's "infinite resources, combined with its isolated position" had made it "master of the situation and practically invulnerable against any or all other powers." It was free to act, or not act, unilaterally and without the advice or approval of any other nation. Regional dominance afforded a tranquillity undisturbed by the normal competitions for power that were common in Europe. "Thus far in our history," Olney explained, "we have been spared the burdens and evils of immense standing armies and all the other accessories of huge warlike establishments, and the exemption has largely contributed to our national greatness and wealth as well as to the happiness of every citizen." Were the European powers ever allowed to establish themselves in the hemisphere, these "ideal conditions" would be destroyed. The United States would have to arm itself "to the teeth" and "convert the flower of our male population into soldiers and sailors." He could not imagine "how a greater calamity than this could overtake us." All that stood in the way of this "grave peril" was the "sure but silent force of the doctrine proclaimed by President Monroe."

Olney's vision of the doctrine was not the Republican vision. Blaine and his colleagues sought primacy to shape the hemisphere in accordance with American principles and interests and to establish the United States as the region's "arbiter," just as Clay, Monroe, and Adams had intended when they first elaborated the Monroe Doctrine. Olney and Cleveland sought primacy in order to avoid involvement in the hemisphere, in the spirit of the doctrine's early opponents. Like Gresham, Olney worried about Americans' penchant for taking on problems that did not concern them, for becoming "wrought up to an active propaganda in favor of a cause." The "age of the Crusades has passed," he insisted, and he advised Americans to attend to "their own security and welfare." His aim was nonintervention, not hegemony. But for the United States to stay out, it was necessary that the Europeans stay out, too.

Olney did not expect the British to accept the application of the Monroe Doctrine to the Venezuelan border dispute, or to accept it even in principle, no matter how narrowly he construed it. British prime minister Lord Salisbury, after expressing "surprise" that Olney had fired an elephant gun at this flea of an issue,[51] rejected the doctrine in toto. Mr. Monroe's "political maxims" must "always be mentioned with respect," he commented, but international law rested on "the general consent of nations" and not on unilateral declarations by one nation, "however powerful." The United States could not claim a right to intervene "in every frontier dispute" that might arise in the Western Hemisphere or even to insist that every dispute be submitted to arbitration. It might or might not have an interest in the particular case of Venezuela, but its claim was in "no way strengthened or extended" by the fact that the dispute involved "some territory which is called American."[52]

Olney agreed, privately, and would have been happy "to drop all reference" to the Monroe Doctrine if the British would simply accept arbitration. But Cleveland would have none of it. He had made the Monroe Doctrine the core of the American case, and now the British had repudiated it. The matter could not be left there. To Congress in December 1895, he insisted that "the doctrine upon which we stand is strong and sound," was meant to "apply at every stage of our national life," and could not "become obsolete while our Republic endures." Even if it had not been admitted "in so many words to the code of international law," it involved principles of a "peculiar, if not exclusive, relation to the United States," which therefore had a right to claim it as international law "as certainly and as securely as if it were specifically mentioned." The president concluded that he was "fully alive to the responsibility incurred" in staking out this position, "and keenly realized all the consequences that may follow." He was, "nevertheless, firm in my conviction that . . . there is no calamity which a great nation can invite which equals that which follows from a supine submission to wrong and injustice, and the consequent loss of national self-respect and honor, beneath which are shielded and defended a people's safety and greatness."[53]

Observers on both sides of the Atlantic assumed Cleveland was ready to go to war. The Republican press cheered. Theodore Roosevelt prepared to enlist in what he hoped would be an invasion of Canada, telling a friend, "If there is a muss I shall try to have a hand in it myself!"[54] Many Democratic politicians were relieved that the president no longer appeared to be a British lackey. But Cleveland and Olney were not looking for or expecting war.[55] They had hoped all along that the British would see reason and help them outmaneuver their domestic critics. When the British proved unhelpful, Cleveland felt betrayed. It would have been "exceedingly gratifying and a very handsome thing for Great Britain to do," he complained, "if in the midst of all this Administration has had to do in attempts to stem the tide of 'jingoism,' she had yielded or rather conceded something . . . for our sake."[56]

Instead, in their attempt to outmaneuver their critics, Olney and Cleveland had "outjingoed the jingoes."[57] And in the process, they had also redefined what constituted a conservative foreign policy. Before the Venezuela crisis, traditional conservative principles had simply called for nonintervention and nonentanglement, even in the Western Hemisphere. Cleveland and Olney now broadened the conservative ambition. They claimed a right to remain "practically invulnerable as against any or all other powers." This was a form of isolationist exceptionalism, but it was an expanded definition of isolationism. Cleveland and Olney now claimed that the United States, alone among the world's powers, had a special right not to have to confront the geopolitical challenges and strategic dangers that all other great powers in history had faced. This was a different kind of reaction to America's increased power from that of Blaine and the Republicans. But it was a response to power. Even isolationists adopted an expanded vision of American needs and interests. Henceforth, isolationism in the United States would mean hemispheric primacy.

The Venezuelan affair was a political victory for Cleveland, but his most loyal supporters felt betrayed. To Thomas Bayard and other members of the cabinet, Olney's policy "was all too reminiscent of the blustering jingoism of Blaine."[58] The president's Wall Street supporters were outraged, fearing confrontation with Great Britain infinitely more than British control of the mouth of the Orinoco.[59] Yale international law professor Theodore S. Woolsey declared, "This is not the Monroe Doctrine. It is dictatorship pure and simple." These were lonely voices, however. Cleveland's most committed foes, and a majority of Americans, applauded what they regarded as his bold challenge to the British. William McKinley declared that the "President's firm and dignified stand will command the approval of the people of Ohio,"[60] and John Hay in London informed an apprehensive British government that the American people were "nearly unanimous in their support of Cleveland's policy."[61]

The British government ultimately settled the boundary dispute and took the opportunity to declare in a more formal manner than ever before that they would cede dominance of the hemisphere to the United States. Arthur Balfour, the Tory leader in the Commons, declared in January 1896 that Britain had no "forward policy" in South America and that it had "never desired" and did not "now desire, either to interfere in the domestic concerns of any South American State or to acquire for ourselves any territory that belongs to them." Instead he made a plea for permanent Anglo-

Saxon friendship and unity. The prospect of war with the United States, he declared, was akin to the "unnatural horror of civil war. . . . We should be fighting our own flesh and blood, speaking our own language, sharing our own civilization." The day would come, he predicted, when "some statesman of authority" would "lay down the doctrine that between English speaking peoples" war was "impossible."[62] This British search for Anglo-Saxon amity was a response not only to Cleveland's belligerence but also to fears of Germany and Russia and to perceived vulnerabilities across the expanse of the British Empire. It was the beginning of a global strategic realignment that would reshape the international system in the twentieth century and that almost immediately raised concerns on the European continent, especially in Germany, about an Anglo-American global dominion.

Those issues lay in the future. In the meantime the British government went so far as to propose a conference to discuss officially codifying the Monroe Doctrine as international law, de jure as well as de facto. But Olney rejected the proposal out of hand. To seek international approval of the Monroe Doctrine might impinge on America's unilateral right to determine its own interests and prerogatives. Olney declared that the United States was "content with existing status of Monroe Doctrine, which, as well as its application to said controversy, it regards as completely and satisfactorily accepted by the people of the Western Continents."[63]

This was hardly the case. America's neighbors in the Western Hemisphere were both appalled by and apprehensive about what they regarded as a new, bolder assertion of American hemispheric primacy. Whatever goodwill might have been earned from helping Venezuela reach a settlement with Britain had been entirely undermined by Olney's refusal to take Venezuelans into his confidence during the negotiations, and by a boundary settlement that gave them much less territory than they believed they deserved. Throughout Latin America, but also throughout Europe, "voices of alarm were raised" by U.S. policies and statements. The German press "strongly objected to U.S. claims under the Olney-Cleveland interpretation of the Monroe Doctrine."[64] In general, worldwide opinion of the United States began to shift and to regard the rising power as more dangerous than previously understood. This had not been Cleveland's and Olney's intention, but it was their legacy.[65]

The Humanitarian War

THE VENEZUELA CRISIS proved but a prelude to the main drama, which was just beginning to brew in Cuba as the confrontation with the British headed toward settlement. In the controversy over what to do about the newly erupted insurgency in Cuba, the Cleveland administration confirmed the essentially conservative and noninterventionist nature of its foreign policy. The nation as a whole confirmed its rejection of that approach.

Americans had paid little attention to Cuba since the *Virginius* crisis of 1873. The Ten Years' War ended in 1878 with a Spanish promise to provide eventual autonomy to Cuba under Spanish sovereignty. Although a series of reforms were enacted on the island, and reformers among the Spanish colonial authorities attempted to govern with a lighter hand, the promise of autonomy had gone unfulfilled. A series of uprisings followed—in 1879, 1883, 1885, 1892, and 1893—but had not amounted to much. Then in February 1895 another rebellion broke out. At first it appeared doomed to fail like the others. But in the fall of 1895 the rebel armies scored some stunning successes, spread their attacks out across the country, and struck at the heart of Cuban wealth in the western part of the island.[66]

The rebels attacked not only Spanish colonial power but the colonial economy. "The chains of Cuba have been forged by its own riches," the leading rebel general, Maximo Gómez, explained, "and it is necessary to put an end to this in order to finish it soon."[67] He decreed that all economic activity on the island must cease: "All sugar plantations will be destroyed, the standing cane set fire and the factory buildings and railroads destroyed." Work itself was "a crime against revolution,"[68] and Gómez decreed that any "worker assisting the operation of the sugar factories . . . will be executed."[69] Winning the war required taking ruthless measures. "What is necessary is to triumph, and the most efficacious and effective means to reach this end, even though they might appear severe, are always the best." The rebel strategy was to destroy Cuba in order to save it. It was "necessary to burn the hive in order to disperse the swarm."[70]

While the destruction of property was primarily a military strategy against Spain, for some it was also part of a revolution against the wealthy property owners in Cuba. Witnessing the "sad and painful disparity" between rich and poor, Gómez exclaimed: "Blessed be the torch." In a decree of July 1896 he ordered rebel forces to "burn and destroy all forms of property" as "rapidly as possible everywhere in Cuba." It was necessary, said one rebel leader, "to destroy the idols before which those stained with blood fall to their knees." How committed the rebels were to social revolution was unclear. The language of class struggle mingled with the language of the Declaration of Independence and the Gettysburg Address. The Cuban Revolution, Gómez declared, would "raise high the banner of a true democracy, of a Republic by the people and for the people." The goal that united the majority of Cubans, though a substantial minority did not share it, was independence.[71]

For Spain, the primary danger was to colonial authority. The rebels' success in crippling the Cuban economy and spreading throughout the island discredited the moderates who had attempted to pursue a policy of conciliation. Power shifted to conservatives, who demanded that the rebellion and its supporters be crushed before they got out of hand.[72] In early 1896 the Spanish authorities appointed General Valeriano Weyler as governor-general of the island to replace the more conciliatory Arsenio Martínez de Campos. Before arriving in Cuba the highly regarded Weyler had criticized Martínez for trying to negotiate an end the conflict: "War should be answered by war." He recognized the futility of trying to defeat the rebels in a straightforward military campaign, however. Even the two hundred thousand troops at his command could not defeat an insurgency that lived off the land, mingled with the rural populace, and melted into the countryside whenever a Spanish force approached. Martínez had already concluded that defeating the insurgency would require "the relocation of the entire rural population away from the zones of insurgent operations to specially constructed fortified centers under Spanish control." But he had rejected the idea as inhumane. Spain would not be able to feed or house the hundreds of thousands of refugees moved into the camps, and "the conditions of hunger and misery in these centers would be incalculable."[73] Weyler, however, saw no alternative.

In early 1896 he launched the policy of "reconcentration." He ordered that the rural population be moved into specially designated zones garrisoned by Spanish forces. Anyone found outside the zones would be considered a rebel and dealt with accordingly. Over the remainder of the year several hundred thousand *reconcentrados,* the majority of them women, children, and older men, were herded into the camps. They brought with them only what they could carry. Weyler ordered the countryside turned into a wasteland that would be incapable of supporting the rebels. "Spanish military forces scoured the countryside in search of all signs of human activity. Villages and planted fields were burned; food reserves were set ablaze, homes were razed, and livestock was seized. Animals that could not be driven to Spanish-held zones were slaughtered." All farming was banned, as was all trade between the country and the cities.[74] Now both sides in the war were bent on destroying the Cuban economy.

Weyler also targeted the political elite in Havana and other cities. He silenced the opposition press and ordered the arrest of politicians known to favor independence or even autonomy and indeed anyone who criticized the government. In July 1896 the American consul counted 720 political prisoners in Havana.[75] Another American reported that "every ten days or so crowds of handcuffed men are driven through the streets of Havana . . . on their way to transport ships which will convey them to penal settlements on the African coast. Many of these men represented the elite of Cuban society." He guessed that "some ten thousand prominent citizens" had been shipped overseas since Weyler's arrival. Weyler did not succeed in defeating the insurgency, however, at least not immediately. Martínez de Campos had predicted that "even the dead will rise against him," and rebel ranks did grow as a result of his repressive policies. "The triumph of the invasion persuaded many previously unsympathetic to separatist goals that the insurrection could succeed; the ruthlessness of Weyler's regime convinced them the insurrection had to succeed."[76]

From the beginning of the rebellion in 1895, President Cleveland had no interest in involving the United States in the Cuban struggle. While both he and Olney knew that American investments on the island were substantial, perhaps $50 million, and that American trade with Cuba was lucrative, they did not consider it enough to warrant entanglement in the messy conflict. Olney's businesslike attitude toward Americans with property in Cuba was that they had taken a calculated risk in a place with a history of instability, and it was not the U.S. government's responsibility to bail them out. Nor did Cleveland have any sympathy for the rebels. He and Olney were outraged by their deliberate brutality, their systematic destruction of private property, and their avowed intention to destroy Cuba in order to save it. Cleveland referred to them, in private, as "the most inhuman and barbarous cutthroats in the world."[77] When Olney met with Cuban junta leaders, he asked them if they approved the rebel strategy of burning crops and plantations. When they replied that it was the only strategy capable of defeating Spain, he said curtly, "There is but one term for such action. We call it arson."[78]

At a broader level, Cleveland, Olney, and many others were convinced that the rebels, and the Cuban people generally, even if they succeeded in defeating Spain, were unfit for democracy and incapable of establishing a stable and reliable government. This view partly derived from Americans' low estimate of Spanish culture and the centuries of oppression that had done so much damage to the Latin character. There was also a substantial degree of racism involved. A large proportion of the rebel army was black, as was one of the three rebel generals. The Spanish government skillfully played on these American fears. The minister in Washington warned Olney that the "negro elements" made up the "most important part" of the revolution. Spanish rule represented "civilization" in Cuba, while a rebel victory meant black equality and perhaps even black domination. Olney in turn warned Cleveland that once Spain was driven out of Cuba, a bloody "war of races would be precipitated."[79]

Cleveland's hostility, however, was only partly based on an assessment of the rebels and their followers. The problem was the rebellion itself and the painful conundrum it raised for American policy and for Cleveland personally. He desperately wanted to avoid involvement in the conflict between Spain and its colony, both because this was his natural inclination and because he feared the effects of a war on the still-reeling American economy. When Olney at one point suggested a closer investigation of the situation, Cleveland demurred. He did not want any investigations. To examine conditions in Cuba would be to acknowledge that the United States had an interest in the matter. He knew this would take him down a path toward eventual entanglement, a possible confrontation with Spain, and in the end responsibility for affairs in Cuba. He wanted no part of any of this. He preferred to ignore Cuba to the extent possible and hoped Spain could bring the conflict to a close quickly. Olney informed the Spanish government that the United States opposed Cuban independence, opposed recognition of the rebels, and supported Spain's efforts to pacify the island. The rest was up to Spain. Throughout the last year of his presidency, Cleveland stuck to this stance, despite mounting public pressures to change course and support the rebels and Cuban independence.

Unfortunately for Cleveland, Spain could not quash the rebellion quickly enough. When the rebels reached the outskirts of Havana, forcing the governor-general to place the Cuban capital under martial law, even skeptics in Washington started to believe that the rebels might succeed, or at least that the Spanish could not defeat them. The sense that the Cuban people were united behind the rebellion gave the movement cachet in the United States. In September 1895 Olney, despite his antipathy toward the rebels, acknowledged that they enjoyed the support of "nine tenths of the Cuban population," including not only the rural campesinos but also significant numbers of the Cuban elite in the cities who were fed up with Spanish misrule.[80]

The Cuban independence movement rapidly developed a wide and enthusiastic following in the United States. To most Americans, the rebels were patriots struggling for independence and republican freedoms, backed by the overwhelming support of the Cuban people. Some questioned whether Cubans were capable of self-government, but no one questioned whether the rebel cause was essentially just and worthy of sympathy. For most, the issue was less the virtues of the rebels than the evil they were fighting against. The revolutionary crisis of 1895 had erupted against a background of long-standing American animosity toward Spain and its presumed history of barbarism and cruelty against peoples in the Western Hemisphere. The "Black Legend" still lived in American imaginations, and it was vividly brought to life in the person of Weyler, "The Butcher." The surprising success of the rebellion seemed to offer proof that the backward Spanish Empire was tottering and could no longer hold Cuba.

The generation that held the reins of power in America, men in their fifties like William McKinley and John Hay, still remembered the *Virginius*. That "mortifying incident" of 1873, one contemporary recalled, "had not been forgotten by the American people; and the memory of it gave poignancy to the anger with which they viewed the barbarities of Weyler."[81] Some remembered the trail of broken Spanish promises that had followed the conclusion of the Ten Years' War in 1878. As Daniel E. Sickles, America's former minister in Madrid, wrote Olney, Spain "has only herself to blame for the present insurrection." It had pledged to provide the Cubans "a large measure of self-government," but Cuba remained "the worst governed spot on this continental hemisphere." America's own independence "was founded on the right of insurrection," and the "heroic struggle made by the insurgents to emancipate themselves and their Island from Spanish rule" deserved sympathy and support.[82]

To capitalize on these American sentiments, the Cubans established a junta in New York to lobby for support. It far surpassed William Scruggs's prodigious efforts on the Venezuela dispute, filling the nation with " 'Sympathy Meetings,' carnivals, theatrical performances, public addresses . . . the publication of its own newspaper, and the systematic preparation and distribution of a deluge of propaganda pamphlets."[83] The junta had a receptive American audience, and its efforts were powerfully aided by an attentive press eager to respond to evident popular interest in the Cuban crisis. As a result, the junta became a significant source of both financing and political influence for the Cuban independence movement.

When the overwhelmingly Republican Congress assembled for the first time in December 1895, it was flooded with petitions from across the country and from broad sectors of American society, from "Ministerial Associations, City Councils, State Legislatures, Veterans' Associations, Mass Meetings, Universities, Boards of Trades, Trade Unions, National Granges, Peace Societies, Professional Men's Organizations, Chambers of Commerce," and every other imaginable civic association. The typical appeal expressed "our sympathy to the Cuban people in their struggle for freedom and independence" and called "on the government to recognize the Cuban rebels" and to take measures to support Cuba's independence from Spanish tyranny.[84]

Members of Congress responded to the public outpouring of sympathy by passing resolutions in the House and Senate in early 1896 calling on the president to recognize a state of belligerency in Cuba and to provide American "friendly offices" to convince the Spanish government to grant the Cubans their independence. The Senate passed its resolution 64–6; the House resolution passed 247–27. The votes revealed support that spanned the political and ideological spectrum. The moderate and generally cautious Republican John Sherman of Ohio, chairman of the Senate Foreign Relations Committee, took the floor to condemn the intolerable conditions in Cuba, warning that the American people would not wait much longer before intervening "to put an end to crimes . . . almost beyond description."[85]

Cleveland quickly became isolated and besieged on the question of Cuba, as he was on many other issues. The only group that seemed to favor his stance of noninterference was the American business community, which was "profoundly hostile to the idea of war" with Spain over Cuba and to any step that might lead to one. Editorials in the business press expressed overwhelming opposition to Cuban independence or recognition of the rebels.[86] Business interests on Wall Street and in other financial centers across the country worried that a conflict would stall recovery from the lingering depression. Those with no interests in Cuba were "fearful that war would disrupt returning prosperity." They were "afraid of its cost and undetermined consequences," and therefore "they wanted peace at almost any price."[87] Businessmen with significant investments in Cuba, like Edwin F. Atkins, had their own reasons for opposing conflict with Spain. Atkins's vast plantations in Cuba "were under special protection of the Spanish government," which would be withdrawn the instant the United States recognized the insurgents. The president of the Spanish-American Iron Company and the representative of Bethlehem Steel's Juragua Iron Company wrote Secretary Olney that "our interests will be jeopardized if belligerency is recognized, as the protection of troops will be withdrawn, which means the immediate closing of our mines, and the probable destruction of our properties, particularly the railway and the dock and harbor improvements."[88] These influential investors lobbied the administration directly, none more effectively than Atkins, a friend of Olney's, who became his main source of information and of advice about the proper course to take.[89] Atkins's influence extended to Congress as well, where representatives of his home state of Massachusetts unanimously opposed pro-Cuban resolutions.[90]

Support from the business community did not compensate for the hostility Cleveland's stance provoked in the press and across the political spectrum, including within his own party. Indeed, it damaged him politically. Business hostility to an interventionist policy in Cuba was so well known that Cleveland's conservative approach to Cuba, like his conservative approach to the economy, was widely assumed to be dictated by Wall Street. When William Randolph Hearst later launched an attack on McKinley's policy, he accused the Republican president of having "yielded to the same influences that have taken President Cleveland captive. . . . He is listening with an eager ear to the big business interests."[91]

As the pressure mounted in the waning months of 1896, Cleveland and Olney looked to Spain for answers. Olney advised the Spanish government to enact political reforms on the island, and above all to make good on the old promise of autonomy. He offered American support if Spain could show progress and predicted the rebels would lose their attraction, both in the United States and in Cuba. He also offered America's services as a disinterested mediator in any negotiation with the rebels.[92] But the Spanish prime minister politely rejected the proposal, insisting there was "no effectual way to pacify Cuba unless it begins with the actual submission of the armed rebels to the mother country."[93] Cleveland despaired of a solution. In his final message to Congress in December 1896, he warned Spain not to assume Washington would remain on a peaceful course forever. "It can not be reasonably assumed that the hitherto expectant attitude of the United States will be indefinitely maintained. While we are anxious to accord all due respect to the sovereignty of Spain, we can not view the pending conflict in all its features . . . without considering that by the course of events we may be drawn into such an unusual and unprecedented condition, as will fix a limit to our patient waiting for Spain to end the contest, either alone and in her own way, or with our friendly cooperation."[94]

The crisis in Cuba unfolded at a time of political turmoil in the United States, and as always, the line between the domestic and the foreign blurred. If the lingering economic depression made businessmen wary of a war that could derail recovery, that same depression had also reshaped Cleveland's Democratic Party, pushing it in a more populist direction. Throughout most of his second term, Cleveland and his conservative "Bourbon" wing of the party were under siege. The depression had thrown millions out of work. Farmers suffered from depressed prices, workers from depressed wages, and this produced a wide array of proposals for social and economic reform to alleviate the pain. Some would prop up farm prices or subsidize farmers. Most contained measures to inflate the currency. All required more active government intervention in the economy. The proposal that rallied the most support across the nation was abandonment of the gold standard and the coinage of silver as a means of inflating the currency and loosening monetary policy. "Silver" Republicans in the western states of Nevada, Colorado, and the Dakotas liked the plan partly because it benefited mining interests. But the biggest effect was on the Democrats. Silver was the platform on which William Jennings Bryan would ride to the party's nomination in 1896.

Cleveland resisted all these measures. He did not believe an inflated currency was the answer to what ailed the economy. Like most Democrats of his generation, he opposed federal spending and believed in limited government. He also shared with many Americans, and with many Republicans, a suspicion and mistrust of new and seemingly radical forces, including the Populists and the burgeoning movement of organized labor. His response to the 1894 Pullman strike in Illinois was to send in federal troops, over the objection of the state's liberal governor, John Peter Altgeld. His actions won support from conservatives but alienated Altgeld and many others, and the whole affair became "a microcosm of the contest within the Democratic party, between angry workers and established social groups and federal and local authority."[95] Cleveland "so aroused laborers and friends of labor that they turned not only against him but temporarily from the Democratic party." In monetary policy, he upheld the gold standard against its many critics. When he vetoed legislation on silver coinage, he split his party wide open and lost most of it. His "refusal to compromise on the money question, and his reluctance to take sufficient positive action in dealing with the depression made his conservatism increasingly unattractive to much of the nation."[96] When he publicly conferred with J. P. Morgan, his opponents cited it as confirmation that he was a tool of the plutocrats. He had become "identified with conservative wealth and nostalgia for a fictitious past; the captive of men 'who put on dress suits and talk at banquets on great subjects.' "[97]

The depression, and to a lesser extent Cleveland's response to it, shifted the American political landscape. The 1894 elections produced "the largest reversal of congressional political strength in American history."[98] The Democrats lost 113 seats in the House and 5 in the Senate, and rebellion in party ranks followed in 1895. While the Republicans were the chief beneficiary of the protest vote, politicians in both major parties were alarmed by the million and a half votes for Populist candidates, almost 50 percent more than in 1892. Republicans had their own quasi-Populist strain in the "Silver" Republicans from western mining states. But the turmoil in the Democratic Party was greater. In the South "the reaction against the Democratic leadership" had enabled the Populists "to recruit independents, dissident elements, and reform-minded groups that had maintained a nominal allegiance to the Democratic party but had long been dissatisfied with its Bourbon character."[99] The Democrats in the West and South would succeed in recapturing the party faithful in 1896, but doing so required nominating the popular Bryan and adopting much of the Populists' rhetoric and some of their proposals.[100] Democrats in the Midwest also responded to the new climate. Governor Altgeld, though no Populist, promised reform and appealed to Populists and workers, as did Nebraska's Bryan. Cleveland's party was changing and leaving him behind. By 1896 the president was "no longer speaking the same language as the people of the South and the West."[101]

Although the Populists were not big winners in elections, the influence of Populist and reformist ideas on both parties and on the future course of American history was significant. As with all broad-based movements in American society, Populism meant different things to different people. It was an amalgam of backward-looking nostalgia for an agrarian past and forward-looking demands for progressive change: "Though the Populists hoped to preserve the values of a by-gone age, they were bent on reversing many old Jacksonian doctrines." On at least one major question—the role of the federal government—many of them departed from traditional conservative Democratic thinking. "We believe that the powers of government . . . should be expanded," the preamble to the 1892 platform declared, "as rapidly and as far as the good sense of an intelligent people . . . shall justify."[102] Emerging leaders of the Democratic Party—the "New Democracy," as it was known, men like Altgeld and Bryan—were perhaps even more committed to the idea of progress and to expanding the role of government to improve society and the lives of people.[103]

Bryan, who would lead the Democratic Party as its presidential candidate for the next dozen years, was no typical post–Civil War Democrat. He paid his respects to the traditions of Jefferson and Jackson, but he also added Lincoln to his political holy trinity. "His belief in the idea of progress" was the "thread running through most of his speeches and writings." It was also "the link between the message he preached and his conception of the mission of America." The "larger the area of our vision," Bryan proclaimed, "the more we see that needs to be done."[104]

Changing political alignments and ideologies influenced the foreign policy debate. Many of the people rebelling against the conservative

Democracy saw echoes of their struggle in Cuba, where workers, farmers, the poverty-stricken, and the common man were also pitted against heartless plutocrats and the forces of conservatism, or so it seemed to many. Populists like Nebraska senator William V. Allen were among the first and loudest supporters of Cuban independence, and he was joined by other Populist senators and by "Silver" Republicans like Colorado's Henry Teller and Utah's Frank Cannon.[105] People in the West and South, who "were disposed to see themselves as underdogs in their own country," also "viewed the Cubans as the oppressed victims of Spanish tyranny." The Spanish government sent troops to put down the workers in Cuba; Cleveland sent troops to put down the workers in Illinois: "In the same breath that they expressed concern with the fate of the Cuban *insurrectos,* the frustrated classes charged aggression by Wall Street."[106] In 1895 the journal of the Knights of Labor called the Cuban Revolution "one of the most righteous ever declared in any country," insisted it be "supported by every lover of liberty and free government in this country," and condemned the Cleveland administration for acting "in the interest of tyranny and oppression, to prevent Cuba from becoming the land of the free and home of the brave." At its 1895 and 1896 conventions the American Federation of Labor passed resolutions supporting Cuban independence and called on the administration to follow "the example of the people of France in giving recognition and aid to the Fathers in their struggle to secure the independence of the colonies."[107] The Populist Party platform in 1896 included a special section devoted to Cuba, offering the "deepest sympathy for their heroic struggle for political freedom and independence" and calling on the United States government to "recognize that Cuba is, and of right ought to be, a free and independent state."[108]

Historians have attributed these expressions of support for the Cuban Revolution to a kind of mass "hysteria" or "psychic crisis" brought on by economic calamity and political failure.[109] But these sentiments crossed all political, economic, and geographical lines. The Knights of Labor and the People's Party employed the same arguments and rhetoric as the moderate Republican senator John Sherman, the steel magnate Andrew Carnegie, the Bostonian Henry Cabot Lodge, and the New York reformer Theodore Roosevelt. Cuba became a national issue in 1896 and could be exploited by both parties for political ends, not because some parts of the nation were gripped by madness but because it struck a chord for a majority of Americans. Indeed, it struck more than one chord. Cuba presented to Americans the picture of a people's struggle for independence against a backward and brutal Catholic tyranny out of step with the "spirit of the age." It offered up a humanitarian tragedy of unprecedented proportions in America's own hemisphere, indeed less than one hundred miles from American shores. And it did so at a time when many saw the United States as a rising, powerful nation, one that had long since proclaimed a right, if not an obligation, to shape at least the Western Hemisphere to conform to American principles.

The significance of the Populist revolt and the overall transformation of the Democratic Party was not that it brought a class-based hysteria to American politics, or that it produced a new impulse toward moralism and activism in American foreign policy. Those impulses had long resided in the Republican Party. The most important effect of the political upheaval of the 1890s was that it brought the Republicans back to power and weakened the conservative forces in the Democratic Party that had long resisted Republican activism both at home and abroad.

The Republicans were the big winners in 1894 and 1896. The depression was "the catalyst that ended the GOP's long search for a national majority." Republicans gained support because the party's economic and political doctrines—the activist state—"seemed more attuned to change" than the old Democratic doctrines and more practicable than those of the Populists. Big federal spending, the infamous "Billion-Dollar Congress," had hurt the Republicans in 1890 and 1892. But in 1894 and 1896, in the midst of the depression, Republicans' spending on soldiers' pensions and internal improvements and their defense of the high tariff were politically popular, especially in contrast to Cleveland's refusal to respond to the economic emergency with government action.[110]

The 1896 election was no Republican landslide. William McKinley won 51 percent of the popular vote and a solid victory in the Electoral College, but Bryan and his followers argued that the Democrats lost a few states by such slim margins that the election could easily have gone the other way. They boasted that Bryan won more votes—6.5 million—than any other candidate in history except McKinley. In Congress 1896 solidified Republican gains from 1894 but did not significantly add to them. The election, however, ended a long stalemate in American politics. Since the 1870s Republican policies had been frequently checked and intermittently rolled back by Democrats in control of one or both houses of Congress, then by Cleveland's two terms in the White House. When in power, Republicans who favored activism both at home and abroad had been forced to move cautiously in a closely divided nation.[111] The Democrats, both in Congress and in the White House, had been the party of the negative, relishing the chance "to slash federal activity, cut expenditures, repeal laws, and end governmental interference in the affairs of private citizens." Cleveland in his two terms had "vetoed over two-thirds of the measures presented to him, more than all his predecessors combined."[112] In foreign policy he had let treaties languish or, as in the case of Hawaii, had tried to reverse the activist policies of his Republican predecessors.

The breaking of the political logjam released "government activism from the restraining effect of the previous era's two decades of political equilibrium." Republican leaders of a "more activist inclination," which included the new Republican president, could begin to glimpse "the broader possibilities for energetic government."[113] McKinley has been viewed by later generations of Americans as a conservative, but for his time he was a moderate liberal in the National Republican mold.[114] He was certainly cautious. Two decades of competing for office in Ohio, where the two parties were in rough balance throughout the 1880s, had impressed upon him the need for compromise and also had made him acutely sensitive to the ebbs and flows of popular attitudes. He was "always reluctant to take a new stand without consulting public opinion." But to consult public opinion in this era was to be a sometime advocate for change and for a larger government role. McKinley favored civil service reform to improve government efficiency and reduce corruption. He favored government intervention in the economy, including that most intrusive form of intervention, the high tariff. He was widely known as a champion of labor and claimed to believe in the high tariff because "it insured prosperity for the worker." It was typical of McKinley's moderate tendencies, however, that he was willing to entertain alternatives to the high tariff. He supported Blaine's attempt to substitute reciprocity treaties, for instance. Nor was he inflexible on currency questions. He had been pro-silver in his early political career and continued to favor "some form of monetary expansion because he thought it expanded the economy." He supported some regulation of business and favored restraints on corporate influence because his idea of national development required harmony among the classes and protection against the excessive power of any single interest or set of interests. McKinley's "idol" was James Blaine, and like Blaine he favored a modernized version of Henry Clay's progressive American System. No less a progressive icon than Robert La Follette considered McKinley a leading representative of "the newer view" in American politics.[115]

In foreign policy McKinley was neither conservative nor radical but a mainstream Republican. Foreign policy was not his principal interest. He had never served on a foreign affairs or military affairs committee in Congress. He said very little about foreign policy during his campaign. He did not utter the word "Cuba" either orally or in writing. He was not known as a "jingo"—early in his presidency he assured Carl Schurz there would be "no jingo nonsense" in his administration. He was not in the circle of eastern intellectuals that included Lodge, Roosevelt, and Henry and Brooks Adams. He regarded Roosevelt as a loose cannon. (Roosevelt returned the compliment, suggesting that McKinley had all the backbone of a "chocolate éclair.") He neither knew nor, apparently, read Mahan. He did not extol the idea of war as beneficial to the nation, the way Roosevelt and some others did. He did not feel the need to prove his mettle in combat, for he had long ago made his reputation as a soldier, and the prospect of war did not excite him. Even after the explosion of the *Maine,* he privately told friends: "I have been through one war. I have seen the dead piled up, and I do not want to see another."[116]

For the foreign policy posts in his cabinet, he picked no firebrands but men who shared his cautious temperament. His key man at the State Department, under the aged John Sherman, was Assistant Secretary William Day, who in turn looked to Alvey A. Adee and John Bassett Moore, both department fixtures and past advisers to the Cleveland administration.[117] He named the cautious and deliberative John D. Long as secretary of the navy and reluctantly agreed to give Roosevelt the post of assistant secretary. Roosevelt wielded little influence either within the administration, where he was constantly frustrated in his efforts to shape policy, or in Congress, where he was regarded by all except Lodge as an "outsider."[118]

If McKinley was the very model of a mainstream Republican, however, this meant that in foreign as in domestic policy he stood for a significantly greater degree of activism than Cleveland and the conservative Democrats. He was an admirer of Blaine's approach to the world and in Congress had worked to support his vision of a panhemispheric political and commercial community, with the United States at its head. The 1896 Republican platform was, as always, "more ambitious and aggressive than the Democratic one" on both foreign and domestic policy. Republicans promised to resume many of the diplomatic initiatives begun under Harrison and Blaine and then halted by Cleveland. These included the annexation of Hawaii, the construction, finally, of a Nicaraguan canal owned and operated by the United States, the purchase of the Danish West Indies, the continuation of the naval buildup, and in Cuba, the use of American "influence and good offices to restore peace and give independence to the island."[119] McKinley's goals in foreign policy were those of his party.[120] He had no grand design and had "never proposed a special global program or strategy." But he "shared with many Republicans a belief that the United States should play a larger role in the world as defined by the issues of the day." Also like many Republicans, and like many Democrats, too, he felt a "deep moral concern" for the "massive civilian suffering in Cuba." He was "genuinely moved by descriptions of starving and diseased women and children in Reconcentration camps."[121]

The burst of American foreign policy activity in the last three years of the nineteenth century has been the source of endless theorizing and speculation by American historians and political scientists. However the best explanation may also be the most prosaic. The election of a mainstream Republican, cautious in his methods but fairly determined in his principles, produced an approach to foreign policy subtly but significantly different from that of the conservative Democrat he replaced. And the defeat of Cleveland's brand of conservatism in the Democratic Party gave wider rein to the moralistic Republican vision that had been nurtured in the messianic struggle of the Civil War.

This shift in course was not immediately obvious on the specific issue of Cuba. McKinley's initial approach to that crisis was typically cautious. He had run as the "advance agent of prosperity" and planned to focus his presidency first and foremost on reviving the economy. He wanted no foreign disruptions, and certainly no foreign war, to distract attention from his domestic economic agenda. In his inaugural address he said little about foreign affairs but made a point of declaring, "We want no foreign wars of conquest; we must avoid the temptation of territorial aggression. Wars should never be entered upon until every agency of peace has failed; peace is preferable to war in almost every contingency."[122] He consulted carefully with Cleveland on the eve of his inauguration, and the outgoing president left the meeting "impressed by McKinley's desire to avoid war."[123] Olney, after a one-and-a-half-hour meeting with the new president, confidently reported to the Spanish minister McKinley's "thorough desire to maintain the same attitude towards your government that the last administration aspired to."[124] McKinley himself told the press in June 1897 that "I anticipate no departure from the policy of my predecessor." As late as July one of his cabinet officers confided that the president had "formed no Cuban policy." His "desire is for the country to enjoy quiet in order that business prosperity may be established. His chief thought is given to securing this one desideratum—quiet."[125]

The Republican Party as a whole was obedient to the desires of its popular new leader, at least at first, and this made for one of those partisan merry-go-rounds so common in American politics. Republican newspapers that had been excoriating Cleveland for inaction on Cuba right up until the last days of the Democrat's term now reversed themselves and backed McKinley's inaction. The small group of Republican barons who directed affairs in the House and Senate were dead set against intervention in Cuba and war with Spain. When Cleveland had been in office, they had let party members loose to criticize the Democrats for betraying the cause of Cuban freedom. But once in power they preferred Cleveland's course. The powerful group known simply as "The Four"—Senators Nelson Aldrich of Rhode Island, William Allison of Iowa, John Spooner of Wisconsin, and Orville H. Platt of Connecticut—joined by McKinley's friend and political adviser Senator Mark Hanna, considered intervention "a dangerous and costly venture into the unknown." They shared the common view of the American business community, for "as men well acquainted with the operations and trends in business, they did not regard war as a reasonable device to facilitate economic expansion."[126] The other leading Republican, Speaker of the House Thomas B. Reed, was virulently opposed to war and had contempt for the Cuban insurgents. He was happy to bottle up any legislation, whether sponsored by Democrats or Republicans, that might force the new president's hand.

The Democrats, meanwhile, released from the burden of defending Cleveland's inaction, now assailed McKinley for pursuing the same course. The National Association of Democratic Clubs demanded "the immediate recognition of the belligerent rights of the Cuban people," and Democrats in Congress took "every opportunity to denounce the wrongs in Cuba and the 'spinelessness' of McKinley's policy." The popular Cuba cause offered Democrats a way to reunite and reenergize the party after the debacle of 1896. Bitterness at Bryan's defeat could be channeled into criticisms of McKinley's refusal to stand up for the downtrodden in Cuba.[127] But it was not all partisan politics. The House Democratic leader, Joe Bailey of Texas, had long been a Cuban sympathizer. With a Republican in the White House he was now freer to vent his feelings. He compared Cuba to the South under Reconstruction and "sympathized with those who lived under military occupation, without political rights and ruled by a distant despotic government."[128]

When McKinley called a special session of Congress to take up the tariff, therefore, the Democrats insisted on taking up Cuba. On April 6, 1897, Alabama senator John T. Morgan introduced a resolution calling for recognition of Cuban belligerence, and Republican leaders in the Senate had to beat back this and other Democratic resolutions. Democrats charged the Republicans with rank hypocrisy for abandoning the "patriotic and humanitarian" statements of their 1896 platform and toadying to big business. Republicans accused the Democrats of playing politics. But they also promised that McKinley would ultimately do right by the Cubans, when and how he saw fit.[129]

That promise revealed an underlying reality, which was that despite McKinley's early success holding his troops in line, his ability to keep them there, even with the help of party leaders, was not unlimited. The president was fully in charge of his own administration. He saw eye to eye with his secretary of state, his secretary of the navy, and his other advisers. There were no renegades pushing him toward war. But outside the administration was a different story. Throughout the months before the outbreak of war with Spain, the president worried constantly about Congress taking control of the Cuban issue out of his hands, and with it control of his presidency. Like Cleveland, he had to work to stay one step ahead.[130]

The problem was that as McKinley took office, the situation in Cuba was taking a dramatic turn for the worse. By the end of 1896 the full, horrific effects of the reconcentration policy began to emerge. As Martínez de Campos had predicted, local authorities in the designated concentration areas were not equipped to house, clothe, feed, or provide medical care for the huge influx of impoverished people from the countryside. The resulting food shortages, unsanitary living conditions, and lack of care had by the beginning of 1897 produced a humanitarian disaster of such magnitude that some critics would call it a genocide. The *reconcentrados* began dying by the thousands as a result of famine and disease. In Santa Clara the U.S. consul reported seventeen deaths per month at the beginning of the year, but then the rate accelerated dramatically. There were 275 deaths in Santa Clara in the first fifteen days of November alone. By late 1897 in Matanzas, where fourteen thousand *reconcentrados* were existing on only nine hundred daily servings of rice, the American consul reported people dying at the rate of eighty per day, mostly from starvation. "The misery and destitution in this city and other towns in the interior are beyond description," he continued. "As I write this, a dead negro woman lies in the street, within 200 yards of the consulate, starved to death; died sometime this morning, and will lie there, maybe, for days." A Boston tobacco merchant returned from Cuba in early 1898 and reported to the Senate Foreign Relations Committee that of the 35,000 *reconcentrados* in Cárdenas in 1897, 26,000 had died.[131]

Observers found the plight of Cuban children especially shocking. "Little children" could be seen "walking about with arms and chest terribly emaciated, eyes swollen, and abdomen bloated to three times the normal size. The physicians say these cases are hopeless." An official American delegation reported, "We saw children with swollen limbs and extended abdomens, that had a dropsical appearance . . . caused by a want of sufficient food." Spanish visitors to the island reported the same human catastrophe. One Spanish visitor outraged by the reconcentration policy reported the condition of the *reconcentrados* in Matanzas and Santa Clara as "horrible" and "frightful." Based on conversations with "priests and soldiers, radicals and conservatives" in early 1898, he reported that "all agree that the war and reconcentration policy have led to the death of a third part, at the very least, of the rural population, that is to say, more than 400,000 human beings," with half again that many deaths likely to follow in the coming months. The war and the reconcentration policy had thus "finished off more than 600,000 lives! What horror!" At a lower estimate of 300,000 deaths, the cost of war and reconcentration by early 1898 was the loss of approximately one-fifth of Cuba's population. An American traveling from Havana to Matanzas in late 1897 reported, "Every house had been burned, banana trees cut down, cane fields swept with fire, and everything in the shape of food destroyed. . . . I did not see a house, a man, woman or child; a horse, mule or cow, not even a dog."[132]

One myth about the American involvement in Cuba in the late 1890s is that politicians and the public were stirred to a frenzy by "sensational" and sometimes fabricated stories of Spanish barbarities disseminated by the tabloid "yellow press" of the day, especially by Joseph Pulitzer's *New York World* and William Randolph Hearst's *New York Journal*. It was true that the press did print some fabrications—sometimes fed to reporters by the Cuban junta—just as it did in every other conflict in American history. But the main thrust of what the press reported about events in Cuba was accurate.[133] Even Hearst could not exaggerate the horrors of the reconcentration camps or tell a story more "sensational" than three hundred thousand Cubans dying of starvation and disease. Even if the American public had received nothing but dry, unemotional, and unembellished accounts, had they seen only the images of women lying dead in the streets and of children with distended abdomens and emaciated limbs, it is unlikely they would have been less outraged than they were by the stories in the yellow press. The pressure on the McKinley administration to take some action in Cuba was not manufactured by publishers looking for a war to sell newspapers. It was the product of Cuban reality and American outrage over actual human suffering.

McKinley had entered office with the situation in Cuba serious but not catastrophic. He had held out some hope for an improvement. The Spanish government insisted Weyler's policies were succeeding in weakening the guerrillas, and American officials wanted to believe that Spain could carry out the reforms on the island necessary to win back a substantial portion of the population. "So far as I can learn at present," John Sherman told reporters in January 1897, "the Spanish government intends granting extensive reforms in Cuba. Thus the insurgents are to have practical autonomy in all matters vital. If this is done, as I am led to believe it will be, that is all that is necessary. The war will be settled."[134] Close observers of the situation in Cuba, however, like the U.S. consul Fitzhugh Lee, believed this hopeful assessment was far too optimistic, and in the early months of the McKinley administration officials began to abandon it. Neither the Cuban rebels nor the Spanish government seemed inclined to compromise, and the likelihood was for a prolonged military stalemate. With the death toll reaching unheard-of proportions and accelerating with each passing day, the situation in Cuba therefore seemed suddenly much more dire and the need for some kind of solution more urgent. Adding to the urgency, American officials and politicians learned from consular dispatches that among the starving in Cuba were some eight hundred American citizens.

The human realities in Cuba increased pressure on McKinley to act, therefore, and so did political realities in the United States. McKinley, whether he liked it or not, was the leader of a party that had declared its pro-Cuban sentiments. He was widely expected to make good on that commitment, especially by many members of his own party. He faced a Democratic opposition in Congress that had seized on the Cuba issue to rally its troops. No one had expected Cleveland to do more on behalf of Cuban independence than he had done, but just about everyone expected McKinley to do more.

Before embarking on any shift in policy, McKinley wanted his own information. In the spring of 1897 he dispatched a political loyalist, William L. Calhoun, to compile a report on conditions in Cuba. Calhoun submitted it at the end of June, and its conclusions were stark. On the one hand, he informed the president, there seemed no reason to hope for a rapid end to the war. The Spanish lacked the capacity to defeat the insurgents in a straightforward military campaign, which was why they had resorted to the reconcentration policy. That strategy might eventually succeed, but only after it accomplished the utter devastation of the island and its population. Meanwhile the preferred solution of both Cleveland and McKinley—the establishment of Cuban autonomy as the necessary reform to end the war—was unlikely to succeed. The rebel leaders insisted that the moment for autonomy had passed. They would accept only independence now, and on this issue they seemed to have most of the population on their side. Calhoun also expressed the view shared by many Americans on the island and by many Cubans of the upper classes that independence would be a disaster for Cuba. The people were uneducated and ignorant, he argued, and were not ready to govern themselves. Independence would likely lead to more warfare, famine, and chaos, including the possibility of racial conflict.

The options for the United States, therefore, were unattractive. One course would simply be to stand back and wait for the conflict to end through the exhaustion of one or both sides. But Calhoun argued that such a policy was unconscionable given the unfolding humanitarian catastrophe. The horrendous condition of the *reconcentrados,* the "destitution and suffering" he witnessed, made his "heart bleed for the poor creatures." There was "no use to dwell on the sad and grewsome [*sic*] picture," he wrote in his report.[135] Yet that sad and gruesome picture was hard to ignore. McKinley also shared the concerns of businessmen that American trade and investments were being severely damaged by the war. Calhoun reported that the "almost total ruin and destruction of both life and property" that would result from continued war included the total destruction of American property and investments. A lucrative American trade would also suffer, at a time when the economy was still feeling the effects of prolonged depression. These were important considerations, but for McKinley they were secondary to the humanitarian crisis. "Basic to all his actions was a deep sense of humanitarianism that made him look with horror on the savage events in Cuba. That they transpired elsewhere than in his own country did not lessen his shock or their importance to his policy."[136]

Soon after receiving Calhoun's report, McKinley, through Sherman, set forth the outlines of a new Cuban policy in a note to the Spanish government and instructions to his new minister in Madrid. Abandoning the more restrained approach of Cleveland and Olney, the president declared he was bound by "the higher obligation" of his office "to protest against the uncivilized and inhuman conduct of the campaign in the island of Cuba." He did so "in the name of the American people and . . . common humanity." He did not insist that Spain cease fighting the rebels. But he did demand that the struggle "at least be conducted according to the military codes of civilization." It was unacceptable that Spain should use "fire and famine to accomplish by uncertain indirection what the military arm seems powerless to directly accomplish."[137] He wanted a solution to the Cuban crisis that was "in conformity . . . with the feelings of our people" and "the inherent rights of civilized man."[138]

McKinley was aware that he was making a rather extraordinary demand of Spain. The Spanish were engaged in an internal struggle on their own territory. No international law or custom forbade a government from mistreating its own citizens, even starving them. But international law and custom certainly forbade the interference of one nation in the internal affairs of another. McKinley was raising a standard of behavior that he claimed was universal and reflected the view of "common humanity," but it was not recognized in the international system of his day.

The Spanish government could readily see that "McKinley's attitude toward Cuba was much harsher than that of Cleveland." Cleveland in his last annual message in December 1896 had also urged the Spanish to bring the war to a speedy conclusion and had expressed concern for the human tragedy in Cuba. He had alluded to circumstances "in which our obligations to the sovereignty of Spain" could be "superceded by higher obligations." But the main thrust of his message had been, as the Spanish minister in Washington reported to Madrid, "to aid Spain in maintaining her sovereignty."[139] McKinley's instructions to the minister in Madrid, on the other hand, "did not explicitly recognize Spanish sovereignty over Cuba, as Cleveland and Olney had always done, and McKinley's position implied that Washington had the right to approve or disapprove a Cuban settlement."[140]

McKinley and his advisers knew they were on shaky legal ground. Therefore, like Harrison and Blaine in their protests to the Russian government over the treatment of Jews, they did their best to identify specific American interests that were allegedly being harmed by Spanish policies and that therefore gave the United States a tangible complaint to justify interference. The fact that there were "a thousand or more of our own citizens among the victims of this policy" gave the United States "the right of specific remonstrance," McKinley declared, even though Calhoun's report insisted that the vast majority of these Americans were naturalized Cubans who had spent little time in the United States. The president suggested that mere proximity gave the United States an interest in Cuba, that a "war, conducted almost within sight of our shores," should at least be conducted in a humane fashion. He brought up the "wanton destruction of the legitimate investments of Americans . . . and the stoppage of avenues of normal trade," though without noting that the majority of that destruction was the fault not of the Spanish government but of the Cuban rebels.[141] "Assuredly," the instruction continued, "Spain cannot expect this Government to sit idle, letting vast interests suffer, our political elements disturbed, and the country perpetually embroiled, while no progress is being made in the settlement of the Cuban problem." McKinley demanded rapid action by Spain, or at least the promise of action, by November 1. The "president's views," relayed by Secretary of State Sherman to the new minister in Madrid, were that the time had come to "put a stop to this destructive war and make proposals of settlement honorable to herself and to her Cuban colony and to mankind."[142]

McKinley and his advisers, in typical American fashion, tried to convince Madrid that what they were demanding was in Spain's own best interest. It was "visionary for Spain to hope that Cuba, even if eventually subjugated by sheer exhaustion, can ever bear to her anything like the relation of dependence and profit she once bore." The methods of warfare Spain had chosen offered "no prospect of immediate peace or of a stable return to conditions of prosperity which are essential to Cuba in its intercourse with its neighbors." If Madrid would pledge to undertake the necessary reforms, the United States would happily "assist her and tender good offices to that end." But if Spain did not undertake the proposed reforms, it should not ask or expect the United States to continue pursuing a "policy of mere inaction." The American minister was instructed not to "disguise the gravity of the situation, nor conceal the President's conviction that, should his present effort be fruitless, his duty to his countrymen will necessitate an early decision as to the course of action which the time and the transcendent emergency may demand."[143]

Despite his calm and affable demeanor, his deliberate and cautious actions, and his sincere desire to avoid war, McKinley knew that when he sent these instructions, war with Spain was a possible if not probable outcome of his policy. Cleveland had told him on the eve of his inauguration that war between the United States and Spain would probably come within the next two years: "Nothing [could] stop it." McKinley had a difficult time recruiting a new minister to Spain because those he approached considered diplomacy futile and war inevitable.[144] Senator Morgan, arguing in favor of his Cuba resolution, candidly declared, "I feel that it makes no difference what steps we take. . . . I contemplate war at the end of any resolution that we pass."[145] Other, less bellicose Democrats, such as Joe Bailey and William Jennings Bryan, did not seek a war with Spain any more than McKinley did. But they knew that their demand for Cuban independence or even for recognition of the Cuban rebels' belligerent status could well lead to war.[146]

Few believed Spain would ever enact reforms sufficient to induce the Cuban insurgents and their followers to settle the conflict peacefully. The American minister in Madrid, voicing the common, jaundiced view of Spanish culture and institutions, did not believe the Spaniards even understood the concept of "real autonomy," at least not as Americans did. Americans understood "that personal freedom and local self-government are inherent, inalienable rights," but even the most liberal Spaniards saw freedom as "a boon to be conferred and to be exercised under Spanish supervision." Beneath the outward courtesy of the Spaniard, he saw "a disposition toward cruel methods . . . and a pride . . . which . . . repeats today the known mistakes of yesterday rather than admit an error and bravely correct it." McKinley's instructions, if they did not necessarily put the United States "on a collision course" with Spain, certainly increased rather than decreased the possibility of a collision. Many foreign observers suspected, not without reason, that Spain would prefer to lose Cuba in a war with the United States than to strike a compromise with the rebels. The American minister in Madrid reported that the Spanish government preferred "the chances of war, with the certain loss of Cuba, to the overthrow of the Dynasty."[147]

McKinley hoped to avoid war. He believed his proposal, if accepted by Spain and the rebels, held out a real prospect of peace. In theory, his plan was coherent enough. If he could press Spain to end the reconcentration policy, relieve the suffering of the *reconcentrados,* broker an agreement for Cuban autonomy, and then press for an armistice on the island that would give time for a new Cuban government to gain legitimacy and authority, McKinley believed the eventual outcome would be Cuba's independence, but achieved peacefully, with Spain's acquiescence, and in a gradual manner more likely to produce stability on the island. Such an approach suited his political style, his lifelong "commitment to incremental success and to compromise." It also offered the best answer to his domestic political problems.[148]

In the months prior to the war, there were occasional, brief moments of guarded optimism. In August 1897 the conservative Spanish prime minister was assassinated—one of a series of assassinations by anarchists that would rock the capitals of Europe and, soon, the United States as well. A liberal government took power in Madrid, and on October 23, ahead of McKinley's November 1 deadline, it sent a note announcing Weyler's recall and promising to conduct a more humane war and to grant Cuba some form of autonomy. In December it decreed a new autonomist constitution.[149] In his annual message in December 1897 McKinley urged Americans to give Spain "a reasonable chance to realize her expectations and to prove the asserted efficacy of the new order of things to which she stands irrevocably committed."[150] He even urged that "Spain be left free to conduct military operations" while the United States for its part would "enforce its neutral obligations and cut off the assistance which it is asserted the insurgents receive from this country."[151]

But in that same message McKinley warned, "The near future will demonstrate whether the indispensable condition of a righteous peace . . . is likely to be attained." If not, "the exigency of further and other action by the United States will remain to be taken." The United States had an "indisputable right and duty" to intervene, McKinley declared, and he would order it "without misgiving or hesitancy in light of the obligation this Government owes to itself, to the people who have confided to it the protection of their interests and honor, and to humanity."[152]

In fact, despite the brief optimism, by the time of the address it was already clear to observers that autonomy had little support in Cuba. The prominent Spanish liberal and future prime minister José Canalejas reported that most Cubans "who at one time had championed autonomy were now unwilling to take up the cause."[153] When Spain sent an emissary to talk to the rebels, Maximo Gómez had him executed, declaring, "We are for liberty, not for Spanish reforms."[154] Conservative and loyalist factions, including Spanish army officers, opposed reforms, too. On January 12, 1898, antiautonomy riots led by Spanish officers broke out in Havana. Adee at the State Department predicted "the beginning of the end" not only for the autonomist government but for Spanish authority in Cuba.[155] Concerned about threats to Americans, he suggested that "it would be well for our naval squadron in the Gulf to be ready for immediate action, for which the emergency may arise any moment. . . . These movements in Cuba are very contagious."[156] The day after the Havana riots Consul Lee requested a warship, and on January 25 the *Maine* arrived in Havana harbor. The mood in Washington had darkened so much that the Spanish minister warned that "any sensational occurrence might . . . disturb the situation."[157]

In fact, two sensational occurrences followed in rapid succession. The first came courtesy of the minister himself, when a private letter he had written to a Spanish colleague was purloined from his office and given to the American press. In the famous "De Lôme letter," splashed across the pages of the Hearst press, the minister described President McKinley as "weak and a bidder for the admiration of the crowd," trying "to leave a door open behind himself while keeping on good terms with the jingoes of his party."[158] These comments were, as the *Raleigh News and Observer* noted, "only in line with what the newspapers of this country say of Mr. McKinley every day."[159] But coming from a Spanish diplomat they were offensive. The minister also expressed a cynical view of reforms in Cuba, suggesting that they were meaningless and that the conflict could only be settled militarily. The explosive revelation for the public was the insult to McKinley; for administration officials it was that Spain seemed bent on a military and not a political solution in Cuba.

No sooner did this controversy begin to fade than on February 15 an explosion sank the *Maine,* killing 266 American sailors. Although some suspected an internal fire had set off the explosion, President McKinley and his advisers believed the explosion was the result of some kind of sabotage. The navy's official monthlong investigation concluded that the explosion came from outside the ship, probably from a submerged mine. McKinley did not believe that Spain was directly responsible for the explosion. He suspected it might be the work of the same conservative, loyalist forces that had led the riots in Havana, however, which only reconfirmed his impression that Madrid was no longer able to control the situation in Cuba. The president told his friend, Republican senator Charles W. Fairbanks, that it was his "duty" to resist pressure for an "avenging blow." The nation would not "be plunged into war until it is ready for it."[160] But the administration did begin making urgent preparations for war. So did the Spanish, who not only considered war inevitable but were all but resigned to their impending defeat. The government took steps to shore up Spain's inadequate fleet in Cuban waters, while at the same time appealing to other European powers to weigh in with the Americans.

American naval officials, led by Roosevelt, watched the Spanish buildup and worried that Madrid was about to augment its fleet through the purchase of two British-made armored cruisers from Brazil. In the beginning of March, therefore, McKinley asked Congress to appropriate $50 million for national defense, to be drawn entirely from the budget surplus and to be used by the president at his discretion. The legislation passed in a day, and the United States used the money to purchase the two warships from Brazil, as well as supply ships, coal, guns, and ammunition.[161] The bold and sudden move "stunned" the Spanish, for not only did it block their acquisition of warships, it demonstrated the vast disparity between the two nations' wealth. It also revealed the domestic support behind McKinley if he chose to take the nation to war.[162]

The *Maine* explosion and subsequent navy report, along with the signs of discord in Cuba, shifted the political balance in favor of war in March. The most dramatic sign of the changing mood came when Senator Redfield Proctor, a moderate Republican known for his loyalty to party leaders and to McKinley, gave a powerful speech on the Senate floor advocating intervention. Proctor, a self-made millionaire from Vermont, had traveled to

Cuba to gather his own impressions of the situation. He had been sympathetic to the Cuban cause but went "with a strong conviction that the picture had been overdrawn; that a few cases of starvation and suffering had inspired and stimulated the press correspondents." He did not believe that two hundred thousand or more Cubans could have died of starvation and disease. What he encountered exceeded his worst imaginings. In the camps he found thousands living in tiny makeshift huts unfit for human habitation. "Torn from their homes, with foul earth, foul air, foul water, and foul food or none, what wonder that one-half have died and that one-quarter of the living are so diseased that they cannot be saved. . . . Little children are still walking about with arms and chest terribly emaciated, eyes swollen, and abdomen bloated to three times the normal size. . . . I was told by one of our consuls that they have been found dead about the markets in the morning, where they had crawled, hoping to get some stray bits of food from the early hucksters." Visiting a hospital in Havana, he saw "400 women and children . . . lying on the floors in an indescribable state of emaciation and disease, many with the scantiest covering of rags . . . sick children, naked as they came into the world; and the conditions in other cities are even worse."[163] Privately, he wrote Assistant Secretary of State Day that "all my conceptions of wrong that could be inflicted on people falls short of this reality." The infamous massacre of "St. Bartholomew's and the Inquisition seem merciful in comparison," he added, revealing how Spain's cruelty in Cuba mingled in his mind with Spanish and Catholic atrocities of the past.[164] In his speech to the Senate Proctor insisted that the issue at hand was not the *Maine* or the need for revenge. It was "the spectacle of a million and a half of people, the entire native population of Cuba, struggling for freedom and deliverance from the worst misgovernment of which I ever had knowledge."[165]

Since Proctor was known as a moderate and not a firebrand, his words carried unusual weight with those not already convinced. For many, it was the first report that had not been filtered or distorted by the American press. To listen to his speech, one senator commented, produced "a raising of the blood and temper as well as of shame that we, a civilized people, an enlightened nation, a great republic, born in a revolt against tyranny, should permit such a state of things within less than a hundred miles of our shore as that which exists in Cuba."[166] Proctor melted hearts in the financial district, too. The *Wall Street Journal* reported that the speech "converted a great many people . . . who have heretofore taken the ground that the United States had no business to interfere in a revolution on Spanish soil. These men had been among the most prominent in deploring the whole Cuban matter, but there was no question about the accuracy of Senator Proctor's statements and as many of them expressed it, they made the blood boil." As one observer of the shift in opinion noted, "With very few exceptions, the most conservative of newspapers now express the opinion that Senator Proctor's careful statement of conditions in Cuba . . . makes intervention the plain duty of the United States on the simple ground of humanity. . . . The situation in Cuba is actually intolerable."[167]

Republican leaders opposed to the war were furious at Proctor and at Illinois senator William Mason, another moderate and longtime friend of McKinley who also came out for war and brought many others with him.[168] But the common assumption was that Proctor and Mason spoke for the president and that Proctor's speech on the Senate floor had been approved at the White House. His central message—that intervention should be for humanitarian purposes, not to avenge the *Maine*—did reflect the president's view. McKinley was already telling associates privately that if war came, it had to be justified on "broader grounds."[169]

McKinley still preferred to avoid war, if he could find a way to stop the suffering in Cuba and win Spain's withdrawal without one. He explored the idea of purchasing Cuba from Spain and taking charge of it long enough to prepare the Cubans to exercise stable and orderly government. He toyed with the idea of establishing Cuban "suzerainty," in which, like the relationship between Tunis and Turkey, the Cubans would pay nominal allegiance to Spain but in practice would be independent. Neither of these ideas proved practicable. The Spanish government would not even consider selling Cuba, a move that would have sparked public outrage and perhaps even a coup. And McKinley rightly suspected that the rebels would not accept suzerainty in place of outright independence. He also devised a plan to seek $500,000 from Congress for relief of the *reconcentrados*. The delivery of the assistance, McKinley believed, would require Spain to stop fighting and open the camps. If Spain refused, he could seek authority from Congress for military action. Under those circumstances, McKinley insisted, "his conscience and the world [would] justify" armed intervention.[170]

McKinley's approach was far from what more determined interventionists would have preferred. To Roosevelt, he appeared to be temporizing unforgivably. Right up until the eve of war, he believed that McKinley was bent on peace.[171] But Roosevelt did not have the president's ear, as evidenced by his tirade at the annual Gridiron Dinner in late March, when he shook his fist at Mark Hanna and declared, "We will have this war for the freedom of Cuba in spite of the timidity of the commercial interests!"[172] He and others learned in frustration that "McKinley dominated the foreign relations of his administration; he established its policies and directed its diplomacy."[173]

This did not mean McKinley was impervious to political pressures, however. The release of the report on the *Maine* at the end of March did push him to act faster than he would have preferred. In the wake of the report rank-and-file Republicans, nervous and exasperated about having to vote against repeated pro-Cuban resolutions offered by the Democrats, threatened to bring up a measure of their own. With the fall elections approaching, the Republicans "wanted their party to assume leadership of the Cuban issue and to dispel the idea that business dictated the party's policies."[174] Lodge warned nervously, "If the war in Cuba drags on through the summer with nothing done, we shall go down in the greatest defeat ever known." He agreed that "to bring on or even threaten war for political reasons is a crime." But "to sacrifice a great party and bring free silver upon the country for a wrong policy is hardly less odious."[175]

The biggest danger for McKinley was not unpopularity, although he could not have enjoyed being burned in effigy and having his picture hissed at in theaters.[176] It was the possibility that Congress would act without him and pass legislation recognizing Cuban independence or calling for war. After barely holding back the Senate at the end of March, Vice President Garret A. Hobart warned the president, "They will act without you if you do not act at once." An angry senator confronted William Day at the State Department and asked, "Don't your president know where the war-declaring power is lodged? . . . Well tell him . . . that if he doesn't do something Congress will exercise the power and declare war in spite of him! He'll get run over and the party with him!"[177] In addition to the embarrassment this would cause, and the damage it would do to McKinley's presidential authority, such action would also destroy any hope of a diplomatic settlement and guarantee war with Spain.

This was not the only reason time was growing short, however. Administration officials believed they needed a settlement before the onset of the Cuban rainy season in May. Once the rains began, Spanish forces would no longer be able to take the offensive, and the war would drag on for another six months at least. In the meantime the hot and humid weather would bring on epidemics of yellow fever and other deadly illnesses in the reconcentration camps. Thus McKinley and his advisers had come to consider May 1 a deadline for action, which meant that Spain and the rebels had to reach some agreement in early April.[178]

At the end of March, therefore, McKinley made what amounted to his final offer. He called on Spain to declare an armistice that would last through October 1. During that time Spain and the rebels would negotiate peace, aided by the "friendly offices" of the United States. If they could not reach agreement, the United States would step in as "final arbiter." In the meantime Spain had to revoke the reconcentration order and authorize distribution of American relief supplies throughout the country. Most significantly, he also insisted that Spain grant Cuba "self-government" with a "reasonable indemnity," which as Secretary Day explained, meant "independence." If Spain agreed, McKinley promised to get the insurgents to agree.[179]

American officials pleaded with the Spanish for a rapid and favorable answer. Day cabled the U.S. minister in Madrid repeatedly: "Important to have prompt answer on armistice matter." "Feeling here is intense." In Washington he told the Spanish minister that if Spain did not agree to McKinley's plan, Congress would force the president to go to war.[180]

The Spanish, however, rejected the offer. While agreeing to revoke the reconcentration order, the Madrid government insisted that the rebels request an armistice before Spain granted one. It was clear from the response, moreover, that Spanish commanders in Cuba would have the right to determine how long the cease-fire would last. As Day put it, what Spain was offering was "not an armistice" but "simply an invitation to the insurgents to submit."[181] The Spanish also insisted that any agreement would have to await the formation of the new Cuban parliament, scheduled for May 4, thus putting off a settlement for at least another month. The Spanish ignored the offer of American "friendly offices." They also conceded nothing with regard to Cuban independence. The president, meeting with assembled advisers and Republican congressional leaders, determined that the Spanish response was inadequate. On April 1 he began preparing for what both Americans and Spaniards assumed was the inevitable war.[182]

Just as the president was preparing his message to Congress, however, the pope and the European powers intervened in a last-ditch effort to prevent war. The Spanish welcomed the international mediation. The pope was sympathetic to Catholic Spain, as were France and Austria. The Spanish, after gaining what they believed was the support of their fellow Europeans, agreed to suspend hostilities if the United States agreed to mediation. The faint sign of possible compromise in Madrid put McKinley in a quandary. The nation was preparing for war, but he was now confronted with an international gesture for peace and the possibility, however remote, that Spain would make the concessions he demanded.

McKinley therefore delayed his message to Congress, for which he was roundly condemned by the Democrats as well as by many rank-and-file

Republicans and much of the national press. The House Democratic leader Joe Bailey declared that "if the President of the United States wants two days, or if he wants two hours, to continue negotiations with the butchers of Spain, we are not ready to give him one moment longer for that purpose." A frustrated McKinley told his closest aide, "The country should understand that we are striving to make our course consistent not alone for today, but for all time. . . . The people must not be unreasonable." On April 6 ambassadors from the major European powers, led by Britain's Sir Julian Pauncefote, met with McKinley in a bit of carefully orchestrated diplomacy. In the *New York World*'s imaginary depiction of the conversation, the diplomats told McKinley: "We hope for humanity's sake you will not go to war," and the American president replied, "We hope if we do go to war you will understand that it is for humanity's sake."[183] In fact, McKinley still hoped to avoid war. Although he had not sought mediation, he welcomed the European diplomatic intervention as a way of calming public opinion and buying more time.[184]

Faced with the possibility that Spain might be relenting and considering an armistice, McKinley turned to the Cuban rebels to gain their acceptance. Spanish officials had on several occasions asked whether the United States could get the rebels to agree to anything. They had been assured by the Americans that the rebels would agree because they depended on American support—an answer that struck the Spanish as bitterly ironic, since Spain had long insisted that the rebellion would collapse without American support.[185] The more complicated truth was that while the rebels did depend on American support, this did not mean McKinley could tell them what to do. The rebel cause was enormously popular in the United States and had overwhelming support in Congress, including among Republicans, as well as in the American press. The rebels knew that Congress might recognize Cuban independence and declare war even over the president's objection. McKinley actually had little influence over them, therefore, unless he was willing to defy Congress and public opinion. As he privately complained, "We will have great trouble in satisfying the insurgents or in getting them to agree to anything—they are more difficult than Spain to deal with."[186]

This was confirmed in early April, when McKinley asked the rebels to agree to an armistice. The Cuban junta member he met with later recalled the president in an impatient mood:

> "You must," he clipped out to me, "accept an immediate armistice with Spain."
> "To what end Mr. President?"

"To settle the strife in Cuba," he cried.

"But is Spain ready to grant Cuba independence?" I asked.

"That isn't the question now," he exclaimed, his voice rising. "We may discuss that later. The thing for the moment is an armistice."[187]

The junta leader explained that an armistice without a promise of independence would be a disaster for the rebel army, which had no means of supplying or quartering itself and would therefore melt away over six months, while the Spanish army, unable to fight during the rainy season anyway, could remain in garrisons without fear of losing ground in the war. The rebels insisted they would accept an armistice only if Spain first recognized the Cuban Republic, granted independence, and began to pull out. McKinley made no further attempt to persuade them.

On April 10 the Spanish government, after consulting with the European powers, offered to declare an armistice. It dropped some but not all of the conditions the U.S. administration had found objectionable. But it still did not agree to Cuban independence. For McKinley, the offer was intriguing, but as a practical and political matter, it was too little and too late to keep him from moving toward war.[188] He did not believe he could delay his message to Congress any longer. On April 11 he formally asked Congress for authorization "to take measures to secure a full and final termination of hostilities between the Government of Spain and the people of Cuba, and to secure in the island the establishment of a stable government, capable of maintaining order and observing its international obligations, insuring peace and tranquility and the security of its citizens as well as our own, and to use the military and naval forces of the United States as may be necessary for these purposes."[189]

The clarity of McKinley's message was muddied a bit by an addendum noting Spain's recent agreement to "proclaim a suspension of hostilities." If "this measure attains a successful result," the president declared, "then our aspirations as a Christian, peace-loving people will be realized. If it fails, it will be only another justification for our contemplated action." Congress was uninterested and on April 19 passed a joint resolution recognizing Cuban independence, demanding Spain's withdrawal from the island, and authorizing the president to use force to accomplish these goals. The next day McKinley forwarded the resolution to Spain, which promptly severed relations with the United States. Congress formally declared war on April 25.

Some of McKinley's close friends and advisers would later insist that he could have avoided war if only he had been given more time. Senator John

Spooner believed that "possibly the President could have worked out the business without a war, but the current was too strong, the demagogues too numerous, and the fall elections too near."[190] McKinley's private secretary later recalled the president himself lamenting that the "declaration of war against Spain was an act which had been and will always be the greatest grief of my life. I never wanted to go to war with Spain. Had I been let alone, I could have prevented the war. All I wanted was more time."[191]

Would more time have made a difference? McKinley and some of his advisers assumed that Spain was moving inexorably toward granting Cuba independence. It needed only time and some face-saving measures in order to ease itself out. Navy Secretary John Long, who shared the frustration at the political pressure for rapid action, privately commented, "You cannot expect [Spain] to get up and get out in five minutes; but, if the history of the last six months means anything, it means constant steps toward her retirement. . . . I honestly believe that if the country and Congress had been content to leave the matter in [the president's] hands, independence would have come without a drop of bloodshed, as naturally as an apple falls from a tree."[192] If McKinley did believe that he could have "prevented war" if only he had more time, this is what he meant: that Spain would ultimately have relented and granted Cuba independence without a war.

There was and is little reason to believe that this was the case, however. There was no evidence whatever that Spain intended to let Cuba go. Spain's willingness to grant an armistice was an attempt to forestall American intervention, not the first step toward granting independence. As the U.S. minister in Madrid constantly reminded Washington, no Spanish government believed it could survive in office if it gave up Cuba without a fight. Today scholars generally agree that "Cuba was not considered a colony but an integral part of the Spanish monarchy, and therefore the predominant ideology prohibited not only the sale of the island to the United States, but also the concession of independence, at least as long as the rebel army remained in existence."[193] The rebels, meanwhile, refused to lay down their arms in the absence of Spain's commitment to independence and withdrawal. McKinley had been unwilling to compel them in early April. It is hard to see why he would have been more willing to do so six months later.

For those opposed to war, and perhaps also for the president, it may have been easier to blame the war on an inflamed public, the yellow press, and congressional "jingoes" than to acknowledge that the president's own policies had made war all but inevitable. If McKinley had wanted peace, and peace alone, there had been a way to accomplish that goal. He could have pursued a policy of nonintervention and noninterference. He could have turned a blind eye to the suffering in Cuba and allowed both Spain and the rebels to prosecute the war as they saw fit until one or both gave up in exhaustion. He could have offered Spain some advice, as Cleveland and Olney had, but he could make no demands and deliver no ultimatums on behalf of "common humanity." War came because McKinley, whatever his misgivings, pursued a policy that had a high probability of producing war. Perhaps he believed he had no choice given public opinion at home, the restiveness of both Democrats and Republicans in Congress, and the approaching midterm elections. But there is little evidence that McKinley was forced to adopt a position that he did not believe was right. While fervently wishing to avoid war, McKinley also insisted with equal fervor that Spain conduct its affairs in Cuba "consistent with humanity and the Christian spirit of this age."[194]

It was not that McKinley wanted war, or the fruits of war, as part of some expansionist or imperialist design. He was not seeking to unite the country or strengthen its character through war. He was not trying to distract attention from economic difficulties at home by fighting a war abroad. He was not trying to fulfill some late-nineteenth-century ideal of masculinity or to save a decaying civilization by instilling "barbarian virtues" through martial glory. He was not "taking up the white man's burden" by intervening in Cuba; nor was he intervening in order to gain access to markets in East Asia. McKinley did not want war at all. But he was prepared to go to war if that was what was necessary to achieve what he regarded as a moral and humanitarian imperative. "In the name of humanity," he declared to thunderous applause in the House chamber, "in the name of civilization, in behalf of endangered American interests which give us the right and the duty to speak and to act, the war in Cuba must stop." As part of a long tradition of American leaders, he appealed to the country's universalist nationalism, and as a member of the Civil War generation and a Lincoln Republican, he insisted it was "no answer to say that this is all in another country, belonging to another nation, and is therefore none of our business. . . . It is specially our duty, for it is right at our door."[195]

McKinley apparently spoke for the majority of the country, for the breadth of support for war by April 1898 was remarkable. The Spanish-American War may well have been the most popular war in American history. A majority of Republicans favored military intervention, not just the Lodges and Roosevelts but Republican moderates and even some conservatives. The tipping point within the party had come when moderate party loyalists like Proctor and Mason declared their support for intervention. Among McKinley's close circle of Republican Party leaders, only Mark

Hanna, Orville Platt, and Thomas Reed remained "absolutely and unqualifiedly opposed to war under all circumstances" right up until the end. The conservative Senator Spooner expressed his "contempt" for "the Masons and Proctors and Co." who had "embarrassed the President in his negotiations" merely "in order to draw attention to themselves." But once diplomacy had failed, Spooner confided to his son, "I am for armed intervention." The situation in Cuba "shocks our humanity, disturbs our trade, destroys our ships and sailors, costs us millions in enforcing our foreign enlistments act, keeps us upon a quasi war footing, and imperils our peace." Senator Allison gave in, too, after reading reports from his home state of Iowa, where the view, "not merely among the hotheads," was that McKinley had tarried too long. Almost everyone "seem[ed] to be anxious for war."[196]

On the other side of the partisan divide, the Democratic leadership in Congress had seized on the Cuba issue and had hoped to run on it in the coming elections. But Democratic support was more than political opportunism. Among Populists, farmers, and laborers sympathy for the Cubans was strong, and their leaders and would-be leaders reflected that sentiment. Former Illinois governor Altgeld insisted war was necessary to satisfy "the moral sense of the civilized world." The *New York Times* opined that there was "no stopping place short of the absolute independence of Cuba." William Jennings Bryan, who had been the choice of six million voters in the 1896 election and who would gain the party's nomination again in 1900, led the cry for war. He declared that "the time for intervention has arrived." War was "a terrible thing and cannot be defended except as a means to an end, and yet it is sometimes the only means by which a necessary end can be secured. . . . [W]ar is the final arbiter between nations when reason and diplomacy are of no avail."[197] When war was declared, Bryan, like Roosevelt, set out to raise a regiment and join the fight.

The war was so popular because it involved American ideals, American interests, American prejudices, and American power. The horrors of the reconcentration policy and three hundred thousand Cuban deaths outraged Americans. This was not unusual or unprecedented. Americans had also been outraged by the massacres in Armenia, the Siberian prison system, pogroms against Jews, and the repression of Poles, Hungarians, Greeks, and others throughout the nineteenth century. The difference this time was the scale of the humanitarian catastrophe and also the proximity. That so much human suffering was being inflicted so close to U.S. shores seemed intolerable, especially because Americans believed they had the power to do something about it. That was another difference from the past.

Ideals and perceived interests converged, but not around a search for markets. Americans' perceived interests were more abstract and intangible. They had arrogated to themselves the leadership of the hemisphere. Spain's conduct of the war in Cuba violated Americans' vision of the peace and harmony that should rule under America's benevolent guidance. It therefore presented something of a challenge to U.S. hemispheric leadership. It mattered a great deal that the perpetrator of the horrors in Cuba was Spain, which Americans considered a benighted, backward, barbaric nation with no legitimate right to hold a colony in the Western Hemisphere. "For me this is not simply a question of Cuba," a prominent Catholic clergyman explained. ". . . [I]t is the question of two civilizations. . . . When Spain is swept off the seas much of the meanness and narrowness of old Europe goes with it to be replaced by the freedom and openness of America."[198] Henry Cabot Lodge from the beginning of the conflict had viewed it through this ideological, civilizational lens. "If that for which the Spanish Empire has stood since the days of Charles V is right," he declared in 1895, "then everything for which the United States stands and has always stood is wrong. If the principles that we stand for are right, then the principles of which Spain has been the great exponent in history are utterly wrong."[199]

There is also no question that the prospect of driving Spain out of Cuba fit within the overall vision, best articulated by Blaine but supported by McKinley, of a hemispheric economic and political system in which the United States should be the dominant partner. Lodge spoke not only of commercial interests on the island itself but of the island's geographical importance to American regional trade and, when a canal was built, trade with Asia as well. The value of investments and trade in Cuba, while they may not have determined the direction of McKinley's policies, certainly increased the salience of the issue. But economic interests alone would not have driven Americans to war. Business leaders generally opposed war when they considered the question from a narrow economic perspective. Business interests and their representatives in Congress came to support the war only when they joined the rest of the nation in outrage at the suffering in Cuba. Powerful Louisiana sugar interests, for instance, staunchly opposed war almost until the bitter end because they feared competition from Cuban sugar producers. But they finally changed their minds when their "humanitarian concerns" took "precedence over any economic concerns."[200]

Americans since the days of Jefferson and John Quincy Adams had believed that Cuba would eventually fall "like a ripe fruit" into their laps, that the "laws of gravity" naturally drew Cuba into the American sphere of influence. As a result of the sectional conflict, northern Republicans like McKinley were no longer interested in southward territorial expansion, and the president opposed annexation. But this long tradition of covetousness did give Americans a sense of proprietary interest in Cuba and a conviction that they had a right and even an obligation to be a dominant influence on the island. There is no evidence that McKinley intervened simply because he feared the impending victory of rebels and some socialist revolution that might threaten American capitalist interests. But there is also no question that McKinley shared a common American view, which was also common among Cuban elites, that the rebels were radical and unreliable, that they had caused a good deal of the suffering in Cuba, and that they would not respect the property rights of those they suspected of being insufficiently supportive during the war. Therefore they could not be trusted to protect American interests, but more importantly they could not be trusted to protect the interests of average Cubans. McKinley and many others believed it would be irresponsible to liberate Cuba and then withdraw without making any effort to create a stable and peaceful government. He was opposed to handing Cuba over to the rebels, therefore, and also to immediate Cuban independence, which he feared would produce chaos and more violence. He believed that the Cuban people would be better off under the firm tutelage of the United States until they were ready to sustain a free and independent government.

The war with Spain was also the product of increased U.S. power. The American public's willingness to go to war had a great deal to do with the fact that most believed the United States capable of winning. Americans may, in fact, have been overconfident. Roosevelt and other navy officials did not believe American superiority guaranteed victory, and as it turned out, bad Spanish luck and bad Spanish decisions made the American victory easier than it should have been. Americans nevertheless believed they would win, and so did President McKinley. This was significant because it gave him the confidence to make the demands that he did of Spain, even though he knew those demands could lead to war. Had he believed America might lose, he would not have chosen the same course.

The belief in their nation's military superiority affected Americans' attitudes in another, more subtle, but perhaps more significant way. The fact that many believed they *could* do something to aid the Cubans helped convince them that they *should* do something, that intervention was the only honorable course. Lodge had given voice to this common sentiment frequently. As he posed the question to his Senate colleagues, "What are the duties of the United States in the presence of this war?" Cuban patriots were being slaughtered by an evil Spanish government, yet "here we stand motionless, a great and powerful country not six hours away from these scenes of useless bloodshed and destruction." The "great power" of the United States was "capable of greater things than that," he insisted. "If that war goes on in Cuba . . . the responsibility is on us; we cannot escape it." It was a question of whether the nation stood for something in world affairs. If the United States "stands for humanity and civilization, we should exercise every influence of our great country to put a stop to that war which is now raging in Cuba and give to that island once more peace, liberty, and independence."[201]

Increased power had changed the perception of Lodge and many others as to what constituted honorable behavior. Such considerations had moved Americans to fight Great Britain in 1812 because, as Calhoun had declared, what a weak America had tolerated a stronger America could no longer tolerate. In the Cuban crisis eight decades later, many people believed they did not have to stand by while Spain brutalized Cuba, and because they did not have to, they had a positive obligation not to. The difference was that in 1812 honor was defined as self-respect and the preservation of American rights. In 1898 honor was defined as the defense of moral principle, and as McKinley declared, it was "no answer to say that this is all in another country . . . [and] therefore none of our business." It was "specially our duty," just as it had been the North's duty to do something for the enslaved blacks in the South.

There were Americans who did not feel this way. The poet E. A. Robinson wrote in April 1898, "My Americanism is not at all rampant—in fact the crudeness and the general cussedness of things American makes me sick." The writer William Dean Howells wrote his sister, "I hope that you will not be surprised to hear that I think we are wickedly wrong."[202] The Speaker of the House, Thomas Reed, was disgusted and lacerated Redfield Proctor, who had made his millions quarrying marble, with the observation that "the war will make a large market for gravestones."[203] Senator Eugene Hale, who had led the fight in Congress for the construction of a new battleship navy, did not consider Cuba the place to use it. He compared the Cuban rebels to the Confederacy.[204] In the socialist journal *Coming Nation* the editors deplored the "hysteria" that they saw gripping the nation and suggested that "every congressman and senator who votes for war should be obliged to join a regiment and go to the front."[205] There were many others who considered war against Spain anything but honorable. And some worried, as Moorfield Storey did, that following a successful war over Cuba, "[w]e would be fairly launched upon a policy of military aggressions, of territorial expansion, of standing armies and growing navies, which is inconsistent with the continuance of our institutions."[206] The voices of conservatism, echoing the earlier warnings of Gresham, joined with progressive voices that spoke of international arbitration and pacifism and believed, with Thomas Reed, that "the time is not far distant when the idea of going to war to settle international difficulties will be thought as strange and out of date as we now consider many other beliefs and practices."[207]

For the much larger number of Americans who favored war, however, defending "humanity" and "civilization" was the honorable course and justified military intervention. Such sentiments had an extraordinarily diverse following. In North Carolina the *New Bern Daily Journal* declared, "The war against Spain has as its basis the real practical events of every day life,—the preservation of honor, the cause of humanity and the adjustment and maintenance of human rights."[208] The socialist editor of the *American Fabian* magazine insisted that no "humane person" could question America's duty to intervene and that history had "no record of so chivalrous and widespread an awakening in behalf of so just a cause." Another *Fabian* essayist observed that while the British "World-Titan could not stop the Armenian massacres or free Crete because of the bonds of her world empire," the United States "could and did dare . . . to redeem and rescue to self-government a sister nation." Hereafter tyrants would "oppress less violently . . . because the young democratic giant of the West" had "overstepped the bonds of its own national concerns."[209] In Cincinnati the *American Israelite,* after commenting of Spain that "a state's treatment of its Jewish population has throughout history served as a sort of moral barometer,"[210] declared for war in order "to advance the sacred cause of humanity, to release the starving people from despotic oppressors; to enlarge the territory of liberty and justice; to draw the Spanish Sennacherib from this new home of freedom and humanity."[211] William Jennings Bryan spoke not just for Populists and Democrats but for a remarkably broad cross section of Americans when he insisted, "Humanity demands that we should act."[212] From the other side of the political and ideological spectrum, the conservative Republican senator John Spooner agreed: "We intervene to put an end to savagery. . . . We intervene . . . to aid a people who has suffered every form of tyranny and who have made a desperate struggle to be free."[213]

Carl Sandburg, the child of Swedish immigrants and twenty years old at the time of the war, later recalled reading the newspapers and learning about the "people of Cuba who wanted independence and a republic. I read about Gómez, García, the Maceos, with their scrabbling little armies fighting against Weyler. They became heroes to me. I tried to figure a way to get down there and join one of those armies. I was going along with millions of other Americans who were about ready for a war to throw the Spanish government out of Cuba and let the people of Cuba have their republic." In 1898 Sandburg did volunteer to serve in the Sixth Infantry Regiment of Illinois.[214]

Within months of the war the nation would be divided in a debate over the acquisition of the Philippines, a debate that has been depicted as pitting "anti-imperialists" against "imperialists." But the decision to intervene in Cuba and to declare war against Spain in April 1898 produced a good deal less division. Some of those who would later become known as leading anti-imperialists joined those who would be labeled imperialists in support of the war. Senator George Frisbie Hoar, who would soon join the anti-imperialist cause against the acquisition of the Philippines, supported a declaration of war against Spain. "It will lead to the most honorable single war in history," he proclaimed. "It is a war in which there does not enter the slightest thought or desire of foreign conquest, or of national gain, or advantage. . . . It is entered into for the single and sole purpose that three or four hundred thousand human beings within ninety miles of our shores have been subjected to the policy intended, or at any rate having the effect, deliberately to starve them to death."[215]

Andrew Carnegie would become the best known and in some ways most important leader of the anti-imperialist movement in the United States, and he had shared the business community's nervousness about war with Spain. But on the eve of the war he joined the condemnation of Spain and declared it America's duty to liberate Cuba.[216] "No power on earth can stop the American people doing what has now become their duty—Cuba must be freed from Spanish oppression," he asserted.[217] Even Carl Schurz, who opposed the war from beginning to end, nevertheless acknowledged that it had come about because the "American people were greatly incensed at the cruel oppression suffered by the Cuban people at the hands of Spain," that it had begun as "a war of liberation, of humanity, undertaken without any selfish motive, . . . a war of disinterested benevolence"—even if it had later, in Schurz's view, degenerated into something more sinister.[218]

While most Americans believed they had gone to war out of the highest of motives, that was not how they were perceived throughout most of Europe, where the combination of American belligerence in the Venezuelan crisis followed by war with Spain produced both anxiety and hostility. Europe was still a continent of monarchies. Kaiser Wilhelm II's "first romantic impulse was to fly to the aid of Maria Cristina in defence of the monarchical principles." Even in republican France monarchists, Catholics, and conservatives sympathized with Spain, as did Russia's Tsar Nicholas II. "Monarchists and privileged social groups" across Europe "perceived U.S. democratic republicanism as a threat to the established order and thus tended to identify more easily with Spain." Even Queen Victoria was outraged at American demands for Cuban independence: "They might just as soon declare Ireland independent!"[219]

Hostility to the United States extended beyond Europe's monarchists and conservatives, however. European commentators of all ideological stripes took the occasion of the war to revive long-standing images of American "materialism, greed, vulgarity, selfishness, hypocrisy and barbarism." Spanish newspapers, of course, reviled the United States "as a nation of immigrant outcasts and avaricious shopkeepers, without culture, without honor, without a soul . . . [and as] hegemonic, materialistic hypocrites." But even outside Spain few accepted American claims that the war was for the liberation of Cuba or to relieve Cuban suffering. This was seen as more rank hypocrisy from a nation that, as German newspapers reminded their readers, had conducted "numerous cruel Indian wars and bloody persecutions of 'Negroes.' " Across Europe there was an "astonishing scarcity" of any discussion of Cuban suffering or aspirations. Coverage of the conflict was marked by "Eurocentrism"; except in Great Britain, the war was perceived as an American war not only against Spain but against all of Europe.[220]

For those liberal Europeans who had been more sympathetic to the United States and its republican and democratic principles, the war was a crushing moment. They perceived the intervention "as a betrayal of American traditions and universal values." The war "brought a sense of loss, of innocence irremediably sullied, as the American myth was shattered before their eyes." Some hoped that American policy did not reflect "the true democratic republican ideals of that nation, but the baneful influence of capitalism and/or McKinley's character." The liberal Spaniard Francisco Pi y Margall, who had opposed Spain's policies in Cuba and had once exclaimed, "Oh, America! You are my hope; it is your destiny to liberate the world," after the peace settlement lamented that this America was no more: "With McKinley's policy the freedom of the world is in danger." There was a great deal of concern in liberal internationalist circles and among peace advocates that the United States, by intervening in the internal affairs of its neighbor, had done severe damage to the international legal order.[221]

Most American historians have been no less condemnatory of the American decision for war. That the United States should have gone to war for abstract reasons—for morality, for humanitarianism, for the liberation of

others, and when "no vital American interests was involved"[222]—has baf-
fled and disturbed commentators, historians, and political scientists for a
century. Most have described the war as "unnecessary,"[223] "totally unnecessary,"[224] or "needless."[225] To explain it, they have invented national psychological disorders—mass "hysteria," "psychic crisis"—or concluded that the
entire nation had succumbed to "an emotional outburst" that "swept away
all reason."[226] Other historians have solved the problem differently, insisting
that American expressions of moral outrage and humanitarian concern were
just a cover for selfish economic interests. Perhaps the business community
did push the country to war after all, surreptitiously, and if not the business
community, then expansionists serving the interests of capitalism by seeking markets in the Western Hemisphere and in Asia. Still others have argued
that the American goal was, above all, to prevent Cuban independence and
thereby gain control of the island; that it was a war, "deliberate and by
design, for the purpose of territorial expansion." This, even though McKinley made it clear he did not want to annex Cuba and even though the United
States did not, in fact, annex it.[227]

It is a commentary on our modern understanding of the behavior of
nations that going to war for honor and in defense of abstract moral principle must be counted as either mad or disingenuous. Yet both for good and
for ill, the pursuit of honor is and always has been among the most common
of human motivations, both for individuals and for nations. Spain was certainly acting primarily for honor, not interest, when it went to war in 1898.
Were Americans so unlike other peoples that they were immune to such
considerations?

To believe that would indeed be to claim that America was exceptional,
and the idea that the war was the result of an irrational hysteria has, in fact,
served to shore up a certain strain of American exceptionalism. It has
allowed many to depict the war as an aberration and a departure from
American traditions rather than as a product of those traditions. The idea
that the United States might move deliberately into a war that was not
necessary to defend "vital interests" contradicts the myth of an isolationist and inherently passive America that responds only when threatened.
The idea that American foreign policy in this era was somehow hijacked
by expansionists or imperialists, or that an emotional and irrational public
was whipped into a frenzy by a yellow press trying to sell newspapers—
such explanations protect this image, too, in their own peculiar way. The
idea that the United States would be led into war not by bellicose "jingoes" but by a moderate, cautious, mainstream Republican who acted and
spoke on behalf of a broad cross section of Americans—such a story

clashes with a popular American self-image.[228] Yet by far the most persuasive interpretation of the war with Spain is that it was indeed undertaken primarily, though not exclusively, for humanitarian purposes, just as McKinley and everyone who supported the war claimed at the time. Americans have a tendency to look for purity of motives, both in themselves and in others. Actions are either purely selfless or purely selfish, based on tangible interests. But national motives, like personal motives, are never that simple. Many human actions originate in some blend of self-interestedness and generosity. Measured against the real world of nations and human beings, the intervention in Cuba had an unusually high degree of selflessness. When John Hay called it a "splendid little war," he meant not only that the fighting itself had been splendid; so, too, he believed, were the goals and purposes for which the war was fought.

THERE IS no good place to divide a two-volume history of American foreign policy. I have chosen to end this volume with the outbreak of the Spanish-American War and to leave the military conflict and its aftermath for the next volume. The war, like all wars, solved one set of problems but unleashed another set. The United States succeeded in putting an end to the civil war in Cuba and to the suffering of the *reconcentrados*. The intervention saved many lives, probably tens of thousands. But it left the United States saddled with the occupation of Cuba for the next four years, an occupation that ultimately produced mixed results that fell far short of most Americans' hopes and expectations when they had entered the war, as well as most Cubans' hopes and expectations. Even more unexpected was the way the war in Cuba led quickly to another, far-from-splendid war in the Philippines. Neither President McKinley nor his advisers nor the vast majority of Americans who supported the war with Spain anticipated acquiring the Philippines as part of the peace settlement, much less having to fight a brutal four-year war against a Filipino army bent on independence.[229] The consequences of America's humanitarian intervention, both intended and unintended, would produce a great debate at the close of the nineteenth century between self-described anti-imperialists and those who believed the retention of the Philippines, as well as the annexation of Hawaii and Puerto Rico, was the only responsible policy for the United States. That debate reflected the tensions and contradictions inherent in the American creed. It echoed similar debates stretching back to the birth of the nation. It also foreshadowed the debates that would recur throughout the twentieth century and into the twenty-first between those who sought to employ America's increasing power to advance American influence and principles, and those who worried about the harmful effect of such an approach both to democratic institutions at home and to peoples and nations abroad. The outbreak of the Spanish-American War launched the United States into a new phase of its history, therefore, marked by greatly increased international power, influence, and involvement, with all the moral and ethical complexities entailed in such a role.

But the war was not only a new departure: it was also a culmination, the not-illogical result of all that had come before it. It was the product of unfolding historical events and forces reaching back to before the founding of the nation. The self-appointed task of historians for the past century has been to explain the departure, to identify what changed in the American character, and a host of theories have been presented, from the economic to the political and social to the psychological. Too few, in my opinion, have seen or perhaps have wanted to see how the war was the product of deeply ingrained American attitudes toward the nation's place in the world. It was the product of a universalist ideology as articulated in the Declaration of Independence. It reflected Americans' view of themselves, stretching back to before the nation's founding, as the advance guard of civilization, leading the way against backward and barbaric nations and empires. It derived from the American experience of the eighteenth and nineteenth centuries and especially from the experience of the Civil War, that great, bloody moral crusade that so many Americans of the late nineteenth century used as their model of a "selfless" war on behalf of "humanity" and "civilization." It grew out of old and potent American ambitions, articulated by Hamilton and Jefferson, Monroe and Madison, Henry Clay and John Quincy Adams, to make the United States the "arbiter" of the Western Hemisphere, the defender of the "sister republics" against the pernicious influences of Europe, and the leader of an American system. It was fueled by the growth of military power, which shifted perceptions both of interest and of honor and of what could and could not be tolerated in the American sphere of influence. The Spanish-American War was, in short, an expression of who the American people were and what they had made of their nation.

NOTES

Introduction

1. Adams to William Plumer, January 17, 1817, in Worthington Chauncey Ford, ed., *Writings of John Quincy Adams*, 7 vols. (1913; reprint, New York: Greenwood Press, 1968), 6:143; Joseph Byrne Lockey, *Pan-Americanism: Its Beginnings* (New York: Macmillan, 1926), p. 159.

2. John Quincy Adams, *Memoirs of John Quincy Adams, Comprising Portions of His Diary from 1795 to 1848* (Philadelphia: J. B. Lippincott, 1875), 4:437–39.

3. J. Fred Rippy, *Rivalry of the United States and Great Britain over Latin America, 1808–1830* (Baltimore: Johns Hopkins University Press, 1929), pp. 92–93.

4. Secret Instructions for the Captain-General of Louisiana, November 26, 1802, quoted in Alexander DeConde, *This Affair of Louisiana* (New York: Scribner's, 1976), p. 150.

5. Baron de Carondelet, "Military Report on Louisiana and West Florida," November 24, 1794, quoted ibid., pp. 57, 59.

6. Quoted in Norman A. Graebner, *Foundations of American Foreign Policy: A Realist Appraisal from Franklin to McKinley* (Wilmington, Del.: Scholarly Resources, 1985), p. xxxii.

7. Quoted in Bradford Perkins, *The Cambridge History of American Foreign Relations*, vol. 1: *The Creation of a Republican Empire, 1776–1865* (New York: Cambridge University Press, 1993), pp. 48, 166.

Chapter 1 / *The First Imperialists*

1. Frederick Merk, *Manifest Destiny and Mission in American History: A Reinterpretation* (New York: Knopf, 1963), p. 3. This is how "mission" was distinguished from "manifest destiny" by Merk in 1963. Thirty-five years later H. W. Brands, in *What America Owes the World: The Struggle for the Soul of Foreign Policy* (Cambridge, U.K.: Cambridge University Press, 1998), distinguished between "exemplarists" and "vindicationists." Brands places Winthrop in the "exemplarist" category. This distinction still animates the debate over the proper course of American foreign policy even in the twenty-first century.

2. Felix Gilbert, *To the Farewell Address: Ideas of Early American Foreign Policy* (Princeton, N.J.: Princeton University Press, 1970), p. 4.

3. Merk, *Manifest Destiny and Mission*, pp. 261–62.

4. Isolation may have been the goal of the "Separatists" who came to Plymouth in 1620; it was not the goal of Winthrop's Puritans, who arrived a decade later.

5. As Perry Miller writes, "Any place in the world would have served. Massachusetts was only a convenient (not too convenient) platform on which the gathering might be enacted." Miller, *The New England Mind: From Colonies to Province* (Cambridge, Mass.: Harvard University Press, 1953), p. 25.

6. The Puritan fathers "were not—despite their analogies with Moses and the tribes of

Israel—refugees seeking a promised land, but English scholars, soldiers, and statesmen, taking the long way about in order that someday they, or their children, or at least their friends, might rule in Lambeth." Ibid., p. 5.

7. Ibid., p. 7.

8. Perry Miller, *Errand into the Wilderness* (Cambridge, Mass.: Belknap Press of Harvard University Press, 1956), p. 11. "[I]f the conscious intention were realized, not only would a federated Jehovah bless the new land, but He would bring back these temporary colonials to govern England."

9. This is in contrast to Gilbert's assertion that the Puritans' utopian mission "favored separation from European affairs," that their "hope of leading a more perfect life on the new continent formed a resistance to involvements with Europe." Gilbert, *To the Farewell Address,* p. 4. "Isolation is not a matter of distance or the slowness of communication," as Miller writes. "It is a question of what a dispatch from distant quarters means to the recipient. A report from Geneva, Frankfurt, Strasbourg, or Leiden might take months to reach John Cotton or Thomas Hooker, but either comprehended it immediately, not as a tale from foreign parts, but as something intimately concerning them." Miller, *New England Mind,* p. 6.

10. "What tormented Winthrop was not that New England failed," Miller notes, "but that the brethren in England rejected the lesson." Miller, *New England Mind,* pp. 8–9.

11. Ibid., pp. 36–37.

12. Bernard Bailyn, *The New England Merchants in the Seventeenth Century* (Cambridge, Mass.: Harvard University Press, 1979), pp. 139–42.

13. Jack P. Greene, *Pursuits of Happiness: The Social Development of Early Modern British Colonies and the Formation of American Culture* (Chapel Hill: University of North Carolina Press, 1988), pp. 195–96.

14. George M. Marsden, *Jonathan Edwards: A Life* (New Haven, Conn.: Yale University Press, 2003), p. 199.

15. "Calvinist revivalists, such as Edwards himself, were part of the eighteenth-century revolution that accentuated individual choice and subverted the authority even of many Reformed churches and clergy." Ibid., pp. 439, 438.

16. Jack P. Greene, *The Intellectual Construction of America: Exceptionalism and Identity from 1492 to 1800* (Chapel Hill: University of North Carolina Press, 1993), p. 114.

17. Greene, *Pursuits of Happiness,* p. 5.

18. Edmund S. Morgan, *American Slavery, American Freedom: The Ordeal of Colonial Virginia* (New York: Norton, 1975), p. 129.

19. There is a historical debate over exactly how "liberal" and "modern" colonial American society may have been. Some historians argue that the colonies were in fact hierarchical, class-conscious, and thus premodern and preliberal prior to the Revolution. For the best explication of this view, see Gordon Wood, *The Radicalism of the American Revolution* (New York: Knopf, 1992).

20. "American foreign policy has a vocabulary all its own, consciously—even ostentatiously—side-stepping the use of terms that would even hint at aggression or imperial domination." Richard W. Van Alstyne, *Rising American Empire* (New York: Oxford University Press, 1960), p. 7. This point was also made by William Appleman Williams, although he was referring chiefly to discussions of twentieth-century American foreign policy. See William Appleman Williams, "The Frontier Thesis and American Foreign Policy," *Pacific Historical Review* 24 (November 1955): 379–95.

21. *The Records of the Virginia Company of London,* ed. Susan M. Kingbury (Washington, D.C., 1906–35), quoted in Morgan, *American Slavery, American Freedom,* p. 47.

22. Philip L. Barbour, ed., *The Jamestown Voyages Under the First Charter, 1606–1609,* Works issued by the Hakluyt Society, 2nd ser., 136, 137 (Cambridge, U.K., 1969), quoted ibid., p. 46. "The Virginia Company thought of the enterprise as something like the

conversion of the primitive Britons by the Romans. Without the civilizing influence of the Romans, England itself would still be populated by heathen savages just as America still was. . . . Although they hoped for profits, theirs was a patriotic enterprise that would bring civility and Christianity to the savages of North America and redemption from idleness and crime to the unemployed masses of England." Morgan, *American Slavery, American Freedom*, p. 47.

23. Greene, *Intellectual Construction of America*, p. 119.

24. Alexander C. Fraser, ed., *The Works of George Berkeley, D.D.*, 4 vols. (Oxford: Clarendon Press, 1901), 4:364–65.

25. Jack P. Greene, "Empire and Identity from the Glorious Revolution to the American Revolution," in *The Oxford History of the British Empire*, vol. 2: *The Eighteenth Century*, ed. P. J. Marshall (Oxford: Oxford University Press, 1998), p. 218; Linda Colley, *Britons: Forging the Nation, 1707–1837* (New Haven, Conn.: Yale University Press, 1992), p. 15.

26. Robert A. Williams, Jr., *The American Indian in Western Legal Thought: The Discourse of Conquest* (New York: Oxford University Press, 1990), quoted in Greene, "Empire and Identity," p. 219.

27. "Part of the mission of New England's 'city on the hill' was to advertise the civility of the English colonists and to hold it in stark contrast with the barbarous cruelty of Spain's conquistadors and the false and blasphemous impiety of France's Jesuit missionaries." Jill Lepore, *The Name of War: King Philip's War and the Origins of American Identity* (New York: Knopf, 1998), p. 9.

28. Richard Hakluyt, "Discourse on Western Planting" (1584), quoted in Jack P. Greene, ed., *Settlements to Society, 1607–1763: A Documentary History of Colonial America* (New York: Norton, 1975), pp. 7–8.

29. Marsden, *Jonathan Edwards*, p. 385.

30. John M. Murrin, "Beneficiaries of Catastrophe: The English Colonies in America," in Eric Foner, ed., *The New American History* (Philadelphia: Temple University Press, 1990), p. 19.

31. Bruce P. Lenman, "Colonial Wars and Imperial Instability," in Marshall, *Oxford History*, 2:152.

32. This was the "great defect in English missions to the Native Americans and why they were so much less successful than their French counterparts. The English were almost always trying to settle the territories where they evangelized. Heroic French Jesuit missionaries who went to live among the Indians presented little immediate threat to the natives' territories or interests." Marsden, *Jonathan Edwards*, p. 407.

33. Greene, *Intellectual Construction of America*, pp. 109, 106, 116.

34. Hans Kohn, *American Nationalism* (New York: Collier Books, 1961), p. 26.

35. For the importance of "honor" and its relationship to property in early American society, see Bertram Wyatt-Brown, *Southern Honor: Ethics and Behavior in the Old South* (New York: Oxford University Press, 1982), pp. 72–73.

36. Stanley Elkins and Eric McKitrick, *The Age of Federalism: The Early American Republic, 1788–1800* (New York: Oxford University Press, 1993), p. 36.

37. James Thomas Flexner, *George Washington: The Forge of Experience, 1732–1775* (New York: Little, Brown, 1965), p. 289.

38. Fred Anderson, *The Crucible of War: The Seven Years' War and the Fate of Empire in British North America, 1754–1766* (New York: Knopf, 2000), p. 739.

39. "If we add up the acreages of western land which Jefferson made at least initial attempts to acquire from 1769 to 1777, we find that they total a substantial amount: about 35,000 acres. . . . All of this land lay west of the Appalachians on waters flowing into the Ohio River." Anthony F. C. Wallace, *Jefferson and the Indians: The Tragic Fate of the*

First Americans (Cambridge, Mass.: Belknap Press of Harvard University Press, 1999), pp. 38–39.

40. Gerald Stourzh, *Benjamin Franklin and American Foreign Policy* (Chicago: University of Chicago Press, 1954), p. 96.

41. Marsden, *Jonathan Edwards,* pp. 466, 467.

42. Ibid., pp. 315, 197.

43. See Richard Koebner, *Empire* (New York: Grosset & Dunlap, 1965), pp. 86–93.

44. "Men like Washington and Franklin . . . would have liked nothing better than to pursue honor, wealth, and power within the British imperial framework." Anderson, *Crucible of War,* p. 745.

45. Stourzh, *Franklin and American Foreign Policy,* p. 44.

46. Koebner, *Empire,* pp. 106–7.

47. David Armitage, *The Ideological Origins of the British Empire* (Cambridge, U.K.: Cambridge University Press, 2000), p. 138.

48. Koebner, *Empire,* p. 86.

49. Colin Jones, *The Great Nation: France from Louis XV to Napoleon* (New York: Penguin, 2002), p. 133.

50. Thomas Gage quoted in Richard A. White, *The Middle Ground: Indians, Empires and Republics in the Great Lakes Region, 1650–1815* (New York: Cambridge University Press, 1991), p. 340.

51. Marsden, *Jonathan Edwards,* pp. 310, 312, 314.

52. Alan Taylor, *American Colonies* (New York: Viking, 2001), p. 426.

53. Stourzh, *Franklin and American Foreign Policy,* p. 43.

54. Ibid., p. 42.

55. Theodore Draper, *A Struggle for Power: The American Revolution* (New York: Crown, 1995), p. 159.

56. Albany Congress, "Representation of the Present State of the Colonies," July 9, 1751, in *The Papers of Benjamin Franklin,* ed. Leonard W. Larabee et al., 28 vols. (New Haven, Conn.: Yale University Press, 1959–), 5:366–74.

57. Stourzh, *Franklin and American Foreign Policy,* pp. 62–63.

58. "Plan for Settling Two Western Colonies in North America, with Reasons for the Plan," in *The Writings of Benjamin Franklin Collected and Edited with a Life and Introduction by Albert Henry Smyth,* ed. Albert Henry Smyth, 10 vols. (New York: Haskell House, 1970), 3:359.

59. Stourzh, *Franklin and American Foreign Policy,* pp. 60, 62, 59, 66.

60. Taylor, *American Colonies,* p. 432.

61. Anderson, *Crucible of War,* p. 412.

62. Marsden, *Jonathan Edwards,* pp. 383, 387, 408–9.

63. Anderson, *Crucible of War,* p. 375.

64. Taylor, *American Colonies,* p. 437.

65. Anderson, *Crucible of War,* p. 373.

66. Stourzh, *Franklin and American Foreign Policy,* p. 70.

67. Draper, *Struggle for Power,* pp. 9–10, 8.

68. Stourzh, *Franklin and American Foreign Policy,* p. 71.

69. Ibid., p. 79.

70. Ibid., p. 81.

71. Draper, *Struggle for Power,* pp. 44, 79, 15.

72. Gordon Wood, following Bernard Bailyn, has attributed the colonists' great fear on this point to their familiarity with a body of thought about the corruption of the English constitution set forth by the so-called commonwealthmen of early-to-mid-eighteenth-century

British politics. See Wood, *Radicalism of the American Revolution,* and also Bernard Bailyn, *The Ideological Origins of the American Revolution* (Cambridge, Mass.: Harvard University Press, 1967).

73. Anderson, *Crucible of War,* p. 571.

74. "The Examination of Doctor Benjamin Franklin &c., in the British House of Commons, Relative to the Repeal of the American Stamp Act, in 1766," in Smyth, *Writings of Franklin,* 4:438–39; Stourzh, *Franklin and American Foreign Policy,* pp. 91–92.

75. Stourzh, *Franklin and American Foreign Policy,* p. 91.

76. Thomas Paine, campaigning for republican revolution a few years later, made a point of arguing that one virtue of independence from England would be to avoid again being "dragged" into any more of Great Britain's wars. "And somehow or other," Richard Van Alstyne writes, "the succession of wars between 1689 and 1763, in all of which American territorial questions had been major issues, went down in American history books as private wars of the kings of England." Van Alstyne, *Rising American Empire,* p. 22.

77. Bradford Perkins, *The Cambridge History of American Foreign Relations,* vol. 1: *The Creation of a Republican Empire, 1776–1865* (New York: Cambridge University Press, 1993), p. 23.

78. Koebner, *Empire,* pp. 206, 207, 225, 234, 215.

79. Draper, *Struggle for Power,* p. 18.

80. Ibid., p. 182.

81. David Ramsay, *The History of the American Revolution,* 2 vols. (Philadelphia, 1789; reprint, ed. Lester H. Cohen, New York: Russell & Russell, 1968), 1:33–34.

82. Andrew Burnaby, *Travels Through the Middle Settlements in North America in the Years 1759 and 1760, with Observations upon the State of the Colonies* (New York: A. M. Kelly, 1970), p. 149.

83. John J. McCusker and Russell R. Menard, *The Economy of British America, 1607–1789* (Chapel Hill: University of North Carolina Press, 1985), pp. 51–60, 280–81.

84. Draper, *Struggle for Power,* pp. 129–30, 451.

85. Quoted in Gilbert, *To the Farewell Address,* p. 106.

86. Richard Middleton, *Colonial America: A History, 1585–1776* (Oxford: Blackwell, 1998), p. 397.

87. Draper, *Struggle for Power,* p. 110.

88. Anderson, *Crucible of War,* p. 740.

89. Peter S. Onuf, *Jefferson's Empire: The Language of American Nationhood* (Charlottesville: University Press of Virginia, 2000), p. 22.

90. Taylor, *American Colonies,* p. 442.

91. Quoted in Langley, *Americas in the Age of Revolution,* p. 14.

92. Benjamin Franklin, "To Lord Kames, 11 April 1767," in Smyth, *Writings of Franklin,* 5:21.

93. Stourzh, *Franklin and American Foreign Policy,* p. 98.

94. John Trumbull, *An Essay on the Use and Advantages of the Fine Arts* (New Haven, Conn.: T. and S. Green, 1770), pp. 13–15.

95. Alexander Hamilton, *The Papers of Alexander Hamilton,* ed. Harold C. Syrett and Jacob E. Cooke, 27 vols. (New York: Columbia University Press, 1961–87), 1:129.

96. Trumbull, *Fine Arts,* pp. 5–7.

97. Hugh Henry Brackenridge and Philip Freneau, *A Poem on the Rising Glory of America* (Philadelphia, 1772), quoted in Ellis, "Culture and Capitalism," p. 174.

98. Stourzh, *Franklin and American Foreign Policy,* p. 99.

99. To understand the Americans' view of their place in the world in the eighteenth century, Ellis notes, it is necessary to "recover a fresh appreciation of the exciting, almost magi-

cal, possibilities that presented themselves when eighteenth-century Americans began to think about the unprecedented productivity that would result if the energies of ordinary Americans were released on the world." Ellis, "Culture and Capitalism," p. 180.

100. Stiles quoted in Edmund S. Morgan, *The Gentle Puritan: A Life of Ezra Stiles, 1727–1795* (New Haven, Conn.: Yale University Press, 1962), p. 214.

101. Ellis, "Culture and Capitalism," p. 174.

102. Thucydides, *The Peloponnesian War,* trans. Rex Warner, 2 vols. (New York: Viking Penguin, 1985), 1:70.

103. Draper, *Struggle for Power,* p. 514.

104. *A Charge on the Rise of the American Empire,* delivered by the Hon. William Henry Drayton, Esq., Chief Justice of South Carolina, to the grand jury for the District of Charlestown (1776), rare book in the Henry E. Huntington Library, San Marino, Calif., quoted in Van Alstyne, *Rising American Empire,* p. 1.

Chapter 2 / *The Foreign Policy of Revolution*

1. As the historian Walter LaFeber has written, "The early quests for wealth, personal salvation, westward empire, control of the world's centers of political and economic power, and supremacy in technology led to both the settlement of America and its rise as the globe's superpower." LaFeber, *The American Age: United States Foreign Policy at Home and Abroad Since 1750* (New York: Norton, 1989), p. 8.

2. See Forrest McDonald, *States' Rights and the Union: Imperium in Imperio, 1776–1876* (Lawrence: University Press of Kansas, 2000), p. 7.

3. Peter S. Onuf, *Jefferson's Empire: The Language of American Nationhood* (Charlottesville: University Press of Virginia, 2000), p. 7.

4. "When the highest English authorities disagreed on what Americans claimed as English rights, and when the Americans ceased to be English by abjuring their King, they were obliged to find another and less ethnocentric or merely historical principle of justification. They now called their rights the rights of man." Robert Roswell Palmer, *The Age of the Democratic Revolution: A Political History of Europe and America, 1760–1800* (Princeton, N.J.: Princeton University Press, 1959), p. 235. As Forrest McDonald puts it, "When the decision for independence was made, all claims to rights that were based upon royal grants, the common law, and the British constitution became theoretically irrelevant." McDonald, *Novus Ordo Seclorum: The Intellectual Origins of the Constitution* (Lawrence: University Press of Kansas, 1985), p. 58.

5. Ron Chernow, *Alexander Hamilton* (New York: Penguin, 2004), p. 60.

6. Hans Kohn, *American Nationalism* (New York: Collier Books, 1961), p. 21.

7. Dexter Perkins, *The American Approach to Foreign Policy* (Cambridge, Mass.: Harvard University Press, 1952), p. 10.

8. Kohn, *American Nationalism,* p. 25.

9. William Appleman Williams, *Empire as a Way of Life: An Essay on the Causes and Character of America's Present Predicament, Along with a Few Thoughts About an Alternative* (New York: Oxford University Press, 1980), p. 41.

10. Quoted in Bernard Bailyn, *The Ideological Origins of the American Revolution* (Cambridge, Mass.: Harvard University Press, 1967), pp. 236, 243–44.

11. Henry Wiencek, *An Imperfect God: George Washington, His Slaves, and the Creation of America* (New York: Farrar, Straus & Giroux, 2003), pp. 192, 244–45, 197, 223.

12. New Hampshire representative William Whipple declared the plan would "lay a foundation for the Abolition of Slavery in America." Ibid., p. 232.

13. Ibid., pp. 220, 272, 352.

14. Joel Barlow, *A Letter to the National Convention of France* (New York, 1793),

quoted in James A. Field, Jr., *America and the Mediterranean World, 1776–1882* (Princeton, N.J.: Princeton University Press, 1969), p. 13.

15. Adams address of July 4, 1821, quoted in Walter LaFeber, ed., *John Quincy Adams and American Continental Empire: Letters, Papers, and Speeches* (Chicago: Quadrangle Books, 1965), p. 45.

16. David Ramsay, *The History of American Revolution*, ed. Lester H. Cohen, 2 vols. (1789; reprint, New York: Russell & Russell, 1968), 1:330–31.

17. Jefferson to Adams, October 28, 1813, in *The Adams-Jefferson Letters: The Complete Correspondence Between Thomas Jefferson and Abigail and John Adams*, ed. Lester J. Cappon (Chapel Hill: University of North Carolina Press, 1988), p. 391.

18. Robert L. Middlekauff, "Why Men Fought in the American Revolution," *Huntington Library Quarterly* 43 (Spring 1980), excerpted in Richard D. Brown, ed., *Major Problems in the Era of the American Revolution, 1760–1791* (Lexington, Mass.: D. C. Heath, 1992), p. 599.

19. Quoted in Edward Handler, *America and Europe in the Political Thought of John Adams* (Cambridge, Mass.: Harvard University Press, 1964), p. 102.

20. See Felix Gilbert, *To the Farewell Address: Ideas of Early American Foreign Policy* (Princeton, N.J.: Princeton University Press, 1970), p. 55.

21. Adams to T. Digges, May 13, 1780, in *The Works of John Adams, Second President of the United States*, ed. Charles Francis Adams, 10 vols. (Boston: Little, Brown, 1850–56), 7:168.

22. Ibid. Handler is quick to warn, "These expressions would be misunderstood . . . if they were taken to imply any sense of obligation to proselytize directly for American liberty among other nations" (*Political Thought of John Adams*, p. 102). This was the singular preoccupation of foreign policy "realists" in the twentieth century.

23. Bradford Perkins, *The Cambridge History of American Foreign Relations*, vol. 1: *The Creation of a Republican Empire* (New York: Cambridge University Press, 1993), p. 9.

24. Palmer, *Age of Democratic Revolution*, pp. 257, 239.

25. Thomas Pownall, *A Memorial most humbly adressed to the Sovereigns of Europe* (London, 1780), pp. 3–4, 77; Gilbert, *To the Farewell Address*, p. 109.

26. The Revolution "showed, or was assumed to show, that ideas of the rights of man and the social contract, of liberty and equality, of responsible citizenship and popular sovereignty, of religious freedom, freedom of thought and speech, separation of powers and deliberately contrived written constitutions, need not remain in the realm of speculation, among the writers of books, but could be made the actual fabric of public life among real people, in this world, now." Palmer, *Age of Democratic Revolution*, pp. 239–40.

27. "It was the American war that precipitated the abortive revolution known as the [Dutch] Patriot movement." Ibid., pp. 325, 242.

28. Simon Schama, *Citizens: A Chronicle of the French Revolution* (New York: Knopf, 1989), p. 48.

29. G. Steiner, ed., *Korrespondenz des Peter Ochs* (Basel, 1927), quoted in Palmer, *Age of Democratic Revolution*, p. 242.

30. Palmer, *Age of Democratic Revolution*, pp. 243, 282.

31. It "provided the Caribbean with a political ideology that struck directly at empire and, by implication, at the social and economic institutions of empire." Lester D. Langley, *The Americas in the Age of Revolution, 1750–1850* (New Haven, Conn.: Yale University Press, 1996), p. 89. Francisco de Miranda, after flirting for several years with the ideology of the French Revolution, ultimately condemned it as "fatal to the peace and progress" of Spanish America. "May God deliver us from Jacobin principles as from the plague!" he wrote in 1796. Quoted in Francisco A. Encina, "The Limited Influence of the French Revolution," in R. A. Humphreys and John Lynch, eds., *The Origins of the Latin American Revolutions, 1808–1826* (New York: Knopf, 1965), p. 107.

32. Langley, *Americas in the Age of Revolution*, p. 162.

33. Willard Sterne Randall, *Thomas Jefferson: A Life* (New York: Holt, 1993), p. 460.

34. Langley, *Americas in the Age of Revolution*, pp. 162–63, 164.

35. Schama, *Citizens*, p. 24.

36. French aid to America proved "profoundly subversive and irreversible." Ibid., p. 47.

37. Randall, *Thomas Jefferson*, pp. 483, 486.

38. Grenville quoted in Lloyd C. Gardner, Walter LaFeber, and Thomas J. McCormick, *Creation of the American Empire* (Chicago: Rand McNally, 1976), p. 50.

39. Adams to Benjamin Rush, August 28, 1811, in C. F. Adams, *Works of John Adams*, 9:635.

40. See Michael H. Hunt, *Ideology and U.S. Foreign Policy* (New Haven, Conn.: Yale University Press, 1988), pp. 95–97.

41. Stanley Elkins and Eric McKitrick, *The Age of Federalism: The Early American Republic, 1788–1800* (New York: Oxford University Press, 1993), p. 309.

42. Hamilton to Washington, September 15, 1790, in Gilbert Lycan, *Alexander Hamilton and American Foreign Policy* (Norman: University of Oklahoma Press, 1970), p. 134.

43. Richard B. Morris, ed., *Alexander Hamilton and the Founding of the Nation* (New York: Dial Press, 1957), p. 124.

44. Washington to Catherine Macaulay Graham, January 9, 1790, in *The Writings of George Washington from the Original Manuscript Sources, 1745–1799*, ed. John C. Fitzpatrick, 39 vols. (Washington, D.C.: U.S. Government Printing Office, 1931–44), 30:497.

45. Elkins and McKitrick, *Age of Federalism*, p. 310. As Garry Wills relates, Pickering, before the Jay Treaty, "had been a Francophile." He "hailed the French Revolution as the legitimate heir to America's revolution—he even approved of the execution of King Louis XVI and Marie Antoinette." He changed his views, according to Wills, because of domestic concerns. "After he saw the tactics used by Jefferson and Madison to sabotage the treaty, he swung violently against the pro-French party in America." Wills, *"Negro President": Jefferson and the Slave Power* (New York: Houghton Mifflin, 2003), p. 31.

46. Adams was "unique among American statesmen in never having given his heart to that Revolution at any point." Handler, *Political Thought of John Adams*, p. 98.

47. As Elkins and McKitrick argue, "There was an odd paradox in Adams's attitude about revolutions in countries other than America. . . . On the one hand, America's experience was unique. No other people could be expected to duplicate it; the French were not wholly prepared for the degree of liberty which the Americans had achieved. On the other hand, if they *should* make an effort in that direction (Adams was certainly not disposed to deny their right to do it), the only imaginable model was America. Whatever they did, then, would somehow be judged by the extent to which it did or did not approximate the American model." Elkins and McKitrick, *Age of Federalism*, p. 313.

48. Handler, eager to protect the "realist" Adams from charges of ideological zeal, writes about this episode, "If he came close in Holland to exerting direct influence on a revolutionary movement, his activity was prompted less by a missionary impulse to propagate revolution than by zeal to promote his country's interests." Handler, *Political Thought of John Adams*, p. 110. What may be more to the point, however, is precisely how congruous were American interests and American ideological affinities at this time.

49. Adams quoted in Handler, *Political Thought of John Adams*, p. 112.

50. "The news that republican principles were exportable ended Americans' sense of isolation and helped legitimate the lawless, indeed treasonable, cause that the Declaration of Independence had sought to defend." David Brion Davis, "American Equality and Foreign Revolutions," *Journal of American History* 76, no. 3 (December 1989): 737, 735.

51. "The [French] Revolution began at the very moment at which America, having already shown the world with its own Revolution what a liberty-loving people could do, was

venturing upon its career as a constitutional republic in 1789, still needing every sanction of legitimacy it could lay hold of for its past and present course, and for its very character." Elkins and McKitrick, *Age of Federalism,* pp. 309, 310.

52. Davis, "American Equality and Foreign Revolutions," pp. 739–41.

53. Quoted in Perkins, *Creation of a Republican Empire,* p. 48.

54. Franklin to the Chevalier de Chastellux, April 6, 1782, in Smyth, *Writings of Franklin,* 8:416.

55. Frederick W. Marks III, *Independence on Trial: Foreign Affairs and the Making of the Constitution* (Baton Rouge: Louisiana State University Press, 1973), p. 23.

56. Adams to Jay, October 17, 1785, in C. F. Adams, *Works of John Adams,* 8:323.

57. Jefferson to Nathanael Greene, January 12, 1785, in *The Writings of Thomas Jefferson,* ed. Paul Leicester Ford, 10 vols. (New York: G. P. Putnam's Sons, 1894), 4:25.

58. Adams to the president of Congress, September 5, 1783, in C. F. Adams, *Works of John Adams,* 8:145.

59. John Jay quoted in Richard B. Morris, *The Peacemakers: The Great Powers and American Independence* (New York: Harper & Row, 1983), p. 306; Norman A. Graebner, *Foundations of American Foreign Policy: A Realist Appraisal from Franklin to McKinley* (Wilmington, Del.: Scholarly Resources, 1985), p. xxxi.

60. Smith and Lee quoted in Marks, *Independence on Trial,* p. 115.

61. Quoted in Samuel Flagg Bemis, *The American Secretaries of State and Their Diplomacy, 1776–1925,* vol. 1: *John Jay, Secretary for Foreign Affairs for the Continental Congress, September 21, 1784, to September 15, 1789* (New York: Knopf, 1927–29), p. 262.

62. Washington to Benjamin Harrison, October 10, 1784, in Fitzpatrick, *Writings of Washington,* 27:475.

63. Marks, *Independence on Trial,* pp. 102–3.

64. The Federalist no. 4, in Clinton Rossiter, ed., *The Federalist Papers: Alexander Hamilton, James Madison, John Jay* (New York: New American Library, 1961), pp. 48–49.

65. Gilbert, *To the Farewell Address,* p. 89. The continuing influence of Gilbert's argument can be seen in the recently published *Cambridge History,* in which Bradford Perkins presents Gilbert's thesis. See Perkins, *Creation of Republican Empire,* pp. 22–23.

66. Paul A. Varg, *Foreign Policies of the Founding Fathers* (East Lansing: Michigan State University Press, 1963), pp. 2–4.

67. Gilbert, *To the Farewell Address,* pp. 17, 89.

68. Quoted in Stourzh, *Franklin and American Foreign Policy,* p. 12.

69. Resolution introduced in the Continental Congress by Richard Henry Lee (Virginia) proposing a Declaration of Independence, June 7, 1776, in *Journals of the Continental Congress, 1774–1779,* ed. Worthington Chauncey Ford (Washington, D.C.: U.S. Government Printing Office, 1905).

70. Few members of Congress agreed with Adams's initial view that French aid could be gained for nothing.

71. Gilbert, *To the Farewell Address,* pp. 44–49.

72. Quoted in Samuel Flagg Bemis, *The Diplomacy of the American Revolution,* rev. ed. (Bloomington: Indiana University Press, 1957), p. 35.

73. American negotiators were instructed to warn France that, should they be deceived in thinking that the United States could not fight on its own, "it will be proper for you to press for the immediate and explicit declaration of France in our Favour, upon a Suggestion that a Re-union with Great Britain may be the Consequence of a delay." Ibid., p. 47.

74. Adams to James Warren, August 4, 1778, in *Warren-Adams Letters: Being Chiefly a Correspondence Among John Adams, Samuel Adams, and James Warren,* 2 vols. (Boston, 1925), 2:40; John Adams to Samuel Adams, July 28, 1778, in *The Revolutionary Diplomatic*

Correspondence of the United States, ed. Francis Wharton, 6 vols. (Washington, D.C.: U.S. Government Printing Office, 1889), 2:668.

75. The argument that Americans meant something different by the term "alliance" is advanced by Gilbert, in *To the Farewell Address,* pp. 44–47.

76. Perkins, *Creation of Republican Empire,* p. 31.

77. Chernow, *Alexander Hamilton,* p. 254.

78. Perkins, *Creation of Republican Empire,* p. 23. According to Perkins, Americans' insecurities about their inability to conduct secret and deceptive diplomacy convinced them that "isolation was the only safe course, the only way to avoid exploitation and perhaps even wars of no real concern to the United States but dangerous to independence and happiness."

79. This point is made well in Graebner, *Foundations of Foreign Policy,* pp. 71–74.

80. See James H. Hutson, "Intellectual Foundations of Early American Diplomacy," *Diplomatic History* 1, no. 1 (Winter 1977): 13.

81. *Warren-Adams Letters,* 2:192, cited ibid.

82. Jefferson to Edward Carrington, December 21, 1787, in *The Papers of Thomas Jefferson,* ed. Julian P. Boyd et al., 24 vols. (Princeton, N.J.: Princeton University Press, 1974), 12:447.

83. Gilbert argues that American views of commerce were shaped by the thinking of the French Physiocrats, who believed, as many European liberals would again in the late nineteenth century, that free trade must create an international harmony of interests, and that mutual interests in increasing wealth would mean "there would be no advantage in enlarging one's own territory and combating one's neighbor." Gilbert, *To the Farewell Address,* pp. 63–64.

84. Merrill Jensen, *The New Nation: A History of the United States During the Confederation, 1781–1789* (New York: Vintage Books, 1962), pp. 154, 156.

85. Chernow, *Alexander Hamilton,* p. 253.

86. Jefferson to G. K. van Hogendorp, October 13, 1785, in Boyd et al., *Papers of Jefferson,* 8:633.

87. Adams to Jay, August 10, 1785, in C. F. Adams, *Works of John Adams,* 8:298–99.

88. Adams quoted in Gerald Stourzh, *Alexander Hamilton and the Idea of Republican Government* (Stanford, Calif.: Stanford University Press, 1970), p. 253.

89. Adams to Jefferson, August 7, 1785, in Boyd et al., *Papers of Jefferson,* 8:354–55.

90. Adams to Jay, December 6, 1785, in C. F. Adams, *Works of John Adams,* 8:357.

91. Jefferson to Charles van Hogendorp, October 13, 1785, quoted in Hutson, "Intellectual Foundations of Early American Diplomacy," p. 8.

92. Adams to Jay, December 6, 1785, in C. F. Adams, *Works of John Adams,* 8:357.

93. The Model Treaty "adopted as ideals the dicta of small-navy belligerents and neutrals" the world over in the eighteenth century. Bemis, *Diplomacy of American Revolution,* pp. 164, 46.

94. Vattel quoted in Stourzh, *Alexander Hamilton,* p. 134.

95. Reginald C. Stuart, *War and American Thought: From the Revolution to the Monroe Doctrine* (Kent, Ohio: Kent State University Press, 1982), p. 16.

96. Chernow, *Alexander Hamilton,* p. 256.

97. Jefferson to James Monroe, November 11, 1784, in Boyd et al., *Papers of Jefferson,* 7:511–13.

98. Graebner, *Foundations of Foreign Policy,* pp. 40–41.

99. John Jay to Marquis de Lafayette, February 16, 1787, in *Diplomatic Correspondence of the United States of America, from the Signing of the Definitive Treaty of Peace, September 10, 1783, to the Adoption of the Cost, March 4, 1789,* 3 vols. (Washington, D.C., 1837), 1:321.

100. Marks, *Independence on Trial,* p. 44.

101. Stuart, *War and American Thought,* p. xiv.

102. Adams to Cotton Tufts, May 26, 1786, in C. F. Adams, *Works of John Adams,* 9:549.

103. See Marks, *Independence on Trial,* pp. 24–25.

104. Chernow, *Alexander Hamilton,* p. 435.

105. Jefferson to Madison, August 28, 1789, in Boyd et al., *Papers of Thomas Jefferson,* 10:367.

106. Adams to Secretary Livingston, February 5, 1783, in C. F. Adams, *Works of John Adams,* 8:35.

107. Gilbert labors to square Adams's desire for a commerce-only relationship with France in 1776, and later in 1783, with his support for an alliance with France in 1778 by suggesting that Adams's understanding of the meaning of "alliance" was more flexible than our own. A more reasonable explanation would be expedience. Adams did not realize how much he would need French help in 1776. He realized it in 1778. And when that help had served its purpose by 1783, he took a different view of the alliance. See Gilbert, *To the Farewell Address,* pp. 44–48.

108. Jay quoted in Marks, *Independence on Trial,* p. 29.

109. Graebner, *Foundations of Foreign Policy,* p. 66.

110. Bradford Perkins, following Gilbert, argues, "This did not mean that Congress rejected Paine's isolationist views, for in contemporary usage the word 'alliance' had a far looser meaning than it does today, encompassing mere treaties of commerce as well as political connections and military guarantees." Perkins, *Creation of Republican Empire,* p. 24.

111. Some historians argue that Hamilton made no such distinction, and for evidence they cite Federalist no. 6. There he takes issue with the Anti-Federalist claim that "the genius of republics" is "pacific," and that the "spirit of commerce has a tendency to soften the manners of men and to extinguish those inflammable humours which have so often kindled into wars." Hamilton attacks these "idle theories" as absurd and insists that commercial republics, like the states, were just as prone to war among themselves as any other type of regime. According to Gerald Stourzh, Federalist nos. 6–9 made up "the very core of Hamilton's theory of the primacy of foreign policy." See Stourzh, *Alexander Hamilton,* p. 149. According to Gilbert, this "section on foreign policy represented a frontal attack on utopianism in foreign policy." See Gilbert, *To the Farewell Address,* p. 112. Hamilton, however, did not consider nos. 6–9 to be a "section on foreign policy." On the contrary, he explains that while the three previous essays by John Jay had been about "the dangers to which we should be exposed, in state of disunion, from the arms and arts of foreign nations," Hamilton intended nos. 6–9 to address the dangers of "dissensions between the States themselves and from domestic factions and convulsions." The "Utopian speculations" he attacked were Anti-Federalist arguments that a stronger government was unnecessary because the states as commercial republics would never go to war with one another. Whether Hamilton really believed democracies were just as likely to fight one another as any other forms of government is far less clear. There is considerable evidence that Hamilton believed liberal nations were less likely to fight one another, a view he made clear during the Napoleonic Wars of the 1790s. For a discussion of Hamilton's views on liberalism and foreign policy, see Chapter 4.

112. Marks, *Independence on Trial,* p. 50.

113. Ibid., p. 19.

114. Ibid., p. 143.

115. Chernow, *Alexander Hamilton,* p. 267.

116. David Ramsay, "Address," in Paul Leicester Ford, ed., *Pamphlets on the Constitution of the United States, Published During Its Discussion by the People, 1787–1788* (Brooklyn, N.Y.: n.p., 1888), pp. 373–77.

117. Marks, *Independence on Trial,* p. 170.

118. For the role of "national honor" in the movement for constitutional reform, see ibid., p. 133.

119. Ibid., p. 195.

120. Wiencek, *Imperfect God,* p. 264.

121. Marks, *Independence on Trial,* p. 140.

122. *The Debates in the Several State Conventions on the Adoption of the Federal Constitution of the United States, 1787–88,* ed. Jonathan Elliot (Brooklyn, N.Y., 1892), quoted in Jonathan Marshall, "Empire or Liberty: The Anti-Federalists and Foreign Policy, 1787–1788," *Journal of Libertarian Studies* 4, no. 3 (Summer 1980): 248–49.

123. Marks, *Independence on Trial,* pp. 196–97, 200–201, 197.

124. Marshall, "Empire or Liberty," p. 249.

125. Pinckney quoted in Stourzh, *Alexander Hamilton,* p. 127.

126. *Massachusetts Gazette* (Boston), January 14, 1788, quoted in Marshall, "Empire or Liberty," p. 240.

Chapter 3 / *Liberalism and Expansion*

1. By "republicanism," I mean simply a nonmonarchical form of government. The broader, ideological meaning that has been given to the term, by Gordon Wood and others, may help explain certain attitudes among the revolutionary generation. But at least when it comes to foreign policy, it is difficult to discern a "republican" foreign policy tradition that is meaningfully different from the "liberal" foreign policy tradition. The engines of American expansion before, during, and after the Revolution were classically liberal pursuits: individual freedom, financial well-being, personal fulfillment, greed, the desire for land and profits. While an attempt has been made to distinguish a Jeffersonian expansionism "in space" aimed at preserving republican virtues, and a Hamiltonian expansion "in time," aimed at building a liberal, commercial, modern state (see Drew R. McCoy, *The Elusive Republic: Political Economy in Jeffersonian America* [Chapel Hill: University of North Carolina Press, 1980]), this is one of those cases where the simplest explanations work best. Jefferson may well have hoped that territorial expansion into the Louisiana territory would help him extend the life of the yeoman farmer in America. But that is not why Americans, and America, expanded into the Louisiana territory. The reasons were much the same as they had been when Anglo-Americans expanded into the Ohio Valley, and later when they moved across the Great Plains and into the Pacific Northwest.

2. Ralph Lerner, *The Thinking Revolutionary: Principle and Practice in the New Republic* (Ithaca, N.Y.: Cornell University Press, 1987), p. 197.

3. Adam Smith, *An Inquiry into the Nature and Causes of the Wealth of Nations* (New York: Modern Library, 1937), p. 22.

4. Hamilton, "Camillus," in *The Works of Alexander Hamilton,* ed. Henry Cabot Lodge, 12 vols. (New York: G. P. Putnam's Sons, 1903), 5:291.

5. Samuel Eliot Morison, Henry Steele Commager, and William E. Leuchtenburg, *The Growth of the American Republic,* 2 vols., 7th ed. (New York: Oxford University Press, 1980), 1:314.

6. Hamilton, "Camillus," in Lodge, *Works of Hamilton,* 5:316.

7. Richard A. White, *The Middle Ground: Indians, Empires, and Republics in the Great Lakes Region, 1650–1815* (New York: Cambridge University Press, 1991), p. 419.

8. Lerner, *Thinking Revolutionary,* p. 153.

9. Alexander DeConde, *This Affair of Louisiana* (New York: Scribner's, 1976), p. 73.

10. John R. Nelson, *Liberty and Property: Political Economy and Policy-Making in the New Nation, 1789–1812* (Baltimore: Johns Hopkins University Press, 1987), pp. 16–17.

11. Hamilton to Harrison Gray Otis, January 25, 1799, in *Works of Alexander Hamilton,* ed. John C. Hamilton, 7 vols. (New York: J. F. Trow, 1850–51), 6:391.

12. The ordinance specifically provided that the region north of the Ohio River would be divided into territories, and when a territory's population reached five thousand adult males, it was to have an elected assembly. When the population reached sixty thousand, it could apply for statehood and legal equality with the rest of the Union. The ordinance provided each territory with the equivalent of a bill of rights, guaranteeing religious freedom and the rights of habeas corpus and trial by jury, as well as a prohibition on slavery.

13. Some historians have ascribed primarily economic motives to the authors of the ordinance, noting that land speculators, among whom were some of the most prominent Americans both in and out of government, "needed to have in the West a liberal form of government which extended as an inducement to Easterners to buy from them land for new farms." Frederick Merk, *History of the Westward Movement* (New York: Knopf, 1978), p. 105.

14. Lloyd C. Gardner, Walter LaFeber, and Thomas J. McCormick, *Creation of the American Empire,* 2 vols. (Chicago: Rand-McNally, 1976), 1:43.

15. "The northern states had been convinced . . . that to relinquish or even to forbear to use the navigation of the Mississippi was dangerous to the future union of East and West." Samuel Flagg Bemis, *Pinckney's Treaty: America's Advantage from Europe's Distress, 1783–1800* (New Haven, Conn.: Yale University Press, 1960), pp. 158, 162.

16. DeConde, *This Affair of Louisiana,* p. 73.

17. "Answers to the questions proposed by the President . . . to the Secretary of the Treasury," September 15, 1790, in *The Papers of Alexander Hamilton,* ed. Harold C. Syrett and Jacob E. Cooke, 27 vols. (New York: Columbia University Press, 1961–87), 7:51–53, and quoted ibid., p. 53.

18. As Emily S. Rosenberg has noted, "[T]hese processes of conquest are still often masked by the disciplinary structures that place 'frontier' history as a subdivision of 'domestic' rather than of 'international' history." Rosenberg, "A Call to Revolution: A Roundtable on Early U.S. Foreign Relations," *Diplomatic History* 22 (Winter 1998): 66. Even as recently as 1996 a respected historian could still label the task of "consolidating control over the North American continent" as an "internal and domestic" matter. See Joseph J. Ellis, *American Sphinx: The Character of Thomas Jefferson* (New York: Knopf, 1996), p. 124.

19. Baron de Carondelet, "Military Report on Louisiana and West Florida," November 24, 1794, quoted in DeConde, *This Affair of Louisiana,* p. 57.

20. Carondelet, "Military Report," quoted ibid., pp. 59, 57.

21. Thomas Jefferson to Archibald Stewart, January 25, 1786, in *The Papers of Thomas Jefferson,* ed. Julian P. Boyd et al., 24 vols. (Princeton, N.J.: Princeton University Press, 1950–), 9:218.

22. Hamilton, "Camillus," in Lodge, *Works of Hamilton,* 5:207.

23. Albert Lycan, *Alexander Hamilton and American Foreign Policy* (Norman: University of Oklahoma Press, 1970), p. 89.

24. Jefferson quoted in Richard W. Van Alstyne, *Rising American Empire* (New York: Oxford University Press, 1960), p. 87.

25. Merk, *Westward Movement,* p. 125.

26. Gardner et al., *Creation of American Empire,* 1:35.

27. Bemis, *Pinckney's Treaty,* pp. 160–61.

28. Merk, *Westward Movement,* p. 140.

29. DeConde, *This Affair of Louisiana,* p. 52.

30. Quoted in Lester O. Langley, *Americas in the Age of Revolution, 1750–1850* (New Haven, Conn.: Yale University Press, 1996), p. 74.

31. "She admitted in effect that she could not maintain her position in the Ohio Valley in the face of American expansionism." DeConde, *This Affair of Louisiana,* pp. 62, 66.

32. Report to Congress, July 18, 1788, in *Journals of the Continental Congress* [hereinafter *JCC*] (Washington, D.C.: U.S. Government Printing Office, 1904–37), 34:342–44, quoted in Reginald Horsman, *Expansion and American Indian Policy, 1783–1812* (Norman: University of Oklahoma Press, 1992), pp. 50–51.

33. Report to Congress, August 3, 1787, in *JCC*, 33:454–63, quoted ibid., p. 40.

34. Report to Congress, July 10, 1787, in *The Territorial Papers of the United States,* ed. Clarence E. Carter, 17 vols. (Washington, D.C.: U.S. Government Printing Office, 1934–), 2:31–35, quoted ibid., p. 36.

35. Horsman, *Expansion and American Indian Policy,* p. 74.

36. William G. McLoughlin, *Cherokee Renascence in the New Republic* (Princeton, N.J.: Princeton University Press, 1986), p. 23.

37. "At Greenville the Americans had drawn a definite boundary between themselves and the Indians," Reginald Horsman notes, "but there seems little reason to suppose that they intended this boundary to be permanent." In the years that followed the treaty American settlers continued their westward expansion across the Ohio. "They were soon pushing up to and across the Greenville line, and all the promises of the early 1790s meant nothing." Horsman, *Expansion and American Indian Policy,* pp. 97, 103.

38. Knox quoted in Walter Lowrie et al., eds., *American State Papers, Indian Affairs* (Washington, D.C.: Gales & Seaton, 1832–34), quoted in McLoughlin, *Cherokee Renascence,* p. 37.

39. Horsman, *Expansion and American Indian Policy,* p. 95.

40. Saul K. Padover, *Thomas Jefferson on Democracy* (New York: Appleton-Century, 1939), quoted in McLoughlin, *Cherokee Renascence,* p. 37.

41. Lerner, *Thinking Revolutionary,* p. 172.

42. Public notice by John Emerson, March 12, 1785, quoted in Lycan, *Hamilton and Foreign Policy,* p. 112.

43. Federalist nos. 11 and 15, in J. C. Hamilton, *Works of Alexander Hamilton,* 11:84, 111.

44. DeConde, *This Affair of Louisiana,* pp. 45–46.

45. Lycan, *Hamilton and Foreign Policy,* p. 88.

46. Lerner, *Thinking Revolutionary,* p. 150.

47. Lowrie et al., *Indian Affairs,* quoted in McLoughlin, *Cherokee Renascence,* p. 36.

48. Hugh H. Brackenridge, *Gazette Publications* (Carlisle, Pa.: n.p., 1793; reprint, 1806), quoted in Joyce Appleby, *Capitalism and a New Social Order: The Republican Vision of the 1790s* (New York: New York University Press, 1984), p. 101.

49. John Quincy Adams, *An Oration, Delivered at Plymouth, December 22, 1802, At the Anniversary Commemoration of the First Landing of our Ancestors at That Place* (Boston: Russell & Cutler, 1802), quoted in Lerner, *Thinking Revolutionary,* p. 165.

50. Appleby, *Capitalism and New Social Order,* p. 101.

51. Lerner, *Thinking Revolutionary,* p. 172.

52. C. C. Eldridge, "Sinews of Empire: Changing Perspectives," in C. C. Eldridge, ed., *British Imperialism in the Nineteenth Century* (London: Macmillan, 1984).

53. Knox to Washington, December 29, 1794, in Lowrie et al., *Indian Affairs,* quoted in Lerner, *Thinking Revolutionary,* p. 159.

54. Report to Congress, June 15, 1789, in Lowrie et al., *Indian Affairs,* quoted in Horsman, *Expansion and American Indian Policy,* pp. 54–55.

55. Instructions to Rufus Putnam in Rowena Buell, ed., *Memoirs of Rufus Putnam and Certain Official Papers and Correspondence* (Boston, Mass.: Houghton Mifflin, 1903), quoted ibid., p. 93.

56. Report to Congress, June 15, 1789, in Lowrie et al., *Indian Affairs,* quoted ibid., pp. 54–55.

57. Report to Congress, August 9, 1787, in *JCC*, 33:477–81, quoted ibid., p. 41.

58. Jefferson to Chastellux, June 7, 1785, in *The Papers of Thomas Jefferson,* ed. Julian P. Boyd et al., 24 vols. (Princeton, N.J.: Princeton University Press, 1950), 8:185.

59. Minutes of the Fort McIntosh Treaty Council, Timothy Pickering Papers, Massachusetts Historical Society, quoted in Horsman, *Expansion and American Indian Policy,* p. 20.

60. "The United States assumed an attitude towards the Indians during this period which ill-reflected actual American power. The victory over England had bred an over-confidence which was to be expiated in a ten-year struggle for the land of the Old Northwest." Horsman, *Expansion and American Indian Policy,* p. 22.

61. Ibid., pp. 41–42.

62. Report to Congress, June 15, 1789, in Lowrie et al., *Indian Affairs,* quoted ibid., pp. 54–55.

63. Knox to Anthony Wayne in Richard C. Knopf, ed., *Anthony Wayne: A Name in Arms* (Pittsburgh: University of Pittsburgh Press, 1960), quoted ibid., p. 61.

64. Knox to James Seagrove (agent to the Creek Nation), August 11, 1792, in Lowrie et al., *Indian Affairs,* quoted in Lerner, *Thinking Revolutionary,* p. 156.

65. Horsman, *Expansion and American Indian Policy,* p. 53.

66. Lerner, *Thinking Revolutionary,* p. 155.

67. Knox to William Blount, April 22, 1792, quoted in Horsman, *Expansion and American Indian Policy,* p. 77.

68. Garry Wills, *"Negro President": Jefferson and the Slave Power* (Boston: Houghton Mifflin, 2003), p. 31.

69. Horsman, *Expansion and American Indian Policy,* p. 54.

70. "The special vulnerability of 'the ignorant Indians' imposed a special responsibility on whites for some nicety in dealing with them." Lerner, *Thinking Revolutionary,* pp. 159–60.

71. Report to Congress, July 10, 1787, quoted ibid., p. 155.

72. James D. Richardson, *A Compilation of the Messages and Papers of the Presidents, 1789–1897* (Washington, D.C.: Published by authority of Congress, 1896–1907), quoted in Horsman, *Expansion and American Indian Policy,* pp. 60–61.

73. Report to Congress, July 7, 1789, in Lowrie et al., *Indian Affairs,* quoted ibid., p. 58.

74. Ibid.

75. Calhoun to Clay, December 5, 1818, quoted in Lerner, *Thinking Revolutionary,* p. 160.

76. Knox in Lowrie et al., *Indian Affairs,* quoted in McLoughlin, *Cherokee Renascence,* p. 36.

77. Report to Congress, July 7, 1789, in Lowrie et al., *Indian Affairs,* quoted in Horsman, *Expansion and American Indian Policy,* p. 58.

78. Speech to Jean Baptiste Ducoigne (a Kaskaskia chief), June 1781, in Boyd et al., *Papers of Jefferson,* 6:60–61.

79. Lowrie et al., *Indian Affairs,* quoted in Horsman, *Expansion and American Indian Policy,* p. 98.

80. See McLoughlin, *Cherokee Renascence,* for a history of Cherokee attempts to adjust to American impositions.

81. Jefferson to Washington, April 17, 1791, in Boyd et al., *Papers of Jefferson,* 20:145.

82. Francis Paul Prucha, *American Indian Treaties: The History of a Political Anomaly* (Berkeley and Los Angeles: University of California Press, 1994), pp. 430–35. As Jay Gitlin points out, "Indian sovereignty was confirmed by treaty in large measure because the United States needed to control an orderly government-to-government transfer of land." Gitlin, "Private Diplomacy to Private Property: States, Tribes, and Nations in the Early National Period," *Diplomatic History* 22 (Winter 1998): 86. Chief among these reasons was to prevent the states from working out their own separate arrangements with the Indians.

83. Knox in Lowrie et al., *Indian Affairs,* quoted in McLoughlin, *Cherokee Renascence,* p. 36.

84. James A. Field, Jr., "All Economists, All Diplomats," in William H. Becker and Samuel F. Wells, Jr., eds., *Economics and World Power: An Assessment of American Diplomacy Since 1789* (New York: Columbia University Press, 1984), p. 21.

85. Douglas North, *The Economic Growth of the United States, 1790–1860* (New York: Norton, 1966), pp. 47–48.

86. Philip Chadwick Foster Smith, essay in Jean Gordon Lee, ed., *Philadelphians and the China Trade, 1784–1844* (Philadelphia: Philadelphia Museum of Art, 1984), p. 28.

87. Morris quoted ibid., p. 63.

88. Field, "All Economists, All Diplomats," p. 21.

89. William Grayson was pleased to relay the news to James Madison that upon their arrival in Canton "our countrymen were treated with as much respect as the subjects of any nation, i.e., the whole are looked upon by the Chinese as Barbarians, and they have too much Asiatic hauteur to descend to any discrimination." Quoted in Tyler Dennett, *Americans in Eastern Asia* (New York: n.p., 1922), p. 7. Dennett is quoted in Margaret Christman, *Adventurous Pursuits: Americans and the China Trade, 1784–1844* (Washington, D.C.: Smithsonian Institution Press, 1984), p. 21.

90. Quoted in Christman, *Adventurous Pursuits,* p. 21.

91. Christman, *Adventurous Pursuits,* p. 24.

92. Smith essay, in Lee, *Philadelphians and the China Trade,* p. 22.

93. Eastern merchants and western farmers thus developed a common "set of concerns about taxation, transportation, access to credit, outlets to the Atlantic trade lanes, and commercial treaties." Appleby, *Capitalism and New Social Order,* p. 44.

94. North, *Economic Growth of United States,* p. 54.

95. These demands crossed partisan boundaries: "Federalists and Republicans alike responded to the economic opportunities opening before America." Appleby, *Capitalism and New Social Order,* p. 49.

96. Thomas Jefferson to Charles Van Hogendorp, October 13, 1785, quoted in James Hutson, "Intellectual Foundations of Early American Diplomacy," *Diplomatic History* 1, no. 1 (Winter 1977): 8.

97. Jefferson to John Jay, August 23, 1785, in Boyd et al., *Papers of Jefferson,* 8:426–27.

98. Field, "All Economists, All Diplomats," p. 14.

99. Jefferson to James Monroe, November 11, 1784, in Boyd et al., *Papers of Jefferson,* 7:511–12.

100. Jefferson to James Monroe, August 11, 1786, ibid., 10:224–25.

101. James Field, *America and the Mediterranean World, 1776–1882* (Princeton, N.J.: Princeton University Press, 1969), p. 35.

102. James R. Sofka, "The Jeffersonian Idea of National Security: Commerce, the Atlantic Balance of Power, and the Barbary War, 1786–1805," *Diplomatic History* 21, no. 41 (Fall 1997): 534.

103. Field, *America and the Mediterranean World,* p. 37.

104. Jefferson to William Cary Nicholas, June 11, 1801, quoted in Sofka, "Jeffersonian Idea of National Security," p. 536.

105. Field, *America and the Mediterranean World,* pp. 50, 52.

106. Madison to William Eaton, August 22, 1802, quoted in Sofka, "Jeffersonian Idea of National Security," p. 540.

107. Quoted in Field, *America and the Mediterranean World,* p. 67.

108. Henry Adams, *History of the United States During the Administrations of Thomas Jefferson and James Madison,* 6 vols. (New York: Albert & Charles Boni, 1930), 1:429.

109. Field, *America and the Mediterranean World,* p. 60.

110. Jefferson to Thomas Cooper, February 18, 1806, quoted in Sofka, "Jeffersonian Idea of National Security," p. 538.

111. Field, *America and the Mediterranean World,* p. 56.

112. Ibid., p. 10. "Awake, Columbians," Humphreys wrote in his "Poem on the Future Glory of America,"

> Progressive splendors spread o'er evr'y clime!
> Till your blest offspring, countless as the stars,
> In open ocean quench the torch of wars:
> With God-like aim, in one firm union bind
> The common good and int'rest of mankind;
> Unbar the gates of commerce for their race,
> And build the gen'ral peace on freedom's broadest base.

David Humphreys, "Poem on the Future Glory of America," quoted ibid., p. 19.

113. Pickering quoted ibid., p. 41.

114. Field, *America and the Mediterranean World,* p. 68.

115. Shaw's report is found in Josiah Quincy, ed., *The Journals of Major Samuel Shaw, the First American Consul at Canton* (Boston, 1847), quoted in Christman, *Adventurous Pursuits,* p. 65.

116. "America was heir to a liberal intellectual tradition already a century and a half old at her founding. This tradition and the ideas it contained constituted the liberal world view that was the ground, the substance, and the very language of the early American leaders. These leaders comprehended the world through the assumptions, definitions, and goals of liberal thought. The structure of their thought represents an intellectual paradigm, visible to them only as specific ideas and perceptions. The whole of it they could not comprehend, for it was their very mechanism of comprehension." Nelson, *Liberty and Property,* p. 1.

Chapter 4 / *To the Farewell Address and Beyond*

1. Stanley Elkins and Eric McKitrick, *The Age of Federalism: The Early American Republic, 1788–1800* (New York: Oxford University Press, 1993), p. 375.

2. Elkins and McKitrick provide the most accurate and comprehensive account; ibid.

3. Ibid., p. 113. As the authors note, "Only when Hamilton's grand design was fully put together would James Madison, upon his return from Virginia in January 1790, receive its full impact and sense its full implications."

4. Madison, "The Union: Who Are Its Friends?," quoted ibid., p. 267.

5. *Annals of Congress,* 3rd Cong., 1st sess. (January 14, 1794), quoted ibid., p. 384.

6. Elkins and McKitrick, *Age of Federalism,* p. 128.

7. Madison's legislation would have placed higher duties on tonnage shipped to the United States by any country with which the United States did not have a commercial treaty. Unlike the French, who had nothing to lose by signing a commercial agreement, the British had understandably, though also somewhat contemptuously, refused to negotiate such a treaty with the Americans. According to Elkins and McKitrick, Madison's aim was neither financial, nor free trade–oriented, nor even intended to benefit American merchants. Rather, "his was no less an object than the dignity of his republic, which Great Britain might be expected to debase in any way she could. Her instrument was now commerce, and as long as the mother country held 'a much greater proportion of our trade than she is naturally entitled to,' she retained that instrument." Ibid., pp. 88–89.

8. *Annals of Congress,* 3rd Cong., 1st sess. (January 29, 1794), quoted ibid., p. 387.

9. Elkins and McKitrick, *Age of Federalism,* p. 338.

10. In 1787, Hamilton had anticipated the time "when others as well as himself would

join in the praise bestowed by Mr. Neckar [the prerevolutionary French reformer] on the British Constitution, namely that it is the only Govt. in the world 'which unites public strength with individual security.' " Gerald Stourzh, *Alexander Hamilton and the Idea of Republican Government* (Stanford, Calif.: Stanford University Press, 1970), p. 170.

11. Elkins and McKitrick, *Age of Federalism*, p. 113.

12. Hamilton, "Americanus," in *The Works of Alexander Hamilton*, ed. Henry Cabot Lodge, 12 vols. (New York: G. P. Putnam's Sons, 1903), 5:94–95.

13. As the French minister Pierre Adet noted, "Mr. Jefferson likes us because he detests England." Pierre Adet to minister of foreign affairs, December 31, 1796, quoted in Joseph P. Ellis, *American Sphinx: The Character of Thomas Jefferson* (New York: Vintage, 1998), p. 124.

14. Jefferson to William Short, January 3, 1793, in *The Writings of Thomas Jefferson*, ed. Paul Leicester Ford, 10 vols. (New York: G. P. Putnam's Sons, 1894), 7:72–76. Even a sympathetic biographer could find in such statements a "revolutionary realism" comparable to that of Lenin or Mao. Ellis, *American Sphinx*, pp. 127, 128.

15. Jefferson to William Short, January 3, 1793, quoted in Willard Sterne Randall, *Thomas Jefferson: A Life* (New York: Holt, 1993), p. 512.

16. Jefferson to Brissot de Warville, May 8, 1793, in Ford, *Writings of Jefferson*, 6:249; Elkins and McKitrick, *Age of Federalism*, p. 358.

17. Jefferson quoted in Bradford Perkins, *The Cambridge History of American Foreign Relations*, vol. 1: *The Creation of a Republican Empire* (New York: Cambridge University Press, 1993), p. 86.

18. Philip S. Foner, ed., *The Democratic-Republican Societies, 1790–1800: A Documentary Sourcebook of Constitutions, Declarations, Addresses, Resolutions, and Toasts* (Westport, Conn.: Greenwood, 1976), quoted in Elkins and McKitrick, *Age of Federalism*, p. 457.

19. In his famous "Camillus" essays published in defense of the treaty in 1795, Hamilton urged Americans to "defer, to a state of manhood, a struggle to which infancy is ill-adapted." Hamilton, "Camillus," in Lodge, *Works of Hamilton*, 5:207.

20. The Republicans had "already identified the domestic conflict as an effort to defend America against corrupting English ways, and it was easy now to see administration policy as an attempt to ally the country with England and the league of despots against liberty and the French." Lance Banning, *The Jeffersonian Persuasion: Evolution of a Party Ideology* (Ithaca, N.Y.: Cornell University Press, 1978), p. 211.

21. As Elkins and McKitrick have observed, "The shadow of conspiracy and subversion that so obsessed Jefferson had its exact counterpart in Hamilton." Elkins and McKitrick, *Age of Federalism*, p. 360.

22. The enemies of his plan for the government, Hamilton declared, had waited and watched "with lynx's eyes" for any chance to discredit it. "A treaty with Great Britain," he stated, had been "too fruitful an occasion not to call forth all their activity." Hamilton, "Camillus," in Lodge, *Works of Hamilton*, 5:190. Hamilton noted that in July Fourth toasts, "wherever there appear[ed] a direct or indirect censure of the treaty, it [was] pretty uniformly coupled with compliments to Mr. Jefferson." The treaty itself had never been considered by its opponents "with candor or moderation" but had immediately "become the instrument of a systematic effort against the national government and its administration; a decided engine of party to advance its own views at the hazard of the public peace and prosperity." Ibid., 5:194–95.

23. Hamilton, "Americanus," in Lodge, *Works of Hamilton*, 5:75–78.

24. Hamilton to Washington, April 14, 1794, ibid., 5:103.

25. Hamilton, "Camillus," ibid., 5:201.

26. Norman A. Graebner, *Ideas and Diplomacy: Readings in the Intellectual Tradition of American Foreign Policy* (New York: Oxford University Press, 1971), p. 4.

27. Joyce Appleby, *Capitalism and a New Social Order: The Republican Vision of the 1790s* (New York: New York University Press, 1984), pp. 57–58.

28. Whether the French stepped up their seizures because of the Jay Treaty or because of the ongoing war with Great Britain is an open question.

29. Hamilton to Washington, July 5, 1796, in Lodge, *Works of Hamilton,* 10:180–81.

30. Washington to Jefferson, July 6, 1796, quoted in Elkins and McKitrick, *Age of Federalism,* p. 497.

31. Matthew Spalding and Patrick Garrity, *A Sacred Union of Citizens: George Washington's Farewell Address and the American Character* (Lanham, Md.: Rowman & Littlefield, 1996), p. 106.

32. According to Perkins, the address was "clearly an appeal to the electorate to defy France by rejecting the Republicans." Perkins, *Creation of Republican Empire,* p. 103. As Alexander DeConde writes, "Although cloaked in phrases of universal or timeless application, the objectives of the address were practical, immediate, and partisan. . . . The valedictory bore directly on the coming election, on the French alliance, and on the status of Franco-American relations in general." DeConde, "Washington's Farewell, the French Alliance, and the Election of 1796," in Burton Ira Kaufman, ed., *Washington's Farewell Address: The View from the 20th Century* (Chicago: Quadrangle Books, 1969), p. 122.

33. Hamilton to Washington, July 5, 1796, in Lodge, *Works of Hamilton,* 10:180–81. The address was indeed published in September 1796.

34. Alexander DeConde, *The Quasi-War: The Politics and Diplomacy of the Undeclared War with France, 1791–1801* (New York: Scribner's, 1966), pp. 446–47. Since the Washington administration had known of these intrigues since the spring of 1796, it is reasonable to assume they were on the minds of both Washington and Hamilton during the drafting of the address.

35. Washington may also have been complaining about Madison's constitutional "innovation," which gave the House a role in ratifying the Jay Treaty.

36. Donald H. Stewart, *The Opposition Press of the Federalist Period* (Albany: State University of New York Press, 1969), p. 230.

37. Spalding and Garrity, *Sacred Union of Citizens,* p. 93.

38. As further demonstration of what he meant, Washington in the Farewell Address hastened to declare that he did not want to be misunderstood, as indeed he was by his Republican opponents and by the French, as proposing "infidelity to existing arrangements." "[L]et those engagements be observed in their genuine sense," Washington argued. "But in my opinion it is unnecessary and would be unwise to extend them."

39. Monroe to Madison, September 1, 1796, quoted in Elkins and McKitrick, *Age of Federalism,* p. 513.

40. Hamilton, "The Warning," in Lodge, *Works of Hamilton,* 6:242, 233–34, 229.

41. Hamilton to Washington, April 14, 1794, ibid., 5:103–4. Hamilton wrote that if there were not a vast portion of the French population ready to welcome in France's enemies, then "human nature must be an absolutely different thing in France from what it has hitherto shown itself to be throughout the globe."

42. Hamilton, "The Stand," ibid., 6:303. Washington agreed that the "overthrow of Europe" by France was no longer inconceivable. Washington to James McHenry, December 13, 1798, in Fitzpatrick, *Writings of Washington,* 37:32–45. And so, too, did Jefferson, though he predictably took a more sanguine view of the matter. While he did not want to "see any nation have a form of government forced upon them," Jefferson mused, "if it is to be done, I should rejoice at its being a free one." Jefferson to Peregrine Fitzhugh, February 23, 1798, quoted in Gilbert Lycan, *Alexander Hamilton and American Foreign Policy* (Norman: University of Oklahoma Press, 1970), p. 331.

43. Ames quoted in Perkins, *Creation of Republican Empire,* p. 85.

44. Washington to Adams, July 4, 1798, Washington to Pickering, October 18, 1798, and

Washington to McHenry, July 11, 1798, quoted in Lycan, *Hamilton and Foreign Policy,* p. 349.

45. Hamilton, "The Stand," in Lodge, *Works of Hamilton,* 6:282.

46. Hamilton, "Americanus," ibid., 5:95, 93.

47. "[T]he interior conduct of the Directory," he noted, "has the same characters with their exterior." Hamilton, "The Stand," ibid., 6:288, 261, 288.

48. "The majority of the Directory foresaw that . . . they judged it expedient to continue in motion the revolutionary wheel till matters were better prepared for creating a new *dynasty* and a new *aristocracy* to regenerate the exploded monarchy of France with due regard to their own interest." Ibid., 6:288.

49. Ibid., 6:266, 261, 267, 288–89 (emphasis added).

50. Hamilton to Washington, May 19, 1798, ibid., 10:284–85.

51. Hamilton, "The Stand," ibid., 6:304.

52. Washington to Timothy Pickering, August 29, 1797, quoted in Lycan, *Hamilton and Foreign Policy,* p. 312.

53. Privately, Washington told his Federalist colleagues that the purpose of negotiations would be to "accumulate proof of French violence and demonstrate to all our citizens that nothing possible has been omitted." Hamilton also proposed sending Jefferson and Madison to France. As he wrote to Washington, "[T]he influence on party, if a man in whom the opposition has confidence is sent, will be considerable in the event of non-success." Hamilton to Washington, January 22, 1797, in Lodge, *Works of Hamilton,* 10:233–34. Washington apparently agreed and favored negotiations with France in part because their likely failure would "open the eyes of all . . . who are not wilfully blind and resolved to remain so." Quoted in Lycan, *Hamilton and Foreign Policy,* p. 325.

54. Hamilton, "The Warning," in Lodge, *Works of Hamilton,* 6:244.

55. Washington to Thomas Pinckney, May 28, 1797, quoted in Lycan, *Hamilton and Foreign Policy,* p. 303.

56. Hamilton, "The Stand," in Lodge, *Works of Hamilton,* 6:283.

57. Robert Liston to Timothy Pickering, November 7, 1798, quoted in Lycan, *Hamilton and Foreign Policy,* p. 386.

58. Bradford Perkins, *The First Rapprochement: England and the United States, 1795–1805* (Berkeley and Los Angeles: University of California Press, 1967), p. 95.

59. Ibid. By April 1797, a mere seven months after the Farewell Address, Hamilton was proposing that the United States "borrow" some ships of the line and frigates from the British navy for use against France; quoted in Karl-Friedrich Walling, *Republican Empire: Alexander Hamilton on War and Free Government* (Lawrence: University Press of Kansas, 1999), p. 234.

60. Even at the height of Britain's war with France, "such protection was not extended to the merchantmen of any other power that did not have a formal military alliance with Britain." Perkins, *First Rapprochement,* p. 98.

61. Ibid., pp. 98–99.

62. Pickering to Edward Stevens, April 20, 1799, quoted ibid., pp. 109–10.

63. Perkins, *First Rapprochement,* pp. 101, 104–5.

64. Hamilton to Harrison Gray Otis, January 26, 1799, in Lodge, *Works of Hamilton,* 10:339.

65. Hamilton to McHenry, n.d., quoted in Lycan, *Hamilton and Foreign Policy,* p. 330.

66. DeConde, *Quasi-War,* p. 117.

67. King to Timothy Pickering, February 26, 1798, quoted in Lycan, *Hamilton and Foreign Policy,* p. 381.

68. King to Alexander Hamilton, July 14, 1798, quoted ibid., p. 382.

69. Hamilton to James McHenry, June 27, 1799, in Lodge, *Works of Hamilton,* 7:97.

70. Hamilton to Rufus King, August 22, 1798, ibid., 10:314–15.

71. Hamilton to Francisco de Miranda, August 22, 1798, ibid., 10:315–16.

72. Hamilton to Rufus King, August 22, 1798, ibid., 10:314–15.

73. John C. Hamilton, *History of the Republic of the United States as Traced in the Writings of Alexander Hamilton and His Contemporaries* (New York, 1857–64), quoted in Lycan, *Hamilton and Foreign Policy,* p. 383.

74. Adams to James Lloyd, March 5, 29, 1815, in *The Works of John Adams, Second President of the United States,* ed. Charles Francis Adams, 10 vols. (Boston: Little, Brown, 1850–56), 10:146–49.

75. Perkins, *First Rapprochement,* p. 105.

76. Hamilton to McHenry, quoted in Lycan, *Hamilton and Foreign Policy,* p. 330.

77. Alexander DeConde, *Entangling Alliances: Politics and Diplomacy Under George Washington* (Durham, N.C.: Duke University Press, 1958), p. 505. As DeConde writes, "Since the Hamiltonians were anti-French, in their view the French alliance was entangling. Ironically, they saw no evil in close connections with Great Britain."

78. Hamilton, *The Papers of Alexander Hamilton,* ed. Harold C. Syrett and Jacob E. Cooke, 27 vols. (New York: Columbia University Press, 1961–87), 5:483–86.

79. Hamilton, "Camillus," in Lodge, *Works of Hamilton,* 5:206.

80. Jefferson to Monroe, November 24, 1801, in Ford, *Writings of Jefferson,* 8:105.

81. Woodrow Wilson, *George Washington* (New York: Harper, 1896), quoted in Kaufman, *Washington's Farewell Address,* p. 32.

82. As Gerald Stourzh points out, "One of his most revealing utterances was his reference, in 1790, to the Spanish possession on 'our right' and the British possessions (Canada) on 'our left'! In other words, Hamilton's inner eye was as a matter of course directed toward Europe!" Stourzh, *Alexander Hamilton,* p. 195.

83. "Hamilton considered himself a leader of an as yet underdeveloped country and that his prime aim was to secure the credit needed to push its industrialization, the essential prerequisite of a truly strong maritime empire." Ibid., p. 199.

84. Craig Symonds, *Navalists and Anti-Navalists: The Naval Policy Debate in the United States, 1785–1827* (Newark: University of Delaware Press, 1980), p. 23.

85. Hamilton, "Camillus," in Lodge, *Works of Hamilton,* 5:489.

86. Hamilton, Federalist no.11, in *The Federalist,* ed. Jacob E. Cooke (Middletown, Conn.: Wesleyan University Press, 1961), p. 72.

87. Quoted in Helene Johnson Looze, *Alexander Hamilton and the British Orientation of American Foreign Policy, 1783–1803* (The Hague: Mouton, 1969), p. 35.

88. Hamilton, Federalist no. 11, in Cooke, *Federalist,* p. 73.

89. Stourzh, *Alexander Hamilton,* p. 265n92.

90. Burton Kaufman has argued that "the Farewell Address can be properly understood only in relation to Washington's concept of his country's imperial future." Kaufman, "A Statement of Empire," in Kaufman, *Washington's Farewell Address,* p. 171.

91. Ibid., p. 183.

92. Hamilton, "Camillus," in Lodge, *Works of Hamilton,* 5:206–7.

93. Hamilton to Rufus King, October 2, 1798, ibid., 10:321. Hamilton's estimates remained roughly consistent over the years. In 1774 he had estimated that in "fifty or sixty years" America would be no longer beholden to Great Britain and "the scale" would begin "to turn in [America's] favour." Quoted in Stourzh, *Alexander Hamilton,* p. 195.

94. As Stourzh asks, "What was the meaning of national greatness as Hamilton envisaged it and as Washington endorsed it? Was it just another word for power? It does not seem so." Rather, this ambition for greatness represented a "positive moral valuation." Stourzh, *Alexander Hamilton,* p. 172.

95. Jack P. Greene, "Empire and Identity from the Glorious Revolution to the American Reolution," in *The Oxford History of the British Empire,* vol 2: *The Eighteenth Century,* ed. P. J. Marshall (Oxford: Oxford Universiy Press, 1998), p. 230.

Chapter 5 / *"Peaceful Conquest"*

1. *New York Evening Post,* January 28, 1803, quoted in Alexander DeConde, *This Affair of Louisiana* (New York: Scribner's, 1976), p. 138.

2. Quoted in Samuel F. Bemis, *John Quincy Adams and the Foundations of American Foreign Policy* (New York: Knopf, 1949), p. 182.

3. Jackson to James Winchester, October 4, 1806, Andrew Jackson Papers, Library of Congress; Robert Vincent Remini, *Andrew Jackson: The Course of American Empire, 1767–1821* (Baltimore: Johns Hopkins University Press, 1998), p. 149.

4. *The Diary and Letters of Gouverneur Morris,* ed. Anne C. Morris (New York: Scribner's, 1888), quoted in DeConde, *This Affair of Louisiana,* p. 177.

5. Jefferson to the chiefs of the Wyandots, Ottawas, Chippewas, Potawatomis, and Shawnees, January 1809, War Department, Secretary's Office, Letters Sent, Indian Affairs, B:412–13, National Archives, Washington, D.C.; Reginald Horsman, *Expansion and American Indian Policy, 1783–1812* (Norman: University of Oklahoma Press, 1992), p. 108.

6. Anthony F. C. Wallace, *Jefferson and the Indians: The Tragic Fate of the First Americans* (Cambridge, Mass.: Belknap Press of Harvard University Press, 1999), pp. 216, 214.

7. Ibid., pp. 236–39.

8. James D. Richardson, ed., *Messages and Papers of the Presidents,* 20 vols. (New York: Bureau of National Literature, c. 1897–1922), 1:386–87, quoted in Horsman, *Expansion and American Indian Policy,* p. 112.

9. Jefferson to John Adams, June 11, 1812, in *The Adams-Jefferson Letters: The Complete Correspondence Between Thomas Jefferson and Abigail and John Adams,* ed. Lester J. Cappon, 2 vols. (Chapel Hill: University of North Carolina Press, 1959), 2:308.

10. John Quincy Adams, *An Oration, Delivered at Plymouth, 22 December 1802, At the Anniversary Commemoration of the First Landing of our Ancestors at That Place* (Boston: Russell & Cutler, 1802), quoted in Ralph Lerner, *The Thinking Revolutionary: Principle and Practice in the New Republic* (Ithaca, N.Y.: Cornell University Press, 1987), p. 165.

11. See Julius W. Pratt, "The Ideology of Expansion," in Avery Craven, ed., *Essays in Honor of William E. Dodd, by His Former Students at the University of Chicago* (Chicago: University of Chicago Press, 1935), pp. 335–53, 344.

12. Adams, *Memoirs of John Quincy Adams, Comprising Portions of His Diary from 1795 to 1848,* ed. Charles Francis Adams, 12 vols. (Philadelphia: J. B. Lippincott, 1874–77), quoted in Walter LaFeber, ed., *John Quincy Adams and American Continental Empire: Letters, Papers, and Speeches* (Chicago: Quadrangle Books, 1965), pp. 36–37.

13. See DeConde, *This Affair of Louisiana,* pp. 64–74.

14. Ibid., p. 66.

15. Joseph Xavier Delfau de Pontalba, quoted ibid., p. 94.

16. Rufus King to James Madison, London, April 2, 1803, quoted ibid., p. 143.

17. Jefferson to Livingston, April 18, 1802, in *The Writings of Thomas Jefferson,* ed. Paul Leicester Ford, 10 vols. (New York: G. P. Putnam's Sons, 1894), 9:363–68.

18. Secret instructions for the Captain-General of Louisiana, November 26, 1802, quoted in DeConde, *This Affair of Louisiana,* p. 150.

19. Irujo to Cevallos, Washington, D.C., January 3, 1803, quoted ibid., p. 142.

20. Pichon to Tallyrand, January 21 and 24, 1803, quoted ibid., p. 156.

21. Georges Henri Victor Collot, quoted ibid., p. 159.

22. Quote attributed to Napoleon in M. J. Louis Adolphe Thiers, *The History of the Con-*

sulate and the Empire of France Under Napoleon (London: Henry G. Bohn, 1875), quoted ibid., p. 157.

23. As Bradford Perkins notes, "Bonaparte's decision to sell Louisiana . . . was influenced by American menace." Perkins, *The Cambridge History of American Foreign Relations,* vol. 1: *The Creation of a Republican Empire* (New York: Cambridge University Press, 1993), pp. 170–71.

24. Livingston to Rufus King, May, 7, 1803, quoted in DeConde, *This Affair of Louisiana,* p. 173.

25. *National Intelligencer and Washington Advertiser,* July 8, 1803, quoted ibid., p. 178.

26. The proclamation is dated November 15, 1803, quoted ibid., p. 204.

27. As Alexander DeConde notes, the "conventional wisdom usually depicts Louisiana as coming to the Jeffersonians unexpectedly, 'out of the blue,' as 'an accident of fate,' a 'diplomatic miracle,' as being suddenly thrust upon 'indifferent hands,' virtually 'forced on the United States,' or tossed 'into the lap of Americans.'" DeConde, *This Affair of Louisiana,* pp. 249–50. Jefferson's contemporary political opponents made this argument. Hamilton and the Federalists, in their partisan efforts to deny Jefferson any share of credit, only strengthened the myth of the immaculate acquisition of Louisiana. It was the "interpositions of an over-ruling Providence," the "fortuitous concurrence of unforeseen and unexpected circumstances," that had delivered Louisiana into American hands, Hamilton insisted, not any "wise or vigorous measures on the part of the American government." *New York Evening Post,* July 5, 1803, quoted in Douglas Adair, ed., "Hamilton on the Louisiana Purchase: A Newly Identified Editorial from the *New York Evening Post,*" *William and Mary Quarterly,* 3rd ser., 12 (April 1955): 274–75; also quoted in DeConde, *This Affair of Louisiana,* p. 179.

28. P. S. Du Pont de Nemours to Jefferson, April 30, 1802, quoted in DeConde, *This Affair of Louisiana,* p. 115.

29. Carlos Martínez de Irujo to Pedro Cevallos, December 1802, quoted ibid., p. 136.

30. Louis A. F. de Beaujour, *Sketch of the United States of North America, at the Commencement of the 19th Century, from 1800 to 1810,* trans. William Walton (London: J. Booth, 1814), quoted ibid., p. 214.

31. Madison to Pinckney, Washington, D.C., October 12, 1803, quoted ibid., p. 202.

32. *The Autobiography of James Monroe,* ed. Stuart Gerry Brown (Syracuse, N.Y.: Syracuse University Press, 1959), quoted ibid., p. 215.

33. Quoted in Lester Langley, *Struggle for the American Mediterranean: United States–European Rivalry in the Gulf-Caribbean, 1776–1904* (Athens: University of Georgia Press, 1976), p. 14.

34. Quoted in William Earl Weeks, *John Quincy Adams and American Global Empire* (Lexington: University Press of Kentucky, 1992), p. 109.

35. Ibid., p. 113.

36. Adams diary, January 14, 1818, in C. F. Adams, *Memoirs of John Quincy Adams,* 4:42.

37. Quoted in Bemis, *Adams and Foreign Policy,* p. 318.

38. Adams diary, November 16, 1819, in C. F. Adams, *Memoirs of John Quincy Adams,* 4:439.

39. Frederick Merk, *Manifest Destiny and Mission in American History* (New York: McGraw-Hill, 1966), pp. 20–21.

40. J. Fred Rippy, *Rivalry of the United States and Great Britain over Latin America, 1808–1830* (Baltimore: Johns Hopkins University Press, 1929), pp. 92–93.

41. Quoted in David M. Pletcher, *The Diplomacy of Annexation: Texas, Oregon, and the Mexican War* (Columbia: University of Missouri Press, 1973), p. 64.

42. Weeks, *Adams and Global Empire,* p. 72.

43. Quoted in Rippy, *Rivalry of United States,* pp. 52, 51.

44. Adams diary, May 6, 1811, in C. F. Adams, *Memoirs of John Quincy Adams,* 2:261.

45. C. F. Adams, *Memoirs of John Quincy Adams,* 4:437–39.

46. Adams diary, November 16, 1819, ibid.

47. C. F. Adams, *Memoirs of John Quincy Adams,* 4:437–39.

48. Adams to Rush, July 22, 1823, quoted in Richard W. Van Alstyne, *Rising American Empire* (New York: Oxford University Press, 1960), p. 96.

49. Adams diary, November 7, 1823, in C. F. Adams, *Memoirs of John Quincy Adams,* 6:178.

50. Quoted in LaFeber, *Adams and Continental Empire,* pp. 128–31.

51. Rippy, *Rivalry of United States,* p. 85.

52. A few months before offering his proposal, Canning had ordered the English naval squadron in the West Indies to make a show of force to keep the Americans at bay. "Whatever they might do in the absence of an English squadron," Canning figured, the Americans "would hardly venture in the face of one to assume the military occupation" of Cuba. Rippy, *Rivalry of United States,* pp. 79–80.

53. For a discussion of the conflict between means and ends in Jefferson's policies, see Robert W. Tucker and David C. Hendrickson, *Empire of Liberty: The Statecraft of Thomas Jefferson* (New York: Oxford University Press, 1990), pp. 157–79.

54. Jefferson warned in 1808 that the "federalist monarchists disapprove of the republican principles & features of our constitution and would I believe welcome any public calamity (war with England excepted) which might lessen the confidence of our country in those principles & forms." Quoted in Roger H. Brown, *The Republic in Peril: 1812* (New York: Columbia University Press, 1964), p. 14.

55. Madison quoted ibid., p. 13.

56. Calhoun quoted ibid., p. 79.

57. "Increasingly, Republican policy sought to sustain national pride against foreign assault. In time this maintenance of pride outweighed protecting commerce for its own sake. The human side of impressments was never lost on the Republicans, but the sailors forced to work on British men-of-war constituted a symbol of violated national sovereignty that the nationalistic republicans could not ignore." Reginald C. Stuart, *War and American Thought: From the Revolution to the Monroe Doctrine* (Kent, Ohio: Kent State University Press, 1982), pp. 106, 127.

58. The Radical Republican Freneau believed that Americans were "despised all over Europe" because their devotion to commerce had made them weak and "cowardly." Steven Watts, *The Republic Reborn: War and the Making of Liberal America, 1790–1820* (Baltimore: Johns Hopkins University Press), p. 84.

59. Ernest R. May, *The Making of the Monroe Doctrine* (Cambridge, Mass.: Belknap Press of Harvard University Press, 1975), p. 19.

60. Watts, *Republic Reborn,* pp. 84, 89.

61. Ibid., p. 61.

62. Brown, *Republic in Peril,* p. 84.

63. Ibid., p. 79.

64. Stuart, *War and American Thought,* p. 136. Adams believed that however Americans might suffer in the conflict they would benefit by recovering "in all their vigor the energies of war." Ibid., p. 137.

65. Watts, *Republic Reborn,* p. 91.

66. Henry Adams, *History of the United States During the Administrations of Thomas Jefferson and James Madison,* 6 vols. (New York: Albert & Charles Boni, 1930), 2:277.

67. Harry L. Watson, *Andrew Jackson vs. Henry Clay* (Boston: Bedford/St. Martin's, 1998), p. 50.

68. Watts, *Republic Reborn,* p. 283.

69. Ibid., p. 318.

70. Richard H. Brown, "The Missouri Crisis, Slavery, and the Politics of Jacksonianism," *South Atlantic Quarterly* 65 (1966): 57.

71. "Logistical problems and economic shortages during the war years greatly intensified Republican commitments to internal improvements, manufactures, and the home market." Watts, *Republic Reborn,* p. 282. "The third important feature of postwar nationalism was the subject of federally financed internal improvements. The war had furnished dramatic evidence to bolster the long-felt need for better communications between the Atlantic Coast and the Mississippi Valley." Norman K. Risjord, *The Old Republicans: Southern Conservatism in the Age of Jefferson* (New York: Columbia University Press, 1965), p. 168.

72. See Robert V. Remini, *Andrew Jackson: The Course of American Freedom, 1822–1832* (Baltimore: Johns Hopkins University Press, 1981), pp. 67–70.

73. Weeks, *Adams and Global Empire,* pp. 46, 47.

74. Risjord, *Old Republicans,* pp. 145, 134.

75. Watson, *Andrew Jackson vs. Henry Clay,* p. 19.

76. Risjord, *Old Republicans,* pp. 242, 153.

77. Charles Grier Sellers, *The Market Revolution: Jacksonian America, 1815–1846* (New York: Oxford University Press, 1991), pp. 74, 76, 82.

78. Ibid., p. 64.

79. Risjord, *Old Republicans,* p. 100.

80. Sellers, *Market Revolution,* p. 70.

81. Ibid., p. 58.

82. Risjord, *Old Republicans,* p. 258

83. Weeks, *Adams and Global Empire,* p. 19.

84. Ronald G. Walters, *American Reformers, 1815–1860* (New York: Hill & Wang, 1997), p. xiii.

85. "America's economic development provided reformers with problems in need of solutions." Ibid., p. 6.

86. Ibid., pp. 22, 3, 32.

87. "In the United States all religions represented have become, to a large extent, 'Americanized.'" Hans Kohn, *American Nationalism* (New York: Collier Books, 1961), p. 16.

88. Joyce Appleby, *Inheriting the Revolution: The First Generation of Americans* (Cambridge, Mass.: Belknap Press of Harvard University Press, 2000), p. 9. According to James A. Field, "The new theology carried more than a touch of Jeffersonianism in its emphasis on the individual and in its confidence in progress." Field, *America and the Mediterranean World, 1776–1882* (Princeton, N.J.: Princeton University Press, 1969), p. 73.

89. Alexis de Tocqueville, *Democracy in America,* 2 vols. (New York: Knopf, 1945), 1:300, 2:126–27.

90. Stuart, *War and American Thought,* p. 155.

91. Anders Stephanson, *Manifest Destiny: American Expansionism and the Empire of Right* (New York: Hill & Wang, 1995), p. 28.

92. Frederick B. Artz, *Reaction and Revolution, 1814–1832* (New York: Harper Torchbook, 1974), p. 3.

93. As Anders Stephanson has put it, American nationalism was "an apparent paradox: a particular (and particularly powerful) nationalism constituting itself not only as prophetic but also universal." Stephanson, *Manifest Destiny,* p. xiii.

94. Thus, as Joyce Appleby notes, early nineteenth-century reformers could direct Americans "toward the moral ends of nationalism." Appleby, *Inheriting the Revolution,* p. 193.

95. Robert V. Remini, *Henry Clay: Statesman for the Union* (New York: Norton, 1991), pp. 286, 225, 174.

96. Bradford Perkins describes Monroe's message as "fifty-one paragraphs long," a "dreary summary of events over the preceding year," and a "series of recommendations on domestic policy." Perkins, *Creation of Republican Empire,* p. 165.

97. Weeks, *Adams and Global Empire,* p. 20.

98. Field, *America and the Mediterranean World,* p. 62.

99. See, for instance, Paul A. Varg, *United States Foreign Relations, 1820–1860* (East Lansing: Michigan State University Press, 1979), p. 14.

100. As Anders Stephanson puts it, the American mission was a "sacred-secular project." See Stephanson, *Manifest Destiny,* p. 28.

101. "The missionary facet of early American life," as James A. Field notes, "had much in common with other projections of American influence overseas." Field, *America and the Mediterranean World,* pp. 89–90.

102. Tocqueville, *Democracy in America,* 1:306.

103. As James A. Field notes, all were "aspects of the American Enlightenment. All had an internationalist bias, all aspired to a better future, all were concerned with man whoever and wherever he might be." Field, *America and the Mediterranean World,* p. 90. Ronald G. Walters also notes the synergy: "Millennial optimism was particularly strong because it interacted with other common attitudes. It merged with the belief that the United States was chosen by God to fulfill a great mission, an old notion given new life in the antebellum period by territorial expansion and religious revivals (sure marks of divine favor). This idea of national destiny was simultaneously accepted and used by reformers. They claimed that America's special place in God's design (a version of what scholars call American exceptionalism) meant that its sins were more heinous than those of other countries and that their reforms were urgently needed. The divine plan—the millennium—depended upon reform. Whatever the merits of the argument, it joined religious and patriotic fervor to make a case." Walters, *American Reformers,* pp. 25–26.

104. Kohn, *American Nationalism,* pp. 24–25.

Chapter 6 / *A Republic in the Age of Monarchy*

1. Frederick B. Artz, *Reaction and Revolution, 1814–1832* (New York: Harper Torchbook, 1974), p. 10.

2. Ibid., pp. 6–7, 146.

3. Ibid., p. 126.

4. Harold Temperley, *The Foreign Policy of Canning, 1822–1827: England, the Neo-Holy Alliance and the New World* (London: G. Bell & Sons, 1925), p. 8.

5. *Memoirs of John Quincy Adams, Comprising Portions of His Diary from 1795 to 1848,* ed. Charles Francis Adams, 12 vols. (Philadelphia: J. B. Lippincott, 1874–77), 6:215.

6. Temperley, *Foreign Policy of Canning,* p. 23.

7. Artz, *Reaction and Revolution,* pp. 164–65.

8. J. Q. Adams to John Adams, August 1, 1816, in *Writings of John Quincy Adams,* ed. Worthington Chauncey Ford, 7 vols. (1913; reprint, New York: Greenwood Press, 1968), 6:143.

9. J. Q. Adams to William Plumer, January 17, 1817, ibid., 6:143; Joseph Byrne Lockey, *Pan-Americanism: Its Beginnings* (New York: Macmillan, 1926), p. 159.

10. Lockey, *Pan-Americanism,* p. 145.

11. J. Q. Adams to John Adams, December 21, 1817, in Ford, *Writings of John Quincy Adams,* 6:275; Lockey, *Pan-Americanism,* p. 172.

12. Samuel F. Bemis, *John Quincy Adams and the Foundations of American Foreign Policy* (New York: Knopf, 1949), p. 356.

13. Quoted in Lockey, *Pan-Americanism,* p. 173.

14. Robert V. Remini, *Henry Clay: Statesman for the Union* (New York: Norton, 1991), p. 175.

15. Bemis, *Adams and Foreign Policy,* p. 346.

16. Remini, *Henry Clay,* p. 174.

17. Bemis, *Adams and Foreign Policy,* p. 356.

18. Remini, *Henry Clay,* pp. 222–23, 160.

19. Bemis, *Adams and Foreign Policy,* p. 342*n.*

20. Arthur Preston Whitaker, *The Western Hemisphere Idea: Its Rise and Decline* (Ithaca, N.Y.: Cornell University Press, 1954), p. 29.

21. Bemis, *Adams and Foreign Policy,* pp. 342–43*n,* 354.

22. Clay quoted in J. Fred Rippy, *Rivalry of the United States and Great Britain over Latin America, 1808–1830* (Baltimore: Johns Hopkins Press, 1929), p. 210.

23. Bemis, *Adams and Foreign Policy,* p. 366.

24. Ibid., p. 358.

25. Adams Address of July 4, 1821, in Walter LaFeber, ed., *John Quincy Adams and American Continental Empire: Letters, Papers, and Speeches* (Chicago: Quadrangle Books, 1965), p. 45.

26. Bemis, *Adams and Foreign Policy,* pp. 362, 356–58.

27. James Madison to James Monroe, November 1, 1823, quoted ibid., p. 384.

28. A. W. Ward and G. P. Gooch, *The Cambridge History of British Foreign Policy, 1783–1919,* vol. 2: *1815–1866* (Cambridge, U.K.: Cambridge University Press, 1923), p. 58.

29. Ibid., p. 61.

30. Quoted in Ernest May, *The Making of the Monroe Doctrine* (Cambridge, Mass.: Belknap Press of Harvard University Press, 1975), p. 72.

31. Adams diary, November 17, 1823, in C. F. Adams, *Memoirs of John Quincy Adams,* 6:190–94.

32. H. W. V. Temperley, "French Designs on Spanish America, 1820," *English Historical Review* 40 (January 1925): 40; Chateaubriand to Talaru, June 9, 1823, quoted in May, *Making of Monroe Doctrine,* p. 105.

33. Rippy, *Rivalry of United States,* p. 117.

34. Bemis, *Adams and Foreign Policy,* pp. 360–61.

35. Quoted in Rippy, *Rivalry of United States,* pp. 120–21.

36. Ibid., p. 122.

37. Temperley, *Foreign Policy of Canning,* p. 79.

38. Ibid., pp. 16, 44.

39. C. F. Adams, *Memoirs of John Quincy Adams,* 6:152.

40. Bemis, *Adams and Foreign Policy,* p. 375.

41. Ibid., pp. 376, 379.

42. Monroe to Jefferson, October 17, 1823, quoted in Norman A. Graebner, *Foundations of American Foreign Policy: A Realist Appraisal from Franklin to McKinley* (Wilmington, Del.: Scholarly Resources, 1985), p. 169.

43. C. F. Adams, *Memoirs of John Quincy Adams,* 6:185.

44. Bemis, *Adams and Foreign Policy,* p. 384.

45. C. F. Adams, *Memoirs of John Quincy Adams,* 6:177, 192.

46. Ibid., 6:185.

47. Edward Meade Earle, "American Interest in the Greek Cause, 1821–1827," *American Historical Review* 33 (October 1927): 44.

48. Ibid., pp. 45, 46.

49. Artz, *Reaction and Revolution,* p. 149.

50. Paul A. Varg, *United States Foreign Relations, 1820–1860* (East Lansing: Michigan State University Press, 1979), p. 58; *The Papers of Daniel Webster,* ed. Charles M. Wiltse, 14 vols. (Hanover, N.H.: Dartmouth College by the University Press of New England, 1974), 1:339.

51. James A. Field, Jr., *America and the Mediterranean World, 1776–1882* (Princeton, N.J.: Princeton University Press, 1969), p. 122.

52. In fact, a translation of Webster's speech circulated widely in Greece, and in 1827 the Greek government thanked Americans for extending "a helping hand towards the Old World." Ibid., p. 126.

53. Robert V. Remini, *Daniel Webster: The Man and His Time* (New York: Norton, 1997), pp. 216–17.

54. May, *Making of Monroe Doctrine,* p. 229.

55. Temperley, *Foreign Policy of Canning,* p. 326.

56. C. F. Adams, *Memoirs of John Quincy Adams,* 6:173.

57. Quoted in May, *Making of Monroe Doctrine,* p. 17.

58. Ibid., p. 20.

59. Harry Ammon, *James Monroe: The Quest for National Identity* (New York: McGraw-Hill, 1971), p. 476.

60. As one Monroe biographer described his thinking, "If it were admitted that the United States had erred in not making such a declaration of policy during the French Revolution, might not the error be compounded by keeping silent? Was it not proper for the United States to encourage nations seeking their freedom while condemning those seeking to deprive others of their liberty?" Stanislaus Murray Hamilton, ed., *The Writings of James Monroe,* 7 vols. (New York: n.p., 1898–1903), 6:310, quoted ibid., p. 483.

61. We know of this first Monroe draft only through Adams's account in his diary. The original first draft was not preserved. Adams diary, November 21, 1823, cited in May, *Making of Monroe Doctrine,* p. 214.

62. Adams diary, November 21, 1823, excerpted in LaFeber, *Adams and Continental Empire,* p. 104.

63. Quoted in May, *Making of Monroe Doctrine,* pp. 215–16.

64. Adams diary, November 22, 1823, excerpted in LaFeber, *Adams and Continental Empire,* p. 105.

65. James Monroe, Annual Message, December 2, 1823, in James D. Richardson, *A Compilation of the Messages and Papers of the Presidents, 1789–1897,* 20 vols. (Washington, D.C.: U.S. Government Printing Office, 1899), 2:209–20, excerpted in La Feber, *Adams and Continental Empire,* p. 111.

66. Ibid., pp. 113, 111; emphasis added.

67. Ibid., p. 113.

68. Quoted in Remini, *Daniel Webster,* p. 211.

69. Quoted in Bradford Perkins, *The Cambridge History of American Foreign Relations,* vol. 1: *The Creation of a Republican Empire, 1776–1865* (New York: Cambridge University Press, 1993), p. 166.

70. Excerpted in La Feber, *Adams and Continental Empire,* p. 112.

71. Adams diary, November 27, 1823, in C. F. Adams, *Memoirs of John Quincy Adams,* 6:211.

72. Varg, *United States Foreign Relations,* p. 14.

73. Robert W. Tucker and David C. Hendrickson, *Empire of Liberty: The Statecraft of Thomas Jefferson* (New York: Oxford University Press, 1990), p. 238.

74. Temperley, *Foreign Policy of Canning,* p. 130.

75. May, *Making of Monroe Doctrine,* p. 245.

76. Temperley, *Foreign Policy of Canning,* pp. 42–43, 49.

77. Rippy, *Rivalry of United States*, pp. 108–10.

78. Temperley, *Foreign Policy of Canning*, pp. 158–59.

79. Rippy, *Rivalry of United States*, p. 184.

80. Harold William Vazeille Temperley, "The Later American Policy of George Canning," *American Historical Review* 11 (1906): 782; Rippy, *Rivalry of United States*, pp. 247–48.

81. Simón Bolívar, "Answer of a South American to a Gentleman of this Island," September 6, 1815, reprinted in R. A. Humphreys and John Lynch, eds., *The Origins of the Latin American Revolutions, 1808–1826* (New York: Knopf, 1965), p. 265.

82. Rippy, *Rivalry of United States*, pp. 186–87.

83. Interview between Bolívar and Captain Thomas Maling in Peru, March 1825, reported in Maling to Lord Melville, March 18–20, 1825, quoted in Temperley, *Foreign Policy of Canning*, pp. 557–60; Rippy, *Rivalry of United States*, pp. 152–53.

84. Rippy, *Rivalry of United States*, p. 154.

85. Ibid., pp. 292–93, 265.

86. Ibid., pp. 173, 166, 210, 192, 195.

87. Perhaps the American decision to tread cautiously in Brazil was due to the fact that Brazil, like the United States, was a slaveholding nation. As we shall see in the next chapter, American slaveholders had a special fear of revolution in slave nations that might spill over into the American South.

88. Rippy, *Rivalry of United States*, p. 176.

89. Varg, *United States Foreign Relations*, p. 18.

Chapter 7 / *The Foreign Policy of Slavery*

1. See Kinley J. Brauer, "The Great American Desert Revisited: Recent Literature and Prospects for the Study of American Foreign Relations, 1815–61," *Diplomatic History* 13 (Summer 1989).

2. Reasons for the neglect of slavery by diplomatic historians are many and varied. For most of the past half century, the majority of historians of American domestic politics and society argued that slavery was not the critical issue in antebellum politics that it had once been portrayed as being. Civil War revisionists, who dominated the field from the 1930s through the civil rights movement of the 1960s, downplayed the significance of slavery, and it is only within the past three decades that historians such as James M. McPherson, Eugene Genovese, Eric Foner, and William W. Freehling have reestablished the centrality of slavery, and the ideological struggle over slavery between the North and South, in our understanding of American politics before the Civil War. Although there have been important exceptions—Frederick Merk has given slavery a prominent place in his explanation of manifest destiny—diplomatic historians, for the most part, have not caught up with their colleagues and have made little effort to link the all-important issue of slavery with the conduct of American foreign policy.

It may also be true, as Kinley Brauer suggests, that modern diplomatic historians have been preoccupied by the search for "useful lessons for the guidance of contemporary foreign policy." Brauer, "The Great American Desert Revisited," p. 399. That has perhaps made them reluctant to address the issue of slavery in nineteenth-century America, since they may believe, wrongly, that the question of nineteenth-century slavery is not relevant to American foreign policy at the end of the twentieth century and the beginning of the twenty-first. This may explain why historians such as Michael Hunt and Thomas Hietala, though more conscious than most of the problem, treat slavery under the broad, unhelpful rubric of "race." Racial prejudices remain prevalent in modern as in antebellum American society. But this attempt to link the past with the present seriously underestimates the very important ideological issues at stake in antebellum America. Slavery was more than racism. It was an entire social structure that gave birth to a coherent ideology, antithetical to what might be called American ideology.

3. See Garry Wills, *"Negro President": Jefferson and the Slave Power* (Boston: Houghton Mifflin, 2003), p. 43.

4. Ibid., pp. 36, 40.

5. Ibid., pp. 43–44.

6. Thomas O. Ott, *The Haitian Revolution, 1789–1804* (Knoxville: University of Tennessee Press, 1973), pp. 195–96. See William W. Freehling, *Prelude to Civil War: The Nullification Controversy in South Carolina, 1816–1836* (New York: Harper & Row, 1966), pp. 54–60, 112.

7. Henry Wiencek, *An Imperfect God: George Washginton, His Slaves, and the Creation of America* (New York: Farrar, Straus & Giroux, 2003), p. 233.

8. Philip S. Foner, *Blacks in the American Revolution* (Westport, Conn.: Greenwood Press, 1975), quoted ibid., p. 234.

9. Winthrop Jordan, *White over Black: American Attitudes Toward the Negro, 1550–1812* (Chapel Hill: University of North Carolina Press, 1968), quoted in Lester Langley, *Struggle for the American Mediterranean: United States–European Rivalry in the Gulf-Caribbean, 1776–1904* (Athens: University of Georgia Press, 1976), p. 33.

10. *Annals of Congress,* 9th Cong., 1st sess., House (February 24, 1806), p. 512, quoted in Linda K. Kerber, *Federalists in Dissent: Imagery and Ideology in Jeffersonian America* (Ithaca, N.Y.: Cornell University Press, 1970), p. 48.

11. Tim Matthewson, "Jefferson and the Nonrecognition of Haiti," *Proceedings of the American Philosophical Society* 140 (March 1996): 35.

12. Ott, *Haitian Revolution,* p. 142.

13. Peter Kolchin, *American Slavery, 1619–1877* (New York: Hill & Wang, 1993), p. 73.

14. British Public Record Office, Foreign Office, Admiralty, Classification No. 1, vol. 506, quoted in J. Fred Rippy, *Rivalry of United States and Great Britain over Latin America, 1808–1830* (Baltimore: Johns Hopkins University Press, 1929), pp. 45–46.

15. J. P. Morier to the Marquis of Wellesley, No. 11, January 24, 1811, F.O. (5), p. 74, quoted ibid., pp. 36–37.

16. John Shy, *A People Numerous and Armed: Reflections on the Military Struggle for American Independence* (Ann Arbor: University of Michigan Press, 1990), pp. 36–37; Wiencek, *Imperfect God,* p. 197.

17. T. Pickering to Stephen Higginson, January 6, 1804, quoted in Kerber, *Federalists in Dissent,* p. 40.

18. Frank Lawrence Owsley, Jr., and Gene A. Smith, *Filibusters and Expansionists: Jeffersonian Manifest Destiny, 1800–1821* (Tuscaloosa: University of Alabama Press, 1997), p. 107.

19. John Quincy Adams to George W. Erving, November 28, 1818, quoted in Samuel F. Bemis, *John Quincy Adams and the Foundations of American Foreign Policy* (New York: Knopf, 1949), pp. 326–27.

20. *Annals of Congress,* 15th Cong., 2nd sess. (1804), quoted in William Earl Weeks, *John Quincy Adams and American Global Empire* (Lexington: University Press of Kentucky, 1992), p. 64.

21. Clay's home state of Kentucky, with its small and dwindling population of slaves, was never considered a reliable part of the South by southerners. And Clay himself was never considered a reliable advocate of southern interests.

22. In 1804 New Jersey was the last northern state to abolish slavery. In Illinois, although slavery had been abolished, many blacks were virtually enslaved as "apprentices."

23. Wiencek, *Imperfect God,* pp. 267–68.

24. "In 1776, in 1800, even as late as 1820, similarity in values and institutions was the

salient fact." James M. McPherson, *Drawn with the Sword: Reflections on the American Civil War* (New York: Oxford University Press, 1996), p. 21.

25. Charles Grier Sellers, *Market Revolution: Jacksonian America, 1815–1846* (New York: Oxford University Press, 1991), p. 139.

26. To counterbalance the higher population of the Northeast, the South at the constitutional convention in 1787 had demanded that its slaves be counted as three-fifths of a citizen for the purpose of apportioning seats in the House. The distribution of two Senate seats to every state regardless of population was also meant to compensate for the South's comparatively sparse population. The fact that votes in the Electoral College were to be distributed according to each state's representation in both the House and Senate ensured the South a powerful influence over the presidency and with it the Supreme Court as well.

27. Quoted in Wills, *"Negro President,"* p. 124.

28. Ibid., p. 120.

29. Kolchin, *American Slavery,* pp. 95, 93.

30. Although slavery "developed many ostensibly capitalist features, such as banking, commerce, and credit," the slave economy was not a capitalist system any more than the institution of serfdom was a capitalist system, despite the existence of banks in tsarist Russia. Eugene D. Genovese, *Political Economy of Slavery: Studies in the Economy and Society of the Slave South,* 2nd ed. (Middletown, Conn.: Wesleyan University Press, 1989), p. 19.

31. By "substituting the physical coercion of the lash for the economic coercion of the market place," southern slaveholders "did violence to the central values implicit in capitalist relations." Kolchin, *American Slavery,* p. 67.

32. Genovese, *Political Economy of Slavery,* p. 23.

33. Eugene D. Genovese and Elizabeth Fox Genovese, "The Slave Economies in Political Perspective," reprinted ibid., p. 297.

34. See, for instance, William H. Pease and Jane H. Pease, *Web of Progress: Private Values and Public Styles in Boston and Charleston, 1828–1843* (Athens: University of Georgia Press, 1994), and Edward Pessen, "How Different from Each Other Were the Antebellum North and South?" *American Historical Review* 85 (December 1980): 1119–49.

35. Alexis de Tocqueville, *Democracy in America,* 2 vols. (New York: Knopf, 1945), 1:362.

36. Ibid., 1:364.

37. Frederick W. Seward, ed., *William H. Seward: An Autobiography from 1801 to 1834* (New York: Derby & Miller, 1891), quoted in Eric Foner, *Free Soil, Free Labor, Free Men: The Ideology of the Republican Party Before the Civil War* (New York: Oxford University Press, 1970), p. 41.

38. Foner, *Free Soil, Free Labor,* p. 42.

39. *Gazette* (Cincinnati), July 31, 1856, quoted ibid., p. 48.

40. Wiencek, *Imperfect God,* p. 360.

41. *The Speech of James McDowell, Jr. (of Rockbridge) in the House of Delegates . . . on the Slavery Question* (Richmond, 1832), quoted in William W. Freehling, *The Road to Disunion* (New York: Oxford University Press, 1990), p. 184.

42. Genovese, *Political Economy of Slavery,* pp. xvi–xvii.

43. Gerrit Smith statement (1823), quoted in Joyce Appleby, *Inheriting the Revolution: The First Generation of Americans* (Cambridge, Mass.: Belknap Press of Harvard University Press, 2000), p. 248.

44. Tocqueville, *Democracy in America,* 1:363–64.

45. Harry L. Watson, *Andrew Jackson vs. Henry Clay* (Boston: Bedford/St. Martin's, 1998), p. 45.

46. J. Q. Adams, May 3, 1820, quoted in William Lee Miller, *Arguing About Slavery: The Great Battle in the United States Congress* (New York: Knopf, 1996), p. 189.

47. Wiencek, *Imperfect God,* p. 268.

48. Tocqueville, *Democracy in America,* 1:362–63.

49. Genovese, *Political Economy of Slavery,* p. xvii.

50. See Gordon S. Wood, "Tocqueville's Lesson," *New York Review of Books* 48, no. 8 (May 17, 2001): 46–49.

51. Foner, *Free Soil, Free Labor,* p. 11.

52. Appleby, *Inheriting the Revolution,* p. 249.

53. J. Q. Adams, *An Oration Delivered at Newburyport . . .* (Newburyport, Mass., 1837), quoted in Daniel Walker Howe, *The Political Culture of the American Whigs* (Chicago: University of Chicago Press, 1979), p. 59.

54. Quoted in Ronald G. Walters, *American Reformers, 1815–1860* (New York: Hill & Wang, 1997), p. 27.

55. Ibid., p. 6.

56. David Brion Davis, *The Problem of Slavery in the Age of Revolution, 1770–1823* (Ithaca, N.Y.: Cornell University Press, 1975), quoted in Sellers, *Market Revolution,* p. 126.

57. Foner, *Free Soil, Free Labor,* p. 39.

58. Kolchin, *American Slavery,* p. 184.

59. McPherson, *Drawn with the Sword,* p. 21.

60. Kolchin, *American Slavery,* p. 185.

61. Southern leaders "instinctively shied away from efforts to tinker with existing institutions, and increasingly came to see reform of any but the tamest sort as heresy that threatened time-tested traditions." Ibid., p. 186.

62. James Henry Hammond, *Selections from the Letters and Speeches of the Hon. James H. Hammond of South Carolina* (New York, 1866), and "Gov. Hammond's Letters on Slavery," *De Bow's Commercial Review of the South and West* 8 (February 1850), both quoted ibid., p. 188.

63. Kolchin, *American Slavery,* pp. 188–89.

64. Adams diary, February 20, 1820, in *Memoirs of John Quincy Adams, Comprising Portions of His Diary from 1795 to 1848,* ed. Charles Francis Adams, 12 vols. (Philadelphia: J. B. Lippincott, 1874–77), 4:529.

65. "For the first of many times, Northerners demanded their own liberation from slaveholders' unrepublican rule." Freehling, *Road to Disunion,* p. 148.

66. "Sway over the entire government was at stake. The less-populated South was already scheduled to wield power disproportionate to its white members in the Senate, for each state, no matter how extensively populated, would elect two senators. In the Electoral College, each state would receive one presidential elector for each senator and representative. Thus extra southern power in the House, when added to extra power in the Senate, would lead to enhanced power in selecting Presidents, which would lead to added control over a Supreme Court nominated by the Chief Executive. Such special leverage, over and above a one-white-man, one-vote basis, denoted that loaded antebellum word, Slavepower." Ibid., p. 146.

67. Ibid., pp. 150, 146.

68. *The Writings of Thomas Jefferson,* ed. Paul Leicester Ford, 10 vols. (New York: G. P. Putnam's Sons, 1894), 10:157–58. "We wish no slave had touched our soil," Thomas Ritchie's *Richmond Enquirer* declared in 1820. "As republicans, we frankly declare before our God and our country, that we abhor its institution." But what was the alternative? "Does not every man, unless he be a fanatic, conceive how difficult it is for us to be rid of it, in a manner consistent with our future peace and tranquility?" *Richmond Enquirer,* February 10, 1820, quoted in Charles S. Sydnor, *The Development of Southern Sectionalism, 1819–1848* (Baton Rouge: Louisiana State University Press, 1968), pp. 122–23.

69. Before 1820 "there was no such thing as a separate and distinct Southern Congres-

sional bloc or southern political platform." Sydnor, *Development of Southern Sectionalism,* p. 156.

70. Thomas Jefferson to John Holmes, April 22, 1820, in Ford, *Writings of Jefferson,* 10:157–58.

71. Bemis, *Adams and Foreign Policy,* p. 416.

72. Adams diary, March 3, 1820, in C. F. Adams, *Memoirs of John Quincy Adams,* 5:4, 11; Adams diary, December 27, 1819, ibid., 4:492.

73. Adams diary, February 24, 1820, ibid., 4:531.

74. Wiencek, *Imperfect God,* p. 352.

75. C. F. Adams, *Memoirs of John Quincy Adams,* 5:205–11.

76. Adams diary, February 24, 1820, ibid., 4:531.

77. Richard H. Brown, "The Missouri Crisis, Slavery, and the Politics of Jacksonianism," *South Atlantic Quarterly* 65 (1966): 59, 55, 58, 60.

78. Jefferson to J. Holmes, April 22, 1820, in Ford, *Writings of Jefferson,* 10:157–58.

79. As William Earl Weeks has noted, this was not true. Had Adams wished, he could have demanded and won a boundary much farther west. Spain after Jackson's armed seizure of Florida was in no position to resist American territorial demands, and "conceding the claim to Texas was not necessary to obtain the Floridas." Weeks, *John Quincy Adams and American Global Empire* (Lexington: University Press of Kentucky, 1992), p. 168.

80. Adams diary, March 31, 1820, in C. F. Adams, *Memoirs of John Quincy Adams,* 5:54.

81. Weeks, *Adams and Global Empire,* p. 167; Adams diary, November 16, 1819, in C. F. Adams, *Memoirs of John Quincy Adams,* 4:278.

82. Brown, "Missouri Crisis," p. 65.

83. James Monroe to Jefferson (May 1820), quoted in Weeks, *Adams and Global Empire,* pp. 167–68.

84. See Freehling, *Road to Disunion,* pp. 259–60. As Mary W. M. Hargreaves has argued, "The heterogeneity that scholars have found in the Jacksonian attack upon the Adams presidency points, not to a lack of conflict over basic issues, but to the myriad forms of its expression. States' rights, as an ideologic ground of concern, was becoming increasingly important in southern regionalism. In the absence of an administration stand on slavery, states' rights surfaced in criticism of the Panama mission, Indian removal, and the domestic program generally." Hargreaves, *The Presidency of John Quincy Adams* (Lawrence: University of Kansas Press, 1985), p. 247.

85. Brown, "Missouri Crisis," pp. 55, 58, 71.

86. Old Republicans like Randolph had "lived long enough to teach the younger generation of Southern statesmen the almost forgotten language of strict construction. Once, before Jefferson became President, the Republicans had professed a belief in strict construction. Most of them abandoned that faith after their party came to power. There were a few, however, who guarded the arsenal of constitutional arguments and passed out weapons to the younger generation of Southerners in the 1820s. Thus it was that Southern opposition to the various phases of the new economic nationalism, an opposition that was chiefly economic, was quickly joined at nearly every point with the doctrines of strict construction and state rights." Sydnor, *Development of Southern Sectionalism,* p. 156.

87. Albert Ray Newsome, *The Presidential Election of 1824 in North Carolina* (Chapel Hill: University of North Carolina Press, 1939), quoted in Sellers, *Market Revolution,* p. 142.

88. Thomas R. Hietala, *Manifest Design: Anxious Aggrandizement of Late Jacksonian America* (Ithaca, N.Y.: Cornell University Press, 1985), p. 15.

89. J. Q. Adams, "First Annual Message," December 6, 1825, quoted in Robert Vincent Remini, *Andrew Jackson: The Course of American Freedom, 1822–1832* (Baltimore: Johns

Hopkins University Press, 1998), pp. 109–11; Nathaniel Macon to Bartlett Yancey, December 8, 1825, quoted ibid.

90. At the same time, over southern objections, more money was poured into the construction of roads and canals.

91. Senator William Smith of South Carolina, chairman of the Senate Finance Committee, in *Register of Debates*, 20th Cong., 1st sess. (April 11, 1828), cols. 645–46, quoted in Hargreaves, *Presidency of John Quincy Adams*, p. 180.

92. David Morris Potter, *The Impending Crisis, 1848–1861* (New York: Harper & Row, 1976), p. 7.

93. Supporters included the economist Matthew Carey, the American System's most effective publicist; Boston's Edward Everett and Thomas L. Winthrop; New York's governor DeWitt Clinton; the author of the nationalist dictionary, Noah Webster; the future president William Henry Harrison; and the philanthropist physician Samuel Gridley Howe. See Edward Mead Earle, "American Interest in Greek Cause, 1821–1827," *American Historical Review* 33 (October 1927): 50.

94. Edward Mead Earle, "Early American Policy Concerning Ottoman Minorities," *Political Science Quarterly* 42, no. 3 (September 1927): 357.

95. Earle, "American Interest in the Greek Cause," p. 63n.

96. George M. Troup, *State Documents on Federal Relations,* ed. Herman Vandenburg Ames (Philadelphia, 1906), quoted in Sydnor, *Development of Southern Sectionalism,* p. 151.

97. Watson, *Andrew Jackson vs. Henry Clay,* p. 45.

98. Henry Clay, *The Life and Speeches of Henry Clay,* 2 vols. (Philadelphia, 1853), quoted in Freehling, *Road to Disunion,* p. 158.

99. This fear distinguished southern realism from John Quincy Adams's realism, for Adams had opposed Clay's and Daniel Webster's ideological exuberance on tactical, not principled grounds—as he proved when as president he carried out both men's policies toward Latin America and Greece.

100. As Langley notes, "The larger issues with which the Monroe Doctrine has always been associated—the hemispheric balance of power, the presence of 'European' political systems in the New World, and the recognition of revolutionary governments—were usually subordinated, or at least rephrased, to conform to the realities of the Caribbean world." Langley, *Struggle for the American Mediterranean,* p. 38.

101. Hargreaves, *Presidency of John Quincy Adams,* p. 156.

102. Senator Macon quoted in Norman K. Risjord, *The Old Republicans: Southern Conservatism in the Age of Jefferson* (New York: Columbia University Press, 1965), p. 261. For John Floyd's statement, see *Register of Debates in Congress,* 19th Cong., 1st sess. (1826), ii, col. 2446, quoted in Dexter Perkins, *The Monroe Doctrine, 1823–1826* (Cambridge, Mass.: Harvard University Press, 1932), p. 147.

103. The American ambassador to Mexico had also used the word "pledge" in conversations with that government. See Perkins, *Monroe Doctrine,* p. 209.

104. Clay to Daniel Webster, February 2, 1826, quoted in Robert V. Remini, *Henry Clay: Statesman for the Union* (New York: Norton, 1991), p. 296.

105. Remini, *Henry Clay,* p. 213.

106. Stephen F. Knott, *Alexander Hamilton and the Persistence of Myth* (Lawrence: University Press of Kansas, 2002), pp. 39–40.

107. Remini, *Henry Clay,* p. 290.

108. A Virginia congressman pointed out that President J. Q. Adams's message on the Panama conference "made the most copious use" of "certain cabalistic phrases" associated with the American System. *Register of Debates in Congress,* 19th Cong., 1st sess. (April 6, 1826), cols. 2079–80, quoted in Hargreaves, *Presidency of John Quincy Adams,* p. 161. Sena-

tor Macon humorously linked Adams's proposal to send delegates to Panama with his plan to build observatories and thus with the overall "attempt to make the constitutional way as wide as the world." Macon to Yancey, April 16, 1826, quoted in Risjord, *Old Republicans,* p. 261. Andrew Jackson, without humor, warned that Adams's Panama project would "destroy the constitutional checks of our government" and "reduce it to a despotism." Jackson to John Branch, March 3, 1826, quoted in Remini, *Jackson: Course of Freedom,* p. 111.

109. Remini, *Henry Clay,* p. 292.

110. Calhoun quoted in John Niven, *John C. Calhoun and the Price of Union: A Biography* (Baton Rouge: Louisiana State University Press, 1988), p. 115.

111. There was irony in this angle of attack against Adams's hemispheric ambitions. Just a few years earlier Secretary of State Adams himself, though a closet abolitionist, had raised the Haitian bogey in arguing against what he considered the premature recognition of South American independence. Greatly exaggerating the "preponderating weight" that blacks were playing in the South American liberation struggles, Adams had convinced many southern congressmen to oppose Clay's proposal to recognize the South American republics on the grounds that it would risk more slave rebellions in the hemisphere and eventually threaten the institution in the United States. A few years later he was the victim of his own cynical device. See Weeks, *Adams and Global Empire,* 98.

112. Adams's Message to the House of Representatives of the United States, March 15, 1826, in Walter LaFeber, ed., *John Quincy Adams and American Continental Empire: Letters, Papers and Speeches* (Chicago: Quadrangle Books, 1965), pp. 135–37.

113. Congressman William C. Rives, Virginia, *Register of Debates,* April 6, 1826, quoted in Albert A. Weinberg, "Washington's 'Great Rule in Its Historical Evolution,'" in Eric F. Goldman, ed., *Historiography and Urbanization: Essays in American History in Honor of W. Stull Holt* (Port Washington, N.Y.: Kennikat Press, 1968), p. 119.

114. Jackson to Branch, March 3, 1826, quoted in Remini, *Jackson: Course of Freedom,* p. 111.

115. U.S. Congress, *Senate Documents,* 19th Cong., 1st sess., no. 68, p. 100, quoted in Hargreaves, *Presidency of John Quincy Adams,* p. 151.

116. Calhoun to Jackson, June 4, 1826, quoted in Remini, *Jackson: Course of Freedom,* p. 112.

117. *Register of Debates,* 19th Cong., 1st sess., quoted in Perkins, *Monroe Doctrine,* pp. 219–20.

118. As Dexter Perkins put it, "One might have thought at the time that it marked the eclipse of the Doctrine itself." Perkins, *Monroe Doctrine,* p. 222.

119. Paul A. Varg, *United States Foreign Relations, 1820–1860* (East Lansing: Michigan State University Press, 1979), p. 59; see also Bradford Perkins, *The Cambridge History of American Foreign Relations,* vol. 1: *Creation of a Republican Empire, 1776–1865* (New York: Cambridge University Press, 1993), p. 167.

120. Freehling, *Road to Disunion,* p. viii.

121. In 1835 fears of a slave revolt in Mississippi led to a record number of lynchings of whites suspected of inciting rebellious slaves.

122. Freehling, *Road to Disunion,* pp. 61, 118.

123. Ibid., p. 154.

124. Sir Charles Kingsley Webster, *The Foreign Policy of Palmerston, 1830–1841: Britain, the Liberal Movement, and the Eastern Question,* 2 vols. (London: G. Bell, 1969), 1:3.

125. Ibid., 2:785.

126. Only constitutional governments, Palmerston insisted, were capable of fully developing "the natural resources of a country" and ensuring "security for life, liberty and property." To Lord Beauvale, Sir Frederick Lamb, January 21, 1841, Broadlands Papers, quoted ibid., 2:786–87.

127. Donald Southgate, *"The Most English Minister": The Policies and Politics of Palmerston* (London: Macmillan, 1966), quoted in Martin Lynn, "British Policy, Trade, and Informal Empire in the Mid-Nineteenth Century," in *The Oxford History of the British Empire,* vol. 3: *The Nineteenth Century,* ed. Andrew Porter (Oxford: Oxford University Press, 1999), p. 102.

128. Lynn, "British Policy, Trade," p. 103.

129. Minute by Palmerston, September 29, 1850, on F[oreign] O[ffice] Memo of September 26, 1850, on Consular Establishments at Foochowfoo and Ningpo, FO 17/173, quoted ibid., pp. 106–8.

130. William Wilberforce, journal [end of 1802], quoted in Abraham D. Kriegel, "A Convergence of Ethics: Saints and Whigs in British Antislavery," *Journal of British Studies* 26, no. 4 (October 1987): 432.

131. Andrew Porter, "Trusteeship, Anti-Slavery, and Humanitarianism," in Porter, *Oxford History,* 3:202.

132. It was no accident that the antislavery crusade initially took hold in "the first nation to achieve a sustained growth of per capita output, a truly industrialized economy, a rapidly urbanized population, and a prosperous middle class." David Brion Davis, *Slavery and Human Progress* (New York: Oxford University Press, 1984), p. 232.

133. *The Later Correspondence of George III,* ed. Arthur Aspinall, 5 vols. (London: Cambridge University Press, 1962–70), quoted in Hugh Thomas, *The Slave Trade: The Story of the Atlantic Slave Trade, 1440–1870* (New York: Simon & Schuster, 1997), pp. 553–54.

134. At the Congress of Vienna, Castlereagh sought and won reluctant support from the assembled great powers of Europe for a declaration condemning the slave trade as "repugnant to the principles of humanity and universal morality." General Treaty signed in Congress at Vienna (London, 1816), quoted ibid., p. 587.

135. Thomas, *Slave Trade,* p. 592.

136. Gerald S. Graham, *Great Britain in the Indian Ocean: A Study of the Maritime Enterprise, 1810–1850* (Oxford: Clarendon Press, 1967), quoted in Porter, "Trusteeship, Anti-Slavery," p. 211.

137. *Foreign Relations of the United States,* 32 vols. [2005] (Washington, D.C., 1915–), 5:72, quoted in Thomas, *Slave Trade,* p. 613.

138. Quoted in Sydnor, *Development of Southern Sectionalism,* p. 152.

139. Andrew Stevenson to John Forsyth, July 21, 1838, Enclosure Stevenson to Palmerston, July 10, 1838. Despatches from London, Roll 41, quoted in Varg, *United States Foreign Relations,* p. 104.

140. Stevenson to Forsyth, November 5, 1838, Enclosure Palmerston to Stevenson, September 10, 1838, quoted ibid., p. 105.

141. Varg, *United States Foreign Relations,* p. 96.

142. Stevenson to D. Webster, August 18, 1841, Enclosure Palmerston to Stevenson, August 5, 1841, quoted ibid., p. 107.

143. See Freehling, *Road to Disunion,* p. 383.

144. Frederick Merk, *Slavery and the Annexation of Texas* (New York: Knopf, 1972), p. 49.

145. Abel P. Upshur to Calhoun, August 14, 1843, quoted in Freehling, *Road to Disunion,* p. 401.

146. Brown, "Missouri Crisis," pp. 69–70.

147. The long hesitation over Texas has led some modern historians to conclude mistakenly that in the two decades between Adams's Transcontinental Treaty and the move to annex Texas, American expansionist tendencies had lain dormant. "The twenties and thirties," according to Norman Graebner, were "years of introspection" during which "the changing

structure of American political and economic life had absorbed the people's energies and directed their thoughts inward." Norman A. Graebner, "Manifest Destiny and National Interests," in Sean Wilentz, ed., *Major Problems in the Early Republic* (Lexington, Mass.: D. C. Heath, 1992), p. 555.

148. The idea that American expansion in the 1840s was prompted by "anxiety" and not, as commonly assumed, by confidence has been well articulated by Thomas Hietala in *Manifest Design*. In trying to provide an overarching thesis that covers both North and South, however, Hietala slights the influence of the slavery question. Like Michael Hunt, Hietala writes of a racial anxiety that existed in both the North and the South. But while racial anxiety existed in the North, it cannot be compared to the unique fears of the South. And it was those fears, not northern anxieties, that led directly to the annexation of Texas, as Freehling has amply demonstrated.

149. Lyon G. Tyler, *Letters and Times of the Tylers,* 3 vols. (Richmond, 1884–85), quoted in Hietala, *Manifest Design,* p. 13.

150. *Report of the Secretary of the Navy, S. Doc.,* vol. 395, no. 1, 27th Cong., 2nd sess. (December 4, 1841), quoted ibid., p. 14.

151. Calhoun to Upshur, August 27, 1843, State Department Record Group 59, Miscellaneous Letters, 1789–1906, National Archives, quoted in Merk, *Slavery and Annexation of Texas,* pp. 21–22.

152. Duff Green to J. Tyler, May 31, 1843, Duff Green Papers, Library of Congress, quoted in Hietala, *Manifest Design,* p. 19.

153. David M. Pletcher, *The Diplomacy of Annexation: Texas, Oregon, and the Mexican War* (Columbia: University of Missouri Press, 1973), p. 121.

154. *London Morning Chronicle,* August 19, 1843, quoted in Freehling, *Road to Disunion,* pp. 397–98.

155. Lord Aberdeen to Richard Packenham, December 26, 1843, quoted ibid., p. 408.

156. As William W. Freehling explains, even if Aberdeen did not press hard for abolition in Texas, slavery in an independent Texas protected by abolitionist Great Britain would be vulnerable. British immigrants would flock to Texas bringing the doctrines of free labor and abolitionism with them. Slave owners would be reluctant to bring their valuable property to a republic where there was even a possibility of some future British-imposed abolition. Freehling, *Road to Disunion,* p. 405.

157. Ashbel Smith to Anson Jones, July 2, 1843, in Pletcher, *Diplomacy of Annexation,* p. 122. See also A. Smith to Calhoun, June 19, 1843, quoted in Harriet Smither, "English Abolitionism and the Annexation of Texas," *Southwestern Historical Quarterly* 32, no. 3 (January 1929): 199–200.

158. Upshur to Beverley Tucker, March 13, 1843, quoted in Freehling, *Road to Disunion,* p. 392.

159. Calhoun to Packenham, April 18, 1844, *Senate Documents,* 29th Cong., 1st sess., pp. 50–53, quoted ibid., pp. 408–9.

160. Upshur to Calhoun, August 14, 1843, quoted ibid., p. 401.

161. Adams diary, May 31, 1843, in C. F. Adams, *Memoirs of John Quincy Adams,* 11:380.

Chapter 8 / *Manifest Destinies*

1. Norman A. Graebner, *Empire on the Pacific: A Study of American Continental Expansion* (New York: Ronald Press, 1955; reprint, Santa Barbara, Calif.: ABC-Clio, 1983), p. 2.

2. William W. Freehling, *The Road to Disunion* (New York: Oxford University Press, 1990), pp. 437–39.

3. Although supporters could be found in the North, "virtually all agitation for annexation had emanated from the South," where southerners "hoped to gain more land, more political power, and more security for the South in general and for slaveholders in particular." Michael Fitzgibbon Holt, *The Rise and Fall of the American Whig Party: Jacksonian Politics and the Onset of the Civil War* (New York: Oxford University Press, 1999), pp. 168–69.

4. Graebner, *Empire on Pacific,* p. vii.

5. Freehling, *Road to Disunion,* p. 452.

6. Ibid., p. 459.

7. Greeley quoted in Holt, *Rise and Fall,* p. 251.

8. *Congressional Globe,* 29th Cong., 2nd sess. (February 19, 1847), p. 454, quoted in Freehling, *Road to Disunion,* p. 462.

9. "The Democratic party . . . had been slowly disintegrating ever since the election of James K. Polk." Avery O. Craven, *The Growth of Southern Nationalism, 1848–1861,* vol. 6 of *A History of the South,* ed. Wendell Holmes Stephenson and E. Merlon Coulter (Baton Rouge: Louisiana State University Press, 1953), p. 314.

10. David Morris Potter, *The Impending Crisis, 1848–1861* (New York: Harper & Row, 1976), p. 17.

11. D. Webster, *The Works of Daniel Webster,* 4 vols. (Boston: Little, Brown, 1877), quoted in Harry V. Jaffa, *Crisis of the House Divided: An Interpretation of the Issues in the Lincoln-Douglas Debates* (Chicago: University of Chicago Press, 1982), p. 80.

12. *The Collected Works of Abraham Lincoln,* ed. Roy P. Basler and Christian Basler, 9 vols. (New Brunswick, N.J.: Rutgers University Press, 1952–55), quoted ibid., p. 219.

13. Eric Foner, *Free Soil, Free Labor, Free Man: The Ideology of the Republican Party Before the Civil War* (New York: Oxford University Press, 1973), pp. 311–12.

14. James M. McPherson, *Battle Cry of Freedom: The Civil War Era* (New York: Oxford University Press, 1988), pp. 91–92.

15. Basler and Basler, *Works of Lincoln,* quoted ibid., p. 187.

16. George Kennan (originally "X"), "The Sources of Soviet Conduct," *Foreign Affairs* 25, no. 4 (July 1947), quoted in John Lewis Gaddis, *We Now Know: Rethinking Cold War History* (New York: Oxford University Press, 1997), p. 37.

17. *Congressional Globe,* 31st Cong., 1st sess., Appendix, quoted in Foner, *Free Soil, Free Labor,* p. 116.

18. *New York Evening Post,* November 10, 1847, quoted in McPherson, *Battle Cry of Freedom,* p. 55.

19. Columbus Delano, *Congressional Globe,* 29th Cong., 2nd sess., quoted in Potter, *Impending Crisis,* pp. 67–68.

20. Potter, *Impending Crisis,* p. 93.

21. *Speeches, Messages, and Other Writings of the Hon. Albert G. Brown, a Senator in Congress from the State of Mississippi,* ed. M. W. Cluskey (Philadelphia: n.p., 1859), quoted in Freehling, *Road to Disunion,* p. 474.

22. William L. Barney, *The Road to Secession: A New Perspective on the Old South* (New York: Praeger, 1972), quoted in McPherson, *Battle Cry of Freedom,* p. 57.

23. "The Late Cuba Expedition," *De Bow's Review* 9 (1850), quoted ibid., p. 106.

24. See Eugene D. Genovese, *Political Economy of Slavery: Studies in the Economy and Society of the Slave South,* 2nd ed. (Middletown, Conn.: Wesleyan University Press, 1989), pp. 256–58.

25. Cluskey, *Speeches, Messages, and Other Writings of Brown,* quoted in Robert E. May, *The Southern Dream of a Caribbean Empire, 1854–1861* (Baton Rouge: Louisiana State University Press, 1973), p. 9.

26. Isaac Holmes, *Congressional Globe,* 28th Cong., 2nd sess. (January 14, 1845), Appendix, quoted in Freehling, *Road to Disunion,* p. 423.

27. George McDuffie in *Niles' Weekly Register* 16 (August 24, 1844):421–44, and *Congressional Globe,* 28th Cong., 1st sess. (June 10, 1844), both quoted ibid., p. 432.

28. *Charleston Mercury,* February 26, 1858, quoted in John McCardell, *The Idea of a Southern Nation: Southern Nationalists and Southern Nationalism, 1830–1860* (New York: Norton, 1979), p. 250.

29. O. C. Gardiner, *The Great Issue* (New York, 1848), quoted in Foner, *Free Soil, Free Labor,* p. 312.

30. Genovese, *Political Economy of Slavery,* p. 250. To accept containment, "the South would have had to abandon its whole ideology." Foner, *Free Soil, Free Labor,* pp. 312–13.

31. See Potter, *Impending Crisis,* pp. 94, 122.

32. Allan Nevins, *Ordeal of the Union,* vol. 2: *A House Dividing, 1852–1857* (New York: Scribner's, 1947), pp. 92–93.

33. Lincoln's famous speech in Peoria, October 16, 1854, quoted in McPherson, *Battle Cry of Freedom,* pp. 128–29.

34. As Harry Jaffa elaborated Lincoln's argument, "a free people cannot disagree on the relative merits of freedom and despotism without ceasing . . . to be a free people. In choosing to enslave other men it is impossible not to concede the justice of one's own enslavement." Jaffa, *House Divided,* p. 336.

35. Lincoln quoted in McPherson, *Battle Cry of Freedom,* p. 129.

36. McPherson, *Battle Cry of Freedom,* p. 125.

37. W. H. Seward, "The Advent of the Republican Party," Albany, October 12, 1855, quoted in Daniel Walker Howe, *The Political Culture of the American Whigs* (Chicago: University of Chicago Press, 1979), pp. 207–8.

38. *Congressional Globe,* 33rd Cong., 1st sess. (May 25, 1854), 31, Appendix, quoted in McPherson, *Battle Cry of Freedom,* p. 145.

39. Atchinson to Robert M. T. Hunter, quoted ibid., pp. 145–46.

40. The term "border ruffians" was coined by Horace Greeley and became popular in Missouri. From Michael Fellman, "Rehearsal for the Civil War: Antislavery and Proslavery at the Fighting Point in Kansas, 1854–56," in Lewis Perry and Michael Fellman, eds., *Antislavery Reconsidered: New Perspectives on the Abolitionists* (Baton Rouge: Louisiana State University Press, 1979), cited ibid., p. 146; John Stringfellow, quoted ibid., p. 147.

41. Freehling, *Road to Disunion,* p. 458.

42. John Ford to John Quitman, July 2, 1855, quoted in May, *Southern Dream,* p. 137.

43. Representative Thomas Bocock of Virginia, *Congressional Globe,* 34th Cong., 1st sess., Appendix, quoted ibid., p. 140.

44. Quitman, *Congressional Globe,* 34th Cong., 1st sess., Appendix, quoted ibid., p. 141.

45. See *Daily Whig,* Richmond, July 18, 1860; C. A. Bridges, "The Knights of the Golden Circle: A Filibustering Fantasy," *Southwestern Historical Quarterly* 54 (1941), quoted in May, *Southern Dream,* p. 150; George Bickley to E. H. Cushing, November 15, 1860, quoted ibid.

46. Samuel Flagg Bemis, *A Diplomatic History of the United States,* 5th ed. (Chicago, London, and New York: Holt, Rinehart & Winston, 1965), p. 324.

47. No. 575, Viscount Palmerston to Lord Howden, October 20, 1854, quoted in McCardell, *Southern Nation,* p. 252.

48. May, *Southern Dream,* p. 31.

49. Freehling, *Road to Disunion,* p. 554.

50. James D. Richardson, *A Compilation of the Messages and Papers of the Presidents,*

1789–1897, 10 vols. (Washington, D.C.: U.S. Government Printing Office, 1899), quoted in May, *Southern Dream*, p. 40.

51. M. J. White, "Louisiana and the Secession Movement of the Early Fifties," in Benjamin F. Shambaugh, ed., *Proceedings of the Mississippi Valley Historical Association for the Year 1914–1915* (Cedar Rapids, Iowa: Torch Press, 1916), quoted in McCardell, *Southern Nation*, p. 254.

52. James Buchanan to William L. Marcy, November 1, 1853, Despatches from London, Roll 61, quoted in Paul A. Varg, *United States Foreign Relations, 1820–1860* (East Lansing: Michigan State University Press, 1979), p. 247.

53. May, *Southern Dream*, p. 47.

54. Varg, *United States Foreign Relations*, p. 246.

55. Potter, *Impending Crisis*, p. 187.

56. Quitman to B. Dill, February 9, 1854, quoted in May, *Southern Dream*, p. 34.

57. Alexander Stephens to Linton Stephens, May 9, 1854, quoted ibid., p. 33.

58. *Richmond Enquirer*, June 20, 1854, in *New York Herald*, June 22, 1854, quoted ibid., p. 39.

59. A. Dudley Mann to Lawrence Keitt, August 24, 1855, quoted ibid., p. 37.

60. Potter, *Impending Crisis*, p. 188.

61. Soulé to Marcy, October 18, 1854, in Philip Shriver Klein, *President James Buchanan: A Biography* (University Park: Pennsylvania State University Press, 1962), p. 238; Buchanan to Marcy, December 22, 1854, quoted ibid., pp. 239–41.

62. Buchanan, the northerner, had tried to restrain even more inflammatory language proposed by Soulé. Klein, *Buchanan*, p. 240. See Roy Franklin Nichols, *Franklin Pierce: Young Hickory of the Granite Hills*, 2nd ed. (Philadelphia: University of Pennsylvania Press, 1958), pp. 368–39.

63. Thomas H. McKee, ed., *The National Conventions and Platforms of All Political Parties, 1789–1900* (Baltimore: Friedenwald, 1900), quoted in May, *Southern Dream*, p. 76.

64. Ivor Spencer, *The Victor and the Spoils: A Life of William L. Marcy* (Providence, R.I.: Brown University Press, 1959), quoted ibid., p. 60.

65. As the *Montgomery Advertiser* (Alabama) put it, Buchanan's position on Cuba was reason enough for "every southern man to cast his vote" for him. *Mobile Daily Register*, June 11, 1856, quoted ibid., p. 72.

66. *Official Proceedings of the Democratic Convention Held in Cincinnati, June 2–6, 1856*, quoted ibid.

67. Henry Cleveland, *Alexander H. Stephens in Public and Private* (Chicago and Philadelphia: National, 1866), quoted ibid., p. 186.

68. *Montgomery Daily Confederation*, March 21, 1860, quoted ibid., p. 179.

69. R. C. Wickliffe in *Tuskegee Republican*, May 13, 1858, quoted ibid., p. 14.

70. "The Destiny of the Slave States," reprinted in *De Bow's Review* 17, no. 3 (September 1854), quoted in Genovese, *Political Economy of Slavery*, pp. 248–49.

71. McPherson, *Battle Cry of Freedom*, p. 194.

72. May, *Southern Dream*, p. 179; see Douglas to A. Stephens, December 25, 1860, in *The Letters of Stephen A. Douglas*, ed. Robert W. Johannsen (Urbana: University of Illinois Press, 1961), p. 506.

73. Basler and Basler, *Works of Lincoln*, 4:150, quoted in Jaffa, *House Divided*, p. 402.

74. Lincoln to Thurlow Weed, December 17, 1860, quoted in McPherson, *Battle Cry of Freedom*, p. 253; Lincoln to W. H. Seward, February 1, 1861, quoted ibid.

75. Lincoln to W. H. Seward, February 1, 1861, quoted ibid., p. 255.

76. New York's Roscoe Conkling predicted that approval of the "hereafter clause" would "amount to a perpetual covenant of war against every people, tribe, and State owning a foot of land between here and Terra del Fuego. It would make the Government the armed

missionary of slavery . . . for purposes of land-stealing and slave-planting, we should be launched upon a shoreless and starless sea of war and filibustering." *Congressional Globe,* January 30, 1861, 36th Cong., 2nd sess., quoted in May, *Southern Dream,* p. 221. Charles Francis Adams predicted to his brother Henry that a southern confederacy "will be aggressive and more slaves and more cotton will be the cry. In spite of England the slave trade will flourish and their system will spread over Mexico and Central America." Charles Francis Adams to Henry Adams, August 25, 1861, quoted ibid., p. 240.

77. *New York Semi-Weekly Tribune,* September 5, 1859, quoted ibid., p. 188.

78. Samuel Walker, "The Diary of a Louisiana Planter," entry for December 19, 1859, quoted ibid., p. 236.

79. James D. Richardson, ed., *A Compilation of the Messages and Papers of the Confederacy, Including the Diplomatic Correspondence, 1861–1865,* 2 vols. (Nashville, Tenn.: United States Publishing Co., 1905), quoted ibid., p. 246.

80. May, *Southern Dream,* p. 247.

81. Jaffa, *House Divided,* p. 408.

82. Adolf Hitler (1933), quoted in Harry V. Jaffa, *A New Birth of Freedom: Abraham Lincoln and the Coming of the Civil War* (Lanham, Md.: Rowman & Littlefield, 2000), p. 73.

Chapter 9 / *Beyond the National Interest*

1. J. Q. Adams to Richard Rush, October 16, 1845, quoted in Samuel Flagg Bemis, *John Quincy Adams and the Union* (New York: Knopf, 1956), p. 479.

2. Quoted in Anders Stephanson, *Manifest Destiny: American Expansionism and the Empire of Right* (New York: Hill & Wang, 1995), p. 39.

3. See, for instance, Robert E. May, *The Southern Dream of a Caribbean Empire, 1854–1861* (Baton Rouge: Louisiana State University Press, 1973), p. 20: "Whigs of both sections were traditionally conservative concerning expansion." The Whigs' "primary concern was the qualitative development of American society, both economically and morally, not its mere quantitative extension." Daniel Walker Howe, *The Political Culture of the American Whigs* (Chicago: University of Chicago Press, 1979), p. 143. According to Frederick Merk, Whigs "objected to continent-wide expansion" and adhered instead "to the philosophy of national authority in a limited area." Merk, *Manifest Destiny and Mission in American History* (New York: McGraw-Hill, 1966), p. 39.

4. Thomas R. Hietala, *Manifest Design: Anxious Aggrandizement of Late Jacksonian America* (Ithaca, N.Y.: Cornell University Press, 1985), pp. 6–7.

5. Daniel Webster, "The Revolution in Greece" (1824), quoted in Howe, *Political Culture of Whigs,* p. 143.

6. Howe, *Political Culture of Whigs,* pp. 210–17.

7. As one Massachusetts Whig put in 1846, "The free state Whigs must dictate the policy of the Party, or the Party had better be defeated and broken up." Henry Wilson to Joshua R. Giddings, February 6 and April 10, 1847, quoted in Michael Fitzgibbon Holt, *The Rise and Fall of the American Whig Party: Jacksonian Politics and the Onset of the Civil War* (New York: Oxford University Press, 1999), p. 266.

8. Robert Toombs to George W. Crawford, February 5, 1846, quoted in John Hope Franklin, "Southern Expansionists of 1846," *Journal of Southern History* 25, no. 3 (August 1959): 337.

9. Frederick Merk, *Slavery and the Annexation of Texas* (New York: Knopf, 1972), p. 10.

10. *Congressional Globe,* 35th Cong., 2nd sess., quoted in May, *Southern Dream,* p. 174.

11. David Herbert Donald, *Charles Sumner* (New York: Da Capo Press, 1996), pp. 303–5.

12. J. Q. Adams to Reverend William Ellery Channing, August 11 and November 21, 1837, quoted in Bemis, *Adams and Union,* p. 360.

13. Webster to Daniel M. Barringer, November 26, 1851, Diplomatic Instructions of the Department of State, Spain, General Records of the Department of State, quoted in Kenneth E. Shewmaker, "Daniel Webster and the Politics of Foreign Policy, 1850–1852," *Journal of American History* 63, no. 2 (September 1976): 313; Webster to Washington Irving, January 17, 1843, quoted ibid.

14. *Congressional Globe,* 32nd Cong., 2nd sess. (January 26, 1853), Appendix, quoted in Paul A. Varg, *United States Foreign Relations, 1820–1860* (East Lansing: Michigan State University Press, 1979), p. 234*n*.

15. W. H. Seward in a speech in Columbus, Ohio (1853), quoted in Ernest N. Paolino, *The Foundations of the American Empire: William Henry Seward and U.S. Foreign Policy* (Ithaca, N.Y.: Cornell University Press, 1973), pp. 7–8; W. H. Seward in a speech in St. Paul, Minnesota (1860), quoted ibid.

16. *Congressional Globe,* 32nd Cong., 2nd sess. (January 26, 1853), Appendix; *The Works of William H. Seward,* ed. George E. Baker, 4 vols. (New York: Redfield, 1853–61), 4:139; and *Congressional Globe,* 33rd Cong., 1st sess. (May 25, 1854), Appendix; all quoted ibid.

17. *Congressional Globe,* 32nd Cong., 2nd sess. (January 26, 1853), Appendix, quoted ibid., pp. 27, 28.

18. *Congressional Globe,* 31st Cong., 2nd sess. (February 27, 1851), and W. H. Seward, in Baker, *Works of Willam H. Seward,* 4:170; both quoted ibid., pp. 25, 27.

19. *Congressional Globe,* 31st Cong., 1st sess. (January 30, 1850), quoted ibid., p. 12.

20. *Congressional Globe,* 34th Cong., 1st and 2nd sess. (August 12, 1856), quoted ibid., p. 37.

21. Baker, *Works of William H. Seward,* 4:320, and *Congressional Globe,* 32nd Cong., 2nd sess. (July 29, 1852); both quoted ibid., p. 29.

22. *Congressional Globe,* 32nd Cong., 1st sess. (April 28, 1852), quoted ibid., p. 34.

23. *Congressional Globe,* 32nd Cong., 1st sess. (April 27, 1852), quoted ibid., p. 32.

24. Baker, *Works of William H. Seward,* 4:166, quoted ibid.

25. As John M. Belohlavek writes, the "advance of commerce" was "the major thrust of Jacksonian foreign policy." Belohlavek, *"Let the Eagle Soar": The Foreign Policy of Andrew Jackson* (Lincoln: University of Nebraska Press, 1985), p. 10.

26. Robert Vincent Remini, *Daniel Webster: The Man and His Time* (New York: Norton, 1997), p. 579.

27. Protocol no. 4, March 25, 1854, enclosed in David L. Gregg to Marcy, no. 64, December 29, 1854, quoted in Merze Tate, "Slavery and Racism as Deterrents to the Annexation of Hawaii, 1854–1855," *Journal of Negro History* 47, no. 3 (January 1962): 3.

28. Paolino, *Foundations of Empire,* p. 9.

29. Rupert B. Vance, "The Geography of Distinction: The Nation and Its Regions, 1790–1927," *Social Forces* 18 (1939), quoted in James M. McPherson, *Drawn With the Sword: Reflections on the American Civil War* (New York: Oxford University Press, 1996), p. 18.

30. Quoted in Stephanson, *Manifest Destiny,* p. 45.

31. *Washington Union,* January 11, 1852, quoted in Robert W. Johannsen, "The Meaning of Manifest Destiny," in Sam W. Haynes and Christopher Morris, eds., *Manifest Destiny and Empire: American Antebellum Expansion* (College Station: Texas A&M University Press, 1998), p. 16.

32. Baker, *Works of William H. Seward,* 3:409, quoted in Paolino, *Foundations of Empire,* p. 11.

33. W. H. Seward, in Baker, *The Life of William H. Seward, with Selections from His Works* (New York: Redfield, 1855), quoted ibid.

34. Clay quoted in William W. Freehling, *The Road to Disunion* (New York: Oxford University Press, 1990), p. 158.

35. Clay speech, May 19, 1821, quoted in Ernest R. May, *The Making of the Monroe Doctrine* (Cambridge, Mass.: Belknap Press of Harvard University Press, 1975), p. 180.

36. Howe, *Political Culture of Whigs,* p. 216.

37. Fillmore to D. Webster, October 23, 1850, quoted in Donald S. Spencer, *Louis Kossuth and Young America: A Study of Sectionalism and Foreign Policy, 1848–1852* (Columbia: University of Missouri Press, 1977), pp. 85–86.

38. Spencer, *Louis Kossuth,* p. 8.

39. Ibid., p. viii.

40. J. B. Syme, "Joseph Kossuth, the Student Chieftain of Republican Hungary," *Burritt's Christian Citizen* (Worcester, Mass.), August 11, 1849, quoted ibid., p. 67. The abolitionists turned against Kossuth when the Hungarian, fearful of alienating the South, equivocated on the subject of slavery.

41. Charles Sumner, "Sympathy for the Rights of Man Everywhere," October 27, 1851, quoted ibid., p. 68.

42. *Congressional Globe,* 29th Cong., 1st sess., quoted ibid., pp. 136–37.

43. Lincoln, *The Collected Works of Abraham Lincoln,* ed. Roy P. Basler and Christian O. Basler, 9 vols. (New Brunswick, N.J.: Rutgers University Press, 1952–55), 2:115–16, quoted ibid., p. 110.

44. *Congressional Globe,* 32nd Cong., 1st sess., quoted ibid., p. 112.

45. *Congressional Globe,* 32nd Cong., 1st sess., Appendix, quoted ibid., p. 140.

46. Spencer, *Louis Kossuth,* p. 103.

47. *Baltimore Clipper,* December 1851, quoted ibid.

48. *Southern Advocate,* February 25, 1852, quoted ibid.

49. Spencer, *Louis Kossuth,* p. 100.

50. James D. Richardson, *A Compilation of the Messages and Papers of the Presidents, 1789–1897,* 10 vols. (Washington, D.C.: U.S. Government Printing Office, 1896–99), 5:116–17, quoted ibid., p. 86.

51. According to Presley Ewings, notes from this meeting were reprinted in many newspapers, including *The Liberator,* February 13, 1852, *Southern Advocate,* February 18, 1852, and *Georgia Telegraph* (Macon), February 24, 1852, quoted ibid., p. 93. See also Glyndon Garlock Van Deusen, *The Life of Henry Clay* (Boston: Little, Brown, 1937), pp. 421–22.

52. Howe, *Political Culture of Whigs,* p. 276.

53. Walter LaFeber, *The New Empire: An Interpretation of American Expansion, 1860–1898* (Ithaca, N.Y.: Cornell University Press, 1963), p. 25; W. H. Seward, *Autobiography of William H. Seward, from 1801 to 1834,* 3 vols. (New York, 1877–91), quoted ibid.

54. Howe, *Political Culture of Whigs,* p. 200.

55. W. H. Seward, "The True Greatness of Our Country," December 22, 1848, quoted ibid., p. 199.

56. Howe, *Political Culture of Whigs,* p. 199.

57. Foner, *Free Soil, Free Labor,* p. 175.

58. Howe, *Political Culture of Whigs,* pp. 281, 280.

59. "The Whig party had been viable as long as northern antislavery feeling had been carefully excluded from the political arena. . . . The task of the new Republicans was to convince northerners that slavery was an important issue, requiring that political steps be taken promptly to halt its spread." Ibid., p. 279.

60. Basler and Basler, *Works of Lincoln,* 2:385, quoted in Harry V. Jaffa, *Crisis of the House Divided: An Interpretation of the Issues in the Lincoln-Douglas Debates* (Chicago: University of Chicago Press, 1982), p. 332.

61. Ibid., pp. 331–32.

62. W. H. Seward, "Freedom in the New Territories," March 11, 1850, quoted in Howe, *Political Culture of Whigs,* p. 204.

63. Jaffa, *House Divided,* p. 321.

64. John P. Diggins, "Slavery, Race, and Equality: Jefferson and the Pathos of Enlightenment," *American Quarterly* 28 (Summer 1976), quoted in Howe, *Political Culture of Whigs,* p. 291; Lincoln, "Speech at Chicago" (1858), quoted ibid.

65. Lincoln, speech in Peoria (1854), quoted in Jaffa, *House Divided,* p. 305.

66. As Harry V. Jaffa summarizes Lincoln's thinking, "Because all men by nature have an equal right to justice, all men have an equal duty to do justice, wholly irrespective of calculations as to self-interest. . . . [O]ur own happiness, our own welfare, cannot be conceived apart from our well-doing, or just action, and this well-doing is not merely the adding to our own security but the benefiting of others." Jaffa, *House Divided,* p. 327.

67. Jefferson Davis, *Jefferson Davis, Constitutionalist: His Letters, Papers, and Speeches,* ed. Dunbar Rowland, 10 vols. (Jackson: Mississippi Department of Archives and History, 1923), 6:357, quoted in McPherson, *Drawn with the Sword,* p. 23.

68. As Eric Foner notes, they saw their struggle against the southern slaveholders as but "one part of a world-wide movement from absolutism to democracy, aristocracy to equality, backwardness to modernity." Foner, *Free Soil, Free Labor,* p. 72.

69. Lincoln, letter to Pierce and others, April 6, 1859, in quoted in Harry V. Jaffa, *A New Birth of Freedom: Abraham Lincoln and the Coming of the Civil War* (Lanham, Md.: Rowman & Littlefield, 2000), p. 73.

70. See David Morris Potter, "The Lincoln Theme and American National Historiography," in Potter, *The South and the Sectional Conflict* (Baton Rouge: Louisiana State University Press, 1968), pp. 151–76; Howe, *Political Culture of Whigs,* p. 296.

71. W. H. Seward to James Maher, March 15, 1844, quoted in Howe, *Political Culture of Whigs,* p. 202.

72. W. H. Seward, October 26, 1848, quoted in Foner, *Free Soil, Free Labor,* p. 72.

73. Quoted in Paolino, *Foundations of Empire,* p. 4.

Chapter 10 / *War and Progress*

1. Frederic Bancroft, *Speeches, Correspondence, and Political Papers of Charles Schurz,* 6 vols. (New York: G. P. Putnam's Sons, 1913), 1:156–58, quoted in Eric Foner, *Free Soil, Free Labor, Free Men: The Ideology of the Republican Party Before the Civil War* (New York: Oxford University Press, 1973), p. 72.

2. James M. McPherson, *Battle Cry of Freedom: The Civil War Era* (New York: Oxford University Press, 1988), p. 248.

3. Foner, *Free Soil, Free Labor,* p. 316.

4. Quoted in James M. McPherson, *Drawn with the Sword: Reflections on the American Civil War* (New York: Oxford University Press, 1996), p. 77.

5. John Keegan, quoted in James M. McPherson, *For Cause and Comrades: Why Men Fought in the Civil War* (New York: Oxford University Press, 1997), p. 94. There is a debate among historians over just how "ideological" soldiers on both sides were. Gerald F. Linderman and others argue that whatever ideals soldiers brought to the battlefield were soon abandoned in the brutality of the situation. See Linderman, *Embattled Courage: The Experience of Combat in the American Civil War* (New York: Free Press, 1987). McPherson's researches are more extensive, however, and more persuasive.

6. Josiah Perry to Phebe Perry, October 3, 1862, Perry Papers, Illinois State Historical Library, Springfield; William H. H. Ibbetson, diary, undated entry sometime in the winter of

1863–64, Illinois State Historical Library; and Robert T. McMahan, diary, September 3, 1863, State Historical Society of Missouri, Columbia, all quoted in McPherson, *For Cause and Comrades,* pp. 112, 113.

7. McPherson, *Cause and Comrades,* pp. 116, 130.

8. Alexander Caldwell to brother, January 11, 1863, quoted ibid., p. 121.

9. Alfred L. Hough to Mary Hough, October 28, 1863, and March 13, 1864, quoted ibid., p. 13.

10. James H. Goodnow to Samuel Goodnow, January 11, 1863, quoted ibid., p. 112.

11. Lincoln, "Meditation on the Divine Will," September 2, 1862, quoted in Daniel Walker Howe, *The Political Culture of the American Whigs* (Chicago: University of Chicago Press, 1979), p. 295.

12. "In the present civil war," Lincoln wrote, "it is quite possible that God's purpose is something different from the purpose of either party—and yet the human instrumentalities, working just as they do, are the best adaptation to effect His purpose." Ibid.

13. There has been a debate over whether the Civil War really meets Clausewitz's definition of "total war." For a summary of the argument, and the case for viewing the Civil War as a "total war," see James M. McPherson, "From Limited to Total War, 1861–1865," in McPherson, *Drawn with the Sword,* pp. 66–86.

14. Quoted in David H. Donald, *Lincoln* (New York: Touchstone, 1996), p. 360. McClellan vehemently opposed what he called Lincoln's "infamous" Emancipation Proclamation and, after being relieved of command, ran for president at the top of the Democratic ticket calling for peace and reconciliation with the unconquered South.

15. Morton Keller, *Affairs of State: Public Life in Late Nineteenth Century America,* (Cambridge, Mass.: Harvard University Press, 1977), p. 15.

16. Russell Frank Weigley, *History of the United States Army* (New York: Macmillan, 1967), pp. 254–55, 252.

17. Quoted in McPherson, *Drawn with the Sword,* p. 83.

18. Weigley, *History of United States Army,* p. 253.

19. McPherson, *Drawn with the Sword,* pp. 64, 184–85.

20. Weigley, *History of United States Army,* pp. 256, 257.

21. The kind of wretchedness seen in the South "belonged to those 'backward peoples' whom the leading imperial powers of Western Europe were in those days seeking to 'develop,' and to whom was applied by common international usage the curious term 'natives.'" C. Vann Woodward, *Origins of the New South, 1877–1913* (Baton Rouge: Louisiana State University Press), p. 109.

22. Keller, *Affairs of State,* p. 47.

23. Woodward, *Origins of the New South,* p. 142.

24. E. Merton Coulter, *The South During Reconstruction, 1865–1877* (Baton Rouge: Louisiana State University Press, 1947), p. 20.

25. According to C. Vann Woodward, an initial "missionary and political phase" in the late 1860s gave way in the late 1870s to a phase of "economic exploitation" when the South and its people "were pictured more and more as opportunities and outlets for economic expansionism." Woodward, *Origins of the New South,* p. 114.

26. Quoted in Michael Perman, ed., *Major Problems in the Civil War and Reconstruction* (Boston: Houghton Mifflin, 1998), p. 408.

27. Quoted ibid., pp. 407, 409.

28. Quoted ibid., pp. 409, 468.

29. Whatever the merits of Johnson and Seward's plans may have been, "any proposal identified with the Johnson administration was sure to meet in Congress with opposition that had no connection with its merits." W. Stull Holt, *Treaties Defeated by the Senate: A Study of*

the Struggle Between President and Senate over the Conduct of Foreign Relations (Baltimore: Johns Hopkins Press, 1933), p. 101.

30. In addition, Radical Republicans hated Reverdy Johnson, the American minister who negotiated the convention, for his part in helping President Johnson survive his impeachment. See Allan Nevins, *Hamilton Fish: The Inner History of the Grant Administration* (New York: F. Ungar, 1957), p. 148.

31. See David Donald, *Charles Sumner and the Rights of Man* (New York: Knopf, 1970), p. 305, and Glyndon G. Van Deusen, *William Henry Seward* (New York: Oxford University Press, 1967), p. 549.

32. Quoted in Keller, *Affairs of State,* p. 58.

33. "He agreed with Charles Francis Adams in 1867 on the need 'for an early restoration of constitutional peace, law, order and progress among ourselves,' and feared that 'centralization, consolidation and [domestic] imperialism' would result from a Radical Republican triumph." Ibid., p. 92.

34. Ibid., p. 59.

35. Edward P. Crapol, *James G. Blaine, Architect of Empire* (Wilmington, Del.: SR Books, 2000), p. 27.

36. Quoted in Edward L. Pierce, *Memoir and Letters of Charles Sumner,* 4 vols. (Boston: Roberts Brothers, 1877–93), 4:620.

37. During the Civil War Lincoln had given Sumner "a virtual veto over foreign policy" almost without precedent in the annals of American history, and Sumner's approval remained the sine qua non for any foreign policy action, great or small, from the end of the war until his equally unprecedented ouster as Foreign Relations Committee chairman in 1870. Donald, *Charles Sumner,* pp. 25, 449, 465.

38. Nevins, *Hamilton Fish,* p. 151.

39. World War II would similarly shape American strategic thinking about overseas bases.

40. Nevins, *Hamilton Fish,* p. 264.

41. Keller, *Affairs of State,* p. 91.

42. As Allan Nevins writes, "the conviction that the annexation scheme had been wild and absurd . . . did not exist in 1869." Nevins, *Hamilton Fish,* p. 272. The acquisition of Santo Domingo, according to Nevins, was "not a whit less defensible than the acquisition of Puerto Rico in 1898, for it was larger, richer, emptier, and of more naval value, while its population was friendlier."

43. The judgment is David Donald's: "Except for Sumner, four carpetbag Senators from the South would hardly have dared to vote against the treaty and . . . Sumner also brought along with him a number of Senators . . . who were strongly under his influence." Donald, *Charles Sumner,* p. 453. Prominent Republican leaders who supported the measure included Zachariah Chandler, Roscoe Conkling, Jacob M. Howard, Oliver O. Morton, William M. Stewart, and Simon Cameron. The defeat of the measure required the united opposition of Democrats. Ibid., p. 452.

44. Quoted in Charles Callan Tansill, *The Foreign Policy of Thomas F. Bayard, 1885–1897* (New York: Fordham University Press, 1940), p. xv; John A. S. Grenville and George Berkeley Young, *Politics, Strategy and American Diplomacy: Studies in Foreign Policy, 1873–1917* (New Haven, Conn.: Yale University Press, 1966), p. 45.

45. James William Park, *Latin American Underdevelopment: A History of Perspectives in the United States, 1870–1965* (Baton Rouge: Louisiana State University Press, 1995), pp. 28–30.

46. Crapol, *James G. Blaine,* p. 27.

47. Robert L. Beisner, "Thirty Years Before Manila: E. L. Godkin, Carl Schurz, and Anti-Imperialism in the Gilded Age," *Historian* 30 (August 1968): 574.

48. Schurz and others also pointed out that some of the people lobbying for Dominican annexation in the late 1860s had lobbied for annexation in the 1850s, when the explicit goal had been to expand the southern slave empire. William Cazneau and his wife, Jane Cazneau, had continued their efforts on behalf of the Confederacy during the war.

49. Speech in the U.S. Senate, January 11, 1871, in *Speeches, Correspondence, and Political Papers of Carl Schurz,* ed. Frederic Bancroft, 6 vols. (New York: G. P. Putnam's Sons, 1913), 2:71–122. That diplomatic historians have generally misunderstood the logic of Schurz's argument shows how little attention most have paid to the context of Reconstruction. Schurz was hardly a racist by the standards of his day, and his argument against the annexation of Santo Domingo was less about race than about Reconstruction. The fear he professed was the fear of excessive power in Washington. The acquisition of more southern territory containing more blacks meant more trouble in the South, which in turn meant more efforts by the North to impose its will by military means. That is one reason Schurz argued that the introduction of mixed races threatened the constitutional order.

This view was common among a small but vocal number of politicians and intellectuals. The editor of *The Nation,* E. L. Godkin, opposed annexation of the Danish West Indies on the grounds that these "semi-civilized additions" to the already semicivilized South would end up costing northerners a fortune and providing "work for forty or fifty thousand soldiers" (Nevins, *Hamilton Fish,* p. 273). The soldiers would be deployed to oppress not West Indian natives but would-be southern slaveholders.

50. Donald, *Charles Sumner,* p. 471; Lester Langley, *Struggle for the American Mediterranean: United States–European Rivalry in the Gulf-Caribbean, 1776–1904* (Athens: University of Georgia Press, 1976), p. 144.

51. Donald, *Charles Sumner,* p. 470.

52. Nevins, *Hamilton Fish,* p. 499. Sumner and Blaine were both dismayed that "President Grant, in his schemes for Caribbean empire, was following the example of his pro-Southern predecessors, Franklin Pierce, James Buchanan, and Andrew Johnson." Crapol, *James G. Blaine,* p. 35. A number of diplomatic historians suggest that Sumner turned against Grant because of the Santo Domingo proposal. But as Nevins long ago demonstrated, hostility to the Grant administration, on the part of Carl Schurz, as well as Sumner and other soon-to-be "Liberal" Republicans, predated the Santo Domingo controversy. See Nevins, *Hamilton Fish,* pp. 294, 322.

53. James G. Blaine, *Twenty Years of Congress: From Lincoln to Garfield,* 2 vols. (Norwich, Conn.: Henry Bill, 1884–86), 2:340.

54. Keller, *Affairs of State,* p. 93

55. Speech in U.S. Senate, January 11, 1871, in Bancroft, *Speeches, Correspondence, and Political Papers of Carl Schurz,* 2:71–122.

56. Blaine, *Twenty Years of Congress,* 2:340.

57. One exception was Schurz, who opposed the annexation of Hawaii in 1893 with the same vehemence that he had opposed the annexation of Santo Domingo in 1868—and with the same arguments. See Beisner, "Thirty Years Before Manila," p. 573.

58. Arthur Alphonse Ekirch, *Ideas, Ideals, and American Diplomacy: A History of Their Growth and Interaction* (New York: Appleton-Century-Crofts, 1966), p. 68.

59. William H. Seward, "The Physical, Moral, and Intellectual Development of the American People," quoted in Akira Iriye, *From Nationalism to Internationalism: U.S. Foreign Policy to 1914* (London and Boston: Routledge & K. Paul, 1977), p. 15.

60. Henry Cabot Lodge, "Outlook and Duty of the Republican Party," *Forum* 15 (April 1893), quoted in William C. Widenor, *Henry Cabot Lodge and the Search for an American Foreign Policy* (Berkeley: University of California Press, 1980), p. 53.

61. Henry Cabot Lodge, *Early Memories* (New York: Scribner's, 1913), quoted ibid., p. 18.

62. Justus D. Doenecke, *The Presidencies of James A. Garfield and Chester A. Arthur* (Lawrence: Regents Press of Kansas, 1981), pp. 22, 47, 25.

63. Keller, *Affairs of State,* p. 379.

64. Richard E. Welch, Jr., *The Presidencies of Grover Cleveland* (Lawrence: University Press of Kansas, 1988), p. 32.

65. H. Wayne Morgan, "Toward National Unity," in Morgan, ed., *The Gilded Age* (Syracuse, N.Y.: Syracuse University Press, 1970), p. 6.

66. Blaine, *Twenty Years of Congress,* 2:673, 675.

67. Keller, *Affairs of State,* p. 4.

68. Widenor, *Henry Cabot Lodge,* pp. 28, 64.

69. Corinne Roosevelt Robinson, *My Brother, Theodore Roosevelt* (New York: C. Scribner's Sons, 1921), and Roosevelt to John Ford Rhodes, November 29, 1904; both quoted in Henry Fowles Pringle, *Theodore Roosevelt: A Biography* (New York: Harcourt, Brace, 1931), pp. 11–12.

70. William Henry Harbaugh, *Power and Responsibility: The Life and Times of Theodore Roosevelt* (New York: Farrar, Straus & Cudahy, 1961), p. 54.

71. H. W. Brands, *T.R.: The Last Romantic* (New York: BasicBooks, 1997), p. 119.

72. Lodge, *Early Memories,* quoted in Widenor, *Henry Cabor Lodge,* p. 21.

73. Harbaugh, *Power and Responsibility,* p. 25.

74. As William C. Widenor has noted, Lodge "never doubted that America would play a moral role if only it could be persuaded to play the part on the world's stage to which its power entitled it. A great nation had its duties and responsibilities and could not be great without them." Widenor, *Henry Cabot Lodge,* p. 74. See also "Senator Lodge's Address," *New York Times,* November 25, 1900, p. 1.

75. Widenor, *Henry Cabot Lodge,* p. 109.

76. David Healy, *James G. Blaine and Latin America* (Columbia: University of Missouri Press, 2001), pp. 4, 5.

77. Crapol, *James G. Blaine,* pp. 19, 5.

78. Keller, *Affairs of State,* p. 86.

79. Ekirch, *Ideas, Ideals,* p. 68.

80. Keller, *Affairs of State,* p. 89.

81. Thomas Andrew Bailey, *America Faces Russia: Russian-American Relations from Early Times to Our Day* (Ithaca, N.Y.: Cornell University Press, 1950), p. 84.

82. Ronald J. Jensen, "The Politics of Discrimination: America, Russia and the Jewish Question, 1869–1872," *American Jewish History* 75 (March 1986): 294; Gary Dean Best, *To Free a People: American Jewish Leaders and the Jewish Problem in Eastern Europe, 1890–1914* (Westport, Conn.: Greenwood Press, 1982), p. 5.

83. Jensen, "Politics of Discrimination," pp. 281, 290.

84. Cathal J. Nolan, "The United States and Tsarist Anti-Semitism, 1865–1914," *Diplomacy and Statecraft* 3, no. 3 (1992): 443.

85. Ibid.; emphasis added.

86. Best, *To Free a People,* p. 12.

87. Jensen, "Politics of Discrimination," p. 292.

88. Nolan, "U.S. and Tsarist Anti-Semitism," p. 442.

89. Bailey, *America Faces Russia,* p. 124.

90. Nolan, "U.S. and Tsarist Anti-Semitism," p. 449.

91. Best, *To Free a People,* pp. 32, 33.

92. Nolan, "U.S. and Tsarist Anti-Semitism," p. 450.

93. Frederick F. Travis, *George Kennan and the American-Russian Relationship, 1865–1924* (Athens: Ohio University Press, 1990), pp. 177, 180.

94. Nolan, "U.S. and Tsarist Anti-Semitism," p. 446.

95. Ibid., p. 447.

96. Richard Hofstadter, *The Age of Reform: From Bryan to F.D.R.* (New York: Knopf, 1955), p. 83.

97. Bailey, *America Faces Russia,* p. 150.

98. Richard William Leopold, *Elihu Root and the Conservative Tradition* (Boston: Little, Brown, 1954), p. 60.

99. Henry Cabot Lodge, "Some Impressions of Russia," *Scribner's Magazine* 31 (1902): 570–80.

100. Letter to Cecil Arthur Spring Rice, 1897, reprinted in Eugene Anschel, *The American Image of Russia, 1775–1917* (New York: F. Ungar, 1974), pp. 176–77.

101. Henry Blumenthal, *A Reappraisal of Franco-American Relations, 1830–1871* (Chapel Hill: University of North Carolina Press, 1959), p. 189.

102. Manfred Jonas, *The United States and Germany: A Diplomatic History* (Ithaca, N.Y.: Cornell University Press, 1984), p. 31.

103. Keller, *Affairs of State,* pp. 86, 87.

104. Clara Eve Scheiber, *The Transformation of American Sentiment Toward Germany, 1870–1914* (Boston: Cornhill, 1923), pp. 12–13.

105. Blumenthal, *Franco-American Relations,* p. 193.

106. Keller, *Affairs of State,* p. 87.

107. Blumenthal, *Franco-American Relations,* p. 190.

108. Keller, *Affairs of State,* p. 87.

109. Blumenthal, *Franco-American Relations,* p. 197.

110. Detlef Junker, *The Manichaean Trap: American Perceptions of the German Empire, 1871–1945* (Washington, D.C.: German Historical Institute, 1995), pp. 19, 11–12.

111. Akira Iriye, *Across the Pacific* (New York: Harcourt, Brace & World, 1967), pp. 22, 28, 21, 24.

112. David M. Pletcher, *The Awkward Years: American Foreign Relations Under Garfield and Arthur* (Columbia: University of Missouri Press, 1973), p. 202.

113. Iriye, *Across the Pacific,* pp. 21, 31, 26, 27.

114. Ibid., p. 24; Jeffrey Dorwart, *The Pigtail War: American Involvement in the Sino-Japanese War of 1894–95* (Amherst: University of Massachusetts Press, 1975), p. 93.

115. Iriye, *Across the Pacific,* p. 32.

116. Warren I. Cohen, *America's Response to China: A History of Sino-American Relations* (New York: Columbia University Press, 2000), p. 41.

117. Leopold, *Elihu Root,* p. 60.

118. Dorwart, *Pigtail War,* p. 94. "Benjamin O. Flower, reformist editor of *Arena* magazine, compared Japan's struggle for recognition with the antebellum abolitionist crusade against slavery in the United States and contended that American support for Japanese progress during the war assisted enlightened and Westernized statesmen in their contest against the remnants of Oriental reaction."

119. Quoted in Norman E. Saul, *Concord and Conflict: The United States and Russia, 1867–1914* (Lawrence: University Press of Kansas, 1996), p. 478, and in Frank A. Ninkovich, "Theodore Roosevelt: Civilization as Ideology," *Diplomatic History* 10 (Summer 1986): 238.

120. Iriye, *Across the Pacific,* p. 22.

121. Dorwart, *Pigtail War,* p. 108.

122. Ninkovich, "Civilization as Ideology," pp. 235, 239.

123. Iriye, *From Nationalism to Internationalism,* p. 16.

124. Ninkovich, "Civilization as Ideology," pp. 232, 240.

125. As Robert Wiebe notes, Roosevelt wanted to check Russia, "which he both distrusted and despised. [But] British influence and Japanese expansion on the continent never

seriously disturbed him." Wiebe, *The Search for Order* (New York: Hill & Wang, 1967), p. 252.

126. Ninkovich, "Civilization as Ideology," p. 231.

127. Ibid., p. 233.

128. "All societies, civilizations, and races stood somewhere in Roosevelt's developmental format. . . . All races could theoretically improve. . . . The stages-of-development scheme then was largely open-ended, full of possibility and chance." Thomas G. Dyer, *Theodore Roosevelt and the Idea of Race* (Baton Rouge: Louisiana State University Press, 1980), pp. 43–44.

129. Iriye, *Across the Pacific*, pp. 6–7.

130. Ibid., p. 10.

131. Edward Caudill, *Darwinian Myths: The Legends and Misuses of a Theory* (Knoxville: University of Tennessee Press, 1997), p. 82.

132. Dyer, *Theodore Roosevelt and Race*, pp. 97, 98.

133. Wiebe, *Search for Order*, pp. 225–26.

134. Cohen, *America's Response to China*, p. 36.

135. Crapol, *James G. Blaine*, p. 38.

136. Keller, *Affairs of State*, p. 6.

Chapter 11 / *From Power to Ambition, from Ambition to Power*

1. Homer E. Socolofsky and Allan B. Spetter, *The Presidency of Benjamin Harrison* (Lawrence: University Press of Kansas, 1987), p. 2.

2. See John A. S. Grenville and George Berkeley Young, *Politics, Strategy and American Diplomacy: Studies in Foreign Policy, 1873–1917* (New Haven, Conn.: Yale University Press, 1966), p. 173.This did not stop some Americans from imagining a war with the British at sea. But British planners anticipated that any war with the United States would immediately turn into a land war for the Canadian territory that so many Americans coveted.

3. Anne Orde, *The Eclipse of Great Britain: The United States and British Imperial Decline, 1895–1956* (New York: St. Martin's Press, 1996), p. 23.

4. Detlef Junker, *The Manichaean Trap: American Perceptions of the German Empire, 1871–1945* (Washington, D.C.: German Historical Institute, 1995), p. 14.

5. Alan Knight, "Britain and Latin America," in *The Oxford History of the British Empire*, vol. 3: *The Nineteenth Century*, ed. Andrew Porter (Oxford: Oxford University Press, 1999), p. 140.

6. Joseph Smith, *Illusions of Conflict: Anglo-American Diplomacy Toward Latin America, 1865–1896* (Pittsburgh: University of Pittsburgh Press, 1979), p. 28.

7. Knight, "Britain and Latin America," p. 140.

8. Charles S. Campbell, *The Transformation of American Foreign Relations, 1865–1900* (New York: Harper & Row, 1976), p. 20.

9. Edward P. Crapol, *James G. Blaine: Architect of Empire* (Wilmington, Del.: SR Books, 2000), pp. 75, 41.

10. Robert V. Remini, *Henry Clay: Statesman for the Union* (New York: Norton, 1991), p. 299.

11. Thomas A. Bailey, *A Diplomatic History of the American People* (Englewood Cliffs, N.J.: Prentice-Hall, 1974), p. 276.

12. Lester Langley, *Struggle for the American Mediterranean: United States–European Rivalry in the Gulf-Caribbean, 1776–1904* (Athens: University of Georgia Press, 1976), p. 148.

13. Crapol, *James G. Blaine*, p. 31.

14. Bailey, *Diplomatic History,* p. 397. In 1884 Blaine's successor, Fredrick Frelinghuysen, negotiated a treaty with Nicaragua providing joint ownership of a canal under U.S. protection, in open violation of the Clayton-Bulwer Treaty.

15. Ibid.

16. Blaine argued that a canal could no more be subject to foreign influence than could America's transcontinental railways. It was "as truly a channel of communication between the Eastern and Western States as our own transcontinental railways," and therefore by extension it had by the same necessity to be placed under America's exclusive control. Crapol, *James G. Blaine,* p. 76.

17. France had little motive to deny Americans access to the moneymaking venture. France and the United States were by the 1880s among the least likely of any two nations to go to war, but even in the unlikely event that France tried to exercise control over a canal in wartime, any such effort would likely have been blocked by the British, who had as much interest in the neutrality of a canal as the United States did.

18. Crapol, *James G. Blaine,* pp. 76, 77.

19. William C. Widenor, *Henry Cabot Lodge and the Search for an American Foreign Policy* (Berkeley and Los Angeles: University of California Press, 1980), p. 90.

20. Orde, *Eclipse of Great Britain,* p. 23.

21. Crapol, *James G. Blaine,* p. 30.

22. Widenor, *Henry Cabot Lodge,* p. 85.

23. Hamilton, Federalist no. 11, in *The Federalist,* ed. Jacob E. Cooke (Middletown, Conn.: Wesleyan University Press, 1982), p. 73.

24. Grenville and Young, *Politics, Strategy and American Diplomacy,* pp. 90–91.

25. "Various sectors of the Chilean press increasingly came . . . to blame earlier acts of American imperialism on the slave states and the Democratic party. Despite the Union's initial defeats, Santiago supported Lincoln throughout the war. Not surprisingly, news of the fall of Richmond sparked spontaneous victory celebrations in Valparaiso; the entire nation rejoiced when the Confederacy finally surrendered." William F. Sater, *Chile and the United States: Empires in Conflict* (Athens: University of Georgia Press, 1990), p. 24.

26. Joseph B. Lockey, "James G. Blaine," in Samuel Flagg Bemis, ed., *The American Secretaries of State and Their Diplomacy, 1776–1925,* 10 vols. (New York: Knopf, 1927–29), 8:169.

27. Josefina Zoraida Vázquez and Lorenzo Meyer, *The United States and Mexico* (Chicago: University of Chicago Press, 1985), pp. 1–2.

28. David Healy, *James G. Blaine and Latin America* (Columbia: University of Missouri Press, 2001), p. 18.

29. Remarks of Allen G. Thurman, *Congressional Globe,* Senate, 41st Cong., 3rd sess., pt. 1, p. 249; James William Park, *Latin American Underdevelopment: A History of Perspectives in the United States, 1870–1965* (Baton Rouge: Louisiana State University Press, 1995), p. 29.

30. Reginald Housman, *Race and Manifest Destiny: The Origins of American Racial Anglo-Saxonism* (Cambridge, Mass.: Harvard University Press, 1981), quoted in Fredrick B. Pike, *The United States and Latin America: Myths and Stereotypes of Civilization and Nature* (Austin: University of Texas Press, 1992), pp. 129–30.

31. E. Taylor Parks, *Colombia and the United States, 1765–1934* (Durham, N.C.: Duke University Press, 1935), p. 91. This anti-Catholic prejudice survived in the United States well beyond the nineteenth century, of course. Even in the presumably more rational and scientific twentieth century political scientists long doubted that democracy could prosper in Catholic nations, and even in the twenty-first century serious American thinkers were still arguing that American democracy was essentially a Protestant phenomenon that could be sustained only by reinvigorating America's Protestant character.

32. Richard H. Bradford, *The Virginius Affair* (Boulder, Colo.: Associated University Press, 1980), p. 13; Park, *Latin American Underdevelopment*, p. 38.

33. Park, *Latin American Underdevelopment*, p. 57.

34. Morton Keller, *Affairs of State: Public Life in Late Nineteenth Century America* (Cambridge, Mass.: Havard University Press, 1977), pp. 90, 91, 94.

35. Crapol, *James G. Blaine*, p. 23.

36. Bradford, *Virginius Affair*, p. 9.

37. Allan Nevins, *Hamilton Fish: The Inner History of the Grant Administration* (New York: F. Ungar, 1957), pp. 350, 247. The naively corrupt Rawlins was one of many holders of Cuban bonds, but few doubted that his sympathy for "poor, struggling Cuba" was greater than his hope of profiting from Cuban independence.

38. In the late 1860s, as later in the 1890s, "the 'hard-money elite' of upper-class North-easterners in both parties fought [against] Cuban recognition." Bradford, *Virginius Affair*, p. 14.

39. Nevins, *Hamilton Fish*, pp. 626, 346.

40. As one Spanish foreign minister put it, "If we lose Cuba by mismanagement and by alienating the affections of the loyal inhabitants, we should be looked upon as traitors; if the United States choose to deprive us of our colony, we may have to yield in the end to superior force, but we shall have preserved our national dignity." Ibid., p. 619.

41. Ibid., pp. 348, 676.

42. Ibid., pp. 186, 198.

43. Kenneth J. Hagan, *This People's Navy: The Making of American Sea Power* (New York: Free Press, 1991), pp. 179–80.

44. In 1869 "the danger of an accidental clash became marked when Admiral Hoff, com-manding the American forces, was instructed to resist the capture of any American vessel by the Spaniards unless she were found actually landing men or contraband of war on the coast of Cuba." Nevins, *Hamilton Fish*, pp. 190–91.

45. Ibid., p. 353.

46. Bradford, *Virginius Affair*, p. 66.

47. Hagan, *People's Navy*, pp. 180–81; Nevins, *Hamilton Fish*, pp. 675–76.

48. Hagan, *People's Navy*, p. 181.

49. Bradford, *Virginius Affair*, pp. xiii, 120.

50. Grenville and Young, *Politics, Strategy and American Diplomacy*, p. 91.

51. David M. Pletcher, *The Awkward Years: American Foreign Relations Under Garfield and Arthur* (Columbia: University of Missouri Press, 1973), p. 36.

52. Healy, *James G. Blaine*, p. 3.

53. Crapol, *James G. Blaine*, p. 87.

54. Grenville and Young, *Politics, Strategy and American Diplomacy*, p. 85.

55. Crapol, *James G. Blaine*, p. 72.

56. Grenville and Young, *Politics, Strategy and American Diplomacy*, p. 91.

57. Jürgen Buchenau, *In the Shadow of the Giant: The Making of Mexico's Central American Policy, 1876–1930* (Tuscaloosa: University of Alabama Press, 1996), p. 6.

58. Healy, *James G. Blaine*, p. 23.

59. Arturo J. Cruz, Jr., *Nicaragua's Conservative Republic, 1858–93* (New York: Pal-grave in association with St. Antony's Oxford, 2002), p. 41.

60. Buchenau, *Shadow of the Giant*, p. 8.

61. Ibid., pp. 15, 11, 15.

62. Vázquez and Meyer, *United States and Mexico*, p. 85.

63. Buchenau, *Shadow of the Giant*, pp. 11, 25, 24.

64. Ibid., p. 19.

65. Ibid., pp. 8, 47.

66. Sater, *Chile and the United States,* pp. 18, 2.

67. Ibid., pp. 18, 20.

68. Buchenau, *Shadow of the Giant,* p. 16.

69. Ibid., pp. 29, 22.

70. Healy, *James G. Blaine,* 28.

71. Ibid., 25, 28, 29–30, 36.

72. Buchenau, *Shadow of the Giant,* p. 33; Healy, *James G. Blaine,* p. 33.

73. Healy, *James G. Blaine,* p. 39.

74. Sater, *Chile and the United States,* p. 2.

75. Healy, *James G. Blaine,* pp. 63, 92, 63.

76. Ibid., pp. 92, 95, 94, 108.

77. Ibid., p. 148.

78. Ibid., pp. 156–57.

79. Ibid., pp. 148, 153.

80. Ibid., pp. 156, 157.

81. Hamilton, Federalist no. 11, in Cooke, *Federalist,* p. 72.

82. Quoted in Helene Johnson Looze, *Alexander Hamilton and the British Orientation of American Foreign Policy, 1783–1803* (The Hague: Mouton, 1969), p. 35.

83. Justus D. Doenecke, *The Presidencies of James A. Garfield and Chester A. Arthur* (Lawrence: Regents Press of Kansas, 1981), p. 56.

84. Crapol, *James G. Blaine,* p. 116.

85. Michael H. Hunt, *The Making of a Special Relationship: The United States and China to 1914* (New York: Columbia University Press, 1983), p. 129.

86. W. Stull Holt, *Treaties Defeated by the Senate: A Study of the Struggle Between President and Senate over the Conduct of Foreign Relations* (Baltimore: Johns Hopkins University Press, 1933), p. 103.

87. Crapol, *James G. Blaine,* pp. 37, 78.

88. Julius William Pratt, *Expansionists of 1898: The Acquisition of Hawaii and the Spanish Islands* (Chicago: Quadrangle Books, 1964), pp. 34, 35.

89. Richard E. Welch, Jr., *The Presidencies of Grover Cleveland* (Lawrence: University Press of Kansas, 1988), p. 169.

90. Pratt, *Expansionists of 1898,* p. 25.

91. Socolofsky and Spetter, *Presidency of Harrison,* p. 205.

92. Akira Iriye, *Across the Pacific* (New York: Harcourt, Brace & World, 1967), p. 42.

93. Warren I. Cohen, *America's Response to China: A History of Sino-American Relations* (New York: Columbia University Press, 2000), p. 14.

94. Iriye, *Across the Pacific,* p. 45.

95. Cohen, *America's Response to China,* p. 27.

96. Iriye, *Across the Pacific,* p. 44.

97. Cohen, *America's Response to China,* pp. 26–27. "When China needed help, the Americans looked relatively friendly and exploitable." Ibid., p. 30.

98. Ibid., pp. 38–39.

99. Milton Plesur, *America's Outward Thrust: Approaches to Foreign Affairs, 1865–1890* (DeKalb: Northern Illinois University Press, 1971), p. 216.

100. Iriye, *Across the Pacific,* pp. 45–46.

101. Walter LaFeber, *The Clash: A History of U.S.-Japan Relations* (New York: Norton, 1997), p. 38.

102. Iriye, *Across the Pacific,* p. 45.

103. Ibid., pp. 46–47.

104. Hunt, *Special Relationship,* pp. 117, 128.

105. Cohen, *America's Response to China,* p. 43.

106. Plesur, *America's Outward Thrust,* p. 211.

107. Hunt, *Special Relationship,* p. 122.

108. Pletcher, *Awkward Years,* p. 198.

109. Hunt, *Special Relationship,* p. 122.

110. Plesur, *America's Outward Thrust,* p. 217.

111. Keller, *Affairs of State,* p. 95.

112. Yur-Bok Lee, *Diplomatic Relations Between the United States and Korea, 1866–1887* (New York: Humanities Press, 1970), pp. 26, 29.

113. Ibid., p. 30.

114. Ibid., pp. 61, 70.

115. Ibid., pp. 70, 58, 117.

116. Ibid., p. 15.

117. Ibid., p. 102.

118. Jeffrey Dorwart, *The Pigtail War: American Involvement in the Sino-Japanese War of 1894–95* (Amherst: University of Massachusetts Press, 1975), pp. 19, 26–27.

119. Ibid., pp. 20, 21, 24.

120. Ibid., p. 26.

121. Although Walter LaFeber is right to note that American businessmen dreamed of doing much better for themselves in Asia and would continue to dream for another century, the economic interests involved were not sufficient to determine American government policies. LaFeber, *The New Empire: An Interpretation of American Expansion, 1860–1898* (Ithaca, N.Y.: Cornell University Press, 1967), p. 45.

122. Dorwart, *Pigtail War,* pp. 73–74.

123. Charles Callan Tansill, *The Foreign Policy of Thomas F. Bayard, 1885–1897* (New York: Fordham University Press, 1940), p. 9.

124. Plesur, *America's Outward Thrust,* p. 199.

125. Tansill, *Foreign Policy of Bayard,* p. 29.

126. Ibid., pp. 47, 53, 54, 62, 69.

127. Ibid., pp. 46, 62, 67, 55.

128. Ibid., pp. 46, 77.

129. Ibid., pp. 70, 71, 73.

130. Ibid., pp. 74, 80, 83, 75.

131. Manfred Jonas, *The United States and Germany: A Diplomatic History* (Ithaca, N.Y.: Cornell University Press, 1984), p. 46.

132. Tansill, *Foreign Policy of Bayard,* pp. 86, 103, 91.

133. Ibid., pp. 104, 101.

134. Bailey, *Diplomatic History,* p. 426.

135. Pratt, *Expansionists of 1898,* p. 27.

136. Tansill, *Foreign Policy of Bayard,* pp. 93, 113–14.

137. Li was also offended and troubled by increasing efforts in the United States to exclude Chinese immigration. But he might have overlooked that problem had the United States been more useful to him in his struggles with Japan and the European powers.

138. Hagan, *People's Navy,* p. 94.

139. Harold Sprout and Margaret Sprout, *The Rise of American Naval Power, 1776–1918* (Princeton, N.J.: Princeton University Press, 1944), pp. 102, 104.

140. Ibid., p. 105. On the day of his retirement in 1837, Jackson changed his mind. After the belligerent confrontation with France in 1835, his Navy Department recommended building twenty-five new ships of the line and twenty-five more ships powered by steam. But the recommendation was not supported by the Congress or by President Van Buren. Ibid., pp. 108, 107.

141. Ibid., p. 113.

142. Ibid., pp. 166, 177.

143. Ivan Musicant, *Empire by Default: The Spanish-American War and the Dawn of the American Century* (New York: Holt, 1998), p. 13.

144. Hagan, *People's Navy*, p. 181.

145. Doenecke, *Garfield and Arthur*, p. 146.

146. Hagan, *People's Navy*, pp. 180, 183, 184.

147. Ibid., p. 185. According to Sprout and Sprout, 1881 was "an historic milestone in the rise of American naval power. The process of naval reconstruction was commenced in that year." Sprout and Sprout, *Rise of American Naval Power*, p. 183.

148. Musicant, *Empire by Default*, p. 13.

149. The ships were "tangible evidence of the physical rebirth of American naval power." Sprout and Sprout, *Rise of American Naval Power*, p. 188.

150. Hagan, *People's Navy*, p. 187; Sprout and Sprout, *Rise of American Naval Power*, pp. 188–89.

151. Hagan, *People's Navy*, p. 187.

152. The armor plate was heavier than that carried by Britain's most powerful battle-ships. According to one British ship designer, the new American battleships were "distinctly superior to any European vessels of the same displacement, and . . . quite a match for any ships afloat." Ibid., p. 197.

153. Ibid., pp. 187–88.

154. Ibid., p. 195. As several historians have labored to point out, this doctrine was not the product of the solitary mind of Alfred Thayer Mahan. Tracy's thinking owed perhaps more to Luce. See, for instance, Grenville and Young, *Politics, Strategy and American Diplomacy*.

155. The chairman of the House Naval Affairs Committee told Luce, "By building such ships, we should avoid the popular apprehension of jingoism in naval matters, while we can develop the full offensive and defensive powers of construction as completely as in foreign cruising battleships in all but speed and fuel capacity." Hagan, *People's Navy*, p. 197.

156. Campbell, *Transformation of American Foreign Relations*, p. 87.

157. Widenor, *Henry Cabot Lodge*, p. 90.

158. Doenecke, *Garfield and Arthur*, p. 150.

159. Grenville and Young, *Politics, Strategy and American Diplomacy*, p. 77; James A. Field, Jr., "American Imperialism: The Worst Chapter in Almost Any Book," *American Historical Review* 83 (June 1978): 667.

160. Thomas Pakenham, *The Scramble for Africa: 1876–1912* (New York: Random House, 1991), p. 13.

161. Plesur, *America's Outward Thrust*, p. 89.

162. Hagan, *People's Navy*, p. 198.

163. Sprout and Sprout, *Rise of American Naval Power*, p. 184.

164. Hagan, *People's Navy*, pp. 198, 206–7.

165. Plesur, *America's Outward Thrust*, p. 89.

166. Grenville and Young, *Politics, Strategy and American Diplomacy*, p. 14.

167. Tansill, *Foreign Policy of Bayard*, p. 103.

168. Secretary of the Navy, *Annual Report*, 1881, p. 3; Secretary of the Navy, *Annual Report*, 1882, p. 32; Fareed Zakaria, *From Wealth to Power: The Unusual Origins of America's World Role* (Princeton, N.J.: Princeton University Press, 1998), p. 78.

169. Hagan, *People's Navy*, p. 203.

170. Grenville and Young, *Politics, Strategy and American Diplomacy*, p. 9.

171. Robert Seager, "Ten Years Before Mahan: The Unofficial Case for the New Navy, 1880–1890," *Mississippi Valley Historical Review* 40, no. 3 (December 1953): 506; Zakaria, *From Wealth to Power*, p. 79.

172. Doenecke, *Garfield and Arthur,* p. 148.

173. Grenville and Young, *Politics, Strategy and American Diplomacy,* p. 93.

174. David F. Healy, *U.S. Expansionism: The Imperialist Urge in the 1890s* (Madison: University of Wisconsin Press, 1970), p. 44.

175. Sprout and Sprout, *Rise of American Naval Power,* pp. 209–10.

176. Healy, *U.S. Expansionism,* p. 44.

177. Even supporters of the new navy called the report a bit of "naval fanaticism." Sprout and Sprout, *Rise of American Naval Power,* p. 211.

178. Fareed Zakaria has referred to "the malleability of the concept of threat," noting that "whenever American leaders decided to expand their country's interests abroad, they quickly discovered foreign threats to the area in question and—sometimes out of genuine belief, sometimes to manipulate the debate—justified their policies as dictated by the nation's dangerously vulnerable position." Zakaria, *From Wealth to Power,* pp. 81–82.

179. Widenor, *Henry Cabot Lodge,* p. 40.

180. Secretary of the Navy, *Annual Report,* 1881, p. 3; Secretary of the Navy, *Annual Report,* 1882, p. 32; Zakaria, *From Wealth to Power,* p. 78. "If we ever expect to have our proper rank among the nations of the earth," declared one typical congressional naval advocate in 1882, "we must have a navy." Representative E. John Ellis, quoted in Seager, "Ten Years Before Mahan," pp. 501–2; Zakaria, *From Wealth to Power,* p. 78.

181. Hagan, *People's Navy,* pp. 194–95.

182. H. Wayne Morgan, *From Hayes to McKinley: National Party Politics, 1877–1896* (Syracuse, N.Y.: Syracuse University Press, 1969), p. 357.

183. Widenor, *Henry Cabot Lodge,* pp. 42, 71.

184. Healy, *James G. Blaine,* p. 207.

185. Ibid., pp. 217, 220, 221.

186. Ibid., pp. 222, 225.

187. Ibid., pp. 227–28, 225, 224.

188. Hagan, *People's Navy,* p. 199.

189. Which helped explain why leaders like Harrison, who as a matter of general policy sincerely wished to build ties of friendship with the nations of the Western Hemisphere, "nevertheless reacted with unnecessary severity whenever they felt the United States had received a slight." Grenville and Young, *Politics, Strategy and American Diplomacy,* p. 100. Grenville and Young go on to suggest, "Their sensitivity was due in part to their apprehensions over Europe's growing influence in Latin America." But that explanation still founders on the fact that Europe's influence was not growing. Blaine's and Harrison's sensitivity was more self-generated than a response to external provocation.

190. Healy, *U.S. Expansionism,* p. 103.

191. Oliver Wendell Holmes, Jr., "The Soldier's Faith," speech at Harvard University, May 30, 1895, in Richard A. Posner, ed., *The Essential Holmes: Selections from the Letters, Speeches, Judicial Opinions, and Other Writings of Oliver Wendell Holmes, Jr.* (Chicago: Chicago University Press, 1992), pp. 87–93.

192. Henry Adams, *History of the United States During the Administration of Thomas Jefferson,* 6 vols. (New York: Albert & Charles Boni, 1930), 2:277.

193. Widenor, *Henry Cabot Lodge,* p. 41.

194. Holmes, "The Soldier's Faith," speech at Harvard University, May 30, 1895.

195. See Chapter 5.

196. As Alfred Thayer Mahan wrote to Rear Admiral Luce, "[T]he energy with which" Harrison had "pushed naval preparations . . . had much to do with the final pacific outcome." Hagan, *People's Navy,* p. 200.

197. Ibid., p. 203.

198. Robert Wiebe, *The Search for Order* (New York: Hill & Wang, 1967), p. 225;

Robert L. Beisner, *From the Old Diplomacy to the New, 1865–1900*, 2nd ed. (Arlington Heights, Ill.: Harlan Davidson, 1986), p. 32; Keller, *Affairs of State*, p. 98. The "revisionist" historians who dissented from this view and depicted the 1880s as "years of preparation," during which American leaders consciously planted the roots of an informal commercial "empire," have been largely repudiated by critics who have demonstrated that no such consistent design shaped American policies. Walter LaFeber argued in his influential work on America's "New Empire" that the 1880s were "years of preparation" for the 1890s, a period when Americans "set out to solve their [domestic economic] problems by creating an empire whose dynamic and characteristics marked a new departure in their history." The 1880s, and indeed the three preceding decades as well, had provided "the roots of empire," though "not the fruit." The "fruit of empire would not appear until the 1890s." LaFeber, *New Empire*, pp. 60–61

199. As James A. Field, Jr., has argued, "One should not, for example, use the 'magnificent naval base at Pearl Harbor' as evidence of vigorous transpacific expansionism twenty years before anyone dredged the mouth of the Pearl River." Field, "Worst Chapter," p. 653.

200. Aaron L. Friedberg, *The Weary Titan: Britain and the Experience of Relative Decline, 1895–1905* (Princeton, N.J.: Princeton University Press, 1988), p. 153.

201. Holger H. Herwig, *Politics of Frustration: The United States in German Naval Planning, 1889–1941* (Boston: Little, Brown, 1976), p. 40.

202. The *Maine*, whose destruction in Havana harbor was a catalyst for the Spanish-American War, was authorized by Congress in 1886. Rear Admiral George Dewey routed the Spanish fleet at Manila Bay in 1898 aboard the *Olympia*, the flagship of the Asiatic squadron, authorized by Congress in 1888. The famous battle at Santiago Bay in 1898, in which the North Atlantic squadron sank or disabled the by-then-badly-outgunned Spaniards, included Rear Admiral William Sampson's flagship, the *New York*, and the battleship *Texas*, both authorized in 1888. The most powerful battleship in the American fleet in 1898, the *Oregon*, which had enough speed to rush from the Pacific Coast to the Caribbean in time for battle, and then enough firepower that it could possibly have defeated the entire Spanish fleet at Santiago by itself, was one of the three world-class battleships authorized by Congress in 1890. A fourth first-class battleship, the *Iowa*, was authorized in 1892. By 1898 these four battleships alone tilted the naval balance in favor of the United States, at least in the waters around Cuba.

203. On this point LaFeber attempts to draw a bright line between the nature of the naval buildup in the 1880s and the "more ambitious" buildup of the 1890s, which he argues was in keeping with the more aggressive search for foreign markets in the latter decade. However, the naval buildup, the origins of the battleship fleet, and the thinking behind them are not so easily divided into pre- and post-1890 phases. See LaFeber, *New Empire*, p. 60.

Chapter 12 / *Morality and Hegemony*

1. John A. S. Grenville and George Berkeley Young, *Politics, Strategy and American Diplomacy: Studies in Foreign Policy, 1873–1917* (New Haven, Conn.: Yale University Press, 1966), p. 34.

2. David F. Healy, *U.S. Expansionism: The Imperialist Urge in the 1890s* (Madison: University of Wisconsin Press, 1970), p. 216.

3. One of the weaknesses of the revisionist account of this era is the tendency to lump Democrats and Republicans together without noting their fundamentally different views of how American foreign policy should be conducted.

4. Richard E. Welch, Jr., *The Presidencies of Grover Cleveland* (Lawrence: University Press of Kansas, 1988), p. 68.

5. C. Vann Woodward, "The Irony of Southern History," in Woodward, *The Burden of Southern History*, 3rd ed. (Baton Rouge: Louisiana State University Press, 1993), p. 190.

6. The party's "Bourbon wing" wielded great influence, and this wing represented a large southern population that "recalled with bitterness how the GOP had attempted to centralize federal authority during and after" the Civil War and that believed, as the southern electorate had believed before the Civil War, that the federal government "played no positive function whatsoever." Justus D. Doenecke, *The Presidencies of James A. Garfield and Chester A. Arthur* (Lawrence: Regents Press of Kansas, 1981), p. 8; Welch, *Presidencies of Cleveland,* p. 12.

7. R. Hal Williams, *Years of Decision: American Politics in the 1890s* (New York: Wiley, 1978), p. 5.

8. Charles W. Calhoun, "The Political Culture," in Calhoun, ed., *The Gilded Age: Essays on the Origins of Modern America* (Wilmington, Del.: Scholarly Resources, 1996), p. 189.

9. Harold Underwood Faulkner, *Politics, Reform, and Expansion, 1890–1900* (New York: Harper & Row, 1963), p. 7.

10. Welch, *Presidencies of Cleveland,* p. 87.

11. William Earl Weeks, *John Quincy Adams and American Global Empire* (Lexington: University Press of Kentucky, 1982), p. 19.

12. Welch, *Presidencies of Cleveland,* p. 14.

13. Ibid., pp. 65, 68.

14. Charles Callan Tansill, *The Foreign Policy of Thomas F. Bayard, 1885–1897* (New York: Fordham University Press, 1940), p. xv; Grenville and Young, *Politics, Strategy and American Diplomacy,* p. 45.

15. Tennant S. McWilliams, *The New South Faces the World: Foreign Affairs and the Southern Sense of Self, 1877–1950* (Baton Rouge: Louisiana State University Press, 1988), pp. 16, 20.

16. Ibid., pp. 18, 35, 44, 35, 21.

17. Welch, *Presidencies of Cleveland,* p. 158.

18. Tansill, *Foreign Policy of Bayard,* pp. xix–xx.

19. Welch, *Presidencies of Cleveland,* p. 159.

20. Tansill, *Foreign Policy of Bayard,* p. xxxvii.

21. Welch, *Presidencies of Cleveland,* pp. 178–79.

22. Charles W. Calhoun, *Gilded Age Cato: The Life of Walter Q. Gresham* (Lexington: University Press of Kentucky, 1988), pp. 6, 135, 155, 134–35.

23. Ibid., pp. 6, 171.

24. Ibid., pp. 6, 135, 138.

25. Ibid., pp. 164, 162.

26. Ibid., p. 166.

27. Ibid., p. 165.

28. McWilliams, *New South Faces the World,* p. 22.

29. Ibid., p. 23.

30. Ibid., pp. 33, 35.

31. Ibid., p. 38.

32. Calhoun, *Life of Gresham,* pp. 148, 151.

33. Ibid., p. 156.

34. Ibid., pp. 153, 154.

35. McWilliams, *New South Faces the World,* p. 41.

36. Calhoun, *Life of Gresham,* pp. 143, 161.

37. Grenville and Young, *Politics, Strategy, and American Diplomacy,* p. 117.

38. See LaFeber, *New Empire,* p. 94.

39. Walter R. Herrick, Jr., *The American Naval Revolution* (Baton Rouge: Louisiana State University Press, 1966), p. 170; James F. Vivian, "United States Policy During the

Brazilian Naval Revolt, 1893–94: The Case for American Neutrality," *American Neptune* 41 (October 1981): 261.

40. Grenville and Young, *Politics, Strategy, and American Diplomacy,* pp. 139, 121.

41. Gerald G. Eggert, *Richard Olney, Evolution of a Statesman* (University Park: Pennsylvania State University Press, 1974), p. 198.

42. Ibid., p. 213. Olney "was trying to quiet the affair as a domestic political issue before the December meeting of Congress by stirring it up as an international incident in July."

43. Ibid., pp. 246, 198, 202, 206.

44. Dexter Perkins, *Hands Off: A History of the Monroe Doctrine* (Boston: Little, Brown, 1941), p. 69.

45. Eggert, *Richard Olney,* p. 203.

46. Perkins, *Hands Off,* pp. 157–58; Tansill, *Foreign Policy of Bayard,* p. 705.

47. Eggert, *Richard Olney,* p. 202.

48. Ibid., p. 204.

49. Tansill, *Foreign Policy of Bayard,* pp. 696–97.

50. Eggert, *Richard Olney,* p. 204.

51. In Salisbury's words, "to present so far-reaching and important a principle . . . in relation to a subject so comparatively small." Tansill, *Foreign Policy of Bayard,* p. 709.

52. Eggert, *Richard Olney,* p. 218.

53. Ibid., pp. 220, 221, 222; Welch, *Presidencies of Cleveland,* p. 185.

54. Eggert, *Richard Olney,* p. 223.

55. Instead of mobilizing the navy, they called for the creation of an independent commission to explore the matter further, which keen British observers correctly saw as a "safety valve" designed to avoid conflict. "Olney and Cleveland substituted the commission as a way to prevent war and apparently made no move whatever to alert the armed forces for either offensive or defensive action." Ibid., pp. 222–23.

56. Ibid., pp. 207, 222. "Cleveland believed that out of good will, Britain should have acceded to arbitration so as to have let his administration off the hook with the domestic jingoes."

57. Tansill, *Foreign Policy of Bayard,* p. 728.

58. Eggert, *Richard Olney,* pp. 209, 224.

59. Tansill, *Foreign Policy of Bayard,* p. 727; Eggert, *Richard Olney,* p. 224.

60. Tansill, *Foreign Policy of Bayard,* pp. 727, 726.

61. Eggert, *Richard Olney,* p. 240.

62. Ibid., pp. 227–28.

63. Ibid., pp. 228–29.

64. Sylvia L. Hilton and Steve J. S. Ickringill, eds., *European Perceptions of the Spanish-American War of 1898* (Bern, N.Y.: Peter Lang, 1999), pp. 10, 16.

65. Eggert, *Richard Olney,* pp. 243–44.

66. Louis A. Pérez, Jr., *Cuba: Between Reform and Revolution* (New York: Oxford University Press, 1988), p. 157.

67. Louis A. Pérez, Jr., *Cuba Between Empires* (Pittsburgh: University of Pittsburgh Press, 1983), p. 133.

68. Ibid., p. 128.

69. Pérez, *Cuba: Between Reform and Revolution,* p. 162.

70. Pérez, *Cuba Between Empires,* pp. 133, 128.

71. Ibid., pp. 136, 135.

72. Pérez, *Cuba Between Reform and Revolution,* p. 158.

73. Pérez, *Cuba Between Empires,* pp. 54, 50–51.

74. Pérez, *Cuba Between Reform and Revolution,* p. 166.

75. Ibid., pp. 167–69.

76. Pérez, *Cuba Between Empires*, pp. 120, 54, 122.

77. Welch, *Presidencies of Cleveland*, p. 198.

78. Philip S. Foner, *The Spanish-Cuban-American War and the Birth of American Imperialism, 1895–1902*, 2 vols. (New York: Monthly Review Press, 1972), 1:184.

79. As Philip S. Foner put it, "It is not surprising that an administration which had 'approved the virtual disfranchisement of the Negro' in the Southern States should have been alarmed by the prospect of a Republic less than a hundred miles off the coast of Florida in which the Negroes would occupy a prominent place." Ibid., 1:194–95.

80. Ibid., 1:179–80.

81. Harry Thurston Peck, *Twenty Years of the Republic, 1885–1905* (New York: Dodd, Mead, 1907), p. 537.

82. Foner, *Spanish-Cuban-American War,* 1:170.

83. George W. Auxier, "The Propaganda Activities of the Cuban Junta in Precipitating the Spanish-American War, 1895–1898," *Hispanic American Historical Review* 19 (August 1939): 288.

84. Foner, *Spanish-Cuban-American War,* 1:185.

85. John L. Offner, *An Unwanted War: The Diplomacy of the United States and Spain over Cuba, 1895–1898* (Chapel Hill: University of North Carolina Press, 1992), pp. 20–21, 19.

86. Jules R. Benjamin, *The United States and the Origins of the Cuban Revolution: An Empire of Liberty in an Age of National Liberation* (Princeton, N.J.: Princeton University Press, 1990), p. 36.

87. H. Wayne Morgan, *William McKinley and His America* (Kent, Ohio: Kent State University Press, 2003), p. 252.

88. Foner, *Spanish-Cuban-American War,* 1:183. "Despite their losses, early in the war U.S. investors saw no alternative to Spanish protection, however inadequate." Benjamin, *Origins of Cuban Revolution*, p. 35.

89. "Mr. Olney," Atkins wrote later, "was always willing to listen to what I had to say upon the Cuban situation and he requested me to make confidential reports to him from time to time. This I did, and one of my reports was embodied almost verbatim in his report to Congress as Secretary of State." Foner, *Spanish-Cuban-American War,* 1:182.

90. "The cautious policy emanating from Washington was sustained for the most part by the business community in the United States." Benjamin, *Origins of Cuban Revolution*, p. 36.

91. J. Rogers Hollingsworth, *The Whirligig of Politics: The Democracy of Cleveland and Bryan* (Chicago: University of Chicago Press, 1963), p. 131.

92. Offner, *Unwanted War,* p. 26.

93. Lewis L. Gould, *The Spanish-American War and President McKinley* (Lawrence: University Press of Kansas, 1982), pp. 25–26.

94. Welch, *Presidencies of Cleveland*, p. 197.

95. H. Wayne Morgan, *From Hayes to McKinley: National Party Politics, 1877–1896* (Syracuse, N.Y.: Syracuse University Press, 1969), p. 470.

96. Hollingsworth, *Whirligig of Politics*, pp. 25, 26.

97. Morgan, *From Hayes to McKinley*, pp. 478–79.

98. Lewis L. Gould, "The Republican Search for a National Majority," in H. Wayne Morgan, ed., *The Gilded Age* (Syracuse, N.Y.: Syracuse University Press, 1970), p. 183.

99. Hollingsworth, *Whirligig of Politics*, p. 30.

100. Faulkner, *Politics, Reform, and Expansion*, p. 136.

101. Hollingsworth, *Whirligig of Politics*, p. 43.

102. Ibid., pp. 62–63.

103. Governor Altgeld, for instance, was "the true precursor of the northern, city-oriented Democratic liberalism of the twentieth century." Morton Keller, *Affairs of State: Public Life*

in *Late Nineteenth Century America* (Cambridge, Mass.: Harvard University Press, 1977), pp. 580–81.

104. Paul W. Glad, *The Trumpet Soundeth: Williams Jennings Bryan and His Democracy, 1896–1912* (Westport, Conn.: Greenwood Press, 1986) pp. 39, 41.

105. Paul S. Holbo, "The Convergence of Moods and the Cuban Bond 'Conspiracy' of 1898," *Journal of American History* 55 (June 1968): 58.

106. Hollingsworth, *Whirligig of Politics,* pp. 130–31.

107. Foner, *Spanish-Cuban-American War,* 1:173–74.

108. Benjamin, *Origins of Cuban Revolution,* p. 27.

109. The phrase "psychic crisis" is Richard Hofstadter's. See Hofstadter, "Manifest Destiny and the Philippines," in Daniel Aaron, ed., *America in Crisis: Fourteen Crucial Episodes in American History* (New York: Knopf, 1952), pp. 173–75. The term "hysteria" is applied by Ernest May, along with "fervor" and "frenzy." See Ernest R. May, *Imperial Democracy: The Emergence of America as a Great Power* (New York: Harper & Row, 1973), pp. 142, 145, 268.

110. Morgan, *From Hayes to McKinley,* p. 479.

111. See Williams, *Years of Decision,* p. 5. "For nearly a dozen years before 1889 the two parties had been so evenly balanced that neither dared take chances. In 1880 the Republicans had won the presidential race by only 7,000 votes out of more than nine million cast; in 1884 they had trailed Grover Cleveland by only 63,000 votes out of ten million. Congressional races were equally close. Less than two percentage points separated the total Republican and Democratic vote for congressmen in all but one election between 1878 and 1888. Such margins affected the party system, making politicians extremely cautious and giving no one the majority needed to govern."

112. Ibid., pp. 5, 6.

113. Calhoun, "The Political Culture," pp. 208–9.

114. Morgan, *McKinley and His America,* p. 45.

115. Ibid., pp. 45, 51, 485.

116. Ibid., pp. 223, 274.

117. Offner, *Unwanted War,* p. 40.

118. Healy, *U.S. Expansionism,* p. 111.

119. Offner, *Unwanted War,* p. 31.

120. "He supported annexation of the Hawaiian Islands, construction of an American-owned Nicaraguan canal, expansion of the merchant marine, greater foreign trade, and reciprocal trade agreements . . . [and had] moderate interest in constructing a larger navy." Ibid., p. 38.

121. Ibid.

122. Hollingsworth, *Whirligig of Politics,* p. 129.

123. Offner, *Unwanted War,* p. 41.

124. Foner, *Spanish-Cuban-American War,* 1:210.

125. Pérez, *Cuba Between Empires,* pp. 141, 140.

126. Horace Samuel Merrill and Marion Galbraith Merrill, *The Republican Command, 1897–1913* (Lexington: University Press of Kentucky, 1971), p. 49.

127. Hollingsworth, *Whirligig of Politics,* pp. 130–31.

128. Offner, *Unwanted War,* p. 43.

129. Ibid., pp. 43–45.

130. "Early in his term he became guarded toward Congress, suspicious of legislative maneuvers capable of infringing on traditional executive prerogatives." Pérez, *Cuba Between Empires,* p. 140.

131. Offner, *Unwanted War,* pp. 112, 81.

132. Ibid., pp. 133, 46–47, 80, 46–47.

133. "Accounts of atrocities resulting from the Spanish treatment of individuals were occasionally fabricated; more often they were verifiable. The horrors of the reconcentration policy were abundantly documented." Gould, *Spanish-American War,* p. 23.

134. Foner, *Spanish-Cuban-American War,* 1:209.

135. Offner, *Unwanted War,* pp. 46–47.

136. Morgan, *McKinley and His America,* p. 254.

137. Offner, *Unwanted War,* p. 48; Gould, *Spanish-American War,* p. 28.

138. Offner, *Unwanted War,* pp. 57–58.

139. Foner, *Spanish-Cuban-American War,* 1:204.

140. Offner, *Unwanted War,* p. 72. See also Morgan, *McKinley and His America,* p. 261: "Though Dupuy de Lôme felt that the new minister was pacific, in retrospect the Madrid government held that his coming ended an era. His first official actions made it clear that the new representative of North America had instructions to approach the Cuban problem with the idea of overshadowing or limiting the sovereignty of Spain."

141. Foner, *Spanish-Cuban-American War,* 1:215; Offner, *Unwanted War,* p. 48.

142. Foner *Spanish-Cuban-American War,* 1:216.

143. Pérez, *Cuba Between Empires,* pp. 142–43.

144. Offner, *Unwanted War,* pp. 41, 54–55.

145. Hollingsworth, *Whirligig of Politics,* pp. 131–32.

146. Offner, *Unwanted War,* p. 43.

147. Ibid., pp. 67, 121.

148. Morgan, *McKinley and His America,* pp. 259–60.

149. Pérez, *Cuba Between Empires,* p. 145.

150. Offner, *Unwanted War,* p. 87.

151. Pérez, *Cuba Between Empires,* p. 147

152. Ibid.

153. Offner, *Unwanted War,* p. 79.

154. Ibid., p. 93; Pérez, *Cuba Between Empires,* p. 149.

155. Gould, *Spanish-American War,* p. 32.

156. Pérez, *Cuba Between Empires,* p. 163.

157. Morgan, *McKinley and His America,* p. 267.

158. Dupuy de Lôme to José Canalejas, undated, in John Bassett Moore, ed., *A Digest of International Law,* 8 vols. (Washington, D.C.: U.S. Government Printing Office, 1906), 6:176; George H. Gibson, "Attitudes in North Carolina Regarding the Independence of Cuba, 1868–1898," *North Carolina Historical Review* 43 (January 1966): 58.

159. *News and Observer,* February 11, 1898, quoted in Gibson, "Attitudes in North Carolina," p. 58.

160. Offner, *Unwanted War,* p. 124.

161. Ibid., pp. 129–30.

162. Morgan, *McKinley and His America,* p. 275.

163. Offner, *Unwanted War,* pp. 131, 132–33.

164. Morgan, *McKinley and His America,* p. 276.

165. Offner, *Unwanted War,* p. 134.

166. Gould, *Spanish-American War,* p. 40.

167. Offner, *Unwanted War,* p. 134.

168. Merrill and Merrill, *Republican Command,* p. 49.

169. Offner, *Unwanted War,* p. 135.

170. Ibid., p. 136.

171. Frank Freidel, "Dissent in the Spanish-American War and the Philippine Insurrection," *Proceedings of the Massachusetts Historical Society* 81 (1969): 171.

172. Morgan, *McKinley and His America,* p. 277.

173. Offner, *Unwanted War,* p. 38. According to Thomas G. Paterson, "The interpreta-tion prevailing in the historiography today is . . . that McKinley dominated American foreign relations." See Paterson, "United States Intervention in Cuba, 1898: Interpretations of the Spanish-American-Cuban-Filipino War," *History Teacher* 29, no. 3 (May 1996): 341–61.

174. Offner, *Unwanted War,* p. 151.

175. Pérez, *Cuba Between Empires,* p. 174.

176. Morgan, *McKinley and His America,* p. 277.

177. Pérez, *Cuba Between Empires,* pp. 174, 173.

178. Offner, *Unwanted War,* p. 144.

179. Pérez, *Cuba Between Empires,* p. 175; Offner, *Unwanted War,* p. 154.

180. Offner, *Unwanted War,* pp. 153–54.

181. Morgan, *McKinley and His America,* p. 281.

182. Gould, *Spanish-American War,* pp. 43–44; Offner, *Unwanted War,* p. 157.

183. Morgan, *McKinley and His America,* p. 282.

184. Offner, *Unwanted War,* pp. 167–68.

185. Ibid., p. 154.

186. Morgan, *McKinley and His America,* p. 286.

187. Pérez, *Cuba Between Empires,* pp. 176–77.

188. "Madrid's action was too vague, and Spain's ability to act effectively was no longer believed in Washington." Benjamin, *Origins of Cuban Revolution,* p. 49. See also Morgan, *McKinley and His America,* p. 283: McKinley "did not believe that Spain was either sincere in her promises or capable of fulfilling them."

189. Pérez, *Cuba Between Empires,* p. 180.

190. Merrill and Merrill, *Republican Command,* p. 51.

191. Pérez, *Cuba Between Empires,* p. 178.

192. Ibid.

193. Sylvia L. Hilton, "The Spanish-American War of 1898: Queries into the Relation-ship Between the Press, Public Opinion and Politics," *Revista Española de Estudios Norte-americanos* 5, no. 7 (1994): 77–78.

194. Offner, *Unwanted War,* p. 59.

195. Gould, *Spanish-American War,* p. 48.

196. Merrill and Merrill, *Republican Command,* pp. 50, 51, 52.

197. Hollingsworth, *Whirligig of Politics,* p. 134.

198. Fredrick B. Pike, *The United States and Latin America: Myths and Stereotypes of Civilization and Nature* (Austin: University of Texas Press, 1992), p. 168.

199. Henry Cabot Lodge, "For Intervention in Cuba," 1896, *Congressional Record,* 54th Cong., 1st sess., pp. 1971–72.

200. Marshall E. Schott, "Louisiana Sugar and the Cuban Crisis, 1895–1898," *Louisiana History* 31 (Summer 1990): 272.

201. Lodge, "For Intervention in Cuba," pp. 1971–72.

202. Elizabeth Hazard, "The *Maine* Remembered: Responses to the Spanish-American War in the Pine Tree State," *Maine History* 37 (Spring 1998): 176.

203. Margaret Leech, *In the Days of McKinley* (New York: Harper, 1959), p. 172.

204. Hazard, "*Maine* Remembered," p. 174.

205. Howard H. Quint, "American Socialists and the Spanish-American War," *American Quarterly* 10, no. 2, pt. 2 (Summer 1958): 135–36.

206. E. Berkeley Tompkins, *Anti-Imperialism in the United States: The Great Debate, 1890–1920* (Philadelphia: University of Pennsylvania Press, 1970), pp. 91–92.

207. Hazard, "*Maine* Remembered," p. 177.

208. Gibson, "Attitudes in North Carolina," p. 63.

209. Quint, "American Socialists," pp. 135, 138.

210. Jeanne Abrams, "Remembering the *Maine:* The Jewish Attitude Toward the Spanish American War as Reflected in *The American Israelite,*" *American Jewish History* 76 (June 1987): 442.

211. Ibid., p. 443.

212. Hollingsworth, *Whirligig of Politics,* p. 134.

213. Louis A. Pérez, Jr., "Incurring a Debt of Gratitude: 1898 and the Moral Sources of United States Hegemony in Cuba," *American Historical Review* 104 (April 1999): 357–58.

214. Ibid., p. 356.

215. Ibid., p. 358.

216. Robert L. Beisner, *Twelve Against Empire: The Anti-Imperialists, 1898–1900* (New York: McGraw-Hill, 1968), pp. 172–73.

217. Joseph Frazier Wall, *Andrew Carnegie* (Pittsburgh: University of Pittsburgh Press, 1989), p. 691.

218. Carl Schurz, "Thoughts on American Imperialism," *Century Magazine* 56 (September 1898): 782–83; Pérez, "Incurring a Debt of Gratitude," p. 357.

219. Hilton and Ickringill, *European Perceptions,* pp. 11, 29.

220. Ibid., pp. 31, 56, 78, 32.

221. Ibid., pp. 66–68.

222. Wililam E. Leuchtenburg, "The Needless War with Spain," *American Heritage* 8, no. 2 (February 1957): 33.

223. James Ford Rhodes, *The McKinley and Roosevelt Administrations, 1897–1909* (New York: Macmillan, 1922), p. 67; Louis A. Pérez, "The Meaning of the *Maine:* Causation and the Historiography of the Spanish-American War," *Pacific Historical Review* 58 (August 1989): 317.

224. Foster Rhea Dulles, *Prelude to World Power: American Diplomatic History, 1860–1900* (New York: Collier, 1971), p. 180; Pérez, "Meaning of the *Maine,*" p. 317.

225. Leuchtenburg, "Needless War with Spain," p. 33; Pérez, "Meaning of the *Maine,*" p. 317.

226. Robert Endicott Osgood, *Ideals and Self-Interest in America's Foreign Relations: The Great Transformation of the Twentieth Century* (Chicago: University of Chicago Press, 1974), p. 43.

227. Pérez, "Meaning of the *Maine,*" p. 321.

228. As the historian Louis A. Pérez, Jr., has observed, the history of the intervention in Cuba has produced "a usable past that serves at once to reflect and reinforce generally shared assumptions" about the "normal" conduct of American foreign policy. Ibid., p. 319.

229. Whether some Americans did, in fact, favor war with Spain partly out of a desire to acquire the Philippines has been a contentious subject for historians. I will address it in the next volume.

BIBLIOGRAPHY

Abrams, Jeanne. "Remembering the *Maine:* The Jewish Attitude Toward the Spanish American War as Reflected in *The American Israelite*." *American Jewish History* 76 (June 1987).

Abrams, Richard M. "United States Intervention Abroad: The First Quarter Century." *American Historical Review* 79 (February 1974).

Adams, Ephraim Douglass. *British Interests and Activities in Texas, 1838–1846.* Baltimore: Johns Hopkins Press, 1910.

———. *Great Britain and the American Civil War.* 2 vols. 1925; reprint, New York: Russell & Russell, 1958.

Adams, Henry. *History of the United States During the Administrations of Thomas Jefferson and James Madison.* 6 vols. New York: Albert & Charles Boni, 1930.

———. *The Life of Albert Gallatin.* Philadelphia and London: J. B. Lippincott, 1879.

Adams, John. *The Works of John Adams, Second President of the United States.* Ed. Charles Francis Adams. 10 vols. Boston: Little, Brown, 1850–56.

———, and James Warren. *Warren-Adams Letters: Being Chiefly a Correspondence Among John Adams, Samuel Adams, and James Warren.* 2 vols. Boston, 1925; reprint, New York: AMS Press, 1972.

Adams, John Quincy. *John Quincy Adams and American Continental Empire: Letters, Papers and Speeches.* Ed. Walter LaFeber. Chicago: Quadrangle Books, 1965.

———. *Memoirs of John Quincy Adams, Comprising Portions of His Diary from 1795 to 1848.* Ed. Charles Francis Adams. 12 vols. Philadelphia: J. B. Lippincott, 1874–77.

———. *Writings of John Quincy Adams.* Ed. Worthington Chauncey Ford. 7 vols. 1913; reprint, New York: Greenwood Press, 1968.

Alfonso, Oscar M. *Theodore Roosevelt and the Philippines, 1897–1909.* Quezon City: University of the Philippines Press, 1970.

Ammon, Harry. *James Monroe: The Quest for National Identity.* New York: McGraw-Hill, 1971.

———. "The Monroe Doctrine: Domestic Politics or National Decision?" *Diplomatic History* 5 (Winter 1981).

Anderson, David L. *Imperialism and Idealism: American Diplomats in China, 1861–1898.* Bloomington: Indiana University Press, 1985.

Anderson, Fred. *The Crucible of War: The Seven Years' War and the Fate of Empire in British North America, 1754–1766.* New York: Knopf, 2000.

Anderson, Stuart. *Race and Rapprochement: Anglo-Saxonism and Anglo-American Relations, 1895–1904.* Rutherford, N.J.: Fairleigh Dickinson University Press, 1981.

Anschel, Eugene. *The American Image of Russia, 1775–1917.* New York: Ungar, 1974.

Appleby, Joyce. *Capitalism and a New Social Order: The Republican Vision of the 1790s.* New York: New York University Press, 1984.

———. *Inheriting the Revolution: The First Generation of Americans.* Cambridge, Mass.: Belknap Press of Harvard University Press, 2000.

Apt, Benjamin L. "Mahan's Forebears: The Debate over Maritime Strategy, 1868–1883." *Naval War College Review* 50 (Summer 1997).

Armitage, David. *The Ideological Origins of the British Empire.* Cambridge, U.K.: Cambridge University Press, 2000.

Arnold, William Thomas. *German Ambitions as They Affect Britain and the United States of America.* New York: G. P. Putnam's Sons, 1903.

Artz, Frederick B. *Reaction and Revolution: 1814–1832.* New York: Harper Torchbook, 1974.

Auxier, George W. "The Propaganda Activities of the Cuban Junta in Precipitating the Spanish-American War, 1895–1898." *Hispanic American Historical Review* 19 (August 1939).

Bailey, Harris Moore, Jr. "The Splendid Little Forgotten War: The Mobilization of South Carolina for the War with Spain." *South Carolina Historical Magazine* 92 (July 1991).

Bailey, Thomas A. "America's Emergence as a World Power: The Myth and the Verity." *Pacific Historical Review* 31, no. 1 (February 1961).

———. *A Diplomatic History of the American People.* Englewood Cliffs, N.J.: Prentice-Hall, 1974.

Bailey, Thomas Andrew. *America Faces Russia: Russian-American Relations from Early Times to Our Day.* Ithaca, N.Y.: Cornell University Press, 1950.

Bailyn, Bernard. *The Ideological Origins of the American Revolution.* Cambridge, Mass.: Belknap Press of Harvard University Press, 1967.

———. *The New England Merchants in the Seventeenth Century.* Cambridge, Mass.: Harvard University Press, 1979.

Banning, Lance. *The Jeffersonian Persuasion: Evolution of a Party Ideology.* Ithaca, N.Y.: Cornell University Press, 1978.

Baton, Harold. "Anti-Imperialism and the Democrats." *Science and Society* 21 (Summer 1958).

Beales, A. C. F. *The History of Peace: A Short Account of the Organized Movements for International Peace.* London: G. Bell, 1931.

Becker, William H., and Samuel F. Wells, Jr., eds. *Economics and World Power: An Assessment of American Diplomacy Since 1789.* New York: Columbia University Press, 1984.

Bedford, Joseph. "Samuel Gompers and the Caribbean: The AFL, Cuba, and Puerto Rico, 1898–1906." *Labor's Heritage* 6 (Spring 1995).

Beisner, Robert L. *From the Old Diplomacy to the New, 1865–1900.* 2nd ed. Arlington Heights, Ill.: Harlan Davidson, 1986.

———. "Thirty Years Before Manila: E. L. Godkin, Carl Schurz, and Anti-Imperialism in the Gilded Age." *Historian* 30 (August 1968).

———. *Twelve Against Empire: The Anti-Imperialists, 1898–1900.* New York: McGraw-Hill, 1968.

Beloff, Max. *The Great Powers: Essays in Twentieth Century Politics.* London: George Allen and Unwin, 1959.

Belohlavek, John. *"Let the Eagle Soar!": The Foreign Policy of Andrew Jackson.* Lincoln: University of Nebraska Press, 1985.

Bemis, Samuel Flagg. *The American Secretaries of State and Their Diplomacy, 1776–1925.* 10 vols. New York: Knopf, 1927–29.

———. *The Diplomacy of the American Revolution.* Rev. ed. Bloomington: Indiana University Press, 1957.

———. *A Diplomatic History of the United States.* 5th ed. Chicago, London, and New York: Holt, Rinehart & Winston, 1965.

———. *John Quincy Adams and the Foundations of American Foreign Policy.* New York: Knopf, 1949.

————. *John Quincy Adams and the Union.* New York: Knopf, 1956.

————. *Pinckney's Treaty: America's Advantage from Europe's Distress, 1783–1800.* New Haven, Conn.: Yale University Press, 1960.

Ben-Atar, Doron. "Nationalism, Neo-Mercantilism, and Diplomacy: Rethinking the Franklin Mission." *Diplomatic History* 22, no. 5 (Winter 1998).

————. *The Origins of Jeffersonian Commercial Policy and Diplomacy.* New York: St. Martin's, 1993.

Benjamin, Jules R. "The Framework of U.S. Relations with Latin America in the Twentieth Century: An Interpretive Essay." *Diplomatic History* 11 (Spring 1987).

————. *The United States and the Origins of the Cuban Revolution: An Empire of Liberty in an Age of National Liberation.* Princeton, N.J.: Princeton University Press, 1990.

Berens, John F. *Providence and Patriotism in Early America, 1640–1815.* Charlottesville: University Press of Virginia, 1978.

Berkeley, George. *The Works of George Berkeley, D.D.* Ed. Alexander C. Fraser. 4 vols. Oxford: Clarendon Press, 1901.

Bernstein, Barton J., and Franklin A. Leib. "Progressive Republican Senators and American Imperialism, 1898–1916: A Re-appraisal." *Mid-America* 50 (July 1968).

Best, Gary Dean. "Financing a Foreign War: Jacob H. Schiff and Japan, 1904–05." *American Jewish Historical Quarterly* 61 (June 1972).

————. *To Free a People: American Jewish Leaders and the Jewish Problem in Eastern Europe, 1890–1914.* Westport, Conn.: Greenwood Press, 1982.

Bhagat, Goberdhan. *Americans in India: Commercial and Consular Relations, 1784–1860.* New York, 1951; reprint, New York: New York University Press, 1970.

Billington, Ray Allen, ed. *The Reinterpretation of Early American History: Essays in Honor of John Edwin Pomfret.* San Marino, Calif.: Huntington Library, 1966.

Blaine, James G. *Twenty Years of Congress: From Lincoln to Garfield.* 2 vols. Norwich, Conn.: Henry Bill, 1884–86.

Blake, Nelson M. "England and the United States, 1897–1899." In *Essays in History and International Relations, in Honor of George Hubbard Blakeslee,* ed. Dwight E. Lee and George E. McReynolds. Worcester, Mass.: Clark University, 1949.

Bloch, Ruth. *Visionary Republic: Millennial Themes in American Thought, 1756–1800.* New York and Cambridge, U.K.: Cambridge University Press, 1985.

Blumenthal, Henry A. *A Reappraisal of Franco-American Relations, 1830–1871.* Chapel Hill: University of North Carolina Press, 1959.

Bostert, Russell H. "Diplomatic Reversal: Frelinghuysen's Opposition to Blaine's Pan-American Policy in 1882." *Mississippi Valley Historical Review* 42 (March 1956).

Bourne, Kenneth. *Britain and the Balance of Power in North America, 1815–1908.* Berkeley: University of California Press, 1967.

Boyd, Julian P. *Number 7: Alexander Hamilton's Secret Attempts to Control American Foreign Policy.* Princeton, N.J.: Princeton University Press, 1964.

Brackenridge, Hugh Henry, and Philip Freneau. *A Poem on the Rising Glory of America.* Philadelphia, 1772.

Bradford, Richard H. *Admirals of the New Steel Navy: Makers of the American Naval Tradition, 1880–1930.* Annapolis, Md.: Naval Institute Press, 1990.

————. *The Virginius Affair.* Boulder: Colorado Associated University Press, 1980.

Braisted, William Reynolds. "The Navy in the Early Twentieth Century, 1890–1941." In *A Guide to the Sources of United States Military History,* ed. Robin Higham. Hamden, Conn.: Archon Books, 1975.

————. *The United States Navy in the Pacific, 1897–1909.* Austin: University of Texas Press, 1958.

Brands, H. W. *T.R.: The Last Romantic.* New York: BasicBooks, 1997.

———. *What America Owes the World: The Struggle for the Soul of Foreign Policy*. New York: Cambridge University Press, 1998.

Brauer, Kinley J. *Cotton vs. Conscience: Massachusetts Whig Politics and Southwestern Expansion, 1843–1848*. Lexington: University of Kentucky Press, 1967.

———. "Economics and the Diplomacy of American Expansionism, 1820–1860." In *Economics and World Power: An Assessment of American Diplomacy Since 1789*, ed. William H. Becker and Samuel F. Wells, Jr. New York: Columbia University Press, 1984.

———. "The Great American Desert Revisited: Recent Literature and Prospects for the Study of American Foreign Relations, 1815–61." *Diplomatic History* 13 (Summer 1989).

———. "The United States and British Imperial Expansion, 1815–1860." *Diplomatic History* 12 (Winter 1988).

Bridge, Francis Roy. "Great Britain, Austria-Hungary, and the Concert of Europe on the Eve of the Spanish-American War." *Mitteilungen des Österreichischen Staatarchivs* 44 (1996).

Brock, Peter. *Pacifism in the United States from the Colonial Era to the First World War.* Princeton, N.J.: Princeton University Press, 1968.

Brooks, Charles W. *America in France's Hopes and Fears, 1890–1920*. 2 vols. New York: Garland, 1987.

Brown, Richard H. "The Missouri Crisis, Slavery, and the Politics of Jacksonianism." *South Atlantic Quarterly* 65 (1966).

Brown, Robert C. "Goldwin Smith and Anti-Imperialism." *Canadian Historical Review* 43 (June 1962).

Brown, Roger H. *The Republic in Peril: 1812*. New York: Columbia University Press, 1964.

Bruchey, Stuart. *Enterprise: The Dynamic Economy of a Free People*. Cambridge, Mass.: Harvard University Press, 1990.

Buchenau, Jürgen. *In the Shadow of the Giant: The Making of Mexico's Central American Policy, 1876–1930*. Tuscaloosa: University of Alabama Press, 1996.

Burnaby, Andrew. *Travels Through the Middle Settlements in North America in the Years 1759 and 1760, with Observations upon the State of the Colonies*. New York: A. M. Kelly, 1970.

Calhoun, Charles C. *Gilded Age Cato: The Life of Walter Q. Gresham*. Lexington: University Press of Kentucky, 1988.

Calvert, Peter. "Great Britain and the New World, 1905–1914." In *British Foreign Policy Under Sir Edward Grey*, ed. F. H. Hinsley. New York: Cambridge University Press, 1977.

Campbell, Alexander E. *Great Britain and the United States, 1895–1903*. London: Longmans, 1960; reprint, Westport, Conn.: Greenwood Press, 1974.

———. "Great Britain and the United States in the Far East, 1895–1903." *Historical Journal* 1, no. 2 (1958–59).

Campbell, Charles S. "Anglo-American Relations, 1897–1901." In *Threshold to American Internationalism: Essays on the Foreign Policy of William McKinley*, ed. Paolo E. Colletta. New York: Exposition Press, 1970.

———. *Anglo-American Understanding, 1898–1903*. Baltimore: Johns Hopkins Press, 1957.

———. *The Transformation of American Foreign Relations, 1865–1900*. New York: Harper & Row, 1976.

Campomanes, Oscar V. "1898 and the Nature of the New Empire." *Radical History Review* 73 (Winter 1999).

Cappon, Lester J., ed. *The Adams-Jefferson Letters: The Complete Correspondence Between*

Thomas Jefferson and Abigail and John Adams. Chapel Hill: University of North Carolina Press, [1959] 1988.

Case, Lynn M., and Warren F. Spencer. *The United States and France: Civil War Diplomacy.* Philadelphia: University of Pennsylvania Press, 1970.

Cashman, Sean Dennis. *America in the Age of the Titans: The Progressive Era and World War I.* New York: New York University Press, 1988.

Castle, Alfred L. "Tentative Empire: Walter Q. Gresham, U.S. Foreign Policy, and Hawaii, 1893–1895." *Hawaiian Journal of History* 29 (Fall 1995).

Caudill, Edward. *Darwinian Myths: The Legends and Misuses of a Theory.* Knoxville: University of Tennessee Press, 1997.

Challener, Richard D. *Admirals, Generals, and American Foreign Policy, 1898–1914.* Princeton, N.J.: Princeton University Press, 1973.

Charles, Joseph. "Hamilton and Washington: The Origins of the American Party System." *William and Mary Quarterly* 12, no. 2 (April 1955).

Chatfield, Charles, with Robert Kleidman. *The American Peace Movement: Ideals and Activism.* New York: Twayne, 1992.

Chenetier, Marc, and Rob Kroes, eds. *Impressions of a Gilded Age: The American Fin de Siècle.* Amsterdam: Amerika Instituut, Universiteit Van Amsterdam, 1983.

Chernow, Ron. *Alexander Hamilton.* New York: Penguin, 2004.

Cherny, Robert W. "Anti-Imperialism on the Middle Border, 1898–1900." *Midwest Review* 1 (Spring 1979).

Christman, Margaret C. S. *Adventurous Pursuits: Americans and China Trade, 1784–1844.* Washington, D.C.: Smithsonian Institution Press, 1984.

Clayton, Lawrence A. "The Nicaragua Canal in the Nineteenth Century: Prelude to American Empire in the Caribbean." *Journal of Latin American Studies* 19 (November 1987).

Clymer, Kenton J. "Checking the Sources: John Jay and Spanish Possessions in the Pacific." *Historian* 48 (November 1985).

Cohen, Naomi W. *Jacob H. Schiff: A Study in American Jewish Leadership.* Hanover, N.H.: University Press of New England for Brandeis University Press, 1999.

Cohen, Warren I. *America's Response to China: A History of Sino-American Relations.* New York: Columbia University Press, 2000.

———. "The History of American–East Asian Relations: Cutting Edge of the Historical Profession." *Diplomatic History* 9 (Spring 1985).

Coletta, Paolo E. *Williams Jennings Bryan.* Vol. 1: *Political Evangelist, 1860–1908.* Vol. 2: *Progressive Politician and Moral Statesman, 1909–1915.* Vol. 3: *Political Puritan, 1915–1925.* Lincoln: University of Nebraska Press, 1964–69.

Colley, Linda. *Britons: Forging the Nation, 1707–1837.* New Haven, Conn.: Yale University Press, 1992.

Contosta, David R. "Whitelaw Reid and the Inadvertent Empire." *Old Northwest* 12 (Spring 1986).

Cooke, Jacob E., ed. *The Federalist.* Middletown, Conn.: Wesleyan University Press, [1981] 1982.

Coolidge, Archibald Cary. *The United States as a World Power.* New York: Macmillan Company, 1908.

Cooling, Benjamin Franklin. *Benjamin Franklin Tracy: Father of the Modern American Fighting Navy.* Hamden, Conn.: Archon Books, 1973.

Cooper, John Milton, Jr. "Progressivism and American Foreign Policy: A Reconsideration." *Mid-America* 51 (October 1969).

Cosío Villegas, Daniel. *The United States Versus Porfirio Díaz.* Trans. Nettie Lee Benson. Lincoln: University of Nebraska Press, 1963.

Craig, John M. *Lucia Ames Mead (1856–1936) and the American Peace Movement.* Lewiston, N.Y.: E. Mellen, 1990.

———. "Lucia True Ames Mead: American Publicist for Peace and Internationalism." In *Women and American Foreign Policy: Lobbyists, Critics, and Insiders,* ed. Edward P. Crapol. Wilmington, Del.: SR Books, 1992.

Crapol, Edward P. *America for Americans: Economic Nationalism and Anglophobia in the Late Nineteenth Century.* Westport, Conn.: Greenwood Press, 1973.

———. *James G. Blaine: Architect of Empire.* Wilmington, Del.: SR Books, 2000.

Craven, Avery O. *The Growth of Southern Nationalism, 1848–1861.* Vol. 6 of *History of the South,* ed. Wendell Holmes Stephenson and E. Merton Coulter. 9 vols. Baton Rouge: Louisiana State University Press, 1953.

———, ed. *Essays in Honor of William E. Dodd, by His Former Students at the University of Chicago.* Chicago: University of Chicago Press, 1935.

Cress, Lawrence D. *Citizens in Arms: The Army and Militia in American Society to the War of 1812.* Chapel Hill: University of North Carolina Press, 1982.

Crook, D. P. *The North, the South, and the Powers.* New York: Wiley, 1974.

Cruz, Arturo J., Jr. *Nicaragua's Conservative Republic, 1858–93.* New York: Palgrave, in association with St. Antony's Oxford, 2002.

Damiani, Brian P. *Advocates of Empire: William McKinley, the Senate and American Expansion, 1898–1899.* New York: Garland, 1987.

Dangerfield, George. *The Era of Good Feelings.* New York: Harcourt, Brace, 1952.

Davis, David Brion. "American Equality and Foreign Revolutions." *Journal of American History* 76, no. 3 (December 1989).

———. *Slavery and Human Progress.* New York: Oxford University Press, 1984.

DeConde, Alexander. *Entangling Alliances: Politics and Diplomacy Under George Washington.* Durham, N.C.: Duke University Press, 1958.

———. *The Quasi-War: The Politics and Diplomacy of the Undeclared War with France, 1791–1801.* New York: Scribner's, 1966.

———. *This Affair of Louisiana.* New York: Scribner's, 1976.

Dement'ev, I. P. "Leo Tolstoy and Social Critics in the United States at the Turn of the Century." In *Russian-American Dialogue on Cultural Relations, 1776–1914,* ed. Norman E. Saul and Richard D. McKinzie. Columbia: University of Missouri Press, 1997.

Dennett, Tyler. *Roosevelt and the Russo-Japanese War: A Critical Study of American Policy in Eastern Asia, 1902–5, Based Primarily upon the Private Papers of Theodore Roosevelt.* Garden City, N.Y.: Doubleday, Page, 1925.

Dennis, Alfred L. *Adventures in American Diplomacy, 1896–1906 (From Unpublished Documents).* New York: E. P. Dutton and Company, 1928.

DeNovo, John A. "The Enigmatic Alvey A. Adee and American Foreign Relations, 1870–1924." *Prologue* 7 (Summer 1975).

Diplomatic Correspondence of the United States of America, from the Signing of the Definitive Treaty of Peace, September 10, 1783, to the Adoption of the Cost, March 4, 1789. 3 vols. Washington, D.C., 1837.

Doenecke, Justus D. *The Presidencies of James A. Garfield and Chester A. Arthur.* Lawrence: Regents Press of Kansas, 1981.

Donald, David Herbert. *Charles Sumner.* New York: Da Capo Press, 1996.

———. *Charles Sumner and the Rights of Man.* New York: Knopf, 1970.

———. *Lincoln.* New York: Touchstone, 1996.

Dorwart, Jeffrey M. "The Independent Minister: John M. B. Sill and the Struggle Against Japanese Expansion in Korea, 1894–1897." *Pacific Historical Review* 44 (November 1975).

————. *The Pigtail War: American Involvement in the Sino-Japanese War of 1894–1895.* Amherst: University of Massachusetts Press, 1975.

Douglas, Stephen A. *The Letters of Stephen A. Douglas.* Ed. Robert W. Johannsen. Urbana: University of Illinois Press, 1961.

Draper, Theodore. *A Struggle for Power: The American Revolution.* New York: Times Books, 1996.

Dull, Jonathan R. *A Diplomatic History of the American Revolution.* New Haven, Conn.: Yale University Press, 1985.

Dulles, Foster Rhea. *Prelude to World Power: American Diplomatic History, 1860–1900.* New York: Collier Books, [1965] 1971.

Dyer, Thomas G. *Theodore Roosevelt and the Idea of Race.* Baton Rouge: Louisiana State University Press, 1980.

Earle, Edward Meade. "American Interest in the Greek Cause, 1821–1827." *American Historical Review* 33 (October 1927).

————. "Early American Policy Concerning Ottoman Minorities." *Political Science Quarterly* 42, no. 3 (September 1927).

Eggert, Gerald G. "Our Man in Havana: Fitzhugh Lee." *Hispanic American Historical Review* 47 (November 1967).

————. *Richard Olney: Evolution of a Statesman.* University Park: Pennsylvania State University Press, 1974.

Einstein, Lewis. "British Diplomacy in the Spanish-American War." *Proceedings of the Massachusetts Historical Society* 76 (1964).

Ekirch, Arthur Alphonse. *Ideas, Ideals, and American Diplomacy: A History of Their Growth and Interaction.* New York: Appleton-Century-Crofts, 1966.

Eldridge, C. C., ed. *British Imperialism in the Nineteenth Century.* London: Macmillan, 1984.

Elkins, Stanley, and Eric McKitrick. *The Age of Federalism: The Early American Republic, 1788–1800.* New York: Oxford University Press, 1993.

Ellis, Joseph. *American Sphinx: The Character of Thomas Jefferson.* New York: Vintage Books, 1998.

————. "Culture and Capitalism in Pre-revolutionary America." *American Quarterly* 31, no. 2 (Summer 1979).

Esthus, Raymond A. *A Double Eagle and Rising Sun: The Russians and Japanese at Portsmouth in 1905.* Durham, N.C.: Duke University Press, 1988.

————. *Theodore Roosevelt and Japan.* Seattle: University of Washington Press, 1967.

Faulkner, Harold Underwood. *Politics, Reform, and Expansion, 1890–1900.* New York: Harper & Row, 1959.

Ferrer, Ada. "Cuba, 1898: Rethinking Race, Nation, and Empire." *Radical History Review* 73 (Winter 1999).

Field, James A., Jr. "All Economists, All Diplomats." In *Economics and World Power: An Assessment of American Diplomacy Since 1789,* ed. William H. Becker and Samuel F. Wells, Jr. New York: Columbia University Press, 1984.

————. *America and the Mediterranean World, 1776–1882.* Princeton, N.J.: Princeton University Press, 1969.

————. "American Imperialism: The Worst Chapter in Almost Any Book." *American Historical Review* 83 (June 1978).

Fifer, J. Valerie. *United States Perceptions of Latin America, 1850–1930: A "New West" South of Capricorn?* New York: Manchester University Press, 1991.

Fischer, David Hackett. *Albion's Seed: Four British Folkways in America.* New York: Oxford University Press, 1989.

Fitzsimons, David M. "Tom Paine's New World Order: Idealistic Internationalism in the Ideology of Early American Foreign Relations." *Diplomatic History* 19, no. 4 (Fall 1995).

Flexner, James Thomas. *George Washington: The Forge of Experience, 1732–1775.* New York: Little, Brown, 1965.

Foner, Eric. *Free Soil, Free Labor, Free Men.* New York: Oxford University Press, 1970.

Foner, Philip S. *The Anti-Imperialist Reader: A Documentary History of Anti-Imperialism in the United States.* New York: Holmes and Meier, 1984.

———. *The Spanish-Cuban-American War and the Birth of American Imperialism, 1895–1902.* 2 vols. New York: Monthly Review Press, 1972.

Ford, Paul Leicester, ed. *Pamphlets on the Constitution of the United States, Published During Its Discussion by the People, 1787–1788.* Brooklyn, N.Y.: n.p., 1888.

Ford, Worthington Chauncey, ed. *Journals of the Continental Congress, 1774–1779.* Washington, D.C.: U.S. Government Printing Office, 1905.

Franklin, Benjamin. *The Papers of Benjamin Franklin.* 28 vols. Vols. 1–15 ed. Leonard W. Larabee et al. New Haven, Conn.: Yale University Press, 1959–.

———. *The Writings of Benjamin Franklin.* Ed. Albert Henry Smyth. 10 vols. New York: Haskell House, 1970.

Franklin, John Hope. "Southern Expansionists of 1846." *Journal of Southern History* 25, no. 3 (August 1959).

Freehling, William W. *Prelude to Civil War: The Nullification Controversy in South Carolina, 1816–1836.* New York: Harper & Row, 1966.

———. *The Road to Disunion.* New York: Oxford University Press, 1990.

Freidel, Frank. "Dissent in the Spanish-American War and the Philippine Insurrection." *Proceedings of the Massachusetts Historical Society* 81 (1969).

Friedberg, Aaron L. *The Weary Titan: Britain and the Experience of Relative Decline, 1895–1905.* Princeton, N.J.: Princeton University Press, 1988.

Fry, Joseph A. "From Open Door to World Systems: Economic Interpretations of Late Nineteenth-Century American Foreign Relations." *Pacific Historical Review* 65 (May 1996).

———. "Imperialism, American Style, 1890–1916." In *American Foreign Relations Reconsidered, 1890-1993,* ed. Gordon Martel. New York: Routledge, 1994.

———. *John Tyler Morgan and the Search for Southern Autonomy.* Knoxville: University of Tennessee Press, 1992.

———. "William McKinley and the Coming of the Spanish-American War: A Study in the Besmirching and Redemption of an Historical Image." *Diplomatic History* 3 (Winter 1979).

Gaddis, John Lewis. *We Now Know: Rethinking Cold War History.* New York: Oxford University Press, 1997.

Gardner, Lloyd C., Walter LaFeber, and Thomas J. McCormick. *Creation of the American Empire.* Chicago: Rand-McNally, 1976.

Garrett, Wendell D. "John Davis Long, Secretary of the Navy, 1898–1902: A Study in Changing Political Alignments." *New England Quarterly* 31 (March 1958).

Gatewood, Willard B., Jr. "Black Americans and the Quest for Empire, 1893–1903." *Journal of Southern History* 38 (November 1972).

———. *Black Americans and the White Man's Burden, 1898–1903.* Urbana: University of Illinois Press, 1975.

Gelber, Lionel M. *The Rise of Anglo-American Friendship: A Study in World Politics, 1898–1906.* New York: Oxford University Press, 1938.

Genovese, Eugene D. *Political Economy of Slavery: Studies in the Economy and Society of the Slave South.* 2nd ed. Middletown, Conn.: Wesleyan University Press, 1989.

Gibson, George H. "Attitudes in North Carolina Regarding the Independence of Cuba, 1868–1898." *North Carolina Historical Review* 43 (January 1966).

Gibson, William. "Mark Twain and Howells: Anti-Imperialists." *New England Quarterly* 20 (March 1947).

Gilbert, Felix. *To the Farewell Address: Ideas of Early American Foreign Policy.* Princeton, N.J.: Princeton University Press, 1970.

Gilderhus, Mark T. *The Second Century: Latin American Relations Since 1889.* Wilmington, Del.: Scholarly Resources, 2000.

Gillette, Howard, Jr. "The Military Occupation of Cuba, 1899–1902: Workshop for American Progressivism." *American Quarterly* 25 (October 1973).

Gitlin, Jay. "Private Diplomacy to Private Property: States, Tribes, and Nations in the Early National Period." *Diplomatic History* 22 (Winter 1998).

Glad, Paul W. *The Trumpet Soundeth: Williams Jennings Bryan and His Democracy, 1896–1912.* Westport, Conn.: Greenwood Press, [1960] 1986.

Goldberg, Joyce S. "Patrick Egan: An Irish-American Minister to Chile." *Eire-Ireland* 14 (Fall 1979).

Goldman, Eric F., ed. *Historiography and Urbanization: Essays in American History in Honor of W. Stull Holt.* Baltimore: Johns Hopkins Press, 1941.

Gould, James W. "American Imperialism in Southeast Asia Before 1898." *Journal of Southeast Asian Studies* 3, no. 2 (1972).

Gould, Lewis L. "Chocolate Éclair or Mandarin Manipulator? McKinley, the Spanish-American War, and the Philippines: A Review Essay." *Ohio History* 94 (Summer–Autumn 1985).

———."The Republican Search for a National Majority." In *The Gilded Age,* ed. H. Wayne Morgan. Syracuse, N.Y.: Syracuse University Press, 1970.

———. *The Spanish-American War and President McKinley.* Lawrence: University Press of Kansas, 1982.

Grabill, Joseph L. *Protestant Diplomacy and the Near East: Missionary Influence on American Policy, 1810–1927.* Minneapolis: University of Minnesota Press, 1971.

Graebner, Norman A. *Empire on the Pacific: A Study of American Continental Expansion.* New York: Ronald Press 1955; reprint, Santa Barbara, Calif.: ABC-Clio, 1983.

———. *Foundations of American Foreign Policy: A Realist Appraisal from Franklin to McKinley.* Wilmington, Del.: Scholarly Resources, 1985.

———. *Ideas and Diplomacy: Readings in the Intellectual Tradition of American Foreign Diplomacy.* New York: Oxford University Press, 1964.

———. "Isolationism and Antifederalism: The Ratification Debates." *Diplomatic History* 11, no. 4 (Fall 1987).

Greene, Jack P. "Empire and Identity from the Glorious Revolution to the American Revolution." In *The Oxford History of the British Empire,* vol. 2: *The Eighteenth Century,* ed. P. J. Marshall. Oxford: Oxford University Press, 1998.

———. *The Intellectual Construction of America: Exceptionalism and Identity from 1492 to 1800.* Chapel Hill: University of North Carolina Press, 1993.

———. *Pursuits of Happiness: The Social Development of Early Modern British Colonies and the Formation of American Culture.* Chapel Hill: University of North Carolina Press, 1988.

———, ed. *Settlements to Society, 1607–1763: A Documentary History of Colonial America.* New York: Norton, 1975.

Grenville, J. A. S. "American Naval War with Spain, 1896–1898." *Journal of American Studies* 2 (April 1968).

———. "Diplomacy and War Plans in the United States, 1890–1917." *Transactions of the Royal Historical Society,* 5th ser., 11 (1961).

————. "Great Britain and the Isthmian Canal, 1898–1901." *American Historical Review* 61 (October 1955).

————, and George Berkeley Young. *Politics, Strategy and American Diplomacy: Studies in Foreign Policy, 1873–1917.* New Haven, Conn.: Yale University Press, 1966.

Griffin, Frederick C. "Protesting Despotism: American Opposition to the U.S.-Russian Extradition Treaty of 1887." *Mid-America* 70 (April–July 1988).

Hagan, Kenneth J. *This People's Navy: The Making of American Sea Power.* New York: Free Press, 1991.

Haines, Gerald K., and J. Samuel Walker, eds. *American Foreign Relations: A Historiographical Review.* Westport, Conn.: Greenwood Press, 1981.

Halle, Louis J. *Dream and Reality: Aspects of American Foreign Policy.* New York: Harper, 1959.

Hamilton, Alexander. *The Papers of Alexander Hamilton.* Ed. Harold C. Syrett and Jacob E. Cooke. 27 vols. New York: Columbia University Press, 1961–87.

————. *The Works of Alexander Hamilton.* Ed. Henry Cabot Lodge. 12 vols. New York: G. P. Putnam's Sons, 1903.

————. *Works of Alexander Hamilton.* Ed. John C. Hamilton. 7 vols. New York: J. F. Trow, 1850–51.

Handler, Edward. *America and Europe in the Political Thought of John Adams.* Cambridge, Mass.: Harvard University Press, 1964.

Hanna, Alfred Jackson, and Kathryn Abbey Kanna. *Napoleon III and Mexico: American Triumph over Monarchy.* Chapel Hill: University of North Carolina Press, 1971.

Harbaugh, William Henry. *Power and Responsibility: The Life and Times of Theodore Roosevelt.* New York: Farrar, Straus & Cudahy, 1961.

Hargreaves, Mary W. M. *The Presidency of John Quincy Adams.* Lawrence: University of Kansas Press, 1985.

Harrington, Fred. H. "The Anti-Imperialist Movement in the United States, 1898–1900." *Mississippi Valley Historical Review* 22 (September 1935).

Hatch, Nathan O. *The Sacred Cause of Liberty: Republican Thought and the Millennium in Revolutionary New England.* New Haven, Conn.: Yale University Press, 1977.

Hazard, Elizabeth. "The *Maine* Remembered: Responses to the Spanish-American War in the Pine Tree State." *Maine History* 37 (Spring 1998).

Headrick, Daniel R. *The Invisible Weapon: Telecommunications and International Politics, 1851–1945.* New York: Oxford University Press, 1991.

Heald, Morrell, and Lawrence S. Kaplan. *Culture and Diplomacy: The American Experience.* Westport, Conn.: Greenwood Press, 1977.

Healy, Ann E. "Tsarist Anti-Semitism and Russian-American Relations." *Slavic Review* 42 (Fall 1983).

Healy, David. *James G. Blaine and Latin America.* Columbia: University of Missouri Press, 2001.

————. *Modern Imperialism: Changing Styles in Historical Interpretation.* Washington, D.C.: Service Center for Teachers of History, 1967.

————. *The United States in Cuba, 1898–1902: Generals, Politicians, and the Search for Policy.* Madison: University of Wisconsin Press, 1963.

————. *U.S. Expansionism: The Imperialist Urge in the 1890s.* Madison: University of Wisconsin Press, 1970.

Heindel, Richard Heathcote. *The American Impact on Great Britain, 1898–1914: A Study of the United States in World History.* Philadelphia: University of Pennsylvania Press, 1940.

Henning, Joseph M. *Outposts of Civilization: Race, Religion, and the Formative Years of American-Japanese Relations.* New York: New York University Press, 2000.

Henson, Curtis T., Jr. *Commissioners and Commodores: The East India Squadron and American Diplomacy in China.* University: University of Alabama Press, 1982.

Herman, Sondra R. *Eleven Against War: Studies in American Internationalist Thought, 1898–1921.* Stanford, Calif.: Hoover Institution Press, Stanford University, 1969.

Herrick, Walter R., Jr. *The American Naval Revolution.* Baton Rouge: Louisiana State University Press, 1966.

Herwig, Holger H. *Germany's Vision of Empire in Venezuela, 1871–1914.* Princeton, N.J.: Princeton University Press, 1986.

———. *Politics of Frustration: The United States in German Naval Planning, 1889–1941.* Boston: Little, Brown, 1976.

Hietala, Thomas R. *Manifest Design: Anxious Aggrandizement in Late Jacksonian America.* Ithaca, N.Y.: Cornell University Press, 1985.

Hilton, Sylvia L. "The Spanish-American War of 1898: Queries into the Relationship Between the Press, Public Opinion and Politics." *Revista Española de Estiodios Norte-americanos* 5, no. 7 (1994).

———, and Steve J. S. Ickringill, eds. *European Perceptions of the Spanish-American War of 1898.* Bern and New York: Peter Lang, 1999.

Hofstadter, Richard. *The Age of Reform: From Bryan to F.D.R.* New York: Knopf, 1955.

———. "Manifest Destiny and the Philippines." In *America in Crisis: Fourteen Crucial Episodes in American History,* ed. Daniel Aaron. New York: Knopf, 1952.

Hogan, Michael J., ed. *Paths to Power: The Historiography of American Foreign Relations to 1941.* New York: Cambridge University Press, 2000.

Holbo, Paul S. "The Convergence of Moods and the Cuban Bond 'Conspiracy' of 1898." *Journal of American History* 55 (June 1968).

———. "Perspectives on American Foreign Policy, 1890–1916: Expansion and World Power." *Social Studies* 58 (November 1967).

Hollingsworth, J. Rogers. *The Whirligig of Politics: The Democracy of Cleveland and Bryan.* Chicago: University of Chicago Press, 1963.

Holt, Michael Fitzgibbon. *The Rise and Fall of the American Whig Party: Jacksonian Politics and the Onset of the Civil War.* New York: Oxford University Press, 1999.

Holt, W. Stull. *Treaties Defeated by the Senate: A Study of the Struggle Between President and Senate over the Conduct of Foreign Relations.* Baltimore: Johns Hopkins Press, 1933.

Horsman, Reginald. "The Dimensions of an 'Empire for Liberty': Expansion and Republicanism, 1775–1825." *Journal of the Early Republic* 9, no. 1 (Spring 1989).

———. *Expansion and American Indian Policy, 1783–1812.* East Lansing: Michigan State University Press, 1967; reprint, Norman: University of Oklahoma Press, 1992.

———. *Race and Manifest Destiny: The Origins of American Racial Anglo-Saxonism.* Cambridge, Mass.: Harvard University Press, 1981.

———. "The War of 1812 Revisited." *Diplomatic History* 5, no. 5 (Winter 1991).

Howe, Daniel Walker. *The Political Culture of the American Whigs.* Chicago: University of Chicago Press, 1979.

Hugo, Markus M. " 'Uncle Sam I Cannot Stand, for Spain I Have No Sympathy': An Analysis of Discourse About the Spanish-American War in Imperial Germany, 1898–1900." In *European Perceptions of the Spanish-American War of 1898,* ed. Sylvia L. Hilton and Steve J. S. Ickringill. Bern and New York: Peter Lang, 1999.

Humphreys, R. A., and John Lynch, eds. *The Origins of the Latin American Revolutions, 1808–1826.* New York: Knopf, 1965.

Hunt, Michael H. *Ideology and U.S. Foreign Policy.* New Haven, Conn.: Yale University Press, 1988.

———. *The Making of a Special Relationship: The United States and China to 1914.* New York: Columbia University Press, 1983.

Hutchison, William R. *Errand to the World: American Protestant Thought and Foreign Missions.* Chicago: University of Chicago Press, 1987.

Hutson, James H. "Intellectual Foundations of Early American Diplomacy." *Diplomatic History* 1, no. 1 (Winter 1977).

————. *John Adams and the Diplomacy of the American Revolution.* Lexington: University Press of Kentucky, 1980.

Iriye, Akira. *Across the Pacific: An Inner History of American East Asian Relations.* New York: Harcourt, Brace & World, 1967.

————. *From Nationalism to Internationalism: U.S. Foreign Policy to 1914.* London and Boston: Routledge & K. Paul, 1977.

————. "Japan as a Competitor, 1895–1917." In *Mutual Images: Essays in American-Japanese Relations,* ed. Akira Iriye. Cambridge, Mass.: Harvard University Press, 1975.

————. *Pacific Estrangement: Japanese and American Expansion, 1897–1911.* Cambridge, Mass.: Harvard University Press, 1972.

Jackson, Andrew. Papers. Library of Congress, Washington, D.C.

Jaffa, Harry V. *Crisis of the House Divided: An Interpretation of the Issues in the Lincoln-Douglas Debates.* Chicago: University of Chicago Press, 1982.

————. *A New Birth of Freedom: Abraham Lincoln and the Coming of the Civil War.* Lanham, Md.: Rowman & Littlefield, 2000.

Jefferson, Thomas. *The Papers of Thomas Jefferson.* Ed. Julian P. Boyd et al. 24 vols. Princeton, N.J.: Princeton University Press, 1950–.

————. *The Writings of Thomas Jefferson.* Ed. Paul Leicester Ford. 10 vols. New York: G. P. Putnam's Sons, 1894.

Jensen, Merrill. *The New Nation: A History of the United States During the Confederation, 1781–1789.* New York: Vintage Books, [1950] 1962.

Johannsen, Robert W. *Stephen A. Douglas.* New York: Oxford University Press, 1973.

Johnson, J. R. "Imperialism in Nebraska, 1898–1904." *Nebraska History* 44 (September 1963).

Johnson, Robert David. *The Peace Progressives and American Foreign Relations.* Cambridge, Mass.: Harvard University Press, 1995.

Johnson, Robert Erwin. *Far China Station: The U.S. Navy in Asian Waters, 1800–1898.* Annapolis, Md.: Naval Institute Press, 1979.

Jonas, Manfred. *The United States and Germany: A Diplomatic History.* Ithaca, N.Y.: Cornell University Press, 1984.

Jones, Colin. *The Great Nation: France from Louis XV to Napoleon.* New York: Penguin, 2002.

Junker, Detlef. *The Manichaean Trap: American Perceptions of the German Empire, 1871–1945.* Washington, D.C.: German Historical Institute, 1995.

Kaplan, Lawrence S. "The Brahmin as Diplomat in Nineteenth-Century America: Everett, Bancroft, Motley, Lowell." *Civil War History* 19 (March 1973).

————. *Entangling Alliances with None: American Foreign Policy in the Age of Jefferson.* Kent, Ohio: Kent State University Press, 1987.

Kaufman, Burton Ira, ed. *Washington's Farewell Address: The View from the 20th Century.* Chicago: Quadrangle Books, 1969.

Keller, Morton. *Affairs of State: Public Life in Late Nineteenth Century America.* Cambridge, Mass.: Harvard University Press, 1977.

Kennan, George F. *American Diplomacy.* Expanded ed. Chicago: University of Chicago Press, 1984.

Kennedy, Paul. "British and German Reactions to the Rise of American Power." In *Ideas into Politics: Aspects of European History, 1880–1950,* ed. R. J. Bullen, H. Pogge von Strandmann, and A. B. Polonsky. London: Croom Helm, 1984.

———. *The Samoan Tangle: A Study in Anglo-German-American Relations, 1878–1900.* New York: Barnes and Noble, 1974.

———, ed. *The War Plans of the Great Powers, 1880–1914.* Boston: Allen and Unwin, 1979.

Kerber, Linda K. *Federalists in Dissent: Imagery and Ideology in Jeffersonian America.* Ithaca, N.Y.: Cornell University Press, 1970.

King, G. Wayne. "Conservative Attitudes in the United States Toward Cuba." *Proceedings of the South Carolina Historical Association* (1973).

Klein, Philip Shriver. *President James Buchanan: A Biography.* University Park: Pennsylvania State University Press, 1962.

Knee, Stuart E., "The Diplomacy of Neutrality: Theodore Roosevelt and the Russian Pogroms of 1903–1906." *Presidential Studies Quarterly* 19, no. 1 (Winter 1989).

Knight, Alan. "Britain and Latin America." In *The Oxford History of the British Empire,* vol. 3: *The Nineteenth Century,* ed. Andrew Porter. Oxford: Oxford University Press, 1999.

Knott, Stephen F. *Alexander Hamilton and the Persistence of Myth.* Lawrence: University Press of Kansas, 2002.

Koebner, Richard. *Empire.* Cambridge, U.K.: Cambridge University Press, 1961; New York: Grosset & Dunlap, 1965.

Kohn, Hans. *American Nationalism.* New York: Macmillan, 1957; New York: Collier Books, 1961.

Kohn, Richard. *Eagle and Sword: The Federalists and the Creation of the Military Establishment in America, 1783–1802.* New York: Free Press, 1975.

Kolchin, Peter. *American Slavery, 1619–1877.* New York: Hill & Wang, 1993.

Kramer, Paul A. "Empires, Exceptions, and Anglo-Saxons: Race and Rule Between the British and United States Empires, 1880–1910." *Journal of American History* 88 (March 2002).

Krein, David F. *The Last Palmerston Government: Foreign Policy, Domestic Politics, and the Genesis of "Splendid Isolation."* Ames: Iowa State University Press, 1978.

Kriegel, Abraham D. "A Convergence of Ethics: Saints and Whigs in British Antislavery." *Journal of British Studies* 26, no. 4 (October 1987).

LaFeber, Walter. *The American Age: United States Foreign Policy at Home and Abroad Since 1750.* New York: Norton, 1989.

———. *The American Search for Opportunity, 1865–1913.* Vol. 2 of *The Cambridge History of American Foreign Relations,* ed. Warren I. Cohen. 4 vols. New York: Cambridge University Press, 1993.

———. "Betrayal in Tokyo." *Constitution* 6 (Fall 1994).

———. *The Clash: A History of U.S.-Japan Relations.* New York: Norton, 1997.

———. "The Constitution and United States Foreign Policy." *Journal of American History* 74, no. 3 (December 1987).

———. *The New Empire: An Interpretation of American Expansion, 1860–1898.* Ithaca, N.Y.: Cornell University Press, 1963.

———. "A Note on the 'Mercantilistic Imperialism' of Alfred Thayer Mahan." *Journal of American History* 48 (March 1962).

———. "That 'Splendid Little War' in Historical Perspective." *Texas Quarterly* 11 (Winter 1968).

———, ed. *John Quincy Adams and American Continental Empire: Letters, Speeches, and Papers.* Chicago: Quadrangle Books, 1965.

Lander, Ernest M., Jr. *Reluctant Imperialists: Calhoun, the South Carolinians, and the Mexican War.* Baton Rouge: Louisiana State University Press, 1980.

Lang, Daniel G. *Foreign Policy in the Early Republic: The Law of Nations and the Balance of Power.* Baton Rouge: Louisiana State University Press, 1985.

Langer, William L. *The Diplomacy of Imperialism, 1890–1902.* 2nd ed. New York: Knopf, 1951.

Langley, Lester D. *America and the Americas: The United States in the Western Hemisphere.* Athens: University of Georgia Press, 1989.

———. "American Foreign Policy in an Age of Nationalism, 1812–1840." In *American Foreign Relations: A Historiographical Review,* ed. Gerald K. Haines and J. Samuel Walker. Westport, Conn.: Greenwood Press, 1981.

———. *The Americas in the Age of Revolution, 1750–1850.* New Haven, Conn.: Yale University Press, 1996.

———. *Struggle for the American Mediterranean: United States–European Rivalry in the Gulf-Caribbean, 1776–1904.* Athens: University of Georgia Press, 1976.

Lasch, Christopher. "The Anti-Imperialists, the Philippines, and the Inequality of Man." *Journal of Southern History* 24 (August 1958).

Latcham, John S. "President McKinley's Active-Positive Character: A Comparative Revision with Barber's Typology." *Presidential Studies Quarterly* 12 (Fall 1982).

Lauren, Paul Gordon. *Power and Prejudice: The Politics and Diplomacy of Racial Discrimination.* 2nd ed. Boulder, Colo.: Westview Press, 1996.

Lee, Jean Gordon. *Philadelphians and the China Trade, 1784–1844.* Philadelphia: Philadelphia Museum of Art, 1984.

Lee, Yur-Bok. *Diplomatic Relations Between the United States and Korea, 1866–1887.* New York: Humanities Press, 1970.

Leech, Margaret. *In the Days of McKinley.* New York: Harper, 1959.

Leffler, John J. "The Paradox of Patriotism: Texans in the Spanish-American War." *Hayes Historical Journal* 8 (Spring 1989).

Leopold, Richard William. *Elihu Root and the Conservative Tradition.* Boston: Little, Brown, 1954.

Lenman, Bruce P. "Colonial Wars and Imperial Instability." In *The Oxford History of the British Empire,* vol. 2: *The Eighteenth Century,* ed. P. J. Marshall. Oxford: Oxford University Press, 1998.

Lepore, Jill. *The Name of War: King Philip's War and the Origins of American Identity.* New York: Knopf, 1998.

Lerner, Ralph. *The Thinking Revolutionary: Principle and Practice in the New Republic.* Ithaca, N.Y.: Cornell University Press, 1987.

Leuchtenburg, William E. "The Needless War with Spain." *American Heritage* 8, no. 2 (February 1957).

Linderman, Gerald F. *Embattled Courage: The Experience of Combat in the American Civil War.* New York: Free Press, 1987.

———. *The Mirror of War: American Society and the Spanish-American War.* Ann Arbor: University of Michigan Press, 1974.

Linn, Brian McAllister. *The U.S. Army and Counterinsurgency in the Philippine War, 1899–1902.* Chapel Hill: University of North Carolina Press, 1989.

Lockey, Joseph Byrne. *Pan-Americanism: Its Beginnings.* New York: Macmillan, 1926.

Lodge, Henry Cabot. "Some Impressions of Russia." *Scribner's Magazine* 31 (1902).

Looze, Helene Johnson. *Alexander Hamilton and the British Orientation of American Foreign Policy, 1783–1803.* The Hague: Mouton, 1969.

Lutzker, Michael A. "The Pacifist as Militarist: A Critique of the American Peace Movement, 1898–1914." *Societas* 5 (Spring 1975).

———. "Themes and Contradictions in the American Peace Movement, 1895–1917." In *The Pacifist Impulse in Historical Perspective,* ed. Harvey L. Dyck. Toronto: University of Toronto Press, 1996.

Lycan, Gilbert. *Alexander Hamilton and American Foreign Policy.* Norman: University of Oklahoma Press, 1970.

Lynn, Martin. "British Policy, Trade, and Informal Empire in the Mid-Nineteenth Century." In *The Oxford History of the British Empire,* vol. 3: *The Nineteenth Century,* ed. Andrew Porter. Oxford: Oxford University Press, 1999.

Mallan, John P. "The Warrior Critique of the Business Civilization." *American Quarterly* 8, no. 3 (Fall 1956).

Marchand, C. Roland. *The American Peace Movement and Social Reform, 1898–1918.* Princeton, N.J.: Princeton University Press, 1973.

Marsden, George M. *Jonathan Edwards: A Life.* New Haven, Conn.: Yale University Press, 2003.

Marks, Frederick W., III. "Foreign Affairs: A Winning Issue in the Campaign for Ratification of the United States Constitution." *Political Science Quarterly* 86, no. 3 (September 1971).

———. *Independence on Trial: Foreign Affairs and the Making of the Constitution.* Baton Rouge: Louisiana State University Press, 1973.

———. "Morality as a Drive Wheel in the Diplomacy of Theodore Roosevelt." *Diplomatic History* 2 (Winter 1978).

———. "Power, Pride, and Purse: Diplomatic Origins of the Constitution." *Diplomatic History* 11, no. 4 (Fall 1987).

Marshall, Jonathan. "Empire or Liberty: The Antifederalists and Foreign Policy, 1787–1788." *Journal of Libertarian Studies* 4, no. 3 (Summer 1980).

Marshall, P. J., ed. *The Oxford History of the British Empire,* vol. 2: *The Eighteenth Century.* Oxford: Oxford University Press, 1998.

Matthewson, Tim. "Jefferson and the Nonrecognition of Haiti." *Proceedings of the American Philosophical Society* 140 (March 1996).

May, Ernest R. *Imperial Democracy: The Emergence of America as a Great Power.* New York: Harper & Row, 1973.

———. *The Making of the Monroe Doctrine.* Cambridge, Mass.: Belknap Press of Harvard University Press, 1975.

———"Response to Harry Ammon." *Diplomatic History* 5 (Winter 1981).

May, Robert E. *The Southern Dream of a Caribbean Empire.* Baton Rouge: Louisiana State University Press, 1973.

McCardell, John. *The Idea of a Southern Nation: Southern Nationalists and Southern Nationalism, 1830–1860.* New York: Norton, 1979.

McCormick, Thomas J. "The 1890s as a Watershed Decade." In *Safeguarding the Republic: Essays and Documents in American Foreign Relations, 1890–1991,* ed. Howard Jones. New York: McGraw-Hill, 1992.

McCoy, Drew R. *The Elusive Republic: Political Economy in Jeffersonian America.* Chapel Hill: University of North Carolina Press, 1980.

McCusker, John J., and Russell R. Menard. *The Economy of British America, 1607–1789.* Chapel Hill: University of North Carolina Press, 1985.

McDonald, Forrest. *Novus Ordo Seclorum: The Intellectual Origins of the Constitution.* Lawrence: University Press of Kansas, 1985.

———. *States' Rights and the Union: Imperium in Imperio, 1776–1876.* Lawrence: University Press of Kansas, 2000.

McKee, Delber L. "Samuel Gompers, the A.F. of L. and Imperialism, 1895–1900." *Historian* 21 (Winter 1959).

McLean, Joseph E. *William Rufus Day: Supreme Court Justice from Ohio.* Baltimore: Johns Hopkins Press, 1946.

McLoughlin, William G. *Cherokee Renascence in the New Republic.* Princeton, N.J.: Princeton University Press, 1986.

McPherson, James M. *Battle Cry of Freedom: The Civil War Era.* New York: Oxford University Press, 1988.

———. *Drawn with the Sword: Reflections on the American Civil War.* New York: Oxford University Press, 1996.

———. *For Cause and Comrades: Why Men Fought in the Civil War.* New York: Oxford University Press, 1997.

McWilliams, Tennant S. *Hannis Taylor: The New Southerner as American.* University: University of Alabama Press, 1978.

———. *The New South Faces the World: Foreign Affairs and the Southern Sense of Self, 1877–1950.* Baton Rouge: Louisiana State University Press, 1988.

Merk, Frederick. *History of the Westward Movement.* New York: Knopf, 1978.

———. *Manifest Destiny and Mission in American History: A Reinterpretation.* New York: Knopf, 1963.

———. *The Monroe Doctrine and American Expansionism, 1843–1849.* New York: Knopf, 1966.

———. *The Oregon Question: Essays in Anglo-American Diplomacy and Politics.* Cambridge, Mass.: Belknap Press of Harvard University Press, 1967.

———. *Slavery and the Annexation of Texas.* New York: Knopf, 1972.

Merrill, Horace Samuel, and Marion Galbraith Merrill. *The Republican Command, 1897–1913.* Lexington: University Press of Kentucky, 1971.

Middlekauff, Robert L. "Why Men Fought in the American Revolution." In *Major Problems in the Era of the American Revolution, 1760–1791,* ed. Richard D. Brown. Lexington, Mass.: D. C. Heath, 1992.

Middleton, Richard. *Colonial America: A History, 1585–1776.* Oxford: Blackwell, [1992] 1998.

Miller, Perry. *Errand into the Wilderness.* Cambridge, Mass.: Belknap Press of Harvard University Press, 1956.

———. *The New England Mind: From Colonies to Province.* Cambridge, Mass.: Harvard University Press, 1953.

Miller, William Lee. *Arguing About Slavery: The Great Battle in the United States Congress.* New York: Knopf, 1996.

Mitchell, Nancy. *The Danger of Dreams: German and American Imperialism in Latin America.* Chapel Hill: University of North Carolina Press, 1999.

———. "Germans in the Backyard: *Weltpolitik* Versus Protective Imperialism." *Prologue* 24 (Summer 1992).

———. "Protective Imperialism Versus *Weltpolitik* in Brazil. Part One: Pan-German Vision and Mahanian Response." *International History Review* 18 (May 1996).

———. "Protective Imperialism versus *Weltpolitik* in Brazil. Part Two: Settlement, Trade and Opportunity." *International History Review* 18 (August 1996).

Moore, John Bassett, ed. *A Digest of International Law.* 8 vols. Washington, D.C.: U.S. Government Printing Office, 1906.

Morgan, Edmund S. *American Slavery, American Freedom: The Ordeal of Colonial Virginia.* New York: Norton, 1975.

———. *The Gentle Puritan: A Life of Ezra Stiles, 1727–1795.* New Haven, Conn.: Yale University Press, 1962.

Morgan, H. Wayne. *America's Road to Empire: The War with Spain and Overseas Expansion.* New York: Wiley, 1965.

———. *From Hayes to McKinley: National Party Politics, 1877–1896.* Syracuse, N.Y.: Syracuse University Press, 1969.

———. *William McKinley and His America.* Kent, Ohio: Kent State University Press, 2003.

———. "William McKinley as a Political Leader." *Review of Politics* 28 (October 1966).

———, ed. *The Gilded Age.* Syracuse, N.Y.: Syracuse University Press, 1970.

Morgenthau, Hans. "The Mainspring of American Foreign Policy." *American Political Science Review* 44, no. 4 (December 1950).

Morison, Samuel Eliot, Henry Steele Commager, and William E. Leuchtenburg. *The Growth of the American Republic.* 7th ed. New York: Oxford University Press, 1980.

Morris, Richard B. *The Peacemakers: The Great Powers and American Independence.* New York: Harper & Row, 1965; Boston: Northeastern University Press, 1983.

———, ed. *Alexander Hamilton and the Founding of the Nation.* New York: Dial Press, 1957.

Murrin, John M. "Beneficiaries of Catastrophe: The English Colonies in America." In *The New American History,* ed. Eric Foner. Philadelphia: Temple University Press, 1990.

Musicant, Ivan. *Empire by Default: The Spanish-American War and the Dawn of the American Century.* New York: Holt, 1998.

Neale, R. G. *Great Britain and United States Expansion: 1898–1900.* East Lansing: Michigan State University Press, 1966.

Nelson, Anna Kasten. "Destiny and Diplomacy, 1840–1865." In *American Foreign Relations: A Historiographical Review,* ed. Gerald K. Haines and J. Samuel Walker. Westport, Conn.: Greenwood Press, 1981.

Nelson, John R. *Liberty and Property: Political Economy and Policy-making in the New Nation, 1789–1812.* Baltimore: Johns Hopkins University Press, 1987.

Nelson, William Javier. *Almost a Territory: America's Attempt to Annex the Dominican Republic.* Newark: University of Delaware Press, 1990.

Nevins, Allan. *Hamilton Fish: The Inner History of the Grant Administration.* New York: F. Ungar, 1957.

———. *Ordeal of the Union.* Vol. 2: *A House Dividing, 1852–1857.* New York: Scribner's, 1947.

Nichols, Roy Franklin. *Franklin Pierce: Young Hickory of the Granite Hills.* 2nd ed. Philadelphia: University of Pennsylvania Press, 1958.

Ninkovich, Frank A. *Modernity and Power: A History of the Domino Theory in the Twentieth Century.* Chicago: University of Chicago Press, 1994.

———. "Theodore Roosevelt: Civilization as Ideology." *Diplomatic History* 10 (Summer 1986).

Niven, John. *John C. Calhoun and the Price of Union: A Biography.* Baton Rouge: Louisiana State University Press, 1988.

Nolan, Cathal J. "The United States and Tsarist Anti-Semitism, 1865–1914." *Diplomacy and Statecraft* 3 (November 1992).

North, Douglass Cecil. *The Economic Growth of the United States, 1790–1860.* Englewood Cliffs, N.J.: Prentice-Hall, 1961; New York: Norton, 1966.

O'Brien, Phillips Payson. *British and American Naval Power: Politics and Policy, 1900–1936.* Westport, Conn.: Praeger, 1998.

O'Connell, Robert L. *Sacred Vessels: The Cult of the Battleship and the Rise of the U.S. Navy.* Boulder, Colo.: Westview Press, 1991; reprint, Oxford and New York: Oxford University Press, 1993.

Offner, John L. "President McKinley's Final Attempt to Avoid War with Spain." *Ohio History* 94 (Summer–Autumn 1985).

———. "United States Politics and the 1898 War over Cuba." In *The Crisis of 1898: Colonial Redistribution and Nationalist Mobilization,* ed. Angel Smith and Emma Dávila-Cox. New York: St. Martin's, 1998.

————. *An Unwanted War: The Diplomacy of the United States and Spain over Cuba, 1895–1898*. Chapel Hill: University of North Carolina Press, 1992.

Olcott, Charles S. *The Life of William McKinley*. 2 vols. Boston: Houghton Mifflin, 1916.

Onuf, Peter S. "The Declaration of Independence for Diplomatic Historians." *Diplomatic History* 22, no. 1 (Winter 1998).

————. *Jefferson's Empire: The Language of American Nationhood*. Charlottesville: University Press of Virginia, 2000.

————, and Nicholas Onuf. *Federal Union, Modern World: The Law of Nations in an Age of Revolutions, 1776–1814*. Madison, Wis.: Madison House, 1993.

Orde, Anne. *The Eclipse of Great Britain: The United States and British Imperial Decline, 1895–1956*. New York: St. Martin's, 1996.

Osgood, Robert Endicott. *Ideals and Self-Interest in America's Foreign Relations: The Great Transformation of the Twentieth Century*. Chicago: University of Chicago Press, [1953] 1974.

Ott, Thomas O. *The Haitian Revolution, 1789–1804*. Knoxville: University of Tennessee Press, 1973.

Owsley, Frank Lawrence, Jr., and Gene A. Smith. *Filibusters and Expansionists: Jeffersonian Manifest Destiny, 1800–1821*. Tuscaloosa: University of Alabama Press, 1997.

Pakenham, Thomas. *The Scramble for Africa: 1876–1912*. New York: Random House, 1991.

Palmer, Robert Roswell. *The Age of the Democratic Revolution: A Political History of Europe and America, 1760–1800*. Princeton, N.J.: Princeton University Press, 1959.

Paolino, Ernest N. *The Foundations of the American Empire: William Henry Seward and U.S. Foreign Policy*. Ithaca, N.Y.: Cornell University Press, 1973.

Park, James William. *Latin American Underdevelopment: A History of Perspectives in the United States, 1870–1965*. Baton Rouge: Louisiana State University Press, 1995.

Paterson, Thomas G. "United States Intervention in Cuba, 1898: Interpretations of the Spanish-American-Cuban-Filipino War." *The History Teacher* 29, no. 3 (May 1996).

Paulsen, George E. "Secretary Gresham, Senator Lodge, and American Good Offices in China, 1894." *Pacific Historical Review* 36 (May 1967).

Pease, William H., and Jane H. Pease. *Web of Progress: Private Values and Public Styles in Boston and Charleston, 1828–1843*. Athens: University of Georgia Press, 1994.

Peck, Harry Thurston. *Twenty Years of the Republic, 1885–1905*. New York: Dodd, Mead, 1907.

Pelz, Stephen E. "Changing International Systems, the World Balance of Power, and the United States, 1776–1976." *Diplomatic History* 15 (Winter 1991).

Pérez, Louis A., Jr. "Between Meanings and Memories of 1898." *Orbis* 42 (Fall 1998).

————. *Cuba and the United States: Ties of Singular Intimacy*. Athens: University of Georgia Press, 1990.

————. *Cuba Between Empires*. Pittsburgh: University of Pittsburgh Press, 1983.

————. *Cuba: Between Reform and Revolution*. New York: Oxford University Press, 1988.

————. "Cuba-U.S. Relations: A Survey of Twentieth Century Historiography." *Review of Inter-American Bibliography* 39 (July–September 1989).

————. "Incurring a Debt of Gratitude: 1898 and the Moral Sources of United States Hegemony in Cuba." *American Historical Review* 104 (April 1999).

————. "The Meaning of the *Maine*: Causation and the Historiography of the Spanish-American War." *Pacific Historical Review* 58 (August 1989).

————. *On Becoming Cuban: Identity, Nationality and Culture*. Chapel Hill: University of North Carolina Press, 1999.

Perkins, Bradford. *Castlereagh and Adams*. Berkeley and Los Angeles: University of California Press, 1964.

———. *The Creation of a Republican Empire, 1776–1865.* Vol. 1 of *The Cambridge History of American Foreign Relations.* New York: Cambridge University Press, 1993.

———. "Early American Foreign Relations: Opportunities and Challenges." *Diplomatic History* 22, no. 1 (Winter 1998).

———. *The First Rapprochement: England and the United States, 1795–1805.* Berkeley and Los Angeles: University of California Press, 1967.

Perkins, Dexter. *The American Approach to Foreign Policy.* Cambridge, Mass.: Harvard University Press, 1952.

———. *Hands Off: A History of the Monroe Doctrine.* Boston: Little, Brown, 1941.

———. *The Monroe Doctrine, 1823–1826.* Cambridge, Mass.: Harvard University Press, 1932.

———. *The Monroe Doctrine, 1826–1867.* Baltimore: Johns Hopkins Press, 1933.

Perkins, Donald. "William Graham Sumner as a Critic of Spanish American War." *Continuity* 11 (Fall 1987).

Perkins, Whitney T. *Constraint of Empire: The United States and Caribbean Interventions.* Westport, Conn.: Greenwood Press, 1981.

———. *Denial of Empire: The United States and Its Dependencies.* Leyden: A. W. Sythoff, 1962.

Perman, Michael, et al. *Major Problems in the Civil War and Reconstruction: Documents and Essays.* Boston: Houghton Mifflin, 1998.

Pessen, Edward. "George Washington's Farewell Address, the Cold War, and the Timeless National Interest." *Journal of the Early Republic* 7, no. 1 (Spring 1987).

———. "How Different from Each Other Were the Antebellum North and South?" *American Historical Review* 85 (December 1980).

Pierce, Edward L. *Memoir and Letters of Charles Sumner.* 4 vols. Boston: Roberts Brothers, 1877–93.

Pike, Fredrick B. *Chile and the United States, 1880–1962: The Emergence of Chile's Social Crisis and the Challenge to United States Diplomacy.* Notre Dame, Ind.: University of Notre Dame Press, 1963.

———. *The United States and Latin America: Myths and Stereotypes of Civilization and Nature.* Austin: University of Texas Press, 1992.

Plesur, Milton. *America's Outward Thrust: Approaches to Foreign Affairs, 1865–1890.* DeKalb: Northern Illinois University Press, 1971.

Pletcher, David M. *The Awkward Years: American Foreign Relations Under Garfield and Arthur.* Columbia: University of Missouri Press, 1973.

———. *The Diplomacy of Annexation: Texas, Oregon, and the Mexican War.* Columbia: University of Missouri Press, 1973.

———. "Reciprocity and Latin America in the Early 1890s: A Foretaste of Dollar Diplomacy." *Pacific Historical Review* 47 (February 1978).

———. "Rhetoric and Results: A Pragmatic View of American Economic Expansionism, 1865–98." *Diplomatic History* 5 (Spring 1981).

Plummer, Brenda Gayle. *Haiti and the United States: The Psychological Moment.* Athens: University of Georgia Press, 1992.

Porter, Andrew. "Trusteeship, Anti-Slavery, and Humanitarianism." In *The Oxford History of the British Empire,* vol. 3: *The Nineteenth Century,* ed. Andrew Porter. Oxford: Oxford University Press, 1999.

———, ed. *The Oxford History of the British Empire,* vol. 3: *The Nineteenth Century.* Oxford: Oxford University Press, 1999.

Portes, Jacques. *Fascination and Misgivings: The United States in French Opinion, 1870–1914.* Trans. Elborg Forster. New York: Cambridge University Press, 2000.

Potter, David Morris. *The Impending Crisis, 1848–1861,* completed and ed. Don E. Fehren-bacher. New York: Harper & Row, 1976.

———. "The Lincoln Theme and American National Historiography." In *The South and the Sectional Conflict.* Baton Rouge: Louisiana State University Press, 1968.

Pratt, Julius. *Expansionists of 1812.* New York: Macmillan, 1925.

———. *Expansionists of 1898: The Acquisition of Hawaii and the Spanish Islands.* Chicago: Quadrangle Books, 1964.

———. "The 'Large Policy' of 1898." *Mississippi Valley Historical Review* 19 (September 1932).

Pringle, Henry Fowles. *Theodore Roosevelt: A Biography.* New York: Harcourt, Brace, 1931.

Prucha, Francis Paul. *American Indian Treaties: The History of a Political Anomaly.* Berke-ley and Los Angeles: University of California Press, 1994.

Quint, Howard H. "American Socialists and the Spanish-American War." *American Quar-terly* 10, no. 2, pt. 2 (Summer 1958).

Ramsay, David. *The History of the American Revolution.* Philadelphia, 1789; reprint, ed. Lester H. Cohen, New York: Russell & Russell, 1968.

Randall, J. G. "George Washington and 'Entangling Alliances.' " *South Atlantic Quarterly* 30 (July 1931).

Randall, Stephen J. "Ideology, National Security, and the Corporate State: The Historiogra-phy of U.S.–Latin American Relations." *Latin American Research Review* 27, no. 1 (1991).

Randall, Willard Sterne. *Thomas Jefferson: A Life.* New York: Holt, 1993.

Rauchway, Eric. "Willard Straight and the Paradox of Liberal Imperialism." *Pacific Histori-cal Review* 66 (August 1997).

Rechner, James R. *Teddy Roosevelt's Great White Fleet.* Annapolis, Md.: Naval Institute Press, 1982.

Remini, Robert Vincent. *Andrew Jackson and the Course of American Empire, 1767–1821.* New York: Harper & Row, 1977.

———. *Andrew Jackson: The Course of American Freedom, 1822–1832* Baltimore: Johns Hopkins University Press, 1998.

———. *Daniel Webster: The Man and His Time.* New York: Norton, 1997.

———. *Henry Clay: Statesman for the Union.* New York: Norton, 1991.

Rhodes, James Ford. *The McKinley and Roosevelt Administrations, 1897–1909.* New York: MacMillan Co., 1922.

Ricard, Serge. "The Anglo-German Intervention in Venezuela and Theodore Roosevelt's Ultimatum to the Kaiser: Taking a Fresh Look at an Old Enigma." In *Anglo-Saxonism in U.S. Foreign Policy: The Diplomacy of Imperialism, 1899–1919,* ed. Serge Ricard and Hélène Christol. Aix-en-Provence: Publications de Université de Provence, 1991.

Richardson, James D. *A Compilation of the Messages and Papers of the Presidents, 1789–1897.* 10 vols. Washington, D.C.: U.S. Government Printing Office, 1899.

Richardson, Leon B. *William E. Chandler, Republican.* New York: Dodd, Mead, 1940.

Rippy, J. Fred. "The European Powers and the Spanish-American War." *James Sprunt His-torical Studies* 19 (1927).

———. *Rivalry of the United States and Great Britain over Latin America, 1808–1830.* Bal-timore: Johns Hopkins Press, 1929.

Risjord, Norman K. *The Old Republicans: Southern Conservatism in the Age of Jefferson.* New York: Columbia University Press, 1965.

Ritcheson, Charles R. *Aftermath of Revolution: British Policy Toward the United States, 1783–1795.* Dallas: Southern Methodist University Press, 1969.

Ronda, James P. *Astoria and Empire.* Lincoln: University of Nebraska Press, 1990.

Roosevelt, Theodore. *Gouverneur Morris.* Boston: Houghton Mifflin, 1888.

Rosenberg, Emily S. "A Call to Revolution: A Roundtable on Early U.S. Foreign Relations." *Diplomatic History* 22 (Winter 1998).

Rossiter, Clinton, ed. *The Federalist Papers: Alexander Hamilton, James Madison, John Jay.* New York: New American Library, 1961.

Rystad, Göran. *Ambiguous Imperialism: American Foreign Policy and Domestic Politics at the Turn of the Century.* Stockholm: Esselte Studium, 1975.

Sater, William F. *Chile and the United States: Empires in Conflict.* Athens: University of Georgia Press, 1990.

———. *Chile and the War of the Pacific.* Lincoln: University of Nebraska Press, 1986.

Saul, Norman E. *Concord and Conflict: The United States and Russia, 1867–1914.* Lawrence: University Press of Kansas, 1996.

Savelle, Max. "The International Approach to Early Anglo-American History, 1492–1763." In *The Reinterpretation of Early American History: Essays in Honor of John Edwin Pomfret,* ed. Ray Allen Billington. San Marino, Calif.: Huntington Library, 1966.

———. *The Origins of American Diplomacy: The International History of Angloamerica, 1492–1763.* New York: Macmillan, 1967.

Schama, Simon. *Citizens: A Chronicle of the French Revolution.* New York: Knopf, 1989.

Schellings, William J. "Florida and the Cuban Revolution, 1895–1898." *Florida Historical Quarterly* 39 (October 1960).

Schieber, Clara Eve. *The Transformation of American Sentiment Toward Germany, 1870–1914.* Boston: Cornhill, 1923.

Schimmelpenninck van der Oye, David. "From Cooperation to Confrontation? Reflections on the Russian-American Encounter on the Pacific." *Itinerario* [Netherlands] 22, no. 3 (1998).

Schmitt, Karl M. *Mexico and the United States, 1821–1973: Conflict and Coexistence.* New York: Wiley, 1974.

Schoenberg, Philip Ernest. "The American Reaction to the Kishinev Pogrom of 1903." *American Jewish Historical Quarterly* 63 (March 1974).

Schoonover, Thomas D. *Germany in Central America: Competitive Imperialism, 1821–1929.* Tuscaloosa: University of Alabama Press, 1998.

———. *The United States in Central America, 1860–1911: Episodes of Social Imperialism and Imperial Rivalry in the World System.* Durham, N.C.: Duke University Press, 1991.

Schott, Marshall E. "Louisiana Sugar and the Cuban Crisis, 1895–1898." *Louisiana History* 31 (Summer 1990).

———. "The South and American Foreign Policy, 1894–1990: New South Prophets and the Challenge of Regional Values." *Southern Studies* 4 (Fall 1993).

Schoultz, Lars. *Beneath the United States: A History of U.S. Policy Toward Latin America.* Cambridge, Mass.: Harvard University Press, 1998.

Schröder, Hans-Jürgen, ed. *Confrontation and Cooperation: Germany and the United States in the Era of World War I, 1900–1924.* Providence, R.I.: Berg, 1993.

Schroeder, John H. *Mr. Polk's War: American Opposition and Dissent, 1846–1848.* Madison: University of Wisconsin Press, 1973.

Schurz, Carl. *Speeches, Correspondence, and Political Papers of Carl Schurz.* Ed. Frederic Bancroft. 6 vols. New York: G. P. Putnam's Sons, 1913.

———. "Thoughts on American Imperialism." *Century Magazine* 56 (September 1898).

Scott, Carole E. "Racism and Southern Anti-Imperialists: The Blounts of Georgia." *Atlanta History* 31 (Fall 1987).

Seager, Robert. "Ten Years Before Mahan: The Unofficial Case for the New Navy, 1880–1890." *Mississippi Valley Historical Review* 40, no. 3 (December 1953).

Seed, Geoffrey. "British Reactions to American Imperialism Reflected in Journals of Opinion, 1898–1900." *Political Science Quarterly* 73 (June 1958).

Selesky, Harold E. *War and Society in Colonial Connecticut.* New Haven, Conn.: Yale University Press, 1990.

Sellers, Charles Grier. *James K. Polk: Continentalist, 1843–1846.* Vol. 2. Princeton, N.J.: Princeton University Press, 1966.

————. *The Market Revolution: Jacksonian America, 1815–1846.* New York: Oxford University Press, 1991.

Shankman, Arnold. "Brothers Across the Sea: Afro-Americans on the Persecution of Russian Jews, 1881–1917." *Jewish Social Studies* 37 (Spring 1975).

Shewmaker, Kenneth E. "Daniel Webster and the Politics of Foreign Policy, 1850–1852." *Journal of American History* 63, no. 2 (September 1976).

————. "The 'War of Words': The Cass-Webster Debate of 1842–43." *Diplomatic History* 4 (Spring 1981).

Shy, John. *A People Numerous and Armed: Reflections on the Military Struggle for American Independence.* Ann Arbor: University of Michigan Press, 1990.

Skinner, Elliott P. *African Americans and U.S. Policy Toward Africa, 1850–1924: In Defense of Black Nationality.* Washington, D.C.: Howard University Press, 1992.

Smelser, Marshall. "George Washington and the Alien and Sedition Acts." *American Historical Review* 59, no. 2 (January 1954).

————. "The Jacobin Phrenzy: Federalism and the Menace of Liberty, Equality and Fraternity." *Review of Politics* 13 (October 1951).

Smith, Adam. *An Inquiry into the Nature and Causes of the Wealth of Nations.* New York: Modern Library, 1937.

Smith, Joseph. *Illusions of Conflict: Anglo-American Diplomacy Toward Latin America, 1865–1896.* Pittsburgh: University of Pittsburgh Press, 1979.

Smith, Shannon. "From Relief to Revolution: American Women and the Russian-American Relationship, 1890–1917." *Diplomatic History* 19 (Fall 1995).

Smither, Harriet. "English Abolitionism and the Annexation of Texas." *Southwestern Historical Quarterly* 32, no. 3 (January 1929).

Socolofsky, Homer E., and Allan B. Spetter. *The Presidency of Benjamin Harrison.* Lawrence: University Press of Kansas, 1987.

Sofka, James R. "The Jeffersonian Idea of National Security: Commerce, the Atlantic Balance of Power, and the Barbary War, 1786–1805." *Diplomatic History* 21, no. 41 (Fall 1997).

Spalding, Matthew, and Patrick J. Garrity. *Sacred Union of Citizens: George Washington's Farewell Address and the American Character.* Lanham, Md.: Rowan & Littlefield, 1996.

Spector, Ronald H. *Professors of War: The Naval War College and the Development of the Naval Profession.* Newport, R.I.: Naval War College Press, 1977.

Spencer, Donald S. *Louis Kossuth and Young America: A Study of Sectionalism and Foreign Policy, 1848–1852.* Columbia: University of Missouri Press, 1977.

Spetter, Allan B. "Harrison and Blaine: Foreign Policy, 1889–1893." *Indiana Magazine of History* 65 (Spring 1969).

Sprout, Harold, and Margaret Sprout. *The Rise of American Naval Power, 1776–1918.* Princeton, N.J.: Princeton University Press, 1944.

Stephanson, Anders. *Manifest Destiny: American Expansionism and the Empire of Right.* New York: Hill and Wang, 1995.

Stevens, Kenneth R. "Thomas Jefferson, John Quincy Adams, and the Foreign Policy of the Early Republic." *Diplomatic History* 19, no. 4 (Fall 1995).

Stewart, Donald H. *The Opposition Press of the Federalist Period.* Albany: State University of New York Press, 1969.

Still, William N., Jr. *American Sea Power in the Old World: The United States Navy in*

European and Near Eastern Waters, 1865–1917. Westport, Conn.: Greenwood Press, 1980.

Stourzh, Gerald. *Alexander Hamilton and the Idea of Republican Government*. Stanford, Calif.: Stanford University Press, 1970.

———. *Benjamin Franklin and American Foreign Policy*. Chicago: University of Chicago Press, 1954.

Strout, Cushing. *The American Image of the Old World*. New York: Harper & Row, 1963.

Stuart, Reginald. *United States Expansionism and British North America, 1775–1871*. Chapel Hill: University of North Carolina Press, 1988.

———. *War and American Thought: From the Revolution to the Monroe Doctrine*. Kent, Ohio: Kent State University Press, 1982.

Stults, Taylor. "Roosevelt Russian Persecution of Jews, and American Public Opinion." *Jewish Social Studies* 33 (January 1971).

Sydnor, Charles S. *The Development of Southern Sectionalism, 1819–1848*. Vol. 5 of *A History of the South*, ed. Wendell Holmes Stephenson and E. Merton Coulter. Baton Rouge: Louisiana State University Press, 1968.

Symonds, Craig. *Navalists and Anti-Navalists: The Naval Policy Debate in the United States, 1785–1827*. Newark: University of Delaware Press, 1980.

Tansill, Charles Callan. *The Foreign Policy of Thomas F. Bayard, 1885–1897*. New York: Fordham University Press, 1940.

Tarragó, Rafael E. "The Thwarting of Cuban Autonomy." *Orbis* 42 (Fall 1998).

Tate, Merze. "Slavery and Racism as Deterrents to the Annexation of Hawaii, 1854–1855." *Journal of Negro History* 47, no. 1 (January 1962).

Taylor, Alan. *American Colonies*. New York: Viking, 2001.

Taylor, Sandra. "The Sisterhood of Salvation and the Sunrise Kingdom: Congregational Women Missionaries in Meiji Japan." *Pacific Historical Review* 48 (February 1979).

Temperley, H. W. V. "French Designs on Spanish America, 1820." *English Historical Review* 40 (January 1925).

———. "The Later American Policy of George Canning." *American Historical Review* 11 (1906).

Temperley, Harold. *The Foreign Policy of Canning, 1822–1827: England, the Neo-Holy Alliance and the New World*. London: G. Bell & Sons, 1925.

Thiesen, William H. "Professionalization and American Naval Modernization in the 1880s." *Naval War College Review* 49 (Spring 1996).

Thomas, Hugh. *The Slave Trade: The Story of the Atlantic Slave Trade, 1440–1870*. New York: Simon & Schuster, 1997.

Thompson, Arthur W., and Robert A. Hart. *The Uncertain Crusade: America and the Russian Revolution of 1905*. Amherst: University of Massachusetts Press, 1970.

Thucydides. *The Peloponnesian War*. Trans. Rex Warner. Introduction and notes by M. I. Finley. New York: Viking Penguin, [1954] 1985.

Tocqueville, Alexis de. *Democracy in America*. 2 vols. New York: Knopf, 1945.

Tompkins, E. Berkeley. *Anti-Imperialism in the United States: The Great Debate, 1890–1920*. Philadelphia: University of Philadelphia Press, 1970.

Trask, David F. "U.S. Historians and the War of 1895–1898: The Influence of International Politics on Scholarship." In *1898: Enfoques y perspectivas [Focal Points and Perspectives]*, ed. Luis E. Gonzáles Vales. San Juan: Academia Puertorriqueña de la Historia, 1997.

Treat, Payson J. *Diplomatic Relations Between the United States and Japan, 1853–1905*. 3 vols. Stanford, Calif.: Stanford University Press, 1932–38.

Trefousse, Hans L. *Carl Schurz: A Biography*. 2nd ed. New York: Fordham University Press, 1998.

Trumbull, John. *An Essay on the Use and Advantages of the Fine Arts.* New Haven, Conn.: T. and S. Green, 1770.

Travis, Frederick F. *George Kennan and the American-Russian Relationship, 1865–1924.* Athens: Ohio University Press, 1990.

Tsvirkun, A. F. "Some Questions on American Foreign Policy in 1898–1914 in the Russian Bourgeois Press." In *Russian-American Dialogue on Cultural Relations, 1776–1914,* ed. Norman E. Saul and Richard D. McKinzie. Columbia: University of Missouri Press, 1997.

Tucker, Robert W., and David C. Hendrickson. *Empire of Liberty: The Statecraft of Thomas Jefferson.* New York: Oxford University Press, 1990.

———. *The Fall of the First British Empire: Origins of the War of American Independence.* Baltimore: Johns Hopkins University Press 1982.

———. *The Imperial Temptation: The New World Order and America's Purpose.* New York: Council on Foreign Relations, 1992.

Ueda, Toshio. "The Russo-Japanese War and the Attitude of the United States." In *Japan-American Diplomatic Relations in the Meiji-Taisho Era,* ed. Hikomotsu Kamikawa. Tokyo: Pan-Pacific Press, 1958.

Vagts, Alfred. "Hopes and Fears of an American-German War, 1870–1915." *Political Science Quarterly* 54 (December 1939).

Van Alstyne, Richard W. *Rising American Empire.* New York: Oxford University Press, 1960.

Van Deusen, Glyndon Garlock. *The Life of Henry Clay.* Boston: Little, Brown, 1937.

———. *William Henry Seward.* New York: Oxford University Press, 1967.

Varg, Paul A. *America, from Client State to World Power: Six Major Transitions in United States Foreign Relations.* Norman: University of Oklahoma Press, 1990.

———. *Foreign Policies of the Founding Fathers.* East Lansing: Michigan State University Press, 1963.

———. *New England and Foreign Relations, 1789–1850.* Hanover, N.H.: University Press of New England, 1983.

———. *United States Foreign Relations, 1820–1860.* East Lansing: Michigan State University Press, 1979.

Vázquez, Josefina Zoraida, and Lorenzo Meyer. *The United States and Mexico.* Chicago: University of Chicago Press, 1985.

Wall, Joseph Frazier. *Andrew Carnegie.* Pittsburgh: University of Pittsburgh Press, 1989.

Wallace, Anthony F. C. *Jefferson and the Indians: The Tragic Fate of the First Americans.* Cambridge, Mass.: Belknap Press of Harvard University Press, 1999.

Walling, Karl-Friedrich. *Republican Empire: Alexander Hamilton on War and Free Government.* Lawrence: University Press of Kansas, 1999.

Walters, Ronald G. *American Reformers, 1815–1860.* New York: Hill & Wang, 1997.

Ward, A. W., and G. P. Gooch. *The Cambridge History of British Foreign Policy, 1783–1919.* Vol. 2: *1815–1866.* Cambridge, U.K.: Cambridge University Press, 1923.

Washington, George. *The Writings of George Washington from the Original Manuscript Sources, 1745–1799.* Ed. John C. Fitzpatrick. 39 vols. Washington, D.C.: U.S. Government Printing Office, 1931–44.

Watson, Harry L. *Andrew Jackson vs. Henry Clay.* Boston: Bedford/St. Martin's, 1998.

Watts, Steven. *The Republic Reborn: War and the Making of Liberal America, 1790–1820.* Baltimore: Johns Hopkins University Press, 1987.

Webster, Sir Charles Kingsley. *The Foreign Policy of Palmerston, 1830–1841: Britain, the Liberal Movement, and the Eastern Question.* 2 vols. London: G. Bell, [1951] 1969.

Webster, Daniel. *The Papers of Daniel Webster.* Ed. Charles M. Wiltse. 14 vols. Hanover, N.H.: Dartmouth College by the University Press of New England, 1974.

Weeks, William Earl. *Building the Continental Empire: American Expansion from the Revolution to the Civil War.* Chicago: Ivan R. Dee, 1996.

———. *John Quincy Adams and American Global Empire.* Lexington: University Press of Kentucky, 1992.

———. "John Quincy Adams's 'Great Gun' and the Rhetoric of American Empire." *Diplomatic History* 14 (Winter 1990).

———. "New Directions in the Study of Early American Foreign Relations." *Diplomatic History* 17, no. 1 (Winter 1993).

Weigley, Russell F. *History of the United States Army.* New York: Macmillan, 1967.

Welch, Richard E., Jr. *George Frisbie Hoar and the Half-Breed Republicans.* Cambridge, Mass.: Harvard University Press, 1971.

———. *The Presidencies of Grover Cleveland.* Lawrence: University Press of Kansas, 1988.

———. *Response to Imperialism: The United States and the Philippine-American War, 1899–1902.* Chapel Hill: University of North Carolina Press, 1978.

———. "William McKinley: Reluctant Warrior, Cautious Imperialist." In *Traditions and Values: American Diplomacy, 1865–1945,* vol. 8: *American Values Projected Abroad,* ed. Norman Graebner. Lanham, Md.: University Press of America, 1985.

Wells, Samuel F., Jr. *The Challenges of Power: American Policy, 1900–1921.* Lanham, Md.: University Press of America, 1990.

Welter, Rush. *The Mind of America, 1820–1860.* New York: Columbia University Press, 1975.

Werking, Richard Hume. "Senator Henry Cabot Lodge and the Philippines: A Note on American Territorial Expansion." *Pacific Historical Review* 42 (May 1973).

Wharton, Francis, ed. *The Revolutionary Diplomatic Correspondence of the United States.* 6 vols. Washington, D.C.: U.S. Government Printing Office, 1899.

Whitaker, Arthur Preston. *The Western Hemisphere Idea: Its Rise and Decline.* Ithaca, N.Y.: Cornell University Press, 1954.

White, John Albert. *The Diplomacy of the Russo-Japanese War.* Princeton, N.J.: Princeton University Press, 1964.

White, Leonard D., with Jean Schneider. *The Republican Era: A Study in Administrative History.* New York: Macmillan, 1958.

White, Richard A. *The Middle Ground: Indians, Empires and Republics in the Great Lakes Region, 1650–1815.* New York: Cambridge University Press, 1991.

Wicks, Daniel H. "Dress Rehearsal: United States Intervention on the Isthmus of Panama, 1885." *Pacific Historical Review* 49 (November 1980).

Widenor, William C. *Henry Cabot Lodge and the Search for an American Foreign Policy.* Berkeley and Los Angeles: University of California Press, 1980.

Wiebe, Robert. *The Search for Order.* New York: Hill and Wang, 1967.

Wiencek, Henry. *An Imperfect God: George Washington, His Slaves, and the Creation of America.* New York: Farrar, Straus & Giroux, 2003.

Wilentz, Sean, ed. *Major Problems in the Early Republic.* Lexington, Mass.: D. C. Heath, 1992.

Williams, R. Hal. *Years of Decision: American Politics in the 1890s.* New York: Wiley, 1978.

Williams, Robert A., Jr. *The American Indian in Western Legal Thought: The Discourse of Conquest.* New York: Oxford University Press, 1990.

Williams, William Appleman. *American-Russian Relations, 1781–1947.* New York: Rinehart, 1952; reprint, New York: Octagon Books, 1971.

———. *Empire as a Way of Life: An Essay on the Causes and Character of America's Present Predicament, Along with a Few Thoughts About an Alternative.* New York: Oxford University Press, 1980.

————. "The Frontier Thesis and American Foreign Policy." *Pacific Historical Review* 24 (November 1955).

Wills, Garry. *"Negro President": Jefferson and the Slave Power.* Boston: Houghton Mifflin, 2003.

Wilson, Major L. *Space, Time, and Freedom: The Quest for Nationality and the Irrepressible Conflict, 1815–1861.* Westport, Conn.: Greenwood Press, 1974.

Winks, Robin W. "The American Struggle with 'Imperialism': How Words Frighten." In *The American Identity: Fusion and Fragmentation,* ed. Rob Kroes. Amsterdam: Amerika Instituut Universiteit Van Amsterdam, 1980.

Wood, Gordon S. *The Radicalism of the American Revolution.* New York: Knopf, 1992.

————. "Tocqueville's Lesson." *New York Review of Books,* May 17, 2001.

Woodward, C. Vann. *The Burden of Southern History.* 3rd ed. Baton Rouge: Louisiana State University Press, 1993.

————. *Origins of the New South, 1877–1913.* 1951; reprint, with a critical essay on recent works by Charles B. Dew, Baton Rouge: Louisiana State University Press, 1971.

Wright, J. Leitch. *Britain and the American Frontier, 1783–1815.* Athens: University of Georgia Press, 1975.

Wright, Louis B. "The Founding Fathers and 'Splendid Isolation.'" *Huntington Library Quarterly* 7 (February 1943).

Young, Marilyn B. "The Quest for Empire." In *American–East Asian Relations: A Survey,* ed. Ernest R. May and James C. Thomson, Jr. Cambridge, Mass.: Harvard University Press, 1972.

Zakaria, Fareed. *From Wealth to Power: The Unusual Origins of America's World Role.* Princeton, N.J.: Princeton University Press, 1998.

ACKNOWLEDGMENTS

I BEGAN WRITING this book ten years ago and have many to thank for their friendship and support. I am deeply grateful to the Carnegie Endowment for International Peace and especially to its president, Jessica Mathews, for her generosity and patience. Paul Balaran, Tom Carothers, and George Perkovich, under whom I have worked at Carnegie, have been valued colleagues. I am also grateful to Mort Abramowitz, who first brought me to Carnegie a decade ago.

I have been fortunate to work with a succession of talented young men and women serving as Carnegie junior fellows, David Adesnik, Mike Beckley, Silvia Manzanero, and Jordan Tama, who helped with research, as well as with two outstanding program assistants, Toula Papanicolas and Indhu Sekar. I am immensely grateful to Chris Henley and Kathleen Higgs, the crack team of librarians at the Carnegie Library, and to Alisa Kramer at American University, who helped with the last phases of the manuscript's production. I owe my agents, Lynn Chu and Glen Hartley, a huge debt of gratitude for their help with this and other projects. It has been a privilege to work with Carol Janeway at Knopf. There is no finer or classier editor.

At American University I have been fortunate to know and learn from an extraordinary group of teachers and scholars: Professors Alan Kraut, Allan Lichtman, Jim Mooney, Roger Brown, Michael Kazin, and the incomparable Valerie French. I cannot begin to repay my debt to Bob Beisner, my adviser and teacher, and my friend. Throughout these years, I have also been lucky to enjoy the comradeship and wise counsel of dear friends Fred Hiatt, Bill Kristol, Leon Wieseltier, Reuel Gerecht, Ed Lazarus, and Joe Rose, all of whom I admire for their integrity and humanity.

A small group of people, including Bob Beisner, showed unparalleled generosity by reading this book in draft form. Craig Kennedy, a valued friend and mentor, has offered encouragement on this and other projects. Strobe Talbott not only read the draft but provided voluminous notes and suggestions on how to improve it. Once again I have benefited from the wisdom and knowledge of Gary Schmitt, from whom I have learned so much over the years.

No one ever had a more loving and supportive family. My brother Fred, and my mother, Myrna, have been lifelong comrades-in-arms. My father, Donald Kagan, who also read through this book in draft, has been the wisest of counselors, the quintessential scholar and teacher. He is my oldest and best friend, and the greatest man I have ever known. I am blessed with two happy, curious, and loving children, David and Leni, who have cheerfully tolerated this book their whole lives. This book is dedicated to my wife, Victoria Nuland, a devoted public servant and loving mother, who is the source of all my happiness.

INDEX

ALSO BY ROBERT KAGAN

"Kagan is in an ideal position to dissect what is wrong in the United States–European relationship and why. He does so with a surgeon's skill, stripping away layer after layer to reveal what in the end is a remarkable conclusion." —The New York Times

OF PARADISE AND POWER
America and Europe in the New World Order

At a time when relations between the United States and Europe are at their lowest ebb since World War II, this brief but cogent book is essential reading. Robert Kagan, a leading scholar of American foreign policy, forces both sides to see themselves through the eyes of the other. Europe, he argues, has moved beyond power into a self-contained world of laws, rules, and negotiation, while America operates in a "Hobbesian" world in which rules and laws are unreliable and military force is often necessary. Tracing how this state of affairs came into being over the past fifty years and fearlessly exploring its ramifications for the future, Kagan reveals the shape of the new transatlantic relationship. The result is a book that promises to be as enduringly influential as Samuel Huntington's *The Clash of Civilizations and the Remaking of the World Order*.

Current Affairs/978-1-4000-3418-5